THE
CAMBRIDGE HISTORY
OF THE BIBLE

VOLUME 1

FROM THE BEGINNINGS
TO JEROME

THE
CAMBRIDGE HISTORY OF
THE BIBLE

VOLUME 1

FROM THE BEGINNINGS
TO JEROME

EDITED BY

P. R. ACKROYD

*Samuel Davidson Professor
of Old Testament Studies
University of London, King's College*

AND

C. F. EVANS

*Professor of New Testament Studies
University of London, King's College*

CAMBRIDGE UNIVERSITY PRESS

CAMBRIDGE

LONDON · NEW YORK · MELBOURNE

Published by the Syndics of the Cambridge University Press
The Pitt Building, Trumpington Street, Cambridge CB2 IRP
Bentley House, 200 Euston Road, London NWI 2DB
32 East 57th Street, New York, NY 10022, USA
296 Beaconsfield Parade, Middle Park, Melbourne 3206, Australia

Library of Congress catalogue card number: 63-24435

hard covers ISBN: 0 521 07418 5
paperback ISBN: 0 521 09973 0

First published 1970
First paperback edition 1975
Reprinted 1976 1978

First printed in Great Britain
at the University Printing House, Cambridge
Reprinted in the United States of America
by Vail-Ballou Press Inc., Binghamton, New York

CONTENTS

Corrections to the text   *page* viii

Preface   ix

Preface to the paperback edition   x

Additions to the bibliography   xi

I   LANGUAGE AND SCRIPT   I

    I   THE BIBLICAL LANGUAGES   I
       by Matthew Black, *Professor of Biblical Criticism and Principal of St Mary's College, University of St Andrews*

    2   THE BIBLICAL SCRIPTS   II
       by the late David Diringer, *formerly Reader in Semitic Epigraphy, Cambridge University*

II   BOOKS IN THE ANCIENT WORLD   30

    3   BOOKS IN THE ANCIENT NEAR EAST AND IN THE OLD TESTAMENT   30
       by D. J. Wiseman, *Professor of Assyriology, University of London*

    4   BOOKS IN THE GRAECO-ROMAN WORLD AND IN THE NEW TESTAMENT   48
       by C. H. Roberts, *Fellow of St John's College, Oxford*

III   THE OLD TESTAMENT   67

    5   THE OLD TESTAMENT IN THE MAKING   67
       by Peter R. Ackroyd, *Samuel Davidson Professor of Old Testament Studies, University of London, King's College*

v

Contents

6   CANONICAL AND NON-CANONICAL   *page* 113
by G. W. Anderson, *Professor of Hebrew and Old Testament Studies, Edinburgh University*

7   THE OLD TESTAMENT TEXT   159
by Shemaryahu Talmon, *Professor of Bible, The Hebrew University of Jerusalem*

8   BIBLE AND MIDRASH: EARLY OLD TESTAMENT EXEGESIS   199
by G. Vermes, *Reader in Jewish Studies, Oxford University*

IV   THE NEW TESTAMENT   232

9   THE NEW TESTAMENT IN THE MAKING   232
by C. F. Evans, *Professor of New Testament Studies, University of London, King's College*

10   THE NEW TESTAMENT CANON   284
by R. M. Grant, *Carl Darling Buck Professor of Humanities, Divinity School, Chicago, Department of New Testament and Early Christian Literature*

11   THE NEW TESTAMENT TEXT   308
by J. N. Birdsall, *Senior Lecturer in Theology, Birmingham University*

12   THE INTERPRETATION OF THE OLD TESTAMENT IN THE NEW   377
by C. K. Barrett, *Professor of Divinity, Durham University*

V   THE BIBLE IN THE EARLY CHURCH   412

13   BIBLICAL EXEGESIS IN THE EARLY CHURCH   412
by R. P. C. Hanson, *Professor of Historical and Contemporary Theology, University of Manchester*

14   ORIGEN AS BIBLICAL SCHOLAR   454
by M. F. Wiles, *Regius Professor of Divinity, University of Oxford*

15   THEODORE OF MOPSUESTIA AS REPRESENTATIVE OF THE ANTIOCHENE SCHOOL   489
by M. F. Wiles

Contents

16 JEROME AS BIBLICAL SCHOLAR   *page* 510
    by H. F. D. Sparks, *Oriel Professor of The Interpretation*
    of Holy Scriptures, Oxford University

17 AUGUSTINE AS BIBLICAL SCHOLAR   541
    by Gerald Bonner, *Lecturer in Theology, Durham*
    University

18 THE PLACE OF THE BIBLE IN THE LITURGY   563
    by J. A. Lamb, *formerly Librarian of New College,*
    Edinburgh

Bibliography   587

Abbreviations   599

Notes on the Plates   601

Plates   *between pages* 608–609

Indexes

    General   609

    Biblical and other references   626

p. 31, par. 2, line 2. Read '*maritimus*'

p. 33, n. 3. For 'p. 75' read 'p. 65'

p. 39, line 10 from end. Read 'anonymity;'

p. 45, line 11 from end. For '*Assyrian*' read '*Babylonian*'

p. 68, n. 2. For '*iuif*' read '*juif*'

p. 165, line 7 from end. For 'eras' read 'era'

p. 185, lines 8 and 2 from end. For 'codices' read 'scrolls'

p. 187, line 14. For '*ante*' read '*anti*'

p. 228, n. 3. For 'London' read 'Oxford'

p. 236, line 8. For 'was only obscured' read 'were only obscured'

p. 301, n. 1. For '*Neutestamenthichen*' read '*Neutestamentlichen*'

p. 312, par. 2, line 9. Read 'patristic'

p. 362, line 3. For 'At about the same time as' read 'Somewhat later than the time when'

p. 362, last 2 lines. Read 'Evagrius then *may* be a person of an earlier time, but two candidates amongst fourth- and fifth-century Christian scholars...'

p. 363, lines 5–6. Read 'Evagrius Ponticus...disciple of Origen and friend of the Cappadocians'

p. 420, line 16. Delete 'Delphi,'

p. 435, lines 7–8. For 'in the second decade of the fourth century' read 'at some point between 318 and 337'

p. 516, lines 3–4 from end. Read '*stolidissimus*'

p. 540, line 9. For 'qipsum' read 'ipsum'

p. 556, last line but one. Add after 'all sinned', 'instead of the correct reading ἐφ' ᾧ πάντες ἥμαρτον – 'because all men sinned,' '

p. 575, line 2. Read διασεσάφηται

p. 601, Note on Plate 3. In line 1 for 'A.D.' read 'B.C.' In line 3 for 'were found in Egyptian refuse heaps' read 'came from mummy cartonage'

The captions for Plates 10 and 12 have been reversed.

PREFACE

The idea of a Cambridge History of the Bible originated within the
University Press and was considered, approved and benevolently
assisted through its early stages by a committee consisting of Professors
M. D. Knowles and Norman Sykes. The two volumes of the original
plan—*The West from the Reformation to the Present Day* and *The West
from the Fathers to the Reformation*—have now appeared (1963 and
1969). This volume represents the logical extension back into the
beginnings of the biblical literature and sets out to trace the essential
features of the process by which the Bible as we know it came into
being, and how it came to be canonised and interpreted under Judaism
and in the early years of the Christian Church.

Like its predecessors, this volume is selective in its treatment of the
subject. Since the chronologically subsequent volume, *From the Fathers
to the Reformation*, was originally conceived apart from any consideration of a volume which should lead up to it, it was planned to take in
matters which properly belong in the present volume and which could
not be omitted from it. Thus the overlap between the two volumes
could not be confined to the point where the one ends and the other
begins (Jerome). The exegesis of the Fathers, which was covered in a
single chapter in the other volume, has necessarily been here examined
in greater detail, while such subjects as the textual criticism of the New
Testament and the texts and versions of the Old Testament have been
treated afresh.

It has seemed proper here to begin from the languages and scripts
used for the actual writing of the biblical books, and to set the biblical
literature in the context of ancient literary activity and book-production.
No complete account could be given in such a work as this of the
processes of formation of all the biblical books, still less of the mass of
literature associated with the Old and New Testaments in the narrower
sense, of the writings of the Old Testament Apocrypha and of the various
works sometimes designated as its Pseudepigrapha (now greatly to be
extended in view of the Qumrân discoveries), and of the writings

associated in some degree with the New Testament. For such matters as these, reference must be made to the literature listed in the bibliographies.

In surveying the place of the Bible in the early Church, the method adopted has been to select a number of outstanding figures and to allow the consideration of exegetical method and of the understanding of biblical authority to centre upon them. This will, we hope, sufficiently indicate the range and variety of early Christian thought on these important questions, and again, the bibliographies point to the context in which these figures are to be understood.

Just as the endeavour has been made to make this volume complete in itself, so too the separate sections are so designed that they can be read independently. At certain points this involves a small amount of overlap between sections, but it has seemed best to allow this degree of freedom to the contributors and also to let it be seen that the evidence may be differently appraised by different scholars. In such an area of study as this, no uniformity of approach or of interpretation can be completely adequate to the complexity of the issues involved.

The editors are deeply indebted to the contributors who have co-operated with such generosity of their time and forbearance in accepting suggestions during the process of the book's formation. In fairness to them it must be added that, since the production of a composite work of this kind inevitably takes time, there is an interval between the submission of contributions and their appearance; at some few points it has been possible to insert references to the most recent literature, but this could not be done as extensively as the editors would have wished.

PREFACE TO THE PAPERBACK EDITION

The publication of a paperback edition of this volume has provided an opportunity to list some few corrections and updatings, in particular to some sections of the Bibliography. No alterations could be made to the text. The editors are grateful to the contributors for their help and to reviewers who have drawn attention to some few inaccuracies in the original printing.

1975

P.R.A.

C.F.E.

ADDITIONS TO THE
BIBLIOGRAPHY

(pp. 587–98)

1. *The Biblical Languages*

Brockelmann, C., *Grundriss der vergleichenden Grammatik der semitischen Sprachen* (Berlin, 1908; reprint 1961).

2. *The Biblical Scripts*

Gelb, I. J., *A Study of Writing* (London, 1952).

3. *Books in the Ancient Near East and in the Old Testament*

I   Material Form

Hunger, H., *Babylonische und assyrische Kolophone* (1968).
Posner, E., *Archives in the Ancient World* (Cambridge, Mass., 1972).

II   The Scribal Art

Williams, R. J., 'Scribal Training in Egypt', *JAOS*, XCII (1972), 214–21.

III   Literature

Pritchard, J. B. ed., *The Ancient Near East: Supplementary Texts and Pictures relating to the Old Testament* (Princeton, 1969); the texts of the supplement are incorporated in the 3rd ed. (1969) of *ANET*.
Simpson, W. K. ed., *The Literature of Ancient Egypt* (New Haven and London, 1972). [An anthology of Stories, Instructions and Poetry in translation.]

4. *Books in the Graeco-Roman World and in the New Testament*

Roberts, C. H., 'The Writing and Dissemination of Literature in the Classical World' (chapter 19 of *Literature and Western Civilisation*, vol. 1, ed. David Daiches, London, 1972).
Turner, E. G., *Greek Manuscripts of the Ancient World* (Oxford, 1971).

Additions to the Bibliography

5. The Old Testament in the Making

General Works

Fohrer, G., *Einleitung in das Alte Testament* (Heidelberg, 1965); English transl. *Introduction to the Old Testament*, by David Green (Nashville, 1968; London, 1970).

Kaiser, O., *Einleitung in das Alte Testament* (Gutersloh, 1969); English transl. *Introduction to the Old Testament* (Oxford, 1975). [A survey of problems and areas of research rather than a formal introduction.]

Form criticism

Hayes, J. H. ed., *Old Testament Form Criticism* (Trinity University, Texas, 1974). [A presentation of the whole field of form critical study and its achievements.]

Koch, K., *Was ist Formgeschichte?* (3rd ed. 1974, with a supplement on 'Linguistik und Formgeschichte').

Cp. also T. L. Thompson, *The History of the Patriarchal Narratives* (*Beihefte ZAW* 133, Berlin, 1974) [see p. 70, n. 1: this volume offers a critical study of the supposed affinities between the patriarchal narratives and the Mari and Nuzi texts].

7. The Old Testament Text

Barthélemy, D., 'A Re-examination of the Textual Problems in 2 Sam. 11: 2 – 1 Kings 2: 11 in the Light of Certain Criticisms of *Les Devanciers d' Aquila*', *Septuagint and Cognate Studies* 2 (Society of Biblical Literature, 1972), 19–89 [see p. 183, n. 3].

Butin, R., *The Ten Nequdoth of the Torah or the Meaning and Purpose of the Extraordinary Points of the Pentateuch* (1906), republished with a Prolegomenon by S. Talmon (New York, 1969) [see p. 171 of text].

Cross, F. M., Jr. 'The Evolution of a Theory of Local Texts', *Septuagint and Cognate Studies* 2 (1972), 108–26. [A re-statement of his theory (see p. 196) with some modifications and additional arguments.]

Jellicoe, S., *The Septuagint and Modern Study* (Oxford, 1968) for an up-to-date comprehensive discussion of issues pertaining to the Septuagint [see p. 168 of text].

Talmon, S., 'Qumran und das Alte Testament', *Frankfurter Universitätsreden* Heft 2 (Frankfurt a/M, 1972), 84–100; *idem*, 'The New Covenanters of Qumran', *Scientific American* 225 no. 5 (November, 1971), 72–83 [see p. 190].

Würthwein, E., *Das Text des Alten Testaments* (4th revised ed., 1973).

Further volumes of *Textus* continue to appear.

Additions to the Bibliography

8. Bible and Midrash: Early Old Testament Exegesis

Heinemann, J., 'Early Halakhah in the Palestinian Targumim', *Journal of Jewish Studies* XXV (1974).

McNamara, M., *Targum and Testament* (Shannon, 1972).

Ménard, J.-E. ed., *Exégèse biblique et Judaïsme* (Strasbourg, 1973).

Schürer, E., – Vermes, G., – Millar, F., *The History of the Jewish People in the Age of Jesus Christ* I (Edinburgh, 1973), 90–114 [The Midrashim–The Targums].

Vermes, G., *Scripture and Tradition* (2nd revised ed., 1973).

Vermes, G., *Post-biblical Jewish Studies* (Leiden, 1975).

9. The New Testament in the Making

For 'Dibelius, M., *Fresh Approach*...' read 'Dibelius, M., *A Fresh Approach*...'

After 'Kümmel, W. G., *Das Neue Testament. Geschichte der Erforschung seiner Probleme* (Freiburg/Münich, 1958),' add 'English transl. of 2nd rev. ed. *The New Testament. The History of the Investigation of its Problems* by S. McLean Gilmour and Howard C. Kee (London, 1973)'.

10. The New Testament Canon

Campenhausen, H. Von, *The Formation of the Christian Bible*. Transl. J. A. Baker (London, Philadelphia, 1972).

Smith, M., *Clement of Alexandria and a Secret Gospel of Mark* (Cambridge, Mass. 1973).

Sundberg, A. C., Jr., 'Canon Muratori: A Fourth-Century List', *HTR* LXVI (1973), 1–41.

11. The New Testament Text

Aland, K., *Die alten Übersetzungen des neuen Testaments, die Kirchenväterzitate und Lektionare* (Arbeiten zur neutestamentlichen Textforschung, Bd. 5, Berlin, 1972).

Colwell, E. C., *Studies in methodology in textual criticism of the New Testament* (Leiden, 1969).

Duplacy, J., *Où en est la critique textuelle du nouveau Testament?* (Paris, 1959), continued in 'Bulletin de critique textuelle du nouveau Testament', *Recherches de science religieuse* L (1962), 242–63, 564–98; LI (1963), 432–62; LIII (1965), 257–84; LIV (1966), 426–76; and then, in collaboration with C. M. Martini, in *Biblica*, XLIX (1968), 515–51; LII (1971), 79–113; LIII (1972), 245–78.

Duplacy, J., 'P75: (Pap. Bodmer XIV–XV) et les formes les plus anciennes du texte de Luc' in *L'Évangile de Luc: Mémorial Lucien Cerfaux* (Gembloux, 1973), 109–26.

Additions to the Bibliography

Klijn, A. F. J., *A survey of the researches into the Western text of the gospels and Acts*: part 1 (Utrecht, 1949); part 2 (Supplements to Novum Testamentum, XXI, Leiden, 1969).

Leloir, L., *Le témoignage d'Ephrem sur le Diatessaron* (CSCO subsidia T. 19, Louvain, 1962).

Martini, C. M., S.J., *Il problema della recensionalità del codice B alla luce del papiro Bodmer XIV* (Analecta Biblica, XXVI, Rome, 1966) [see p. 328].

13. Biblical Exegesis in the Early Church

Evans, E., *Tertullian, Adversus Marcionem*, edited and translated, 2 vols. (London, 1972).

de Lubac, H., *Histoire et Esprit* (Paris, 1950).

Meijering, E. P., *Orthodoxy and Platonism in Athanasius* (Leiden, 1968).

16. Jerome as Biblical Scholar

For 'Holworth' read 'Howorth'

Under Rahmer, for '*hebräische*' read '*hebräischen*'

Add Kelly, J. N. D., *Jerome* (London, 1975)

17. Augustine as Biblical Scholar

(Cp. p. 543, n. 7)

Berrouard, M. F. ed., *Homélies sur l'Évangile de saint Jean* (Bibliothèque August-inienne 71, Paris, 1969); *id.* 'La date des "Tractatus I–LIV in Iohannis Evan-gelium" de Saint Augustin', *Recherches Augustiniennes* VII (1971), 105–68.

La Bonnardière, A.-M., *Recherches de chronologie augustinienne* (Paris, 1965) (re-viewed by D. F. Wright, *JTS* NS XVII (1966), 182–6.)

Wright, D. F., 'The Manuscripts of St Augustine's *Tractatus in Evangelium Iohannis*', *Recherches Augustiniennes* VIII (1972), 55–143, esp. 100–6.

18. The Place of the Bible in the Liturgy

Daniélou, J., *The Bible and the Liturgy*. (Notre Dame University Press, 1956).

Martimort, A. G., *L'Eglise en prière* (3rd edition. Tournai); English transl. *The Church at Prayer* (Irish University Press, Shannon. Part I, 1968. Part II, 1971).

Constitutio de sacra Liturgia (1964). There are several English translations, with notes. Lietzmann, H., *Messe und Herrenmahl* (Bonn, 1926); English transl. *Mass and Lord's Supper*, by D. Reeve with Introduction and Supplementary Essay by R. D. Richardson, in fascicles, from 1953 onwards (Leiden). (One part still to come.)

CHAPTER I

LANGUAGE AND SCRIPT

1. THE BIBLICAL LANGUAGES

With the exception of several chapters of Daniel and Ezra,[1] which are written in Aramaic, the language of the Old Testament is Hebrew. The Creation story (cf. Gen. 2: 19 ff.) and the story of the tower of Babel (Gen. 11) imply that Hebrew was the original language of mankind. When we turn from folk legend to linguistic origins, however, Hebrew does not appear to have been the original language of the Hebrews themselves, but the language of the inhabitants of Canaan who were conquered and partly displaced by Joshua; it is more accurately described once in the Old Testament (Isa. 19: 18) as 'the language of Canaan' (it is usually referred to by the Old Testament writers as 'Jewish', e.g. Isa. 36: 11; 2 Chron. 32: 18). The more primitive nomad desert tribes from across the Jordan appear to have been gradually assimilated to the culture and civilisation of the conquered Canaanites and to have adopted their speech as well as much in their culture, if not their manner of life; we do not know the precise nature of the original language of the Hebrew invaders, but it was probably a tribal dialect of the Old Aramaic, with possibly close affinities with the speech of Canaan[2] (cf. Deut. 26: 5 RSV). The name 'Hebrew' to describe the language of the Old Testament is derived from the ancient name of the Israelites *'Ibriyyim*, explained in the Old Testament as a patronymic (Gen. 10: 21). The name, in the form *Habiru*, is now known from Mari (second millennium B.C.) and many other second-millennium cuneiform sources. Various modern etymologies explain the word as 'the dwellers beyond the River', i.e. either the Jordan or (more probably) the Euphrates. (Abraham was born 'beyond the River' in this latter sense.) Other explanations are that it was a term applied to freebooters and mercenaries in Palestine and its neighbourhood (e.g. in the Tell-el-Amarna letters, 1400 B.C.); another

---

[1] Dan. 2: 4–7, 28; Ezra 4: 8—6: 18; 7: 12–26.
[2] See further, below, p. 5.

proposal is that the word means 'those who pass over boundaries', i.e. nomads, and was a social classification.[1] The early nomadic tribes of the Patriarchs may have been so named for their customs and manner of life. (The name Israel came to be applied, after the conquests of Joshua, to the invading nomad tribes, not necessarily all *Habiru*, forged into a nation by the conquest and settlement in Canaan.) The application of the name to the Hebrew language appears first in the Greek adverb Ἑβραϊστί, 'in (the) Hebrew language', in the prologue to ben Sira; it is also found in the New Testament, e.g. Rev. 9: 11, in Josephus and, less frequently, in the Talmud (the rabbis prefer the description 'the holy tongue').

Other Near Eastern languages are sporadically represented by a few isolated words and glosses in the Old Testament. There are, for instance, some Persian words in Daniel and Esther, and a few Greek words in Daniel. Gen. 41: 43, 45 gives the Egyptian form of Joseph's name and an Egyptian exclamation *'abrēk*, EVV 'Bow the knee!' (perhaps simply 'Attention'). At Gen. 31: 47 Laban uses the Aramaic expression *yᵉgar sahᵃdūtā*, Jacob its Hebrew equivalent *galʿēd*, 'heap of witness'. Jer. 10: 11 was possibly written in Aramaic as an injunction to be delivered to other nations.

Hebrew and Aramaic are two of the main representatives of the Semitic family of languages, named after Shem, the reputed ancestor of the Semitic peoples (Gen. 10: 21 ff.).[2] These languages were once spoken in an area extending roughly from the Mediterranean to the other side of the Euphrates and Tigris, and from the mountains of Armenia to the horn of Africa. More precisely, the ancient habitat of the Semitic languages may be defined as Mesopotamia, Syria–Palestine, Arabia and Ethiopia. The living descendants of this ancient Semitic family are still to be found in this same extensive area; they are Hebrew in Israel (a modern revival of the classical language and its descendant, namely rabbinical, particularly Mishnaic, Hebrew), Syriac, Arabic— the most widely spoken modern Semitic language—and Ethiopic. The different branches of the ancient Semitic family are usually distin-

---

[1] This suggestion comes to me from Dr John C. L. Gibson of the University of Edinburgh. But cf. also F. F. Bruce in *Archaeology and Old Testament Study*, ed. D. W. Thomas (Oxford, 1967), p. 15.

[2] For a fuller account of these languages consult S. Moscati, *An Introduction to the Comparative Grammar of the Semitic Languages*, Porta Linguarum Orientalium (Wiesbaden, 1964).

guished by the geographical areas where they mainly flourished, though this is in some respects less important than genealogical relationships or linguistic 'next of kin', which may or may not belong to the same area. The main branches are nowadays defined as North-East Semitic (Mesopotamia), North-West Semitic (Syria–Palestine) and South-West Semitic (Arabia and Ethiopia).[1] The North-East branch is represented by Akkadian, which replaced the non-Semitic Sumerian in the second millennium B.C., Babylonian, the dialect of the southern part of the region, and Assyrian, the dialect of the northern part. Some scholars have concluded that an even earlier Semitic language, to which they have given the name Old-Amorite, existed in this linguistic area in the second half of the third millennium B.C. North-West Semitic embraces Canaanite and Aramaic. Canaanite, which includes Hebrew, Phoenician and Punic, and Moabite, represents the non-Aramaic linguistic phenomena of the Syro-Palestinian area, from the second millennium B.C. onwards. Ugaritic, the language of the Ras Shamra texts (fourteenth, thirteenth centuries B.C.), is variously placed in the North-West or North-East branch. Aramaic represents a widespread linguistic group going back to the beginning of the first millennium B.C.[2] Arabic and Ge'ez or Ethiopic belong to the South-West Semitic group, the latter being a descendant of the old southern Arabic known from inscriptions. It used to be claimed that Arabic was one of the 'purest' of Semitic languages, i.e. the least contaminated by foreign influences and, therefore, the closest to the earliest form of Semitic speech. The latter rôle, however, nowadays would probably be accorded to Akkadian.[3] Ancient Ethiopic first appears in epigraphic materials of the first Christian centuries and in the Aksum inscriptions of the fourth century A.D. It is the language of an extensive Ethiopian Christian literature. The modern Semitic languages of Ethiopia are represented by Tigriña, Tigre, Amharic, Harari and Gurage.

On the whole, these broad geographical divisions correspond tolerably well (with some exceptions) with the distribution of gross linguistic features. East Semitic exhibits quite independent characteristics from West Semitic and these become more marked in the course

[1] See Moscati, *Introduction to the Comparative Grammar*, esp. p. 4.
[2] See further, below, p. 5.
[3] 'Purity' of Arabic can also refer to the classical Qur'anic type of language; the language of the Qur'an is an artificial and scholastic one, based on one of the oldest dialects, presumably that of Mecca.

of time; differentiation, however, is not so clearly evident in the archaic phases. Current opinion regards, for instance, the second-millennium languages, Amorite, Ugaritic and Tell-el-Amarna 'Canaanite' as largely an undifferentiated collection of dialects; some scholars even refuse to recognise a division between 'Canaanite' and Aramaic till the first millennium.[1] The relationship between the members of this widely diffused family, each with its own distinctive features, the result of factors such as isolation, foreign influences, culture 'drift', etc., is much the same as that within the Germanic group of languages, German, Norse, Danish, Swedish, etc., or the Slavonic group, Lithuanian, Russian, Polish, Serbian, etc.

Classical Hebrew, by definition, is the language of the Old Testament scriptures. This is a comparatively narrow range of literature, dealing with a restricted area of topics, so that many other fields are totally neglected. The result is that Hebrew lexicography to a large extent reflects the interests of the redactors of the classical literature rather than the full range of the literary language, much less the spoken language of the classical period. The situation has to some extent been remedied by modern discoveries. Evidence for the proto-Hebrew of the Canaanites has been supplied by place-names and the Canaanite glosses on the Tell-el-Amarna letters (fifteenth to fourteenth centuries B.C.). (These glosses are composed in a form of Akkadian but contain many 'Canaanite' expressions.) The Ras Shamra epics (fourteenth to thirteenth centuries B.C.), written in Ugaritic, are particularly important no less for their literary style and poetic structure than for their language. The Lachish letters of the sixth century B.C., inscriptions, like the Gezer Calendar, the Siloam inscriptions, etc., have all added substantially to our knowledge of the ancient Hebrew language. This has also been extended forwards, so to speak, as well as backwards, by the extensive Hebrew discoveries known as the Dead Sea Scrolls. Rabbinical and Mishnaic Hebrew build on the classical language and prepare the way for modern spoken Hebrew.

Structurally, Hebrew and Aramaic are relatively simple and uncomplicated languages—in word-stems, word-formation, syntax and grammar. Semitic word-stems are generally triliteral, i.e. they consist of three consonants only, though many of these were originally biconsonantal stems, the third letter having been added later as a 'modi-

---

[1] See further, below, p. 5.

fier': e.g. out of the biliteral root h m, two triliteral roots are formed, n h m and r h m, each representing different aspects of the basic idea of 'compassion'. There are very few words with four consonants, and compounds and polysyllabic words are virtually unknown in Semitic languages, except where borrowed from other languages. Differences of meaning are in the main conveyed by ringing certain changes in the consonantal stem, by gemination or the doubling of a letter, by the use of preformatives, etc.; or again, semantic differences are conveyed in pronunciation by the vocalisation of the consonantal stem. Originally in Hebrew the vowels were not represented in writing: later certain weak consonants, e.g. h, y, were used to represent vowels, and a complicated system of vowel points was introduced, placed in some cases above but usually below the consonants. Syntax and grammar are fundamentally of a simple character; parataxis predominates over hypotaxis in the structure of the sentence. The verb and its modifications, especially in its so-called 'tense' forms, plays a very important rôle. The 'tenses', Perfect, Imperfect, express kinds or modes of actions, especially as incomplete and continuous (Imperfect) or as finished and complete or as describing a state or condition (Perfect). In the noun, where semantic differences are also conveyed by gemination, preformatives, etc., there are two genders, masculine and feminine, the former without any special ending, the latter often ending in the morpheme t or ah.

With the help of Akkadian cuneiform inscriptions the existence of Aramaic-speaking tribes in the Mesopotamian basin can now be traced to the beginnings of the first millennium B.C.; records of their language in its earliest discoverable form—the 'Old Aramaic'—are extant in inscriptions from Damascus, Hamath, Arpad, Šam'al and Assyria, dating from the tenth to the eighth century B.C. The 'Old Aramaic', in its spoken types, probably consisted mainly of a number of tribal dialects, with close affinities, in an earlier period, with 'Canaanite' dialects.[1] Its successor was the classical or so-called Imperial Aramaic (*Reichsaramäisch*) of the Achaemenid chancelleries, the official language

---

[1] Cf. above, p. 1. Two of the Šam'al inscriptions contain a specially important type of Aramaic known as Yaudic (from the name of the state of Šam'al, Ya'udi). Dr Gibson (in a letter) writes that, from his work on these and other Old Aramaic inscriptions, he finds that 'it is very difficult to differentiate scientifically' between 'Aramaic' and 'Canaanite': there are links between 'Aramaic' and Moabite, between Hebrew and Yaudic, and 'Yaudic' is not easily classified as either 'Aramaic' or 'Canaanite'.

of the Persian Empire and the international medium of cultural and commercial intercourse from the Euphrates to the Nile, even in countries possessing no indigenous Semitic culture. The Imperial Aramaic flourished from the seventh century till the close of the Persian period, into the third and possibly even the second century B.C. Most of our information about the official language comes from papyri discovered at Elephantine in the Upper Nile, documents consisting of letters and official correspondence with the central government in Persia.[1] This Imperial Aramaic served also as a literary language in this period: the story of the Persian sage Ahikar, one of the most popular tales of oriental antiquity, was composed in Aramaic in the fifth century B.C. The Aramaic portions of Daniel and Ezra—biblical Aramaic—belong to the literary Aramaic of the classical period, though there are already indications in biblical Aramaic, in particular in orthography, of features which belong to, or more correctly anticipate, later forms of Jewish Aramaic. The so-called Aramaic *Apocryphon*, an early pre-Christian Jewish midrash, along with other fragments in Aramaic from Qumrân (e.g. substantial portions, in several recensions, of the Aramaic Enoch), also belong to this literary Aramaic of the classical period, though the Jews probably continued to write this form of Aramaic until early in the Christian period. Nabataean and Palmyrene are forms of West Aramaic found in inscriptions and papyri from Petra, Palmyra and elsewhere (Nabataean papyri have been found at Qumrân). Both these states (Petra and Palmyra) flourished between the first and the third centuries B.C.: the population was ethnically Arab. Palmyrene inscriptions are said to have been found in England.[2] Some scholars are inclined to class this 'later' West Aramaic with the Old Aramaic.

Towards the beginning of the Christian era, some think earlier, others later, Aramaic split into two main branches or dialects, West and East Aramaic, the latter an amalgam of older eastern dialects. The former was a more direct continuation of the Imperial Aramaic and the forerunner of the later Aramaic of the post-Christian Jewish rabbis, of the Talmud (Palestinian), some Midrashim and the Targums. Jewish Palestinian Aramaic was spoken and written in Palestine in the time of Christ and during the first centuries of the Christian era; Dalman

[1] Other sources, in addition to inscriptions, are Assyrian and Babylonian texts, Pahlavi (Persian), Egyptian ostraca, etc.

[2] Cf. Moscati, *Introduction to the Comparative Grammar*, p. 11.

detected within it two distinct dialects, a Galilaean (cf. Matt. 26: 73) and a Judaean. The Babylonian Talmud is composed in a Jewish form of the East Aramaic. East Aramaic was to provide the Christian Church with one of its main and distinctive media of literary expression, namely Syriac. Aramaic speech still survives in debased forms in the neighbourhood of Damascus, and in villages around Lake Urmiah and Mosul. A special form of Syriac was used mainly for liturgical purposes by Christian communities in Palestine; this 'Palestinian' Syriac was nearer the Jewish Aramaic of the synagogue and the Aramaic Targums or paraphrases of scripture than was classical Syriac. The liturgies and Targum to the Pentateuch of the Samaritans are composed in a similar form of Aramaic (not earlier than the fourth century A.D.).

The New Testament is written in a form of biblical Greek, the language of the Greek Old Testament and related writings, which is itself a deposit of the widely diffused hellenistic language, usually designated the Koine, i.e. the general (lit. common) form of the Greek language in the post-classical or hellenistic era. Strictly speaking the term Koine applied chiefly to spoken Greek, but it has come to be widely used to describe the literary Greek of this period, which is itself largely an amalgam of the spoken Koine and the old literary language.[1] The discovery in Egypt of masses of Greek papyri in the early decades of this century, written mainly in the unliterary spoken Koine, led at the time to the claim that the main feature of New Testament Greek was that it was the ordinary vernacular Greek of the period. No one nowadays is disposed to deny the presence of such elements in the New Testament or that the Greek papyri have made an important contribution to New Testament linguistic studies. Even before the discovery of the papyri the view that the New Testament contained a colloquial or vernacular type of language was gaining ground; in Mark, it was claimed, spoken Greek, even Greek as spoken by the lower classes, had made its entry into literature.[2] On the other hand, it is equally impossible to ignore the markedly Semitic cast and colouring of the style and language of the Septuagint or of other types of Jewish Greek, vernacular or literary, or the fact of translation of Semitic, Hebrew or Aramaic sources. Mr E. K. Simpson's *Words Worth Weighing in the*

---

[1] Cf. A. Thumb, 'Hellenistic and Biblical Greek', *Dictionary of the Apostolic Church*, I (Edinburgh, 1915).

[2] So J. Wellhausen, *Einleitung in die drei ersten Evangelien* (Berlin, 1905), p. 9.

Greek New Testament[1] has shown how many important words there are on which the papyri shed no light at all, but which receive their true explanations in the literary hellenistic usage of the period; and the close attention now being paid to biblical semantics no less clearly underlines the fundamentally Semitic ways of thought, impressed on language and idiom, which have passed into the New Testament.

Among the more important contributions which have been made to the discussion of this problem in recent years are those of Nigel Turner,[2] H. S. Gehman[3] and K. Beyer.[4] Dr Turner, who carried on to its completion the *Syntax* volume of Moulton's famous *Grammar* (volume III), took a different view of the character of New Testament Greek from that of his distinguished predecessor in volume I: Dr Turner claims that biblical Greek, as a whole, 'is a unique language with a unity and character of its own' (p. 4), and that this unique quality was imparted to it by Semitic influences, first on the translators of the Septuagint, and then on the New Testament writers whose style was moulded by the Septuagint, though they themselves may have been unacquainted with Semitic speech or idiom. Dr Turner also subscribes to the theory of the existence of a literary and unliterary or spoken type of Jewish Greek influencing the New Testament; and he also fully allows for Semitic, more specifically Aramaic, influence, through the use by the New Testament writers, in particular in the gospels, of Aramaic sources. Dr Gehman sought to advance the hypothesis of Jewish Greek: he argued that there existed, in certain places and for certain periods, a vernacular 'Jews' Greek': in bilingual areas the masses did not keep both languages separate; Greek-speaking Jews spoke, and wrote, Greek with a pronounced 'Semitic cast'.

Dr Klaus Beyer's *Satzlehre* is a first part only of his projected Semitic syntax of the New Testament: in this volume the author is concerned exclusively with the structure of the New Testament

---

[1] Tyndale Lecture (London, 1946).

[2] J. H. Moulton, *A Grammar of New Testament Greek*, III, *Syntax*, by Nigel Turner (Edinburgh, 1963), especially Introduction, pp. xi ff. Dr Turner's views are set out more fully in his article on 'The Language of the New Testament' in the new *Peake's Commentary* (London, 1962), pp. 659 ff. Cf. also 'The Unique Character of Biblical Greek', *VT*, v (1955), 208 ff.

[3] *VT*, I (1950), 90; IV (1954), 347. Cf. also Peter Katz, 'Zur Übersetzungstechnik der Septuaginta' in *Welt des Orients*, II (1956), 272 ff.

[4] *Semitische Syntax im Neuen Testament*, I, *Satzlehre*, Teil I (Göttingen, 1961).

sentence which he shows has a predominantly Semitic character in the Synoptic Gospels, in the Johannine writings and in the Epistle of James.

Two illustrations which may be given from the vocabulary of the New Testament are the words ὑπόστασις and παρουσία, both of which, it has been claimed, receive their correct explanation from the usage of the papyri, the first, especially in its use at Heb. 11: 1 in the meaning 'title-deeds', and the second in the sense of a royal 'coming' or 'presence'.[1] According to Moulton–Milligan (*Vocabulary*, p. 660), while the varied uses of ὑπόστασις in the papyri are somewhat perplexing, in all cases there is the same central idea of something that underlies visible conditions and guarantees a future possession; they draw attention to one instance where ὑπόστασις stands for the whole body of documents bearing on the ownership of a person's property, deposited in the archives, and forming the evidence of ownership. Consequently at Heb. 11: 1 they suggest the translation: 'Faith is the title-deed of things hoped for...' Both words have been undeniably illumined by the usage in the papyri, but the usage in Jewish and biblical Greek is no less important. In biblical Greek ὑπόστασις is used as the equivalent of the Hebrew *tōḥeleṯ* in the sense of 'hope' with the emphasis on an attitude of patient and confident waiting for something, a state of confident expectation; and this may well be the true sense of Heb. 11: 1. Josephus employs παρουσία in defining a diaphanous mist which surrounded the Tabernacle (probably the Shekhinah is in his mind) as the παρουσία of God, i.e. the *presence* of God in this theophany.[2] This is even closer to New Testament usage than the use in the papyri.

A distinctive Semitic type of syntax is the *Zustandsatz* or circumstantial clause,[3] a clause introduced by a noun or pronoun, describing circumstances attendant on but subordinate to the action of the main verb: the idiomatic equivalent in Greek is the genitive absolute construction or a temporal or other subordinate clause. A typical example from the Greek Bible will be found at 2 Sam. 20: 8, rendered by the RSV as 'When they were at the great stone which is in Gibeon, Amasa came to meet them'. The Hebrew (and its literal Greek translation) has simply 'and they (καὶ αὐτοί) were at the great stone which is in

---

[1] See especially A. Deissmann, *Light from the Ancient East* (London, 1910), pp. 372 ff.

[2] *Ant.* III, 203.   [3] A. Deissmann, *Semitische Syntax*, pp. 115 ff.

9

Gibeon...'. Dr Beyer has drawn attention to the frequency of this construction in Luke,[1] as I had also done,[2] though ascribing it to Aramaic influence: it may be due, however, in Luke, to the influence of the Septuagint.[3]

It is only very rarely possible to determine in relation to a Greek Semitism whether it is the result of Hebrew or Aramaic influence; whether we are dealing with Septuagint influence or source or translation phenomena. For the sayings and teaching of Jesus, however, there is little doubt that the bulk of Semitisms are translation phenomena, and have arisen in the process of translating and paraphrasing the *verba ipsissima* of Jesus. We can be sure of this, not only on the *a priori* ground that Jesus spoke Aramaic, but from those few distinctive Aramaisms which are to be detected in the translation Greek of the gospels. It can be taken as certain that an Aramaic tradition (oral or written) lies behind the sayings of Jesus (in the Fourth Gospel as well as in the Synoptics), and possibly in the tradition of the words of the Baptist, and the speeches in Acts.[4]

There is one New Testament book, Revelation, whose crude Greek is particularly stained by 'Semitisms'. Like Mark's Gospel, Revelation has been explained as 'spoken Koine' Greek, the colloquial speech of the market-place: if it is, then those who spoke and wrote it were manifestly Jews. No New Testament book has a better claim to be written in 'Jews' Greek' than Revelation. In spite of its crudities, however, it probably belongs to the 'literary' rather than to the spoken Jewish Greek of its period. Apart altogether from the problem of sources—and the writer or final editor is plainly drawing on prior tradition, Jewish or Jewish–Christian, written or oral—the book is composed in the same kind of Greek as the Jewish–Greek apocalypses, such as the Greek Enoch or the Testaments of the Twelve Patriarchs.[5]

---

[1] *Ibid.*

[2] *An Aramaic Approach to the Gospels and Acts* (Oxford, 3rd ed. 1967), p. 83.

[3] For a possible example of this clause as an explanation of the notorious *crux interpretum* at Heb. 11: 11, see my article on 'The Semitic Element in the New Testament', *ET*, LXXVII, no. 1 (Oct. 1965), 20 ff. and in *Apophoreta, Festschrift Ernst Haenchen* (Berlin, 1964), pp. 39 ff., and *An Aramaic Approach*, 3rd ed., pp. 83 ff.

[4] See my *An Aramaic Approach*, 3rd ed. The investigation of Semitic sources in Acts has been carried an important step further by Dr Max Wilcox in his book *The Semitisms of Acts* (Oxford, 1965).

[5] Cf. N. Turner, 'The Testament of Abraham: Problems in Biblical Greek', *NTS*, 1 (1955), 222 ff.

We do not know when the Greek translations or redactions of these very popular writings were made, and in their final form they underwent severe Christian re-editing, but it seems highly improbable that the only literary activity of Greek-speaking Judaism prior to the Christian era was confined to the Septuagint. Revelation almost certainly belongs to this category of Jewish–Greek 'literary' compositions, probably typical of its kind in that it incorporates or re-edits previous traditions, Hebrew or Aramaic.

It is impossible to comprehend or characterise within a single formula the complex nature of the language of the New Testament. A substantial portion of the gospels, certainly the 'sayings-tradition', has been transmitted in translation-Greek, but more often in versions more literary than literal;[1] the influence of the Greek Bible has been profound, especially in Luke, but also throughout the epistles, in Hebraic concepts like 'justification', 'propitiation', etc.; it has also left its mark on New Testament style and idiom, the type of hellenistic Greek employed by the authors of the New Testament scriptures. Some portions of these are written in the ordinary vernacular Greek of the period. But even this kind of Greek was probably 'Jews' Greek'; and this applies especially to the Greek of Revelation, though the latter may have been of the 'literary' variety of Jewish Greek. Since the latter was almost exclusively concerned with 'sacred' or biblical themes, we are led to look rather to the language of the Greek-speaking synagogue, possibly itself a spoken 'Koine' Greek, as the *matrix* of New Testament Greek. And this language, like the Hebrew of the Old Testament which moulded it, was a language apart from the beginning; biblical Greek is a peculiar language, the language of a peculiar people.[2]

2. THE BIBLICAL SCRIPTS

This section is subdivided into four: (1) Early Hebrew, (2) Square Hebrew, (3) Greek and (4) Latin, and three minor sections: (5) Syriac, (6) Coptic, (7) Ethiopic.

[1] Cf. *An Aramaic Approach*, 3rd ed., pp. 274 ff.

[2] N. Turner, *Grammar*, III, p. 9: '...the strongly Semitic character of Biblical Greek, and therefore its remarkable unity within itself, do seem to me to have contemporary significance at a time when many are finding their way back to the Bible as a living book and perhaps are pondering afresh the old question of a "Holy Ghost Language".'

EARLY HEBREW

This term is employed in distinction from that of 'Square Hebrew' (see pp. 16 f.) which was the parent of the modern Hebrew alphabet. The Early Hebrew alphabet is the original script of nearly the whole of the Old Testament. It was the script of the Hebrew kings and prophets, and was employed by the ancient Hebrews in the pre-exilic period, that is, in the first half of the first millennium B.C., but its use in a limited measure continued into the fifth to the third centuries B.C., and lingered on till much later times. The writing on Jewish coins and the Samaritan alphabet were direct derivatives of the Early Hebrew script.

Accurate knowledge of the Early Hebrew alphabet is an achievement of the last decades. Winckler, Naville, Benzinger, Jeremias, Grimme, and other eminent scholars of the last hundred years argued that cuneiform was the official mode of writing of the ancient Hebrews up to the time of Hezekiah (c. 700 B.C.). Some parts of the Bible were supposed to have been written in cuneiform characters on clay tablets, and certain biblical terms have been interpreted accordingly. Some scholars even denied that alphabetic writing was practised in Palestine before the Persian period. Cowley, for instance, suggested that it was Ezra who, with the assistance of his colleagues, translated the cuneiform documents into Hebrew, and wrote the result down in simple Aramaic characters.

Jewish savants, on the other hand, suggested that the Square Hebrew alphabet was employed unchanged from the time of Moses. The Jewish Italian scholar Azariah de' Rossi was the first to assert—on the basis of several statements in the Talmudic literature—that the Torah was originally written in the Old Hebrew script, the *keṯāḇ 'iḇrī*.

It has to be emphasised that until relatively recent times epigraphical remains of ancient Israel were very scarce. Up to the present no Israelite stela of victory has been unearthed, similar to those of the Egyptians or Babylonians or Assyrians or even of the Moabites or Aramaeans. David, Solomon, Jeroboam, Hezekiah, Isaiah, Jeremiah, and all the other kings and prophets of Israel or Judah are known to us primarily from the biblical record. There can be no doubt, however, that many Early Hebrew documents existed, but the vast majority, probably written on leather or papyrus, could not be expected to have survived until our time.

The biblical data about writing fit in with the general picture: while, for instance, in the *Iliad* writing is referred to only once, and in the *Odyssey* not even once, in the Bible we find as many as 429 references to writing or written documents.

The Early Hebrew and the Phoenician alphabets were two branches from the Canaanite stem, which was a continuation of the North-Semitic. This was the original alphabet, the prototype of the numerous alphabets still in use and of those which have fallen out of use in the long history of the alphabet. The scripts of the Moabites, the Ammonites, and the Edomites were directly connected with the Early Hebrew alphabet.

During the past sixty years there has been a considerable amount of research on Early Hebrew inscriptions. In his outstanding *Text-book of North-Semitic Inscriptions*,[1] G. A. Cooke included only one Early Hebrew inscription and three seals. Thirty-one years later, about 300 Early Hebrew inscriptions, ostraca, seals, jar-handle-stamps, weights, and so on, were published by the present writer (*Le iscrizioni antico-ebraiche palestinesi*).[2] In the last thirty years many more Early Hebrew written documents have been discovered and published, and indeed, the Early Hebrew alphabet has become familiar to the ordinary reader.

Through the results of excavation and research, the development of the Early Hebrew alphabet can now be traced for more than a thousand years. We may assume that about 1000 B.C., after the united kingdom had been established and its centralised administration organised by King David with a staff of secretaries (see, for instance, 2 Sam. 8: 17 and 20: 25), the Early Hebrew alphabet had begun its autonomous development.

The Gezer Calendar, a small soft-stone tablet, discovered in 1908 at Gezer, contains a list of eight months with their agricultural operations; it is generally assigned to *c.* 1000 B.C., that is, to the period of Saul or David. According to some scholars, it was the work of a peasant; according to others it was a schoolboy's exercise tablet. Among casual scribblings discovered in 1938 on the palace steps at Lachish were the first five letters of the Early Hebrew alphabet; this places the earliest archaeological evidence for the letter-order of the Hebrew alphabet and of its systematic teaching in the ninth–eighth centuries B.C.

---

[1] (Oxford, 1903). [2] (Florence, 1934).

In the development of the Early Hebrew alphabet (in contrast to, say, forty years ago, when even the term 'Early Hebrew' alphabet was unknown), it is now possible to distinguish at least five styles.

(a) *Monumental or Lapidary*

The Siloam tunnel inscription, discovered by chance in June 1880 by some schoolboys and now preserved in the Museum of Antiquities at Istanbul, is the main monumental inscription of ancient Israel, though it contains only six lines. It records the labour of those who dug the tunnel, which is probably that described in the Bible (2 Kings 20: 20; 2 Chron. 32: 3 f., 30; 33: 14) as having been constructed by King Hezekiah. Hence, it is generally assumed that the Siloam inscription was cut about 700 B.C.

Several other inscriptions, mainly short ones, were discovered in the Arab village of Silwan (not far from the Siloam tunnel), at Hazor (Upper Galilee), and at other sites. The lapidary style was also suitable for smaller objects, such as jar-handle-stamps (about 600 'Royal' and private impressions have been found), inscribed weights (about 100), and personal seals, of which about 150 are known.

(b) *Cursive or Current Style*

In this style, the chief consideration is speed and utility. The letters naturally assume a less precise form, strokes become slurred, angles become more and more curved. The Samaria ostraca, of the ninth or eighth century B.C., are the earliest documents written in Early Hebrew current or running hand. About eighty of them were discovered in 1910 at Sebastîye, ancient Samaria.

The cursive style reaches its climax in the Lachish ostraca (known as the Lachish Letters) at the beginning of the sixth century B.C. The twenty-one documents, found in 1935–8, are probably a very small remnant of a large correspondence and of a cache of other written documents. Indeed, although only a small part of Lachish has been excavated, hundreds of other jar fragments were found there, but owing to their burnt and decayed condition it is impossible to say whether they had been inscribed. The script of the Lachish ostraca is a fluent cursive, and appears to have been the work of scribes well accustomed to such writing. This script makes us realise, as indeed one scholar has pointed out, that the ancient Israelites could write quickly and boldly in an artistic flowing hand, with the loving penmanship of those who enjoy writing.

Several other ostraca—belonging to the eighth–sixth centuries B.C.—have come to light at Ophel (East Jerusalem), at Samaria, at Tell Qasile (north of Tel Aviv), at Hazor, and at many other sites.

(c) *Literary or Book-hand*

Several biblical fragments (from Leviticus and Deuteronomy), found among the Dead Sea Scrolls, are written in the Early Hebrew script, in a style which probably represents a beautiful Early Hebrew literary hand, the first of its kind ever discovered. The fragments probably belong to the fourth or third century B.C. The words are separated by dots or short strokes (as in the Siloam inscription, the Samaria and Lachish ostraca, and so on). The letters are mainly short, squat and wide. It is interesting to note that in some other Dead Sea Scrolls, written in the Square Hebrew character, the *Tetragrammaton* or the word *'el* (= God) are written in the Early Hebrew character. Indeed, even some early Greek copies of the Bible have preserved the *Tetragrammaton* in the Early Hebrew script, though in a very stylised form.

(d) *Jewish Coin-Script*

A few extant Jewish coins of the fifth–fourth centuries B.C. contain the word *Yᵉhûd*, 'Judaea', probably indicating, as was suggested by Sukenik, the small autonomous state set up under Persian sovereignty. The script of these coins may be regarded as transitional between the Early Hebrew and the Jewish coin-script (of the Maccabaean and Bar-Kochba's war periods, *c.* 135 B.C.–A.D. 132–5), suggesting that the Maccabaean and Bar-Kochba coin-script was a direct derivative of the Early Hebrew, and not an artificial revival, as has been suggested by several scholars.

(e) *Samaritan Script*

This is the only direct descendant of the Early Hebrew alphabet which is still in use today. It is an attractive, neat and symmetrical form of writing, employed for purely liturgical purposes by the few hundred Samaritans living at Shechem or Nablus (in Jordan) and Holon (near Tel Aviv), who represent all that remains of a once-flourishing sect.

SQUARE HEBREW

This is the ancestor of the modern Hebrew alphabet. There can be little doubt that the Square Hebrew alphabet derives from the Aramaic script. It is generally, but not quite correctly, believed that the Early Hebrew alphabet was completely superseded by the Aramaic during the Babylonian exile. At any rate, a distinctive Palestinian Jewish type of script, which we can definitely regard as the Square Hebrew script, can now be traced from the third or the second century B.C.

A focus of world interest from 1947 onwards has been the sensational discovery of the Dead Sea Scrolls and many other written documents more or less contemporary with them. They are mainly written in the Square Hebrew character. Discussion of their date, their theological, biblical and philological significance, continues unabated and there is now an extensive literature on the various problems. From the point of view of the script, however, the main contribution is the fact, many times emphasised by the present writer, that there were many written documents in ancient Israel which have not come down to us.

Before the discovery of the Dead Sea Scrolls, several Square Hebrew inscriptions were known, belonging mainly to the first century B.C. and the succeeding centuries. They were found in Palestine, Syria, North Africa and Italy. Some are in monumental or lapidary style, some in a semi-cursive style (for instance, the *graffiti* on ossuaries), while *dipinti*, or painted inscriptions, are in a cursive style. The earliest literary documents were: the Nash Papyrus (preserved in Cambridge University Library) of the second or first century B.C.; some fragments at the Bodleian Library at Oxford, of the third–fifth centuries A.D.; the Dura Europos roll-fragment of *c*. A.D. 245, and so on. The earliest extant datable Hebrew biblical manuscripts, apart from the Dead Sea Scrolls, belong to the ninth and tenth centuries A.D. Some hundred thousand fragments of Hebrew biblical and non-biblical manuscripts come from the famous Cairo *geniẓah*.

The (Square) Hebrew alphabet became standardised just before the Christian era and took the form which, with insignificant changes, we have now. The minute rules laid down by the Talmud as to calligraphy and consonantal orthography made further *essential* developments of the formal Hebrew character impossible. Thus, the standardised script of the Torah scrolls is in fact, in all its essentials, the same script which was used two thousand years ago.

So far as the details in the shapes of the letters are concerned, three types of writing can be traced in the two thousand years of the history of the Hebrew alphabet. (*a*) The Square or formal script, which gradually developed into the neat, well-proportioned printing-type of modern Hebrew; (*b*) the cursive literary or bookhands, also known as

	GEZER	MONUMENTAL	CURSIVE	BOOK-HAND	COIN-SCRIPT	SAMARITAN	MODERN HEBREW	*Phonetic value*
1							א	ʾ
2							ב	b
3							ג	g
4							ד	d
5							ה	ḥ
6							ו	w
7							ז	z
8							ח	ḥ
9							ט	ṭ
10							י	y
11							כ	k
12							ל	l
13							מ	m
14							נ	n
15							ס	s
16							ע	ʿ
17							פ	p
18							צ	ṣ
19							ק	q
20							ר	r
21							ש	sh
22							ת	t

A. Early Hebrew styles of writing.

rabbinic styles or Rashi-script, which were the hands employed by the medieval Jewish savants in Spain, Italy, France, Germany, the Levant, and so on; and (*c*) the current hands, of which the Polish–Yiddish form, with some insignificant changes, became the current Hebrew hand of today.

The Hebrew alphabet consists of the ancient twenty-two Semitic letters, which are all consonants, though four of them (ʾ*ālep̱*, *hē̱*, *waw* and *yō̱d̠*) are also used to represent long vowels, particularly at the end of a word. The absence of vowel-letters was not very strongly felt in Hebrew any more than it was in the other Semitic languages. (Indeed, it must be emphasised that the Semitic languages are mainly based on consonantal roots.) On the other hand, as Hebrew speech passed out of daily use, and familiarity with biblical Hebrew steadily declined, it became necessary to introduce some form of vocalic distinction so that the Torah could be read and explained correctly.

Three main vowel systems are known: the 'Babylonian', the 'Palestinian', and the 'Tiberiadic' or 'Tiberian'. The last finally gained general acceptance, while the others gradually fell into oblivion. The Tiberian vocalisation system, which consists of dots and little dashes, has seven notation marks, which denote long and short vowels, as well as semi-vowels; other marks denote the word-tone and secondary stresses.[1]

THE GREEK ALPHABET

Out of the troubled darkness which shrouded the transition from the Mycenaean civilisation of the Late Bronze Age, in the twelfth century B.C., to the Early Greek primitive geometric art of the Iron Age, in the tenth–ninth century B.C., there came the remarkable invention of the Greek alphabet, the earliest fully developed alphabetic system of writing, containing both consonants and vowels. The North-Semitic origin of the Greek alphabet is accepted by all serious scholars. It is proved by these facts: (1) the shapes of nearly all the early Greek letters and of the derivative Etruscan clearly recall their Semitic origin; (2) the phonetic value of the majority of the early Greek letters was the same as that of the Semitic; (3) the order of the Greek letters corresponds, with a few understandable exceptions, to the order of the Semitic letters; (4) the direction of writing in the early Greek script

---

[1] On the vocalisation, cf. also below, pp. 26, 29, 160.

and in the derivative Etruscan writing was from right to left as in the Semitic; and (5) the Greek letter-names are meaningless in Greek, while their Semitic equivalents are generally words in Semitic languages.

Much more difficult is the chronological problem. There are many conflicting opinions concerning the date of borrowing of the Greek alphabet: they range between the fourteenth and the seventh centuries B.C. Various inferences point to about 1000 B.C. Like the Semitic scripts, the earliest Greek was written from right to left, a style which was later superseded by the *boustrophedon* (= alternate lines from right to left and left to right). After *c.* 500 B.C. Greek writing regularly proceeded from left to right, the lines running from top to bottom.

The Greek alphabet occupies in many ways a unique place in the history of writing. Although the Greeks did not invent the alphabet, they improved it to such a degree that for three thousand years it has furnished the most convenient vehicles of communication and expression for the thoughts of many peoples, creeds and tongues. They also gave to the alphabet symmetry and art.

There were several local Greek alphabets, but they gradually moved in the direction of uniformity. In 403 B.C. the Ionic alphabet of Miletus was officially adopted at Athens, and in the following half-century this action was followed by the other mainland states as well. By the middle of the fourth century B.C. almost all the local alphabets had been replaced by the Ionic, which thus became the established, classical Greek script of twenty-four letters.

After this time the development of the Greek alphabet was almost wholly external, in the direction of greater utility, convenience, and above all beauty. The classical style was retained as a monumental or lapidary script. From it there sprang: (1) the Greek uncial script— which is the writing of the beautiful biblical codices and of many codices of classical Greek literature; (2) the Greek cursive hands which have developed into the modern Greek minuscule; and (3) the Greek minuscule, consciously adapted as a bookhand about A.D. 800, after which date the Greek uncial characters quickly went out of use for books.

The numerous Greek inscriptions (decrees, annals, codes of laws, votive inscriptions, and so on) are of paramount importance for history; they form the subject of Greek epigraphy. The many thousands of Greek codices (ancient and medieval) are the subject of Greek palaeography. Through its direct and indirect descendants in western Europe (the Etruscan and the Latin alphabets) and in eastern Europe (the Cyrillic alphabet), the Greek alphabet has become the progenitor of all the European alphabets, which indeed have spread all over the world.

The capitals of modern Greek handwriting are partly borrowed from Latin handwriting.

The opinion once commonly held, even by leading scholars, was that the Latin alphabet was derived directly from the Greek in the form used by the Greek colonists in Italy. Recently, however, it has been shown that, on the whole, this theory is improbable and that the Etruscan alphabet was the link between the Greek and the Latin. Most of the Latin names of the letters, which have descended into English, as into the majority of modern alphabets, were also taken over from the Etruscans.

The oldest Latin record extant is the Praeneste fibula, a gold brooch, dating probably from the seventh century B.C.; it is still written from right to left, and the sound *f* is expressed by the letters *wh*. Another early inscription, known as that of Duenos, is on a vase found in Rome near the Quirinal, and seems to belong to the sixth century B.C. The direction of writing is also from right to left. Much more important is a sixth-century B.C. inscription from the Roman Forum, which preserves the oldest text written in Latin. It contains the word *recei* (or *regei*, connected with *rex* (?)) which apparently links it with the monarchic period of Rome. The inscription is written vertically on the four faces of a *cippus*, in *boustrophedon* style.

It is a somewhat curious fact that the Latin or Roman alphabet, which has had such tremendous importance in the history of civilisation, is very poorly attested during the first five or six centuries of its existence. It is only from the first century B.C. onwards that Latin inscriptions, too numerous to count, are found all over the areas of Roman influence.

Of the twenty-six Graeco-Etruscan letters the Romans adopted only twenty-one. The early Latin alphabet contained the letter C for the sounds of *g* and *k*, the Greek *zeta* in its original place (that is, as the seventh letter of the alphabet), the letter I as a vowel and consonant, the letter V as vowel *u* and consonant *v*, and the letter X as the last letter of the alphabet. At a later stage, the *zeta* was dropped (because there is no such sound in Latin) and was replaced by a new letter, G (for the sound *g*). In the first century B.C., after the conquest of Greece, the symbols Y and Z, adopted for the transliteration of Greek sounds, were placed at the end of the alphabet.

The subsequent history of the Latin alphabet consisted essentially in the external transformation of the single letters, especially in the cursive or current styles of writing. (In the Middle Ages the signs U/V were differentiated and W was added; I/J were also differentiated.) The external transformation of the Latin letters was due mainly to two considerations: the nature of the writing material employed and the desirability of speed.

Originally there was only one style, the monumental or lapidary. The chief considerations were permanence, beauty, proportion, evenness. The main material was stone; the main tool, the chisel. There were no 'minuscules'. The main materials employed for cursive scripts were waxen tablets, papyrus and parchment; the main tools, the stylus, the brush, the reed pen and the quill; the chief considerations, speed and utility. Indeed, the transformation of the monumental writing into the modern script is due entirely to the technical qualities of the tools, primarily the brush, the quill, and the pen, and to the materials of writing, primarily papyrus and parchment. It was the stylus, the brush, the quill, and the pen, which eliminated the angular forms; it was wax, papyrus and parchment, which made the curves possible.

There were in Imperial Rome three main varieties of the monumental or lapidary script: (1) the lapidary capitals; (2) the elegant book-capitals; (3) the rustic capitals. At the same time there were several varieties of cursive or current scripts: (1) the majuscule cursive; (2) the minuscule cursive; (3) the semi-cursive minuscule. Between the monumental and the cursive scripts there was a whole series of varieties: (1) the lapidary and the literary semi-cursive script; (2) the early semi-uncial script, being a mixture of capitals, cursive letters, and uncials; (3) a derivation of this script, the beautiful uncial script which appeared in the third century A.D., and in the fourth–eighth centuries was the main Latin bookhand. The semi-uncial script, easier than the uncials, was another offshoot of the early semi-uncials, and was frequently employed as a bookhand in the fifth–ninth centuries.

In the Middle Ages several 'national' hands or rather 'national' styles of the Latin cursive minuscule assumed distinctive features, and there thus developed, on the European continent and in the British Isles, the five main hands, known as Italian or Roman cursive, Merovingian (in France), Visigothic (in Spain), Germanic, and Insular. Each of them gave rise to several varieties. The most beautiful and the most important of all these 'national' styles were the 'Insular' or Anglo-Irish hands. They did not originate, as the Continental hands did, from the cursive minuscule. Their origin, which was more complex, has not yet been definitely established. Apparently they developed from the semi-uncial bookhand of the early Christian missionaries to the British Isles.

There were two principal varieties of the Insular style: (*a*) The Irish hand, which was already in use during the sixth century, and which according to some scholars was introduced from Gaul by St Patrick himself. It continued to be employed throughout the Middle Ages and developed into the modern Irish script. (*b*) The Anglo-Saxon semi-uncial style which developed from the Irish hand in the seventh and eighth centuries, at the time when the Roman uncial script was still predominantly employed for the writing of manuscripts and codices. It was used for writing Latin until about 940 and for Anglo-Saxon until after the Norman conquest.

At the end of the eighth century, probably under Charlemagne or perhaps earlier, the beautiful, widely spaced and rounded letters known as the Caroline minuscule were formed in the Frankish Empire. The precise part which Charlemagne and Alcuin of York played in its creation is uncertain, but there is no doubt that the Anglo-Irish style influenced its invention to a considerable extent. In the ninth and tenth centuries the script became the principal bookhand of western Europe, and was responsible for the blending of majuscules and minuscules in modern European scripts. It was the official script of the Carolingian imperial government and (for a time) of the Chancery of the Holy Roman Empire, and was widely employed until the twelfth century. It developed into Frankish, Italian, German and English varieties; the most important of the latter was the Winchester School hand, a particularly clear and legible form.

In the course of the following centuries various bookhands, court-hands or charter-hands and other cursive scripts developed from the Caroline. The most characteristic of these descendants was the 'Black

NORTH SEMITIC				GREEK				ETRUS-CAN		LATIN			MODERN CAPS		
EARLY	EARLY HEB	MOAB	PHOEN	EARLY	EAST	WEST	CLASS	EARLY	CLASS	EARLY	MONUM	CLASS	BLACK LETTER	ITAL	ROMAN

B. Development of the alphabet.

Letter', known as 'Gothic' writing, employed in north-western Europe, including England, until the sixteenth century. In this literary or bookhand the letters gradually assumed angular shapes, due to the pen being held so as to make a slanting stroke. German printers took over the 'Black Letter' hand as their principal typeface; as a result, it continued to be used in Germany as the 'national hand' after the sixteenth century and indeed until quite recent times.

In Italy both the 'Black Letter' and the round hand were used, and during the fifteenth century a new cursive minuscule, the round, neat, humanistic or Renaissance style, was introduced in Florence and employed for literary productions, while a secondary form was used to meet the needs of everyday life. This Renaissance style developed into two principal varieties: (1) the Venetian minuscule now known as *italics*, which is probably the most perfect and legible typeface ever invented; and (2) the Roman type of lettering, which was perfected in northern Italy, chiefly at Venice, and used at printing presses there from the end of the fifteenth century, spreading thence to Holland, England, Germany, France and Spain. From these two forms have developed all the typefaces ordinarily used by printers in the West today.

SYRIAC ALPHABETS

The terms 'Aramaeans' and 'Syrians', 'Aram' and 'Syria', are synonymous. The Hebrew *'aram* is rendered in the Septuagint by 'Syria'. However, the term 'Syriac' denotes the ancient Semitic language and literature of the 'Syriac' Christians, but is not synonymous with 'Christian inhabitants of Syria'; it roughly denotes those Christians who employed the Syrian descendant of Aramaic or were part of the Syriac Church under the influence of Syriac thought and hellenistic culture. Syriac was then the language and script of the extensive Syriac literature, which is a Christian literature in a very special sense, consisting entirely of original documents dealing exclusively with Christian subjects. The city of Antioch of Syria was one of the most important centres of early Christianity and it was there that 'the disciples were for the first time called Christians' (Acts 11: 26). But Antioch was also the centre of Greek culture.

Edessa (in Syriac Ur-Hai, now Urfa), in north-western Mesopotamia, was the first centre of Christianity in the Syriac-speaking world, and it became its principal focus. Indeed, it was the only centre of early Christian life where the language of the Christian community was other than Greek. Here the native Aramaic or Syriac dialect had already been used for some time as a literary language, even before Christianity gained influence in the country. Christianity was preached in Edessa already in the second century, and thence it spread to Persia. The Edessan dialect became the liturgical language of the Syriac Church, the literary language of the Christian Aramaeans of Syria and of the neighbouring countries, even of Persia. Syriac literature flourished mainly in the fourth to seventh centuries.

With the great schism in the seventh century between the Nestorians (or East Syrians) and the Monophysite Jacobites (or West Syrians) a separation took place, which implied a severance of tradition in the literature which emanated from the two sects. The Melkites, or 'Royalists', continued to carry on in union with Constantinople; whereas the Maronites, who were originally Monophysites or Mono-thelites, about 1102 became united to the Church of Rome. After the Arab conquest, the Nestorians and the Jacobites began a remarkable period of missionary expansion throughout Central Asia. For some time in the Middle Ages there were 150 Jacobite archbishoprics and bishoprics. The Nestorian faith became the official religion of the then flourishing Persian Church, and the city of Seleucia became the seat of their Patriarch, or *Catholicos*. In the seventh and eighth centuries, Nestorian missionaries preached Christianity in China, and in the eighth century a Nestorian bishop of Tibet was appointed. In 1265 there were twenty-five Asiatic provinces, with seventy bishoprics, in Persia, Mesopotamia, Khorasan, Turkistan, India and China.

At one time it looked as though the Mongol emperor Qubilay Khān (1216–94) might adopt Christianity; his brother Hūlāgū Khān, who in 1258 captured Baghdād and put an end to the Abbāsid caliphate, and was the first to assume the title of Il-Khān, had a Christian wife; he accorded special favours to the Nestorian patriarch and to his Church. Half a century later, the seventh Khān chose Islām as the state religion. Gradually all the activities of the Syrian Churches ceased and very little remained to tell the glorious tale, except the numerous sepulchral and other inscriptions, the illuminated Church service-books in various parts of central and eastern Asia, and particularly the paramount influence—directly or indirectly exerted by Nestorian culture and book production upon Central Asia and the Far East—upon the Mongolian and Manchurian alphabets.

The Syriac alphabet was the last important descendant of the Aramaic branch; it was an offshoot from a cursive Aramaic script, perhaps from the Palmyrene cursive in its early stage. It originated in the first half of the first century A.D. The Syriac alphabet consists of the twenty-two old Semitic letters, all of them having consonantal values. The order of the letters is the same as in Hebrew, but the names of some of them are slightly different (*'ālap* for *'ālep*, *gāmāl* for *gimel*, *dālāt* or *dālād* for *dālet*, *lāmād* for *lāmed*, *mīm* for *mēm*, *semkat* for *sāmek*, etc.). Moreover, in the later Jacobite or West Syrian alphabet some letter-names were changed again (into *'ōlap*, *gōmal*, *dōlat* or *dōlad*, *yūd*, *lōmad*, *nōn*, *rīš*, etc.). The letters *b, g, d, k, p, t* (cf. the modern Hebrew pronunciation) had a twofold pronunciation, one being hard (like English *b, g, d, k, p, t*), the other soft, aspirated or sibilated (*v, gh, dh* or *th* as in 'the', *kh* as the Scottish *ch*, *ph*, and *th* as in 'thank').

As in the Arabic alphabet, the majority of the Syriac letters have different forms in accordance with their positions in a word, whether at the beginning, middle or end, and whether they stand alone or are joined to the others, on the right or on the left, or on both sides. As in other Semitic languages, the consonants *'alāp*, *w* and *y* came to be employed to express vowel sounds. The insufficiency of such a representation of vowel sounds in the transcription of Greek words, especially for theological purposes, on the one hand, and (at a later period) the fact that in the seventh century Arabic began to replace Syriac as the language of daily life, were the main reasons for the introduction of fixed forms of vocalic distinction. On the whole, three main vowel systems developed: (1) the Nestorian, consisting of a combination of the consonants *w* and *y* and the dot (placed above it or below it) or two dots (placed above or, more often, below the consonants to be vocalised); (2) the Jacobite, consisting of small Greek letters, placed above or below the line; and (3) the late West Syrian system, consisting of a combination of the diacritical vowel marks and the small Greek letters. Direction of writing was mainly horizontal, from right to left.

There were several types of Syriac writing. The most important was *Estrangelo* or *Estrangela*, in two styles: (*a*) a very beautiful current hand, known as majuscule, and (*b*) the lapidary style. The split of the Syriac Church produced other varieties of the Syriac script—the Nestorian or East Syrian; the Western, known as *Serta* or *Serto* 'linear', which again developed into two varieties, the Jacobite and the Melkite. The Melkite script—more properly known as Christian Palestinian or Palestinian Syriac—has some characteristics which are not found in the other varieties. Two styles can again be distinguished: (1) a kind of Uncial Melkite, of lapidary, inscriptional type, and (2) the more cursive style of the late Palestinian Syriac manuscripts (eleventh to fourteenth centuries).

COPTIC SCRIPT

The term 'Copt' (from Arabic *qopt, qubt, qibt*, a corruption from Greek *Aigyptios-gyptios*) is employed nowadays to indicate the indigenous population of Egypt who, after the Arabic conquest of that country in A.D. 641, maintained their Christian monophysite faith, i.e. the 'Coptic religion'. They continued to use the 'Coptic' language (that is, the last stage of Egyptian) and script as their spoken and written language until the seventeenth century; later it remained as the liturgical language of the Coptic Church, when Arabic had been adopted as the speech of everyday life. In ancient times Coptic was essentially the non-cultivated speech of Egypt, for the Egyptian 'aristocracy' was already thoroughly hellenised. Coptic itself has a large admixture of Greek elements, especially in all that belongs to Christian doctrine, life and worship.

Coptic literature is almost exclusively religious; it consists for the most part of translations from Greek, and includes versions of the Bible (Old and New Testaments), apocrypha of the Old Testament and of the New Testament, the apocryphal legends of the apostles, the *Martyrdoms* and the *Lives* of the Saints, and so on. Although the earliest Coptic manuscripts extant belong to the fourth century, there is no doubt that the translation of the biblical books into the native Egyptian dialects was accomplished much earlier. The Sahidic version of the Old Testament books was probably made before the end of the second century; the Bohairic somewhat later. The Sahidic New Testament version may be assigned to the late second century; the Bohairic version, to the first half of the third century. Versions of the New

Testament have been identified in manuscripts written in all the main Coptic dialects (the Akhmimic, the Memphitic, the Fayyûmic, the Sahidic, and the Bohairic).

The Coptic alphabet consisted of thirty-two letters, twenty-five borrowed from the Greek uncial script, and seven taken over from a particularly cursive variety of the Egyptian demotic writing to express Coptic sounds which did not exist in the Greek language. The ancient Nubian Christians, occupying the territory south of Egypt, adopted the Coptic script, but in adapting it to their own language they took over from the cursive Meroitic writing three signs for sounds which could not be expressed by Coptic letters.

ETHIOPIC WRITING

From the fourth century onwards, after the conversion of the Aksumite Empire (northern Abyssinia) to Christianity—according to tradition, by Syrian missionaries—there came into being a literature which was essentially Christian, more especially because of the intensification of Christian propaganda by many Syrian monks, who introduced Greek and Syriac influences. At that time, the literary and ecclesiastical language of Ethiopia was Ge'ez (*lesana ge'ez*). The Ge'ez literature consists largely of translations of ecclesiastical works from Greek and—after Arabic superseded Greek and Coptic in Egypt—from the Christian Arabic literature, which then flourished in Egypt. In addition, there is the important and interesting Ethiopic version of the Old Testament. Two books, Jubilees and Enoch, which have no place in our Old Testament or our Apocrypha, are preserved in their entirety in classical Ethiopic.

The Ethiopic script originated in the first half of the fourth century A.D., from the Sabaean or South Semitic alphabet. It consists of twenty-six characters; of the twenty-eight Sabaean letters, four have been abandoned, and the letters *pait* and *pa* have been added. The letters became more and more rounded. The direction of writing, originally from right to left, became—probably under Greek influence—from left to right. The letter-names are in great part different from the Hebrew, Syriac and Greek letter-names. The order of the letters differs completely. An interesting peculiarity is Ethiopic vocalisation. The vowel following each consonant is expressed by adding small appendages to the right or left of the basic character, at the top or at the bottom, by shortening or lengthening one of its main strokes, and by other differentiations. There are thus seven forms of each letter, corresponding to the consonants followed by a short *a* or *e*, or a long *u*, *i*, *a*, *e*, *o*. Four consonants (*q*, *ḫ*, *k*, *g*) have five additional forms when they are followed by a *u* and another vowel.

CHAPTER II

BOOKS IN THE ANCIENT WORLD

3. BOOKS IN THE ANCIENT NEAR EAST AND IN THE OLD TESTAMENT

The discovery of more than half a million documents spanning the period of the Old Testament now enables a comparison to be made between the various contemporary literary forms in use within the ancient Near East. Such a study is an essential preliminary to any adequate critical study of the Old Testament, itself a collection of books and writings brought together over many centuries.

MATERIAL FORM

Papyrus

The loss of original or early manuscripts of the Old Testament books is almost certainly due to the use of perishable writing materials. Throughout Palestine the most common may well have been papyrus (*Cyperus papyrus* L.: Egyptian *ṯwfy*, called in Hebrew *sûp*) which grew freely in shallow lakes in Egypt and Syria. Since large quantities were used and transhipped from the Syrian port of Byblos it is surmised that the Greek word for books (τὰ βιβλία) derives from that place-name though the Greek word for papyrus-reed (hence the English 'paper') may itself be of Egyptian origin ('that of (belonging to) Pharaoh').

The reeds were stripped and cut lengthwise into thin narrow slices before being beaten and pressed together into two layers set at right angles to each other. When dried the whitish surface was polished smooth with a stone or other implement. Pliny refers to several qualities of papyri and varying thicknesses and surfaces are found before the New Kingdom period when sheets were often very thin and translucent. Though a papyrus sheet was somewhat thicker than modern writing paper it could be rolled easily. The maximum dimension of any sheet was governed by the usable height of plant-stalk from which it was made (47 cm). This dimension is, however, only found in papyri used for rough accounts; the length of an individual sheet varied between 42–38 cm (Middle Kingdom) and 20–16 cm (New Kingdom), allowing for trimming or cutting. The most common height for a scroll was 42 cm (Middle Kingdom and Hyksos periods) with half that height used for literary works and even shorter papyri (6–9 cm) for business texts. A number of papyri joined with a slight overlap, the standard number being twenty pasted sheets (Greek κόλλημα), built up a roll of up to 6 metres long. Writing in columns[1] was first upon the horizontal fibres ('recto') and then on the vertical fibres parallel with the joins ('verso'), the whole being rolled with the horizontal fibres inside. When the 'inside' of the roll was completed the scribe would either paste on additional sheets or, more easily and thus more frequently, continue on the 'outside' or back (as Ezek. 2: 10). Shorter communications, such as a letter, would be written and then cut from a single sheet.

The 'scribe's pen' (Jer. 8: 8) was a brush fashioned from rushes (*Juncus maritimis*) about 6–16 in. long, the end being cut to a flat chisel-shape to enable thick and thin strokes to be made with the broad or narrow sides. The reed-pen was in use from the early first millennium in Mesopotamia from which it may well have been adopted, while the idea of a quill pen seems to have come from the Greeks in the third century B.C. Ink was made by damping dried cakes of fine carbon-black or red-ochre mixed with gum. Ezekiel's scribe had a 'writing case' at his side (9: 2–3, 11; Heb. *qeset*; Egypt. *gsti*), probably the hollowed reed or wooden palette which held the brushes, pens, inks and, hanging from it, a rag for erasing errors by washing (cf. Num. 5: 23) or a penknife used for trimming pens or papyri (Jer. 36: 23). Red ink, rarely employed in the Old Kingdom, was sometimes used in the second millennium for dates, headings, the opening words ('title') and beginnings of new sections ('rubrics'), concluding phrases, for marking the correct division, accentuation or pagination (Papyrus Ebers) of a text or for entering corrections above the line or in the margin. Illustrations were added after completion of the texts. There would seem to be little change in the technical development of the papyrus 'book' from its inception *c.* 3000 B.C.

The Assyrian and Babylonian scribes of the first millennium also

---

[1] The Heb. *d'latôt* '(door)-leaves' in Jer. 36: 23 could refer to the sheet or column of writing.

employed scrolls of papyrus (*ni'aru*)[1] or leather ([*mašak*] *magillatu*) for Aramaic inscriptions. Since prepared skins of goat or sheep would be readily available to the Israelites the 'scroll of the book' (*mᵉgillaṭ sēper*; Ps. 40: 7; Ezek. 2: 9; Jer. 36: 2) was probably made from one of these accessible materials. Though the 'book' of the Old Testament (Heb. *sēper*) was often a roll or scroll, the term like its Mesopotamian counterpart (*šipru*) could denote writing in any form on any smooth surface, whether a document, book, letter (2 Kings 5: 6) or decree (Esther 1: 22).

Clay tablets

The cheapest and most durable writing material was clay prepared and dried in the sun or, for documents of more than passing import, in a kiln. The size of tablet was governed by the content and thus the writing-space required. It was usually rectangular and varied from about ¼ in. square to 18 × 12 in. The cuneiform inscription (see pp. 34 f.) normally ran in unruled lines from left to right parallel to the short side. The text was inscribed on the obverse (flat) side, across the lower edge, down the reverse (often convex) side, across the upper edge and then, if necessary, along the left and right edges. On a large tablet the text would be written in columns running left to right on the obverse and right to left on the reverse. A few large and bulky tablets were read in columns and turned over as one would the folios of a modern book. Some contracts were safeguarded by the repetition of the text (later of a summary only) on a sealed clay envelope which could be 'opened' if directed by a judge. There were local variations in the shape and colour of tablets, as in the ductus and characteristics of the script, but the basic form never changed from its inception *c.* 3100 B.C. till clay tablets were finally superseded *c.* A.D. 100 by other materials.

Where a large number of lines was required for historical, building or similar lengthy reports, or the size of tablet became too cumbersome to handle without danger of breaking, a larger surface was obtained by use of prisms, cones or barrel cylinders of baked clay. Illustrative matter—diagrams, plans and the impressions of cylinder or stamp seals left by witnesses—was added after completion of the inscription. The scribe wrote his wedge-shaped (cuneiform) signs with a stylus of reed

[1] R. P. Dougherty, 'Writing upon parchment and papyrus among the Babylonians', *JAOS*, XLVIII (1928), 109–35.

(*qân ṭuppi*), wood or other material using the long or short edge for horizontal or vertical wedges and the corner for the corner shaped stroke. The surface could be smoothed by the stylus to erase an erroneous sign or the surface of a new tablet cleaned off by a damp cloth before the clay had hardened. A fine string or straight edge was used to draw the lines marking divisions or columns. Space was reserved in the last column of certain texts for the insertion of the colophon. This, like the title-page of a modern book, might include the title of the work according to its opening words, the name of the scribe (sometimes with his patronym), the name of the owner and sometimes the date and category or purpose of the composition.[1] If the text was but one tablet or 'chapter' (*ṭuppu*) in a longer work the colophon would indicate this by giving the number of the tablet within the series (Akkadian *eškaru*; Sumerian *éš.gàr*) thus: 'sixth tablet of "He who has seen the Depth", series Gilgamesh'. 'He who has seen the Depth' is the title and opening phrase of the whole work. As a check the catch-line or first line of the following tablet and the total number of lines in the tablet may also be given. Sometimes the 'book', that is the 'series' or 'collection of tablets', may be subdivided into sections or 'parts' (*pirsu*) and thus bear a double system of numbering. Alternatively it may be stated that the text is but an extract (*nisḫu*) from a given series. A necessary part of many of these ancient book-plates was the curse invoked on any who should 'alter, put it in the fire, dissolve it in water, bury it, destroy it by any means, lose or obliterate'[2] the copy, and the blessing on the reader who would preserve the text—'let him who loves Nabū and Marduk preserve this and not let it leave his hands'.[3] A literary work could consist of any number of tablets; one astrological omen series (*Enuma Anu Ellil*) required 71 tablets to accommodate its *c.* 8,000 lines. The Epic of Gilgamesh took up twelve, originally eleven, tablets.

Tablets were usually stored on shelves in a special archive room or in wooden or clay boxes or jars (as Jer. 32: 14) or in reed baskets. Similarly the Hebrews, as the Egyptians with their scrolls, seem to have used a special wooden storage box for texts of great importance

---

[1] E. Leichty, 'The Colophon', *Studies presented to A. Leo Oppenheim* (Chicago, 1964), pp. 147–54.

[2] D. J. Wiseman, *The Vassal-Treaties of Esarhaddon* (London, 1958), p. 60.

[3] D. J. Wiseman, *Chronicles of Chaldaean Kings* (London, 1956), p. 75.

(Exod. 25: 16; 1 Kings 8: 9). Storage containers were provided with labels or tags of clay inscribed with a summary of their contents. The Babylonian invention of reverse-engraved brick stamps and seal inscriptions enabled them to make exact replicas of brief formal inscriptions on clay. The short step from this to the mass production or 'printing' of other texts was, however, never taken.

Where an inscription was required to be of a permanent monumental and religious character, stone or a durable material was chosen. Thus the Decalogue (Exod. 24: 12) and the copy of it on the altar (Josh. 8: 32) were inscribed on stone. Metal tools, available throughout the Near East in the literate period, were used to engrave any smooth surface, stelae, obelisks or cliff-faces. The iron stylus as used by Isaiah (8: 1, *heret*) or the pen of Jeremiah (17: 1, *'ēt*) are thought to be hard pointed instruments used for writing on bronze or other metals, possibly iron or lead.[1] So far such pens have not been identified beyond question among artifacts discovered.

Temporary notes, letters and accounts were often written with a mixed carbon and iron ink on potsherds (ostraca). Trade memoranda or tax accounts from Samaria, letters from besieged Lachish *c.* 589 B.C. and one complaining about the confiscation of a cloak (cf. Exod. 22:26) illustrate the use of this readily accessible and cheap writing material. The brick or tile on which Ezekiel drew a plan of Jerusalem (4: 1) was probably similar to paintings on bricks of a type known from Assyria and Babylonia.

Writing-boards

While the Hebrew word 'tablet' (*lûah*) may denote a clay tablet, of which examples of the late second millennium have been found at Gezer, Megiddo, Jericho, Ta'anach and Beth-Shemesh among other Palestinian sites, this is by no means certain. The word in Akkadian (*lē'u*) is used of the rectangular writing-boards made of ivory and wood. These differ from simple flat boards used in Egypt for exercises and other texts in that they have a recess to hold an inlay of wax mixed with some coloured and granulated substance, carbon-black or yellow sulphide of arsenic, to take the impression of a stylus. The examples found at Calah in Assyria were made in 711 B.C. to take a total of more than 5,000 lines of minute cuneiform script in two columns on each side of

---

[1] G. R. Driver, *Semitic Writing* (London, 1954), p. 84 n. 11; p. 230, considers that '*ēt* was originally a reed-pen.

16 boards (12·5 × 31·3 cm). The boards were hinged together to form a continuous folding 'book' and thus had the advantage that any length of writing surface could be supplied. The Assyrian sculptures show scribes holding a diptych or polyptych while they make inventories of spoil. Boards of this type were used also by the Hittites and Etruscans and in Babylonia could have been used to write either the cuneiform script or the Aramaic alphabet. Since the surface did not harden like the more cumbrous clay tablet, additions and alterations could be made at any time. Only a few examples of wooden writing-boards have been discovered at any site, none as yet from Palestine, owing to the perishable nature of the materials. Nevertheless, these boards may well have been the type of 'tablet' used by Isaiah (30: 8) or Habakkuk (2: 2).

THE SCRIBAL ART

Education and literacy

The varied and numerous documents and writing materials presuppose persons skilled in writing. From *c.* 3100 B.C. in Mesopotamia, and soon thereafter in Egypt, Anatolia and Elam, scribes were at work in the principal cities and centres of government. In the third millennium, it is generally assumed, Egyptian schools were controlled by the priests whose primary aim was the preservation of 'the word of god' or 'divine words'—the sacred writing. Manuscripts were kept in the scriptorium or 'House of Life' and from this store, copies and selections of standard texts (Pyramid, Coffin Texts or the Book of the Dead) were made. However, no description or remains of a priestly school has been identified and evidence rests upon the finished product. The scribal art was also passed from father to son, for a text (probably dating from *c.* 2300 B.C. of which copies are extant from 1900 B.C.) gives examples of advice (*sebayet*; 'teaching and discipline') to a young man to follow this most noble 'white-kilt' profession. The bureaucracy of the Middle Kingdom led to the establishment of government schools to supply the growing number of secretaries and clerks required. The profession was highly considered for 'if you want to rise high and have a non-manual job, stick to your classes in school and you will get ahead'.[1] The students first learned the hieroglyphic and hieratic scripts

[1] J. A. Wilson in *City Invincible*, ed. C. H. Kraeling (Chicago, 1960), p. 104.

and then moved on to exercises and extracts from traditional texts, the *Story of Sinuhe*, *Teaching of Amenhetep I*, *Hymn to the Nile* and the *Satire on the Trades*. The memorising and copying of lists of the names of deities, professions and places (*onomastica*) were included.

More is known of education in ancient Babylonia where, in Sumerian times, boys attended the 'tablet-house' (*é.dub.ba*) and as its pupils or 'sons' were apprenticed to the master ('father') much as were young boys in any manual trade. Under his direction preceptors ('older brothers') taught the complicated cuneiform script used for Sumerian and Akkadian. All education, like the higher culture, was bilingual until the mid-second millennium when the main centre of learning moved to Babylon and education fell into the hands of individual families who proudly traced their ancestry in the trade-guild back some ten or more centuries. The curriculum was traditional; after the learning of signs the students quickly moved on to copy lists of words, synonym lists and vocabularies, and to extracts, written from memory (*idû*) rather than from dictation. A distinction was made between dictation (*liginna qabû*) and 'taking dictation' (*liginna šaṭāru*) in the later schools. In this way the student copied more than 30,000 lines and most of the standard literary and other forms of text before qualification as a specialist. Examinations included calligraphy, grammar, translation into and from Sumerian and Akkadian, vocabulary, phonetics, epigraphy, as well as special studies in accountancy, mathematics, the technical jargon used by various crafts and groups, occult-writing, music and singing.[1] The latter, like rhetoric, seemed to be closely linked with the work of a scribe. 'The scribal art is the mother of speakers, the father of scholars.'[2] Scribes were often poets and could rise high in any profession; among those listed the Secretary of State is commonly found—such an official as Ezra may have been, with special responsibility for Jewish affairs. In Assyria the office of Head of the Royal Chancery was held through five generations by a single family of savants (*ummānu*) who spanned the period from *c.* 900 B.C. to the fall of Assyria *c.* 612 B.C. Such scribes specialised in languages (e.g. Egyptian, Aramaic) or professions—law, medicine, technology, the majority being laymen—or the priesthood.[3] From Old Babylonian

---

[1] B. Landsberger in *City Invincible*, pp. 94–100.

[2] S. H. Langdon in *AJSL*, xxviii (1911), 232.

[3] Holding government appointments. A Sumerian proverb says that 'a disgraced scribe becomes a man of spells'.

times many scribes, the poor aristocracy, would sit and wait for custom from the illiterate in the street or at the city-gate.

In general there was a low level of literacy. A few monarchs, Shulgi of Ur, Lipit-Ishtar of Isin, Ashurbanipal of Nineveh and Darius I of Persia, claimed to be able to read and write but were exceptional in this. One agricultural centre, Alalakh in Syria, boasted seven scribes among a population of more than 3,000 persons in *c.* 1700 B.C. The abundance of inscribed tablets, with the indication of other perishable materials in use, would show a significant and influential class of scribes throughout the near East.

The 200 Amarna letters penned in Palestine after the middle of the second millennium by Canaanite scribes to Egyptian kings betray the local dialect they spoke, even though they employed the Babylonian cuneiform script learned in a formal scribal training. In these small towns, as well as in the major trade-centres like Ras Shamra, native scribes had learned the cumbersome script to write the Amorite Akkadian used as a diplomatic *lingua franca*. By the time of Moses eight different languages were recorded in five different writing-systems.[1] The development of a simple 22-letter system must soon have led to widespread literacy. It is therefore not surprising to find the first attributions of literacy ascribed to this time. Moses himself, tutored at the Egyptian court (cf. Acts 7: 22), is said to have recorded laws and legal decisions (Exod. 24: 3–7; Deut. 31: 24–6), a song (Deut. 31: 22), curses (Exod. 17: 14) and memoranda connected with the Israelite journeys. Under administrative pressure he appointed literate officials (*šōṭᵉrîm*) to record decisions and order affairs (Deut. 1: 15; cf. Exod. 18: 21–2).[2] Since parents were responsible for their own children's education (Gen. 18: 19; Deut. 6: 7) it is likely that the literate, and especially the scribes, readily passed on their art.[3] Inscriptions engraved on altar-stones (Josh. 8: 32) or on gems and metal plates by seal cutters (Exod. 39: 14, 30) require both writers and readers. By the time of Gideon even a village lad could spell out the

[1] G. E. Mendenhall, 'Biblical History in Transition' in *The Bible and the Ancient Near East*, ed. G. E. Wright (London, 1961), p. 50 n. 23.

[2] Cf. Akkadian *šaṭāru* 'to write'. The idea of the appointment of administrative officials may have derived from Egypt (cf. Exod. 5: 14).

[3] The Shechem tablet may have been written by a schoolmaster complaining that a boy's tuition fees had not yet been paid (W. F. Albright, *BASOR*, LXXXVI, 1942, 30). B. Landsberger, however, interprets this as a reference to pederasty (*JCS*, VIII, 1954, 54).

names of persons (Judg. 8: 14). While in Israel there would be several who could 'handle the writer's pen' (or 'staff' of office, Judg. 5: 14), there are indications that a Kenite family descended from Caleb long continued to be noted for this (1 Chron. 2: 55). Between Moses and David there is given an unbroken list of those who guarded the ark which contained, or had with it, the Torah or basic 'state' documents (Deut. 31: 24–6). From David to Josiah the names are given also of state scribes, an office of high order, who ranked before the Chronicler (*mazkîr*) who kept the numerous state records (2 Sam. 8: 16; 1 Kings 4: 3). The Chief Scribe was a royal adviser and some, like Shebna, rose to be Chief Minister. Other scribes were employed on military or census duties under their own chief (2 Kings 25: 19; Jer. 52: 25) and senior scribes had their own rooms in the palace or temple (Jer. 36: 10, 12–21). Until the Exile the scribal profession was largely separate from the priesthood which had its own secretaries and scribes, and in this Israel was in line with her neighbours.

No account of a specific school has survived, but with the establishment of local sanctuaries young male students (*limmûdîm*) were doubtless taught writing (and rhetoric) by the prophets (1 Sam. 10: 11–13; Isa. 10: 19). The alphabet was learned by oral repetition or by question and answer.[1] The tradition of a Temple school goes back to the first Temple (1 Chron. 25:8) and of a more general education perhaps to the second. In Judah Simon ben-Shetah introduced elementary education for all boys in 75 B.C. There were, of course, literates and illiterates at all ages (Isa. 10: 19; 29: 12) and if a king could not copy out the law for himself as directed (Deut. 17: 18) he would have at hand a scribe to read or write it (2 Chron. 34: 18) or to take a dictated letter (2 Kings 10: 1). The prophet Jeremiah employed Baruch in this manner. Among secular scribes, such as Daniel is described to be, were many who could read both Babylonian and Aramaic as the result of a local court education. State correspondence in the Achaemenid era (cf. Ezra 5: 6; 6: 1; Dan. 5: 7) is in keeping with contemporary style.

Authors and editors

In Egypt, Mesopotamia and Israel literary works were generally anonymous. The later Babylonians and Assyrians knew of famous

---

[1] Isa. 28: 10; G. R. Driver translates as *s* after *ṣ*, *s-ṣ*, *q-q*, *q-q*: *Semitic Writing*, p. 89. But cf. more recently G. R. Driver in *Words and Meanings*, ed. P. R. Ackroyd and B. Lindars (Cambridge, 1968), pp. 53–6.

authors like Arad-Ea of the fourteenth century B.C. who had earlier composed a named work. Such information is inserted in the colophon of a later copy of a text. In one, the Irra Epic, we are told that 'Kabti-ilāni-Marduk, son of Dabibi, was the compiler of its tablets. It was revealed to him in the night and when he spoke it in the morning he did not leave out a single line, nor did he add one to it.'[1] This implies only early editorial work. To one Enlilmuballiṭ (*c.* 1800 B.C.) is ascribed the composition of a series of medical texts but, since elements of the series are known in earlier dated texts, it must be presumed that here again we have a stage in the collection or transmission of the work. Once an author's name is inserted in an acrostic within a poem, and frequently authors are known only from their mention in catalogues listing titles and the names of scribes to whom authorship, compilation or copying is ascribed. Often this was to a scholar (*ummānu*) of a particular early city in the third (Eridu) or second millennium (Babylon). Several works were ascribed to antediluvian sages, notably the first Adapa-Oannes; others are marked as of divine origin without any human intermediary named, though Ea, the god who plays a special rôle as interpreting or revealing the divine mind to man, figures the most frequently in Babylonian texts. In Egypt this applied especially to law and ritual. Berossus' assertion that 'from that time (the Flood) nothing new has been discovered' is not dissimilar to the Rabbinic tradition that all divine revelation is to be found in the Torah.[2] However, in general, the scribes were well aware of the traditional authority associated with many of the texts they copied. This authority lay not in anonymity, for these scribes 'antiquity of authorship implied authority with divine authorship implying the greatest authority'.[3] Thus wherever feasible a scribe would strive to copy or collate an original written text. Where a variety of text traditions was consulted the scribe aimed to keep close to the earliest recension available. The care with which copies were made is also to be seen in the check made on the number of lines in a text, the total being added in some colophons. In addition a text may have the note added to the effect that it had been 'checked against the original'. Where a defective text had been consulted a scribe would mark the presence of lacunae by

[1] W. G. Lambert, 'A catalogue of Texts and Authors', *JCS*, XVI (1962), 70.

[2] Cf. P. Schnabel, *Berossus und die babylonisch-hellenistiche Literatur* (Leipzig, Berlin, 1923), p. 253.

[3] W. W. Hallo, *IEJ*, XII (1962), 16.

inserting the word 'broken' (*ḫepi*) and no attempt was made at restoration of the defective or missing signs or passages. There were at the same time local and indigenous compilations and adaptations of major traditional texts (the Gilgamesh and Creation epics) or collections of one class of texts (hymns, medical diagnoses or astrological omina) by a local practitioner. An analysis of the major archives, the Sumerian at Nippur, Hittite at Boghazköi or the Assyrian 'library' collections of Ashur (1100 B.C.), Nineveh (800–650 B.C.) and Nimrud (705–614 B.C.), reveals comparable editorial methods. In Mesopotamia oral tradition played only a limited part in the transmission of literary texts after 2700 B.C., the scribe using an oral source ('from the mouth of an expert') only when all else failed.[1] Such use of oral transmission was constantly corrected against the written tradition and, as in early Islam, served as a commentary. In Mesopotamian law and science descriptions of methods used are absent, probably being verbally discussed, while the deductions or results are always given in writing. Comparison of early and late omina, a genre notably absent from the Old Testament, shows a gradual tendency to enlarge in a creative, if sometimes artificial, manner. Reference works (*tamirtu*) were readily available, a skilled scribe copying out his own books; and there is some evidence that excerpts from different texts were made in such a way as to imply an accepted list of 'classical' or 'canonical' texts and a standard order in which they were to be read or studied. As with the Jewish scribes, emphasis was placed on the continuity of the tradition and their responsibility was conceived as the copying, checking and preservation of the written word. They had to hand the word on undiminished to their successors.[2]

LITERATURE

This highly specialised scribal activity implies the existence of diverse literary genres. Although never classified in general categories the literature of the ancient Near East may, like that of the Old Testament itself, conveniently be considered under three main headings—History, Law, and other writings.

[1] J. Laessøe, 'Literacy and Oral Tradition in Ancient Mesopotamia', in *Studia Orientalia Ioanni Pedersen* (Copenhagen, 1953), pp. 212–13.

[2] The extent to which there was a process of 'canonisation', comparable with biblical writings, is much debated; cf. W. W. Hallo, *IEJ*, xii (1962), 23 ff. and W. G. Lambert, 'Ancestors, authors, and Canonicity', *JCS*, xi (1957), 1–14.

Epic and early historiography

There is a general parallelism in subject matter between the early Sumerian literature of the so-called 'Heroic Age' *c.* 2400 B.C. and the introductory chapters of the Old Testament (Gen. 1–11). Sumerian cycles of individual 'heroes'—the early rulers Enmerkar, Lugalbanda and Gilgamesh—have plots based on historical fact though with some poetic embellishments. In form they incorporate speeches, descriptive narrative and lengthy repetitions. More than one account of the creation of the universe and of man, of paradise and the flood is to be found. Early disputations reflect the 'Cain–Abel' motif, while the dispersion of mankind as well as the idea of the organisation of the earth, of a personal god, divine wrath, natural catastrophe, death and punishment find their earliest expression in poetry and prose.[1] In later Egyptian stories early cosmological ideas are adapted to the theological viewpoint of the local editor. By the early second millennium one Semitic epic of Atrahasis ('the very devout') links together events from the Creation to the Deluge in a single account. To do this it makes use of summary 'king-lists' or genealogies (Heb. *toledot*). Such lists were the common basis of all Mesopotamian science and subsequent historiography.[2] In Egypt one such list of the forebears of a local ruler, Ukhotep, spans some 600 years with the names of 59 predecessors in genuine chronological order from the fourth dynasty to the twelfth-dynasty king Amenemhat II (i.e. *c.* 2500–1925 B.C.). Among others, Ankhef-en-Sekhmet traces 60 generations over 1,300 years to *c.* 750 B.C. with names of contemporary kings and nomenclature which leaves the genuineness of the record in no doubt.[3] 'History is the intellectual form in which a particular civilisation renders account to itself of the past.'[4] All civilisations are aware of the past but record it in different ways. That the Egyptian and Mesopotamian epics and historiography could have been known to the Hebrews cannot be doubted, for a

[1] S. N. Kramer, 'Cuneiform Studies and the history of Literature: the Sumerian Sacred Marriage Texts', *Proceedings of the American Philosophical Society*, CVII (1963), 486–9.

[2] So J. J. Finkelstein, 'Mesopotamian Historiography', *Proceedings of the American Philosophical Society*, CVII (1963), 461–72.

[3] K. A. Kitchen, 'Some Egyptian Background to the Old Testament', *The Tyndale House Bulletin*, V (1960), 14–18.

[4] Quoted in J. J. Finkelstein, 'Mesopotamian Historiography', p. 462.

fourteenth-century B.C. copy of the Gilgamesh epic was found at Megiddo; other literary Babylonian texts of approximately the same period were found at Ras Shamra and Alalakh. They may well have been known at the Egyptian court also. The similarities and differences between the Babylonian and Hebrew accounts of Creation and the Flood have been much discussed and the view that the latter must be dependent in some way on the former is by no means unanimously held.[1]

Laws and records

In Mesopotamia and Israel the overriding cultural factor was the concept of law and authority which ensured the vitality, stability and continuity of a highly developed civilisation. Since the human ruler had no absolute authority he was held to be responsible to the gods who charged him with the maintenance of truth and justice (*mešārum ù kittum*), both of which express eternal verities (as do Heb. *'emet*, 'truth'; *mêšār*, 'uprightness, equity' and *ṣedāqā*, 'righteousness'). The trend was from theocracy to democracy and man was servant, never author, of law. The individual's inalienable rights were guaranteed since laws embodying the truth were timeless. Law was also thought to be inseparable from religion and ethics. It behoved a man to observe all legal commitments into which he had entered, for they were ultimately enforceable by divine sanction. To be valid these solemn obligations had to be recorded in writing. The basic premise whereby the divine cosmic law and order was reflected on earth was one of Mesopotamia's most influential concepts, spreading with its scribes, script and literature to the Hittites and Syria (Ugarit, Alalakh and Mari), to Palestine and eventually to Greece and the West.[2]

By contrast the religion and government of Egypt was authoritarian in that the pharaoh was himself regarded as a god and was thus the supreme authority. Since he could not be in competition with any other authority, personal and impersonal, this may explain the absence of recorded laws from that country. Babylonia and Assyria have left no statement of law directly comparable with the 'I–thou' character of the Sinai covenant with its Ten Commandments or stipulations. Yet the form of the latter is fundamentally identical with the Mesopo-

[1] Cf. W. G. Lambert, *JTS*, XVI (1965), 288–300; A. Heidel, *The Epic of Gilgamesh and Old Testament Parallels* (Chicago, 1949), pp. 260–9.

[2] E. A. Speiser, 'Early Law and Civilization' in *The Canadian Bar Review* (1953), 863–77 = *Oriental and Biblical Studies* (Philadelphia, 1967), pp. 534–55.

tamian suzerainty treaty whereby an overlord imposed his will on a vassal. In this a specific historical situation is stated or implied, then the stipulations are listed in the form 'thou shalt (not)....'. These Laws or 'Directions' are given orally but recorded in writing before witnesses including deities. The recipients had to acknowledge publicly that they would keep the terms. This was often done by calling out 'Amen' after each provision had been read out. They also undertook to read and reaffirm the stipulations or 'law' at stated periods. The vassal swore allegiance to the sovereign's deity on pain of invasion and deportation should he revoke his word. He had to teach the covenant to 'his sons, his son's sons and his seed for ever'. Curses concluded the document, calling the divine wrath on any who failed to keep the stipulations (*adē*) and blessings on any who did so. This type of document was laid up in the national shrine (cf. 1 Sam. 10: 25) to be taken out and read at stated times. It is noteworthy that similar literary elements, sometimes in identical phraseology, are to be found in the Old Testament covenantal forms (cf. Exod. 19–24; Josh. 24; Deut. 6). While the basic literary form was unchanged over two millennia, the survival of texts in which extracts from one part or other of these 'treaty' documents were made shows that the ancient historians freely made abstracts or summaries of parts of the whole text (as was done in Deuteronomy). International covenants between equals (parity treaties) followed a similar outline but with provision of mutual concern—the extradition of runaway slaves (Alalakh nos. 2–3, cf. Judah and Philistia 1 Kings 2: 39–40; Deut. 23: 15–16), boundary disputes, confiscation of property on the death of evil-doers (cf. 1 Kings 21), and similar matters.

The collections of legal decisions (sometimes inaccurately referred to as 'codes' of law) are closely related to these 'covenants'. A number of laws are extant from Sumer (Ur-Nammu, Lipit-Ishtar), Babylonia (Eshnunna, Hammurapi) and Assyria (Middle Assyrian collection). These are all summaries of cases, of both evidence and decision, which were brought together as an illustration of the way the individual king had maintained the traditional 'law and order'. They were, in effect, reports to the deity on the exercise of the divinely given royal 'wisdom'. As in the case recorded of Solomon they were often of unusual or abstruse decisions (1 Kings 2: 6; 3: 16–28). The many legal summaries collected in Deuteronomy probably belong to this genre.

Since much stress was placed on the unbroken continuity of the law, a king on his accession was required to issue a *mešārum*-edict to announce the form of tradition he would maintain. This edict would be accompanied by any necessary supporting economic and religious reforms. In Israel such public statements, perhaps reflected in the historian's verdict 'he did the right (*hayyašār*) in the eyes of Yahweh', imply the maintenance of the Torah and presuppose its existence in written form. Despite prophetic urgings only a few kings, David, Asa, Jehoshaphat, Azariah and Josiah, are recorded as taking this step, though all failed to implement it fully. The beginning of a reign was often the time for public protest and demand for legal and economic changes (Josh. 9: 23–5; 1 Kings 12: 1–15).[1]

The mass of legal documents in Egypt and Mesopotamia, and therefore presumably in Israel, comprised the individual contracts of sale, loans, adoptions, redemption, marriage and divorce. In many cases it is possible to compare the terminology and format of those in the Old Testament with texts from neighbouring places and periods. Thus the comparison of patriarchal customs with eighteenth- to fifteenth-century B.C. Old Babylonian (Mari, Alalakh) or Hurrian (Nuzi) texts has led to a detailed appraisal of that period. Abraham's purchase of Machpelah (Gen. 23) or Jeremiah's contract for the field of Hanameel at Anathoth (Jer. 32: 7–25) conform to contemporary usage. All this legal business depended upon, and resulted in, a manifold bureaucracy. The Hebrews, like their neighbours, did not lack census lists, lists of citizens by name, household, occupation or class; landowners, administrative boundaries, military rolls, records of booty, itineraries or geographical memoranda (cf. Num. *passim*; Gen. 5: 1; 10; Neh. 11–12). Each of these is classified as 'a writing' (Heb. *sēper*), a term used also for any written record or, at Ugarit, for a dossier (*spr*).

The Sumerians adapted their writing first for the classification of observed phenomena rather than the expression of abstract thought. Lists were arranged in varying, including chronological, order and were soon used for recording daily events or facts behind a given situation. Thus 'king-lists', year formulae and other data necessary to the law became the basis of historical writing. The description of a dispute between the cities of Umma and Lagash by a scribe *c.* 2500 B.C. is a detailed and interpretative history of the struggle with due regard

---

[1] D. J. Wiseman, 'The Laws of Hammurabi Again', *JSS*, VII (1962), 166–8.

to political and economic motives.[1] From such early records the step to annals and chronicles was not long delayed. Thus from the late second millennium written reports made to the national god and to the nation, like the vivid account by Sargon II of his eighth campaign near Lake Van, were recorded contemporaneously with the events described. Annals, of which chronicles are but a synopsis for a given purpose, were sometimes written after a single campaign or edited according to a geographical rather than chronological framework on the basis of several such accounts. Each successive edition during a long reign might require the rewriting or paraphrasing of part of the history to adapt it to the purpose required.[2] The same methods were used by the Egyptians though their major historical records, as those of the later Babylonian kings, now survive only in monumental texts. Despite a tendency to traditional style and formulae, which may be accounted for by the religious nature of many of these texts, there is evidence of original composition and of journals meticulously kept a day at a time. From these were drawn up chronicles for precise purposes, religious or secular, the Babylonian court scribes keeping note of the dates of all public events, accessions, deaths, mutinies, famines and plagues, major international events, wars, battles, religious ceremonies, royal decrees and other pertinent facts. Such records were available to any in search of precedents (as Cyrus in Ezra 5: 17) in these subjects. Thus a chronicle of a given number of years could select only those factors relevant to the political relations of two states (*Assyrian Chronicle of Years* 680–626 B.C.), of events in the religious calendar or those facts required to relate the history of the king or state to contemporary events in other realms. Daily records included astronomical observations, the weather, prices of staple commodities and the height of the river on which the irrigation system and thus the economy depended.[3] Extracts were often made without reference to the source, though the Hebrew historians frequently did so, as can be seen in their allusions to records which are no longer extant—*The Book of the Wars of Yahweh* (Num. 21: 14), *The Book of the Chronicles of the Kings of Israel* (1 Kings 14: 19) or *of Judah* (1 Kings 14: 29), etc., which may have had abbreviated titles as *The Book of the Kings*

[1] S. N. Kramer, 'Sumerian Historiography', *IEJ*, III (1953), 217–32.

[2] A. T. Olmstead, *Assyrian Historiography* (The University of Missouri Studies, Social Science Series III, 1. Missouri, 1916).

[3] D. J. Wiseman, *Chronicles of Chaldaean Kings* (London, 1956), pp. 1–5.

of Israel (1 Chron. 9: 1) or have appeared in a composite edition as *The Book of the Chronicles of the Kings of Judah and Israel* (2 Chron. 16: 11). Like her neighbours the Hebrews kept the data for individual reigns, those of Asa and Jehu being mentioned. Nathan and Shemaiah the prophets, Iddo the seer and Ahijah the Shilonite all kept records of the acts of Solomon and other kings in 'books', 'chronicles', 'prophecies' and 'visions' (2 Chron. 9: 29; 12: 15) or historical writings (cf. 1 Kings 11: 41).

Other Writings

It has become customary to refer to other Hebrew 'writings' as 'Wisdom literature'. This genre includes essays, proverbs, precepts, fables, riddles, dialogues and some psalms. Books or collections of proverbs were made by the Sumerians, Babylonians and Hittites. The Hebrew Proverbs (as also Ecclesiasticus and Wisdom of Solomon) are closest to the precepts or instructions (Egyptian *sebayet*) which range from the Old Kingdom writings of the Egyptian sages Imotep, Hardidief and Ptahhotep to the New Kingdom collections of Ani, Amennakhte and Amenemope and are scattered throughout the literature. Despite much discussion there is no indisputable evidence that the Old Testament collections depend on the Egyptian any more than on the Mesopotamian.[1] All may well draw from a common stock with local variations. Biographical instructions as in the Middle Kingdom *Teaching of Mentuhotep* and the Babylonian *Advice to a Prince* are found in Prov. 4; 31. The book of Job wrestles with the problem of the righteous suffering undeserved punishment which had been discussed in earlier Sumerian texts and in the lengthy eleventh-century Babylonian poems *ludlul bēl nēmeqi* and '*Theodicy*'. Pessimistic literature such as Ecclesiastes finds its counterpart in Sumerian compositions, the Akkadian *Dialogue of Pessimism* and the Egyptian *Dialogue of a man tired with life with his soul,* in which the personal conflict reaches the brink of suicide. *The Admonitions of Ipuwer* also treats of the breakdown of society. There are Sumerian parallels to the later Aesopic Fables. The brief glimpses of this genre afforded in Judges (9: 8–15) and Isaiah (10: 15; 29: 16) show that in Israel, as in late Egypt, this mode of teaching was popular. Disputations and dialogues such as the *Eloquent*

[1] K. A. Kitchen, 'Some Egyptian Background to the Old Testament', *The Tyndale House Bulletin*, v (1960), 14–18.

Peasant's nine rhetorical speeches within a narrative prose prologue and epilogue—a mode employed in Job—call for social justice. Parables (as in 2 Sam. 12 : 1–4; Isa. 28 : 4) and allegories (Isa. 5 : 1–7) have not as yet been traced in Sumerian, Akkadian or Ugaritic documents.

From earliest times vast and highly sophisticated collections of hymns, psalms (and some prayers) are to be found in many cult centres. Some were composed in praise of gods or kings with the special purpose of uniting the people in a common allegiance. In Egypt Hymns to Sesostris III and earlier in Babylonia more than a hundred compositions ascribed to the kings of Ur, Isin, Larsa and Babylon (2100–1700 B.C.)— with as many as thirty in honour of Shulgi alone—attest the vitality of this form. There are strong indications that, while most were composed during the reign of the king so honoured, other 'extra-canonical' renderings of the standard style and format were made according to local historical conditions. Psalms of this type re-appear in the Qumrân texts. A. L. Oppenheim has shown that at least one Assyrian priest-poet had command of various *topoi* which could be drawn upon at will. Some are found in Sumerian and Akkadian texts dated many years apart.[1] A constructive poet would create ever new combinations of phrases, lines and stanzas for new compositions. Examples of this are also to be found in the biblical psalms. Catalogues of incipits show that many hymns and psalms have not survived. The Hebrew 'Book of Jashar' must also have contained poems, now lost (Josh. 10: 13; 2 Sam. 1: 18).

Long before the 'Song of Songs' or Canticles was published the Egyptians composed passionate and rhapsodic cultic love-songs, and dirges like Lamentations had their precursors in Sumerian poems bewailing the destruction of the great temple-cities of Nippur and Ur. In one dirge Lugaldingirra bemoans the death of his father and wife in elegiac verse comparable only with David's words concerning Saul. Yet humour too was not lacking. The vivid Assyrian seventh-century *Tale of the Poor Man of Nippur*, based on a third millennium original, has been shown to have survived in Arabic folk-lore in the *Supplemental Nights* to *The Book of the Thousand Nights and a Night*. Another old Babylonian story of a man and a cleaner at Ur may well have been written to be mimed. It is assumed that these represent a sizeable body of *belles-lettres* of which much has perished.

[1] A. L. Oppenheim, *Analecta Biblica*, XII (Rome, 1959), 282–301.

Predictive prophecy was known and exercised by both the Egyptians and Babylonians. In such works as the *Admonition of Ipuwer* (twenty-third to twenty-second century B.C.), the *Teaching of Merikarē* and the *Prophecy of Neferty* (*c.* 1990 B.C.) there are allusions to the future, while the Babylonians cast descriptions of the reigns of unnamed kings in the form of prediction much as did Daniel (8: 23–5; 11: 3–14). Yet it is the rarity of this and other literary forms which contrasts with much of the Old Testament writings and with the unusual unity of theme and purpose in the selections there made. Against a literary background in which omina, astrology and myth play perhaps the largest rôle, their absence in the Old Testament is the more remarkable. The evidence of so rich and varied a literature throughout the Ancient Near East makes comparison and contrast with the biblical writings essential for the understanding of both. Moreover, it requires new approaches in our study of the Old Testament literature.

4. BOOKS IN THE GRAECO-ROMAN WORLD AND IN THE NEW TESTAMENT

The world into which Christianity was born was, if not literary, literate to a remarkable degree; in the Near East in the first century of our era writing was an essential accompaniment of life at almost all levels to an extent without parallel in living memory. In the New Testament reading is not an unusual accomplishment; Jesus can clinch an argument with his opponents with 'Have you not read...?' (Matt. 12: 3; 19: 4; cf. 21: 42), and reading may be assumed to have been as general in Palestine as, from the vast quantity of papyri of all kinds and descriptions, we know it to have been in up-country Egypt at this time. The hellenisation of the Near East contributed powerfully to the more general use of the written word; but although where books were concerned the sophisticated Judaism of Alexandria was influenced by the hellenic elements it sought to proselytise (as can be seen in Philo), a widespread use of the book was something that hellenism and Judaism, even in its more ultramontane forms, had in common. Both Greeks and Jews used the roll as the vehicle for their literature, although the latter tended to prefer skin·to papyrus for copies of the Law read in synagogues, while to the Greek the use of papyrus was one of the marks of civilisation. Both used the waxed tablet for elementary instruction in school as well as for memoranda. The discoveries at Qumrân and Murabba'ât have shown that certain scribal practices such as methods of cancellation or paragraphing by means of spacing were common to both, though probably Greek in origin.

Together with the widespread use of writing and reading, even though the reading list of the pious Jew was severely limited, went a distrust of the written word among Greeks and Jews alike. Plato's criticisms of the written word,[1] or at least of its abuse—that so far from helping memory, it destroys it, that it is no substitute for a true dialectic, or an exchange of minds between teacher and taught, that the profoundest truths cannot be put down in black and white—were frequently echoed in antiquity and (the Law always excepted) can be paralleled in Judaism. Some such attitude, as well as jealousy for the priority of the written Law, lay behind the prohibition on recording the oral Law in writing, or at any rate on transmitting or publishing it in written form; it was an attitude that powerfully influenced the early Church. Publication, in literary circles in Rome or Alexandria and equally in Christian circles, was always by public recitation. The story of the minister of Queen Candace whom Philip heard reading the book of Isaiah to himself (Acts 8: 28, 30) reminds us that reading in the ancient world, even solitary reading, invariably meant reading aloud.

But, as always with the Jews and usually with the Christians, it is the differences from the pagan world rather than the resemblances to it that impress. What we know as the Old Testament—and generally speaking its content was effectively fixed before the Christian era—occupied a place in Jewish national life, worship and sentiment to which classical antiquity offers no parallel. Greeks and Romans were acquainted with sacred books, whether those of minority groups such as Orphics or Pythagoreans or, as in Rome, belonging to the state, but the physical object was not treated with the same veneration nor the text itself so scrupulously protected as was the case with the Jewish Law. The strictest rules governed the handling, the reading and the copying of the Law. Multiplication of copies by dictation was not allowed; each scroll had to be copied directly from another scroll; official copies, until A.D. 70 derived ultimately from a master copy in the Temple, were kept at first in a cupboard in each synagogue, later

---

[1] *Phaedrus,* 274 f.

in a room adjoining it. The cupboard faced towards Jerusalem, and the rolls within it were the most holy objects in the synagogue.

This reverence was not confined to the Hebrew text. Hellenised Jews regarded the Septuagint as a work of inspiration, an attitude that the story of its miraculous origin in the Letter of Aristeas reinforced, as it was surely intended to do. Thus for the Jews of the Diaspora and consequently for Christians, inspiration was not limited to the Hebrew tongue nor to a distant past; it was only after the Septuagint had been adopted by Christians as the text of the Old Testament that it fell into disfavour with the Jews and was replaced by other versions. For the earliest Christians it was both a datum of their religious life and a model for what in course of time became the New Testament. With this attitude went a concern for preserving the precise wording of the translated text; the Jewish rule that the sacred books must be read, not recited after being learnt by heart (as was the case with the uncanonised oral Law), itself contributed to the safeguarding of the text. The Church knew no such ban, but the general attitude to the sacred writings whether of the old or of the new dispensation was much the same.

The discoveries at Qumrân show that in the first century B.C. the text of Isaiah, for example, was faithfully transmitted; the widely varying interpretations that might be placed on the text by Jews as well as later by Christians, so far from leading to frequent variant readings, may well have defended it from them. An attitude to the text which regarded its careful reproduction almost as an end in itself implied a continuing process of transmission, control and supervision, something that in the Greek world could be found, and then with very different presuppositions, only in the small circle of professional scholars and writers.

The institutions in Judaism that at once enshrined this attitude to the Law, protected, and actively encouraged it, were the synagogue and the school, often closely associated, both devoted to the education of the nation in its religion.[1] The *lector* and the interpreter of the scriptures would have been no less familiar figures in the early churches than was

---

[1] Cf. Philo's picture of the Essene synagogues (*Quod omn. prob.* 81–2): 'these holy places are called synagogues, and there the young sit and are instructed in age groups by their elders, attending with suitable decorum. One takes the books and reads them aloud, another more learned comes forward and instructs them in what they do not know.' For the synagogue in general see G. F. Moore, *Judaism* (Harvard, 1927): I, I, ch. v and in particular the other passages from Philo quoted on p. 306.

the διδάσκαλος or teacher, as important in early Christian life as he was in Judaism. Paul's commission (1 Tim. 2: 7) was to be the teacher of the Gentiles, a commission executed directly when he is present, in his absence through his letters (1 Thess. 5: 27). In the church at Antioch (Acts 13: 1) there were teachers as well as prophets; in 1 Cor. 12: 28 teachers rank directly after apostles and prophets and in Eph. 4: 11 they are coupled with pastors as a recognised 'order' in the Church. The specific function of the teacher is as clearly recognised in the Apostolic Fathers.[1] Though the teacher himself need not be a writer of books any more than Jesus himself was, yet his activity implied that books were readily available. Christianity grew up with the idea, quite alien to the pagan world, that books were an essential part of religion. The growth of Christian literature and teaching and in due course of the Canon can only be understood in the light of practices inherited from Judaism.

Thus while a Jewish convert or sympathiser of the first generation would have found nothing strange in the attitude to and use of books, a Gentile convert would have been struck by the divergences from pagan practice. The physical object, however, would have been equally familiar to both. The Jewish preference for rolls of skin, instead of papyrus, remained, but except for certain cultic purposes it seems not to have been more than a preference. At Murabba'ât rolls, or parts of rolls, of the Old Testament have been found written both on leather and papyrus; and two pre-Christian rolls of the Septuagint from Egypt, both of Deuteronomy and in fine professional hands, are written on papyrus. A roll when complete would not normally have exceeded 35 feet, long enough to be a clumsy and unwieldy object; there were no rules governing the length of lines or the number of lines to a column and no numeration of columns. In the last there would have been little point, given the difficulty in a roll of making a quick reference. The detailed prescriptions for the manufacture and writing of rolls of the Law preserved in rabbinic sources should probably not be read back into the times of the Second Temple, and certainly have no analogue in Greek practice.

In the New Testament writings the book is a familiar object, under the names of βίβλος, the roll of papyrus and its diminutive βιβλίον, used both of books and documents. Thus it is the roll of Isaiah that

---

[1] *Did.* 13: 2; 15: 2; *Ep. Barn.* 1: 8; 4: 9; Hermas, *Vis.* III, 5, 1; *Sim.* IX, 15, 4.

Jesus opens and reads from at Capernaum (Luke 4: 17); the βιβλία mentioned by the writer of the second epistle to Timothy may be assumed to have been rolls of the Old Testament (2 Tim. 4: 13). The sealed roll of Rev. 5: 2 alludes to the practice of sealing important documents such as wills. Metaphors from books and writing are evidence, if any were needed, of their universality; the most striking is that in which Paul, following a long tradition in Greek and Jewish literature (and in particular Prov. 3: 3), contrasts the word engraved on stone or wood with that written in the human heart. The bizarre passage in Revelation (10: 8 ff.) where an angel holds open a small roll and John takes and eats it echoes Ezek. 2: 8—3: 3 and is the only allusion to an opisthograph roll—one written on both sides—in the New Testament, occasionally, as here, with the same text running continuously from one side to the other. Nothing makes plainer the position held by the Old Testament than the use of γραφή, γραφαί, *writing*, *writings* without the addition of *holy* to denote *tout court* the Old Testament or its constituent books (see especially John 19: 37, *another writing*); the word may be classed among the relatively few religious *termini technici* in the New Testament.

Christian literature began, as did Christian preaching, with the interpretation of the Old Testament in the light of Christian experience (Acts 18: 28). It is significant that in the account of the post-Resurrection appearance to the eleven in Jerusalem the revelation of the true meaning of the scriptures ('Moses and the prophets and the psalms') is directly linked with 'these...my words': the holy writings of the past with the holy writings of the future (Luke 24: 44 f.). We find the same association between *the scripture and the word which Jesus had spoken* in John (2: 22); here and in the preaching of Apollos in Achaia (Acts 18: 28) we can see at work the process by which the Christian interpretation of the scripture, associated as it usually was with the remembered words of the Lord, became as important and as indispensable as the scripture itself.

The literature of the earliest Church, in as far as we can picture it from the New Testament, is with two exceptions what might have been predicted from its Jewish origins: the sacred books of Judaism and some interpretations of those books in the light of Christian experience. The New Testament itself is composed of three classes of book. First, the gospels (and for this purpose Acts may be classified with them) which, whatever the claims made for their central figure, make no claim *as books* to be on a par with the Old Testament and whose purpose is succinctly stated in John 20: 31, 'that you may believe that Jesus is the Christ, the Son of God, and that believing you may have life in his name'. Secondly, the Epistles which (with the possible exception of Hebrews) do not set out to be literature, but originated as *pièces d'occasion*, half-way between ordinary correspondence and literature proper. Lastly, Revelation, the only work in the New Testament that claims inspiration, a claim deriving principally from the genre to which it belongs, partly perhaps from the late date of its composition.

The two exceptions, both of them clues to later developments, are the references to the *words of the Lord*, frequent enough to suggest that the authority they claim would eventually be recognised in a form permanent and independent of the Old Testament, and the seemingly trivial allusion in 2 Tim. 4: 13 to 'parchments'. The relatively few Latin words that occur in the New Testament are used to denote something peculiarly Roman, e.g. πραιτώριον for which there is no obvious Greek equivalent; the use of μεμβράναι in this passage in place of the Greek διφθέραι (which would denote parchment or skin *rolls*) suggests a difference in the object. *Membranae* is found in Latin from the first century B.C. onwards for a parchment notebook (in which, for example, a poet might write his first drafts). This extension of the familiar wax tablet seems to have been a Latin invention; there is no evidence, literary or archaeological, for it in the Greek East.

What the notebook in question contained is a matter for conjecture; and what our conjecture is may depend on whether this section in the Epistle is considered to be Pauline and, if not, at what date it was written. There are good reasons for thinking that the first Christian book was a book of Testimonies, that is, of select passages from the Old Testament which could be interpreted as forecasting or confirming the gospel. Before gospel or even epistle was written the *searching of the scriptures* which Jesus attributes to the Jews with the comment 'it is they that bear witness to me' (John 5: 39) was actively pursued. Thus at Beroea sympathetic Jews 'received the word with all eagerness, examining the scriptures daily to see if these things were so' (Acts 17: 11), and in Achaia Apollos, after he had been instructed by Priscilla and Aquila in Ephesus, 'powerfully confuted the Jews in public, showing by the scriptures that the Christ was Jesus' (Acts 18: 28). So Philip in Acts 8: 35 when he found Candace's minister reading aloud to himself 'beginning with this scripture [Isa. 53: 7–8] told him the good news of Jesus'. Some leaves from a papyrus codex containing just such a collection of *testimonia* have been discovered in Egypt, though the particular copy is not earlier than the fourth century. More significant because earlier is the discovery of a collection of proof texts about the Messiah in Cave IV at Qumrân,[1] a close parallel to New Testament usage, though the need for such a collection is sufficiently obvious for one not to have been the source of the other. In some of the Qumrân manuscripts, e.g. in one of the copies of Isaiah, special signs were employed to indicate passages of messianic significance; to this there is no parallel among the earliest Christian manuscripts.

Such collections of proof texts might not, at any rate at first, rate as books but would correspond to the notes or ὑπομνήματα sometimes kept of the teaching of rabbis or to the notebooks kept by an antiquarian such as the Elder Pliny. This would be one reason for the format denoted by μεμβράναι; another might be the ease of reference that a notebook, whether wooden tablet or parchment, offered to the travelling missionary.

The question posed by the frequent mention of *the words of the Lord* is both more important and more difficult to answer. That they were widely known and accepted as authoritative is clear from the New Testament, but it gives us no clue to the means of transmission, still less to the process by which or the date at which this material became fixed and began to constitute one of the principal elements in the gospel. Before it could be circulated (even though not published) in a regular written form, the objections felt in Judaism and consequently, we may suppose, in the earliest Christian communities, had to be overcome. This goes some way to explain the long-lived preference for the oral tradition that we find, for example, in Papias, bishop of Hierapolis in Asia Minor at the beginning of the second century. 'I thought', he wrote, 'that it was not so much what was taken from books that would help me as that which came from a living and still present voice' (referring to what he had heard directly from John the elder).[2] Eusebius following Clement and Papias compares Mark's Gospel with 'the un-

---

[1] See G. R. Driver, *The Judean Scrolls* (Oxford, New York, 1965), pp. 19, 527 f.
[2] Eus. *H.E.* III, 39, 4.

written teaching of the *kerygma* of God',[1] reflecting a time when for some churches there was a choice between the two. No doubt the oral tradition was reinforced, as it was in Judaism, with notes; the contrast here is with a genuine book. The word ὑπόμνημα can be applied to a treatise as well as to notes; too much emphasis should not therefore be laid on Eusebius' allusion to the ὑπομνήματα[2] of the Lord's discourses, especially as a little later he refers to Mark and Luke 'having made publication of their gospels', using the word ἔκδοσις, the standard term for the public dissemination of any writing.

Nothing in this account obliges us to think of—for example—Mark's Gospel having grown by degrees out of the private notes used for the Jewish oral Law; equally 'publication' need not imply activity by the book trade so much as widespread distribution within the Church. We may surmise that even when some Gospels existed in the form known to us they were still not accepted as texts having the same authority as the Old Testament; that stage may well have coincided with the selection of the four as the final and complete record of the Church. A single inspired book, or group of books, was not in the first two generations felt to be necessary for the 'instruction in Christ' provided by the living tradition handed on from mouth to mouth, reinforced by circular letters from the leaders of the Church. Collections of such letters may have been second only to the collection of *testimonia* in the history of Christian literature.

If we were dependent on the few references in ancient authors, we would assume that the earliest Christian books were much the same in appearance as those in use in Jewish or Greek circles and might further infer, as many scholars since Harnack[3] have done, that the Old Testament remained the only sacred scripture of the early Church until the second half of the second century. Both these views, which are closely connected, have been challenged by the discovery of Christian manuscripts, often very fragmentary, among the Egyptian papyri in the last 75 years. Towards the end of the nineteenth century and in the first thirty years of the twentieth, Christian papyri had been published, some of which, e.g. the so-called *Logia*, now known to be part of the Gnostic *Gospel of Thomas*, excited great attention because

[1] *H.E.* II, 15, 1.
[2] *H.E.* III, 24, 5–7; cf. V, 8, 2–4 (quoting Irenaeus).
[3] *Bible Reading in the Early Church* (Eng. trans. London, 1912), p. 41.

of their content; when, as was often the case, they were written not on rolls, but in codex form, this was sometimes regarded as a ground for dating them later than the strictly palaeographical evidence would require, in ignorance or at any rate neglect of the allusions in pagan literature of the later first and early second century A.D. to the existence of the codex in the West. In the 1930s the publication first of the great series of Chester Beatty papyri containing very substantial parts of books of the Old and New Testaments together with some non-canonical works, followed by that of the Egerton Gospel in the British Museum and of the Rylands St John—all of them on papyrus, all codices—put the problem in a new perspective. Since then a collection hardly less important than that of Sir Chester Beatty, that of M. Bodmer in Geneva, together with other minor texts (among which may be mentioned some early fragments of the First Gospel divided between Magdalen College, Oxford, and Barcelona)—again all papyrus codices —have reinforced the conclusions to which the discoveries of the years before 1914 had in fact pointed. (It is possible, though not proven, that the Chester Beatty and Bodmer codices may have formed part of a single church library, accumulated over two centuries or more, and eventually deposited, in the Jewish fashion, in a Geniza; if this is so, it does not weaken their evidence.)

The evidence for dating the hands of literary papyri, consisting partly of exactly dated documents found together with and sometimes quite closely resembling the literary hands, partly of literary papyri for which a *terminus ante* or *terminus post* could be established, was now considerable. Though a precise and infallible dating is not possible, on all the criteria generally accepted by palaeographers certain of these Christian manuscripts—notably the Chester Beatty Numbers and Deuteronomy, the Egerton Gospel and the Rylands St John—were written in Egypt in the first half or about the middle of the second century, and the number of Christian manuscripts plausibly assigned to that century is now not less than twelve. They are not just notebooks, but parts of substantial books, some when complete running to a hundred pages or more; some were clearly professional productions. In passing it should be observed that there is no instance in Egypt of a papyrus notebook, i.e. folded sheets of papyrus equivalent to a multi-leaved tablet and used for memoranda, before the fourth century A.D., and none from Syria before the third.

The contrast with pagan texts is striking. An analysis of pagan literary manuscripts from Egypt made some years ago gave the proportion of codices to rolls as 2·3% in the second century, 2·9% among those assigned to the border between the second and third centuries, 16·8% in the third, 48·1% on the borderline between third and fourth, 73·95% in the fourth. Subsequent publications have if anything increased the ratio of rolls in the second and third centuries. (A fair proportion of the earliest codices are what might be called sub-literary —technical or professional texts.) A survey of biblical texts from Egypt made at the same time yielded 99 codices and 12 rolls, and on closer examination even those 12 provided insecure evidence for the roll as a vehicle of the Bible in the early Church. Five were opisthograph—that is, on the verso of a roll already used for some other purpose, whether literary or documentary. Here the writer of the biblical text had no choice but to employ the roll form and the employment of such material is no evidence of the choice of the roll form as such: it was an obvious and much-used economy. Of the remainder three are certainly and six possibly Jewish. Only one is indubitably Christian, and that is a roll of the Psalms. No early manuscript of the New Testament known to us was written on the recto of a roll. All Christian manuscripts of the Bible, whether of the Old Testament or the New Testament, attributable to the second or the earlier third century, are codices, all written on papyrus.

Thus it is not so much a question of a preference for the codex as a deliberate and almost exclusive choice of it where the Bible was concerned. With Christian manuscripts other than biblical, practice varies; some, possibly because they were candidates for the Canon, others more probably on the analogy of the biblical texts, are in codex form; others, and not only scholarly treatises when pagan practices might be expected to be followed, but texts such as Tatian's *Harmony of the Four Gospels* (found at Dura Europos and so written before the destruction of the city in A.D. 256) and one of the Logia papyri, are in roll form. Although the parchment notebook was well established in Rome and though an enterprising publisher attempted to popularise the parchment book as a vade-mecum for travellers at the end of the first century A.D., legal writers in the middle of the third century could still dispute whether the definition of a book covered a codex. It was probably in consequence of strong Greek influence in cultural circles that only the roll was fully a book until at least the middle of that century. At this period there is no Greek word for codex; both the name and the object it denotes are unmistakably Western.

Various theories have been advanced to explain this odd addiction on the part of the early Church (or at least on that of the Egyptian church, since there is no comparably early evidence for the rest of the world) for a novel form of book. In that both sides were fully and conveniently used, the codex was more economical than the roll; the early Church was not wealthy. On this ground we might expect a preference, hardly an addiction; nor does this theory adequately explain either the abandonment of the roll for the Old Testament scriptures or its retention for some non-biblical texts. And in the earliest manuscripts, though not *éditions de luxe*, the writing is well spaced and the letters of normal size; nothing suggests that the scribe's first objective was to get the maximum of text into the minimum of space. Again, it has been urged that the greater capacity of the codex was an attraction, especially in the period when the Canon was being formed. But the earliest codices do not seem to have been of unusual capacity, though one held both Numbers and Deuteronomy, another Luke and John; the earliest of all probably carried the Fourth Gospel only. This consideration would hardly have carried weight before the establishment of the fourfold canon of the gospel; further, this theory too fails to explain the transfer of the Old Testament books from roll to codex by Christians. Thirdly, it has been rightly said that the codex was more convenient than the roll for the traveller and the missionary, with its numbered pages easier to consult, in its compact shape perhaps easier to conceal. But pagan teachers and Jewish missionaries did not abandon the roll (as the Testimony roll from Qumrân illustrates). Convenience may have been a factor; it cannot have been decisive.

Another hypothesis may be found in the Roman origin of the codex. The earliest Christian congregations in Rome who would have been literate, but hardly literary in their interests, would have needed, apart from the sacred rolls of the Old Testament or letters from apostles or other churches, some notes for the day-to-day teaching of converts, whether *testimonia* from the Old Testament or records of what was later incorporated in the gospels. In their ordinary business life the tablet, both in waxed wood and in parchment, would have been familiar. This may well have been the form in which, according to the account recorded by Papias and transmitted by Eusebius, Mark reduced to writing Peter's reminiscences, not long after Peter's death. The work, intended for private circulation among the faithful, may well have kept the form of the parchment notebook (cf. μεμβράναι in 2 Tim. 4: 13), even if later elaborated into what we know as the Second Gospel. (Incidentally, the last leaf of a codex is far more likely to be torn or lost than the last column of a roll, protected by being on the inside.) Certainly the papyrus codex of Egypt must have had a parchment predecessor; since papyrus is hardly a natural material for this format (and notebooks of papyrus are unknown at this period), it is difficult to see where, if not at Rome, this could have originated.

A tradition that goes back to the second century associates Mark with the foundation of the Church of Alexandria, a minor founder figure for a major church. This may point to some early connection between Rome and Alexandria, probable enough on other grounds; the theory that Mark's Gospel at a very early date was accepted in Alexandria and consequently throughout Egypt as a fundamental statement of faith might account for the facts. For, once in Egypt, it would have been copied and recopied on the native material, papyrus,[1] and some of the respect and authority attributed to the content must have been accorded to the form. The next stage was reached when the codex was established as the proper form not only for this Gospel, but for all the texts that later formed the New Testament and, significantly, for Christian copies of the Old Testament as well.

It is this latter development that is the more striking, as it marks the independence of the Church from Jewish traditions and practices and points the way to the formation of the Christian Canon. We possess codices of Old Testament books, or fragments of them, from the first half of the second century, and consequently this break with the past, which must have seemed impious to a Jew, probably took place not much later than the turn of the century. The adoption of the codex for specifically Christian texts (including for example the Third Gospel and Acts, which, being addressed to the Graeco-Jewish world and having some literary pretensions, would naturally have been published in roll form) would have occurred somewhat earlier, the authority attached to Christian texts being such that they determined the format

[1] Only two classical MSS. from Egypt on parchment and probably antedating the third century are known.

of the Old Testament books used in the Church rather than vice versa. This process must have begun—not necessarily in Egypt—well in the first century; some complementary evidence of this may be found in the papyri themselves.

In Jewish copies of the Greek versions of the scriptures it was usual for the name of God, Yahweh, to be written in Hebrew letters (the name itself being pronounced Adonai, Lord, in reading aloud), sometimes by a second hand, the place for it being indicated by spacings or dots. This treatment of the Tetragrammaton provided a precedent for what palaeographers know as *nomina sacra* in Christian manuscripts. Certain words of religious significance were singled out for special treatment by scribes (except of course where the word occurred in a secular context, e.g. θεός of pagan gods or πνεῦμα in the sense *wind*). The ordinary Greek habit of indicating the symbols for numerals, ordinal and cardinal, and other non-words by a line placed over the letter or letters concerned, as a warning to the reader necessary in texts with no word division, was wedded to the Hebrew practice of omitting the vowels (in Greek, the vowels of the stem). The *nomina sacra* are thus contracted by the omission of certain vowels and sometimes of consonants and the contraction indicated by a line placed above it, a construction unknown to Greek or Hebrew writing. The four key words are θεός, κύριος, Ἰησοῦς and χριστός. The last two are invariably contracted (with the non-significant exception of the very rare scribal error); with the other two confusion occasionally arises because of their secular as well as their religious connotation. The system was extended to other words, but the degree of consistency in usage varies; it need not concern us here, any more than the theological significance of the selection of some words and the omission of others for such treatment.

The system must first have been applied to specifically Christian manuscripts, in keeping with the interest in symbolism of which there are traces in the New Testament. As a second stage it was used in Christian manuscripts of the Old Testament; it is already found in some of the oldest Christian papyri of the Old Testament (in others the surviving fragments are too small to yield instances of the relevant words), notably in the Chester Beatty Numbers and Deuteronomy. In this codex written in the first half of the second century the words contracted include not only κύριος and Ἰσραήλ but Joshua = Jesus. The habit of contracting the name Jesus as a mark of reverence must have been very well established for a scribe to slip into using it as a matter of course when the same name occurred in an Old Testament book. That the practice of *nomina sacra* reaches back into the first century is strongly suggested by a passage in the anti-Jewish *Epistle of Barnabas* (written towards the close of the century). Here the number (318) of Abraham's followers as given in Gen. 14: 14 is explained on the ground that the Greek letter *tau* = 300 stands for the Cross, while the letter for 18 (*iota* followed by *eta*) stands for the name Jesus. This is one of the forms of the *nomen sacrum* for Jesus.

The transference of the Law from its sacrosanct form to a format of no antiquity and little regard, sanctioned only by its use for the Gospels, must have seemed to the Jew an act of sacrilege; the further step of employing the *nomina sacra*, of not inserting the Hebrew name in the Greek text and of treating other names with equal reverence must have seemed blasphemy. At this point, some time in the first century, we may place the beginnings of the Christian Canon. With this appropriation of the Hebrew scriptures as the true inheritance not of Judaism, but of the Church, and their assimilation to the form and scribal patterns of the new religion, would naturally go an independence in the choice of what constituted scripture; the fact that some book or books—which we do not know—provided a model for the transcription of the Old Testament suggests that a Christian Canon was beginning to take shape.

It would however be a mistake to suppose that the development of the Christian Bible was straightforward and simple. Some books of the Old Testament, especially the Law and the Psalms, would have been the essential equipment of any church from the earliest days; for the sayings of the Lord a prejudice in favour of the direct oral tradition as a reliable and living witness lingered in some circles at least for a long time. Just as Irenaeus memorised what Polycarp told him of his direct knowledge of John, recorded 'not on papyrus but in my heart',[1] so Papias preferred the oral to the written record. None the less, Papias wrote a commentary on the sayings of the Lord[2] (which surely assumes the existence in writing of the *logia* in question), just as the gospel was a datum for Irenaeus. The earliest Christian missions relied on eye-witness accounts; this was their strength and goes far to explain the persistence of the oral tradition.

[1] Eus. *H.E.* v, 20, 7.   [2] *Ibid.* ii, 39, 1 f.

Our earliest Christian manuscripts have much in common. All (with a single exception from the third century) come from Egypt; all were found by excavation. There are twelve plausibly assigned to the second century; ten of these carry texts of the Bible, seven of the Old Testament, three of the New Testament. All ten are written on papyrus, all are codices. The New Testament texts are a fragment of the Fourth Gospel (probably the earliest manuscript of them all), a much more extensive though later manuscript containing most of the same Gospel in 108 pages, and a fragment of the Epistle to Titus. Of the Old Testament texts two are of the Psalms, two of Genesis, one of Exodus; while the sixth contained both Exodus and Deuteronomy, the seventh Numbers and Deuteronomy. It is no surprise that the Pentateuch and the Psalms were of all Old Testament books the most read in the early Church; with Isaiah they are the most quoted books in the New Testament. Of the two remaining manuscripts in this oldest group one is the Egerton Gospel, written about the middle of the century on a papyrus codex; the other is a text of the *Shepherd* of Hermas, written on the back of a local government register from the Fayûm, probably a copy made locally for the church in Arsinoe, the capital of the Fayûm; it has been specially marked for reading aloud. Of manuscripts on the borderline between the second and third centuries there may be mentioned a fragment of Irenaeus' *Adversus Haereses* written on a roll in a fine literary hand, a papyrus codex of Matthew, again a professional production, two more manuscripts of the Psalms, the Chester Beatty Pauline epistles (a codex that when complete ran to 208 pages) and the two *logia* manuscripts now known to belong to the Gospel of Thomas.

Not many generalisations can usefully be made about this earliest group of manuscripts. But it is noticeable that many of them, though well and clearly written, are the work not of professional literary scribes, but of fluent writers who, used to writing, tried hard for the most part to write in bookhands, but betray the documentary styles with which they were more familiar, frequently in the use of ligature, sometimes in letter forms. Since precisely dated documents survive in abundance from the first three centuries, this is an aid to dating. It is significant that the scribe of the Chester Beatty Numbers and Deuteronomy, when he comes to write the Greek for centurion, uses the abbreviation familiar in military and official documents, while the

Baden Deuteronomy, the style of which is of all the closest to that of contemporary documents, was found together with a document written in the same hand. (It is also worth noting that we do not know of a single case of the same scribe writing a Christian and a secular manuscript.) This confirms what in any case might have been guessed, that the earliest manuscripts were the product not of the book trade but of communities whose members included businessmen and minor officials well used to writing. A few however are in an unmistakable literary hand with only occasional documentary reminiscences such as can also be found in secular manuscripts.

These books have no uniform format, but there are two which are favoured, one in which the height of the page is nearly twice the width, the other in which the page makes approximately a square, either of six inches or of eight. All are eminently practical books. Pages are usually numbered, but even in the best manuscripts the number of lines to a page varies considerably. The hands are not cramped and do not suggest a desire for economy; as far as we can tell, none of these early codices contained more than two books of the Pentateuch, whereas in the third century more capacious codices, that for example of the Chester Beatty four Gospels and Acts, are frequent. The oldest of all, the Rylands St John, would have had to consist of 132 pages, whether in separate quires or, as was often the case, in a single quire, to take the whole Gospel. Codices were not composed of separate leaves already written; their make-up, the varying number of lines to the page and the fact that pages are not planned to end with a section or a sentence, all tell against the view that particular features in the books as we know them can be explained by transposition of pages.

With few exceptions the New Testament is composed of books that either are anonymous or are explicitly non-literary; whose status as books is conferred on them by time and use. Our early copies of them are no more private copies than they are book trade copies; not addressed to the world at large, they were the products of a community, and the community saw to their dissemination. (In classical literature some analogy may be found in the circulation of Aristotelian or Epicurean texts.) In Colossians we read of letters being exchanged and copied between Colossae and Laodicea;[1] at this stage there is no thought of the formation of a library, but when the same practice is alluded to

[1] Col. 4: 16.

in Polycarp[1] and Ignatius,[2] we may be sure that the Church regarded such copies as part of their archives, if not of their libraries. The clearest reference to the 'publication' of Christian texts is to be found in the *Shepherd* of Hermas:[3] 'You shall write then', says the Lady to Hermas in his vision, 'two little books and you shall send one to Clement and one to Graptē. Clement shall then send them to the cities overseas, for that is his duty; Graptē shall admonish the widows and the orphans; but in this city [Rome] you shall read them yourself together with the priests that have the charge of the Church.'

On the rapid circulation of literature among the churches and on its regular and public reading much of the coherence of the early Church must have depended; libraries and archives would have been as essential an element in them as they were in the synagogues. The remarkably uniform system of *nomina sacra* discussed above suggests that at an early date there were standard copies of the Christian scriptures, much as before the destruction of Jerusalem the authoritative copy of the Law was preserved in the Temple. The unvarying use of the codex, so marked in the Egyptian church, may have been the result of direct Roman influence and, for all we know, may not have extended beyond Egypt until the third century; the uniformity in *nomina sacra* may point to a more general rule.

Community control may explain the relative absence of 'wild' texts among New Testament manuscripts, very marked if we compare them with those of the *Acta Pauli* or of *The Shepherd*. M. Dibelius[4] has suggested that the existence of the marked divergences in the readings of the Western Text of Luke and Acts (more striking in these books than in any others) is explained on the ground that there were two editions: one sold through the book trade and addressed to the sympathetic hellenised Jew or pagan, the other circulating in the Christian communities; since the text of Acts was adapted for liturgical purposes later than that of Luke, it is wilder because it was later in gaining the protection of community use and control. We might add that persecution may have prevented the trade edition from enjoying a prolonged circulation and that the text of Luke may have suffered less because it was protected relatively early by the single codex of the four Gospels. This is guesswork; we have to admit that we know as little of the

---

[1] *Phil.* 13: 2. [2] *Smyrn.* 11: 3; *Philad.* 10: 1; *Mart. Pol.* 27, 2.
[3] *Vis.* 2 end. [4] *JR*, XXI (1941), 421 f.

organisation and circulation of early Christian literature as we do of the finances of the early Church.

If we ask who was responsible for copying, and on the whole copying accurately, the Christian scriptures, the answer is again largely a matter of surmise; matters taken for granted are rarely recorded. Remains of a scriptorium have been found at Qumrân and of that community it has been said 'copying was the earliest and principal task of the Community, as of Christian monks'.[1] The Church in the world was in a different situation but the obligation may have been felt to be no less heavy than it was in orthodox Judaism.

In the early second century the variety in the types of hands and the documentary influence visible in some of them tell against the hypothesis of central scriptoria. In the latter part of the century radical changes in this as in other spheres of Church life took place. We can infer from Celsus and Lucian that Christian books were accessible enough; with the establishment of the Catechetical School in Alexandria, a lay institution, the techniques of classical scholarship, mingled with the tradition of Jewish exegetes, began to be applied to Christian texts. To it would have been attached a scriptorium which was probably the model for that which Origen established with the help of a wealthy friend at Caesarea and for the library in Jerusalem founded by Bishop Alexander some time after A.D. 212. Eusebius' account of Origen's scriptorium at Caesarea—surely the first reference on record to the employment of women stenographers[2]—suggests that in its use of shorthand it looked back to the ancient world, as in its specialised and enclosed activity it foreshadowed the cathedral scriptoria of the Middle Ages. His assistants were skilled not only in shorthand but in calligraphy; from now on Christian book production was on a level with that in the pagan world. The purpose of the scriptorium was to produce copies of the Bible and biblical commentaries; the earliest liturgical books among the papyri are nearly a century later.

Details of scribal procedure—punctuation, quotation marks, signs of omission and deletion—were much the same in Greek and Jewish manuscripts and were naturally adopted in Christian books. What was peculiar to the Jews was the veneration for the manuscript as the incarnation of the Law and consequent on this, especially after the

[1] G. R. Driver, *The Judaean Scrolls* (Oxford, New York, 1965), p. 359.
[2] *H.E.* VI, 23, 2.

destruction of the Jewish state, scrupulous care in the minutest detail of its production. Though Jewish scrupulosity is not paralleled in the early Church and we know of no minute regulations governing the production of the text, something of respect for the text and the manuscript was transmitted to the Church. Just as the pious Jew never lived far from a copy of the Law, so Abercius Marcellus, bishop of Hieropolis in Phrygia towards the close of the second century, in his famous inscription[1] claims that Paul, i.e. the Pauline epistles, was his travelling companion and praises the Church as the teacher of 'sound writings'. Evidence for the care taken in copying and correcting can be found both in early writers[2] and in the early papyri themselves, though we cannot be sure if equal care was taken with Christian records and books before they were set on the path to ultimate canonisation; the first years of any book's life are always the most dangerous for the text.

Christian culture and education were bookish through and through; reliance on the book, initially a legacy from Judaism, was soon a weapon of the Church in its fight against paganism. This ensured that the specifically Christian preaching would be transmitted in writing at an early date, but it was transmitted with a difference. *Tertium genus dicimus*:[3] the history of Christian manuscripts in the first three centuries mirrors in small the relation of the Church to Judaism on the one hand and to hellenism on the other, a relationship of alternate repulsion and attraction, of derivation as well as of originality. 'We are so accustomed', wrote A. D. Nock,[4] 'to the Church as a fact of life that we do not always realise how remarkable a phenomenon it was—differing from synagogue and from pagan cult group; the total novelty of the Church manifested itself early...the Christian movement from the beginning shows both continuity and cultural break.' On that text the manuscripts of the first three centuries, written occasionally on rolls as well as in codices, employing the usual scribal conventions as well as *nomina sacra*, offer an apt gloss.

---

[1] *Reallexikon f. Antike u. Christentum*, I, *s.v. Aberkios*.
[2] E.g. Eus. *H.E.* v, 20, 2.   [3] Tertullian, *Ad Nationes*, 8.
[4] In *JBL*, LXVII (1948), 257.

CHAPTER III

THE OLD TESTAMENT

5. THE OLD TESTAMENT IN THE MAKING

THE PROBLEM OF ORIGINS

At one end of the process are the necessarily nebulous beginnings of Israel's literature. Since our concern is to understand something of the whole range of ways by which the material now in the Old Testament came into being, some definition must be made of the starting point in time. And this definition is as difficult to make as is the decision where to begin a history of Israel or a study of Israel's religion. It may be convenient for the former to determine the point in time at which it is proper to speak of Israel as an entity rather than as a loose agglomeration of small elements, and to decide on this basis that the history of Israel in the true sense begins with the monarchy, or with the tribal amphictyony, or with the Exodus; the decision will be made by each historian on his own terms. But inevitably he must also assess the available evidence for the pre-history of those elements which were ultimately to become explicitly Israel. Similarly the study of Israel's religion involves a decision on starting point, but again, whatever the choice, the pre-settlement religion or the pre-Mosaic religion comes under discussion however uncertain of interpretation the evidence may be. Israel's literature, naturally enough, is so tied in with both history and religion that a comparable decision about origins has to be made. But the lines have to be drawn from there back into the remoter past, just as—again as with religious and institutional problems—the origins of literary types which appear at a later stage have also to be investigated. The search for origins must be undertaken if we are to understand the literature as it developed within Israel; but the discovery of origin does not by itself explain the nature of the literary type as we find it in the Old Testament. For that its precise context and the use to which it is put must be considered. Ideally we might hope to trace the origins and history of development of each literary type, as Hermann Gunkel attempted to do in regard to psalmody.[1] But the attempt remains no more than that—productive though it has been of much of the modern development of psalm study and in particular of form-critical study—for on the one hand the relation between literature and life is much more complex than can be expressed in terms of single-line developments, and on the other hand, the information is lacking for any full-scale historical treatment. For this reason, too, any attempt at writing a study of the historical development of Old Testament literature, as undertaken for example by Adolphe Lods,[2] remains inevitably unsatisfactory. Not only are there too many uncertainties about the dates of many Old Testament books and passages—though some may be fairly closely dated and much general chronological ordering may be undertaken—but there are also too many problems of interpretation which are bound up with questions of date and provenance, as we may see in the presence within any particular section of Old Testament material of elements of its later exegesis. Every passage has to be read at more than one level.

The psalms, whether in the Psalter itself or scattered about in the historical and prophetical books,[3] did not owe their origin simply to the activities of Israelite or Judaean authors, poets who were officials of the sanctuaries or even private individuals. However much of specifically Israelite motif and allusion now appears in them, their sources lie much further back, as may be seen from the existence of ancient Canaanite poetry in the Ugaritic documents from Ras Shamra, dating from *c.* 1400 B.C., or from the wealth of psalmody from Egypt and Babylonia, closer to or more remote from Old Testament psalmody in its style and content.[4] It may well be doubted if it is possible to prove direct adaptation, as has, for example, been suggested for Ps. 29; the argument that such a psalm contains many Canaanite elements in language and style may in reality derive more from the fact that we are now able to enlarge our understanding of Hebrew language and style by comparison with the Ras Shamra texts: Hebrew may, after all, be not unreasonably described as a Canaanite dialect. Yet it is appropriate to recognise that many of the elements and themes and stylistic con-

---

[1] *Einleitung in die Psalmen*, completed by J. Begrich (Göttingen, 1933).

[2] *Histoire de la littérature hébraïque et juive depuis les origines jusqu'à la ruine de l'état iuif* (135 *après J.-C.*) (Paris, 1950).

[3] E.g. Exod. 15: 1–18; 1 Sam. 2: 1–10; 2 Sam. 22 (= Ps. 18); Mic. 7: 7–20; Hab. 3.

[4] Cf. the examples in *ANET*, pp. 365 ff.; *DOTT*, pp. 111 ff., 142 ff.

ventions of psalmody belong to an earlier age than that of Israel's full monarchical organisation. The community evidently took over important elements in the culture and religious practice of the peoples among whom it settled. It could, for example, at certain periods at least, be regarded as entirely proper to utilise the familiar title Ba'al, 'lord', 'husband', now well known to us from the Ras Shamra texts, as applicable to Israel's own god YHWH.[1]

Israel also made some at least of the ancient sanctuaries of the land its own. It is a reasonable assumption therefore, quite apart from the clear literary affinities which point to the same conclusion, that psalmody, part of the liturgical material which belonged to sanctuary observance, was also taken over and in course of time became by adaptation and reinterpretation an element in Israel's own inheritance.

Literary developments are to be seen also in the narratives associated with the taking over of sanctuaries. Part of the tradition of a sanctuary often appears to have been the legend associated with its origin, the moment when a special revelation of a deity marked out that particular place as holy and indicated that worship to the deity there, by the name then revealed, would be acceptable and proper. So we have sanctuary legends associated with Bethel (Gen. 28: 11–22), Sinai (Exod. 3: 1–6), and a high place at Jebus (Jerusalem, 2 Sam. 24) subsequently rightly or wrongly identified with the site of the Jerusalem temple (1 Chron. 21—22: 1).[2] The Bethel sanctuary legend, being fuller than some of the others, provides a good example of the process by which an ancient tradition, obviously pre-Israelite, has been taken over and baptised into Israelite use. It relates how the ancient name of the place Luz was replaced by a new name Bethel, 'house of God' (El). It associates this renaming with the visit there of Jacob, the forefather of the Israelite tribes. The story is complex, containing elements of different traditions; thus it is evident that one tradition describes a revelation in terms of a 'ladder' between heaven and earth (Gen. 28: 12); the other tradition almost certainly conceives of YHWH standing 'beside him' (i.e. Jacob, Gen. 28: 13 RSV margin), as is recorded also in Samuel's call

[1] Cf. the names of Saul's son Ishbaal (2 Sam. 2: 12, the *ba'al* part of the name having been subsequently replaced by *bōšet* 'shame'; cf. 1 Chron. 9: 39 Eshbaal); Gideon/Jerubbaal (Judg. 6: 32); the remarkable name Bealiah = 'Yah is Baal' (1 Chron. 12: 5); and names on the Samaria ostraca, cf. *DOTT*, pp. 204 ff.

[2] The identification must remain uncertain, and indeed suspect, since the Chronicler also identifies the same site with Mount Moriah (2 Chron. 3: 1, cf. Gen. 22). Cf. pp. 89 f

experience (1 Sam. 3: 10). Jacob is depicted as realising the presence of YHWH, God of Israel, but the new place-name Bethel (Gen. 28: 17) does not quite accord with this, since it uses the general word El for the deity and not the personal name YHWH. This word El is itself known as an ancient divine appellative and indeed virtually as a personal name (*'Il*) in the Ras Shamra texts. It is clear that an older sanctuary legend, associated with the holy place at Luz—and possibly the use of the term *māqôm* 'place' for Jacob's resting place in Gen. 28: 11 indicates an awareness that it was in fact of more ancient origin, since the term, though not always used so technically, often denotes a 'holy place' in the Old Testament—and describing the revelation of El as the deity of the place, has now been taken over by Israel as part of the process by which Canaanite sanctuaries became hallowed as Israelite places of worship, associated now with a personal revelation of God under his name YHWH.

Equally it is clear that Israel's legal literature, now so largely co-ordinated around the person of Moses, goes back to an origin much more remote than the historical moment to which it is attached, though at the same time there are many later elements combined with the older. Parallels between patriarchal customs and those of more or less contemporary societies, evidenced in the Mari and Nuzi texts,[1] show that the ancestors of Israel shared in the common legal heritage of the area. The later more strictly legal material, embodied in the books of Exodus, Leviticus, Numbers and Deuteronomy, while revealing at every point the distinctive emphases and interpretations characteristic of Israelite thinking, bears enough likeness to more ancient and more closely contemporary law collections to show that at each stage the development of the legal literature owed much to common trends within the area. Even where the actual content of the laws differs significantly, as is often the case, the forms in which legal precepts are stated, apodictic or casuistic,[2] reveal the common origin of the types.

At a more evidently theological level, that of the Creation and other

[1] Cf. above, p. 44, and for a brief discussion, with examples, H. H. Rowley, 'Recent Discovery and the Patriarchal Age' in *The Servant of the Lord* (London, 1952; 2nd ed. 1965). The material needs to be used with caution.

[2] Cf. A. Alt, *Die Ursprünge des Israelitischen Rechts* (Leipzig, 1934), E.T. 'The Origins of Israelite Law' in *Essays on Old Testament History and Religion* (Oxford, 1966), pp. 79–132.

primeval stories, there is the same evidence of contact between the traditions which the Old Testament preserves and those found elsewhere. The Old Testament material was eventually formulated in a unified scheme in Gen. 1–11 out of earlier presentations which may be associated with different strands in the Pentateuchal material; allusions appear elsewhere as motifs in the poetry of psalmists, prophets and the wise,[1] often in a more primitive form than in Genesis. Elsewhere such traditions are to be found either directly as parts of long epic accounts, as in the Gilgamesh epic, or indirectly in the allusions to divine conflicts and ordering of life such as are to be found in the Ras Shamra poems. The relationship is not to be explained simply in terms of direct literary dependence, though it may well be that Babylonian forms of the material were actually known in Palestine;[2] nor can the similarities be explained as resulting from entirely independent formulation of the same problems. The relationship is too close for the latter, the differences too significant for the former. But the fact that we may discern that the two Creation descriptions (Gen. 1: 1—2: 4a; 2: 4b–25) belong to two strands, often for convenience' sake described as P (Priestly) and J (Jahwistic), the latter earlier in formulation than the former, does not allow us to conclude that at a given moment Israel either spontaneously created such material or naïvely took over already existing traditions. There is a much larger and more complex tradition of Creation and of primeval man which stretches back beyond any precisely definable historical moment. The beginnings lie back in the ages of speculation about the world and God and man, long before precise accounts were set out; the subsequent development reaches the realm of literary articulation only as a result of considerable rethinking and no doubt of substantial influence from the traditions of contemporaries and neighbours.

In each of these examples, here only briefly adduced, we may detect the origins of particular types of literature; but we cannot possibly delineate those origins precisely, nor necessarily distinguish with accuracy between elements which belong to the earlier stages and those which reflect later ways of thought and action. Subsequently[3] we may investigate how far it is possible to trace origins, not in the sense of

[1] Cf. e.g. Ps. 74: 12–17; Isa. 51: 9–11; Job 38; Prov. 8: 22–31.
[2] Cf. the reference on p. 42 to the fragment of the Gilgamesh epic found at Megiddo.
[3] See below, pp. 79–85.

starting points, but in the sense of situations, and consider how far such a procedure enables us to arrive at a better understanding of the nature of the material and hence at its interpretation.

If the search for origins must always in some measure be left open, the other end of the process of the formation of the Old Testament is sufficiently fixed. This is not to ignore the many problems and uncertainties which surround the fixation of the Old Testament text,[1] or those which concern the defining of which books are canonical and which are not.[2] For a considerable period both text and canon were as yet undefined in the strict sense. Yet there came a point at which, apart from minor variations, the text was fixed; and the canon of the Old Testament was recognisably closed, even if in some religious communities a somewhat wider selection of books was given canonical authority or at least something approaching it. While it is of immense importance to the study of the literature that we can now at certain points penetrate behind the final forms of both text and canon, the primary material for our investigation is the familiar Old Testament, with what is now known as the Apocrypha forming a closely connected body of literature which itself cannot be satisfactorily investigated in complete isolation from certain other works of the so-called intertestamental period. These last are often known as pseudepigrapha,[3] a term covering a loosely defined group, but it needs now to be broadened to include the Qumrân literature and a good case can also be made out for including some of what was eventually incorporated in later rabbinic compilations.

The real starting point for the study of the literature must of necessity be the final formulation, the only stage fully known to us. Some assistance towards discerning earlier stages of the material is provided by the evidence of different forms of the text, as in the case of the Septuagint version of Jeremiah which offers both a different arrangement of the text—placing the foreign nation oracles of chapters 46–51 in the middle of chapter 25—and also a somewhat shorter

---

[1] See III, 7.   [2] See III, 6.

[3] Cf. R. H. Charles (ed.), *Apocrypha and Pseudepigrapha* (2 vols. Oxford, 1913, reprinted 1963).

recension of the book. The survival at Qumrân of a fragment of what may be regarded as an alternative form of the narrative contained in Dan. 4—the 'Prayer of Nabonidus'[1]—enables us to detect something of the process by which older traditions, deriving from Babylonian Jewry though not necessarily of Jewish origin,[2] were re-used in the book of Daniel and also possibly independently. At many points details of textual variation and differences of order may point the way to a fuller understanding of the evolution of the literature. But for the most part we are limited to what actually stands in the Old Testament books, and any speculation about the processes involved in the formation of these books must be such as to provide an explanation of how the material came to be as we now have it. All the time we have to argue back from what is now there, but in such a way as to be able to trace the line forward again to what eventually came to be fixed. The analysis must begin from the text; but from analysis we must indicate a possible line of development to the final form.

An example from a familiar area—that of Pentateuchal criticism—may serve to illustrate the twofold problem of explaining the literature. Over a period of more than two centuries—and deriving in fact from a much longer period of awareness of the presence of the problem—the analysis of various strands of material in the opening books of the Old Testament, the Pentateuch or often the Pentateuch together with the books which follow it, has been taken to a point at which it is clearly recognised that the books as we now have them are made up of different elements, not all of one piece. Opinions differ as to the point in the material to which clearly separable strands can be traced. To some scholars the strands may be detected into the books of Kings; others would wish to make a clear division between the first four books, the Tetrateuch, in which at least the three strands known as J, E and P can be traced, and the Deuteronomic History, the series of books from Deuteronomy to 2 Kings which present a unified view of Israel's history from the wilderness to the exile, a survey utilising much earlier material and probably also already existing documentary matter. Opinions differ too as to how far it is appropriate in this discussion to

[1] For a translation see G. Vermes, *The Dead Sea Scrolls in English* (Harmondsworth, 1962), p. 229.
[2] The traditions utilised in 1 Esdras 3–4 are probably not Jewish in origin; those in Esther may in part be alien.

think in terms of written documents already in existence as sources for these books. There is no question that such documents existed in Israel,[1] but it is not easy to be certain where documents have been used and where there is dependence upon formulated oral tradition. Thus other scholars would wish to allow a much larger place to the influence of oral traditions, to picture the development of the various strands rather in terms of gradual elaboration in use and to allow for the influence upon later forms of the material of traditions which had not been recorded in writing but remained as part of the popular heritage.

There are also substantial differences of estimate as to the date at which the various strands came together. Those who still maintain in some form, often very much modified, the ancient view that Moses was responsible for the Pentateuch, may well allow the existence of various types of material on which he drew.[2] Those who maintain on the basis of clear evidence in the material that its final form must belong to a substantially later date, however much of early tradition or documentary information is incorporated, endeavour to trace the influence of various lines of thought and of various historical situations and hence to arrive at an assessment of the point or points to which the Pentateuch as we now have it belongs.

In all these varied ways the attempt is made to explain the divergences within the material. An adequate solution must meet all the essential requirements. It must explain the inconsistencies of language, style, theological presentation and the like; it must also demonstrate by what processes the present condition of the material can have been reached.

Thus, we have already noted that there are two Creation accounts (Gen. 1: 1—2: 4a; 2: 4b–25). The differences of style, language and theological conception are such as to make unsatisfactory the various attempts which have been made, both more anciently among rabbinic writers and more recently in reaction against source analysis, at explaining away the differences and seeking to regard the two as really only one. Even such attempts, as for example that of Rashi and of those moderns who have followed him, perhaps unconsciously, at showing

---

[1] Cf. D. J. Wiseman, in II, 3.

[2] The title of one of the great pioneer works of Pentateuchal criticism may serve to illustrate this: *Conjectures sur les mémoires dont il paroit que Moyse s'est servi, pour composer le livre de la Genèse*, by Jean Astruc, published in 1753.

that the differences of divine names in the two accounts can be explained from the theological emphasis (rather than from differences of source), at least reveal the awareness of a problem which has to be faced.

But the problem of differences is much broader than this, and what is here observable may be traced again and again in other parts of the Pentateuch, making it probable that we are concerned not with isolated fragments, nor with the changes imposed on a single writer by the nature of his subject matter, but with consistent and delineable traditions or sources. But when the analysis has been made and the two accounts are seen to lie side by side, the further question has to be asked: how and why did these come together? Part of the answer lies in the recognition that this material is not narrative in a narrow sense, but is theologically motivated—it is indeed difficult to find any part of the Old Testament, however apparently secular, which does not carry such an element. If, as is probable, the material has passed through generations and even centuries of use before reaching its present form, it has come to possess in the process what we may not unreasonably call 'canonical' authority. The material has been preserved because it enjoyed a status in the people's faith. The different traditions may represent different areas—the common association is of J with the south and E with the north—or different strata—as the proposed association of Deuteronomic material with Levitical circles—within the life of the people. So in the course of time, as a result of the welding together of various groups and of the later historical circumstances through which Israel (or that part of it which survived) rethought its nature as people of God and re-evaluated its traditions, we should expect that what had come down from the past, belonging to more than one constituent part of the eventual community, should come together into a literary unity. But a further stage must also be recognised. The two accounts now stand together, and not only analysis is necessary for their understanding: they are to be read as complementary, as shedding light on one another, if we are to enter into the minds of those who brought them together and who used them together.

The situation is more difficult where analysis—as in the Flood narratives of Gen. 6–9—shows that the strands are closely interwoven. The same comments may here be made in regard to 'canonicity' and to the combining of traditions belonging to different groups within the community. But here a greater problem exists in regard to the mechanics of the matter. By what kind of process did the strands come to be combined? This is a problem which faces the literary analysis over and over again in the Pentateuchal material. Various types of approach are possible. We may think that a basic narrative has in each case been 'glossed' by the insertion into it of elements belonging to another or more than one other tradition. Or we may point to the analogy of Tatian's *Diatessaron* in the second century A.D., a harmony of the Gospels produced by the device of taking small pieces from each Gospel and weaving them together into a coherent narrative. Criticism of such a view that it is too modern and inapplicable to the Old Testament—a dismissal of it as mere 'scissors and paste'—must take account of this Gospel harmony from a relatively early date. Nor is this the only evidence for redactorial activity of this kind. It is by a somewhat similar process that the author (or authors) of the great work Chronicles–Ezra–Nehemiah—usually referred to by the shorthand name 'the Chronicler'—has taken over material which is to some extent already known to us in a prior form, whether in the Pentateuch from which he has drawn much of his genealogical material and ordered it into a consistent pattern, or in the historical books, into which he has inserted other information, some of it probably of good historical quality. He has also at times felt free to rearrange the order to obtain what was evidently for him a more significant theological interpretation, as in his placing of the narrative of 2 Sam. 24 = 1 Chron. 21.[1] It is possible that some part of this selecting and re-ordering process had already taken place before the Chronicler compiled his form of the work; it is clear that he did not use the books of Samuel and Kings as we have them. But this does not affect the point. Someone, and probably a whole series of persons, was responsible for adding, cutting, rearranging, reinterpreting already existing literary material to make a new entity.

The Chronicler's work provides us with the most extensive example of duplicate texts in the Old Testament, but in this it is by no means unique. Ps. 18 has already been noted as equivalent to 2 Sam. 22; the small deviations in the text are of considerable interest, though it is doubtful if it can be established that one form of the text is preferable to the other. This psalm was evidently regarded by the compiler(s) of the books of Samuel as suitable for its position among the various

---

[1] Cf. below, pp. 86–90.

addenda which constitute 2 Sam. 21–4; it stands side by side with another psalm, the so-called 'Last words of David' (2 Sam. 23: 1–7). The fact that it does so may suggest that both were taken from an already existing collection of psalms associated with the name of David. The psalm was also included in the Psalter whose composition presents us with a different series of problems, since some earlier collections can with reasonable certainty be traced within it (cf. e.g. Ps. 72: 20: 'The prayers of David, the son of Jesse, are ended'). It is impossible now to tell what is the precise relationship between these two forms of the same text; what seems clear is that neither text has been taken directly from the other.[1]

More significantly, we find duplicate forms of prophetic oracles, as in Isa. 2: 2–4; Mic. 4: 1–4, differing in detail, here both in wording and in the division of units, and now offering alternative modes of interpretation. It is no longer possible to determine with certainty whether this was an oracle of one of the two prophets to whom it is ascribed or whether it belongs to neither; some degree of overlap between the oracular traditions associated with both prophets suggests the possibility that their words were handed down in the same or closely connected circles. In each case, the oracle occupies a theologically intelligible position, commenting in Isaiah on the gloomy and hopeful oracles on Jerusalem in Isa. 1,[2] and in Micah on the doom of the city pronounced in the last verses of chapter 3. Here analysis, which must separate out this oracle from its context, can be complemented by the recognition that, however the oracles actually came into their present positions, and whoever was responsible for this, the resultant form of the material is theologically intelligible.

The same principle has to be applied to all those cases where it appears likely that the text has been glossed by a later editor or scribe. It is important for full understanding not only to mark those passages which are of later origin and interrupt the smooth line of the material, but also to consider, so far as the evidence allows, for what purpose the original passage was glossed. That there may sometimes be elements of chance here is not to be denied. It is conceivable that the awkwardly

---

[1] Cf. also the duplicate occurrence of the psalm: Ecclus. 51: 13 ff. and 11QPsᵃ, cols. XXI–XXII (J. A. Sanders, *The Psalms Scroll of Qumrân Cave 11* (11QPsᵃ) (Oxford, 1965), esp. pp. 79–85.

[2] I would ignore the 'title' of 2: 1, cf. *ZAW*, LXXV (1963), 320 f.

placed phrase in Gen. 4: 7, 'its desire is for you, but you must master it', is a corrupted (or modified) form of the similar phrase in Gen. 3: 16, 'your desire shall be for your husband, and he shall rule over you'.[1] Could the phrase—which appears to belong much more properly in 3: 16—have been accidentally omitted at some stage by a copyist, added in the margin[2] and inadvertently regarded as belonging also to 4: 7 which in the particular manuscript happened to occur in the same line in the adjacent column? Such an explanation can never be more than hypothetical—unless a manuscript is found to confirm it—and many scholars would be quite unwilling to accept it as being too far-fetched.

In Isa. 3: 1 it has been argued that the original phrase 'stay and staff', explained in *vv*. 2 ff. in terms of leadership, has been glossed by the words 'the whole stay of bread and the whole stay of water' which interrupt the sequence of thought. If so, we may reasonably postulate that such a gloss belongs to a time of siege—whether of Isaiah's own time, i.e. 701 B.C. when Sennacherib besieged Jerusalem, or perhaps more probably 588–587 B.C., the time of the Babylonian siege. The latter would fit in with some other indications in the opening chapters of Isaiah which suggest that the words of the eighth-century prophet were reinterpreted in the early years of the exile because they were then understood as relevant to the new situation: the message of the prophet in all its grimness was now seen to be fulfilled in total disaster. Here the attempt is made both to analyse the text and to explain some stages at least of its evolution.

It must be admitted that sometimes a phrase which appears intrusive is only so to a modern eye, because a greater logic of thought is looked for than the ancient writer provides: not a few of the psalms are difficult to us because they change subject and change grammatical construction with an apparently unnecessary abruptness. It sometimes happens too that a difficult phrase has been wrongly interpreted, and that a better understanding of the Hebrew language in relation to its cognates enables a consistent interpretation to be offered. We must always be chary of accepting as a gloss something which does not in some way

---

[1] The Hebrew text shows more clearly the closeness of the two:

| 3:16 | wᵉʾel ʾišēk | tᵉšûqātēk | wᵉhûʾ | yimšol | bāk |
| 4:7 | wᵉʾēlêkā | tᵉšûqātô | wᵉʾattā | timšol | bô |

[2] For such marginal additions, the Qumrân MSS. may be compared, e.g. 1QIsᵃ, cols. XXVIII, XXXII, XXXIII.

explain the supposed original text; not a few commentaries on the Old Testament books offer skilful analysis, pointing to glosses which it is suggested now impede the understanding of the original text, but which leave the reader totally in the dark as to what process, other than sheer carelessness, could have created the present form of the text complete with its supposed glosses. We must work always with one eye firmly on the resultant text, for this is, for the most part, the only fixed point in relation to which we can operate.

With this caution we may, however, consider how far we can legitimately get behind that text to discover more original forms and the processes involved in its formation.

LITERATURE AND LIFE

It may be asked whether in fact the term 'literature' ought to be applied to the Old Testament writings at all. If the term is used very broadly it will, of course, include such works as these; but if a narrower definition, in terms of literary, artistic works is intended, then it is extremely doubtful if it is justified. The Old Testament is a collection of religious writings which, whatever their individual origins, are in their final form directed to the maintenance of the life of a community which thought of itself as being in a special sense the people of God. The resultant 'literature' is not a collection of the best writings of ancient Israel, a sort of *Golden Treasury* of a people's prose and poetry. Equally it would be wrong to define it in terms of what happened to survive, since it is likely that a much wider range of writings existed—some of which are known to us by name, others by fragmentary survivals in post-biblical and extra-biblical works, as for example the 'Prayer of Nabonidus' already mentioned, and others by allusion to broader traditions which appear later in Targum and Midrash, as is shown in G. Vermes' discussion in this volume.[1] It is a corpus, partly unconsciously and partly deliberately defined as a 'canon'.[2]

Yet this corpus of writings can neither be understood in isolation, apart from its environment in ancient Near Eastern culture and writing, nor be assessed adequately in its final form unless we take account of the laws which govern the formation and development of the particular literary types to be found here. (This use of the term 'laws' must not

[1] Cf. chapter III, 8.   [2] Cf. chapter III, 6.

be interpreted too strictly, as if there were external canons imposed on literary development, but only as a reference to generalisations deduced from the forms of the literature itself.) The same patterns can be observed in the literatures of Israel and of other ancient cultures of the area. The earlier and later examples of the same types can be shown to follow closely similar structures and often to make use of stereotyped language. The tracing of origins and of literary forms always involves both a consideration of the Old Testament examples and of those which can be adduced from the surrounding lands, and it involves the recognition of the persistence of conventions within which individual authors, prophets or wise men or others, operate and to which traditions, legal or historical or psalmodic, conform.

An example may serve to illustrate and clarify the point. A simple reading of the opening of Isa. 6, the so-called 'Call of Isaiah' (though in fact nowhere definitely specified as the initial prophetic experience), would suggest that we have here a straightforward narration of a particular visionary and auditory experience, datable by its opening to a precise moment in the people's history, the year of Uzziah's death in the prophet's lifetime. But further examination shows that there is more to it than that. In the Old Testament itself, a parallel narrative is to be found in 1 Kings 22: 19–22. A further parallel may be adduced from Assyria, in a series of exorcism texts, from which the relevant phrases may be quoted:

The God (Anu) and the goddess (Antu) have commissioned me: Whom shall I send to Bêlit of the field with the command?

I am commissioned, I go: I am sent, I speak. Against the power of my wizard and witch, Marduk, lord of exorcism, has sent me.[1]

An examination of the two Old Testament narratives shows a series of points of similarity—the scene in the heavenly court, YHWH sitting upon his throne, the host of heaven, the divine question, the acceptance of the commission. Differences are, however, sufficiently apparent to make it extremely unlikely that one is copied from the other. The Isaiah passage is much fuller and introduces other elements—the heavenly song of praise, the prophet's act of confession and his cleans-

[1] K. L. Tallqvist, 'Die assyrische Beschwörungsserie Maqlû', *Acta Societ. Scient. Fennicae*, xx (1895), 35; cf. p. 121: partly quoted by I. Engnell, *The Call of Isaiah* (Uppsala, 1949), p. 42. Engnell does not draw the full consequences of the parallel.

ing. Furthermore, in the one case, Micaiah describes a heavenly scene of which he was witness—as prophet he has access to the heavenly court;[1] in the other case, Isaiah is himself involved in the drama, as can be seen also in other prophetic experiences (e.g. Ezek. 9; Zech. 3; 4). The similarity, though not identity, of other prophetic narratives of their experience of commissioning (e.g. Ezek. 1–3; Jer. 1; Amos 7: 14 ff.; Exod. 3: 1—4: 17), as well as the partial parallel to the Isaiah and Micaiah passages in the Assyrian texts, indicates that we are dealing with a particular 'literary' form, what we might term the 'prophetic commissioning' (though not so narrowly limited to prophets in the strict sense). This may well itself be derived from other experience, not necessarily religious. The prophet's experience may be understood from different viewpoints. There is clearly a basic question concerning the nature of the contact between God and man which such an experience raises; this forms the content of the section, but its examination is not here our concern. There is further the question of the relationship between experience and form: religious experience is in any society governed at least in part by the presuppositions of the community to which the individual belongs. What Isaiah here says about God cannot be understood in isolation—indeed the use of the term 'king' and the hymnic utterance of the heavenly beings point to important elements in the conception of the divine nature which demand a much wider background of study. The nature of the experience is also conditioned by contemporary beliefs concerning the relationship between the heavenly dwelling and the temple as its earthly counterpart. The experience and its description are governed by the 'situation' in which the prophet belongs, both religious and literary. From the limited amount of material of this kind available within the Old Testament and its near environment, some features of the 'form' may be clearly seen; in some measure, where the evidence is sufficiently datable, we may trace the form through a period of years, though we know too little to engage in writing a history of it. From the point of view of study of the content, it is important to see the place of an individual example of the form within the group to which it belongs; for the interpretation of phraseology and vocabulary, the form-critical analysis

[1] Cf. Jer. 23: 22, and compare also Zech. 3: 7; Amos 3: 7, where the word translated 'secret', *sôḏ*, is the same as that rendered 'council' in Jer. Cf. L. Koehler, *Hebrew Man* (E.T. London, 1956), pp. 99 ff. for the analogy upon which such a concept of the heavenly sphere is based.

may enable a better understanding. Thus in the example under discussion, the Isaianic 'Here am I ! Send me' (6: 8) may be better understood as a response to a sense of divine commission (the comparable phrase in the Assyrian text is used by a presumably professional exorcist), or as a renewed recognition of divine commission, rather than, as has sometimes been thought, as an indication of the prophet as volunteer. The contrast sometimes drawn on this basis between Isaiah and Jeremiah may be seen from a form-critical standpoint to be unwarranted.

A great deal of attention has been paid in recent years to form-critical analysis of Old Testament material. This was applied at first especially to the psalms, the types of which were traced initially by Gunkel and subsequently further developed; analysis of psalms outside Israel revealed the same patterns of construction. Such analysis was at one and the same time an attempt at understanding the literary structure and a search for the original situation of the type, and in relation to the psalms has led to a much deeper appreciation of the liturgical aspects of psalm composition and use, particularly in the work of Mowinckel. From the point of view of the understanding of the content much was gained, though the risk was always present— and still is—that the analysis which points back to an original situation is then used, sometimes legitimately, sometimes not, to postulate a continued existence of such an original situation at a later stage. Thus the analysis of prophetic call narratives—at which we have just briefly looked—has been thought to lead to the conclusion that there was a regular commissioning ceremonial for prophets, though no direct evidence is available for this; and much of the debate concerning whether or not there was a New Year ritual in Israel, in which the king was deeply involved, turns on the question how far we may legitimately deduce from allusions in the psalms the actual practice in Israel of rituals which exactly corresponded to what was being recited. Such views affect the discussion of the formation of the Old Testament in that this would suggest a longer active life for the forms in their original context rather than an evolution of them in new settings. This latter may in some cases at least be more clearly demonstrated.

We are not here concerned with these wider questions which form-critical analysis has raised and to the discussion of which it has contributed much; but rather with the way in which older forms continued to be used, and the modification which later interpretation and use then brought about in them. Thus a form-critical analysis of the Song of Hannah in 1 Sam. 2: 1–10 reveals it to be a royal psalm; in the examination of royal psalmody and discussion of that particular literary type it takes its place alongside other material, for example Pss. 72 and 89. In its content it may provide some clues to the nature of Israel's beliefs about her kings and their place in God's relation to his people. But the present position of the psalm reveals other levels of use and shows that a psalm originally belonging to one situation may in course of time be applied after reinterpretation to another quite different situation. For now this poem is used to express the piety of a particular individual and shows how in a later stage of religious and literary development what originally applied to the king could be adapted for the purposes of worship by the ordinary individual. When it was included in the narrative we cannot know, though it is clear that it must be at least Davidic in date and may well be later; for the psalm to be reinterpreted suggests that some time is likely to have elapsed. The choice of this particular psalm could have been due to the presence in it of a reference to the 'barren' who 'has borne seven' (*v.* 5); but it is also possible that we can detect another aspect of the literary development. Samuel as he is eventually depicted in the narratives concerning him is a complex figure, enshrining priestly, prophetic and judicial (almost royal) elements. The victory over the Philistines attributed to him in 1 Sam. 7 is of doubtful historicity, if we may judge by the over-all picture of the Philistine threat provided in 1 Samuel. Here he acts as a great military leader, a great religious judge and not unlike a king. The eventual form of the narrative includes criticism of the institution of monarchy, and Samuel's view of it as apostasy. The choice of the psalm for Hannah could be seen as one more link in the creation of the over-all picture of Samuel by the eventual compiler of the material.

The example makes it clear that a consideration of the origin of a particular literary form and the assigning to that group of appropriate compositions is only of limited use. Much more illuminating alongside this is the evaluation of present context and of the interpretation subsequently placed upon the unit, and this may not only be of more use in understanding its meaning but also give some insight into the structure of the larger literary units.

In discussions of the literary types—as for example in the first part of Otto Eissfeldt's *The Old Testament: an Introduction*[1]—it is often rightly observed that a large number of the 'secular' types of literary composition—harvest songs, wedding poems, watchmen's and other workmen's songs (though in some of these the 'secular' not infrequently involves something of what we should term the religious)—are known to us not directly from actual settings in the harvest field or at the bridal party, but only from their use in other contexts, notably in the prophetic literature. Thus in Isa. 21: 11 f. we have a watchman's song indicated; in Isa. 23: 15 f. a harlot's song. Such occurrences reveal to us that Israel had a much larger literature—or oral tradition— than has survived in the Old Testament itself. There must have been much, both poetry and prose, which was in use, possibly over centuries, which has left no direct trace. But at the same time, we are aware that the literature which does survive represents in many cases not the original use and interpretation of a literary unit, but a subsequent reapplication of it to a new situation, that of prophetic judgement in the two examples just mentioned. That the prophet could think of himself as watchman we know from Ezekiel (3: 17–21; 33: 7–9); the image is clearly one appropriate for the prophetic function. But it contains again a warning against reading back from the forms to actual situations in the prophet's experience; it is a literary use of the watchman's song in Isa. 21, not a performing of watchman's functions in any other than a metaphorical sense.

Thus an important element in the understanding of Israelite literature consists in recognising the existence of older forms, which must go back into the most ancient stages of the people's life and indeed, as was indicated earlier, cannot really be defined as beginning at any precise point in time since they themselves evolved gradually out of the actual situations of life, including religious practice. But to a large extent what we now have in the literature is not those original forms, nor even in most cases the original settings, but the adaptation and reinterpretation of the material in newer ways, to bear wider and deeper meanings. We may not unreasonably guess from the riddle propounded by Samson at his wedding:

> Out of the eater came something to eat,
> Out of the strong came something sweet (Judg. 14: 14)

[1] (E.T. Oxford, New York, 1965), pp. 9–127.

that the posing of riddles belonged to wedding festivities in Israel, though also to other settings as the story of the queen of Sheba's visit to Solomon shows (1 Kings 10). Yet unless we are to suppose the guests at the wedding to have been gifted with second sight, the chance of their guessing that the correct answer was

> What is sweeter than honey,
> What is stronger than a lion? (Judg. 14: 18)

would seem to have been extremely remote, for they did not know of Samson's exploit against the lion related earlier in the same chapter (14: 5–9). Or are we perhaps to suppose that there is underlying the riddle and its answers a connection not now discernible by us—some subtlety of words and meanings, perhaps, as has been suggested, connected with marriage? And has this in its turn led to the juxtaposition of this narrative element in the Samson tradition with that other element, that of his exploit with the lion? The whole problem of literary structure here moves over from the consideration of the nature of the individual unit into that of the larger section; here it is particularly complex since it is likely that, while some elements in the narratives belong to the situation of the Danites in the Shephelah under pressure from the Philistines, other elements are more probably derived from mythological or legendary accounts, not unlike those associated with the figures of Gilgamesh and Hercules. The literary and the historical problems here, as so often, interact.

It is possible to see, even in the examination of a small literary unit, something of the complex literary processes involved in its formation and eventual use—the term 'literary' again here must be kept sufficiently loosely defined to allow for the development of traditions both orally and in writing, and for the possible influence on written or orally fixed traditions of others which are variants on them or which are unrelated but similar pieces of material.

As a next stage we may examine some passages of different literary types, to see how within them both original individual units of material and also more complex structures may be detected, and thus to trace some of the processes involved in the formation of the larger sections.

FROM THE UNITS OF MATERIAL TO THE LARGER STRUCTURES

Narrative

We consider first a narrative which appears twice in the Old Testament, in 2 Sam. 24 and 1 Chron. 21. The double occurrence enables us to examine the way in which the same material is differently treated by different compilers, both as regards details of presentation and also in relation to the wider purpose of the compilers in including and placing this particular section. By analogy with other narratives, we may also attempt to look behind the present forms to see what evidence there is of earlier structure in which different elements in the section may have had separate existence.

We are not here concerned with questions of historicity, but inevitably such questions impinge on literary study at many points, and in this particular instance the elements in the narrative may possibly belong to distinct historical situations. Sometimes, as for example with the threefold occurrence of the narrative of a man who conceals the fact that the woman accompanying him is his wife (Gen. 12: 10–19; 20; 26: 6–11), we may see how a narrative motif—which may or may not have historical foundation—can be utilised within a larger context not merely with reference to one situation but to several. To postulate three separate historical instances of the same event is much less probable in this case than to recognise that motifs can readily be transferred from one character to another, and in particular there is a marked tendency for traditions to be attached to notable characters of history or legend. The motif of the concealment of a child at birth from danger threatening its life is common in the ancient world: it is therefore not surprising that similar forms of this motif may be found applied to Sargon of Akkad[1] as well as to Moses (Exod. 2: 1–10). The transfer of motifs is a normal part of the formation of traditions; the weaving together of originally separate elements may then be utilised to give a presentation which, in the Old Testament, is of a theological rather than a historical nature.

The narrative in 2 Sam. 24 contains three elements: the census

[1] In the second half of the third millennium B.C. For the text cf. Pritchard, *ANET*, p. 119.

(*vv.* 1–9), the plague (*vv.* 10–17), the purchase of the threshing floor (*vv.* 18–25). It is possible that these three elements represent stages in one historical sequence; certainly as they now appear there is a closely knit structure, and the division of verses just indicated does not sufficiently show the degree of overlap which is present. Verse 10 provides a link between the census and the plague, and verse 16*b*, 'And the angel of Yahweh was by the threshing floor of Araunah the Jebusite', anticipates the third element. At the same time there are loose ends in the material which suggest that the three may originally have been independent: thus the relationship between the statement of divine mercy in the staying of the plague in verse 16 and the plea of David for judgement solely on himself and his own dynasty is not clear. It may be that we have here three originally independent narratives, now skilfully woven together to make a unified and powerful statement.

The taking of the census—of those who are 'valiant men who drew the sword' (*v.* 9)—suggests a military purpose, though bound into this is a theme, expressed in the words of Joab (*v.* 3), that there is something impious in what is being undertaken.[1] Whatever the origin of the story it is now so interpreted as to lead up to judgement, and explained furthermore as being itself due to the intention of God to bring judgement (*v.* 1). Here is a presentation of an originally presumably normal instrument of government within the theological framework of divine will and judgement, the reason for divine anger being indicated at the outset no more than in the Moabite Stone (*c.* 830 B.C.):[2] 'Chemosh was angry with his land.' But it moves rapidly over into another atmosphere with its indication of awareness of the danger of the procedures being adopted (*vv.* 3, 10).

The second element, the plague, is an example of a natural disaster of a not uncommon kind; a similar calamity overtook the Philistines (1 Sam. 5–6) and a comparable case may underlie the narrative of the Assyrian withdrawal in the time of Hezekiah (cf. Isa. 37: 36; 2 Kings 19: 35; Herodotus, *Hist.* II, 14). The original event underlying this may have been of relatively local occurrence, as in the Philistine example; it has now been given a wider range, covering all Israel

---

[1] Cf. E. A. Speiser, 'Census and Ritual Expiation in Mari and Israel', *BASOR*, CXLIX (Feb. 1958), 17–25 = *Oriental and Biblical Studies* (Philadelphia, 1967), pp. 171–86.

[2] For a recent discussion and translation, cf. E. Ullendorff in *DOTT*, pp. 195–8, with plate.

'from Dan to Beer-sheba' (*v.* 15) and, still more significant, set in the context of a prophetic narrative in which the prophet Gad is instructed to offer a choice of disasters to David as punishment. Here again the original material has been given a theological interpretation, and it is doubtful how far theological meaning and original narrative may be satisfactorily disentangled.

The third element is the sanctuary legend concerning the threshing floor of Araunah (cf. above, pp. 69 f. on Jacob at Bethel). It has its own interest in its description of business dealings, the conventions of polite negotiations for a purchase (cf. Gen. 23: 3–18): even this element in the story has acquired theological emphasis (*v.* 24). The story culminates in the building of an altar and the offering of sacrifices. Whatever judgement is made on the problem of the relationship between these three elements and the degree of historicity which can be discerned behind them, it is clear that the presentation we now have is highly stylised, both in its separate elements and its totality. The narrators of the original stories, the compiler or compilers of the eventual form, reveal a high degree of literary and artistic skill, expressed within forms familiar in their particular cultural tradition.

An examination of the second form of this material in 1 Chron. 21 reveals some interesting differences of detail, such as the vivid presentation of the angel with the drawn sword (*v.* 16) which has been thought to suggest the appearance of a comet; the much larger numbers in the census story (*v.* 5) and in the purchase price (*v.* 25); and the significant variant that Levi and Benjamin were excluded from the census. Some of the detail is reduced (e.g. in verse 4 which has an abbreviated description of the taking of the census); as has already been indicated, in such points as these we cannot now determine how far changes of detail may already have appeared in the form of the Samuel text known to the Chronicler,[1] but this does not affect the main point of interest, which is that the literary processes in the formation of the Old Testament involve many such gradual modifications of earlier material which may actually appear in a later form or may in fact have been so known and appear only obliquely in later allusions to them.[2]

Two major differences must be noted. The initiation of this series

[1] Cf. p. 76. This is true of the detail of verse 16 which appears in the text of 4QSam[a].   [2] Cf. S. Talmon, below, p. 164; G. Vermes, below, p. 209.

of events is attributed not to the anger of God but to the activity of 'Satan'—the name appears here without the definite article and perhaps therefore as a proper name, whereas elsewhere the word appears either in normal use meaning 'adversary' (1 Kings 11: 14) or with the definite article as 'the Satan', probably better to be rendered 'the adversary', evidently a functionary of the heavenly court (Job 1–2; Zech. 3: 1 f.). Although no indication is given of the relationship between God and 'the Satan'—in Job 1–2, he acts clearly under divine authority—and no suggestion is made that the responsibility of David is reduced, a major theological difficulty of the earlier narrative is in some measure resolved. The problems raised by this figure of 'the Satan' remain.

Even more important is the change brought about partly by the changed position of the narrative in relation to other material and partly by the explicit statement with which it concludes (1 Chron. 22: 1). 2 Sam. 24 is one of a number of passages which now form a complex appendix to the books of Samuel (2 Sam. 21–4). The Chronicler places this narrative in a coherent context, having also utilised other sections of this appendix material, viz. the list of David's heroes (2 Sam. 23: 8–39) in 1 Chron. 11: 10–41 (with which the Chronicler includes material not in our 2 Sam. text), and details of the Philistine campaigns (2 Sam. 21: 18–22) in 1 Chron. 20: 4–8, immediately before this narrative. The literary processes underlying both the formation of the appendix in 2 Sam. 21–4 and the presentation of parts of this material in 1 Chron. are evidently very complex. What is clear, however, is that the Chronicler sees this narrative in 1 Chron. 21 as providing an appropriate introduction to his account of how David prepared for the building of the Temple by Solomon (1 Chron. 22: 2–19; 28–29: 9. The intervening section, chs. 23–7, may well be a later insertion, but it too illuminates the ideas concerning David's organising of the worship of the Temple). Whereas the 2 Sam. narrative makes no link with the building of the Solomonic Temple—and this strongly suggests that the narrative originally had to do with another sacred place—the Chronicler identifies the site precisely (22: 1), explains why David could not go to Gibeon where the Tabernacle was (21: 29–30), and subsequently also identifies this site explicitly with the Mount Moriah of Gen. 22 (2 Chron. 3: 1), an even more improbable identification, though fully intelligible in the light of the growth of tradition concerning the Jerusalem Temple and its importance in the period to which the Chronicler belonged.

Thus in this example we may trace some of the original elements and the stages in the formation of the final forms in 2 Sam. and 1 Chron. It must, however, be noted that the passage cannot be understood in isolation. In its first occurrence, as part of the appendix to 2 Sam., it helps to illuminate the richness of the David traditions, additional to those which appear in the main body of the work; how many other such traditions existed which did not find any place in the canonical books? It also reveals aspects of the structure of the context in which it stands—between 1 and 2 Sam. and 1 and 2 Kings; for there is no natural break between these now divided books—they form a continuous complex narrative work. At some stage in their formation it was possible for this and other passages to be inserted in the work. Indeed, the content of 2 Sam. 21–4 points to a threefold process of amplification—or a three-stage development of a small separate collection then inserted as a whole; 2 Sam. 21: 1–14, a narrative revealing certain similarities of interest and theological interpretation with chapter 24, and 2 Sam. 24 mark the first stage; into this was inserted material concerning the Philistine war and David's heroes (2 Sam. 21: 15–22; 23: 8–39), and in this was further inserted the poetic passage consisting of two psalms, 2 Sam. 22 and 23: 1–7. In the occurrence in 1 Chron. we can see, in the presentation and placing of this same narrative, some indications both of the literary methods and of the theological viewpoint of an author whose work represents the most complete and consistent over-all presentation of Israel's history in the Old Testament, running as it does from creation to Ezra–Nehemiah.

What significance does this example have for the understanding of the formation of Old Testament literature? It shows us two clear stages in the evolution of particular traditions. Behind these lie the earlier processes, in which the units themselves are formed, processes only partly discernible and in part to be inferred from other comparable material. Study of the pre-literary stages must inevitably be tentative. When we look at the present form of the material, in this case in its two presentations, it is evident that we have only some of the links in the chain. Others are likely to have existed, whether in written or in oral form. It is clear too that for a long time there is no absolute fixity in the material; it can be shaped and reshaped, provided with new motives and interpretations. It is part of a living tradition, capable of being used over and over again in the presentation of different ways of understanding the workings of God in Israel's affairs. The consciousness of such action of God is often the real motive force underlying the transformations, and to a limited extent we can detect the changes in theological understanding, the deepening of theological sensitivity, which make possible the rehandling of older material. If we were merely to try to dovetail the various forms of the material, producing a sort of 'harmony' like Tatian's harmony of the Gospels, in the hope of discovering a simple historical event, we should do far less than justice to the different presentations and to those who stand behind them.

Narrative material in fact belongs to various settings in the life of a community. There is the more official type of transmission which belongs to courts—the periodical recording of the events of a king's reign (cf. Esther 2: 23; 6: 1), records of the kind referred to as sources for further information regarding a particular ruler (cf. e.g. 1 Kings 14: 29). There is the transmission, oral or written, which belongs to a sanctuary, handing down and interpreting the foundation tradition, and no doubt also significant moments of re-ordering (cf. the account of the building of the Solomonic Temple in 1 Kings 6–8, elaborately developed in its last section; and 2 Kings 16: 10–18). Although there is no direct reference to storytellers in the Old Testament, it is reasonable to suppose that traditions concerning the people's origin and history, and particularly fortunes of tribes and families, formed material popularly as well as more officially handled. The interaction of different forms of the same material may be seen in the partly official, partly more popular presentations of the early history found in the two main early strands of narrative, known as J and E, in the first books of the Old Testament, and ultimately presented in the context of a much later structure, known as P, which itself undoubtedly contains very early elements as well.

The study of the individual units in the tradition, the tracing of the processes by which these have been built up into larger wholes, involves both form-critical examination and literary analysis. But alongside this is the need to understand the nature and purpose of the various stages—to what situation, for example, was the so-called 'Succession History of David' (2 Sam. 9–20; 1 Kings 1–2) directed

before it became part of the larger work in which it now stands?—
and in particular to take account of the final presentations. This is
much more elaborate in the Old Testament than, so far as we know,
elsewhere in the ancient Near East. There are literary works which are
comparable to parts of the material, but not to the major theological
presentations of the history—the Tetrateuch (or the Priestly Work),
the Deuteronomic History, the Work of the Chronicler—all of which
present, from different viewpoints and covering differing ranges, an
over-all interpretation of the nature and significance of Israel conceived
as people of God. They all contain material which is of importance for
the study of Israel's history, as well as of her law and worship, custom
and tradition; but they are concerned fundamentally not with providing
this information but with offering an interpretation of it. This interpretation does not remain static, and it is therefore proper to see that
the eventual formation of a fixed canonical body of literature does not
in fact close the process; the Old Testament remains open-ended,
capable of reinterpretation subsequently by various religious traditions
for which the literature is in some sense normative.

Law

Our next two examples may be taken from what is most simply
described as legal material. One of them represents an example of an
actually established law, for which no occasion is indicated, namely the
law of the dividing of the spoils of war in 1 Sam. 30. The other is an
example of the enunciation of a directive, strictly a *tôrāh*,[1] by the
priests, the indication of a ritual expression associated with a specific
occasion described in Hag. 2.

The legal ruling made by David after the battle described in 1 Sam.
30 was designed to cover the case of a dispute over the sharing of
spoils between the actual fighting men and those who guarded the
baggage. A similar principle is to be found in Josh. 22: 8 and in Num.
31: 27. We have no means of determining whether the decision of
David was an original one, in the sense that it had not so been ruled
before; or of deciding whether the reflection of a similar practice in

---

[1] The term means a directive, a decision in a particular case, an oracular response; it
may thus be used in both the singular and the plural. It comes to be used also for a whole
collection of law (so Deut. 4: 44), and eventually for the first five books of the Old
Testament, the *Tôrāh*. (Cf. B. Lindars, 'Torah in Deuteronomy' in *Words and Meanings*, ed. P. R. Ackroyd and B. Lindars (Cambridge, 1968), pp. 117-36.)

the other two passages is to be regarded as deriving from an earlier period—and so to provide a foundation for the Davidic decision—or to a later period, and so, in the case of the Numbers passage, to represent the incorporation of the Davidic decision into a later body of law. The present form of both Josh. 22 and Num. 31 is certainly later than David, but this does not preclude the probability that they contain much earlier material.

From the way in which in much ancient Near Eastern law the same decisions or similar cases are recorded in different collections of laws, it would seem likely that we should regard the Davidic case as being a firm ruling in a case in which there was frequent evasion of the law or, bearing in mind the practice attested for some ancient rulers,[1] an example of the kind of standard of justice to which David committed himself. No such statement of law is associated with the anointing of David as king, either by the southern tribes at Hebron (2 Sam. 2: 4) or subsequently by the tribes of Israel, also at Hebron (2 Sam. 5: 1–3), though in the latter case the covenant mentioned could have included some statement by the king of the standards he accepted.

The narrative of 1 Sam. 30 enunciates the basic principle of justice that all should be treated alike. But there were some, 'all the wicked and base fellows among the men who had gone with David' (*v.* 22), who did not wish to see such equality and would not be prepared to allow any booty to those who had not actually fought. The implication is that David was not alone in his recognition of the rightness of the principle; he came down firmly on the side of law and custom, and his decision, without being new, was sufficiently memorable to be quoted subsequently as an indication of both the rightness of the law and the propriety of David's conduct. In this particular example, we have both this narrative and another incident described in Josh. 22 where verse 8 alludes to the division of battle-spoils, and a similar injunction is set out as a command to Moses in Num. 31: 25 ff. This passage also introduces a further point concerning the allocation of a part of the spoil as an offering to God. It would seem from these passages that in the Old Testament, as in other ancient Near Eastern laws, the primary factor in the evolution of law is the particular occasion, the case which serves both to maintain and to establish legal principle and which may be preserved as an illustration of the application of the principle to an

[1] Cf. D. J. Wiseman on p. 44.

actual situation. The community builds up its legal heritage on the basis of such case-law, the remembering of previous cases which are similar—and so we find the elders of a village responsible for the conduct of legal proceedings (cf. e.g. Ruth 4)—the particular enactment designed to clarify a legal situation. A law code in the sense of a compilation designed to cover all aspects of life would appear to be a later development; what appears in the Old Testament is, for the most part at any rate, collections of laws, associated perhaps with particular rulers or particular localities—though these associations are now in large measure lost—set out as descriptive of normal practice, and providing in this respect a momentary indication of the state of law rather than a complete description of its coverage.

Hag. 2: 10–14 records how the prophet consulted the priests on a point of ritual law, the nature of the contagious quality of holiness and uncleanness. The *tōrāh*, the directive given by the priests, cannot be exactly paralleled elsewhere in the Old Testament, though similar principles are enunciated in Lev. 22. We cannot here trace any precise development of the Law; we do not know how far this particular decision influenced subsequent thinking within the Old Testament period, though there is no good reason for believing that the whole case is a purely hypothetical one, with no foundation in fact. The decision was real, whether or not we suppose that the prophet already knew what the answer would be; the priests, being consulted, gave their directive presumably in accordance with established custom. In so far as there may have been something new or unusual in the inquiry, the decision will have conveyed an extension of existing principle. Subsequent decisions did not have to follow exactly the same point, though cumulatively the effect of such decisions will have been to clarify the precise interrelationship of differing legal principles, just as in a famous case David was able to overrule the conflicting principles of blood revenge and family preservation (2 Sam. 14: 4–11). The point is that here again we have a living presentation of the mode by which law came into being in a particular form, a glimpse into the real processes, the activity of those, kings or priests, whose functions included the giving of laws or directives to set out in detail the application of certain underlying principles or already established customs.

But this is not the end of the process. On the one hand we have ample evidence from the later Jewish material, the great rabbinic compilations, to show that the Old Testament law is only one stage. It is incomplete, it requires fuller exposition to make clear the nature of man's obligations in all those situations which are not immediately covered by formulated laws. On the other hand, the Old Testament itself shows us law no longer presented simply in the form of groups or collections of single laws, but expounded in the light of general principles of understanding and more particularly in relation to highly developed theological thinking. What are often conveniently called the 'Law Codes'—the Book of the Covenant (Exod. 20: 22—23: 33), the Holiness Code (Lev. 17–26), the Deuteronomic Code (often limited to 12–26, 28, though more properly described as including at least 4: 44—11: 32, or indeed as consisting of virtually the whole of Deuteronomy)—are not really codifications of law in the modern sense, nor merely collections of laws from particular situations, associated perhaps with some king or other leader, but expositions of law. They are directed towards the demonstration, in relation to legal material, of the theological principles underlying the very existence of Israel conceived as people of God, and exemplifying the kind of behaviour which belongs within that particular theological context.

One of the important moments, known to us because we have a narrative which describes it, was the acceptance as part of a reforming movement of a law book discovered in the Temple in 621 B.C. (2 Kings 22: 3–20). Another important moment is described in Neh. 8, the reading of the law by Ezra, which shows not only reading but also expounding of the law. It is likely that there is a fairly close relationship between the law described in the first instance and Deuteronomy, though this apparent relationship may be in part due to the belief of the narrator that the law which he regarded as authoritative must have been used as the basis of the reform. Determining what law was read by Ezra is extremely difficult. But the important point is that in both cases we have a clear indication of exposition of law rather than legal material pure and simple, for even in the former case it is plain that words of judgement were included with the law (2 Kings 22: 13, cf. the curses of Deut. 27). The full description of these two moments suggests that there was recognised to be something special about them, they were significant within the community's history. Yet they do not stand entirely alone, and if the injunction of Deut. 31: 10–13 was in fact carried out—and there is no reason to doubt that it reflects actual practice—there was at least in some areas a seven-year recital of law and acceptance of it which gives a context for the place occupied by the Law in the people's life. It is law expounded, shown to be the basis of life in the covenant relationship with God, which is set out in the various collections, and it is particularly intelligible therefore that a great deal of the compiling and expository activity appears to be most naturally associated with that period of the people's life, the exile, in which a rethinking of the nature of the covenant and of the meaning of obedience and of the need to maintain the people as people of God was especially urgent. Deuteronomy and the Holiness Code and the compilation of material, including law, which makes up the Priestly Work all belong in their final form either more strictly to the period of exile or relatively shortly after it.

We may also note the picture of the psalmist whose ideal is the man whose life is blessed as he meditates in the law day and night (Ps. 1, cf. Pss. 19 and 119 especially), to whom the law is a whole delight. When we recall that eventually for the Old Testament the term *tôrāh* comes to be extended to cover the whole of the first five books, the Law in its fullest sense, then we may realise that such meditation on the law is not a contemplation of its detail—though even this has its place in the total working out of Israel's life—but a glorification of the God whose wonderful works are declared both in creation and redemption in the deliverance from Egypt, and also in the creation of that people Israel whose supreme function was to be his people and to offer him worship for ever. This means that when we consider Old Testament law as it is finally presented, we are not in the first instance concerned with legalism, but with the presentation of a theology, an understanding of God whose action is the context for what men are to do by way of response in worship and obedience. The preservation of the law is only partly concerned with the setting out of a legal code; it is very much concerned with showing forth the whole nature and purpose of God, and in this respect particularly Old Testament law differs sharply from its counterparts in the ancient Near East.

Prophecy

A third variety of Old Testament literature is provided by the prophetic books, containing an immense wealth of material of many different kinds. From the point of view of content, no completely sharp division can be made between the prophetic literature and other parts of the Old Testament. There are oracles of judgement and promise incorporated in the prophetic narratives in the books of Samuel and Kings. The prophetic books contain, equally, historico-biographical sections which correspond closely in style and content to material in those narrative works, and at certain points a clear overlap may be observed. Isa. 36–9 provides an almost complete duplicate text of 2 Kings 18: 13—20: 21, though the Isaiah form of the material includes a psalm, the Prayer of Hezekiah (38: 9–20), not found in 2 Kings; Jer. 52: 1–27, 31–4 provides a slightly variant form of 2 Kings 24: 18—25: 21 and 27–30. The intervening section in 2 Kings 25: 22–6 provides a much briefer version of Jer. 40: 7—43: 7, and in fact not a little of the narrative material in this part of the book of Jeremiah is closely similar in style and content to the narratives of 2 Kings. So, too, the prophetic books contain psalms, closely resembling those of the Psalter, and in one case, Hab. 3, complete with opening and closing rubrics identical with titles found in the Psalter.[1] Wisdom elements— proverbial sayings such as Isa. 28: 27–9—reveal an overlap with another kind of literature well known in the Old Testament. In addition, as has already been noted, the prophetic books preserve for us examples of other literary forms not otherwise attested and here used for particular theological purposes.

The prophetic books represent larger and smaller collections of oracles, psalms, narratives—autobiographical and biographical; within the literature we have many indications of use and re-use of the same prophetic oracles, by the same prophet or by his successors. Thus we are told that Jeremiah dictated a scroll of prophecies 'in the fourth year of Jehoiakim' (605 B.C.), a collection of all his messages over the previous twenty years, now seen to be relevant to the situation in which the life of Judah was threatened by the newly victorious power of Babylon (ch. 36). The original reference of such messages is unlikely to have been to Babylon; now they can be understood in a new light. Similarly we find that the same prophetic oracle may occur more than once but in quite different contexts and associated with different prophets. We have already noted an example of this in Isa. 2 and Mic. 4. Such a double occurrence need not surprise us, nor that the same words appear to be ascribed to more than one prophet. For the prophetic

---

[1] It is still uncertain what these titles or rubrics really are.

tradition is much richer than merely a record of the activities of a small number of named individuals speaking their oracles and recording their messages. There is evidence of a much greater amount of prophetic activity; named and unnamed prophets appear in the historical books, and the prophetic books themselves, when analysed and related to historical situations so far as may be, reveal that the names associated with particular books are not in fact those of authors but rather of inspirers of a particular line of prophetic tradition. The number of the unknown is substantial, and some among them were men of great stature. Indeed what to many would appear to be the major contribution of Old Testament prophecy (Isa. 40–55) cannot be properly attributed to a known individual, but rather to an unnamed successor, standing in the line of the known prophet Isaiah of Jerusalem. With this name has come to be associated the whole wealth of material which makes up the book of Isaiah, in spite of the very evident fact that within it 40–55 constitutes a section to be associated with the later years of the Babylonian exile (*c.* 550–540 B.C.), and other parts of the book (notably 24–7 and some parts probably of 56–66) may well be of still later origin. Yet to understand this as due to some artificial cause—space on a scroll which had to be filled with other material which lay to hand—does insufficient justice to points of relationship of thought between the various component parts. The book is the product of a long and complex but extremely lively prophetic tradition.

The prophetic literature is a deposit from a movement in which there is a continual interplay between great individuals—some known by name and others not—men whose highlighted experience contributes much to the development of Old Testament religious thought, and the continuum of religious witness and protest, of worship and oracular utterance, which maintains the life of the community over the centuries. The prophets who stand out as individuals are intelligible only within the context of that continuum; the life of the continuum is nourished and made what it is by the impact upon it of the minds of those whose depth of experience has left their mark, but at the same time that experience is commented upon, and applied to different situations, within the life of the community. The words of the eighth-century prophets have been seen by their successors early in the sixth century to be meaningful in the context of the final disaster to the Judaean monarchy and to the Jerusalem Temple. Such reinterpretation was not simply a matter of glossing an established text: it was a recognition of the living quality of the divine word which, once uttered in a particular situation, retained its validity and could be seen, perhaps with a change of context or a change of wording or the addition of an explanatory phrase, to be still meaningful to a new generation.

The whole process of the formation of the prophetic books is a very complex one. Virtually every section of them reveals what at first sight appear to be collocations without principle of arrangement. Closer investigation sometimes reveals the principles involved, though this is by no means always the case. Thus it has been suggested that the arrangement of the oracles in Isa. 40–55 (Deutero-Isaiah) is based upon the 'catchword principle'—a word in one oracle becomes the point for the attachment of another. Such a principle may indeed not infrequently be operative in such collections, for it has a mnemonic element which would make it intelligible. In so far as the words of a prophet are preserved orally among his disciples and successors, it would be natural to find that they are linked in the mind by small points of contact which to a modern reader seem to be less important than they are likely to have been to one who saw similarities of wording, or even the same word with quite distinct meanings, as pointing to ways in which the material could be elucidated. In Isa. 40–55, while such a principle may operate, there may well be other, more profound, exegetical considerations involved too. Similarly, what appear at first sight to be relatively confused passages—as for example Jer. 10: 1–16 —may be seen on closer investigation to be closely knit and ordered not logically but out of an association of ideas, in this example the contrasting of the themes of idolatry and of the glorification of the one and only creator. The inclusion of psalm material in the prophetic books which sometimes results in the climax of a section being reached in a hymn of praise—as for example in Isa. 1–12 (Isa. 12 consists of psalm passages) or Habakkuk (where chapter 3 is a psalm)—suggests the probability that sections of prophecy were used in liturgical contexts or that the influence of liturgical practice was felt in the ultimate arrangement of the material, whether by the prophets themselves or by their followers and expounders.

The place of exposition is indeed very important. The first chapter of Isaiah—often described as a sort of introductory summary of the prophet's message—is in fact rather to be viewed as an exposition of the faithless and faithful Zion. It centres around the past and present experience of the city and its people; their failure, both in social life and in worship; the prospect of a restoration to purity as at the first, to be again the city of righteousness. There lies behind this the kind of thinking which we can associate with a number of psalms—for example Ps. 87—in which the idea of the city as the dwelling place of God is a source of rich meditation and anticipation of divine blessing. Herein lies one of the sources for the whole range of eschatological thinking concerning the future of Jerusalem, the 'new city' concepts which are to be found so richly expressed in Ezek. 40–8 and in the New Testament in the book of Revelation (cf. also Isa. 62; Zech. 8: 1–8)—an element which came to be of very great importance in both Jewish and Christian thought. The real fulfilment of the conception of Jerusalem as the faithful city is to be found in the oracle which opens Isa. 2, and a similar structure is to be found in Micah. Here the problems of the prophetic tradition are complicated by the fact that Jer. 26: 16–19 paints a picture of Micah as a prophet of utter judgement, and from this it has been argued that the genuine Micah material is to be found substantially in Mic. 1–3, and such other oracles as are solely of judgement. Yet it is more appropriate to recognise that, whatever we may have to say about the genuineness or non-genuineness of particular oracles in the book, its present structure shows an appreciation of the relationship between the Jerusalem that is a faithless city, doomed to destruction (so especially 3: 9–12), and that Jerusalem which is the centre of the world's life which is expressed most clearly in the oracle which follows in 4: 1–5 and also appears in Isa. 2: 2–4.

Another example of clearly definable prophetic structure may be seen in Amos 7: 1—8: 3. Here a group of vision experiences has been built together with a biographical narrative in 7: 10–17 into a unity. The four visions, 7: 1–3; 4–6; 7–9 and 8: 1–3 are similar in structure, the first two more closely so than the others. The third vision, culminating in the judgement on the house of Jeroboam, provides a convenient point for the biographical section which deals with the effect of Amos' prophecy of judgement and includes a fragment of a judgement oracle in verse 11 which in part duplicates the oracle in verse 9. After the interruption of the series of visions, the form reappears in 8: 1–3. The wide difference in content of the visions suggests that they belong to different contexts in the prophet's experience.

Whether Amos himself brought them together by way of explaining the nature both of his authority and of his message, or whether they were linked in the handing down of the prophetic tradition and eventually, with their expansion, combined with other material to form the prophetic book, we cannot know. We can see that there is a linkage of thought also with the biographical section, for this too is concerned with the nature of the prophet's authority. A further examination of the book reveals that there are overlaps of material between the oracles of 8: 4–14 (introduced by 'Hear') and oracles in other sections of the book, inviting comparison with the series 'hear this word' in 4: 1—5: 17 and the 'woes' of 5: 18—6: 8—these series themselves providing evidence of stylised structure. Clearly no simple process is involved, and equally clearly it is unlikely that we can now discover all the stages in the process. More important is the evident fact that the words of Amos have been handed down over a period of time, and that they have been reinterpreted by the addition of the oracles of hope in 9: 11–15 which almost certainly belong to the exilic period or later.

We may also trace, with some measure of greater precision, the use of particular phrases. One of the clearest is the prophecy of seventy years of captivity in Jer. 25: 11 f. and 29: 10, and used subsequently in Zechariah, in the Chronicler and in Daniel. This begins as a presumably conventional phrase, a symbolic figure to denote a captivity beyond which none will survive of those taken into exile. It is possible, though not quite certain, that the phrase is already an interpretative comment in Jer. 29, and that from there it has also been included in the similar material of Jer. 25. Subsequently the phrase is understood more precisely, perhaps already in Zech. 1: 12, where it becomes a term to cover the years of judgement on the cities of Judah, and it is noteworthy that a period of approximately seventy years elapsed between the destruction of the Temple and its rebuilding. It is possible that the dating of the rebuilding has been conformed to this prophetic date. This date is not referred to precisely in Zechariah though it is clear that the prophecies of Zech. 8 in part presuppose that rebuilding is complete, but is provided only in the Chronicler's account in Ezra 6. Certainly elsewhere, in 2 Chron. 36: 21, the Chronicler made use of the Jeremianic prophecy, combining it with a phrase from Lev. 26: 34, 43 (in the peroration of the Holiness Code of Lev. 17–26), so as to explain the exile as a period of Sabbath rest for the land. And this

Sabbath interpretation is the one which has evidently influenced the author of Daniel, for in Dan. 9 there is a precise reapplication of this prophecy and its interpretation in terms not simply of ordinary years but in terms of groups of seven years so as to cover the whole period from the fall of Jerusalem to the moment of writing. Possibly also this seventy-year period, which contrasts with Ezekiel's statement of a forty-year captivity (4: 6), has had its effect in the opening verse of the book of Ezekiel; the problematic mention of a 'thirtieth year' there could perhaps most easily be explained on the assumption that a later scribe sought to reconcile the two divergent prophecies of the length of the exile by explaining that Ezekiel had begun his work thirty years after Jeremiah's prophecy—chronologically an impossible statement, but of a reconciling kind which can be traced not only within the biblical material but increasingly in post-biblical handling of it.[1]

This example shows something of the way in which a particular element, even of a minor kind, may be used by later writers to explain the events of their own time. It is important also because it enables us to see the way in which earlier material is coming to have an authoritative status. What the prophets said must be fulfilled; the interpretation of their words is therefore to be seen in the light of current experiences. It is only a step from this to the Qumrân *pēšer* with its precise application of individual sayings to contemporary events, and from this to the New Testament which equally understands events in terms of fulfilment.

Wisdom

A fourth type of Old Testament material is represented by wisdom writings, in which contact with the literature of this kind throughout the ancient Near East appears often to be particularly close. We can trace such writings in Egypt and Babylonia to the second or third millennia, and although it is clear that due allowance must be made for the different cultural milieus and presuppositions, so that phrases sounding similar in translation do not necessarily carry the same meanings, there are many points of contact in style and thought between Israel's wisdom writings and those of the surrounding peoples. The closest relationship has been seen between the Teaching of Amenemope, which may date from the end of the second millennium, and one section of the book of Proverbs, 22: 17—24: 22. The exact nature of the

---

[1] For other aspects of this cf. G. Vermes, pp. 209 ff.

relationship is difficult to determine and the closeness has at times been exaggerated. Yet this is only one example of relationship, and it has been rightly observed that the Old Testament wisdom writings often have a much less national character and are more universal in style and scope than other Old Testament literature.

What place this kind of material occupied in the life of the community is uncertain. Connections with education, as elsewhere in the ancient Near East, are likely. It is not difficult to suppose that the training of scribes would make use of such material in the process of learning in Israel too.[1] Popular proverbial sayings are likely to have been used by the people themselves on many occasions; L. Koehler has suggested, perhaps rather too imaginatively, that such sayings were a staple part of the conversation between men in the village communities.[2] But we know also of some more official status accorded to the wise; the counsel of Ahithophel was as the 'oracle of God', and this indicates the degree of his influence. Jer. 18: 18 and Ezek. 7: 26 place the 'counsel of the wise' (Ezek. has 'elders') alongside the word of the prophet and the *tôrāh*-directive of the priest. In the ordering of public and private affairs there was here evidently an important class of person, though we do not know how far in the earlier stages they formed a separable group. Wisdom writings ultimately become in Israel, as elsewhere, the vehicle for profound questionings and affirmations, a vehicle for apologetic and exposition, sharing in the interpretation of the experiences which the community underwent in its later contacts with the outside world. It provides one element in the teaching of the New Testament, particularly in the letter of James, as also elsewhere.

A very early stage is marked by the double occurrence of the proverbial saying: 'Is Saul also among the prophets?' (1 Sam. 10: 11 f.; 19: 24). Two quite different explanations are given of the saying, associating its origin in each case with a band of prophets, perhaps the same band though the occasions are quite differently described. The interpretation of such a saying is not easy. The first occurrence might seem to suggest that surprise is being expressed that a respectable man of good family should be associated with a band of ecstatic prophets whose behaviour might well be of somewhat doubtful quality. But this

---

[1] Cf. D. J. Wiseman, pp. 35–8.
[2] *Hebrew Man* (E.T. London, 1956), pp. 101–7.

implies a judgement on these prophetic bands which does not fit in entirely with other impressions of their status and influence, and the second occurrence shows such a band (perhaps the same one) under the leadership of Samuel; elsewhere such bands are associated particularly with Elijah and Elisha. It is conceivable that the saying had a quite different meaning: 'What! Saul, the failed king, a member of the prophetic order?' Or it may be that we should recognise that, as with the proverbial sayings of many communities, the original meaning has been entirely lost to sight, and the Old Testament having preserved two explanations, we should not necessarily expect them to be identical.

This difficulty of interpretation often faces the reader where isolated sayings appear. There are many such, in the prophets (e.g. Jer. 8: 7; Isa. 28: 23 ff.) and in the psalms (especially in Ps. 119), and in still larger numbers in Job, Proverbs, and Ecclesiastes, and in the apocryphal and pseudepigraphical writings, particularly in Ecclesiasticus (The Wisdom of Jesus ben Sira) and the Wisdom of Solomon. But in such works, although there are often simple collections of proverbial sayings, there are more often groupings for particular purposes and more significant still the use of proverbial sayings for the expression of theological ideas which take the sayings out of their original context and often make it difficult to discover their original meaning. The richness of the transmission, the duplicate occurrences common in the book of Proverbs, the accumulation of such sayings in other works, show us how large a place this kind of literature occupied in the life of the people and how it was found natural to express much of their profoundest thinking in such a style. For the expression of the deeper truths about God and man, as appears clearly in the two most philosophical works of the Old Testament, Job and Ecclesiastes, the allusive style of the wisdom literature, the pictures which it draws, the ease with which it may set contrasting and complementary notions side by side, show how Old Testament writers could recognise the hazards of expressing in too sharply defined a manner truths which inevitably tax the normal mechanisms of human expression. We may note too that there is some evidence of a tendency to interpret Old Testament material of quite other kinds in the light of wisdom thinking, as is shown by the position of the wisdom psalm, Ps. 1, which sets the tone for a particular kind of psalm interpretation, and the reflective colophon to the book of Hosea (14: 9) which points to the prophetic words as a way of life or of death.

The wise to whom the secrets are revealed come to the fore also in apocalyptic writings. 2 Esdras 14: 46 informs us that of the 94 books revealed to Ezra, 70 were to be preserved for the wise. It seems likely that these are primarily the apocalyptic works, of which 2 Esdras is itself one, those writings which claim to reveal through dreams and visions and descriptions something of the nature of the hidden world. This is a natural extension of that function which belongs to wisdom of expressing the problems of life and of the nature of God, though here it is mingled with much that belongs to other types of literature, and in particular it is combined with exegetical activity, the expounding of already known and accepted older writings.

THE FORMATION OF THE OLD TESTAMENT

It would be possible to go further and examine yet other varieties and examples, exploring their origin and nature and tracing, so far as may be, the processes involved in their being developed from original forms to their present use. But sufficient has been said for the purpose of this introductory discussion to reveal some part of what is involved. At every point, if we wish to understand the literature, we are compelled to investigate the probable sources, to trace the interpretation and reinterpretation, to assess the pointers towards the present form of the material.

But, as has already been indicated, the units are built together not simply into groups, small complexes composed of oracles or sayings, into now unified though originally separate narratives, collections of poems and the like. The Old Testament consists of larger units still, in some cases coincident with what are there marked off as books, in other cases overlapping what are evidently artificial divisions. In these larger units earlier material has been brought together and given what may be regarded as a definitive form. In some cases such larger units have survived virtually intact; in other cases they have themselves become parts of yet other works; sometimes both survive side by side.

If we seek to discover the nature of these works, we are bound to take into account both the possibility that they were produced as a result of the activity of men of genius and also the probability that, as in other cultures, the impulse to produce a literary work is linked to historical circumstances and pressures, governed by moments of crisis or need. The Old Testament has its own explanation of these points. It speaks of men raised up by God to give Israel a law or a divine word. It implies that law is ultimately derivable from such inspiration, through the person of Moses. Similarly, by its association of other parts of the Old Testament with particular persons—an association in some cases made fully explicit only later (e.g. the responsibility of David for all the psalms)[1]—it stresses this same recognition of the place of the great individual in the formation of the literature. The Old Testament also speaks in terms of divine action, in judgement and salvation, at particular moments of history. The description of the formation of the literature of a community which so understood its life cannot be undertaken unless such views are taken seriously. The Old Testament literature is theologically orientated. Nor can we adequately interpret it without the recognition that, unlike other ancient literatures of the area—those of Babylonia and Assyria, for example—the Old Testament has been continuously a live part of a religious tradition from which those who belong to the Jewish or Christian or Islamic communities cannot detach themselves. What we may do here is describe what can be learned of the processes and recognise that the theological interpretation of these processes and the assessment of its validity fall strictly outside the scope of our present inquiry.

More than once in this discussion there has been reference to narrative sources—sometimes called 'documents'—traceable in the opening books of the Old Testament. The precise nature of these sources, whether they are to be seen as continuous documents once actually existing or as traditions not necessarily set down in writing, is often difficult to define. The dates and provenance of the sources too are matters in which no certainty is available. What is clear is that no explanation of the present form of the material is possible without the recognition of the presence of divergent elements—overlaps, duplications, and even contradictions within the material point to this.

The formation of these first books—the Pentateuch and those which

---

[1] This is not implied by all the titles of the psalms even if they are regarded as indicative of authorship. Ps. 90 is thus attributed to Moses and others are also 'non-Davidic'. Yet the tendency was strong to ascribe all to David, as may be seen from 11QPs[a] (Sanders, *The Psalms Scroll of Qumrân Cave* 11, see col. XXVII, p. 48, pl. XVI).

follow to 2 Kings—has been much discussed during the past century and more. In general we may recognise certain widely accepted pointers to the nature of their compilation. It is held by most scholars that there are three main strands of material in the narratives of Genesis to Numbers, designated J, E and P. Some scholars, noting that such a source as J is not completely unified, have seen within it further separable strands, and similar subdivisions have also been made in E and P. It is probably better to recognise that all three strands are the result of a complex structural development, while at the same time each has a certain unity of language, style and presentation. The book of Deuteronomy, in which dependence can be seen upon some of the same material as is known from the preceding books—though not necessarily dependence upon the books as we know them—stands very much on its own, since virtually no traces of its distinctive language and style are to be seen in Genesis to Numbers. The final structure of the books Joshua to 2 Kings, however, clearly owes much to writers who thought and wrote very much in the style of Deuteronomy. The material underlying this second group of books, Joshua to 2 Kings, described in the Hebrew canon as the 'Former Prophets', bears a close relationship to the material of J and E; many scholars believe that it is possible to trace here the original continuation of those sources. Material bearing affinity to P is less easy to discover, though it may perhaps be seen, for example, in the territorial allocations described in the second part of the book of Joshua which bear a resemblance to the thought of P in regard to the nature of Israel's occupation of the promised land. Within Joshua to 2 Kings there are sections which are marked out by their own particular interests and mode of presentation. Thus 2 Sam. 9–20 with 1 Kings 1–2—perhaps together with some other passages—make up a coherent and theologically significant work, setting out the nature of Davidic kingship and succession. Its markedly theological viewpoint made it very appropriate for inclusion within the larger work of which it now forms a part. Similarly the cycles of narratives concerning Elijah and Elisha, perhaps formed as a result of a dovetailing of two overlapping groups of stories, also form an appropriate part of the final work, though in certain respects differing from it in viewpoint. It is indeed one of the characteristics of such complex works as these that earlier material was frequently preserved even where its original intention did not accord with that of the eventual compiler. Such earlier material could, in effect, be neutralised by being set in a new context; thus the second Creation narrative in Gen. 2 is neutralised by the presence of the first, and the description of Jeroboam II as a 'saviour' in 2 Kings 14: 23–9 is neutralised within the book's over-all negative judgement upon the northern kingdom.

Much discussion turns on the question whether these books together should be seen as the result of one long and complex editorial process, a work which may be termed the 'Enneateuch' covering the nine books from Genesis to Kings,[1] subsequently divided into two, Pentateuch and 'Former Prophets'; or whether a division should be made into two great theological, historical works, the Tetrateuch (Genesis to Numbers, the Priestly Work as it may be described from the viewpoint and interests of its final compilers), and the Deuteronomic History (Deuteronomy to Kings). The two approaches are not necessarily completely mutually exclusive. The virtual absence of Deuteronomic influence from the Tetrateuch makes it most appropriate to treat that work as a unity, though it is quite possible that its original ending has been displaced—perhaps appearing in part at the end of Deuteronomy and some passages perhaps in Joshua—as a result of its being linked with the Deuteronomic History. At the same time it is proper to see within the latter work much that belongs closely with the material known to us as J and E in the Tetrateuch and this suggests that underlying the particular form of the material which we have, there may be detected earlier works whose range was not identical with the interests of either the Priestly or the Deuteronomic writers. The two great works have much in common. They offer different presentations of the theological interpretation of Israel's history; in the one case, in the Priestly Work, from the Creation to the moment of Israel's Entry into the Promised Land, in the other case, in the Deuteronomic History, from the Exodus to the collapse of the kingdom of Judah and its aftermath. But behind them lie earlier presentations, and we may not unreasonably suppose that the foundation of Israel's monarchy and the glorious years of David and Solomon provoked thinking about the nature of God's purpose with his people in bringing them to such unity and power. It may be that J provides just such a presentation.

[1] The subdivisions of Samuel and Kings are much later than biblical times. Cf. pp. 136 f.

It must, however, be remembered that in ancient literary works, where each copy has to be made separately—and lavish copying was not likely in the relatively small kingdoms of Israel and Judah—the forms of the literature which we now have are not likely to have been the only ones which existed. What we now have may not unreasonably be seen as representing the attempts of the theologians of the sixth and possibly fifth century B.C. at reassessing the older traditions and literature of their people in the light of the new needs of their own time.

As this material has come down to us, a sharp division has been made within it. The earliest forms of Israel's traditions about her experience in the Exodus period are likely to have included some indication of the nature of God's demand, i.e. law. This element became of increasing importance because the relationship between God and people was interpreted in covenant terms which naturally included legal provisions. So with theological developments, traceable also in prophetic teaching and in the psalms, in which the normative nature of the Exodus period was stressed as the moment of divine–human encounter, it was not unnatural that that part of the literature which described and expounded the Exodus period (including Sinai and the wilderness) should have been separated off as the *Tôrāh*, the Law in which the Jewish community of the period after the exile saw both the nature of God's revealing of himself in creative and redemptive power and also the obligation which rested upon Israel as the people of God. The books from Joshua to Kings thus came, as a truncated section, to be seen as part of that commentary on the subsequent history which could be found also in the prophetic books, and not at all inappropriately came to be described as the 'Former Prophets', i.e. those which stand first in the order of the books.

The 'Former Prophets'—the four books Joshua, Judges, Samuel and Kings—came to be matched by four corresponding books of 'Latter Prophets', i.e. those which stand after.[1] The four books here are all themselves complex structures. We have already looked at some indications of the processes by which prophetic oracles and other material associated with such figures came together into groups and complex wholes. Each of the four prophetic 'books' has its own

---

[1] Neither of these descriptions can be purely of date, though Joshua antedates the 'Latter Prophets' in time and the last prophetic books postdate 2 Kings. But there is also much overlap between the books of Kings and the prophetical books chronologically.

particular problems. The book of Isaiah contains not only a structure of oracles and other material associable with the Isaiah after whom the book is named, a prophet of Judah of the latter half of the eighth century B.C., but also much evidence of later reinterpretation and the addition of large sections of prophecy from later dates, notably the so-called Deutero-Isaianic prophecies of Isa. 40–55. Other parts of the book may be of still later origin. Yet a certain degree of unity of thought—which must not, however, be exaggerated—suggests that we have here a series of deposits of prophetic material, indications of its use and re-use, within one important circle in the community. The book of Jeremiah also contains separate and overlapping elements, though its whole content is more closely linked with one figure. But it offers not only a collection like that of other prophetic books (1–24 (25)), but also a series of highly stylised narratives and historical passages (26–45) which are perhaps more concerned with the interpretation of the last years of Judah and hence with their meaning for the future than with the presentation of the prophet. Different again is the book of Ezekiel in which prophetic oracles and other material are brought together into a form now organised as a series of dated sections, giving the appearance of very careful workmanship and highly stylised presentation. Not improbably this book too represents much more than the teaching of a single prophet: it provides evidence of another rich tradition of thought associated with a particular name. The last of the four prophetic 'books', the 'Book of the Twelve'— commonly known as the 'Minor Prophets' by reason of their size— is not really a book at all as it consists of small collections associated with a number of named prophets—Hosea, Amos, Micah, etc.—as well as a prophetic legend, associated with the Jonah named in 2 Kings 14: 25, and at the end three collections of anonymous prophecy, Zech. 9–11, 12–14 and Malachi (this last being not the name of a prophet but simply a title 'my messenger', cf. Mal. 3: 1), though some links between Zech. 9–14 ('Deutero-Zechariah') and Zech. 1–8 (the collection associated with the prophet Zechariah) may suggest a continuity of prophetic tradition here too. This collection of four prophetic 'books', including the 'Twelve', we know to have been familiar to Jesus ben Sira in the early second century B.C.[1]

The third part of the Hebrew Old Testament consists of the remain-

[1] Cf. Ecclus. 48: 17—49: 10, and below, p. 128 on the Canon.

der of the books, and here much less evidence of literary grouping is to be seen. The Psalter is a collection in itself and reveals both the survival and reinterpretation of early psalmody at a later date and also the existence of earlier collections incorporated in it (cf. Ps. 72: 20). If the titles were fully understood, other indications of grouping might appear, but although some of them—e.g. Asaph—show links with guilds of singers (cf. 1 Chron. 16: 4 f.), it is uncertain whether these necessarily indicate that the psalms so headed formed part of an actual separate collection. The discovery of collections of psalms at Qumrân in which the order is different and other poems are included[1] shows that, whether or not such collections had authority, psalms could be arranged differently, probably for liturgical purposes. It is reasonable to suppose that the biblical Psalter owes its arrangement at least in part to some kind of liturgical demands.

The book of Job clearly stands as a work on its own, having its own structural problems in view of the presence of both a prose narrative (1–2 and 42: 7–17) and an elaborate poetic dialogue; if not necessarily all the work of one author, it has a unity of purpose which enables us to treat it as a unity. The book of Proverbs is a collection of collections of sayings (cf. the titles in 1: 1; 10: 1; 24: 23; 25: 1, etc.); the existence of a much wider range of such material is indicated both by similar elements in the book of Job and by the later collections in the Wisdom of Ben Sira and the Wisdom of Solomon. An early liturgical grouping is seen in the five '*m^egillôt*' or rolls—Song of Songs, Ruth, Lamentations, Ecclesiastes, Esther—books differently placed in the Greek and English Bibles; their traditional association with festal occasions has brought them together, but each has its own independent history. Daniel is *sui generis*, a compilation clearly referring to the religious persecutions of the period of Antiochus Epiphanes (*c.* 167–164 B.C.), but clearly also containing much that is likely to be of earlier origin.

The one great coherent work remaining is in the Hebrew Old Testament divided into two in such a way that its last section, the books of Ezra and Nehemiah in the English Bible, stands before its first section, the books of Chronicles. Not inappropriately the Greek Old Testament (and hence the English) placed them side by side with Kings, for this is another great theological history of Israel. As we have seen, it is at times quite radical in its reshaping of the material at its author's (or

[1] Cf. esp. 11QPs^a (see above, p. 77 n. 1).

authors') disposal. It surveys the whole history from Creation to the time of Ezra, laying particular stress on the significance of the exile for the understanding of the contemporary situation of the community, and laying great emphasis also on the normative character of the period of David rather than on the period of the Exodus as in the earlier accounts.

This brief survey is designed simply to draw together in quite summary fashion the formation of the Old Testament books. It is only rarely that we can point to individuals as authors—the author of Job, the author of Ecclesiastes perhaps, and a few more; more often we can point to compilers, single figures or schools—the Deuteronomists, the Priestly Writers, and the Chronicler whose work has undergone some substantial amplification in the same spirit. Again we may point to great men whose personality and vision lie behind collections—and above all here the figures of the great prophets and other leaders around whom tradition has gathered. The Old Testament is not, on the whole, greatly concerned about authorship: it is more concerned about authority.

Equally significantly we can see at certain points the relationship between major historical events and crises and the formation of the literature. The Exodus was perhaps less productive of literature than of the theology which at many points dominates the literary presentation of the early history. The period of David and Solomon was evidently a high moment for literary activity, as we might expect with the development of scribal life and at a moment of national triumph. The periods of crisis—the fall of Samaria (722 B.C.), the fall of Jerusalem (587 B.C.) above all—were moments for reassessing and reordering older material. The crisis of the exile, indeed, appears to have exerted a very great influence on the rethinking of older ideas and the reshaping of older writings. The later crisis in which the Chronicler was involved is only partly known to us, mainly in so far as it may be deduced from his work; we may detect the presence of the Samaritan schism and the asking of the question: what constitutes membership of the community as it now is? A new impetus to literary activity, taking us in the main beyond the Old Testament proper, came with the tensions of the last two centuries B.C., as may be seen in the wealth of what is loosely called 'the intertestamental literature'.

But to be aware of such great crises only allows a very rough and ready relating of literature to history. Concealed within the pages of the Old Testament and not easy to detect because of the elusiveness of the persons and the allusiveness of the language, are the moments of day-to-day experience and thought in which generation after generation of the community's sensitive religious leaders thought and rethought their experience, read and re-read their literature, attempted to understand their faith and to apply it to their own times and needs. Whatever has been lost—and is to be regretted because of the many gaps in our knowledge—there remains a rich testimony to the vitality of faith and the continually renewed life of a community which, unlike so many of its contemporaries, did not have to be rediscovered by the archaeologist, but could be approached directly through a literature still read and cherished.

6. CANONICAL AND NON-CANONICAL

Difficult as is the task of tracing the growth of Old Testament literature and disentangling the strands of the several traditions which preceded the written records, that of reconstructing the processes by which the Old Testament Canon emerged is still more complex. It is salutary to recall that even within the Christian Church, with its reiterated appeal to canonical scripture as authoritative for faith and practice, either apart from or in conjunction with ecclesiastical tradition, the understanding of the nature of canonical authority and the definition of the contents of the Canon vary in different communions today, and have varied over the centuries. Accordingly, any attempt to discover how the Old Testament Canon was formed must reckon not only with the fact that the evidence available is far from complete, but also with the possibility that different conceptions of canonicity were presupposed at different stages in the process and in different regions and communities. These difficulties are aggravated by the lack, during the period under review, of a clear and consistent conception of canonicity and of unambiguous terminology with which to express it.

In the present survey the subject will be treated under the following main sections: (1) a consideration of the terms used to describe the canonical writings and of the definition of canonisation and canonicity within the relevant period; (2) a discussion of the evidence for acts of canonisation by which the several sections, and finally the collection as a whole, came to be recognised as canonical; (3) an account of the contents of the Canon and of their varying enumeration and arrangement; (4) an inquiry into the possibility that different attitudes to the Canon were adopted in different communities; (5) some account of the relation between canonical and non-canonical literature.

THE DEFINITION OF CANONICITY

The terms 'Canon' and 'canonical books' belong to Christian usage and first appear in patristic writings of the fourth century. In the Mishnah the scriptures are referred to as 'the sacred writings' (*kiṯᵉḇê hakkōḏeš*) and are said to 'defile the hands' (*mᵉṭammᵉᵉîm 'eṯ-hay-yāḏayim*).[1] The latter phrase in effect indicates canonical status. Of the various interpretations of it which have been offered the most probable is that the books so described were, so to say, impregnated with a contagious quality of holiness which had to be washed away so that it might not be conveyed to mundane objects. Contemporary Jewish terminology is reflected in the New Testament in general expressions such as 'the scriptures'[2] and 'the sacred writings';[3] but these are so general as to shed little or no light on the way in which the authority of the scriptures was understood.

A famous passage in Josephus provides both a descriptive terminology and a definition of the nature of the Canon as it was understood in his time.[4] Josephus is concerned to maintain that the inspired Jewish scriptures are neither unduly numerous nor mutually contradictory but circumscribed and self-consistent. They comprise five books of Moses, thirteen prophetic books, and four others containing hymns to God and moral precepts. At a later stage it will be necessary to consider more closely the implications of this reference to a threefold division and the problems raised by the numbers of the books contained in the second and third divisions. For our present purpose it is important to note that Josephus indicates that there are chronological as well as arithmetical limits to the sacred collection. The prophetic section is said to span the period from the death of Moses to the reign of Artaxerxes. Records of the later period do indeed exist; but they are not accorded the same credence, because by then the authentic prophetic

[1] Yadaim 3, 5. [2] Matt. 21: 42.
[3] 2 Tim. 3: 15. [4] *C.Ap.* I, 38–42.

succession had ceased. The Artaxerxes referred to is the first of the name (465–424 B.C.). Thus the period of time within which the contents of the entire Canon were produced extends from the lifetime of Moses to the age of Ezra and Nehemiah for, although the four books in the third section are not explicitly assigned to any period, what is said about the failure of prophetic succession in the time subsequent to Artaxerxes makes it improbable that Josephus supposed that they had been written then. No reason is given for the earlier chronological limit. It might indeed be supposed that none was needed. The dominating position of Moses as lawgiver and as recorder of patriarchal tradition made his lifetime the appropriate starting point. But it is evident that the recognition of this upper limit effectively excluded from the authoritative sacred collection those apocalyptic works which purported to be the work of pre-Mosaic figures such as Enoch. The lower limit is associated not only with the beginning of a period in which it was felt that the gift of prophetic inspiration had been withdrawn, but with the status accorded to Ezra in Jewish literature and tradition as a second Moses, communicating the sacred scripture to God's people a second time after the havoc wrought by the fall of Jerusalem and the Exile. The most colourful expression of this view of Ezra is found in 2 Esdras 14 (roughly contemporary with Josephus), a legendary narrative which tells how Ezra prayed for the inspiration of the Holy Spirit, so that he might rewrite the text of the scriptures which had been destroyed by fire. He subsequently dictated to five amanuenses, during a period of forty days, what had been revealed to him, amounting in all to ninety-four books: twenty-four for general publication and use, seventy to be reserved for 'the wise among your people'. The smaller group of writings is evidently to be equated with the books which, at least from the end of the first Christian century onwards, were accepted as forming the authoritative scriptures of Judaism (five books of the Law, eight books of the Prophets, and eleven books of the Writings). The larger group, being esoteric in character, must presumably have consisted of apocalyptic books, read and understood only by the initiated. The immediate relevance of this account for the present discussion is that it emphatically and explicitly represents Ezra as receiving in a new revelation all that had formerly been recorded in the scriptures. The implication is that none of these books originated after his time. A similar view is implied by the conclusion of the extraordinary series of statements in the Talmudic tractate Baba Bathra:

Moses wrote his own book, and the section about Balaam and Job. Joshua wrote his own book, and eight verses in the Torah. Samuel wrote his own book, and the books of Judges and Ruth. David wrote the book of Psalms at the direction of the ten elders, the first man, Melchizedek, and Abraham, and Moses, and Heman, and Jeduthun, and Asaph, and the three sons of Korah. Jeremiah wrote his own book, and the book of Kings and Lamentations. Hezekiah and his company wrote Isaiah, Proverbs, Song of Songs, and Ecclesiastes. The men of the Great Synagogue wrote Ezekiel, and the Twelve, Daniel, and the Roll of Esther. Ezra wrote his own book and the genealogies in Chronicles down to his own time.[1]

Here, as in Josephus, Moses is the *terminus a quo* and Ezra the *terminus ad quem*.

The assertion that a particular collection of writings belongs to a defined period of time may seem to be far removed from any attribution to it of canonical status; but it is precisely the acknowledgement that the collection is in a special sense authoritative and therefore distinct from other writings that underlies this particular chronological demarcation.

Josephus makes other assertions about the Jewish scriptures which bring out in a more theological fashion their peculiar status. There is, he says, inbred in all Jews the conviction that these writings are decrees of God,[2] by which they ought to abide and for which they should be prepared to die gladly. Moreover, although the documents have been transmitted over a long period of time, no one has dared to add to them, to delete any part of them, or to change the text in any way.[3]

If in these statements of Josephus we detect more than a trifle of the exaggeration of the partisan advocate, it is nevertheless true that this idealised account of the transmission of the Jewish scriptures and of the instinctive and unswerving devotion to them of every member of the Jewish people conveys a fairly rigorous conception of their canonical status. That status is indicated by four characteristics: the books are accepted as of divine authority; the number of them is fixed; the period of time within which they originated is expressly limited; their text is regarded as unaltered and unalterable.

---

[1] Baba Bathra 14*b*–15*a*.   [2] Θεοῦ δόγματα.
[3] *C.Ap.* I, 42, 43.

If, as has been argued by Hölscher[1] and others, the recognition of these characteristics is indispensable for the existence of a canon, then the emergence of any sort of canonical corpus must be dated relatively late, probably at some time between 100 B.C. and A.D. 100. But, apart from other considerations which will be noted later in this discussion, such a definition is unreasonably and unrealistically narrow. Precise textual uniformity had certainly not been attained at the time when Josephus wrote. His sweeping claims and their somewhat rhetorical formulation are no doubt to be explained in part by his apologetic purpose in the *Contra Apionem*. The substance of his statements about the distinctive nature of the canonical scriptures is in all probability to be attributed to his Pharisaic connections; and his enumeration of the contents of the scriptures, though beset by some difficulties of interpretation, almost certainly corresponds with the books contained in the tripartite Canon which was confirmed in the debates of the rabbis at the end of the first Christian century.

But the recognition that the canonical corpus was so understood and defined in the period of its final formulation does not commit us to the view that before such characteristics as chronological limitation, textual accuracy and inviolability, and an absolute *numerus clausus*, were acknowledged there was no canonical collection of writings at all and no acts of canonisation had taken place. Without resorting to an anachronistic application of later ideas of canonicity, it may legitimately be claimed that the beginnings of the history of the Canon may be traced in the Old Testament period. But two important distinctions must be observed. The growth of the Canon is not identical with the growth of the literature, even if the two processes are not wholly separable. Further, the fact that any utterance, literary composition, or collection of writings is recognised as divinely inspired does not necessarily imply that there is accorded to it the kind of authority which may properly be regarded as canonical. It is when a document is accepted as normative for the religious life of a community that the idea of canonicity emerges. When Josephus enumerated the features which, in his view, demonstrated the divine authority of the scriptures, the worship and life of the Jewish community had already been regulated for centuries by a normative corpus. An

---

[1] G. Hölscher, *Kanonisch und Apokryph. Ein Kapitel aus der Geschichte des alttestamentlichen Kanons* (Leipzig, 1908).

attempt must now be made to trace the successive stages by which the corpus was accepted, its scope enlarged, and its limits finally determined.

ACTS OF CANONISATION

The claim to divine inspiration is not synonymous with the assertion of canonical authority; but the one may be the preparation for the other. This is manifestly so in the Old Testament, where explicit claims that laws were uttered, dictated, or written by God point forward to and provide a justification for the subsequent canonisation of the larger documents in which these laws were incorporated. The Decalogue is introduced by the assertion, 'And God spoke all these words, saying ...';[1] it is said to have been written by Yahweh on tables of stone,[2] and after they had been broken to have been written again by Moses.[3] Similar claims recur in varying forms throughout the legal parts of the Pentateuch. They are reinforced by the command not to add to the text of the divine commands or to suppress any part of them.[4] But though such claims and safeguards may seem to have a special appropriateness to the Law, they are inseparable from the presentation of Moses as a prophetic figure, a man to whom God spoke face to face.[5] There is, accordingly, a link between them and the formulae, 'The word of the LORD came to...', 'Thus says the LORD', 'Hear the word of the LORD', and the like, which recur throughout the prophetic literature, and with the conviction that the true prophet has 'stood in the council of the LORD' and has had disclosed to him the LORD's 'secret'.[6] Like the laws, though in a different way, the prophetic oracles disclose to Israel the divine will: even oracles concerned with foreign nations form part of the prophetic testimony to Israel. By contrast with the laws, which are of permanent application, prophecy is related to the changing situations of history. But the fact that the prophetic teaching was remembered, recorded and interpreted, and that some interpretations were embodied in the prophetic texts, is an

[1] Exod. 20: 1.
[2] Exod. 24: 12; cf. 32: 15 f.; Deut. 9: 9, 11, 15.
[3] Exod. 34: 1, 28; cf. Deut. 10: 1–5.
[4] Deut. 4: 2; 12: 32.
[5] Exod. 3: 1—4: 17; 24: 1, 15–18; 33:7–11; 34: 5–7; Num. 12: 1–8; Deut. 18: 15–19.
[6] Jer. 23: 18, 22; Amos 3: 7. The words 'council' and 'secret' both render the Hebrew word *sôḏ*, which can mean both 'intimate circle' and 'counsel' or 'secret plan'.

indication that it was held to be authoritative not only for the generation to which it was uttered but for later ages; it provided guidance for the continuing life of the people of God.

A similar normative factor is present within the context of worship. The Torah-liturgies, or liturgies of approach, enunciate the character required in those who come to worship Yahweh in his sanctuary.[1] Further, embedded in a number of psalms there are passages which exhibit the style and quality of prophetic utterance and which, it is reasonable to infer, were spoken or chanted in the context of worship by persons who performed prophetic functions.[2] These oracular passages present, alongside the summons to worship Yahweh, emphatic reminders of his requirement of wholehearted obedience and warnings of the dangers of disobedience and disloyalty.

Such declarations of Yahweh's requirements of his worshippers are in some contexts linked with rehearsals of his past goodness, and in particular of how he delivered them from Egypt and brought them into the promised land. The same combination of historical recital with command and admonition is found in a number of important passages in the prophetic literature, sometimes with lapidary brevity, as in 'Hear this word that the LORD has spoken against you, O people of Israel, against the whole family which I brought up out of the land of Egypt: "You only have I known of all the families of the earth; therefore I will punish you for all your iniquities"',[3] and elsewhere at greater length.[4] It provides the pattern of certain important speeches in the historical records.[5] It appears in the Decalogue,[6] of which the prefatory divine self-description is an integral part: 'I am the LORD your God, who brought you out of the land of Egypt, out of the house of bondage.' It may also be traced *in extenso* in the present structure (whatever may have been its original form) of Deuteronomy, with its narrative and hortatory prolegomena, its core of laws, and its epilogue of curses and blessings. This combination of the recital of divinely ordered events, which were held to be constitutive of the community's very existence, with the enunciation (by command, reproof, warning, or appeal) of the divine will which is regulative of the community's

---

[1] Pss. 15; 24: 3–6.   [2] E.g. Pss. 50: 7–23; 81: 6–16; 95: 7*b*–11.
[3] Amos 3: 1 f.   [4] E.g. Amos 2: 6–16; Mic. 6: 1–8.
[5] E.g. Josh. 24: 1–28; 1 Sam. 12: 6–15.
[6] Exod. 20: 1–17; Deut. 5: 6–21.

life, and the relation of both these elements to the community's worship, help to account for the shaping of much of the literary material contained in the Canon.

It is, then, evident that from early times there existed in Israel oral or written formulae which were regarded as divinely inspired and normative. Further, according to a widely held view, passages such as Josh. 24: 1–28 indicate that the Israelite tribal confederacy or amphictyony regularly enacted a ritual in which Yahweh was acknowledged, the covenant was renewed, and the divinely given laws of the covenant community were proclaimed and accepted. But the presence in the Pentateuch of different codes of laws, such as the so-called Yahwistic Decalogue[1] and the Book of the Covenant,[2] indicates some degree of variation at different times and presumably also in different regions.

The discovery of the book of the Law in the Temple at Jerusalem in the eighteenth year of the reign of Josiah (621 B.C.) led to a decisive development in the emergence of the Canon. Josiah had already reversed the process of extreme syncretism which had characterised the religious life of Judah for nearly half a century before his accession. But the discovery of the book of the Law gave a new impetus to his programme of reform,[3] which involved not only a thoroughgoing purification of the national religion from alien elements but also the centralisation of sacrificial worship. The close correspondence between the reforms of Josiah and the standards laid down in Deuteronomy make it virtually certain that the book found in the Temple was at least a substantial part of Deuteronomy. Not only was the document accepted as of divine authority: its provisions were applied throughout the land by royal mandate. There is also evident a strong emphasis on the unity of the nation, corresponding to the unity of God which Deuteronomy proclaims[4] and the unification of worship by the restriction of sacrifice to the one legitimate centre, Jerusalem. The Deuteronomic emphasis on *all* Israel is matched by Josiah's policy of incorporating in his realm the central and northern parts of the country which had been lost to the house of David three centuries previously. The enacting of the reforms was not simply the sweeping away of abuses. It was in some sort a reconstitution of the nation as

---

[1] Exod. 34: 12–26.
[3] 2 Kings 22 f.; 2 Chron. 34.
[2] Exod. 20: 22—23: 33.
[4] Deut. 6: 4.

the people of God. This was marked by the solemn celebration of the feast of Passover.[1] Since we can date the events with reasonable precision and have the document on which the reform was based, even if we cannot exactly determine its limits, this formal acceptance of the book of the Law as the rule of the community's life is an important stage in the history of the Canon. Indeed, the idea of canonical scripture appears with a distinctness to which there is no earlier parallel.

But this formal enforcement of the standards of the book of the Law was not, in fact, such as to preclude further modification and amplification. The Deuteronomic code was itself modified in at least one particular when it was applied in practice in the reform: the provision that priests from the now suppressed local sanctuaries should be allowed to officiate at the central sanctuary in Jerusalem proved to be impracticable, as the narrative of the reform indicates.[2] It is evident from the comments of the Deuteronomistic historian on the reigns of Josiah's successors, and also from the implications of the relevant parts of the book of Jeremiah, that there were far-reaching lapses from Josiah's religious policy. The fall of Jerusalem, the destruction of the Temple, and the deportation of a considerable part of the population might have been expected to relegate Deuteronomic standards into the realm of the ineffective, since the place which God had chosen for his sanctuary had been devastated, and the people whom he had chosen had been thus tragically divided. But Deuteronomic standards survived the Exile, as is clear from such evidence as we have of the ideals of the community of returned exiles in and around Jerusalem. This may be in part explained by the fact that among the predominantly upper-class exiles there were many from families which, in Josiah's time, had actively co-operated in the royal policy. Further, it is not unreasonable to suppose that the official acknowledgement of its divine origin and normative authority had given to the document found in the Temple an unprecedented status and permanence. It did not, however, have such finality as precluded the formulation of other codes. Ezek. 40–8 contains detailed regulations for the organisation of the life and worship of the returned community. Though parts of these chapters may come not from Ezekiel himself but from his disciples, the section may at all events fairly be taken as providing one answer to the need

---

[1] 2 Kings 23: 21–3; 2 Chron. 35: 1–19.
[2] Contrast 2 Kings 23: 9 with Deut. 18: 6–8.

felt in exilic circles for prescribed standards in the restored community. A closely related code which (though its date of origin is much debated) probably comes from the same general period is Lev. 17–26, the Holiness Code. In its concern for holiness (as in many points of detail) it resembles Ezek. 40–8; in its restriction of sacrifice to one sanctuary it resembles Deuteronomy; but in its emphatic prohibition of the slaughter of oxen, sheep, and goats elsewhere than at the sanctuary it reads like a counterblast to Deuteronomy.[1] The Holiness Code is now incorporated in the Priestly Code, to which is assigned the rest of Leviticus, and the bulk of the legislative material in the latter part of Exodus and in Numbers, with which are allied a sequence of narratives and narrative fragments in Genesis and Exodus. Parts of its contents may well be of great antiquity; but the period of its compilation is generally inferred to have been the later sixth or early fifth century. It can hardly have been officially adopted at so early a date by the restored community in Jerusalem, however, for even Malachi (*c.* 470–460 B.C.) betrays practically no knowledge of its requirements in his appeals for the reformation of worship, and seems rather to reflect Deuteronomic usage. But we can say with reasonable certainty that it must have been adopted no later than, and perhaps before, the next decisive step which is recorded in the development of the Canon.

It appears to have been through the work of Ezra that these various codes, now amalgamated (with the exception of Ezek. 40–8), were established in the Palestinian Jewish community, and thus ultimately in the whole of Judaism. Ezra is said to have been 'a scribe skilled in the law of Moses which the LORD the God of Israel had given' and to have 'set his heart to study the law of the LORD, and to do it, and to teach his statutes and ordinances in Israel'.[2] Some time after his arrival from Babylonia he carried out, with the help of assistants, a solemn public reading of 'the book of the law of Moses which the LORD had given to Israel' on an occasion which was followed by the celebration of the feast of Booths.[3] As the narrative now stands, Ezra's arrival appears to have taken place a few years before the beginning of Nehemiah's first governorship, and the reading of the Law to have followed the establishment by Nehemiah of secure conditions of community life in Jerusalem and its immediate neighbourhood. Some

[1] Contrast Lev. 17: 1–9 with Deut. 12: 15–28.   [2] Ezra 7: 6, 10.
[3] Neh. 8: 1—9: 37.

of Nehemiah's reforms are related to the Deuteronomic law.[1] But the celebration of the feast of Booths after Ezra's reading of the Law corresponds with the directions given in the Priestly Code.[2] In all probability, then, Ezra's book of the Law was the completed Pentateuch, and not simply the Priestly Code: and the Pentateuch was formally accepted as normative in 444 B.C. But strong arguments have been advanced against accepting the order in which the events are related in Ezra–Nehemiah and against the chronology thus implied. According to Ezra 7: 7 f., Ezra came to Jerusalem in the seventh year of Artaxerxes. If the king referred to here was the second of the name (an assumption which alleviates some difficulties in the biblical record and which also accords better with external evidence from the Elephantine papyri) then Ezra's arrival in Jerusalem will have taken place in 398 B.C., the narrative of Neh. 8–9 will have been wrongly inserted in its present context, and it will follow that there was no direct link between Nehemiah's reforms and the promulgation of the Law by Ezra. Acceptance of this later date for Ezra strengthens the general probability that his book of the Law consisted not only of the Priestly Code but of the entire Pentateuch, though as yet the text was by no means finally fixed in every detail. If Neh. 8–9 does not in fact refer to the promulgation of the entire Pentateuch as the normative document for the restored Jewish community, then no record of such promulgation has survived. Arguments from silence are notoriously weak; but it would be a strangely deformed tradition which described for us the solemn acceptance of the Priestly Code but failed to preserve any record of an event so momentous as the canonisation of the Pentateuch as a whole.

A further consideration which has usually been advanced to clinch the argument that the entire Pentateuch had been accepted early in the fourth century B.C. concerns the position of the Pentateuch in the Samaritan community. The five books of Moses are the only part of the Jewish Canon accepted by the Samaritans. It cannot well be supposed that they adopted these books as canonical after the decisive breach between the Samaritan and Jewish communities, or indeed after the embitterment of relations between them. Dates suggested for the breach have varied between the fifth and first centuries B.C.; but the

[1] Cf. Neh. 13: 1 ff. with Deut. 23: 3 ff. and Neh. 10: 31 with Deut. 15: 2.
[2] Cf. Neh. 8: 13–18 with Lev. 23: 39–43.

majority opinion has favoured the latter part of the fourth century. Fresh light has been shed in recent years on the history of the Samaritan community by excavations at Shechem[1] and by the discovery of fourth-century Aramaic papyri at Wâdi Dâliyeh,[2] and on the history of the Samaritan form of the text of the Pentateuch by the Qumrân material.[3] It now seems highly probable that the Samaritans re-established their community life at Shechem towards the end of the fourth century B.C., at about the time when their temple on Mount Gerizim was completed, but that the emergence of a distinctive Samaritan text of the Pentateuch (and hence the *terminus ad quem* for the dating of a decisive breach between the Samaritan and Jewish communities) cannot well be dated before the Maccabaean or early Hasmonaean periods.[4] But if the final breach has to be dated at so late a period, it is also apparent that a common Palestinian textual tradition of the Pentateuch had been current in both Jerusalem and Samaria for a considerable time. Moreover, since the Samaritans did not include in their canon the prophetic corpus which, as will be seen below, was probably accepted by the Jews as part of the scriptures by the end of the third century B.C., relations between the two communities must by then have been severely strained, and what they held in common must have been of fairly long standing. The fact that the Septuagint translation of the Pentateuch dates from the middle of the third century points in the same direction. The middle of the third century is about as late a date as can reasonably be assigned to the work of the Chronicler. Many would regard a fourth-century date as more probable. The narrative of Neh. 8–9 indicates that, at the time when he wrote, it was believed that 'the book of the law of Moses which the LORD had given to Israel' had been promulgated by Ezra as the constitutive document of the restored community in Jerusalem.

The second section of the Hebrew Canon, as described by Josephus, and as it exists today, is prophetic. The total of thirteen books mentioned by Josephus raises questions which will be discussed at a later point in this chapter. He ascribes the recording of post-Mosaic history to the

[1] See G. Ernest Wright, *Shechem: The Biography of a Biblical City* (London, 1965), pp. 170–81.
[2] F. M. Cross, 'The discovery of the Samaria Papyri', *BA*, XXVI (1963), 110–21.
[3] See chapter III, 7.
[4] F. M. Cross, 'The History of the Biblical Text in the light of discoveries in the Judean Desert', *HTR*, LVII (1964), 281–99.

prophets; and there is at least this correspondence between his state-ment and the present arrangement of the Canon that the latter consists of history (Joshua, Judges, 1 and 2 Samuel, 1 and 2 Kings) as well as of prophetic books in the narrower sense (Isaiah, Jeremiah, Ezekiel, and the twelve Minor Prophets: Hosea, Joel, Amos, Obadiah, Jonah, Micah, Nahum, Habakkuk, Zephaniah, Haggai, Zechariah, Malachi). Both the assertion of Josephus and the implication of the arrangement of the Canon as it has been transmitted in its Hebrew form indicate that the history is in some sort prophetic.

Unfortunately, there is relatively little evidence to enable us to determine when this group of writings came collectively to be regarded as canonical. The narrative books came into existence by a complicated process, by which materials of widely different kinds were woven into a history dominated by the Deuteronomistic outlook, interpreting the nation's life as 'judged by the law of the Lord, and in the light of the spirit of prophecy'.[1] Accordingly, it was natural that they should be regarded not only as a record of the past but as a testimony to later ages. The prophetic books in the narrower sense were also the result of a long and complex development. The prophet was the man of the spoken word, authoritative but directed to the specific occasion rather than intended to be permanently normative. But the fact that the prophetic words were preserved in the memory of disciples and repeated to later generations was assuredly something more than an exercise in the compilation of oral memoirs and arose from the sense of the continuing authority and power of the divine word com-municated through the prophet. But for such recollection and oral repetition, much of the prophetic literature would have been lost and never recorded in writing. The natural milieu for such transmission was the circle of the prophet's disciples. The relationship between the prophet and a single personal disciple and also that between an out-standing individual prophet and circles or groups of disciples are exemplified in the stories told of Samuel, Elijah, and Elisha.[2] No refer-ence is made to disciples of Amos and Hosea; but it is reasonable to infer that it was through such agency that their teaching was trans-mitted. In spite of some difficulties of interpretation, Isa. 8: 16 brings

[1] H. E. Ryle, *The Canon of the Old Testament* (London, 1892), p. 100.
[2] 1 Sam. 19: 18–24; 1 Kings 19: 19–21; 2 Kings 2: 1–18; 4: 12, 25–31, 38–44; 5: 19–27; 6: 1–17; 8: 4 f.; 9: 1–10.

together the spoken word, the written record, and the prophetic disciples: 'Bind up the testimony, seal the teaching among my disciples.' Earlier in the same chapter there is an instance of the spoken word being committed to writing and attested, so that its subsequent fulfilment cannot be gainsaid;[1] but in 8: 16 the message which most have rejected is entrusted in written form to the circle of responsive disciples. Jer. 36 describes how, in a special situation, prophecies which Jeremiah had uttered during the first twenty years of his ministry were, by express divine command, recorded in writing and, when the manuscript had been destroyed, rewritten and enlarged. The narrative is illuminating in a number of ways. It implies that the prophet's primary medium of communication was the spoken word, and that the written record was for a specific purpose and in accordance with divine direction. Further, the scroll contained utterances from earlier situations which were now directed to the need of the hour; and thus it exemplified the applicability of the prophetic word to occasions beyond the one in which it was originally imparted. The rewriting of the scroll is another indication that the validity of the prophetic revelations extended into the future. It is also reasonable to suppose that this document, whatever its extent, formed the nucleus of the book of Jeremiah. The embodying of prophetic revelation in written form is vividly expressed in the account of the call of Ezekiel, in which the prophet is commanded to eat a scroll on which there are written 'words of lamentation and mourning and woe'.[2] Ezekiel's commission, like that of his predecessors, was primarily to be a spokesman; but this feature in his call indicates that the written record was thought to be appropriate to prophetic revelations and further underlines the idea that their validity extended beyond the situation in which they were uttered.

It is evident, however, that at first the validity of the teaching of prophets like Amos, Hosea, Isaiah, Micah, Jeremiah, and Ezekiel was recognised only by the faithful disciples who learned from them and transmitted the traditions of what they had said and done. By its very nature prophetic teaching did not as yet receive the wider public acknowledgement which was accorded to the codes of law. But in the exilic and post-exilic periods this wider acknowledgement increasingly became a reality, and the record of prophetic teaching was no longer the special inheritance of circles of prophetic disciples. Deuteronomy

[1] Isa. 8: 1–4.   [2] Ezek. 2: 8—3: 3.

combines a solemn warning about the danger of disregarding the message of a true prophet with a simple test of the divine origin of that message: 'when a prophet speaks in the name of the LORD, if the word does not come to pass or come true, that is a word which the LORD has not spoken; the prophet has spoken presumptuously, you need not be afraid of him'.[1] But the prophecies of judgement did come true when Jerusalem fell and Judah became a Babylonian dependency, with many of its inhabitants in exile. This provided a powerful argument for applying to the life of the restored community the teaching which in the period of the monarchy had been rejected by the mass of the people.

Be not like your fathers, to whom the former prophets cried out, 'Thus says the LORD of hosts, Return from your evil ways and from your evil deeds.' But they did not hear or heed me, says the LORD. Your fathers, where are they? And the prophets, do they live for ever? But my words and my statutes, which I commanded my servants the prophets, did they not overtake your fathers?[2]

So long as prophecy was still a living force, the various collections of prophetic teaching continued to be preserved and enlarged. It is evident that this involved not only the addition of new material but also the adaptation and interpretation of older prophecies in such a way as to apply them to new situations. As we have seen, this process is already present in Baruch's copying out of Jeremiah's oracles. A quite explicit addition made to an older prophecy in order to meet a new situation appears in Isa. 16: 13 f.: 'This is the word which the LORD spoke concerning Moab in the past. But now the LORD says...' Less obvious additions and adaptations appear elsewhere. Behind this process lie two convictions: that the prophetic revelation is authoritative, and that it is a continuous process into the present. These two convictions appear with special clarity in Isa. 40–55, and in particular in the passages which pour scorn on diviners, idol-worshippers, and their deities: the God of Israel alone can foretell events; what he has declared in the past has come true; and he alone makes plain through the prophetic revelation what is now coming to pass.[3]

But prophecy did not continue as a living force. The desolating sense of the withdrawal of prophetic revelation, characteristic of a period

---

[1] Deut. 18: 22; see the whole passage, *vv.* 15–22.   [2] Zech. 1: 4–6.
[3] Isa. 41: 21–9; 43: 9; 44: 24–6, etc.

of religious decline,[1] threatened as divine punishment for unfaithfulness,[2] and felt with peculiar intensity at a time of national disaster,[3] became a normal feature during the two centuries before the beginning of the Christian era. Writing at the beginning of the second century, Jesus ben Sira, the original author of Ecclesiasticus, can write of his own writings as if they issued from an inspiration comparable to that of the prophets.[4] But, if 1 Maccabees may be taken as a trustworthy witness, the lapse of prophetic inspiration had become an acknowledged fact before the middle of the century.[5] The most important literary production of that period, the book of Daniel, indicates clearly that if the living voice of prophecy was now silent, the prophetic teaching of an earlier age was not only preserved in accessible literary form, but was established as authoritative scripture: 'I, Daniel, perceived in the books the numbers of years which, according to the word of the LORD to Jeremiah the prophet, must pass before the end of the desolations of Jerusalem, namely, seventy years.'[6] Though the reference here is only to Jeremiah, it is clear that at least a generation earlier the contents of the prophetic part of the Canon had substantially been assembled, and that it had taken its place alongside the Pentateuch as a collection of sacred scriptures whose limits had been defined though its text had not yet been finally fixed. In the familiar passage in which Jesus ben Sira celebrates the famous men of Israel's past,[7] the account of the patriarchal and Mosaic ages is followed by references, with varying degrees of detail, to the contents of the books of Joshua, Judges, Samuel, and Kings, and to Isaiah, Jeremiah, Ezekiel, and 'the twelve prophets'.[8] No enumeration of the 'twelve' is either given or hinted at; but the references to Jeremiah and Ezekiel, though brief, reveal knowledge of the text of the books; and the eulogy of Isaiah includes the statement, 'By the spirit of might he saw the last things, and comforted those who mourned in Zion. He revealed what was to occur to the end of time, and the hidden things before they came to pass.'[9] This is clearly both a general allusion to passages in Isa. 40–55 such as 42: 9 and also a quotation of Isa. 61: 2 f. indicating a knowledge not only of the account of Isaiah given in Kings or even of the tradition of the teaching of the

---

[1] 1 Sam. 3: 1. [2] Amos 8: 11 f. [3] Ps. 74: 9; Lam. 2: 9.
[4] Ecclus. 24: 33; 39: 12; 50: 27.
[5] 1 Macc. 4: 46; 9: 27; 14: 41. [6] Dan. 9: 2.
[7] Ecclus. 44–50. [8] Ecclus. 48: 20–5; 49: 6–10.
[9] Ecclus. 48: 24 f.

prophet preserved in the first part of Isaiah, but acquaintance with the later part of the book as we now have it. Although the evidence falls short of actual demonstration, it seems highly probable that the prophetic section of the Canon had been established by 200 B.C. If its limits had remained undetermined for a few decades longer, the book of Daniel (which was written about 165 B.C. and early exercised wide influence) would certainly have been accorded a place in it. There is, indeed, an arrangement of the Canon which links Daniel with the prophetical books. Of this more must be said below. But in the line of development represented by the evidence so far surveyed, Daniel remains outside the prophetic corpus; and the most natural explanation of this fact is that it appeared too late to be included.

In ben Sira's eulogy of famous men there are signs that he took account of books outside the Pentateuch and the Prophets (in the wider sense of the term). The statement that David made arrangements for temple choirs and for the due observance of the festivals appears to be based on two passages in Chronicles.[1] The references to Zerubbabel and Jeshua[2] may be dependent on the books of Haggai and Zechariah rather than on Ezra. Of Ezra there is no mention. Nehemiah's work in rebuilding the walls of Jerusalem is commemorated, thus implying knowledge of the material embodied in the latter part of the Chronicler's history. Thus, while there are these slight indications of knowledge of a wider range of literature referring to Israel's past, there is no solid ground for the supposition that ben Sira regarded any writing or group of writings outside the Pentateuch and the Prophets as of comparable authority. The generally accepted dating of the books of Daniel and Esther provides a sufficient explanation of his failure to refer to the leading characters in them. It is harder to explain his silence about Job and Ezra, unless the writings referring to them were unknown to him.

In the Prologue of Ecclesiasticus, written about 130 B.C. by ben Sira's grandson and translator, there are more specific allusions to a third corpus of sacred writings alongside the Pentateuch and the Prophets: 'Whereas many great teachings have been given to us through the law and the prophets and the others that followed them ...', 'the law and the prophets and the other books of our fathers...',

---

[1] Cf. Ecclus. 47: 9 f. with 1 Chron. 16: 4; 23: 31.
[2] Ecclus. 49: 11 f.

'the law itself, the prophecies, and the rest of the books'. In later times, the third section of the Canon was (and is) known as the Writings (*keṯûḇîm*) or the Hagiographa. But it is generally assumed that the terms used by ben Sira's grandson refer to an incipient and perhaps ill-defined third group of writings and not to the completed collection of Hagiographa.

As subsequently embodied in the Jewish Canon, the Hagiographa consist of: Psalms, Proverbs, Job, the Song of Songs, Ruth, Lamentations, Ecclesiastes, Esther, Daniel, Ezra and Nehemiah, 1 and 2 Chronicles. The important place occupied by the Psalms in Temple worship doubtless ensured that they would have a place in the third corpus. The general references which the Chronicler makes to the arrangements for music and song in worship reflect that liturgical use; and this is done more specifically in the catena of psalm passages inserted into the narrative after 1 Chron. 16: 7. More to our purpose, however, is the citation of Ps. 79: 2 f. at 1 Macc. 7: 16 f., introduced by the formula 'in accordance with the word which was written'. Liturgical song has become Holy Scripture. There is a similar implication in the statement in 2 Macc. 2: 13 that Nehemiah 'founded a library and collected the books about the kings and prophets, and the writings of David, and letters of kings about votive offerings'. Here the Psalter is set alongside what appears to be a reference to the two parts of the prophetic corpus ('the books about the kings and prophets') and followed by what may be an allusion to the royal decrees and letters embodied in the book of Ezra. For our present purpose it is unnecessary to discuss either the vexed question of the relationship of this part of 2 Maccabees to the main body of the work or the historicity of the statement about Nehemiah. The passage is at least a testimony from the first century B.C. to the ranking of the Psalms with other sacred writings. A more emphatic statement is made in Luke 24: 44, where the united testimony of scripture is described by the risen Christ as 'everything written about me in the law of Moses and the prophets and the psalms'. Here the tripartite structure of the Canon is unmistakably presupposed. But it is still not clear how much is assigned to the third section. 'The psalms' may mean simply what it says; for the Psalter was a rich source of Christological *testimonia*. On the other hand, the title of the most familiar and most widely used book in the third corpus may be taken to serve as a designation of the whole, or of that part of the whole which had so far been compiled. The statement in Matt. 23: 35 and Luke 11: 50 f. is generally understood to indicate with greater precision the limits of the Jewish Canon as they were finally determined. The persecution of the righteous servants of God is said to have extended from Abel to Zechariah, i.e. from the fratricide described in Gen. 4 to the assassination of Zechariah in the court of the Temple as recorded in 2 Chron. 24: 20–2. If the passage is rightly so understood, it is a reference to the whole span of scripture, and points to the completion of the Hagiographa, with Chronicles as the closing book. But the Zechariah mentioned in 2 Chron. 24: 20–2 was the son of Jehoiada; whereas Matt. 23: 35 speaks of the son of Barachiah. This has been taken to be an erroneous addition arising from confusion with the canonical prophet, Zechariah the son of Berechiah.[1] But it has been suggested that the reference is to Zechariah the son of Bareis (or, according to other readings, of Baruch or of Bariscaeus) whose judicial murder in the Temple precincts by the Zealots is described by Josephus in his account of the revolt against the Romans (A.D. 66–70).[2] This suggestion, which is based on the assumption that the words in Matthew and Luke are not an authentic saying of Jesus but originated a generation or more after his death, means that the span indicated is a historical one and not that from the first book to the last in the Canon. It is, however, most unlikely that the death of the later Zechariah would be laid at the door of the Scribes and Pharisees, when the Zealots were in fact responsible, or that that Zechariah, not being a priest, would have been between the Temple and the altar; furthermore, the Zechariah of 2 Chronicles is the subject of a number of rabbinic traditions, and therefore the story of his death was presumably a not unfamiliar part of scripture. Accordingly, it may fairly be argued[3] that the parallel passages in Matthew and Luke point to the completion of the structure and contents of the Canon, though there may still have been room for discussion about specific books. General support for this view is afforded by the fact that in the New Testament there are quotations from all the books of the Hagiographa except Ezra–Nehemiah,

---

[1] Zech. 1: 1.

[2] *B.J.* IV, 334–44.

[3] It should perhaps be added that the above argument presupposes an *order* of books, and that it is difficult to assume a fixed order (except where narrative sequence requires it) when the scriptures were written on scrolls and not on codices. There appears to be no evidence for the existence of Hebrew codices at so early a date.

Esther, the Song of Songs, and Ecclesiastes. But acknowledgement of Chronicles presupposes acknowledgement of Ezra–Nehemiah; and no *argumentum e silentio* of any consequence can be based on the absence from the New Testament of citation from or allusion to the other three books.

There is a fair amount of circumstantial evidence indicating that the final discussions about the contents of the Canon took place towards the end of the first Christian century. Certain general considerations are of obvious relevance. The existence of the Dispersion for several centuries had made Judaism increasingly a 'religion of the Book'. The work of the returned exiles in rebuilding the Temple, the splendour bestowed upon it by Herod's grandiose and costly reconstruction, and the legal restriction of sacrificial worship to that one sanctuary, could not outweigh the fact that for very many Jews the practice of their religion had to be carried out far from Jerusalem. Thus the practical importance of the scriptures was enhanced not only because of the place which they occupied in the worship of the Synagogue but because of the guidance and inspiration which they afforded to the individual Jew. The final destruction of the Temple in A.D. 70 provided the dramatic culmination of this long process. Deprived finally of its historic sanctuary, Judaism had to turn with renewed urgency to its sacred writings and to the interpretation and application of them. In this situation it was necessary that any doubt or disagreement about the contents of the Canon should be removed.

This need was reinforced by the existence of the apocalyptic writings. Almost all of these were pseudonymous in character; and their pseudonymity implied a claim that they were the products of inspired men in earlier ages, such as Enoch, Abraham, the sons of Jacob, and Daniel. It is a matter of dispute how seriously and in what sense this attribution was intended to be understood. It has been argued, with no great cogency, that only by such claims could the apocalyptists secure a hearing, since prophetic inspiration had ceased, and further that since the scope of the canonical corpus had now been in large measure determined, the apocalyptic teaching could not secure adequate recognition unless it was presented as the work of great religious figures of the past.[1] In all probability this view is to be rejected. It is, indeed,

---

[1] It would be out of place to discuss fully here the nature of pseudonymity or the reasons for its adoption as a device.

evident that the apocalyptic writings are intended to be regarded as the media of special revelations. But such orthodox Jewish teaching as they contain is blended with a considerable amount of material derived from non-Jewish sources. At a time when the old foundations of Judaism had to be laid with a new precision it was important to make clear whether such writings were authoritative. They had a considerable vogue, as is shown, for example, by the Qumrân discoveries; but in later times they had no place in the main stream of Jewish teaching. It is less likely that their claims to inspiration were an attempt to get behind the middle wall of canonical partition than that the limits of the Canon were defined in order to exclude most of them. Only the book of Daniel secured a place, presumably because its standing had already been established for a considerable time.

A third factor was the rise of Christianity, a vigorous and expanding movement with a growing literature of its own. Since, however, the specifically Christian scriptures appealed to the testimony of the Law, the Prophets, and the Hagiographa, and since subsequent Christian apologetic made a similar appeal, the precise definition of the Canon was an insufficient safeguard against the new movement and its teaching. The conflict was extended into the field of the interpretation of the scriptures which the two communities had in common.

These general factors, together with the evidence about the growth of the Canon which has been outlined above, rule out of serious historical consideration the statement in 2 Esdras 14 that Ezra promulgated the complete Canon. They also refute, if refutation is needed, the later form of that view which was presented by the Jew, Elias Levita (1472–1549), in his work *Massoreth ha-Massoreth*, to the effect that Ezra and his associates collected the scriptures and arranged them according to the threefold grouping of Law, Prophets, and Hagiographa, and not in the order in which Prophets and Hagiographa are referred to in Baba Bathra (see above, p. 116). Elias Levita identified the associates of Ezra with the men of the Great Synagogue, an assembly whose nature and historicity is not easily to be determined from the references to it in rabbinic tradition, of which the basis is probably Neh. 8–10.

But the assembly which probably was responsible for the last major stage in the delimitation of the Canon was the so-called Synod of Jamnia, which is said to have met during the last decade of the first Christian century. At the time of the fall of Jerusalem, Rabbi Johanan ben Zakkai obtained from the Romans permission to establish an assembly of religious teachers at Jamnia, not far from Joppa, in the coastal plain. This body was regarded as in some sort a replacement for the Jerusalem Sanhedrin, but did not possess the same representative character or national authority. Unfortunately, the evidence for decisions relating to the scriptures is far from clear.

The records of discussions among the rabbis show that there had been differences of opinion about the status of certain books. Somewhat surprisingly, Ezekiel was one of the books about which questions were raised. The discrepancies between the regulations in the last nine chapters and those in the Torah gave rise to concern, not unnaturally in a period when there was scrupulous attention to regulations. It is recorded that Rabbi Hananiah ben Hezekiah, having obtained a supply of 300 measures of oil, worked day and night to dispose of the discrepancies. Doubts seem also to have been felt about Proverbs and Esther. But it was chiefly around Ecclesiastes and the Song of Songs that there was controversy. Ecclesiastes was suspect because it appeared to contradict itself (e.g. 4: 2; 9: 2) and because it was alleged to contain heretical teaching (e.g. 1: 3). How these difficulties were overcome is not clear. Perhaps the attribution of the book to Solomon, together with the presence in it, and at its close, of expressions of traditional orthodoxy and piety, secured its place in the Canon. The Song of Songs owed its final acceptance to allegorical interpretation. Literally interpreted it is an expression of the love between man and woman. But as in later Christian interpretation it was understood as an expression of the love of Christ for the Church or for the soul of the believer, so there were rabbis who maintained that it expressed God's love for Israel. Its doughtiest defender was Rabbi Aqiba, who said of it, 'God forbid that any men of Israel should deny that the Song of Songs defiles the hands; for all the ages are not worth the day on which the Song of Songs was given to Israel. For all the scriptures are holy; but the Song of Songs is holiest of all.'[1]

These and other records of debate among the rabbis presuppose the existence of an authoritative collection of sacred books whose limits had already been substantially determined; and this, too, is the presupposition of rabbinic discussions on other subjects during the same period. Differences of opinion about books whose canonical status

[1] Yadaim 3, 5.

had been questioned may have persisted into the second century; but in spite of the nebulous character of the evidence relating to the Synod of Jamnia, it is difficult to doubt that both the tripartite structure of the Canon and its precise contents had been settled soon after A.D. 100, if not earlier. The Mishnah, which presupposes that the contents of the authoritative corpus of scripture had been determined, was given written form by the end of the second century, but its contents had already been systematised in the process of oral transmission. Thus its testimony corroborates what on other evidence (circumstantial rather than precise) appears most probable: the final definition, not later than the first quarter of the second century, of a collection identical with that which we now have in the Hebrew Bible.

THE ENUMERATION AND ARRANGEMENT OF THE CONTENTS OF THE CANON

The history of the Canon as outlined above is a process in three main stages, corresponding to the three principal sections of the Hebrew Bible as it exists today and has existed for centuries. The threefold division into Law (*tôrāh*), Prophets (*nᵉbî'îm*), and Writings (*kᵉtûbîm*) constitutes a total of twenty-four books. The Law contains the five books, Genesis, Exodus, Leviticus, Numbers, and Deuteronomy. There are eight books of the Prophets, subdivided into two groups of four: the Former Prophets (*nᵉbî'îm rišônîm*), and the Latter Prophets (*nᵉbî'îm 'ahᵃrônîm*). The Former Prophets are Joshua, Judges, Samuel, and Kings; and the Latter Prophets are Isaiah, Jeremiah, Ezekiel and the Twelve (i.e. the Minor Prophets: Hosea, Joel, Amos, Obadiah, Jonah, Micah, Nahum, Habakkuk, Zephaniah, Haggai, Zechariah, and Malachi). The Writings are eleven in number: Psalms, Proverbs, and Job (traditionally classed as the poetical books); the Five Scrolls (*mᵉgillôt*): the Song of Songs, Ruth, Lamentations, Ecclesiastes, Esther; Daniel, Ezra–Nehemiah (one book), and Chronicles. In this enumeration the books of Samuel, Kings, Ezra–Nehemiah, and Chronicles each count as one book and not as two; and the twelve Minor Prophets are also reckoned as one.

The absence of the tripartite structure is one of a number of features, to which fuller reference must be made later, which distinguish the Septuagint (and the versions derived from it) from the Hebrew Bible.

But the evidence for the antiquity of the tripartite structure is strong. It is attested by the Prologue to Ecclesiasticus, in its references to 'the law and the prophets and the others that followed them', 'the law and the prophets and the other books of our fathers,', and 'the law itself, the prophecies, and the rest of the books'. It is fairly clearly implied by the allusion in Luke 24: 44 to 'the law of Moses and the prophets and the Psalms'. From a somewhat later period comes the dictum of Rabbi Judah the Prince: 'They brought before us the Law, the Prophets, and the Writings united together and we approved them.'[1] At first sight it is natural to assume that the same arrangement is pre-supposed by the statement of Josephus already mentioned, that the scriptures are twenty-two in number: five books of Moses, thirteen prophetic books, and four others containing hymns to God and moral precepts.[2] The books are indeed classified in three groups; but problems are raised by the total (twenty-two, and not twenty-four), and by the number of books assigned to the second and third sections. It has been inferred that the four books which Josephus assigns to the third section are Psalms, Proverbs, the Song of Songs, and Ecclesiastes. Presumably, then, the middle section, which he describes as prophetic histories of the period from the death of Moses until the reign of Artaxerxes, consists of the remaining books of the Hagiographa together with the Former and Latter Prophets. But in order to obtain a total of thirteen, it is generally assumed that Ruth is treated as part of Judges (to which it is a natural sequel) and that Lamentations is similarly bracketed with Jeremiah, and further that, as in the enumeration followed in the Hebrew Bible, Samuel, Kings, Ezra–Nehemiah, Chronicles, and the Twelve Prophets are each reckoned as one book. If these inferences are correct, then the contents of the Canon presupposed by Josephus must have been identical with those of the Hebrew Bible as we know it, and as it appears to have been established in the Jamnia period. But although he presents a threefold structure, Josephus seems to indicate an arrangement of the books markedly different from that of the Prophets and the Hagiographa, but which bears some resemblance to the general pattern found in the Septuagint. Yet the Septuagint contains additional books of which Josephus takes no account, and differs from him in some details of enumeration.

Although different manuscripts exhibit detailed differences of

[1] Baba Bathra 13 *b*.   [2] *C.Ap.* I, 39–42.

arrangement, the main groups in the Septuagint are narrative (beginning with the five books of the Law), poetical, and prophetic. The narrative section includes Ruth, Chronicles, and Ezra–Nehemiah (2 Esdras), all of which belong to the Hagiographa in the Hebrew arrangement. Ecclesiastes and the Song of Songs are included in the poetic section; and Daniel and Lamentations appear among the prophets. Samuel and Kings are divided into four books of 'Kingdoms' or 'Reigns'; and Chronicles is divided into two. There are also additional books or parts of books (those now commonly classed as apocryphal), the character and status of which will be discussed in a later section of this chapter. Thus the points of similarity between the Septuagint and the arrangement which is thought to be presupposed by the statement of Josephus are considerably less impressive than the differences.

The general grouping followed in the Septuagint is presupposed in a list of books of the Old Testament quoted by Eusebius from Melito, bishop of Sardis, though it is noteworthy that this list does not include the additional books contained in the Septuagint.[1] Eusebius also reproduces a similar list recorded by Origen, in which the names of the books are given in Greek, followed by the Hebrew names in transliteration and translation.[2] Origen explains that the four books of 'Kingdoms' or 'Reigns' appear in Hebrew as one book of Samuel and one book which he calls 'the Kingdom of David', and that what appear as two books of Chronicles and two books of Esdras in Greek are each one in Hebrew. Not only does he place Ruth immediately after Judges, but he asserts that in the Hebrew reckoning they count as one book. He takes Lamentations and 'the Letter' (i.e. of Jeremiah) together with the book of Jeremiah as one book. Within the canonical list 'the Letter' is the one addition from the books contained in the Septuagint but not in the Hebrew; but Origen mentions the books of the Maccabees as 'outside these'.

Origen explicitly stated that the total number of canonical books is twenty-two; and if Melito (from whose list Esther is missing) reckoned Ruth as separate from Judges, his total also is twenty-two. Origen and some other Fathers explain this number as corresponding to the number of the letters in the Hebrew alphabet. In his *Prologus galeatus* Jerome gives the total number of the canonical books as twenty-two, and draws the same numerical parallel with the Hebrew alphabet. He

---

[1] *H.E.* IV, 26, 14.   [2] *Ibid.* VI, 25, 2.

points out, however, that five letters have an alternative form which is used when they occur at the end of a word, and that correspondingly there are five books each of which may be reckoned as two: Samuel, Kings, Jeremiah–Lamentations, Chronicles, Ezra (i.e. Ezra–Nehemiah). This gives a total of twenty-seven, which is also mentioned by Epiphanius[1] as an alternative to twenty-two, though with differences of arrangement. In spite of such perplexing variations, it is evident that the total twenty-seven is simply another way of reckoning the twenty-two books. Furthermore, Jerome remarks at a later point in the *Prologus galeatus* that Ruth and Lamentations are reckoned by some among the Hagiographa, thus giving the total twenty-four. His testimony throughout this passage is a curious blend of the arrangement and enumeration of the books in the Hebrew Bible on the one hand and of those in the Greek and Latin Bibles on the other. He presents the tripartite arrangement, which characterises the former, and takes cognisance of the total twenty-four; but his reference to the division of each of the five books into two is characteristic of the latter. It is also noteworthy that although he states that Judges–Ruth is treated both as one book and as two, he does not include it in his list of 'double books'.[2] Had he done so, he would have had more double books than there are Hebrew letters with final forms, and his alternative total to twenty-two would have been not twenty-seven but twenty-eight. In his preface to Daniel, Jerome presents the Hebrew enumeration and arrangement with unmistakable clarity: 'among the Hebrews, Daniel is not reckoned with the Prophets, but with those who wrote the Hagiographa. For by them all scripture is divided into three parts, the Law, the Prophets, and the Hagiographa, that is, into five, and eight, and eleven books.' The incongruity of his various statements can probably best be accounted for if we infer that he gives the number twenty-four as the canonical total on the basis of that first-hand knowledge of Jewish sources which he assiduously sought as a preparation for his work of translation, but that the totals twenty-two and twenty-seven which he also mentions are derived from the Greek and Latin Bibles and from similar enumerations and lists found in other patristic sources.

The persistence of the number twenty-two (or alternatively twenty-seven) in lists derived from such early Christian sources has often been

---

[1] *Pan. haer.* VIII, 6, 2; *De mens. et pond.* 23.   [2] 'libri duplices'.

thought to indicate, together with the evidence of Josephus, that this was the original reckoning of the total contents of the canonical corpus, and thus to show that the current Hebrew arrangement, with its total of twenty-four, is a later and artificial scheme. But, even when such lists include the Hebrew names of the books in Greek transliteration, they appear to be based primarily on the Greek Bible. Furthermore, those lists which state or imply the total twenty-two involve the reckoning of Ruth as one book with Judges and of Lamentations as one with Jeremiah. Such a reckoning is not difficult to understand on the broad principle of arrangement by literary character or subject matter which is characteristic of the Septuagint. But if so obviously appropriate a juxtaposition had been original, it is hard to see why Ruth and Lamentations should subsequently have been separated from Judges and Jeremiah and relegated to the third section of the Canon. On the other hand, if the three sections of the Hebrew Canon correspond to three main stages in the process of canonisation, as outlined above, then it is not unnatural to suppose that in a later arrangement, influenced by considerations of content, Ruth and Lamentations came to be linked with Judges and Jeremiah, particularly if, as seems evident, the arrangement of books other than the five books of Moses varied considerably. The basis of the total given by Josephus remains somewhat uncertain. If we accept as correct the assumption noted above about the contents of his prophetic section of the scriptures, then presumably Judges–Ruth and Jeremiah–Lamentations were each reckoned by him as one book. Alternatively it has been suggested that he may have omitted two of the books which were the subject of dispute during the first century. At all events we have from the same period the independent evidence of 2 Esdras 14: 45 that the authoritative scriptures for general use consisted of twenty-four books (see above, p. 115). It must be admitted, however, that on this subject modern scholarly opinion remains divided. Some hold that the total of twenty-four books is original, that the number twenty-two is an artificial adaptation of the reckoning of the books to accord with the number of the letters in the Hebrew alphabet, and that this is derived from Alexandrian Judaism, i.e. from the Septuagint. Others maintain that even in Palestinian Judaism the total twenty-two is the earlier, and that the linking of Ruth with Judges and of Lamentations with Jeremiah came before the stage at which they were ranked as separate books in the Hagiographa.

A closer examination of the order of the books reveals some interesting variations in the Hebrew tradition and a bewildering diversity in the Greek Bible. No variation is found in the order of the books of the Pentateuch. This is doubtless to be attributed to the fact that their canonical status was recognised throughout Judaism at a relatively early date. In Hebrew manuscripts the four Former Prophets occur invariably in the order Joshua, Judges, Samuel, Kings, as is, indeed, required by the chronological sequence of the narrative which runs through them. The order which has become accepted for the Latter Prophets (Isaiah, Jeremiah, Ezekiel, and the Twelve) is derived from manuscripts of Spanish origin. In French and German manuscripts, however, we find the order Jeremiah, Ezekiel, Isaiah, the Twelve. This accords with a Talmudic assertion that 'the order of the Prophets is Joshua, Judges, Samuel, Kings, Jeremiah, Ezekiel, Isaiah, the Twelve'.[1] Various explanations of this order have been offered. The sequel to the passage just quoted accounts for it on the ground that Kings, which ends with desolation, is appropriately followed by Jeremiah, which is all desolation, and that in turn by Ezekiel, which begins with desolation and ends with consolation, leading to Isaiah, which is all consolation (a somewhat undiscriminating description). More probably the reason for this arrangement was the general affinity in period and subject matter between the closing part of Kings and the book of Jeremiah and, in turn, between Jeremiah and Ezekiel. Thus Isaiah was left in appropriate juxtaposition with the earliest of the Twelve. Other variations of order which occur are Jeremiah, Isaiah, Ezekiel, the Twelve; and Ezekiel, Isaiah, Jeremiah, the Twelve. The arrangement of the Twelve is intended to be chronological. Hosea, Joel, Amos, Obadiah, Jonah, and Micah represent the eighth century, though the overwhelming weight of modern critical opinion would place Joel, Obadiah, and Jonah at considerably later periods. Nahum, Habakkuk, and Zephaniah belong to the closing decades of the seventh century. Haggai, Zechariah, and Malachi come from the Persian period.

Still wider diversity of order is found in the Hagiographa. The arrangement which has been adopted in printed Hebrew Bibles is: Psalms, Job, Proverbs (or, Proverbs, Job), the Song of Songs, Ruth, Ecclesiastes, Lamentations, Esther, Daniel, Ezra–Nehemiah, (1 and 2) Chronicles. Of these, the first three have traditionally been classed as

[1] Baba Bathra 14*b*.

the poetical books (though of course much poetry is found in other parts of the Old Testament) and have been collectively referred to by the Hebrew word *'emet* (truth), of which the consonants are the initial letters of the names of the three books, Job, Proverbs, Psalms, in that order. The Psalter has come to be established in the first place because it is the most important book in the group and also in the Hagiographa; but, as we shall see, it was sometimes preceded by Ruth or Chronicles. The fact that Job sometimes precedes Proverbs is attributed to the fact that it was held to be of Mosaic authorship and therefore superior to Solomon's work. The five books which follow form a group known as the Megilloth, or Scrolls. Each of them has a special place in the calendar of synagogue worship: the Song of Songs at Passover, Ruth at Pentecost, Lamentations at the commemoration of the destruction of Jerusalem on the ninth of Ab, Ecclesiastes at the feast of Tabernacles, and Esther at the feast of Purim. In the manuscripts they appear in several variations of order. In particular, Lamentations sometimes precedes and sometimes follows Ecclesiastes. The following three books (Daniel, Ezra–Nehemiah, Chronicles) have been classed as narrative, a description which is not wholly appropriate to Daniel. The above general arrangement has been adopted in printed editions of the Hebrew Bible from manuscripts of German origin. In many Spanish manuscripts, and also in the famous Leningrad Codex B 19 A (L), the first book in the Hagiographa is Chronicles. In the passage in Baba Bathra to which reference has already been made, the order of the Hagiographa is given as follows: Ruth, Psalms, Job, Proverbs, Ecclesiastes, the Song of Songs, Lamentations, Daniel, Esther, Ezra (i.e. Ezra–Nehemiah), Chronicles. Presumably Ruth, with its account of David's ancestry, was regarded as an appropriate prologue to the Davidic Psalter, and Esther was put between Daniel and Ezra–Nehemiah for chronological reasons.

Since the Septuagint was produced primarily for Alexandrian Jewry, it has generally been inferred that both in its contents and in its arrangement it represents the standards and usage of that community. The question whether the more extensive range of its contents represents an Alexandrian canon differing from the Palestinian canon, as represented by the Hebrew Bible, will be discussed in the next section of this chapter. Its arrangement is difficult to describe except in the most general terms, since even the oldest codices exhibit significant differences from one another, and other variations occur in the lists which appear in patristic sources. But the following general features may be noted. The Former Prophets are usually separated from the Latter Prophets and classed with the histories. Of the Hagiographa, Ruth is linked with Judges in the historical group and Lamentations with Jeremiah in the prophetical group, Ecclesiastes and the Song of Songs appear with Psalms, Proverbs, and Job in the poetical group, Daniel ranks with Isaiah, Jeremiah, and Ezekiel as a Major Prophet, and Chronicles and 2 Esdras (Ezra–Nehemiah) are among the histories. In Codex Sinaiticus (ℵ) and Codex Alexandrinus (A) the prophets follow the histories and precede the poetical books; but in Codex Vaticanus (B) the prophets come last, and the poetical books come between the main histories and a smaller group of narrative books. The order of Codex Vaticanus is widely supported by the lists given in patristic sources and has been generally adopted in printed editions of the Septuagint. It is as follows (the titles of books not in the Hebrew Bible being italicised): Genesis, Exodus, Leviticus, Numbers, Deuteronomy, Joshua, Judges, Ruth, 1–4 Kingdoms (1 and 2 Samuel, 1 and 2 Kings), 1 and 2 Chronicles, 1 *Esdras*, 2 Esdras (Ezra–Nehemiah), Psalms, Proverbs, Ecclesiastes, the Song of Songs, Job, *the Wisdom of Solomon*, *Ecclesiasticus*, Esther, *Judith*, *Tobit*, Hosea, Amos, Micah, Joel, Obadiah, Jonah, Nahum, Habakkuk, Zephaniah, Haggai, Zechariah, Malachi, Isaiah, Jeremiah, *Baruch*, Lamentations, *the Epistle of Jeremy*, Ezekiel, Daniel. Here not only have the Twelve Minor Prophets been put before the Major Prophets, but the order of the first six Minor Prophets is different from that found in the Hebrew Bible. Probably Jonah comes at the end of the six because of its manifestly different character (a prophetic narrative rather than a record of prophetic utterances), and the other five have been arranged in descending order, according to their length.

THE CANON IN DIFFERENT JEWISH COMMUNITIES

In what has been said above about the enumeration and arrangement of the canonical books in the Septuagint, it has been evident that a comparison with the Hebrew Bible is complicated by the presence in the Septuagint of additional books. This fact has given rise to the assumption that there was an Alexandrian canon which was more extensive in its scope than the Palestinian canon as represented by the books in the Hebrew Bible. Whether or not this assumption is justified, it is appropriate to inquire whether there is any evidence that in different communities the extent of the canonical corpus varied. Three such communities come into consideration: the Samaritans, Alexandrian Jewry, and the Qumrân sectaries.

Concerning the extent of the Samaritan canon there is no question. It consists solely of the five books of Moses. Although in the post-biblical period a considerable body of Samaritan religious literature was produced, no part of it attained canonical status. Nor did any of the Former or Latter Prophets, or of the Hagiographa. The critical attitude to the Northern tribes and the Northern Kingdom which is adopted in many passages in the Former Prophets would in itself be sufficient explanation of the omission of these books. Similarly, the general neglect of northern affairs in Chronicles and the light in which the Samaritans are presented in Ezra–Nehemiah would rule these books out as candidates for admission to a Samaritan canon. But, such considerations apart, the principal reasons for the limitation of the Samaritan canon to the Pentateuch are presumably historical.

According to 2 Kings 17, the Samaritans are descended from immigrants from Babylon, Cuthah, Avva, Hamath, and Sepharvaim, who were brought by Assyrians to colonise northern Israelite territory after the fall of Samaria in 722 B.C. They acquired their knowledge of Israelite religion from an exiled priest whom the Assyrians repatriated expressly for this purpose; but their practice of it was defaced and distorted by the alien cults which they had brought with them and which they never really abandoned. This was the community with which, at later periods, Zerubbabel and Jeshua, Ezra and Nehemiah, found themselves in conflict when they undertook the work of restoring the Temple, rebuilding Jerusalem, and reintroducing the ordered worship and service of the God of Israel in accordance with the Law of Moses.

The Samaritan account is very different. According to it, the decisive breach took place in the time of Eli who, in order to achieve his ambition to be High Priest, established a new sanctuary at Shiloh to rival the true sanctuary on the site chosen by God on Mount Gerizim. This act of apostasy involved the establishment at the new sanctuary of the priestly line of Ithamar, from whom Eli was descended, whereas the Samaritans regarded the line of Phineas as the authentic priesthood. For our present purpose it is unnecessary to trace in detail the Samaritan account of the consequences of this schism and of the varying fortunes of their own community over the centuries. By contrast with the Jewish account, it is recorded that the plight of the land after the fall of Samaria and the deportation was met when an Assyrian king brought back the exiled Samaritans and worship was restored on Mount Gerizim.

To this community and its sanctuary, the rebuilding of the Temple at Jerusalem and the restoration of worship and of community life there constituted a challenge. The books of Ezra and Nehemiah describe something of the tensions and conflicts to which the enterprises of Zerubbabel and Jeshua and of Nehemiah gave rise.[1] But in the Samaritan records Ezra appears as the arch-enemy. According to them it was he who tampered with the text of scripture. Although the overwhelming majority of the 6,000 differences between the Samaritan Pentateuch and the Massoretic Text belong to the minutiae of textual criticism, some reflect the rival claims of the two communities. Of these the most important are the following. After Exod. 20: 17 and Deut. 5: 21 (Hebrew 5: 18) the Samaritan text has a commandment that an altar should be built on Mount Gerizim and sacrifices offered there; and at Deut. 27: 4, where the Massoretic Text has 'And when you have passed over the Jordan, you shall set up these stones, concerning which I command you this day, on Mount Ebal, and you shall plaster them with plaster', the Samaritan text reads 'Gerizim' instead of 'Ebal'. It is generally held (though we cannot be certain of this) that in the latter passage the Samaritan text gives the true reading and that the change to 'Ebal' was made in the interest of anti-Samaritan polemic. On the other hand, there can be little doubt that the addition to the Decalogue found in the Samaritan text is a partisan insertion, supporting the Samaritan claims for Mount Gerizim, and by implication designating the sanctuaries at Shiloh and Jerusalem as schismatical. A similar feature occurs at Gen. 22: 2, where the place of the attempted sacrifice of Isaac, Mount Moriah (identified in Jewish tradition with Mount Zion), appears in the Samaritan text as Moreh and thus is identified with Shechem (cf. Gen. 12: 6). Since in Jewish tradition it was Ezra who reintroduced the Law, it is not surprising that the

---

[1] Ezra 4: 1–5; Neh. 2: 10, 19; 4; 6.

Samaritans attributed to him the falsification of its text for partisan purposes, though it may well be that Samaritan bitterness against him also originated in part in the separatist policy which he advocated. But when full account has been taken of the textual differences and of the rival claims to which they are related, it is clear that the Samaritan attitude to the Pentateuch was essentially conservative. They preserved it in an archaic script and devoted great pains to the task of transmitting it accurately. They claimed for themselves the title *šām^erîm* ('keepers', i.e. of the Law), rather than *šōm^erōnîm* ('inhabitants of Samaria'); but their ideal of strict observance of the Law did not lead to the development of legal interpretation and commentary, as in rabbinic Judaism; nor did they recognise any other religious document as of comparable authority. The fact that the Samaritans, though bitterly hostile to the main stream of Judaism, prized the Law so highly and accorded to it a quite unique status, is a pointer not only to the conservative character of their community but also to the firm entrenchment of the five books of the Law as holy scripture among all who were heirs of the ancient Israelite tradition.

It has been widely held that the Jews of Alexandria and of the hellenistic Diaspora generally represented a position at the opposite extreme to that of the Samaritans, and included within their canon not only the five books of the Law and the additional nineteen books contained in the second and third sections of the so-called Palestinian canon but also the other works which subsequently came to be known as the Apocrypha. The basis of this view is that since (as has been noted above, p. 141) the Septuagint was produced within, and primarily for, Alexandrian Jewry, it seems reasonable to suppose that the additional books in the Septuagint were translated and added to the Palestinian collection because they were recognised in Alexandria (and perhaps further afield) as authoritative. But the argument is far from cogent. As a collection of sacred writings, the books in the Septuagint have been transmitted within the Christian Church; and we have no direct evidence that the collection was acknowledged as such by any Jewish community, though the individual books come from Jewish sources. There is, in fact, little evidence to enable us to infer whether any distinctive views about the canon were entertained in the hellenistic Diaspora during the period before the Synod of Jamnia. Such indications as there are about the canonical corpus accepted by

Alexandrian Jewry suggest almost without exception that it consisted only of the Pentateuch.

The Septuagint rendering of the five books of Moses is characterised by a faithfulness and consistency which are not found in the other books. The point has been effectively put by Ryle: 'The want of uniformity, the inequalities and inaccuracies which characterise the rest of the translation, show that its execution was not part of a sacred duty, nor even carried out in deference to any official requirement.'[1] This is reinforced by a consideration of the pseudepigraphical document, *The Letter of Aristeas*, which purports to tell how the Septuagint originated, when Ptolemy II Philadelphus, on the suggestion of his librarian Demetrius Phalereus, arranged for the translation of the Jewish Law. In response to the king's request, the Jewish High Priest Eleazar sent to Alexandria seventy-two elders who completed the task in seventy-two days. It is generally agreed that the letter is not, as it claims to be, of third-century origin, but more probably comes from the latter part of the second century B.C., that very many of the details in it are fictitious, and that, in particular, the assertion that the translation was made by Palestinian Jews does not accord with its linguistic character which, in spite of Hebraisms, suggests an Alexandrian origin. It may fairly be regarded, not indeed as wholly unhistorical, but as primarily an apologetic or propaganda document. For our present purpose two points are specially noteworthy. First, the translation to which *The Letter of Aristeas* refers is that of the five books of Moses, and not the entire contents of either the Palestinian canon or the Septuagint as now known to us. This is emphasised by Josephus, who states that Philadelphus did not acquire the entire corpus of the Jewish records but only the part which contained the Law.[2] Secondly, emphasis is laid by Aristeas on the concern that the translation should be scrupulously preserved without alteration, addition, or omission:

After the books had been read, the priests and the elders of the translators and the Jewish community and the leaders of the people stood up and said, that since so excellent a translation had been made, it was only right that it should remain as it was and no alteration should be made in it. And when the whole company expressed their approval, they bade them pronounce a curse

[1] H. E. Ryle, *The Canon of the Old Testament* (London, 1892), p. 147.
[2] *Ant.* I, 12.

in accordance with their custom upon any one who should make any alteration either by adding anything or changing in any way whatever any of the words which had been written or making any omission.[1]

This solemn emphasis on the absolute inviolability of the text corresponds to the fourth of the marks of canonicity enumerated by Josephus.[2] While it is arguable, and has indeed been argued,[3] that the point of the imprecation is to maintain the status of the *translation* as authoritative, the clear implication of the narrative is that the document as such was authoritative and regulative for the community. There are no indications of similar concern about the maintenance of an inviolably accurate rendering of the other books in the Septuagint.

We have already noted (above, pp. 129 f.) that ben Sira's grandson shows knowledge of a tripartite collection of sacred writings, though the third section was in all probability still incomplete. It is also clear from his Prologue that he was familiar with Greek renderings of the books in all three sections:

For what was originally expressed in Hebrew does not have exactly the same sense when translated into another language. Not only this work [i.e. the book written in Hebrew by his grandfather and now translated into Greek], but even the law itself, the prophecies, and the rest of the books differ not a little as originally expressed.

Thus one who had come to Egypt, as he himself tells us, in the thirty-eighth year of Ptolemy VII Euergetes (132 B.C.) was aware of the existence of Greek translations of not only the Law but other parts of the scriptures, but still thought of them in terms of the grouping appropriate to the Palestinian canon. He gives no indication either of a different arrangement or of a more extensive canonical collection.

Some account has been given (above, pp. 136 f.) of the difficulties raised by the description of the Jewish scriptures which Josephus gives in the *Contra Apionem*. These difficulties concern both the arrangement and the enumeration which he presupposes. But in spite of these difficulties, and even if, as has been suggested, the number twenty-two

---

[1] *Letter of Aristeas*, §§ 310, 311. Translation by H. T. Andrews in R. H. Charles (ed.), *The Apocrypha and Pseudepigrapha of the Old Testament* (Oxford, 1913), II, 121.

[2] Cf. above, p. 116.

[3] See, above all, P. Kahle, *The Cairo Geniza* (2nd ed. Oxford, 1959), pp. 209–18.

is to be explained by the omission of two of the disputed books, it remains sufficiently clear that it is about the contents of the Palestinian canon that Josephus is writing. This is the more significant, since there are many indications in the language and subject matter of the *Antiquities* that he was familiar with the Septuagint, including 1 Esdras and the Greek additions to Esther. Knowledge of the wider range of literature is not accompanied by any acceptance of an extended canonical corpus.

More to the point is the evidence of Philo, the quintessential representative of Alexandrian Jewry. His numerous quotations from the scriptures provide important evidence about the history of the Greek text of the Old Testament and also about Alexandrian hermeneutical method. Although he does not expressly frame a clear definition of the limits of the Canon, it is evident that for him the Law is the supreme documentary authority. He quotes from all the books in the other two divisions of the Palestinian canon except Ezekiel, Song of Songs, Ruth, Lamentations, Ecclesiastes, Esther, and Daniel. These omissions may well be accidental. It may of course be argued that if Ruth was linked with Judges and Lamentations, citations from the larger works would imply knowledge and acknowledgement of the lesser. It is also noteworthy that Ezekiel, Song of Songs, Ecclesiastes, and Esther were all books about whose canonical status there were doubts, and further, that the Greek additions to the text of Esther and Daniel may indicate a somewhat lax attitude in the hellenistic Diaspora to their contents. Although there are similarities in diction and subject matter between passages in Philo and certain of the books of the Apocrypha, it has been maintained that these do not indicate direct citation. At all events it does not appear that Philo quotes any apocryphal book as holy scripture. Contrary to the view which was prevalent in Palestinian Jewry (cf. above, pp. 127 f.), Philo did not think of divine inspiration as confined to an earlier age; but this does not seem to have led him to assume any extension of the limits of the Canon. The great preponderance of his quotations from and allusions to scripture are derived from the five books of Moses; and thus the evidence is that if he had a view of the Canon which differed from that held in Palestine, it was more restricted and not more extensive.

Accordingly, it may be inferred that in the first Christian century and at least the two preceding, the Law was firmly established in

Alexandrian Jewry as authoritative. This is what one would expect during that period in any Jewish community with the slightest claim to religious faithfulness. If there was any recognition of the inspired character of at least some of the books contained in the second and third sections of the Palestinian canon, it appears to have been less well defined. There is no definite evidence that any book not in the Palestinian canon was accepted as canonical in Alexandria or elsewhere in the hellenistic Diaspora; and accordingly there is no ground for the claim, which has often been made, that there was an Alexandrian canon which was more extensive than that of Palestinian Jewry. If there was a different conception of the canon in Alexandria, it was more restricted; or, at all events, there was a less definite attitude to the sections of the canon outside the Law. If the Prophets and the Writings were less clearly marked off as canonical, it is not difficult to understand how other narrative and didactic books, written in or translated into Greek, might have come to be associated with them. But we have no definite evidence of any such process in Alexandria during the period before the Septuagint was taken over by the Christian Church.

Although the documentary discoveries made in the Judaean desert since the end of the Second World War have provided abundant materials for the study of the history of the Old Testament text, it is difficult to elicit from them specific evidence of the extent of the canonical corpus which the sect recognised. There are, however, three general considerations which suggest that the documents might be expected to shed fresh light on the formation of the Canon. First, on any reasonable view of the history of the Qumrân community, it may be assumed that it extended from the second century B.C. into the latter part of the first Christian century, a period of decisive importance for the final definition of the Old Testament Canon. Secondly, the Qumrân sectaries were ardent biblicists. They devoted great care to the preservation and transmission of the biblical texts and to the interpretation and application of them. Thirdly, the documents discovered include material not found in the Palestinian canon. The documents which are relevant to our purpose may be roughly classified as follows:[1] (*a*) texts of canonical books of the Old Testament in the original; (*b*) texts of canonical books of the Old Testament in Greek or Aramaic

[1] Cf. Otto Eissfeldt, *The Old Testament: An Introduction* (trans. Peter R. Ackroyd. Oxford, 1965), pp. 640–1.

translation; (*c*) Hebrew and Aramaic texts of apocryphal and pseud-epigraphical works hitherto known only in other languages; (*d*) extra-canonical writings hitherto unknown, being either works specially related to the life and beliefs of the community or works generally similar to the previously known apocrypha and pseudepigrapha.

The fact that the sect withdrew from the main body of Judaism in the latter half of the second century B.C. raises the question whether among the distinctive features which marked them off may not have been a different estimate of the extent of the Canon. About the status of the Law and the Prophets there can be no real doubt. Both the abundance of textual material representing the full range of these sections of the Canon and the existence of commentaries on parts of them indicate that they were accepted without question as authoritative documents, both as laying down patterns of life and worship and also as predicting, when rightly interpreted, the outworking of the purpose of God in the age in which the community existed. The only book in the Hagiographa which is not directly represented in the Qumrân documents is Esther. The book is so short that it would be hazardous to infer that it was either not known or not valued by the community, the more so since it has been claimed that there are some oblique allusions to the text of Esther in the sectarian scrolls. The other *m^egillôt* (Song of Songs, Ruth, Lamentations, Ecclesiastes) are all represented both by fragmentary manuscripts and by possible allusions in the sectarian literature; but there is no clear case of citation of any of them as scripture. There are fragmentary manuscripts of Job and also part of a hitherto unknown Aramaic Targum, as well as some possible allusions in the sectarian literature. In addition to manuscript evidence of Proverbs and literary allusions to it, there is a specific citation of Prov. 15: 8, introduced by the formula 'for it is written', in the *Damascus Document*,[1] which, though it came to light in Old Cairo some half a century before the Qumrân discoveries, clearly belongs to the literature of the same community. Chronicles and Ezra–Nehemiah are meagrely represented by manuscript fragments and relatively few echoes have been detected in the sectarian scrolls. The rotation of priestly duties[2] is obviously based on 1 Chron. 24: 1–19, though the number of courses is not twenty-four, as in Chronicles, but twenty-six, to fit the solar calendar which the community followed.

---

[1] *CD*, XI, 20–1.   [2] E.g. at 1QM II: 1–4.

There is no definite evidence against the assumption that all of the books of the Hagiographa hitherto mentioned were accepted as canonical by the Qumrân community, though for some of them the indications of their canonical status are general and circumstantial rather than explicit. Paradoxically, it is in connection with two books which were extensively used and highly esteemed in the Qumrân community that serious questions arise concerning the extent of the Canon which the community acknowledged. The books are Daniel and the Psalter.

Fragments of at least seven different manuscripts of Daniel have been discovered. There are also several allusions and quotations, including some introduced by the formula, 'as it is written in the book of the prophet Daniel'.[1] This last feature might determine beyond reasonable question the canonical status of Daniel. But two objections have been raised. Some of the fragments are of papyrus, whereas leather was normally used for canonical books. Again, the Daniel fragments come from manuscripts in which the height and breadth of the columns were almost equal, whereas most of the manuscripts of canonical books were written in columns of which the breadth was half the height. Neither objection is cogent. It is not the case that the larger type of scroll (i.e. having a column of greater height) was invariably and exclusively used for canonical texts; and there is clear evidence that at Qumrân a canonical text might be written on papyrus. It seems, therefore, reasonable to conclude that the Qumrân community not only used and highly valued the book of Daniel, but recognised it as having canonical authority. It is also noteworthy that the texts of Daniel which have been discovered appear not to have included the additions to the book which are found in the Greek text (the stories of Bel and the Dragon and of Susanna, and the Song of the Three Holy Children).

It is also evident that the book of Psalms was extensively used by the community. This is evident from the number of Psalms manuscripts which have come to light and by the fact that the Thanksgiving Hymns (*hôdāyôt*) are modelled on the biblical Psalms and contain numerous quotations from and allusions to them, but seem always to have been kept separate from them. It is also significant that there are fragments of commentaries on parts of the Psalter. But the question of the canonical status of the Psalter and also of its delimitation as a canonical corpus is raised by evidence that at Qumrân at least two manuscripts

1 J. T. Milik, *Ten Years of Discovery in the Wilderness of Judaea* (London, 1959), p. 41.

containing canonical psalms also included 'apocryphal' psalms and that one of these manuscripts contained other extra-canonical material. The first of these is the Psalms Scroll from Qumrân Cave 11 (11QPs^a), acquired by the Palestine Archaeological Museum in 1956 and published in 1965.[1] Four fragments which clearly belong to this scroll contain parts of Pss. 101, 102, and 109. Another fragment, acquired independently by Y. Yadin, contains parts of Pss. 104, 105, 118, 147.[2] The main scroll includes practically the whole of Pss. 118–50, with some variation from the normal order, and the Hebrew text of nos. 1, 2, and 3 of five apocryphal psalms, previously known in Syriac, of which the first appears in the Septuagint as Ps. 151. It also contains Ecclus. 51: 13–30, three other poetical passages (labelled by the editor 'Plea for Deliverance', 'Apostrophe to Zion', and 'Hymn to the Creator'), and a prose passage enumerating King David's literary output. Fragments of the second manuscript (4QPs^f) were found in Cave 4, containing parts of Pss. 22, 107, and 109, of the 'Apostrophe to Zion' and of three other similar poems.[3] It is unnecessary for our present purpose to consider the literary and textual features of these apocryphal compositions. What is of immediate interest for the study of the Canon is the existence of manuscripts containing both what we know as canonical psalms and also other similar compositions. Three possibilities suggest themselves. (1) The Qumrân community may have accepted as canonical a collection of psalms containing poems additional to those which had been accepted by the main body of Judaism. (2) The existence at Qumrân of a Psalter with this additional material may point to a stage at which the contents of the canonical Psalter had not yet been definitely fixed and when, therefore, collections of psalms were in circulation which contained items which were ultimately to be rejected from the canonical corpus. (3) The contents of the canonical Psalter may have already been both established in the Jewish community at large and also accepted by the Qumrân community. In that event, the manuscripts referred to above will have been liturgical anthologies, embodying compositions which were accepted

[1] J. A. Sanders, *The Psalms Scroll of Qumrân Cave 11 (11QPs^a)*, *Discoveries in the Judaean Desert of Jordan*, IV (Oxford, 1965).

[2] Y. Yadin, 'Another Fragment (E) of the Psalms Scroll from Qumrân Cave 11', *Textus*, V (1966), 1–10.

[3] J. Starcky, 'Psaumes apocryphes de la grotte 4 de Qumrân (4QPs^f VII–X)', *RB*, LXXIII (1966), 353–71.

as canonical and also other material suitable for liturgical or devotional use. Any conclusion drawn from the evidence at present available must clearly be provisional; but the balance of probability seems to lie with the third of these possibilities.[1] It should be noted that we do not know whether the manuscripts in question contained all of the canonical psalms; accordingly they may well have been deliberately selective. Moreover, although the psalms in 11QPs^a depart from the canonical order, knowledge of that order seems to be presupposed. One of the disarrangements is the placing of Ps. 133 separately from the other 'Songs of Ascents' (Pss. 120–34), between Pss. 141: 5–10 and 144: 1–7; but Ps. 133 nevertheless carries the superscription, 'A Song of Ascents'. It has also been pointed out that the existence of a special 'Qumrânic' canonical Psalter would be a unique phenomenon, since no comparable 'Qumrânic' form of any biblical book has hitherto been brought to light.[2] On the other side, it has been claimed that the prose enumeration of David's writings which comes near the end of 11QPs^a implies that the entire collection is Davidic and canonical. But no such assertion is explicitly made in the prose passage, which states the extent of David's poetical production and the fact that some of his poems were used for particular cultic occasions. How far the ascription of Davidic authorship may be taken to imply canonical status is not clear. In this connection we may note that in another manuscript from Cave 11 (11QPsAp^a) one canonical psalm (91) is included in a group of apocryphal psalms, one of which is attributed to David.[3] All in all, it may be said that there is no positive evidence of any weight that the Qumrân community had its own canonical Psalter, differing in contents from that of orthodox Jewry, and that, on the whole, the presence of apocryphal psalms among those which we know as canonical, or the inclusion of a canonical psalm in a group of apocryphal ones, can best be explained by the view that the manuscripts are parts of liturgical collections. The combination of canonical and non-canonical material in such collections has many obvious parallels in subsequent Jewish and Christian use.

[1] Cf. M. H. Goshen-Gottstein, 'The Psalms Scroll (11QPs^a): A Problem of Canon and Text', *Textus*, v (1966), 22–33; P. W. Skehan, 'The Biblical Scrolls from Qumrân and the Text of the Old Testament', *BA*, XXVIII (1965), 100.

[2] M. H. Goshen-Gottstein, *op. cit.* p. 28.

[3] J. van der Ploeg, 'Le psaume XCI dans une recension de Qumrân', *RB*, LXXII (1965), 210–17.

Relatively few of the books of the Apocrypha are represented in the Qumrân documents: a fragment of the Greek text of the Letter of Jeremiah, one Hebrew and four Aramaic manuscripts of Tobit, and some fragments of Ecclesiasticus in addition to the passage included in 11QPsᵃ, as noted above. There appears to be no specific evidence that any of these works was accorded canonical status.

Of the documents which were produced within the community for the regulation of its common life and for the instruction of its members there is none for which canonical authority can fairly be claimed. The *Manual of Discipline* and the *Damascus Document* presumably had a status analogous to that of handbooks of ecclesiastical constitution and order in churches which accept the scriptures as the supreme rule of faith and practice. Nor is there any indication that the War Scroll or the Hymns (*hôdāyôt*) had canonical status, however much they may have been prized and however extensively they may have been used.

The great wealth of fragments representing scores of pseudepigraphical writings does not supply any definite evidence that there were at Qumrân special additions to the Canon. The number of fragments representing 1 Enoch and Jubilees indicates the esteem in which these books were held. This is not surprising, since the Qumrân community followed the solar calendar which is referred to in these books. This fact may imply that Enoch and Jubilees carried a special authority at Qumrân. More than that we cannot say.

Special interest attaches to the references[1] to the '*Book of Study*', or '*Meditation*' (*spr hhgw/y*). There is no agreement about the meaning of this title or about the work to which it refers. Clearly it was a work of fundamental importance for the life of the community, since those holding positions of responsibility were required to be instructed in it. One plausible suggestion is that the *Book of Meditation* is to be identified with the canonical scriptures.[2]

Certainly the scriptures were of fundamental importance for the Qumrân community. It differed from the main stream of Judaism on matters connected with the calendar, the organisation of the life of its members, the legitimacy of the priesthood, and possibly the interpretation of scripture; but there is no clear indication of any major departure from the canonical corpus accepted by contemporary Palestinian

[1] E.g. *CD*, x, 4 ff.; xii, 22—xiii, 4; xiv, 6–8.
[2] I. Rabinowitz, 'The Qumrân Authors' *spr hhgw/y*', *JNES*, xx (1961), 109–14.

Jewry, unless a special authority was accorded to 1 Enoch and Jubilees. About the Law and the Prophets there can be no question. Their authority was securely established within orthodox Judaism itself. There was, as we have seen, continuing discussion about some books in the Hagiographa until at least the end of the first Christian century; and it is about the extent to which this part of the Canon was recognised at Qumrân that there is some doubt. The existence of commentaries on parts of the Psalter indicates that it was recognised as authoritative; but we cannot be sure of the extent of the Qumrân Psalter. Such doubt as there is about the status of other books of the Hagiographa arises from a lack of positive evidence.

CANONICAL AND NON-CANONICAL

An examination of the relationship between canonical and all non-canonical books would be an immense and probably unprofitable task. Our concern is not with such non-canonical Jewish works as the writings of Philo and Josephus, but with those which are loosely described as apocrypha and pseudepigrapha.

The word 'apocrypha' is the neuter plural of a Greek adjective meaning 'hidden'. Books might be hidden or withheld from general circulation because they contained esoteric lore, suitable only for the initiated. This thought appears in Dan. 12: 4, 9: 'But you, Daniel, shut up the words, and seal the book, until the time of the end.' 'Go your way, Daniel, for the words are shut up and sealed until the time of the end.' It finds its clearest and most illuminating expression in Esdras 14: 45–7 (cf. above, p. 115): 'Make public the twenty-four books that you wrote first and let the worthy and the unworthy read them; but keep the seventy that were written last, in order to give them to the wise among your people. For in them is the spring of under-standing, the fountain of wisdom, and the river of knowledge.' In such a context the secret knowledge reserved for the few is something to be prized. The claim to reveal hidden knowledge is one of the main characteristics of apocalyptic literature. When the Canon was finally fixed, practically the whole of this literature was excluded, and therefore such hidden lore was more likely to be regarded as dangerous.

But in Jewish usage 'hidden' was not necessarily used in a pejorative sense to describe books excluded from the Canon. A Hebrew synonym of 'apocrypha' is the plural participle *gᵉnûzîm*. This word, and the verb *gānaz*, are used in connection with the hiding or storing away (in a Genizah) of books which for external reasons were unfit for public use: e.g. copies of scripture which were badly worn, or which had in some way been defectively copied. But the terms are also used of books whose canonical status was disputed. In the tractate Aboth of Rabbi Nathan (ch. 1) it is said that at first Proverbs, the Song of Songs, and Ecclesiastes were said to be hidden (*gᵉnûzîm*) because of the symbolical or fictitious language which they contained, and that this lasted till the Men of the Great Synagogue resolved the difficulties. In the tractate Shabbath in the Babylonian Talmud there is recorded (30*b*) a similar attempt to have Proverbs treated as 'hidden' because it contained contradictions. According to Shabbath 13*b* the book of Ezekiel would have been 'hidden' had it not been for Rabbi Hananiah ben Hezekiah, whose scholarly industry resolved the seeming contradictions between Ezekiel and the Law. But such attempts to declare certain books *gᵉnûzîm* related to some which were already highly esteemed and had a strong claim to inclusion in the Canon. Works regarded as heretical (such as Christian writings) were called not *gᵉnûzîm* but *sᵉpārîm ḥîṣônîm* (extraneous books). Although this latter term, and the opprobrium associated with it, were sometimes extended to all works outside the canonical twenty-four, in general three classes of books were recognised: those that defile the hands (i.e. canonical books; cf. above, p. 114), hidden books, which might not be used in public worship, and extraneous books, which might not be read at all. The books noted above as having been threatened with inclusion among the *gᵉnûzîm* in fact remained in the class of those that defile the hands. It may well be that some of the books now known to us as Apocrypha were at one time classed as *gᵉnûzîm*, but later lapsed into disuse or were relegated to the extraneous books. The high esteem in which Ecclesiasticus was held is attested not only by the fragments discovered at Qumrân and Masada but also by the freedom with which it was quoted by the rabbis as late as the third or even the fourth century A.D. It may well be that the Christian use of that and some other books of the Apocrypha led ultimately to their being classed among the extraneous books. Origen[1] states that the Jews had hidden Susanna and other

---

[1] *Ep. ad Afric.*

books from the people, and that they had told him that Judith and Tobit were not even included among their hidden books. The extreme position of Jewish exclusiveness on this subject is effectively expressed in the quaint saying in Midrash Koheleth 12: 12: 'Whoever brings together in his house more than twenty-four books [i.e. the canonical scriptures] brings confusion.'

In Greek and Latin usage the word 'apocrypha' also undergoes marked changes of meaning. In circles in which esoteric lore was highly regarded, 'apocryphal' was a favourable adjective to apply to books, and was so applied to the book of Revelation. But in a less favourable sense it was applied to books excluded from the Canon. It is so used by Jerome in the *Prologus galeatus* when, after referring to the tripartite structure and the contents of the Canon, he mentions as apocryphal books Wisdom, Ecclesiasticus, Judith, Tobit, the Shepherd of Hermas, and 1 and 2 Maccabees. The word also came to be used of spurious or heretical writings. But in common usage the term 'Apocrypha' has come to refer to fourteen or fifteen documents, some of which are books whereas others are additional parts of books in the Canon. These documents are derived from the Greek and Latin Bibles. To the question of their status we must return.

The term 'pseudepigrapha', which should denote books bearing a false title or books which purport to be by someone other than the actual author, could be appropriately applied to the canonical books of Daniel and the Song of Songs, and to the books of Wisdom and Baruch, the letter of Jeremiah, and the Prayer of Manasseh in the Apocrypha. It is, however, generally applied collectively to a large number of writings from the period 200 B.C. to A.D. 200. They include wisdom and apocalyptic works, legendary narratives, and psalmody. Many of them are associated with the names of persons mentioned in the Old Testament, such as Enoch; but by no means all of the 'pseudepigrapha' are pseudepigraphical. Clearly they enjoyed a considerable popularity in different circles in Judaism, including the Qumrân community. Indeed, it is evident from the fragments found at Qumrân that the extent of this literature was considerably greater than had previously been realised. Some of the 'pseudepigrapha' were valued and used in different Christian communities, and thus came to be preserved (sometimes with Christian interpolations) in Greek, Syriac, Ethiopic, and other versions. The application of the word 'pseudepigrapha' to this extensive and varied literature can only be regarded as a semantic misfortune.

Our immediate concern is to inquire which, if any, of the books not included in the Palestinian canon were serious candidates for canonical status or were accorded such by the early Church. As we have seen, rabbinic evidence relating to discussions of the canon refers to books whose canonical status was challenged but which were nevertheless retained. Ecclesiasticus was valued, even in orthodox rabbinic circles; but there is no evidence that it or any other book was considered for inclusion in the Palestinian canon and rejected.

In the New Testament, in which the tripartite structure is presupposed and all the books in the Palestinian canon are quoted except the Song of Songs, Ecclesiastes, and Esther, the ideas and imagery found in much of the extra-canonical literature (particularly the apocalypses) are often present; but the only extra-canonical text which is expressly cited is 1 Enoch 1: 9 at Jude 14–15.

The Greek-speaking Christian Church took over the Septuagint, which contained other works and in which, moreover, some of the canonical books included additional sections. One representative list has been given above (p. 142) with an indication of the books additional to the Palestinian canon. The extra material which is not found in the Hebrew and Aramaic texts of canonical books consists of a total of 107 verses inserted at six places in Esther, and in Daniel the Song of the Three Holy Children, the story of Susanna, and the story of Bel and the Dragon. But in fact the contents of the Septuagint are notoriously difficult to define; and it is evident that much of the literature which is loosely described as the pseudepigrapha circulated in Greek in the Christian Church. The evidence relating to the varying esteem in which this additional literature was held and to the process by which attempts were made to define its relationship to the contents of the Palestinian Jewish canon is both confused and incomplete. But the following general facts should be noted. First, the early Christian Fathers quote extensively from this additional literature. Secondly, when patristic writers try to enumerate the contents of the Old Testament Canon (cf. above, pp. 137 f.) their almost unanimous adherence to the total 22 (24), even when they also mention additional books, indicates that the Palestinian canon (with the possible exception of Esther) was accepted without question. Thirdly, the earlier form of the Peshiṭta, a daughter version of the Septuagint, seems to have omitted the additional books and Chronicles. If it was of Christian origin, this would be a pointer to the restriction of the canonical list within the Church. From this it may be argued that the entire Palestinian canon had become so firmly established in Judaism even before its formal ratification in the Jamnia period, that it was automatically accepted by the Christian community in spite of Jewish–Christian controversies. An alternative view is that in the period immediately before Jamnia the third section of the Palestinian canon was still somewhat nebulous in Judaism, and what the Church accepted without question was the securely accepted corpus of Law and Prophets, and that the further definition of the Christian Canon was carried out within the Church itself. The tracing of the subsequent Christian debate and of the different conclusions reached in different parts of the Church lies outside the scope of this chapter; but in all the complexities of the development and the diversities of ecclesiastical decision, the impressive fact remains that whatever additions may be made the contents of the Palestinian canon are common to all systems.

7. THE OLD TESTAMENT TEXT

I

We shall examine here the first stages in the history of the transmission of the Old Testament text over a period of approximately 500 years, starting with *c.* 300 B.C. For the preceding phases in the history of the text woefully little historical evidence is available, and none of it is contemporary. Any account of the development of the text prior to *c.* 300 B.C., i.e. in the Persian period, not to mention the periods of the Babylonian Exile or of the First Temple, must perforce rely upon conjecture and, at best, upon deductions and analogies derived from later literature and later manuscripts.

The beginning of what may properly be called the history of the Old Testament text roughly coincides with the final phases of the canonisation of the Old Testament books, a subject which has been discussed in the preceding section. During the period under review, the Jewish scribes and sages decided on, and carried out, the minute fixation of the consonantal text of the scriptures in the original Hebrew tongue.

Concurrently, the Old Testament books were translated into other Semitic languages—Aramaic and Syriac—and also into non-Semitic languages—Greek, and subsequently Latin. This intense activity of editing and revising resulted, at the end of this period (first half of the third century A.D.), in the first comprehensive scholarly enterprise, Origen's *Hexapla*.[1] In its six columns Origen presented a synoptic view of the then current Hebrew text of the Old Testament and its Greek translations: (1) The Hebrew Old Testament in Hebrew letters; (2) this same text transcribed in Greek letters; (3–6) the Greek versions of Aquila, Symmachus, the Septuagint and Theodotion.[2]

The work of the Jewish scribes affected, as we have said, only the Hebrew consonantal text. To the best of our present knowledge, no fully fledged system of recording vowels in Hebrew had yet been invented, with the exception of the use of some consonants as *matres lectionis*, i.e. as indicators of a few basic long vowel values. The pronunciation of Hebrew words, as it was current in that period, can, however, in some cases be ascertained by means of retroversion from their rendering in translations, and in some instances from their transcription into the vocalised Greek or Latin alphabets.

The absence of vowels meant that many a Hebrew consonant group could be differently pronounced, and from this resulted the fact that a variety of meanings could be attached to one and the same word in the original. When ultimately vowels were introduced into the Hebrew text of the Bible, these pronunciation variants sometimes became the bases of *variae lectiones*.

The lack of any system of interpunctuation in written Hebrew at that time was another factor which gave rise to different interpretations of many passages. These diverging interpretations may also in the end turn up as variants in versions which are based on fully interpunctuated manuscripts.

The full establishing of these features of the text which are complementary to the basic Hebrew consonantal text, namely the vowel system(s), interpunctuation, and the subdivision of the text into paragraphs (*seḏārīm* and *pārāšōṯ*), was carried out by the various schools of Massoretes, vocalisers and interpunctuators who flourished in the last

[1] Cf. v, 14.
[2] For a short presentation of the salient characteristics of these versions, cf. B. J. Roberts in *Cambridge History of the Bible*, Vol. 2, ed. G. W. H. Lampe, pp. 13–26.

quarter of the first millennium A.D. These late aspects of the textual transmission of the Bible do not come within the orbit of our present exposition.[1]

II

There is probably no other extant text, ancient or modern, which is witnessed to by so many diverse types of sources, and the history of which is so difficult to elucidate as that of the text of the Old Testament. The task of the scholar who endeavours to trace the antecedents of the text as we know it today is further complicated by the fact that he is concerned with sacred literature, every word of which is considered to be divinely inspired and therefore infallible. However, having been handed down by human agents for more than two millennia, the text of the scriptures suffered from the shortcomings of man. It became faulty to a greater or less degree and even at times distorted. It must therefore be subjected to scholarly critical analysis like any other ancient literary document.

The Old Testament books were handed down, as has been said, not only in their original Hebrew or, in some passages, Aramaic tongue, but also in a variety of translations into Semitic and non-Semitic languages. All these textual traditions, as we know them today, differ from one another. What is more, even the witnesses to one tradition, in the original language or in a translation, often diverge from one another. As a result, the scholar who takes a synoptic view of all the sources at his disposal is confronted with a bewildering plethora of *variae lectiones* in the extant versions of the Old Testament books. This fact obviously does not become apparent in the common editions of the Old Testament, in Hebrew or in translation, which are in every-day use. However, it should be borne in mind that the printed editions represent the end of a long chain of textual development and of editorial activities which were aimed at unifying the sacred texts. These late editions can in no way be taken to exhibit faithfully the autographs of the biblical authors. In fact not one single verse of this ancient literature has come to us in an original manuscript, written by a biblical author or by a contemporary of his, or even by a scribe who lived immediately after the time of the author. Even the very earliest manuscripts at our disposal, in Hebrew or in any translation language,

[1] On this subject cf. B. J. Roberts, *op. cit.* pp. 1–26.

are removed by hundreds of years from the date of origin of the literature recorded in them.

Even a cursory perusal of the sources available immediately reveals
that not one tradition and not one manuscript is without fault. Each
and every one patently exhibits errors which crept into it during the
long period of its transmission, in the oral stage, when written by hand,
and even, though to a lesser degree, when handed down in the form
of printed books.

It should, however, be stressed that these errors and textual divergences between the versions materially affect the intrinsic message
only in relatively few instances. Nevertheless this may occur. Some
examples of variants significant from a theological or ideo-historical
angle may in fact be found. In most instances the differences are of a
linguistic or a grammatical nature, which resulted either from the
unpremeditated impact of the linguistic peculiarities of successive
generations of copyists, or from their intentional attempts to adjust
the wording of scripture to changing concepts of linguistic and stylistic
norms.

The above remarks do not, however, absolve us from accounting
for the fact that the further back the textual tradition of the Old Testament is followed, i.e. the older the biblical manuscripts perused, and
the more ancient the records which come to the knowledge of scholars,
the wider is the over-all range of textual divergence between them. The
existing variants, therefore, cannot be simply explained as having
arisen solely from the cumulative effect of imperfect copying and
recopying of the text over many centuries. The very earliest biblical
manuscripts known—and in this respect the biblical scrolls from
Qumrân[1] are of decisive importance—exhibit practically all types of
variants found in later witnesses. This fact indicates that variation as
such in the textual transmission cannot be laid exclusively at the door
of careless scribes, or of sometimes unscrupulous, and sometimes well-
meaning, emendators and revisers. One has to consider the possibility,
as scholars have indeed done, that individual variants, and also groups
or even types of variants, which have been preserved in the ancient
versions, both in Hebrew and in translations, may derive from divergent
pristine textual traditions. That these divergent traditions are today
represented in the extant witnesses only in what amount to haphazard

[1] See below, pp. 182–7.

remains, can be explained as resulting from the endeavour of later generations to establish for each version one officially acclaimed standard text. After the establishment of such an official standard, new copies would have been based from the very start on the *textus receptus*. In the course of time, earlier non-standard manuscripts would also have been emended to conform to it. In the ensuing process of unification, which was inspired both by religious-dogmatic and scholarly motives, divergent texts almost automatically went out of circulation, or were more or less systematically suppressed. After a given period in the history of the text, a period which differs from version to version, all manuscripts of a version can be reduced to a very restricted number of prototypes. In some instances, as is the case with the Massoretic and the Samaritan Hebrew texts, all manuscripts conform to one basic text form. In other words, the later the witnesses which are reviewed, the more pronounced their conformity, and the fewer their divergences, both in number and type.

The scholar whose interest lies in tracing the history of the text cannot rely upon the end products, but must turn for information to the earliest sources available. In doing so he is faced with an *embarras de richesse* of variant and often conflicting readings even in the most ancient witnesses to the text. It now becomes his task not only to sketch the lines of these developments, but also to attempt the reconstitution of the original wording, or wordings, of the text. He will sift the available evidence, and discard from the outset obvious faults and errors. He will try to establish manuscript families, as far as this is possible. All manuscripts which can be affiliated with each other will then be considered as one composite witness to a reading found in them. Any decision with regard to the importance of a reading cannot be based merely on counting manuscripts. They have to be assessed and their intrinsic value taken into account. At the apex of this long and complicated process of collation and critical analysis, the investigator may carefully conclude that with the available evidence no 'first' text form can be established. Or else, more optimistically, he may attempt to reconstitute the presumed pristine texts of each of the major versions individually. It then still remains to be debated whether these proto-texts of the extant versions can be reduced to one common stem, or whether, at least in part, they must be considered to represent intrinsically independent textual traditions. Even if by retracing the steps of textual development we may be able to arrive at the *Ur-text* of this version or that, the question still remains open whether we shall ever be able to recover the *ipsissima verba* of a biblical author.

III

In pursuing the chain of development of the Old Testament text, we may discern four distinct main stages in its transmission between its initial inception at a time varying from book to book, and its form in the days of Origen.

The initial stage, that of the not provable but highly probable oral phase of the biblical literature, lies outside the scope of our present investigation, since by its very nature it precedes written documentation. It should, however, be pointed out that originally oral variations may ultimately turn up as textual variants between duplicate texts within the Old Testament. Such instances are found in two versions of one and the same psalm embedded in a book of the Former Prophets and Psalms (e.g. 2 Sam. 22 = Ps. 18), in Chronicles and Psalms (e.g. 1 Chron. 16: 8–36 = Ps. 105: 1–15; 96: 1–13; 106: 1, 47–8), or in the Book of Psalms itself (e.g. Ps. 31: 2–4*b* = 71: 1–3; 60: 7–14 = 108: 8–14).[1] Again, we meet with two or even three presentations of a piece of biblical literature in parallel passages in the Former and Latter Prophets (2 Kings 18: 13—20: 19 = Isa. 36: 1—38: 22 = 2 Chron. 32: 1–20; 2 Kings 25: 1–22 = Jer. 39: 1–10 = 52: 4–27; 2 Kings 25: 27–30 = Jer. 52: 31–4). To some extent also quotations from an earlier book in a later one may exhibit textual variants. However, in these cases literary licence and a possible tendency towards intentional variation or rephrasing on the part of the writer who is borrowing may lie at the root of the present divergences.

It goes without saying that in using the term oral tradition we do not exclude the transmission of some biblical books or parts of them in manuscript form even at this stage. The question rather is one of the relative preponderance of the two vehicles of transmission of literary material, the oral and the written. For this reason it is completely unwarranted even to attempt, with the means currently available, to delineate what cannot be known—namely the process of transition from the stage of mainly oral tradition to that of preponderantly

---

[1] On this theme cf. also pp. 185 ff.

written transmission. In all likelihood the process was gradual, with the weight progressively shifting from the former to the latter. Without aiming at precision, in view of the foregoing remarks, it may be said that the period of the Babylonian Exile after the destruction of the First Temple, i.e. the middle of the sixth century B.C., could be taken as a rough dividing line. The definite shift of emphasis from oral to written transmission of the biblical books would thus have become clearly apparent during the period of the Return, i.e. at the end of the sixth and in the fifth century B.C., in what, from a wider historical viewpoint, may be termed the Persian period. These considerations indicate, as will be further shown, that in attempting an elucidation of the history of the text we cannot concern ourselves exclusively with literary issues, but have to look out also for social and political phenomena whose impacts made themselves felt in its development.

The preponderance of written transmission of Old Testament books after the return from the Exile still does not make this second phase of development a ready subject for textual study in the strict sense of the term, since it is not yet represented by manuscript evidence. Any conclusions with regard to the history of text at that time lack a documentary basis. They are grounded solely on inference from subsequent phases of development and on theoretical considerations rooted in other fields of biblical research and transferred from them to the study of the text. Textual study proper commences in the next stage with the appearance of accessible manuscripts of Old Testament books.

The third phase begins, according to the present state of our knowledge, in the early third century B.C. For several reasons this phase must be considered the pivot around which any investigation into the history of the Bible text turns. At this stage, the written transmission of biblical literature finally and, to all intents and purposes, completely replaced oral tradition. With this transition went the gradual formal sanctification of the books which were accepted as scripture, culminating at the end of this phase, i.e. by the turn of the eras, in the establishment of the complete and closed Old Testament Canon. The very fact that an attempt was made to compile a definite codex of the sacred lore of the community shows that those who undertook it sensed that a period in the history of Israel and of its literature had come to a close, and that a new era of basically different literary standards and norms had begun. In instigating the canonisation of those books, they intended to ensure the faithful preservation of the spiritual heritage of preceding generations. At the same time they purported to draw a definite line between this acknowledged body of written sacred literature and contemporary non-sacred books on the one hand, and on the other hand between it and the emerging new type of rabbinic literature which was to be only orally transmitted. Again, as has been shown in the section on the Canon, we are concerned with a gradual process, of which many aspects still cannot be adequately examined for lack of reliable evidence. Yet it would appear that the progressive demarcation of the books accepted as scripture over against all other writings extant at that period was a prerequisite for the ensuing preoccupation with the exact wording which aimed at guaranteeing an unimpaired textual transmission. No such tendency is apparent in the preceding phase. It seems that only with the emerging concept of a clearly circumscribed canon of inspired literature could there develop this concern for the exact preservation of its wording. We have no reason to suppose that much heed was paid to the text of non-sanctified writings, nor does the traceable textual history of writings of this kind, such as Ecclesiasticus, substantiate such an assumption. Since they had no claim to have been conceived under divine inspiration, variants in their transmitted wordings were regarded as of no consequence.

IV

The internal Jewish trends outlined above were intensified by another set of factors. In the period under review, Israel was drawn into the orbit of hellenistic culture, which heavily influenced contemporary Jewish culture. The resulting contact with the Greek world of letters had a decisive impact on the transmission of the Old Testament. Jewish scribes emulated Greek scribal techniques and terminology, and adopted their insistence on exactitude in handing down written records and literary works.[1]

This development occurred at an opportune moment in the history of the Old Testament text, when its translation into other languages was first undertaken. The demand for a translation of the Hebrew scriptures into Aramaic probably arose during the Babylonian Exile or immediately after the return of the exiles to Palestine, i.e. in the

[1] Cf. S. Lieberman, *Hellenism in Jewish Palestine* (New York, 1950), pp. 3–46.

Persian period. Aramaic being the *lingua franca* of the time, it was adopted by many Jews in their intercourse with the non-Jewish world. Being a Semitic language, closely related to Hebrew, it eventually achieved the status of a sister tongue to Hebrew even in the internal life of the Jewish people, especially in the Babylonian Diaspora, but also in Palestine. At first, the translation of the scriptures into Aramaic was most probably sporadic and undirected. It was left to the individual communities to tend to the needs of their members by providing a vehicle which would make the message of the sacred writings understandable also to those whose command of the mother tongue had become insufficient for this purpose. Lacking authorised supervision, the resulting translation often assumed the form of a somewhat free paraphrase of the original, rather than of an accurate rendering into the translator's language. But even when a word-by-word translation was attempted, divergence from the Hebrew *Vorlage* was inevitable. Translation from one language into another always produces inaccuracies since there is no exact correspondence between the vocabulary and the syntax of the two, even if they belong to the same language family. Moreover, the probably divergent first renderings of the Hebrew scriptures into Aramaic were based on originals which may well have differed among themselves to a smaller or larger degree, for reasons set out above.

The same considerations apply with additional force to the translation of the Old Testament books into Greek, a non-Semitic language. This translation was required, for reasons similar to those mentioned above, by Jews living within the sphere of hellenistic culture, whether in Ptolemaic Egypt, where the Jewish community of Alexandria was the focal point, or in Palestine. Tradition maintains that in this case official non-Jewish agents also showed interest in rendering the Old Testament into Greek, and instigated a properly supervised scholarly translation. This tradition will be further discussed subsequently. The pseudepigraphic *Letter of Aristeas* credits King Ptolemy II Philadelphus (285–246 B.C.) with having inaugurated the translation of the Pentateuch into Greek by seventy sages. As a result of their concerted effort, the Septuagint, commonly designated LXX, was in the Pentateuch less open to the uncontrolled impact of translators' idiosyncrasies. It contains indeed fewer deviations from the Hebrew text here than in the renderings of the other books. But it is still open to discussion whether this reputedly official undertaking is to be considered the first attempt at translating the Old Testament or parts of it into Greek and to have provided the impetus to further ventures of the same kind, or whether it should rather be viewed as an event which ,crowned a long series of previous diffuse attempts with a standardised version.

The first wave of translation of the Hebrew Old Testament into other languages, Semitic and non-Semitic, perforce resulted in the creation of variants and types of variants in the then extant witnesses to the text. The ensuing embarrassing textual diversity of the versions of the sacred books soon called for the application of the methods of textual analysis and textual criticism to remedy this deficiency. As stated above, the ground for this new approach had been laid by the conjunction of scholarly norms borrowed from the Greeks with the care for the accurate transmission of the inspired literature which had developed within Judaism. This attitude towards the text characterises the fourth period of its history.

v

We have already indicated that the fourth phase in the textual history of the Old Testament may be reckoned to extend from the end of the last century B.C. to the beginning of the third century A.D. It is marked by a vigorous process of textual standardisation which affected practically all versions. In order to include within this time-span the activities of Jewish and Samaritan scribes who applied themselves to the stabilisation of the Hebrew text, and of Christian, and to some extent also of Jewish, scribes and scholars who dealt with the Greek Bible, the upper and lower limits have been chosen with some latitude. The dates could be lowered by half a century or so at both ends as far as the Hebrew text is concerned. Also in this phase we have to take into account the impact of socio-political events on the history of the text, especially the emergence of Christianity and the destruction of the Second Temple in A.D. 70. The finalisation of the rift between the Synagogue and the Church which was incomparably more important and decisive than any preceding clash of the main stream of Judaism with deviating movements, and the insistence of both Jews and Christians on basing the cardinal tenets of their conflicting beliefs on the sacred scriptures, necessitated the clear definition of the text on which these claims were grounded. Further, the destruction of the

Second Temple seriously impaired the social cohesion of Jewry which had previously ensured some unity of the text, or at least had prevented its dissolution into innumerable streamlets of textual tradition. The renewed dispersion of Jews over a large geographical area, the disruption of existing socio-religious centres and the creation of new pivotal agencies with the possible resulting diversification of the biblical textual traditions, required counteraction. The propagation of one, universally recognised text form was considered indispensable for ensuring the continuity of the national unity. Rabbinic literature, Hebrew fragments of the Old Testament from after A.D. 70 such as those from Wadi Murabba'at and Massada,[1] and some subsidiary evidence from the ancient versions, witness to the emergence of a Hebrew *textus receptus*, the prototype of the Massoretic text which was finally established almost a millennium later.

Correspondence between the developments of the Hebrew and non-Hebrew versions terminates somewhere at the end of the first century A.D. By then the division between them is in fact no longer a division along linguistic lines, but reflects the schism between the Synagogue and the Church and their different attitudes to the text. The process of textual unification referred to above affected not only the rabbinic Hebrew Bible and the Samaritan Hebrew Pentateuch but also seems to be observable in the Jewish Aramaic translations of the Old Testament books, especially in the Targum Onkelos to the Pentateuch. As against this, if we may judge by Origen's enterprise, and by some preceding Greek evidence from Qumrân, Christian scholars were indeed also bent on editing, and probably on stabilising, the various extant Greek translations, but apparently did not attempt to weld them into one solely acceptable textual tradition. This interpretation of the available evidence is borne out by the subsequent fate of the Greek Bible which after Origen's time was also subjected to recurrent revisions which in practice sometimes amount to new translations. This state of affairs brought about the renewed efforts of Jerome some two centuries later to provide the Church with a new Latin version, the Vulgate, based on the then extant form of the *hebraica veritas*.[2] The Vulgate was intended to supersede the Old Latin version then in use, itself derived from the Greek and therefore presenting in many cases readings which deviated considerably from the current Hebrew text. True, there is

---

[1] See below, pp. 182–6.   [2] See v, 16 in the present volume.

no comparable evidence on hand for the Jewish-Hebrew text in the period under review. At the beginning of the second century manuscript Hebrew evidence comes abruptly to an end, and the text remains unattested for some seven centuries until the appearance of the earliest medieval Hebrew manuscripts. However, the basic similarity between the Hebrew textual traditions at the two extreme points of this time-span, which is not impaired by the persistence of individual variants or even the emergence of new ones, bears out the above statement that after the first century A.D. one single Hebrew text type gained the upper hand and that deviant types practically went out of circulation.

VI

At this point of our investigation we have to turn our attention to the history of biblical textual research as it has developed since the rediscovery of the Samaritan Hebrew Pentateuch by Pietro della Valle in 1616. The Samaritan text was made available to scholars shortly afterwards when Morinus first printed it in 1632 alongside the other versions in the Paris Polyglot. Its many deviations from the Massoretic text, later estimated at about six thousand, were soon observed. It was further established that approximately one third of these *variae lectiones* could be traced also in the Septuagint. This concurrence enhanced the doubts which had been raised concerning the veracity of the Massoretic text. It was maintained that, having been revised by the rabbis after the destruction of the Temple, in the first half of the second century A.D., it did not represent the *ipsissima verba* of the divinely inspired message, but a faulty text, resulting from *incuria librariorum* or from wilful malicious tampering with it on the part of the Jews. As against this it was claimed that the Septuagint had never been subjected to such interference, and therefore represented the biblical text in its pre-revision stage. If it was not altogether a true image of the pristine form of the divine word, it certainly came closer to it than any other version. The alignment of the Hebrew Samaritan version with the Greek in so many instances seemed to strengthen the position of the defenders of its accuracy. True, the history of the Samaritan community remained to a large extent shrouded in mystery, but its seclusion throughout more than a millennium appeared to imply that its version of the Pentateuch had been safeguarded from the impact of the biased Jewish revision. It was therefore accepted as a true reflection of the Hebrew Pentateuch as that had been extant before the rabbis exerted their influence on it.

It hardly needs stressing that the discussion at that time, and into the eighteenth century, arose almost exclusively from theological considerations and not from detached scholarly observation. Textual criticism was employed in order to prove the claim that the Greek Bible adopted by the Church was the only true manifestation of the divine message. Accordingly, the Hebrew text of the Synagogue was relegated to an inferior status. The Reformation had, however, instigated a counter movement. Its reliance on the Hebrew text accorded the latter a new place of honour in biblical studies. It was indeed agreed that the Massoretic text exhibited a text form which had been fixed and codified by numerous successive generations of Jewish scribes and sages, and that it bore the imprint of their redactional activities. But, it was argued, this very preoccupation of those early scholars with the accurate preservation of the text, and the uninterrupted supervision of its transmission, had saved it from the corroding impact of insufficiently controlled copying which had been the lot of the other versions. Collations of the available Hebrew manuscripts which were prepared at the end of the eighteenth century by Kennicott and de Rossi, and which superseded all previous endeavours, proved their basic identity.[1] The rich crop of individual variants which were recorded in the apparatus of these works at first sight appeared to disprove the compactness and stability of the Hebrew text. However, closer scrutiny more and more strengthened the conviction that almost all of them can and should be classified as intentional or unintentional secondary scribal alterations. In any case, they could not offset the clear impression that the consonantal text of practically all Massoretic manuscripts showed no deviation of any consequence. All exhibited a tradition which was identical to the smallest *minutiae*, even in recording anomalous phenomena such as the *puncta extraordinaria*, and the unconventional spelling or pronunciation of certain words. The lesson to be drawn from Kennicott's, de Rossi's and other such collations was summarised at the end of the eighteenth century by E. F. C. Rosen-

---

[1] M. H. Goshen-Gottstein has recently provided us with new insights into the phase of research into the history of the Massoretic text which is briefly discussed here. See his 'Hebrew Biblical Manuscripts', *Biblica*, XLVIII (1967), 249–77.

mueller as follows: 'This whole range of variants...leads moreover to the simple recognition that all surviving codices are relatively late in relation to the *originals*...they all represent *one recension*, all stem from one *source*...'[1] It is imperative to underline Rosenmueller's reference to *originals* (in the plural), and his conclusion that all medieval Hebrew manuscripts derive from one single recension, i.e. a revised text source. They are therefore to be regarded as one composite witness. Moreover, they can in no way be viewed, without further analysis, as a faithful reflection of the original Hebrew text. Their collation can only help us to reconstitute or recapture the prototype of the Massoretic recension, not the pristine Hebrew Bible.

This line of argument by which the extant *variae lectiones* in Massoretic manuscripts were shown to be of secondary origin was further elaborated in the early nineteenth century to include also the Samaritan Pentateuch text. In his dissertation *De Pentateuchi Samaritani Origine* (1815), W. Gesenius subjected this version for the first time to a proper textual analysis, leaving aside theological considerations. After collecting and categorising the variant readings in the Samaritan, comparing them whenever possible with parallel readings in other non-Massoretic sources, he concluded that in the overwhelming majority of cases these variants resulted from a Samaritan revision of the same basic text exhibited by the Massoretic text, and therefore cannot be considered to present evidence for an original independent text tradition. Even the concurrence of the Samaritan in so many instances with the Septuagint could not affect this conclusion. Gesenius' successors did not materially add to his findings, but only put in sharper relief the dependence of the Samaritan Version on the Massoretic text, and thus further diminished the former's text-critical value. Z. Frankel defined the Samaritan as a faulty recension full of mistakes and scribal redactions, based on the Massoretic text,[2] a view subscribed to by S. Kohn in numerous publications, and summed up by him as follows:

The Samaritan and the Massoretic text are not two divergent copies of one book, but the Samaritan is related to the Massoretic text in the way that a new edition, carefully revised, is related to an older one; it not only improves

---

[1] E. F. C. Rosenmueller, *Handbuch der biblischen Kritik und Exegese*, I (Göttingen, 1797), p. 244; quoted by E. Preuschen, *ZAW*, IX (1889), 303. (Translation by the editors.)

[2] Z. Frankel, *Ueber den Einfluss der palaestinischen Exegese auf die alexandrinische Hermeneutik* (Leipzig, 1851), p. 242.

on it in content—though in this instance it is mainly the opposite of improvement—but it is also modernised in regard to language and orthography.[1]

Rosenmueller's well-balanced 'one-recension' theory which, it is to be noted, he had applied to the Massoretic text only, was pushed into the background by the more sweeping 'archetype theory' propounded by P. de Lagarde about a century ago. In Lagarde's formulation all Hebrew manuscripts derived from one single exemplar, not one recension. This hypothetical manuscript admittedly did not faithfully mirror the original text, but patently contained numerous deviations from it which had been faithfully transmitted and preserved in all extant manuscripts: 'The result is that our Hebrew manuscripts of the Old Testament all go back to one single exemplar, and have even faithfully reproduced as corrections the correcting of its scribal errors and taken over its fortuitous imperfections.'[2] It was tacitly assumed or even expressly conceded, e.g. by J. G. Sommer, that that unique proto-Massoretic manuscript either derived directly from the Temple or else was based upon a copy of the complete Canon which had been kept there before the fall of Jerusalem in A.D. 70, although it achieved its final form only somewhat later.[3]

Lagarde widened the scope of his investigation by applying a similar method to the Greek tradition. He argued that all the available Greek manuscripts could be reduced to the three basic local recensions of Origen, Hesiod and Lucian, from which scholars could trace their way back to the original Septuagint. Taken as a whole the Greek tradition represented a textual family which differed from the Massoretic text. Although it must be viewed as an unsatisfactory translation of the original, this tradition can be employed, by way of comparison, to go behind the archetype which underlies the Hebrew manuscripts: 'We could only penetrate behind this archetype of the Massoretic text by conjecture, were it not for the fact that the Greek version of the Old Testament opens up the possibility of making use of at least a poor translation of a manuscript belonging to a different family.'[4]

---

[1] S. Kohn, 'Samaritikon und Septuaginta', *MGWJ*, xxxviii (1895), 60. (Translation by the editors.)

[2] P. de Lagarde, *Anmerkungen zur griechischen Uebersetzung der Proverbien* (Leipzig, 1863), p. 2. (Translation by the editors.)

[3] J. G. Sommer, *Biblische Abhandlungen* (Bonn, 1846), p. 79; further: J. Olshausen, *Die Psalmen* (Braunschweig, 1853), pp. 15–17.

[4] P. de Lagarde, *ibid.* n. 18. (Translation by the editors.)

The various manifestations of the Old Testament text could, according to this theory, be likened to the branches of a tree, all of which had grown from one stem in diverse stages of bifurcation. There remained little doubt that an analysis and comparison of the main versions, chiefly of the Massoretic text and the reconstituted Septuagint buttressed by the Hebrew Samaritan Pentateuch version, would lead scholars to the very *Ur-text* common to all. The Greek tradition was deemed especially valuable for the purpose of purging the Old Testament of anti-Christian falsifications which allegedly had been introduced into the Massoretic text by the rabbis. This consideration, more theological than textual, fixed the *terminus non ante quem* of the reputed Jewish *Ur-exemplar*. It could not precede the emergence of Christianity, indeed not the first centuries A.D., since one had to allow some time for the Jewish–Christian controversy to develop.[1] The final fixation of the proto-Massoretic text was soon connected with the members of the Sanhedrin of Jamnia that flourished in the days of the Emperor Hadrian (first half of the second century A.D.), and especially with Rabbi Aqiba, probably the most prominent rabbi of the early Christian era. In some such formulation Lagarde's *Ur-text* theory, which was incorrectly considered an elaboration of Rosenmueller's 'one recension' theory, carried the day. Scholars differed in their opinions as to how the basic Massoretic text had been established—whether a deliberate choice had been made by some official Jewish body (Olshausen), or whether, rather haphazardly, a readily available manuscript had been made the basis of the standard text (Noeldeke).[2] But they concurred on the basic issue—the presupposed existence of an archetype. The situation was succinctly summarised at the end of the nineteenth century by F. Buhl:

Of the style and manner in which this authorized text was constructed we unfortunately know nothing definitely. This much only is plain, that the very conception of such an authorized form of text implies the existence of a definite standard manuscript, which was pronounced the only allowable one. In so far, the relatively recent but already widespread theory, that all extant manuscripts point back to one single archetype, is decidedly correct.[3]

---

[1] For a summary of Lagarde's views see A. Rahlfs, *P. de Lagardes wissenschaftliches Lebenswerk* (Göttingen, 1928), pp. 75–82.

[2] Th. Noeldeke, *Alttestamentliche Literatur*, I (Leipzig, 1868), pp. 22–5.

[3] F. Buhl, *Canon and Text of the Old Testament*. Translated by J. Macpherson (Edinburgh, 1892), p. 256.

Buhl subscribed to the idea that this standard text was officially pro-claimed, and soon pushed its way

in a remarkably short time wherever the Pharisaic influence extended. On the other hand, the equally widespread theory that this primitive codex obtained this position by mere arbitrary choice, or by the manuscripts of the several books that by chance were at hand being bound together into one standard Bible, is by no means certain.[1]

But he was less sure than Lagarde that we can reach back behind this archetype by comparing the Hebrew version with the extant Greek. It is important, he says,

to determine the exact relation between the Massoretic text and the Arche-typal texts of Aquila, Symmachus, and Jerome. In a remarkable way the Hebrew manuscripts, which were certainly derived from the most diverse regions, seem to form a unity over against those translators, because the variations present in these are only extremely seldom repeated in any one manuscript. Evidently the rigid stability of form which resulted from the labours of the Massoretes called into being new standard texts, on which the manuscripts are directly dependent, which, however, were themselves collateral with the manuscripts used by those translators.[1]

VII

The validity of some of Lagarde's arguments was questioned already in his lifetime. Within thirty years after the inception of the *Ur-text* theory the onslaught on it from various quarters forced its adherents to modify their rigid position, and ultimately resulted in the conception of new rival hypotheses. P. E. Kahle drew attention to Hebrew manu-scripts from the Cairo Geniza stemming from the end of the first and the beginning of the second millennium A.D. which exhibited variants in the secondary phenomena of the Hebrew text (vocalisation, punctua-tion, etc.). These derived from different Massoretic systems, and seemed to indicate that the Hebrew tradition was less solidified than Lagarde had assumed.[2] But since these manuscripts were much too late, and their variants did not really affect the consonantal text, their evidence could not be adduced to disqualify the *Ur-text* hypothesis.

[1] Buhl, *ibid.*
[2] P. Kahle's work of a lifetime is summarised in his *The Cairo Geniza*. The Schweich Lectures of the British Academy 1941 (London, 1947; 2nd ed. Oxford, 1959).

More decisive were the strictures raised by V. Aptowitzer. His collection of biblical quotations in rabbinic literature, a field which had not been explored at all by earlier scholars, brought to light a wealth of variant Hebrew readings, which were sometimes reflected also in one or another of the versions.[1] In spite of attempts to diminish the value of this evidence, by explaining the variations as arising from quotation by heart, or from intentional alteration of the original on the part of the quoting authors, it stands to reason that it severely undermines the theory of a single Jewish *Ur-text*. It would be hard to explain the persistence of variants in rabbinic literature, even when these occur merely in quotations, if indeed the text of that one manuscript had ousted all others since the days of Rabbi Aqiba.

The very existence of variant quotations in rabbinic writings and in their exegetical comments, particularly in Midrash literature, which mirror a text that deviates from the Massoretic text, dealt a severe blow not only to the *Ur-text* hypothesis, but also to the less rigorous 'one recension' theory. Rival theories were now put forward. All of these set out to account for the co-existence of divergent text traditions of the Old Testament in the pre-Christian rabbinic and the early Christian period, in Hebrew as well as in Aramaic, in Greek and possibly also in Latin translations, as are exemplified in: (*a*) divergent textual traditions exhibited in quotations in rabbinical literature; (*b*) parallel Aramaic translations of the Pentateuch, which indeed stem from a period later than the one under discussion here, but most probably derive from pre-Origenic prototypes, namely Targum Onkelos which possibly originated in Babylonia, and certainly was redacted there, Pseudo-Jonathan, of Palestinian origin, and a third Aramaic version which until recently had been known only from excerpts, and therefore had been named the Fragment Targum, but now has been proved to represent in fact a fully fledged Jerusalem Aramaic translation;[2] and

[1] V. Aptowitzer, *Das Schriftwort in der rabbinischen Literatur: Prolegomena. Sitzungsberichte der Kaiserlichen Akademie der Wissenschaften, philosophisch-historische Klasse,* Band 153, Abhandlung VI (Vienna, 1906). The 'Prolegomenon' was followed by a detailed investigation into quotations from the Former Prophets in rabbinic literature, published in four separate instalments. Cf. further I. Abrahams, 'Rabbinical Aids to Exegesis' in *Essays on Some Biblical Questions of the Day. By Members of the University of Cambridge* (London, 1909), pp. 172 ff.

[2] See A. Diez Macho, 'The recently discovered Palestinian targum: its antiquity and relationship with the other targums', *Supplements to Vetus Testamentum,* VII, Congress Volume Oxford 1959 (Leiden, 1960), 222–45.

(c) the propagation of diverse Greek translations exhibited in an almost codified form in the parallel columns of the *Hexapla*, and sometimes preserved in the form of variant-quotations from the Old Testament in the Apocrypha, the New Testament and the writings of the early Church Fathers, and also in Jewish hellenistic literature, especially in the works of Flavius Josephus.

The most extreme of the new theories was that of the 'vulgar texts' proposed by Paul Kahle which may be considered the very opposite of Lagarde's *Ur-text* hypothesis, and with some qualifications also of the 'one recension' theory. As stated, both these hypotheses take for granted that all extant versions of the Old Testament books, and also most of the intra-versional textual variants, can in the last analysis be reduced, at least in theory if not always in practice, to one common text base which was the only acclaimed, or possibly even the only extant, text form of the Old Testament at the beginning of the Christian era. Though differing as to the characterisation of the 'archetype' as a 'recension' or as a single manuscript, neither of these two hypotheses seems to have taken into consideration the antecedents of the presupposed archetype. It would, in fact, appear that in both the respective archetype was believed to have represented the very first text form of the Old Testament books, not preceded by any divergent predecessors. In other words, all present divergences in the extant versions must be considered to have arisen after the archetype had been established and had been officially accepted. The archetype is viewed, as it were, as a riverhead running off into numerous rivulets, all of which, however, can be retraced to the original source.

Now, it may be said that Kahle would be prepared to subscribe to such a description of the issue as far as the latter part of the simile is concerned, namely the diversification of the Old Testament text tradition in the post-Jamnia period. He would also agree that many variants in the diverse versions are of a secondary nature, resulting from intentional or accidental scribal alterations. But on the other hand he would maintain that on the whole the more important witnesses to the Old Testament text, such as the primary Hebrew Massoretic and Samaritan versions, and the basic Greek and Aramaic translations, represent in essence text forms which preceded Lagarde's model-codex or Rosenmueller's arch-recension. The 'vulgar texts' school does not consider the archetype to be the riverhead, but rather the confluence of preceding varying text traditions. These pristine traditions were unified to a considerable degree by the endeavour of generations of tradents within the Jewish, Samaritan and Christian communities who established the (proto)-Massoretic *textus receptus*, the Samaritan consolidated version of the Pentateuch and the Septuagint respectively. But they never fully succeeded in completely suppressing older and purer, i.e. non-revised, 'vulgar' texts within their own official tradition, which was determined by linguistic peculiarities and religious dogma, nor could they ever establish one common archetype of the Old Testament books.[1]

It is the great merit of Kahle that he attempted to push the inquiry into the history of the text in all its ramifications beyond the *terminus non ante quem* which his predecessors had tacitly or explicitly considered as the starting point for their investigations, namely the end of the Second Commonwealth or the beginning of the period after the destruction in A.D. 70. In his understanding of the matter, the then already extant *textus receptus* of each single version marked the apex of a long chain of development in the course of which divergent text-traditions had been progressively abolished. The creation of the Septuagint as portrayed in the pseudepigraphical *Letter of Aristeas*, the compact Aramaic Targums, the Massoretic text and the Samaritan Version are the crowning events in a process of textual unification which had been set on foot by the needs of socio-religious organisations: the Synagogue, the Samaritan community and the Church.

Without, to the best of my knowledge, stating so explicitly, Kahle in fact applied to the research into the history of the Old Testament text ideas and principles which concurrently emerged in the study of biblical stylistics and literature. Quite correctly, he considered textual history as a phenomenon of a socio-religious kind and endeavoured to map out its place in actual communal life, i.e. to establish, in Gunkel's terminology, its 'Sitz im Leben'.

It follows that in many instances an ancient variant, or a Bible quotation which differs from the authoritative texts, exhibits a *wirkliche Variante*, i.e. a true variant which is a remnant of a pristine text-tradition that had escaped the levelling influence of the official redactions. Inter-version variants may have resulted from the fact that the

[1] Similar ideas had been already presented *in statu nascendi* by A. Geiger. See e.g. his remarks on the Samaritan text in: *Nachgelassene Schriften*, IV (Berlin, 1876), 67.

individual versions finally crystallised at different stages of the textual transmission of the Old Testament. Variant quotations survived predominantly in texts which did not come under the scrutiny of the official revisers. They should be considered sediments of 'vulgar', i.e. popular traditions that had been in use before the introduction of each respective *textus receptus*.

VIII

It hardly needs stating that by virtue of its being the very antithesis to the *Ur-text* and the *Ur-recension* theses, Kahle's theory of 'vulgar texts and *textus receptus*' was from the outset rejected by the followers of Lagarde and Rosenmueller. But scholars who were inclined to embrace the new idea also called for the correction of some of its constituent elements. They fully recognised a diversity of the textual traditions of the Old Testament as already existing in the very first stages of its manuscriptal transmission—the point on which Kahle had based his arguments—and they accepted his attempt to account for this diversity by trying to retrace the steps of the textual development before the emergence of a standard text. It was nevertheless considered imperative to smooth out some features of his theory which had justifiably evoked criticism. Kahle had brought into clear focus the natural, uncontrolled transmission of the 'vulgar' traditions, thus freeing them from the rigidity of a conception which supposes the *Ur-text* or the *Ur-recension* to be scholarly creations. Yet he postulated that very same 'academic' setting for the Massoretic *textus receptus*. His presentation of the process by which this model text came about suffers from all the misconceptions which led the *Ur-text* thesis to postulate an abstract scholastic procedure—a procedure for which there is little evidence that it corresponded with socio-historical realities. His assumption that the *textus receptus* should be viewed as resulting from the concerted efforts of a rabbinic academy, especially that of Jamnia, and that its exclusive status was achieved by what amounts to a wholesale *auto-da-fé* of all diverging manuscripts, is neither substantiated by any historical evidence nor plausible. The emergence of the *textus receptus* should be conceived of as a protracted process which culminated in its *post factum* acclamation in the first or at the latest in the second century A.D., as has been stated previously.

179

Some of the opposition to the *Vulgärtexte* theory, when not attributable to dogmatic rather than rational, scholarly motives, probably has its roots in the reluctance of scholars to accept the bewildering 'disorderliness' implied by that thesis in place of the much more systematic theory of an *Ur-text*. But its impact on the issue under review was soon felt. As normally in scholarly discussion and evaluation, some novel intermediate theories were produced which, by way of synthesis, combined salient features of the opposing schools. It may be said that basically, the attempt was made to bring some method into the madness of the uncontrolled vulgar texts, and at the same time little was needed to square Kahle's *textus receptus* with Lagarde's Hebrew *Ur-text* or Rosenmueller's *Ur-recension*, all of which in fact were considered to be mirrored with some deviations in the present Massoretic text.

We shall consider here two propositions which purport to take into account the diversity of the actual textual traditions from the very moment at which they become known to us in manuscript form or in quotations in early post-biblical Jewish and Christian literature, and to avoid at the same time the disturbing diffuseness of the vulgar texts if seen as pristine independent traditions.

Setting out from Kahle's premises, and probing into the antecedents of the various text forms in which the Old Testament is extant, in Hebrew as well as in translations, and especially in Greek, A. Sperber attempted to reduce all versions in their variations to two basic textual traditions: one is supposedly derived from Judah and is represented most clearly by the Massoretic text; the other stems from Ephraim, and is best recognised in the Samaritan Hebrew Pentateuch. Both have their offshoots in the major Greek textual families, in manuscripts A and B.[1] The admitted initial dichotomy of the biblical text-tradition, carried back by Sperber's hypothesis into pre-exilic times, is fundamentally opposed to the 'one *Ur-recension*' and the 'one *Ur-text*' theories. The difference between one textual tradition and two is qualitative, and not merely quantitative. On the other hand Sperber invalidated to a high degree the originality of the 'vulgar texts', which Kahle had assumed, by presenting them as derivations from a preceding

---

[1] Sperber's criticism of the archetype theory may be found in his *Septuagintaprobleme* (Stuttgart, 1929). For a presentation of his own views see 'New Testament and Septuagint', *JBL*, LIX (1940), 193–293.

pristine textual tradition which diverged from the prototype of the present Massoretic text. Sperber further introduced into the discussion the idea of 'local traditions' which figures prominently in the most recent theory, yet to be described, perceiving in the Samaritan not merely the product of a late dissident Jewish group, but rather the best-preserved representative of a North-Israelite (namely Ephraimite) text type, and in the Massoretic text its South-Israelite (Judaean) counterpart.

In the same manner as Kahle had applied, as was suggested, Gunkel's exclusively literary concept of the 'Sitz im Leben' to the sphere of biblical textual history, so Sperber appears to have transferred to the study of the text the notion of a geographical dichotomy of the pentateuchal literature inherent in the sigla J and E which, according to some views, are taken to represent the Judaean–Jahwistic and the Ephraimite–Elohistic traditions respectively. At the same time he abandoned the evaluation of the diverse text types which is concomitant with Kahle's very terminology, 'vulgar texts' versus *textus receptus*, and repaired to a purely descriptive division of the extant representatives of the text.

S. Liebermann,[1] on the other hand, took up the qualitative differentiation between the witnesses to the text, applying it, however, not to 'textual traditions', but to types of manuscripts which were extant in the crucial period of the last one or two centuries B.C. and the first one or two centuries A.D. His division between manuscripts as 'base' (φαυλότερα), 'popular' (*vulgate* or κοινότερα) and 'excellent' (ἠκριβω-μένα) also has some 'local' affiliations, since the first were supposedly unworthy copies found mainly in the hands of uneducated villagers, the second class was widely used in cities for study purposes, even in schools and rabbinic academies, whereas only the third type had binding force and was meticulously transmitted by the learned sages of Jerusalem. It goes without saying that only the latter group can be taken to represent faithfully the pristine text of scripture, whereas the others must be judged inferior, their variants being in the nature of secondary deviations. Here Lieberman, without stating so expressly, obviously presupposes the existence of some basic text of exclusive validity which is best mirrored in the manuscripts.

It is important, again in reference to later theories pertaining to the

---

[1] Cf. *Hellenism in Jewish Palestine.*

history of the text which are yet to be discussed, to put in relief Liebermann's threefold division of biblical manuscripts at the end of the Second Temple period, and the assumption that the three types were anchored and transmitted in different localities. One may also detect in his system a sociological dimension in so far as the above types are affiliated with different strata of Jewish society: illiterate or semi-illiterate country people on the one hand, and 'academicians' on the other hand, with an intermediate, less precisely delineated group including city dwellers of all kinds.

IX

At this stage of our investigation we turn to the presentation of some issues which have caused novel developments in the theories about the history of the text.

It was said above that the third phase in the early history of the text, which coincides approximately with the hellenistic and the early Roman period, i.e. the last three centuries B.C., must be considered crucial for our investigation. The final and complete transition from oral tradition to written transmission, the gradual canonisation of the books which were deemed holy, the emerging processes of translation of the Hebrew Bible into other languages, and the impact of hellenistic literary norms and techniques, make this stage the very centre of our inquiry.

To the above considerations must be added one other factor which looms very large in contemporary research into the issue under review. It necessitates, in fact, a reopening of the discussion on the history of the text, and a re-evaluation of theories which had been formed at the end of the nineteenth and in the first half of the twentieth century. We refer to the collection of manuscripts and fragments from the Judaean Desert, also known by the misnomer 'The Dead Sea Scrolls', which include numerous scrolls and thousands of fragments of biblical books. Since 1947 when the new finds were first reported, an incessant stream of discoveries, so far only published in part, illuminates that phase in the history of the text.

The above documents are of two groups, quite disparate from the standpoint both of chronology and of their sociological provenance. One group hails from Qumrân which is situated some five miles south of Jericho and two miles west of the shores of the Dead Sea. It precedes the destruction of the Second Temple (A.D. 70)—so important an event for the textual history of the Old Testament—and derives from the dissident Jewish sect of the 'New Covenant'.[1] The other consists of scattered manuscript finds from the region to the south of Qumrân, Wadi Murabba'at (halfway between Jericho and 'Ein Gedi), Naḥal Ze'elim and Massada, and exhibits the textual tradition of what has been styled by G. F. Moore 'normative' Judaism.

The latter fragments, which date from the Bar-Kochba revolt (middle of the second century A.D.), do not shed much light on our problem because they provide evidence for only some sections of a few Old Testament books, and because they present a text which had already been almost wholly adjusted to the prevailing *textus receptus*.[2] These documents therefore do not bear on the phase of textual development at present under review. The biblical manuscripts from Qumrân, on the other hand, some of which are dated by scholars in the third and many in the second and first centuries B.C., have added a new dimension to the criticism of the biblical text and to the study of its history, both in the original Hebrew and in the earliest ancient versions, especially in Greek.[3] Some of these manuscripts are quite extensive. Thus in the case of the First Isaiah Scroll (1QIs^a), we have a virtually complete copy of the biblical book. This, like many other manuscripts from Qumrân, precedes the oldest extant manuscripts of any part of the Old Testament in the Hebrew Massoretic tradition by more than a millennium, and those in Greek or any other translation by several centuries. They are thus of unsurpassed importance for an investigation into the third phase of the history of the text, and into the processes of its transmission.

The new material often helps in elucidating the genesis and the history of individual variants in which one or more of the ancient versions differ from the Massoretic text. They also open up new possibilities for the recovery, or the reconstruction, of the factors which underlie textual variation. The sifting of these cases, their

[1] The reader will find a valuable summary of the literature and the ideology of this group in F. M. Cross, jun., *The Ancient Library of Qumrân* (revised edition, New York, 1961).

[2] See Y. Yadin, *The Finds from the Bar Kokhbah Period in the Cave of Letters* (Jerusalem, 1963).

[3] See D. Barthélemy, O.P., 'Les Devanciers d'Aquila', *Supplements to Vetus Testamentum*, x (Leiden, 1963).

classification, and a statistical assessment of the frequency of their appearance, may make possible the systematic presentation of the processes which can be proved empirically to have been conducive to the emergence of *variae lectiones*. The pertinent information gained from these first-hand sources, because of their scope and their primacy, should enable scholars to improve on previous attempts along these lines.

Prior to the discovery of the Qumrân Scrolls, observations on the skill and the peculiarities of the ancient copyists of the text could be inferred only from the analysis of variants which are found in medieval Hebrew manuscripts, or had to be abstracted from deviating translations in the ancient versions. With the pre-Christian Hebrew Scrolls from Qumrân at our disposal, we are now in a position to verify principles established by inference, and to put them to a practical test. The Scrolls afford us a completely new insight into ancient scribal craft and give us an unparalleled visual impression of the physical appearance of the manuscripts in which the biblical *variae lectiones* arose. We can now observe at close range, so to say *in situ*, scribal techniques of the Second Temple period which left their impression on the text in subsequent stages of its history. We can perceive the conditions which were the breeding ground of the variants that crop up in the extant witnesses to the text of the Old Testament.

There is nothing specifically sectarian in the external appearance of the Qumrân Scrolls, in the scribal customs to which their copyists adhered, or in the majority of the deviant readings found in them. The impression of dissent that goes with the biblical Scrolls from Qumrân derives from the secession of their scribes from normative Judaism, and has no roots in the manuscripts as such. That is to say, it must be attributed to the socio-historical processes which engulfed these Scrolls, but in no way to their textual or manuscript character. Genetically the biblical texts from Qumrân are 'Jewish'. They became 'sectarian' in their subsequent history.

What makes the evidence of the Scrolls especially valuable is the fact that they present not just a horizontal cross-section of one stabilised version, such as is the Massoretic *textus receptus*. Because of their diversity, the kaleidoscope of the textual traditions exhibited in them, their concurrence here with one, here with another of the known versions, or again in other cases their exclusive textual individuality, the biblical manuscripts found at Qumrân, in their totality, present in a nutshell, as it were, the intricate and variegated problems of the Hebrew text and versions. The concentration of processes which obtain in the history of the text in a comparatively small corpus of manuscripts, small in comparison with the bulk of Hebrew (Massoretic and Samaritan), Aramaic, Syriac, Greek, Latin, etc., manuscripts which have to be sifted, collated and compared in the course of the critical work on the text—a corpus which moreover is relatively homogeneous with respect to time and provenance—make the Qumrân Scrolls an ideal subject for a study of these processes. Although the results gained from an analysis of the Qumrân material cannot be applied without qualification to the wider field of comparative research into the Massoretic text and the versions, we may derive from them certain working hypotheses which have then to be verified by application to the wider problem.

Thus the situation at Qumrân reflects on a basic issue in Old Testament textual research, namely the debated problem of the very establishment of a Hebrew *textus receptus*. The coexistence of diverse texttypes in the numerically, geographically and temporally restricted Covenanters' community, the fact that some or most of the conflicting manuscripts had very probably been copied in the Qumrân scriptorium and that no obvious attempts at the suppression of divergent manuscripts or of individual variants can be discovered in that voluminous literature, proves beyond doubt that the very notion of an exclusive *textus receptus* had not yet taken root at Qumrân.

We have no reason to doubt that this 'liberal' attitude towards divergent textual traditions of the Old Testament prevailed also in 'normative' Jewish circles of the second and first centuries B.C. According to rabbinic testimony, even the model codices that were kept in the Temple precincts—the ‘*ăzārāh*—not only exhibited divergent readings, but represented conflicting text-types.[1] Phenomenologically speaking, the situation that prevailed in the ‘*ăzārāh* of the Temple may be compared, though with qualifications, with the one that obtained in the scriptorium at Qumrân. The difference consists in the fact that in the end the Temple codices were collated, probably in the first century A.D. and, what is more important, that rabbinic Judaism ultimately

---

[1] See S. Talmon, 'The Three Scrolls of the Law that were Found in the Temple Court', *Textus* (*Annual of the Hebrew University Bible Project*), II (1962), 14–27.

established a model text and strove to banish deviant manuscripts from circulation. But at this stage the comparability of Jewish 'normative' with Qumrân practice breaks down. The active life-span of the Covenanters' community ends some time in the first century B.C., although sporadic attempts at restoration have repercussions in the first and possibly into the second century A.D. However, even the latest manuscripts from Qumrân which provide evidence of the local history of the text in the crucial period, the last decades before the destruction of the Temple, do not give the slightest indication that even an incipient *textus receptus* emerged there, or that the very notion of a model recension was ever conceived by the Covenanters.

The coexistence of varying text forms of the Old Testament, and the absence of any noticeable attempt at establishing one universally recognised recension of binding force, must have confronted the Qumrân scribes with the problem of what attitude to take towards these conflicting textual traditions, which had not yet been assessed and evaluated. The individual scribe could solve this problem by adhering faithfully to the manuscript which he had chosen, or had been assigned, as the *Vorlage* for his own copy. In a reasonable number of instances he could perpetuate parallel readings which he found in other manuscripts that were at his disposal, by noting them in the margins or between the lines of his own copy, or sometimes by integrating them in his text-base, in which case he would create a double reading.[1] Now these devices, which were a common stock-in-trade of the ancient Bible scribes regardless of their socio-religious affiliations, are mere practical expedients that may work fairly well, up to a certain point, for the individual copyist, but cannot satisfactorily solve the problem of the community's disposition towards divergent, but equally well-documented, readings. In manuscripts which are intended for public use, critical annotations must be kept to a practical minimum. In fact, even these relatively few marginal entries will tend to disappear at subsequent copyings by sheer routine omission, unless they are absorbed into the text proper. Even where authoritative guidance is absent we may find a spontaneous tendency towards the simplification and the stabilisation of the textual traditions of scripture and other hallowed books. This process cannot be expected to culminate in

[1] See S. Talmon, 'Double Readings in the Massoretic Text', *Textus*, I (1960), 144–84.

complete unification but it will effectively circumscribe the scope, and reduce the number, of textual types which are allowed a continued existence until, if ever, conscious official redactional activities set in.

The impending gradual disappearance of variant readings, which on objective grounds could not be declared to be intrinsically inferior to those which happened to have taken root in the predominant textual traditions, may well have been viewed with misgivings by those concerned with the preservation of scripture. The practical advantage of acquiring a fairly standardised text-type for communal-cultic purposes was offset by an understandable apprehension for the—to all intents and purposes—irrecoverable loss of valid and venerated textual traditions of the biblical books, which perforce would result from the process outlined above. Contradictory as it may sound, such *pro* and *ante* deliberations seem to have produced diverse manuscript and non-manuscript techniques of variant preservation which helped to balance the scale which was tipped in favour of the text-tradition(s) that became increasingly predominant, to the exclusion and practically complete suppression of less favoured *variae lectiones*.

Here again, a comparison with attitudes and techniques that were current in other communities is in order. In rabbinic circles, the prevalence of such trends of thought may have been responsible for the perceptible latitude in the employment of the text in scholarly discussion which conspicuously contrasts with the unceasing efforts to establish an exclusive *textus receptus* for public worship and for official text-transmission. Whereas deviant readings were banned from the books which were earmarked for these latter categories, they were readily accepted and used as bases for midrashic exposition.[1] At times it appears that such an officially discarded variant was not employed merely as a convenient peg upon which to hang a midrash that was to hand, but rather that the midrash in question was constructed on a variant that had been barred from the *textus receptus*, in order to give it a non-manuscript lease of life. This supposition especially applies to the specific type of the '*al tiqrē*' midrash in which an established reading is suspended as it were, and another reading becomes the point of departure for an ensuing midrashic comment, by means of the introductory formula: 'do not read...but rather read...'. A famous case

[1] See S. Talmon, 'Aspects of the Textual Transmission of the Bible in the Light of Qumrân Manuscripts', *Textus*, IV (1964), 125–35.

in point is the *'al tiqrē'* midrash (Bab. Tal. Berak̲ot 64 *a*) which hinges on reading in Isa. 54: 13 *bōnayik̲* = 'thy builders', instead of *bānayik̲* = 'thy sons' (cf. τέκνα; Targum *bānāk̲*), a variant which now has turned up in 1QIsᵃ as an emended reading *bᵒnayk̲ī*. Similarly the midrash 'do not read (the flesh of) his arm but (the flesh of) his offspring' (Bab. Tal. Shab. 33 *a*) can be anchored in the different text traditions of Isa. 9: 19. Here the Massoretic text (= 1QIsᵃ) reading: 'they shall eat every man the flesh of his own arm' = *zᵉr(ō)ʻō* is abandoned for the variant reading *zarʻō* = 'his offspring' which underlies the Aramaic paraphrastic rendering: 'they shall plunder everyone the goods of his neighbour', and Symmachus' τοῦ πλησίον αὐτοῦ. Both readings were apparently conflated in the main stream of the Septuagint tradition: τοῦ βραχίονος τοῦ ἀδελφοῦ αὐτοῦ.

We do not mean that every extant *'al tiqrē'* midrash can be shown to have arisen from an already identifiable textual variant. This certainly is not the case. *Variae lectiones* which supposedly triggered off the emergence of many midrashim of this type have been lost for us together with the (suppressed) manuscripts which exhibited them. Moreover, this specific type of midrash progressively degenerated. The *'al tiqrē'* formula was then often employed even when the midrash in question could not be related to an actually extant reading, though this had originally been by definition a *sine qua non* requirement. Ultimately it became a mere exegetical *Spielelement*.[1] Conversely, the introductory formula of a genuine *'al tiqrē'* midrash was often dropped, so that now the same exposition is sometimes preserved both with and without that formula.

In a majority of cases the textual variations involved are of the simplest and most common types: interchange of graphically similar letters or of auricularly close consonants; haplography or dittography; continuous writing of separate words or division of one word into two; *plene* or defective spelling (as in the cases adduced above); metathesis; differences of vocalisation, sometimes entailing a change of verb conjugations. Some cases of more complicated textual phenomena do not materially affect the over-all impression.

The ambivalence of the request for a generally recognised standard

---

[1] See I. L. Seeligmann, 'Voraussetzungen der Midraschexegese', *Supplements to Vetus Testamentum*, I. Congress Volume Copenhagen, 1953 (Leiden, 1953), 150–81, and III, 8 in the present volume.

text of scripture, and the concomitant apprehension over the resulting loss of possibly valuable readings, may have produced yet another technique of variant preservation in the early Church. The recording of different text-traditions in the parallel columns of Origen's *Hexapla* was a way out of this dilemma. On the one hand it ensured the continued preservation of probably widely accepted text forms. On the other hand, with the help of a system of critical symbols by which omissions or additions in the Greek in comparison with the Hebrew text could be indicated, the basis for the establishment of an officially acknowledged and critically guaranteed text was created. In this case, as also in the case of the rabbinic *'al tiqrē'* formula, the critical symbols were subsequently not properly recorded in copies made of or from Origen's work. This may have resulted simply from scribal carelessness. However, in view of our foregoing remarks it is reasonable to surmise that this apparently merely technical deficiency was helped along, so to say, by the postulated disinterestedness of the Church in the centuries after Origen in establishing one exclusive, binding text-tradition of scripture.

We seem to be able to discern three main types of technique intended to counterbalance the impact of standardisation which affected the textual transmission of the Old Testament in all its ramifications in various degrees of intensity and at various stages of its development:

(1) Internal manuscript notation of variant readings, either in the text-base, leading to the emergence of double-readings, or else in the margins, as exhibited, e.g., in the Qumrân Scrolls and probably also in some *qerē* readings in the Massoretic text.[1]

(2) The preservation of variant readings in parallel text-traditions. In its earliest form this technique may be observed in the retention of *variae lectiones* in parallel passages in the Former Prophets and Chronicles, etc., and from it may have been derived the basic idea which underlies Origen's *Hexapla*.

(3) Extra-manuscript preservation of variants in midrashic-homiletic exegesis.

x

The situation which obtains at Qumrân holds out one more possibility of comparison in respect of another aspect of the history of the text.

---

[1] See the chapter by B. J. Roberts (vol. 2, pp. 1–10).

In conformity with a basic characteristic of Second Commonwealth Judaism, the Covenanters' religious concepts were Bible-centred. Their original literary creations, such as the War-Scroll, the *Hōdayōt*, the Sectarian Manual, and the Zadokite Documents, swarm with verbatim Bible quotations, paraphrases and allusions. Their most fundamental beliefs and practices reflect the attempt to recapture, and typologically to re-live, biblical Judaism. This scriptural piety produced the *pēšer* technique,[1] so indicative of the Covenanters' system of Bible hermeneutics, by the aid of which biblical history was actualised, and made existentially meaningful. In this unceasing process of quotation, interpretation and adaptation, the text at Qumrân was exposed to a fate which is comparable to that which the *hebraica veritas* experienced on a wider scale in rabbinic Judaism and in the orbit of Jewish and Christian communities that had recourse to translations of the Hebrew original. The deliberate insertion of textual alterations into scripture for various reasons of style and dogma, the uncontrolled infiltration of haphazard changes due to linguistic peculiarities of copyists or to their characteristic concepts and ideas, which may be observed in the wider transmission of the text, have their counterparts in the 'Qumrân Bible'. The study of these phenomena at Qumrân is again facilitated by the comparative compactness of the material and by the decidedly more pronounced manner in which they are manifest. We thus encounter in the Qumrân writings developments of biblical text-transmission which may be considered prototypes of phenomena that emerge concurrently and subsequently in the text-history of the Old Testament in Jewish and Christian tradition, albeit in less concentrated form, and at different grades of variation.

That the sum total of the biblical documents from Qumrân may be seen to present the issue of the 'Massoretic text and the versions' in miniature, derives further support from one more characteristic of that material. The Qumrân manuscripts exhibit, as already stated, a basic homogeneity with regard to time and provenance. There are no grounds to doubt that these manuscripts were written in Palestine, and that a great majority, if not all, were copied at Qumrân. It may also be considered as established that, with the exception of some odd items, the bulk of the manuscripts in the Qumrân library was copied within a span of not much more than three hundred years, approxi-

---

[1] On the *pēšer*, cf. also pp. 225 ff.

mately from the beginning of the third century B.C. to the middle of the first century A.D. In view of these circumstances, the marked diversity of textual traditions which can be observed in these scrolls presumably derives from the temporal and/or geographical heterogeneity of the *Vorlagen* from which the Qumrân manuscripts, or some of them, were copied. Thus, in addition to the horizontal cross-section view of the text at Qumrân during the last phases of the Second Commonwealth period, this material also affords a vertical cross-section view of the transmission of the text, which reflects different chronological layers, geographical areas and social strata. These circumstances further enhance the similarity of the problems relating to the text at Qumrân with those appertaining to the wider issue of the relations of the Massoretic text and the versions and, therefore, give rise to new definitions of their historical development.

XI

Before presenting in detail the impact of the Judaean Desert Scrolls on existing theories of the text-history of the Old Testament and their importance for the formation of new theories, it may be useful to summarise the main conclusions which can be drawn from the material published up to the present.

(1) Different books of the Old Testament differ in their textual history and furnish different sets of problems. Restraint should therefore be exercised in subjecting textual processes observed in one book to an analysis which is based on the analogy of issues which obtain in another book. In the last resort, the textual development of almost each individual book must be viewed separately. Thus we can observe in the Hebrew tradition of the Pentateuch at Qumrân the same relative textual compactness, and the same relative sparseness of variant readings, which have already been pointed out in the Septuagint Pentateuch. On the other hand the extant copies of the book of Isaiah, and above all the complete First Isaiah Scroll (1QIs^a), present us with a veritable crop of *variae lectiones*. It has moreover become quite clear that, e.g., the book of Samuel and the book of Jeremiah were current at the time in clearly discernible deviant Hebrew text-traditions. All this goes to show that the text of these and similar books was still in a state of flux. Only a careful synopsis of the results achieved by a detailed analysis

of the individual books may ultimately lead to more general conclusions with regard to the over-all history of the Old Testament text.

(2) The Hebrew scrolls from Qumrân prove beyond doubt the actual existence of variant readings in the biblical books of the hellenistic and Roman periods which until their discovery had been beyond the scope of textual research proper. They have added a kaleidoscopic wealth of individual readings for practically all books of the Old Testament, represented in the Qumrân library whether by substantial manuscript finds or sometimes even by only small fragments. Some of these *variae lectiones* are to be found also in:

(*a*) the textual traditions of the main versions, in Hebrew or in translation;

(*b*) quotations in post-biblical writings (Apocrypha, early Christian, hellenistic-Jewish and rabbinic literature); and even

(*c*) medieval Hebrew manuscripts.

In view of the arguments presented earlier, we may assume a genetic relationship between Qumrân variants and identical or similar readings found in the first two sets of the above witnesses which precede the final stabilisation of the Hebrew text. As against this it is probable that the comparatively rare congruence of *variae lectiones* in the third group, i.e. in medieval Hebrew manuscripts or in medieval Jewish commentaries with Qumrân readings, is merely accidental. In most instances the similarity seems to have been caused by the equal but independent impact of the same scribal habits on widely separated sets of manuscripts.

(3) All the extant major versions of the Old Testament, as we know them today, are already represented in Qumrân manuscripts, not only in individual readings, but also in the form of prototypes of their textual traditions. This observation applies principally to the Hebrew Massoretic and the Samaritan (Pentateuch) versions, and to the Septuagint. But manifold affinities with the Aramaic Targums, the Syriac Peshiṭta, and in rare cases even with Jerome's comparatively late Vulgate (end of fourth century A.D.) can also be observed. It is self-evident that this circumstance will weigh heavily in the appreciation of the individual development of these sources and of their common history.

XII

In view of the foregoing presentation of the manuscript finds from Qumrân, it can hardly cause surprise that these discoveries required a reopening of the inquiry into the history of the Old Testament. The resulting scholarly discussion of this issue, and not a mere comparative textual research into the diverse versions, brought about a renewed confrontation of the rival theories of Rosenmueller in Lagarde's version of it, and of Kahle. On the one hand it was claimed with full justification that the presence of the prototype of the Massoretic text among the Qumrân manuscript finds, e.g. in fragments of the Pentateuch or the Second Isaiah Scroll (1QIs^b) and others, proved the existence of an early precursor of the *textus receptus* at a time which considerably preceded the date presupposed by the followers of the *Ur-recension* and the *Ur-text* schools. On the other hand it was argued that the 'vulgar texts' theory is fully vindicated by the host of textual variants and also of clearly discernible different textual traditions in the bulk of the Qumrân material. The stalemate that resulted from the *pro* and *contra* arguments which could now be buttressed by tangible evidence, unlike the situation which obtained in the stage of the discussion referred to above, again became the point of departure for the conception of a novel theory.

The foundations for a new interpretation of the available material were laid by W. F. Albright.[1] His ideas were soon embraced by a group of predominantly American scholars, and were further developed and succinctly summarised by F. M. Cross:

Any reconstruction of the biblical text before the establishment of the traditional text in the first century A.D. must comprehend this evidence: the plurality of text-types, the limited number of distinct textual families, and the homogeneity of each of these textual families over several centuries of time. We are required by these data...to recognize the existence of *local texts* which developed in the main centers of Jewish life in the Persian and hellenistic age.[2]

[1] W. F. Albright, 'New Light on Early Recensions of the Hebrew Bible', *BASOR*, 140 (1955), 27–33.

[2] F. M. Cross, jun., 'The Contribution of the Qumrân Discoveries to the Study of the Biblical Text', *IEJ*, XVI (1966), 85. The author's preceding studies of this problem are listed in the notes to that article.

After at first accepting Albright's terminology, Cross is to be commended for subsequently introducing a significant change of terms into the system advocated by Albright who had referred to 'local recensions'. Says Cross:

Against Albright, we should argue, however, that the local textual families in question are not properly called 'recensions'. They are the product of natural growth or development in the process of scribal transmission, not of conscious or controlled textual recension.[1]

These considerations are in line with the arguments presented above, and disclose a welcome recognition of the fallacy of the concept of a 'scholastic-academy recension', a concept which haunted practically all preceding theories about the history of the text. However, notwithstanding this difference, the 'local recensions' theory in its 'local texts' variation absorbed some prominent features of its predecessors which it built into its own system, as will be shown. The following quotation summarises the basic concepts of the new school:

Three textual families appear to have developed slowly between the fifth and first centuries B.C., in Palestine, in Egypt, and in a third locality, presumably Babylon. The Palestinian family is characterized by conflation, glosses, synoptic additions and other evidence of intense scribal activity, and can be defined as 'expansionistic'. The Egyptian text-type is often but not always a full text. In the Pentateuch, for example, it has not suffered the extensive synoptic additions which mark the late Palestinian text, but is not so short or pristine as the third or Babylonian family. The Egyptian and Palestinian families are closely related. Early exemplars of the Palestinian text in the Former Prophets, and pentateuchal texts which reflect an early stage of the Palestinian tradition, so nearly merge with the Egyptian, that we are warranted in describing the Egyptian text-type as a branch of the Old Palestinian family. The Babylonian text-type when extant is a short text. Thus far it is only known in the Pentateuch and Former Prophets. In the Pentateuch it is a conservative, often pristine text, which shows relatively little expansion, and a few traces of revision and modernising. In the books of Samuel, on the contrary, it is a poor text, marked by extensive haplography and corruption.[2]

An analysis of the above quotation discloses the dependence of the 'local texts' theory on its predecessors. It may be described as a new synthesis, arrived at by sifting the major contentions of earlier views,

[1] *Ibid.* note 21.   [2] *Ibid.* p. 86.

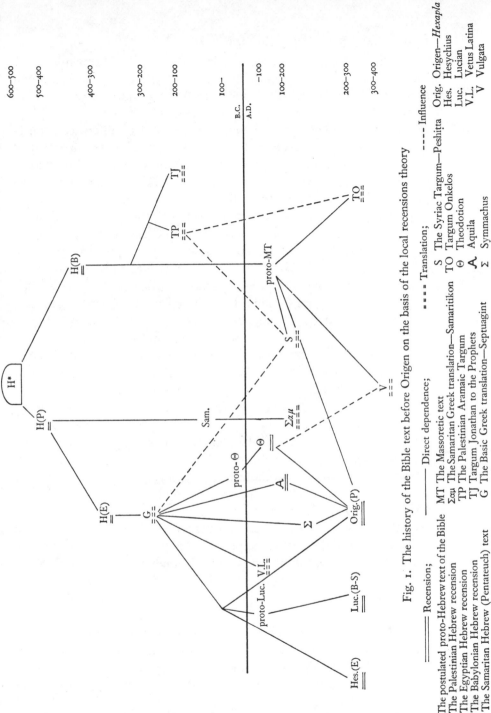

Fig. 1. The history of the Bible text before Origen on the basis of the local recensions theory

═══ Recension;   ──── Direct dependence;   ╌╌╌ Influence   ■■■ Translation;

H*   The postulated proto-Hebrew text of the Bible
H(P) The Palestinian Hebrew recension
H(E) The Egyptian Hebrew recension
H(B) The Babylonian Hebrew recension
Sam. The Samaritan Hebrew (Pentateuch) text

MT   The Massoretic text
Σαμ   The Samaritan Greek translation—Samaritikon
TP   The Palestinian Aramaic Targum
TJ   Targum Jonathan to the Prophets
G   The Basic Greek translation—Septuagint

S   The Syriac Targum—Peshitta   Orig. Origen—Hexapla
TO   Targum Onkelos   Hes.   Hesychius
Θ   Theodotion   Luc.   Lucian
A   Aquila   V.L.   Vetus Latina
Σ   Symmachus   V   Vulgata

discarding some items and maintaining others, and subsequently welding them into a novel structure. It is interesting to remark that although initially the conceivers of the 'local recensions/texts' theory seemed to view themselves as being in line with the basic ideas of the Lagarde–Rosenmueller school, in later presentations of it no reference is made to the *Ur-text/Ur-recension* theory. The very concept of solidified textual traditions, however, whatever term may be applied to characterise them, is apparently tacitly accepted. Further, the assumption of *three* 'local recensions' or 'traditions' is not intrinsically opposed to the 'one recension/manuscript' theory. Of the presupposed three textual recensions or families, in fact only one, namely the Palestinian, has some claim to having been presented by the proponents of the 'three local texts' school as an independent, fairly clearly circumscribed entity, recognisable by specific textual peculiarities. The so-called 'Egyptian' text-type is regarded as derived from the Palestinian, and is presumed to have broken off from it at some time in the early fourth century to begin its independent development. The definition of the third family is not too clear either and its locale can be defined only as being 'presumably Babylon'. This text also obviously originated in Palestine, but had come into final form in Babylon in the sixth century. It is assumed that it had developed there during the interval between the fifth and the second centuries B.C., was reintroduced into Palestine some time after the Maccabean period, and by the end of the first century A.D. had established itself as the dominant or standard Jewish text.[1] Without stating it explicitly, the 'local texts' theory appears to presuppose the existence of an *Ur-text* in Palestine at some time before the Babylonian Exile from which the two major types, the Babylonian and the Palestinian, and the latter's derivative, the Egyptian, emerged at later stages in the post-exilic period. It appears that as a result of the now available material, which is several hundred years older than the material on which scholars of the 'pre-Qumrân' generations could base their arguments, the date of the implied *Ur-text* is also pushed back by some centuries.

In a way, the new theory in its major aspects also resembles Sperber's parallel-transmission system. Both assume different locales for the emergence of the different traditions: here post-exilic Palestine and Babylon; there pre-exilic North and South Palestine. Again we are

[1] *Ibid.* p. 91.

transported into the realm of purely hypothetical statements, arrived at by deductions and reconstructions which lack any material, i.e. manuscript, basis.

The very idea of 'local' texts underlies not only Sperber's 'two traditions' theory, but also the system of 'three manuscript types' elaborated by Lieberman, who had not only already posited a tripartition of the biblical textual tradition, but had also affiliated the diverse manuscript types with different types of localities, though in Palestine. One further point is to be noted, namely that the differentiation in value between a standard/received and a vulgar text, introduced into the discussion by Kahle, had been taken up with significant variations in Lieberman's distinction between 'inferior local school texts', 'Jerusalem vulgar manuscripts', and the 'most exact copies of the temple'. Such a value judgement is now applied again by Cross to characterise his three local families: the Palestinian text is conflate and expansionistic, the Egyptian is presented as a predominantly full text, and the Babylonian, in the main, as a short pristine tradition. The shortcomings of this characterisation become apparent when it is applied in detail to the textual tradition of different biblical books in the families thus distinguished. It then transpires that, as if refusing to submit to the scholar's natural quest for order, in the books of Samuel, for example, the Babylonian, somewhat unexpectedly, 'is a poor text, marked by extensive haplography and corruptions'.

One cannot help suspecting that the proposed tripartition of the Old Testament text tradition into a Palestinian, a Babylonian and an Egyptian family in some way echoes the widely accepted three-pronged transmission of the New Testament text in Palestinian, Antiochian (Syrian) and Egyptian versions. Though in itself such a transfer of theories is certainly permissible and could be constructive, it remains doubtful whether in the present case it can be justified in view of the differing attitudes which the Synagogue and the Church took towards the text transmission of their holy scriptures. It has been pointed out above that whereas the former strove gradually to abolish deviant readings and text-types, the latter, possibly because of its heterogeneous composition, attempted to accommodate the diverse traditions that had emerged in the main daughter churches. An unqualified application of a theory which arises from an investigation into the history of the New Testament text to the history of the Old Testament text perforce results in a distortion of the issue and in yet-to-be-proved, or unprovable, hypotheses.

Summing up, we may say that in spite of its appeal the 'three local texts' theory cannot really explain satisfactorily the 'plurality of text-types' at the end of the pre-Christian era. It could indeed account for the 'limited number of distinct textual families' extant at that time. But one is inclined to attribute this feature of the text transmission to two factors: (*a*) historical vicissitudes which caused other textual families to disappear; (*b*) the necessary socio-religious conditions for the preservation of a text-tradition, namely its acceptance by a sociologically integrated and definable body. It is this latter aspect of the problem which safeguarded the preservation of the (proto-)Massoretic text which ultimately became the standard text of the Synagogue, the Samaritan Hebrew Pentateuch version which gained authoritative status in the Samaritan community, the Greek Bible that was hallowed by the Church, and the diverse textual traditions saved for us by the Judaean Desert Covenanters in a form from before standardisation. This tradition complex should be viewed as representing the remains of a yet more variegated transmission of the Old Testament books. Contradictory as it may sound, one is almost inclined to say that the question to be answered with regard to the history of the Old Testament text does not arise from the extant 'plurality of text-types' but rather from the disappearance of other and more numerous textual traditions.

These considerations do not necessarily call for an unqualified acceptance of Kahle's theory of a '*textus receptus* and vulgar texts' which, as already stated, suffers from the over-emphasis put on presupposed but unsubstantiated conscious, official redaction processes. All we can say is that from the very first stage of manuscript transmission of the Old Testament text the material which is available to us witnesses to a wide variety of textual traditions which seemingly mirror fairly exactly the state of affairs which obtained in the pre-manuscript state of transmission. In other words, the extant evidence imposes on us the conclusion that from the very first stage of its manuscript transmission, the Old Testament text was known in a variety of traditions which differed from each other to a greater or less degree. As a result of undirected, and possibly in part also of controlled, processes of elimination, the majority of these variations went out of use. The remaining traditions achieved by and by the status of a *textus receptus* within the socio-religious communities which perpetuated them. These standardised texts were preserved for us in the major versions of the Hebrew Bible and its translations.

8. BIBLE AND MIDRASH: EARLY OLD TESTAMENT EXEGESIS

Although intertestamental and rabbinic Judaism may correctly be defined as a 'religion of the Book', religion in which practice and belief derive from the study and interpretation of scripture, it would be false to assume that biblical exegesis itself is essentially and necessarily a post-biblical phenomenon. No one familiar with the Old Testament can fail to observe the repeated emphasis laid by some of its authors on the obligation to meditate on, recite, and rethink the Law. It was no doubt a midrashic process such as this which was partly responsible for the formulation of the more recent legal codes, the Deuteronomic and the Priestly, and its influence becomes even more apparent in post-exilic literature (Chronicles and Daniel) and certain of the Apocrypha (Ecclesiasticus). Post-biblical midrash is to be distinguished from the biblical only by an external factor, canonisation. By common though mysterious consent, and using criteria which largely elude us, the Palestinian religious authorities decided, probably at about the end of the third century B.C., to arrest the growth of sacred writings and establish a canon. With one exception, Daniel, their policy was successfully carried through, and from then on the nation's religious and moral guidance was entrusted not to writers but to interpreters. Yet the old tendency to express all fresh insight in the form of new compositions did not vanish without putting up valiant resistance, as is manifest in the Septuagint canon (by nature more receptive than the Palestinian) and to a lesser extent in the integration of commentary and scripture found, for instance, in the Palestinian Targums, some of the Pseudepigrapha, and Josephus' *Jewish Antiquities*.

In order to understand the nature and purpose of midrash, it is necessary to glance briefly at those biblical passages which foreshadow and prompt the discipline of exegesis. The earliest relevant material appears in the Deuteronomic corpus. As the book of Deuteronomy itself takes the form of a repetition of the Law by Moses before his death, it is not surprising that the school which transmitted and developed its message should have attached prime importance to a renewed study of the Torah. It was to be the Book of Meditation for every pious Jew, great and humble. Believed in its time to offer the most complete and up-to-date version of the 'Mosaic' code, it was to be the daily *vade mecum* of the king.

And when he sits on the throne of his kingdom, he shall write for himself in a book a copy of this law, from that which is in charge of the Levitical priests; and it shall be with him, and he shall read in it all the days of his life, that he may learn to fear the LORD his God, by keeping all the words of this law and these statutes, and doing them. (Deut. 17: 18–19)

Again, the Deuteronomic preface to the book of Joshua records a divine command according to which the Law was to remain permanently on the lips of Moses' successor and the subject of his uninterrupted meditation.

Only be strong. . . being careful to do according to all the law which Moses my servant commanded you. . . This book of the law shall not depart out of your mouth, but you shall meditate on it day and night, that you may be careful to do according to all that is written in it; for then you shall make your way prosperous, and then you shall have good success. (Josh. 1: 7–8)

Soon the same admonition was extended to all Israel, and the righteous man, characterised negatively by the Psalmist as one who 'walks not in the counsel of the wicked', is described positively as a Torah student whose 'delight is in the law of the LORD', on which 'he meditates day and night' (Ps. 1: 1–2 f. Cf. Josh. 1: 7–8; 1 QS VI, 6–7). His familiarity with that Law, later identified by ben Sira as the eternal and creative divine Wisdom itself (Ecclus. 24: 23), implied a real contact with God and insight into the mysteries of heaven.

In time, this wide preoccupation with the Bible created a demand for authoritative interpreters, and a particular class of men emerged from the ranks of the priests and Levites whose whole business was professional exegesis. According to ben Sira, who was one of them, the *sopher*, or scribe, is

he who devotes himself to the study of the law of the Most High. . . If the great Lord is willing, he will be filled with the spirit of understanding. He will pour forth words of wisdom and give thanks to the Lord in prayer. He will direct his counsel and knowledge aright and meditate on his secrets. He will reveal instruction in his teaching, and will glory in the law of the Lord's covenant. (Ecclus. 39: 1–8)

The most famous of the scribes was Ezra, and it is in connection with him that scripture interpretation as such is first mentioned in the Bible. His celebrated reform was inaugurated by a solemn and public reading of the 'book of the law of Moses which the LORD had given to Israel' (Neh. 8: 1), followed by an exposition delivered by Levitical scribes who 'read from the book, from the law of God, clearly (or "with interpretation"); and they gave the sense, so that the people understood the reading' (Neh. 8: 7–8). If it is true that by that time the Babylonian exiles spoke Aramaic, such an interpretation may also have entailed a translation into the vernacular. In any case, rabbinic tradition sees in this episode the origin of a new institution, Targum, or translation-interpretation.[1]

The public recitation of scripture which was part of Temple worship became the essential feature of synagogal liturgy already in pre-Christian times and appears in the New Testament as a well-established custom (cf. Luke 4: 16 ff.). According to Mishnah Megillah 3, the Pentateuch was read section by section, i.e. continuously, from Genesis 1 to Deuteronomy 34, and each recitation was followed by an appropriate passage, known as the *haphtarah*, chosen from the Former and Latter Prophets. Both Torah and *haphtarah* were accompanied verse by verse by an Aramaic Targum. Whether the hellenistic communities used a parallel Greek Targum is still open to question. In short, the Bible, correctly interpreted, became the legal charter of national life, the foundation of public worship, the unique source of inspiration for individual piety, and a text-book for the schooling of young and old. Judaism's most treasured possession, its study and observance were thought to constitute at all times, during the eschatological age also, the quintessence of religion. No counsel among the Sayings of the Fathers (*Pirke Aboth*) is urged more pressingly than meditation on the Torah, and in apocalyptic and Qumrân thought it was a return to this study that was to herald the onset of the final age.

In those days, children shall begin to study the laws and to seek the commandments, and to return to the path of righteousness. (Jub. 23: 26)

---

[1] Cf. Y. Meg. 4, 74*d*.

And when these become members of the Community, they shall. . . go into the wilderness to prepare the way of Him; as it is written, Prepare in the wilderness the way of (YHWH); make straight in the desert a path for our God (Isa. 40: 3). This (path) is the *midrash* of the Law which He commanded by the hand of Moses, that they may do according to all that has been revealed from age to age, and as the Prophets have revealed by His holy spirit. (1 QS VIII, 12–16)

This brief discussion of the origins of Bible interpretation will have given some general idea of the nature of the demand to which creative midrashic literature responded between the third century B.C. and the fourth century A.D. To understand it more exactly it is necessary to take a closer look at the intellectual and religious needs of early post-biblical Jewry. What sort of problems was the interpreter expected to handle?

Some arose from linguistic difficulties and from real or imaginary gaps in the original Hebrew text. Others resulted from a failure on the part of the compilers of the laws to unify and harmonise contradictory excerpts selected from sources of diverse historical and geographical origin. Again, the development of ideas and evolution of customs often rendered the scriptural record of earlier times not only unacceptable but offensive. Matters such as these were dealt with by what may be termed 'pure' exegesis.

Another type of problem sprang from the conviction that the Bible conveys the full divine message to Israel and that every possible question is given its answer there. Religious teachers, therefore, confronted with new situations unforeseen by the legislators, found themselves faced with the task of associating them with that message and of giving them scriptural relevance. In addition, Palestinian Jewry was divided, from the second century B.C. to the end of the Second Temple, into separate and rival groups (Pharisees, Sadducees, Essenes, Judaeo-Christians) each of which slanted its interpretative system to justify the biblical authenticity of its beliefs and way of life. Here then were two other demands: exegesis was required to adapt and complete scripture so that it might on the one hand apply to the present time, and on the other, satisfy the requirements of polemics. The resulting form of interpretation, which is not primarily concerned with the immediate meaning of the text but with the discovery of principles providing a non-scriptural problem with a scriptural solution, may be called 'applied' exegesis.

Since the historical study of midrash, and particularly of haggadah, is still in its infancy, I have chosen to avoid dogmatic generalisations in the present discussion. I have also judged it wisest, bearing in mind that to many this is unfamiliar territory, to proceed by way of examples intended to illustrate the various facets of ancient Jewish Bible exegesis. It is hoped that as a whole they will project a sufficiently clear image of a highly complex reality.

At this juncture it should be remembered that the ancient versions of the Bible are themselves also part of exegetical literature. A considerable amount of interpretative material found its way into the Septuagint, the Palestinian Targums, and occasionally the Peshiṭta, only to be more or less thoroughly eliminated in the subsequent revisions or translations of Aquila, Symmachus, Theodotion and Onkelos. Needless to say, we are concerned exclusively with these non-literal elements.

'PURE' EXEGESIS

As has been shown, from the point of view of its *Sitz im Leben* 'pure' exegesis owes its existence to four principal causes: (i) a scriptural passage contains a word whose exact meaning escaped the interpreter; (ii) it lacks sufficient detail; (iii) it seems to contradict other biblical texts; (iv) its apparent meaning is unacceptable.

(i)

The most obvious instance of philological difficulty requiring specific exegesis is the presence in the Hebrew text of an unfamiliar foreign term. Two such words occurring in Genesis 41 greatly disconcerted ancient readers. In verse 43 we read that when Pharaoh appointed Joseph as his viceroy and sent him, seated in his second chariot, to tour the capital, 'they cried before him, '*abrēk*', an Egyptian phrase variously translated by modern scholars as 'Attention'[1] or, on the assumption that the Egyptians borrowed the Semitic root *brk*, 'Pay homage'.[2]

With the exception of Aquila and Jerome, who by rendering '*abrēk* as 'genuflect' derive the meaning directly from the Hebrew *bārak*

[1] W. Spiegelberg, 'Correspondences du temps des rois-prêtres', *Notices et extraits des manuscrits de la Bibliothèque Nationale*, XXXIV, 2 (1895), 261.

[2] J. Vergote, *Joseph en Égypte* (Louvain, 1959), pp. 138–40.

(and thereby, if Vergote is right, obtain a correct answer from a false premise), all the interpreters base their guesses either on the immediate context of the sentence in which the word appears, or on the general framework of the Joseph story. In the first case it is thought that the person calling out before the chariot must be a herald and we consequently read κῆρυξ and *praeco* in the Septuagint and the Vulgate. In the second, *'aḇrēḵ* is taken to be a title given to Joseph by Pharaoh. Jubilees 40: 7, for example, recognising in *'br* of *'aḇrēḵ* the Hebrew word *'abbîr*, mighty, renders it, 'God, God, and the mighty one of God', the 'mighty one' being the chief magician according to R. H. Charles,[1] a fitting description of a successful dream-interpreter. Targum Neofiti, on the other hand, reads: 'Long live the father (*'āḇ*) of the king (cf. Gen. 45: 8), who is great in wisdom, young in beauty, tender (*rakkîḵ*) in years. And he appointed him master and ruler over the whole land of Egypt.' This interpretation is founded on a separate exegesis of the two syllables *'ab* and *rēḵ* inserted into a summary of the Joseph narrative. In Targum Onkelos and the Peshiṭta we find an abridgement of the Palestinian version, namely: 'This is the father of the king', and 'Father and ruler'.[2]

In the second passage, Gen. 41: 45, Joseph's new name, Zaphenath-paneah, is expounded similarly, though with even more imagination. The Septuagint and Jubilees 40: 10 wisely leave it alone and remain content with a more or less accurate transliteration.[3] But although the Palestinian targumists and their disciples and imitators—Josephus, Onkelos and the Peshiṭta—are also unable to make head or tail of 'paneah', they understand 'Zaphenath' to derive from *spn*, to hide, and deduce that the title is another allusion to Joseph's activities as interpreter of dreams. Hence, 'the man to whom secrets are revealed' (Targums and Peshiṭta), and 'discoverer of secrets' (Josephus).[4]

But it was not foreign words alone that presented the midrashist with a stumbling-block. Sometimes an unusual or archaic Hebrew idiom proved no less troublesome. For instance, in Gen. 4: 7 God, seeing that Cain's countenance has fallen because his sacrifice has not

---

[1] *The Apocrypha and Pseudepigrapha of the Old Testament*, II (Oxford, 1913), 71.

[2] G. Vermes, 'Haggadah in the Onkelos Targum', *JSS*, VIII (1963), 162.

[3] The LXX transcription ψονθομφανήχ is interpreted by Philo as 'mouth which judges in answer' (*De Mut. Nom.* 91).

[4] *Ant.* II, 91.

been accepted, addresses him thus: 'If you do well, *śeʾēṯ*. And if you do not do well, sin is couching at the door.' As it stands, the text makes no sense because of the elliptical use of *śeʾēṯ*, lifting up. The Septuagint sees in it a reference to a sacrificial rite and reads, 'If you make an offering rightly'; but the others hesitate. Some (Aquila, Theodotion, the Peshiṭta, the Vulgate, Gen. R. 22, 6) render it as 'you will receive a reward', thus implicitly adding *pānîm*, face, and understanding the phrase to mean that God raises his countenance towards Cain in sign of approval. In others (the Palestinian Targums, Symmachus, and to a lesser extent Onkelos), where we find, 'your transgressions will be pardoned', the implicit supplement to *śeʾēṯ* is *ʿāwôn*, sin. Targum Neofiti, for example, translates the verse: 'If you perform your deeds well in this world, it shall be loosed and forgiven you in the world to come. But if you do not perform your deeds well in this world, your sin shall be retained for the day of the Great Judgement.'

(ii)

To the second category of biblical texts demanding a midrashic solution belong those in which the writer provides only an outline of the essential features of his composition. Whatever its nature, whether juridical or narrative, the reader is left with many unanswered questions. If juridical, he is bound to inquire into the particular applicability of laws formulated in general terms. 'Thou shalt do no work on the Sabbath day.' But what is work? He will also wonder which general principle underlies a particular case-law. If narrative, he will wish to give density to the author's apparently thin story.

In the legal sphere, the law of divorce is perhaps the example *par excellence* of the necessity for halakhic midrash. On this highly important topic the Pentateuch gives no direct and general ruling at all. Deut. 24: 1–4, the only scriptural text relating to it, is a case-law envisaging not divorce as such (its existence and legality are taken for granted), but the unlawfulness of remarriage between a man and his former wife if she has married again and been divorced by her second husband or has been widowed. The actual procedure of divorce is merely hinted at, as it were accidentally, in verse 1: 'When a man takes a wife and marries her, if she then finds no favour in his eyes because he has found some indecency in her, and he writes her a bill of divorce and puts it into her hand and sends her out of his house...' In other words, a husband was obliged to deliver a written document to his wife before he ordered her to leave the matrimonial home. But his grounds for doing so—'if she finds no favour in his eyes because he has found in her *'erwat dāḇār'*, literally, a nakedness of a thing—remain most vague. To judge by the use of the same phrase in Deut. 23: 12 ff., where it is said that latrines should be situated outside the camp 'so that God may not see *'erwat dāḇār* among you',[1] the expression appears to convey the sense of something unbecoming or indecent. But what sort of indecency could constitute sufficient grounds for a man to divorce his wife?

The imprecise rendering of the Septuagint, and historical evidence available from the first century A.D., tend to suggest that the earliest exegesis of the law was very elastic. Josephus gives the following paraphrase: 'He who desires to be divorced from his wife...for whatever cause (καθ' ἁσδηποτοῦν αἰτίας), and with mortals many such may arise...' (*Ant.* IV, 253). Again, recounting his own matrimonial troubles, he writes: 'At this period, I divorced my wife, being displeased at her behaviour' (*Vita*, 426). Rabbinic sources ascribe the same happy-go-lucky outlook to the school of Hillel. In the Mishnah we read that a husband may divorce his wife 'even if she has spoiled his dinner'.[2] Aqiba too is recorded in the same passage as remarking with even more cynicism that a wife ceases to 'find favour', and thereby gives her husband lawful cause for divorce, 'if he encounters another woman prettier than she'. At the beginning of the Christian era, however, a much more stringent interpretation was introduced by Shammai, who submitted that one reason alone justified divorce, namely immorality. He arrived at this by understanding the biblical phrase *'erwat dāḇār* as a synonym of *d‘ḇar 'erwāh*, a matter of nakedness.[3] It is worth noting in this context that the Targums, and perhaps the Peshiṭta, also follow the Shammaite opinion when they render *'erwat dāḇār* as 'something sinful' or 'immoral'. The Gospel of Matthew echoes the dispute between the schools of Hillel and Shammai. The question put by a group of Pharisees to Jesus, 'Is it lawful to divorce one's wife *for any cause*?' (Matt. 19: 3), is formulated in Hillelite terms and receives a Shammaite response: no, 'except for unchastity' (Matt. 19: 9; 5: 32). Philo also appears to have held a view not unlike

---

[1] See LXX and 1JT. Cf. also Deut. 24: 1(LXX).
[2] Gitt. 9, 10.   [3] *Ibid.* Cf. Deut. 22: 13 ff.

that of Jesus.[1] Clearly, a conflict developed between religious teachers favouring the maximum amount of latitude and those desiring to tighten the law. For the latter, the general principle of 'immorality' needed to be defined. What exactly was meant by *dᵉbar 'erwāh*? It was not to be understood as adultery, a crime calling for death. It must therefore be of a milder kind, such as the display by a married woman of uncovered head or arms.[2] The argument of the lenient was no doubt that the vagueness of Deut. 24: 1 ff. was deliberate, and that if the Lawgiver had wished to impose a more severe rule, he would have done so. For their opponents that same vagueness called for amplification and definition.

A patchy and incomplete biblical narrative required exegesis of quite a different kind to the one just described. Gen. 12: 10–19, presenting the story of Sarah's unpleasant adventure in Egypt, confronts the reader with a number of uncertainties. How did Abraham know that his life would be endangered if the Egyptians learnt that his companion was his wife? What actually happened to Sarah in Pharaoh's harem? How did Pharaoh discover the cause of the calamities which befell his house? To the first of these questions, haggadah gives two answers, one rational, the other tinged with the supernatural.

The rational explanation appears in Josephus' account: Abraham decided to take precautions because he was aware of the Egyptian lust for women,[3] proverbial in midrash. We read, for instance, that if the Pharaoh of Exodus allowed newly born Israelite girls to live whilst the boys were to die, this was 'because the Egyptians were carried away by carnal passion'.[4]

The supernatural interpretation is found, in a somewhat mutilated context, in the Qumrân Genesis Apocryphon, where the story is told of Abraham's dream on the night of his arrival with Sarah in Egypt.

I saw in my dream a cedar tree and a palm tree... Men came and sought to cut down the cedar tree and to pull up its roots, leaving the palm tree alone. But the palm tree cried out saying, 'Do not cut down this cedar tree, for cursed be he who shall fell (it).' And the cedar tree was spared because of the palm tree and (was) not felled. (1QGA XIX, 14–17)

Abraham who, according to Jewish legend, was a miracle-worker and

---

[1] *De Spec. Leg.* III, 30 f.   [2] Y. Gitt. 9, 50*d*.
[3] *Ant.* I, 162.   [4] Exod. R. I, 22.

an interpreter of dreams, immediately realised the significance of his vision and made appropriate arrangements.

As for the infinitely more delicate subject of Sarah's fate in Pharaoh's house, the reassuring answer is given everywhere that she escaped untouched; but the details differ greatly. Josephus, with his inclination towards the natural, asserts that Sarah's virtue was saved by an 'outbreak of disease and political disturbance';[1] but in another version of the story even he introduces the supernatural by stating that Abraham's prayer secured for her an invincible Protector, and that anyway her absence only lasted for one night.[2] Rabbinic exegesis follows in the same vein with an account of a guardian angel armed with a whip with which to keep the king at a safe distance during that one night.[3] Genesis Apocryphon goes still further, explaining that although the unfortunate woman remained in the royal palace for two full years, 'an evil spirit' sent by God continued to scourge Pharaoh during that time so that 'he was unable to approach her and he knew her not'. (1QGA XX, 16–18)

The third question—how did Pharaoh discover that Sarah was a married woman?—leaves tradition deeply divided. In a late haggadah ascribed to Rabbi Levi (c. A.D. 300), the secret was disclosed by Sarah herself: 'She told him repeatedly, I am a married woman; but he would not leave.'[4] But hellenistic Jewish exegesis provides the story with a backcloth of Egyptian priests or magicians. Josephus recounts that when Pharaoh decided to offer sacrifice in order to discover a cure for the plague, 'the priests declared that this calamity was due to the wrath of God because he had wished to outrage the stranger's wife' (*Ant.* I, 164). Eupolemus also credits the magicians of Egypt with the revelation of Sarah's true identity.[5] The author of Genesis Apocryphon, on the other hand, mentions the 'magicians and healers', not in relation to Sarah but as failing to cure the king. It is because of their inadequacy that Abraham is appealed to for help by Pharaoh's envoy, who learns the truth from Lot.[6]

However naïve some of these interpretations may appear to readers accustomed to modern methods of criticism, they correspond to real lacunae in law or narrative. It is impossible to say when the need for them first arose; the date of the sources in which they are preserved

---

[1] *Ant.* I, 164. [2] *B.J.* V, 380–1. [3] Gen. R. 40 (41), 2.
[4] *Ibid.* [5] Eus. *Praep. ev.* IX, 17. [6] 1QGA XX, 22–3.

may indicate simply a *terminus ante quem*. Whether Bible interpretation occasionally originates in unwritten tradition going back to biblical times cannot be proved, but a few facts are worth considering.

First, biblical law was part of the real life of the community before, as well as after, the Exile. As such it was bound to be accompanied by a legal commentary, especially when the wording of the law itself is imprecise. This commentary was not affected by the canonisation of the Torah, and the earliest exegetical traditions doubtless derive from, and may sometimes even be identical with, the immediate pre-canonical understanding of the Bible.

Secondly, is it not reasonable to assume that a great many gaps in the narrative sections, similar to those considered above, are due to the redactional activity of scribes responsible for the final 'edition' of the Pentateuch? If so, they themselves knew what they had omitted and they may, to say the least, have handed down the necessary supplements by way of exegesis. Would it be too extravagant to suggest that the permissive interpretation of the divorce law, or the comment that Sarah's absence lasted for only one night, may belong to the pre-Ezra period? The following section will, it is hoped, add substance to this tentative hypothesis.

(iii)

The first and foremost of all exegetical imperatives was harmonisation and reconciliation. A religion which recognised the totality of its scriptures as word of God and rule of life could not accept that some legal and historical biblical passages disagree, and even flatly contradict one another.

The laws relating to the status of the Israelite slave-woman provide an illuminating example of disparities in biblical legislation and the manner in which they were resolved. According to the Code of the Covenant, the earliest of the sources, a male Hebrew slave has the right to obtain his freedom during the Sabbatical year, but he may instead choose to remain in servitude for life (Exod. 21: 2–6). This right to liberty does not, however, extend to the slave-woman. Exod. 21: 7 expressly states: 'If a man sells his daughter as a slave, she shall not go out as the male slaves do.' Deuteronomic law reiterates the male slave's possible choice between going free and remaining a 'bondman for ever', but adds that he may not be sent away empty-handed but must be recompensed liberally with grain, wine and livestock to the amount of half the wages for six years of a 'hired servant' (Deut. 15: 12–18). So far, therefore, there is no great difference between this and the earlier Code. But when Deuteronomy goes on to award equal status to the woman slave, the divergence is marked. In what is obviously a gloss, her eventual freedom is foreseen as well as that of the man. 'If your brother, a Hebrew man, *or Hebrew woman*, is sold to you...you shall let him go free from you' (*v.* 12). It is also said that the ceremony transforming the slave into a perpetual bondman is to be similarly performed for the woman (*v.* 17).

The Priestly legislation takes over and liberalises further the Deuteronomic rule. Though no special reference is made to Israelite women, it is clear from the whole tone of the paragraph that both sexes are to be employed as hired servants and not as slaves proper. They are to be released from their bond, probably each seventh year, but certainly in each year of Jubilee. The superior status of the temporary Israelite servant appears in relief against that of the lifelong Gentile slave, the permanent property of his master's family:

You may buy male and female slaves from among the nations...You may bequeath them to your sons...to inherit as a possession for ever. You may make slaves of them, but over your brethren...you shall not rule, one over another, with harshness. (Lev. 25: (39) 44–6)

Faced with three versions of the one law, what were the interpreters to think? They found no great difficulty in combining Deuteronomy and Leviticus since they supplement one another,[1] but how were they to reconcile them with the rigorous directive appearing in Exodus, according to which the woman slave is to be used differently from her male counterpart and 'shall not go out as the male slaves do'? Since their life was governed by the more recent law, they concluded that it was the text of the older legal concept that needed reinterpretation.

Z. Frankel[2] and A. Geiger[3] pointed out more than a century ago that a deliberate distinction tending to suppress the contradiction between Exodus and Leviticus–Deuteronomy appears already in the Septuagint version of the Exodus passage, where a Hebrew female

[1] See, e.g., Jos., *Ant.* IV, 273.
[2] *Ueber den Einfluss der palästinischen Exegese auf die alexandrinische Hermeneutik* (Leipzig, 1851), p. 91.
[3] *Urschrift und Uebersetzungen der Bibel in ihrer Abhängigkeit von der innern Entwickelung des Judenthums* (Breslau, 1857), pp. 187–8.

slave is rendered as οἰκέτις, housemaid, and not δούλη, slave-woman. The inference seems to be that 'she shall not go out as the male slaves do' means, not that a Hebrew maidservant is never to be freed, but that the rules concerning her liberation differ from those affecting the Gentile slave, *'ebed* or δοῦλος: a Jewish servant would be termed a *śākîr* or μισθωτός.[1]

If this assumption is correct, as I believe it is, the oldest exegetical evidence reasons as follows. Deuteronomy postulates that the Hebrew slaves, men and women, are to 'go out' in the seventh year. The Code of the Covenant does not contradict Deuteronomy: it merely appears to do so. In fact, the conflict vanishes as soon as it is understood that Exod. 21: 7 contrasts the lot of the Hebrew woman-servant with that of a Gentile, and not an Israelite, slave.

Such an exegesis provokes a new question. If Exod. 21: 7 refers to Gentile slaves, how can their 'going out' be reconciled with Leviticus, according to which they are to be 'bondmen for ever'? The answer is incorporated in the Mekhilta[2] and the Targum of Pseudo-Jonathan. Slaves, says Exod. 21: 26–7, are to receive their liberty in compensation for the loss of an eye or a tooth. Since it is inconceivable that a fellow-Jew should be treated so harshly, this law must apply to the non-Israelite slave. The liberation of Hebrew slaves, the commentaries continue, is regulated by Leviticus and Deuteronomy: they 'go out' in Sabbatical and Jubilee years.

This argument was nevertheless not entirely satisfactory and another interpretation came into being in which the text of Exodus is understood to allude to Hebrew slaves. For this meaning to be rendered acceptable, the exegetes had to find some special occasion, additional to the customary years of release, for the emancipation of the Israelite slave-woman. For motives not wholly clear, this was recognised to be the onset of puberty or the attainment of the girl's majority at the age of twelve years, whichever came first—implying, incidentally, that a father was entitled to sell his daughter only while she was a minor. The custom has all the appearance of being secondary in relation to scripture: i.e. of deriving not from interpretation proper but from legal reasoning.[3]

The latter exegesis is almost certainly the more recent of the two.

[1] See Lev. 25: 40; Philo, *De Spec. Leg.* II, 85.   [2] Ed. Lauterbach, 3, 24.
[3] *Ibid.* 3, 18–19.

But whereas the Mekhilta includes them both, keeping them separate, the Mishnah repeats only the later one, stating that in addition to being released during Sabbatical and Jubilee years, 'The Hebrew bondmaid acquires her freedom also through the tokens'.[1] In Targum Pseudo-Jonathan on Exod. 21: 7, the two arguments are skilfully amalgamated:

If a man, a son of Israel, sells his daughter, a minor, to be a bondmaid, she shall not go out as do the Canaanite slaves who gain liberty through a tooth and an eye, but in the years of Release, through the tokens, at the Jubilee, the death of her master[2] and through payment of money.[3]

Here, the harmonisation of all the relevant biblical laws, and the two types of interpretation, reaches perfection and the task of exegesis is completed.

Reconciliation of contradictory narratives entails a process not unlike that used in relation to problematic legal texts and is illustrated briefly in the following summary of an analysis published elsewhere[4] of the exegesis of the Balaam story.

As is known, together with the older JE account (Num. 22–4; Mic. 6: 5) the Bible preserves an additional series of Deuteronomic and Priestly fragments (Num. 31: 8, 16; Deut. 23: 5–6; Josh. 13: 22; 24: 9–10; Neh. 13: 2). The two collections present very different portraits of the principal figure. In the earlier tradition (with the exception of two probable glosses (Num. 22: 22; 24: 1)), Balaam is exonerated from blame and Balak and the Moabites appear as the chief culprits. The prophet refuses to accept their invitation unless authorised by God and is unwilling to utter a word without the prompting of the divine spirit. He expresses his readiness to return home after his meeting with the hostile angel. Throughout his mission, and despite the pressure brought to bear on him by the Moabites, he remains faithful to his original words: 'Though Balak were to give me his house full of silver and gold, I could not go beyond the command of the LORD my God' (Num. 22: 18. Cf. 22: 35; 23: 3, 26; 24: 12 f.). The narrative contains no criticism or reproach; its final words read, 'Then Balaam rose and went back to his place' (Num. 24: 25). Although the Deuteronomic

---

[1] Kidd. 1, 2. Cf. Rashi on Exod. 21: 7.   [2] Cf. Lev. 25: 45–6.
[3] Cf. Exod. 21: 8.
[4] G. Vermes, *Scripture and Tradition in Judaism* (Leiden, 1961), pp. 127–77.

supplements are also mainly anti-Moabite, they adopt a more partisan approach than Num. 22–4. Balaam comes to Moab with the intention of cursing Israel but is prevented by God from accomplishing his plan (Deut. 23: 5 f.; Josh. 24: 9 f.; Neh. 13: 2). In the Priestly tradition, the story is given a very different slant. Balaam is held responsible for the wicked advice to Balak that he should seduce the Israelites and lead them into sin by means of the Moabite women, and also for the death of the twenty-four thousand who perished of the subsequent plague (cf. Num. 25). It was in revenge that the Israelites 'slew Balaam the son of Beor with the sword' (Num. 31: 8, 15 f.; Josh. 13: 22).

The Priestly tradition with its emphasis on Balaam's guilt, for the interpreters the most 'modern' of the three, was the one they selected as source of inspiration. In their resulting exegesis, everything Balaam says or does is viewed with disfavour. He accepts the Moabite invitation because of his greed and vanity. He delights in curses and longs to pronounce a malediction on Israel. As one of Pharaoh's counsellors, he has already tried unsuccessfully to destroy the Israelites in Egypt and welcomes the new opportunity. He deliberately refuses to understand the divine injunction not to anathematise those blessed by God and persists in asking for permission to go to Moab even after a categorical divine refusal. Neither the miracle of the speaking ass, nor the appearance of the angel, make him see that his journey is displeasing to God, and when he is finally compelled to bless those whom he wishes to annihilate, he retaliates by providing Balak with an idea which put into practice will destroy the Hebrews. Balaam in fact becomes the arch-villain, *Bil'ām hā-rāšā'*. Once more, exegetical tradition, represented not only by Talmud, Targum and Midrash, but also by Philo, Josephus and the New Testament, solves the dilemma arising from conflicting accounts by integrating them.

Sometimes the harmonisation is merely partial. Pseudo-Philo, for instance, although familiar with the Priestly tradition concerning Balaam's fateful advice, abstains from altering the sense of Num. 22–4. His Balaam is no enemy of Israel and no friend of Moab. He is not the fortune-seeker depicted by the majority of exegetes, but truly obedient to God's will. He commits no sin but makes two mistakes. First, he should have refused outright to accompany Balak's envoys since he knew that Israel was God's elect. Secondly, he should not have offered sacrifice on behalf of the Moabites. Moved by pity for Balak and his hopeless cause, and slow to recognise that he has been employed to persuade God to change his plans, he brings his own ruin and the loss of his gift of prophecy upon himself. His advice to Balak is an act of despair, of spiritual suicide. In short, the Balaam of *Liber Antiquitatum Biblicarum* 18 is a tragic hero.

Pseudo-Philo, a man of individual views and convictions, deliberately kept himself apart from the main stream of interpretative tradition, but those who followed it appear to have obeyed a principle of biblical origin. The implicit reinterpretation of earlier accounts in the light of current ideas was part of the redactional activity for which the members of the Priestly school, the compilers of scripture, were responsible. Their successors, the exegetes of the Bible, merely rendered such reinterpretation explicit by injecting into the antiquated recensions the sense of the final version. Jewish exegesis is thus seen to be in direct continuity with the Bible, and midrash the lawful heir of scriptural tradition.

Apart from the task of explaining away biblical discrepancies, the ancient interpreter was also expected to pronounce on one further enigma: scriptural superfluity. What sense did he make of the literal repetition of laws? In the three appearances in the Pentateuch (Exod. 23: 19; 34: 26; Deut. 14: 21) of the precept forbidding the boiling of a kid in its mother's milk he saw an indication that this specific law embraces a general rule; namely, that no meat whatever might be cooked in milk.[1] Halakhah later asserts that the prohibition is threefold because it alludes to three kinds of meat, and finally forbids Jews not only to cook meat in milk but even to eat the two together.[2] In Targum Onkelos, the exegesis, 'You shall not eat flesh with milk', is substituted for the original biblical wording.

(iv)

To the final category of biblical texts demanding 'pure' exegesis belong those which for practical or doctrinal reasons were unacceptable in their literal meaning. With the passing of time, certain laws inevitably grew so obsolete that their very appearance scandalised the reader; others permitted customs considered untenable by some

[1] See 1JT; Hull. 8, 1.   [2] Cf. Mekh. (ed. Lauterbach, 3, 188); Hull. 8, 4.

branches of Jewry; others condemned practices which under new and often external influences had become part and parcel of the world of the midrashist. Again, the ordinary Jew was taught to avoid as grievous sins some of the deeds ascribed in biblical history to the Patriarchs and Moses; to associate them with the saints of the past struck him as nothing less than sacrilege. The methods adopted by the interpreters to deal with such cases vary from the sensible and rational to the desperate and drastic.

Let us consider as an example the law prohibiting child sacrifice to Molekh: 'Thou shalt not give any of thy seed to pass (it through the fire) to Molekh' (Lev. 18: 21; 20: 2). This was not only without practical significance in post-exilic Israel; the very idea that it was ever necessary must have filled the interpreters with revulsion. Consequently, Palestinian commentators advanced at an early stage various allegorical interpretations of the passage.

In the oldest of these, the biblical words *ʒeraʻ*, seed, and Molekh, are both recognised as metaphors, the first signifying 'sons', and the second, 'pagan religion'. The original injunction is thus extended to prohibit an Israelite father to cause or allow his sons to become apostates. This exegesis survives in Targum Neofiti on Lev. 20: 2, where we read: 'Any man of the sons of Israel who shall permit any of his sons to pass to idolatry, shall surely be put to death.' The Septuagint on 18: 21, 'And of thy seed thou shalt not give to serve Archon', appears to include the same interpretation: if, that is, λατρεύειν ἄρχοντι is understood to mean 'to worship the God-King', and not 'to serve a ruler'.[1] Such a rendering is in harmony with the essence of the biblical law and expresses itself in terms meaningful to the hellenistic era in particular, and also to later ages.

The second allegorical exegesis is founded on the general context of Lev. 18, a chapter occupied with sexual matters. Molekh is again accepted as a symbol of idolatry, but 'seed' and 'to pass to' are understood as 'semen' and 'to impregnate' (cf. Lev. 18: 20; Job 21: 10). The law is consequently construed into a ban on fornication with non-Jewish women:[2] an Israelite shall in no circumstances risk fathering a child bound to swell the ranks of idol-worshippers. The pure form of

[1] Cf. A. Geiger, *Urschrift und Uebersetʒungen der Bibel*, pp. 302–3. See also the Samaritan version of Lev. 18: 21 and Deut. R. 2, 33.
[2] Cf. Lev. 20: 5 ('*whoring* after Molekh'); Sanh. 9, 6.

this type of interpretation is preserved in Targum Pseudo-Jonathan on Lev. 18: 21: 'Thou shalt not use thy seed with a daughter of the nations, impregnating her to the benefit of idolatry.'[1] The antiquity of both teachings is guaranteed by a formula quoted with disapproval in the Mishnah, 'Thou shalt not give of thy seed to impregnate within heathendom', and expounded by Rabbi Ishmael, a famous early second-century A.D. exegete: 'This is one who takes a heathen wife and raises sons out of her; he raises enemies to God.'[2] The Mishnah itself[3] prefers the older anti-idolatry exegesis echoed somewhat clumsily by Targum Onkelos: 'Thou shalt not give any of thy sons transferring them to Molekh.'

Interpreters were also expected to pronounce on biblical customs long since become obsolete. The legitimacy of polygamy, for instance, is so much taken for granted by the Old Testament that it does not even require special legislation—neither Abraham, Jacob, nor David, to name only the most famous, was monogamous—but the practice was generally dropped in post-biblical times, mainly because it was beyond the means of most people. Yet though monogamy became the rule, Jewry as a whole preferred to allow biblical marriage to remain undebated. Not so the Qumrân community. The sectaries believed that polygamy was not only impracticable but also unlawful, and that by marrying two women a man falls into the first of the 'nets of Belial', fornication. Appealing to scriptural exegesis, they proclaim that the principle of matrimony laid down by God since the time of the creation is '(One) male and (one) female created he them' and that this principle was observed by those who were saved from the Flood: Noah and his sons each had only one wife (Gen. 1: 27; 7: 7). Furthermore, since the law forbids even the king to 'multiply wives to himself' (Deut. 17: 17; i.e. to marry more than one), the same must *a fortiori* concern the ordinary citizen.[4] David's contravention is excused on the grounds that he was ignorant of 'the sealed book of the Law which was in the ark, for it was not opened in Israel from the death of Eleazar and Joshua...'.[5] The example of the patriarchs is passed over in silence. In fact, the whole argument is illogical. The Qumrân commentator wished to proscribe polygamy and did so.

[1] Cf. T. Neof.marg on Lev. 20: 2 and Peshiṭta (Lev. 18: 21; 20: 2).
[2] Meg. 4, 9; Y. Meg. 4, 75 c.
[3] Sanh. 7, 7.   [4] CD IV, 19–v, 2.   [5] CD v, 2–6.

By contrast, it is interesting to examine the exegetical justification of a custom solemnly forbidden in scripture. The Decalogue prohibits both the making and the worshipping of images (Exod. 20: 4–5; Deut. 5: 8–9). In post-exilic times the commandment was strictly obeyed, and continued to be observed during the intertestamental period. It is, declares Josephus, unlawful for a Jew to make or possess images of persons or animals.[1] Attempts by Herod and Pilate to erect a Roman eagle in Jerusalem or to bring in their military signa encountered violent resistance.[2] Again, Petronius when he was sent to Judaea to set up the effigy of Gaius Caligula in the Temple was told that Jews 'were forbidden to place an image of God, much less of a man, not only in their sanctuary, but even in an unconsecrated spot throughout the country'.[3] None the less, by the beginning of the second century A.D. a change of attitude is to be noticed in Jewish Palestine. When reproached for frequenting a public bath in Acco containing a statue of Aphrodite, Gamaliel II is said to have distinguished between cult and decoration and to have remarked that the Jew is not expected to avoid a place in which statues fulfil the role of ornament.[4] Whether this episode belongs to history or fiction is immaterial; the fact is that although an authority quoted in the Mekhilta of Rabbi Simeon ben Yoḥai continues to forbid an Israelite to make for himself a molten god even for decorative purposes,[5] already in the Tannaitic era a certain breach had been made in the rule. It is unnecessary to travel to the centres of syncretism in the Diaspora, to the Jewish catacombs of Rome or the synagogue of Dura Europos, to discover the wide use of figurative representation of both animals and human beings; they appear also in Palestine itself in the necropolis of Beth Shearim and on synagogue floors. This would have been impossible without at least the tacit acquiescence, if not positive support, of the rabbinic authorities, and in effect the Palestinian Talmud cites Rabbi Yoḥanan (mid-third century) and Rabbi Abin (around A.D. 300) as passively accepting the embellishment of buildings with frescoes and mosaics.[6] When biblical sanction was sought, the exegetes found

[1] *Ant.* XVII, 151.   [2] *B.J.* I, 648–70; *Ant.* XVII, 151.
[3] *B.J.* II, 184 ff.   [4] A. Zar. 44*b*.
[5] Ed. J. N. Epstein and E. Z. Melamed (Jerusalem, 1955), p. 222 on Exod. 34: 17. See also E. E. Urbach, 'The Rabbinical Laws of Idolatry in the Second and Third Centuries in the Light of Archaeological and Historical Facts', *IEJ*, IX (1959), 149–65; 229–45.   [6] Y. A. Zar. III, 42*d*.

a suitable opening in the final clause of Lev. 26: 1: 'You shall make for yourselves no idols and erect no graven image or pillar, and you shall not set up a figured stone in your land, *to bow down to them.*' Their conclusion as it appears in the Palestinian Targum is:

You shall make for yourselves no idols nor erect images or pillars *for worship*; you shall place in your land no sculpted stone *to bow the knee before it.* But you may lay upon the ground of your sanctuaries a mosaic pavement engraved with images and likenesses, *but not to worship it.*[1]

A no less difficult task confronted the haggadist when he was called on to expound some of the more scandalous events recorded in the Bible. Unable to conceive the notion of legal development, his mind was equally closed to the idea of evolution in the realm of morals. For him, the great figures of Israel's past were models of piety and perfection and biblical allusions seeming to detract from their greatness must at all costs be explained away. His simplest course, and one for which there is biblical precedent in the Chronicler's treatment of the life of David, would have been that of silence (cf. 1 Chron. 20 and 2 Sam. 11). But this, save for rare exceptions, such as the omission of the episode of the golden calf by Josephus, interpreters were reluctant to practise. They preferred to ascribe a favourable meaning to the incriminating passage or rewrite it completely. As will be seen, the relatively strict rules of legal exegesis do not apply in haggadic matters.

Abraham, father of the nation, elect and lover of God, was considered by the Jew of the post-biblical era as the supreme example of holiness; yet he was told by the book of Genesis that the patriarch married his own sister, or at best his half-sister (cf. Gen. 12: 13; 20: 12; Jub. 12: 9). Now the law of Moses not only condemns such a union (Lev. 18:9): it declares that both culprits 'shall be cut off' (Lev. 20: 17). It would have been impossible to accept the Genesis story literally because it imputed not only guilt to the patriarchal couple but an incestuous origin to Israel. All the exegetes agree therefore to weaken the meaning of the term 'sister' by substituting another degree of close kinship, one that constitutes no obstacle to lawful marriage, and as Gen. 12 and 20 give them little opportunity to do so, they attach the new interpreta-

[1] 1JT on Lev. 26: 1. Cf. A. Zar. 1: 8. See also M. Simon, *Verus Israel* (Paris, 1964), pp. 35–46; J. Gutmann, 'The Second Commandment and the Image of God', *HUCA*, XXXII (1961), 161–74; E. R. Goodenough, 'The Rabbis and Jewish Art in the Greco-Roman Period', *ibid.* 269–79.

tion to Gen. 11: 29: 'And Abram and Nahor took wives; the name of Abram's wife was Sarai, and the name of Nahor's wife, Milcah, the daughter of Haran, the father of Milcah and Iscah.' In Midrash, Iscah and Sarai are identical and Sarai thus becomes Abraham's niece. Already traditional in the first century A.D., this exegesis is adopted by Josephus when he writes: 'Aran left a son, Lot, and daughters Sarra and Melcha...Nachor married his niece Melcha, Abraham his niece Sarra' (*Ant.* I, 151). In Targum Pseudo-Jonathan, the same interpretation is appended by means of a brief gloss to the end of verse 29: '...the father of Milcah and Iscah—she is Sarai.' It is repeated also in the Talmud[1] and is taken over by Rashi in his exposition of the Genesis passage.

That Abraham married his brother's daughter was, it seems, a satisfactory explanation except for those who, like the members of the Qumrân group, held that in forbidding a nephew to marry his aunt Leviticus also prohibits the uncle–niece alliance.[2] Unfortunately, the Dead Sea Scrolls have not revealed their own solution but I would venture to suggest that it may have taken the form of that preserved in the Targum of Pseudo-Jonathan on Gen. 20: 12, where Abraham describes Sarah as his first cousin: 'Indeed, she is my sister, the daughter of my father's brother, but not of the kindred of my mother.'

Another disconcerting story is that of the abduction of Sarah told in Gen. 12. Abraham, it is said, was forced by famine to migrate into Egypt but foresaw that his wife's beauty would endanger his life. He therefore provided for his safety by persuading her to conceal her real identity. Events took the expected turn; Sarah was led off to the palace and Abraham was well treated by Pharaoh on account of his 'sister', even to the point of becoming very rich. Must one deduce that the ancestor of Israel was a selfish, cowardly and unscrupulous man?

The laconic brevity of the scriptural account may already testify to profound embarrassment. Early exegesis tackles the problem from two different angles: it denies Abraham's voluntary collaboration with the Egyptians, and it dissociates his wealth from Sarah's transfer to the house of Pharaoh. Thus according to Jub. 13: 11–14, Abraham had spent five years in Egypt before his wife was 'torn away from him'.

---

[1] Meg. 14*a*; Sanh. 69*b*.
[2] CD v, 7–11. Cf. C. Rabin, *Qumrân Studies* (Oxford, 1957), pp. 91–3.

Pharaoh 'seized' Sarah and was punished for doing so by plagues. And then, as though quite unconnected with what has gone before, there follows a description of the patriarch's riches. The Qumrân Genesis Apocryphon emphasises the violence used by Pharaoh's emissaries and Abraham's sorrow: 'And I, Abram, wept aloud that night...because Sarai had been taken away from me by force. I prayed...and said in my sorrow while my tears ran down..."I cry now before Thee...against Pharaoh...because of my wife who has been taken from me by force"' (1QGA xx, 10–14). Following the pattern set in Gen. 20: 14 ff., the mention of Abraham's wealth is postponed until after the healing of Pharaoh by the patriarch (*ibid.* xx, 28–33). Josephus' point of view is almost the same. It is at the time of Sarah's return to her lawful husband that Abraham receives compensation from Pharaoh.[1] Presented in this light, the story ceases to scandalise. Abraham, if guilty of anything, shows merely a lack of foresight; knowing the Egyptians, he should never have journeyed to that country. A consideration of the same kind must have prompted the strange haggadah preserved by Josephus in another place,[2] in which Sarah is taken prisoner by an Egyptian army invading the land of Canaan. Moved by her husband's prayer, God compels Pharaoh to return her immaculate, but not before showering them both with silver and gold.

Enough has been said of the origins of 'pure' exegesis and the purposes it served. In brief, the aim of primitive midrash was to render every word and verse of scripture intelligible, the whole of it coherent, and its message acceptable and meaningful to the interpreters' contemporaries. 'Pure' exegesis is organically bound to the Bible. Its spirit and method, and in more than one case the very tradition it transmits, are of biblical origin or may be traced back to a period preceding the final compilation of the Pentateuch. So scripture as it were engendered midrash, and midrash in its turn ensured that scripture remained an active and living force in Israel.

[1] *Ant.* I, 165. [2] *B.J.* v, 379–81.

'APPLIED' EXEGESIS

Whereas at first midrash was primarily required to eliminate obscurities in the biblical text, by the beginning of the Christian era other demands were being made of it. The point of departure for exegesis was no longer the Torah itself, but contemporary customs and beliefs which the interpreter attempted to connect with scripture and to justify. The result was an evolving closely reasoned corpus of systematic exegesis which eventually determined the whole orientation of individual and social life.

This new form of halakhic Bible interpretation seems to have accompanied the rise of the religious parties, and in particular of the Pharisaic movement. As has been noted, in the early centuries of the post-exilic age it was the priestly and Levitical scribes who, as the professional and authoritative teachers of the people, were responsible for the transmission and exposition of scripture. Even the Qumrân 'Essenes' remained faithful to the old system despite their break with the Jerusalem priesthood, relying entirely on the guidance of the sons of Aaron within their ranks.[1] Pharisaism, on the other hand, recruited its followers mainly from the progressive branch of the traditional Jewish laity. Its leaders were therefore unable to claim authority by reason of hereditary status or professional training and wherever their doctrine departed from the accepted norm they were obliged to defend it with argument solidly backed by scripture. Out of this necessity a technique of exegesis soon arose which conformed to well-defined rules, the *middôt*.[2] Hillel, so rabbinic tradition informs us, compiled a list of seven, these being subdivided into thirteen by Rabbi Ishmael in the early second century A.D., and increased to thirty-two, according to medieval authorities, by Rabbi Eliezer ben Yose the Galilaean.[3] In principle, if not always in application, the *middôt* of Hillel and Ishmael are commonsense rules of logic and literary criticism demanding *a fortiori* or analogical inference, confrontation of the general statute with the particular, comparison of parallel passages, and study of the context.

Although the *middôt* were often employed in a scholarly demonstra-

[1] 1QS IX, 7. [2] Cf. pp. 383 ff.
[3] Cf. H. L. Strack, *Introduction to the Talmud and Midrash* (Philadelphia, 1945), pp. 93–8.

tion of the validity of traditional exegesis, they were principally useful to the interpreter seeking to forge a link between the 'written Torah' and the 'oral Law', the latter embracing immemorial customs whose scriptural antecedents had long since been forgotten. These two sources together were considered to represent authentic Judaism, and when on the fall of the Second Temple the Pharisees emerged as the sole authorities in religious matters, they embarked on a large-scale programme intended to amalgamate the one with the other. They set out their findings in the Tannaitic Midrashim, the Mekhilta, Siphra and Siphre, and afterwards codified and systematised them in the Mishnah, which took on the form of a practical summary of biblical law unaccompanied by scriptural evidence.

In parenthesis, it may be of interest to note that as a further development this same system of 'applied' exegesis was later employed in connection with the Mishnah itself. The result was the Gemara of the two Talmuds. In the process, the rabbis created a large body of terminological minutiae[1] and a system of dialectics; but these are the concern of the talmudist rather than of the student of midrash.

Mishnah Beṣah 1: 6 provides the first of two selected examples of 'applied' exegesis. Num. 15: 17–21 imposes on the Israelite the duty to bring as a dough-offering a cake made of the first coarse meal. Deut. 18: 3 determines 'the priests' due from the people, from those offering a sacrifice'. The Hillelites and the Shammaites, the two leading schools of the first century A.D., disagreed on the implications contained in the conjunction of these two passages. The Mishnah records the Shammaites as maintaining that it is forbidden to carry these offerings to the Temple on a feast-day. They argue in the form of *gᵉzērāh šāwāh*, analogy, as follows: 'Dough-offering and priests' dues are a gift to the priest, as is also a heave-offering (Num. 18: 11 f.). As they may not bring a heave-offering, neither may they bring priests' dues.' The Hillelites, by contrast, permitted the gifts in question to be brought to the Sanctuary on feast-days because in their opinion the texts quoted are not in fact analogous. The second illustration is taken from the Mekhilta,[2] where the law in Exod. 21: 7 relating to Israelite bondwomen is chosen as the premise of a *ḳol wāḥômer* (*a*

---

[1] Cf. W. Bacher, *Die exegetische Terminologie der jüdischen Traditionsliteratur* (Leipzig, 1899, 1905); M. Gertner, 'Terms of Scriptural Interpretation: A Study in Hebrew Semantics', *BSOAS*, xxv (1962), 1–27.   [2] Ed. Lauterbach, 3, 21.

fortiori or *a minori ad maius*) inference. Does the passage, which proclaims a father's right to sell his daughter, also entitle him to betroth her? The answer is yes. 'You must argue: if he has the right to transfer her from the state of potential betrothal to that of servitude, how much more from potential to actual betrothal.' The establishment and adoption of 'applied' halakhah in the schools created a dichotomy in legal exegesis of which the rabbis were fully aware. They therefore took care to distinguish between a *pᵉšaṭ* or plain sense, and a *dᵉraš* or derived sense of scripture. *Pᵉšaṭ* is, however, by no means always a literal understanding of the Bible. It may be, we are told by good authorities, 'pure' midrash has become traditional and identified with the teaching of scripture itself.[1]

'Applied' exegesis was not confined to halakhah; it also played a vital rôle in doctrinal controversy and determined the validity or otherwise of all sectarian claims.

According to biblical tradition, the Temple is the chosen dwelling-place of the Shekhinah, the divine presence, and sacrificial worship the focal point of the religion of Israel. In the intertestamental era, the Sadducaean priests in charge of the Sanctuary were more than content with the letter of scripture which appeared to confirm them as leaders of the nation appointed by heaven. Not surprisingly, their complacent attitude was rejected by all the other religious parties—the priests of the Onias temple in Egypt, the Pharisees, the Qumrân sectaries, and the Pauline Church. The first of these groups, the followers of Onias, contended that the temple built by their founder in the district of Heliopolis in the first half of the second century B.C. was Jerusalem's equal. Josephus reports that Onias tried to justify his revolutionary claim by emphasising that the erection of a temple on Egyptian soil was in conformity with the prediction of Isa. 19: 18–19.[2] In fact, it is clear that the Heliopolitans adopted a particular reading of this text and that it is preserved in the Septuagint: 'In that day, there shall be five cities in Egypt...swearing by the name of the Lord of hosts; one of them shall be called the city of ἀσεδεκ. In that day, there shall be an altar in the land of Egypt...' ἀσεδεκ is obviously a transliteration of

[1] Cf. J. Z. Lauterbach, 'Peshat', *Jewish Encyclopedia*, IX, 652 f.; R. Loewe, 'The "Plain" Meaning of Scripture in Early Jewish Exegesis', *Papers of the Institute of Jewish Studies, London*, I (1964), 140–85. [2] *Ant.* XIII, 68; *B.J.* VII, 432.

ha-ṣedeḳ, righteousness. The terminology of Isa. 1: 26, where Jerusalem is described as 'the city of righteousness', is introduced to underline the case of the protagonists of the Onias temple, which is thus indirectly given equal status.

The Sadducee response is unknown though not difficult to imagine, but the attitude of mind of the other Jewish groups is revealed in the textual variants appearing in Hebrew and in the ancient translations, and also in the Mishnah and Tosephta. Symmachus and one of the Qumrân scribes,[1] unwilling to express an opinion on the Heliopolitan claim, are content to read *ha-ḥeres*, 'city of the sun'. The Massoretic reading, 'city of *ha-ḥeres*', ruins, reflects the Pharisaic understanding of the passage soon after the destruction of the Egyptian sanctuary by the Romans, probably in A.D. 73. Originally, the name did not convey a total condemnation of that institution; in fact, the Mishnah expressly states that participation in the cult offered in the 'house of Onias' is, though illicit, not basically wicked.[2] But later, long after the fall of the temple in Egypt, Pharisee opinion took on a sharper tone. The Tosephta sees in that worship a crime worthy of excommunication,[3] and when the Targum on Isaiah translates the verse as 'the city of Beth Shemesh (House of the Sun) which is destined to be destroyed', it not only conflates the two readings but implies that the ominous name, 'city of ruins', points to the ungodliness of the place.[4]

But the real concern of the Pharisees was not so much the unique sacredness of the Temple of Jerusalem, which they took for granted, as the inclusion of their own cultic stronghold, the synagogue, within the sphere of the Shekhinah. To prove their contention that the divine presence was to be found there also, they turned to Exod. 20: 21 (24): 'In every place where I cause my name to be remembered, I will come to you and bless you.' They did not, of course, regard this passage as authorising several sanctuaries, but as evidence that Jews are allowed to worship lawfully in more than one place. According to the Fragmentary Targum, every prayer-assembly is favoured with the presence of God: 'Wherever you call upon my holy name, my Memra will reveal itself above you and will bless you.'[5] With the destruction of the Sanctuary, these Temple polemics came to an end. The synagogal

---

[1] Cf. 1QIsaᵃ.   [2] Men. 13, 10.   [3] T. Men. 13, 12–13.
[4] Cf. I. L. Seeligmann, *The Septuagint Version of Isaiah—A Discussion of its Problems* (Leiden, 1948), .p. 68.   [5] The other Targums read *šᵉkintâ* instead of *mêmrâ*.

presence of the Shekhinah was accepted;[1] indeed, God was thought to be wherever ten,[2] and even two,[3] men were gathered together to study the Torah.

In short, whatever their particular emphasis, the Sadducees, Pharisees, and followers of Onias agreed in recognising Jerusalem as the holy and enduring centre of Jewish religion. The Qumrân Covenanters, however, took a different view. In their belief, the Temple had been temporarily deprived of its sanctity because of the wickedness of its priests, and the election and holiness of Jerusalem had been transferred to the 'Council of the Community', their own supreme institution. This complex biblical argument is seen in their interpretation of Hab. 2: 17, 'For the violence done to Lebanon shall overwhelm you', which reads: 'Lebanon is the Council of the Community.' In ancient exegetical writings, the word 'Lebanon' is employed as a symbolical name for the Temple. The author of the Habakkuk Commentary, familiar with this 'pure' exegesis, proves his point that the Council of the Community is now the true substitute for the Sanctuary in Jerusalem—until the reconquest of the city—by identifying the Council as Lebanon: a classic example of 'applied' exegesis.[4]

Pauline Christianity, by contrast, held that Jerusalem had been permanently supplanted by the community of faithful Christians, that it was itself a 'holy temple' and 'dwelling-place of God', and even that every member of the Church was to offer 'spiritual worship' by presenting his own body as a 'living sacrifice' (cf. Eph. 2: 20–2; Rom. 12: 1).

Another type of 'applied' exegesis is that of fulfilment-interpretation, found particularly, though not exclusively, in the Qumrân Scrolls and the New Testament. Its subject-matter is biblical prophecy in its widest sense, its prerequisite an eschatological outlook, and its model the book of Daniel.

The chief biblical precedent appears in Dan. 9, where the seventy years of exile foretold by Jeremiah are said to mean, in reality, seventy weeks of years. Furthermore, the author's own epoch is understood to coincide with the last few years immediately preceding the 'appointed

[1] Cf. Mekh. (ed. Lauterbach, 2, 287).   [2] Ab. 3, 6.   [3] Ab. 3, 2.
[4] Cf. 1QpHab xii, 3 ff.; 1QS viii, 4–6. See G. Vermes, *Scripture and Tradition*, pp. 32–3.

end' of the 'desolator', Antiochus Epiphanes.[1] Following this pattern, the Qumrân *pēšer* assumes (*a*) that biblical prophecy possesses, beyond its obvious sense, a hidden allusion to the 'last days'; (*b*) that these last days have already begun; (*c*) that the Community represents the elect of the *Endzeit*. Thus the Qumrân commentators read in the scriptural text a detailed account of the past, present and future history of their sect, and simultaneously prove its predestination. The Habakkuk Commentary interprets the predictions of the prophet concerning the coming of the Chaldeans as announcing also the approach of the Kittim-Romans. The persecution of the just man by the wicked is seen to be finally fulfilled in the story of the Teacher of Righteousness and the Wicked Priest. Habakkuk's words, 'The righteous shall live by his faith', prophesy the destiny of the faithful members of the sect, whom God will save 'because of their suffering and because of their faith in the Teacher of Righteousness'.[2]

The same sort of exegetical argument survives here and there in rabbinic literature also. In ancient Jewish tradition, Num. 24: 17, 'A star shall come forth out of Jacob', is commonly expounded as heralding the future Messiah.[3] Already aware of this interpretation, Rabbi Aqiba changes the name of Ben Kosiba to Bar-Kochba, 'Son of the Star', to proclaim the leader of the Second Revolt as Israel's saviour in accordance with prophecy.[4] A similar exegetico-doctrinal reasoning is manifest in the title 'Star' given to Jesus in the New Testament, and also in the Matthaean story of the Magi (Rev. 22: 16; Matt. 2: 1–12).

'Applied' exegesis has one further important function. Whereas we have noticed its influence on the recasting of Jewish law when altered historical circumstances demanded a new definition of observances, it is also important to consider its impact on the consequent changes in religious thought. This phenomenon is illustrated by the evolution of the haggadah relating to Exod. 4: 25–6. It appears from the extant commentaries that during the last centuries of the Second Temple, Judaism insisted on the saving and quasi-sacrificial virtue of the actual blood of circumcision, arguing that it was this blood which delivered Moses from the hand of the angel come to punish him. The Palestinian Targum, quoting Zipporah's thanksgiving, epitomises this

---

[1] In addition to ch. 9, see also Dan. 11: 30. Cf. Num. 24: 24 and *Scripture and Tradition*, pp. 168–9.   [2] 1QpHab *passim* and especially VIII, 1 ff.
[3] Cf. the Targums.   [4] Y. Taan. 4, 68*d*.

point of view: 'How beloved is the blood of circumcision which has saved my husband from the hand of the Angel of Death!'[1] But when in the second century A.D. Hadrian banned Jewish circumcision on pain of death, the doctrine had to be reviewed. The need then was to stress not the redemptive virtue of the blood, but the obligation to obey the commandment of circumcision no matter what the cost. The teachers of that time did not therefore attempt to diminish Moses' guilt as their predecessors had done, but rather insisted on it, asserting that even he would have perished for neglecting the circumcision of his son had it not been for his wife, who herself performed the rite.

Rabbi Joshua ben Karḥa says: Great is circumcision, for not even the merit of Moses could suspend punishment for the delay of an hour.
Rabbi (Judah the Prince) says: Great is circumcision, for all the merits of Moses were unavailing when he was in trouble because of it. He went to bring Israel out of Egypt, yet because he delayed circumcision for one hour, the angel sought to kill him.[2]

As a postscript, attention should be drawn to a particular type of Bible interpretation familiar among Jews of the hellenistic Diaspora. The Septuagint translation made scripture accessible, especially in Egypt, to non-Jewish readers who often sought in it ammunition for their anti-semitic propaganda. Distorting the account of the sojourn in Egypt and of the exodus, Greek writers represented the Israelites as responsible for all the evil which befell that country. Countering such allegations, and to give themselves reassurance, Jewish apologists inserted purely fictional features into the rewritten version of the Bible in order to demonstrate that far from being a nuisance, their ancestors bequeathed to the Egyptians the benefits of their superior civilisation.[3] Artapanus, whose work 'On the Jews' was written around 100 B.C., is quoted by Eusebius as describing Abraham as the man who initiated the Egyptians into the science of astrology.[4] Moses, he writes, was the inventor of, among other things, ships, weapons, irrigation and philosophy.[5] To prove that Jews were not unpatriotic, he makes of Moses an army general who saved Egypt from an Ethiopian invasion.[6] Other

[1] 2JT on Exod. 4: 26. Cf. *Scripture and Tradition*, pp. 179–84.
[2] Mekh. (ed. Lauterbach, 2, 169–70).
[3] Cf. G. Vermes, 'La figure de Moïse au tournant des deux Testaments', *Moïse, l'homme de l'alliance* (Paris, 1955), pp. 64–74.   [4] *Praep. ev.* IX, 18, 1.
[5] *Ibid.* IX, 29, 4.   [6] *Ibid.* IX, 29, 7. Cf. Jos., *Ant.* II, 238–53.

Jewish authors, from Aristobulus[1] to Josephus, anxious to impress the cultivated hellenists, insist on the outstanding philosophical value of Moses' work, the source of wisdom of all the celebrated sages of Greece. Josephus remarks:

That the wisest of the Greeks learned to adopt these conceptions of God from principles with which Moses supplied them, I am not now concerned to argue...Pythagoras, Anaxagoras, Plato, the Stoics who succeeded him, and indeed nearly all the philosophers, appear to have held similar views concerning the nature of God. (*C.Ap.* II, 168)

Philo also believed firmly that the hellenistic ideal of a philosopher-king was eminently fulfilled in the person of Moses.[2] In fact, to judge by the considerable impact which Judaism made on the upper classes of the Graeco-Roman world, and also by Galen's attempt to deny explicitly any philosophical character to the work of Moses,[3] the exegetes would seem to have succeeded in their task.

At the outset of this inquiry, it was pointed out that a society which adopted the Bible as its fundamental charter necessarily required exegesis to respond to its every practical, apologetical and doctrinal need. We have now examined Jewish Bible interpretation in its various forms and have classified and assessed them. If the critical method employed in these pages is valid, scripture interpretation turns out to be the most basic and vital expression of the post-biblical mind, and its study, if properly conducted, likely to offer to Old Testament scholars, and to students of Judaism and the New Testament, a profound insight into Jewish life in its manifold aspects.

Interpreters of the Hebrew Bible cannot fail to benefit from the work of their predecessors in antiquity. Not only will they discover which biblical texts were thought to demand particular interpretation: they will also notice that the midrashist's problems often coincide with their own, and may be surprised to see that 'modern' solutions to scriptural difficulties are not infrequently foreshadowed in these ancient writings. But beyond any immediate exegetical assistance, midrash is by nature apt to provide the closest historical link with Old Testament tradition itself. Scholars not misled by the analytical tendency of

[1] *Praep. ev.* XIII, 12, I.   [2] *De Vita Mos.* II, 2-3.
[3] Cf. R. Walzer, *Galen on Jews and Christians* (London, 1949), pp. 18 ff.

the literary-critical school will fully appreciate the importance of primitive midrash to a proper understanding of the spirit in which scripture was compiled.

The historian of the legal, social and religious ideas of post-biblical Judaism, seeking to make decisive progress towards a reconstruction of their complicated evolution, will in his turn find in Bible exegesis that precious thread of Ariadne which will lead him safely through the literary labyrinth of Targum, Midrash, Mishnah and Talmud. He will also discover there the unifying bond which ties biblical and post-biblical Judaism together. There, too, lies the answer to a great many real problems confronting the New Testament scholar. Since the Christian *kerygma* was first formulated by Jews for Jews, using Jewish arguments and methods of exposition, it goes without saying that a thorough knowledge of contemporary Jewish exegesis is essential to the understanding (and not just a better understanding) of the message of the New Testament and, even more, of Jesus.

Insistence on an historical approach to midrash, the *sine qua non* of comparative study, raises the following fundamental questions, a brief discussion of which will provide an appropriate ending to the present study. Since the bulk of the sources of Jewish exegesis belong to rabbinic literature which received its final form between the third and fifth centuries of the Christian era, is it possible to distinguish the new from the old among the traditions incorporated there? If so, can they be placed in precise chronological sequence?[1]

Approached from this angle, the problem of midrash is not unlike that of the Bible, which nineteenth- and twentieth-century critics tackled and, to a large extent, solved. It is, in fact, considerably less exacting, owing to the shorter time-gap between the origin of an exegetical tradition and its recording in writing, and to the greater wealth of sufficiently well-dated intermediary material, such as the Septuagint, Pseudepigrapha, Qumrân Scrolls, New Testament, Philo, Josephus, etc. Moreover, it is to be borne in mind that in the field of halakhah the major codification, to which the Tannaitic Midrashim and the Mishnah bear witness, occurred within a century of the

[1] Cf. Renée Bloch, 'Note méthodologique pour l'étude de la littérature rabbinique', *Recherches de Science Religieuse*, XLIII (1955), 194–227; 'Midrash', *Supplément au Dictionnaire de la Bible*, v, 1263–80; J. Heinemann's review of *Scripture and Tradition in Judaism*, *Tarbiẕ* (1965), 84–94 (in Hebrew).

catastrophe of A.D. 70. The changes necessitated by the fall of the Sanctuary and its related institutions make it possible to distinguish traditions appertaining to the *ancien régime* from those of a more recent date. From further comparison of the former with intertestamental sources may emerge not only a reasonably clear picture of the line of evolution followed between 200 B.C. and A.D. 70, but also a pointer to the genesis of a given halakhah.

The dating of haggadah is more delicate because this kind of exegesis, concerned with ideas and beliefs rather than with laws and customs, was less quickly influenced by political and social factors. Consequently, in the absence of parallel pre-Christian or first-century A.D. sources, no one can be sure to which historical period any interpretation may belong. From the analyses included in this chapter and in my *Scripture and Tradition in Judaism*—though admittedly the examples have been chosen in such a way that external comparative material has always been available—it would appear that in general the Palestinian Targums preserve, untouched or retouched, Bible exegesis in its earliest form. Is one therefore entitled to rely on the antiquity of targumic tradition as a whole? In particular, to what extent may one depend on Pseudo-Jonathan, which is known to have received additions as late as the Byzantine and Arab periods?

The answer to these questions may be illustrated in one final example. Exod. 2: 5 informs us that Moses was saved from the river by one of the attendants of Pharaoh's daughter. Despite the Massoretic text, confirmed by the Septuagint and Josephus,[1] Pseudo-Jonathan declares that the child was brought to safety by the princess herself. Was this interpretation created by the targumist, or did he rather borrow it from the Babylonian Talmud, completed at the end of the fifth century, where in an exegetical discussion Rabbi Judah ben Ilai, who flourished in the middle of the second century A.D., voices the same exegesis?

The answer to both alternatives is no. The targumic view was so much part of common tradition that the artist responsible for the scene depicting Moses' infancy in the synagogue of Dura Europos substituted it for the Exodus account. We see there Pharaoh's daughter standing in the Nile and holding the child on her arm. But this implies that even on the distant shores of the Euphrates the Bible story was

[1] *Ant.* II, 224.

seen in the middle of the third century A.D. through the eyes of the Palestinian Targum.[1] If this was so, and remembering that biblical interpretation requires a relatively long time to become tradition, the exegesis in question must have originated not later than the middle of the second century A.D. In truth, however, the haggadah on Exod. 2: 5 may be traced as far back as Ezechiel the tragic poet,[2] who lived in the second century B.C. Furthermore, there is good reason to believe that even Ezechiel was not its inventor but merely bore witness to it. How old then can it be?

The student of midrash may deduce that he is entitled to begin his investigation with the following working hypothesis: unless there is specific proof to the contrary, the haggadah of the Palestinian Targums is likely to antedate the outbreak of the Second Jewish Revolt in A.D. 132.

[1] Cf. C. H. Kraeling, *The Synagogue: The Excavations at Dura-Europos, Final Report VIII, Part I* (New Haven, 1956), pp. 176–8, 351–4.
[2] *Praep. ev.* IX, 28, 2.

CHAPTER IV

THE NEW TESTAMENT

9. THE NEW TESTAMENT IN THE MAKING

Christianity is unique among the world religions in being born with a Bible in its cradle. The limits of the Old Testament may not have been finally fixed by the New Testament period, but there was already sufficient definition for its books to be referred to collectively as 'scripture' (ἡ γραφή) or 'the scriptures' (αἱ γραφαί), and to be further specified as 'the law (Moses) and the prophets', or in one instance, possibly reflecting liturgical usage, as 'the law of Moses and the prophets and the psalms' (Luke 24: 44). There was nothing quite like this phenomenon in the civilised world, and its effects, both positive and negative, on the first Christians were far-reaching. As their only literature and as their principal frame of reference, its positive effect was to evoke and direct their theological thought and eloquence; and in the case of Gentiles to introduce them to not only the foreign substance but also the foreign idea of an authoritative Bible, to a habit of mind which expected the issues of life to be decided by appeal to it, and to a familiarity with its text in the often inaccurate Greek (Septuagint) version sufficient for them to recognise indirect allusions as well as direct citations. It would be a distortion to picture Christians as everywhere engrossed in the study of the Old Testament, for most would be incapable of it and the scriptures would rarely be the possession of the individual, but the claim already present in the probably pre-Pauline formula of 1 Cor. 15: 3 f. that the gospel was 'in accordance with the scriptures' (κατὰ τὰς γραφάς—an all-embracing expression without exact parallel in the rabbis, who generally referred to particular passages), or, which comes to the same thing, that it was 'according to the definite plan and foreknowledge of God' (Acts 2: 23), argues at least among some of their leaders and in some of their assemblies a considerable activity of biblical research and debate. For this a wide range of exegesis, both rabbinic and possibly that of less orthodox expositors also, would lie to hand, while there were certain features of the Christian tradition itself which would give rise to new approaches to the Old Testament and to fresh ways of handling it. Such, for example, would be the criticism of Pharisaism and of some Old Testament laws in the teaching of Jesus, Paul's critique of the Law as such, the crisis for Israel in a message of a crucified and risen messiah, the peculiarly intense sense of fulfilment which distinguished the message (cf. the community at Qumrân), and the recrudescence of inspired prophetic utterance which it engendered in the Church. On the hypothesis of J. Rendel Harris the first essay in Christian literature was a direct outcome of this activity, in the form of a testimony book or anthology of Old Testament proof texts which was already available to New Testament writers.[1] The hypothesis has not, however, won wide acceptance. Nevertheless, the use of the Old Testament continued to play a great part in Christian writing as it had done previously in Christian speech (see IV, 12).

On the other hand the existence of an authoritative Bible would have had the negative effect of inhibiting any thought of producing fresh books, and there is more than a suggestion in the early Church of a reluctance to write. With the exception of the Pauline letters the New Testament writings were relatively slow in appearing, and a high proportion of them are anonymous. Even when they do appear they are marked less by literary characteristics than by the preservation to a notable degree in written works of the personal mode of address, and by qualities belonging to the spoken word. Precisely because of its possession of written scriptures Pharisaic Judaism had already placed great emphasis on an oral law as explicatory of them, and neither the Baptist nor Jesus, unlike Muhammad and other founders of religions, appears to have written anything. The eschatological urgency of their message and mission to 'this generation' required as its instrument the short prophetic utterance, and almost precluded the more impersonal and protracted medium of writing. This urgency passed to the early Church in a commission not to write but to proclaim and teach, and Paul's 'Woe to me if I do not preach the gospel!' (1 Cor. 9: 16), or his 'my speech and my message were not in plausible words of wisdom, but in demonstration of the Spirit and power' (1 Cor. 2: 4), as well as his conception of the Spirit as the promise of the glory soon to come, hardly envisage the possibility of a written gospel or of a new holy

[1] *Testimonies*, I (Cambridge, 1916), II (1920).

book. Even his letters, though judged 'weighty and strong' by others, are not those of one who looked on himself as an author, but were rather an inferior substitute for his presence with his converts (Gal. 4: 20; 2 Cor. 13: 10; 1 Cor. 11: 34; cf. 2 John 12; 3 John 13). Papias may thus have been speaking for many of his contemporaries and predecessors when he could still say (*c.* 130?) with reference to his inquiries about the discourses and traditions of the elders, 'I supposed that things out of books did not profit me so much as the utterances of a voice that lives and abides' (Eus. *H.E.* III, 39, 4). The same kind of sentiment is heard in Justin's observation that Christ's sayings 'were short and concise, for he was no sophist, but his word was the power of God' (*Apol.* I, 14). The only New Testament book which appears to have been written self-consciously as if for canonical status (but only until the imminent end) is Revelation, with its solemn blessing on those who read and hear it and its threat of damnation on anyone who adds to or subtracts from it, but this is because writing had become a solemn and mysterious act in the apocalyptic tradition, and it is significant that Revelation, though a mosaic of Old Testament phrases and allusions, nowhere makes any explicit citation from it.

So long as Christianity stood close to Judaism, or was predominantly Jewish, scripture remained the Old Testament, and this situation can be seen persisting in such a document as 1 Clement, with its frequent and almost exclusive appeal to the Old Testament text. The elevation of Christian writings to the position of a new canon, like those writings themselves, was primarily the work of Gentile Christianity, whose literature also betrays a feeling that the very existence of the Old Testament was now a problem to be solved, and that there was need of some new and specifically Christian authority. More than one solution of these problems was, however, possible. Harnack listed seven forms which Christian writings could have taken as a supplement to the Old Testament, once the earlier position of an oral tradition as a fulfilment of, or comment upon, it had been left behind, and he contended that each of these forms had at some time been actual in some area of the Church.[1] In fact none of these arrangements maintained itself, and what eventually took place was precisely what in the earliest days of the Church could hardly have been conceived, namely, the creation of a further Bible to go along with that already in existence,

[1] A. von Harnack, *The Origin of the New Testament* (London, 1925), Appendix II.

which was to turn it into the first of two, and in the end to relegate
it to the position of 'old' in a Bible now made up of two testaments.
The history of the development of the New Testament Canon is the
history of the process by which books written for the most part for
other purposes and from other motives came to be given this unique
status; and the study of the New Testament is in part an investigation
of why there were any such writings to canonise, and of how, and in
what circumstances, they came to possess such qualities as fitted them
for their new rôle, and made it impossible for them to continue simply
as an expansion of, or supplement to, something else.

This study has of necessity become one largely of internal criticism
of the New Testament documents themselves, because such external
evidence on matters of origin, authorship, sources and date as has
come down from the second and succeeding centuries is very meagre,
and, when itself subjected to critical examination, turns out to be of
dubious value, if not worthless. In its battle with what it considered to
be false teaching the Church of the second century held apostolicity
to be the hallmark of authority and truth, and came to believe that in
its New Testament it possessed a book which was an apostolic unity
through and through, being the work of six apostolic figures—
Matthew, Peter as the author of two epistles and as standing behind
Mark's Gospel, Paul as the author of fourteen epistles and as standing
behind Luke–Acts, John as the author of three epistles, a Gospel and
Revelation, James and Jude. The effect of historical criticism has been
to multiply these authors to perhaps a dozen, and to question the
apostolic status of most of them in any literal sense of the word
'apostolic'. Attention has thus been turned from the supposed authorship of the books as a guarantee of their contents to the books themselves, to the variety of traditions in the churches represented in them
which the creation of the Canon forged into a unity of the one Church,
and to those elements of new creation both in form and substance
which make them the books they are. For, while the Old Testament
supplied the basis of early Christian thought, it did not supply the
models for its writing, and in the matter of literary forms the New
Testament is remarkably independent of the Old. A parallel has been
drawn by writers both ancient and modern between the gospels (the
Lord) and the epistles (the Apostle) on the one hand and the law and
the prophets on the other, but the parallel is mistaken. Not only is the

relation between the two constituents different in either case, but the gospels, even if influenced by the themes and even at times by the structure of the Pentateuch, are not really like it, and the epistles, even if written by men who display some of the qualities of the prophets, are not at all like the prophetic books. New and unexpected forms of writing came into being in the Church as expressions of a new substance. The εὐαγγέλιον (gospel) was a new genre, whose nature and relation to the Church which produced it was only obscured by Justin's attempt to bring it within the current category of 'memoirs'; πράξεις (Acts) does not fit Luke's second volume, and has led to misunderstanding and misuse of it; Paul created something new out of the letter, and others blended the letter with homily or tract in a variety of forms; Revelation is as unlike as it is like other apocalypses. F. Overbeck denied that the New Testament writings were Christian literature at all, which began in the strict sense of the word with the apologists and Clement of Alexandria, and he wished to give them the name 'proto-literature' on the grounds that 'Gospel, Acts and Apocalypse are historical forms which from a quite definite point of time disappeared within the Christian Church'.[1] This creative period was of comparatively short duration. The New Testament was not, like the Old Testament, the result of a long and gradual growth over the centuries, and the virtual formation of the Canon by the end of the second century, which prevented it from being such, also revealed the limited amount of material available for canonisation.

THE PAULINE EPISTLES

Some of these features are already apparent in what are the earliest, as they are also the most unexpected, of the surviving writings of the apostolic Church, the Pauline epistles. As writings these are *sui generis*. Once they had become documents in the Canon they naturally came to be treated as source books of Pauline theology and ethics, and to be assimilated to those 'epistles', treatises in fact and epistolary only in form, which were common in the ancient world as a literary genre for the communication of philosophical, moral or religious truth (cf. the Epistles of Seneca, Epicurus, etc.). By their intensely personal and circumstantial character, however, they are bound to resist such treat-

[1] Quoted by E. Hennecke, *New Testament Apocrypha* (London, 1963), I, 27.

ment, and the discovery in this century of so many genuinely private letters among the papyri has established the Pauline epistles as real letters. There are parallels not only in form (address and greeting, thanksgiving, profession of prayer on behalf of those addressed, special contents, personal salutations, conclusion by the sender), but also in phraseology—with 'I beseech and exhort you' and 'I want you to know' in the papyrus letters may be compared 'We beseech and exhort you in the Lord Jesus' and 'I want you to understand' in 1 Thess. 4: 1; Rom. 11: 25, etc. 'Paul had better work to do than the writing of books, and he did not flatter himself that he could write scripture; he wrote letters, real letters, as did Aristotle and Cicero, as did the men and women of the Fayyûm.'[1] The matter cannot, however, be left there, for what has still to be explained is why no one previous to Paul had written letters of this kind, and why no one was to do so after him. We have no other examples of a man, even a Christian missionary, entangling himself with others in such a way as to produce an exchange of letters of this kind. As Wilamowitz put it, 'The style of the letters is Paul, no one but Paul. They are not private letters, nor are they literature, but something in between, inimitable, though repeatedly imitated.'[2] By 'Paul' here is to be meant not simply a private or public individual with his own characteristic temperament and style communicating with personal disciples and confidants, but one who writes in pursuance of what he believes to be a strictly unique vocation in a unique situation, and who unconsciously creates out of it a new form of literary expression. When in place of the customary '*A* to *B* greeting (peace)' he addresses the Corinthians with 'Paul, called by the will of God to be an apostle...to the church of God which is at Corinth... called to be saints...Grace to you and peace from God our Father and the Lord Jesus Christ', it is because he is writing neither as a private person to private persons, nor as a public official to his constituency, but with the weight and authority of an apostle, or accredited representative, of the Jewish king-messiah or lord, who embodies in himself the ultimate purposes of God for the Jewish race, and by implication—and this Paul believed to be his special insight—for the whole world; and those he addresses are the saints, the community of the last days, who are to assist this messiah in the final judgement of

[1] A. Deissmann, *Bible Studies* (Edinburgh, 1901), p. 44.
[2] *Die Kultur der Gegenwart*, I, Abt. VIII (1905), 157.

the world. These special circumstances created their own medium, with the result that a Pauline letter is generally much longer than the majority of papyrus letters, can at times approximate to the solemn court style of the royal missive, can open with a variegated form of thanksgiving as an overture in which the main themes of the letter are introduced, and can include in its main part the scriptural argumentation of a rabbi, the style of the hellenistic diatribe, the elevated language of prophecy, and formulations already traditional in the Church—all this without ever ceasing in the process to be a real letter. Even the private letter to Philemon and his house church is distinctive.

What had produced these special circumstances was, to use a word which Paul employs more than all the other New Testament writers put together, 'the gospel'. Yet although the letters are in some measure an extension of preaching, and derive something of their content and rhetorical style from it, they are not immediately instruments of this gospel, but rather of what had resulted from it. Only very rarely is it possible to glimpse from them what Paul's missionary preaching had been when he had visited a place for the first time; what is more clearly discernible is his conception of his mission. This seems to have been as follows: in the limited time before the parousia (1 Cor. 7: 29; 1 Thess. 4: 15–17; Phil. 1: 6–10) the plan of God, to which Paul was privy, was to be accomplished in the preaching of the gospel, by others to Israel and by himself and his colleagues to the Gentiles (Gal. 2: 7–9), not indeed to all men individually but to the whole civilised world representatively in its principal nations and regions, the part standing for the whole ('the full number of the Gentiles', Rom. 11: 25), so that with his work done in the East, when he has evangelised the chief towns as far as Illyricum, he contemplates turning to the West, which means Spain, with only a passing visit to Rome, where the gospel has already been preached (Rom. 15: 18–28). The letters are pastoral instruments of this mission. This is evident from the terms by which the recipients are designated in greeting and salutation, from the autobiographical passages, which are seldom concerned with personal revelations or private life but only with the mission, from the frequent mention and justification of his work, plans and movements (1 Thess. 1–3; Gal. 1–2; 2 Cor. 1–2, 7; Phil. 1: 3–20), from his references to money, hospitality and support, and from the place assigned to the collection for the saints as a symbol and bond of union between Jewish and Gentile Christians. But it is also to be seen in what makes up a considerable part of the letters, the struggle to maintain the churches in the faith and sanctity which would enable him to present them to Christ at the end (1 Thess. 3: 11—4: 18; 1 Cor. 4–6; 2 Cor. 11: 2; Gal. 3–5; Phil. 3: 17—4: 9). Since this was indeed a struggle the letters are pastoral–polemical writings, and along with much of the rest of the New Testament they reflect the extent to which the new faith, by reason of its peculiar love–hate relationship with Judaism and its openness to the diverse currents of hellenistic religious thought, was beset from the beginning, and to a greater extent than most religions, with controversy, and was brought to a fuller understanding of itself and to literary expression through conflict and debate. In Paul's case the controversy was predominantly domestic, arising within the Pauline communities, so that while the letters have much in common as writings of Paul they are also diverse in virtue of the different communities and situations addressed, and within the general pattern there are considerable variations in length and shape, and in content, tone and style. What the questions at issue were has frequently to be deduced from the answers given, and interpretation may depend upon the ability to identify Paul's opponents, and to detect how far the controversy arose from their understanding of what he had previously said and from his belief that they had misunderstood it. If, nevertheless, there is a unity pervading the epistles, it proceeds from a certain remarkable unity of perception in Paul himself which governed his conduct of controversy, and from his confidence that once a situation had been seen in its true light the gospel of the crucified and risen Lord would prove to be the key to it. His conviction that the gospel and the Church, and his own person and work, stood at the heart of things, not only fulfilling the Old Testament promises but superseding its dispensation (2 Cor. 3), brought forth fresh and creative statements of Christian truth, and it was not surprising that it came to be recognised that his letters, however circumstantial in origin and limited to a particular occasion and audience, could not be excluded from any canon of Christian scriptures which was to be the possession of the whole Church.

Further elucidation of the Pauline letters as documents in the Church is faced by three not unconnected problems, their formation into a corpus, their unity and authenticity, and their chronology; and in each case the data are insufficient for a solution. How did it come about that a letter written to a local church for its particular needs became the property of any other church, and that a fixed corpus of such letters became the property of the whole Church, so as then to exercise a literary and theological influence upon it? What process lies between on the one hand 1 Clement (*c.* 96?), whose author, apart from the letter to his own church, Romans, knows one letter only to the Corinthians (and possibly Galatians and Philippians), and on the other hand Marcion's collection (*c.* 140?) of ten letters, the collection—in a different order from Marcion's—of thirteen letters in the Muratorian canon (Rome, *c.* 200), where their inclusion is justified on the spurious ground that since they were written to a sacred number of seven churches they were, despite their local origin, addressed to the whole Church, and the collection—in a different order still—of ten letters, including Hebrews, in $\mathfrak{P}^{46}$ (Egypt, early third century)? The usual explanation is that it was a process of exchange, first between the Pauline churches, in which letters had not been given a single reading when first received (1 Thess. 5: 27; Col. 4: 16), like letters sent from Jerusalem to the synagogues, but had been treasured and constantly re-read; and then between Pauline and other churches, resulting first in the creation of smaller collections (hence the differences in the order), and eventually by accumulation in the possession of all available letters by the entire Church. Or, as a variant, that there was for some time no circulation of letters, whose contents concerned only their original recipients, until at a certain point the idea got abroad that they might be of value to others, and a movement was set afoot to collect them.[1] These are natural explanations, and may well be correct, but they fail to account for certain features of the Pauline correspondence as it came to be preserved. The letter referred to in 1 Cor. 5: 9 has not survived (2 Cor. 6: 14—7: 1 may be a fragment of it), as also the letter 'from Laodicea' (Col. 4: 16), unless this is to be identified with Philemon or Ephesians. It is widely held that 2 Corinthians is made up of parts of two or more separate letters now arranged out of order, and that Philippians either consists of two letters (1: 1—4: 9 and 4: 10–20), or has been interpolated. Textual evidence requires that the words 'in Ephesus' were originally absent from Ephes. 1: 1, the destination of the letter being unknown, and that Romans once had a

---

[1] A. von Harnack, *Die Briefsammlung des Apostels Paulus* (Leipzig, 1926).

different ending, ch. 16 being possibly part of a letter of greeting to Ephesus.[1] If these judgements are correct they might suggest that some at least of the letters, so far from being preserved intact by constant use, had been allowed to fall into oblivion, had lost their context through neglect, and were in a state of some disarray until a particular arrangement was imposed upon them when they were given currency as a collection—by someone unknown, by a Paulinist who wrote Ephesians as an introduction to the corpus (so E. J. Goodspeed), by Onesimus, bishop of Ephesus, who was responsible for the inclusion of the purely private letter to Philemon (so J. Knox), by Marcion, who is at least known to have had his reasons for a Pauline corpus as an instrument of his theological position. Paul's injunction to read his letter to the congregation (1 Thess. 5: 27; Col. 4: 16) need not imply that the process was repeated, nor the possible use of eucharistic language in 1 Cor. 16: 20 ff. that the letter was intended for reading at the eucharist.

Were the letters, however they may have been collected, all from Paul's hand? Hebrews already appears as such in 𝔓⁴⁶, but its Pauline authorship, which was resisted by the West until overborne by the East, is now everywhere abandoned. The Pastorals, which were absent from Marcion's canon either because he did not know them or because he rejected them, form a unit so distinctive in vocabulary, style and thought that those who defend their authenticity have to do so by liberal use of the hypothesis of an amanuensis, thought of as one who had been given *carte blanche* to write on the apostle's behalf. Pauline authorship of Ephesians has been widely questioned on the cumulative grounds of its lack of real epistolary character, its declamatory and florid style, and its close connection with Colossians, where parallelism of wording combined with the use of similar terminology to express somewhat different ideas might be held to suggest the work of an imitator rather than the use by the apostle of a previous letter. 2 Thessalonians presents a problem, whether written soon or long after 1 Thessalonians, in being a shadow of that letter. The possibility has thus to be allowed that Paul's epistolary output was both originally greater than the loss of some letters now allows us to perceive, and

[1] For both 1 and 2 Thessalonians as made up of two letters, see W. G. Kümmel in *Zeit und Geschichte*, ed. E. Dinkler (Tübingen, 1964), pp. 295 ff., who considers that all the Pauline letters except Galatians have suffered redaction.

also less than the Pauline corpus now makes it appear, and that along-side the direct, immediate or subsequent influence of the letters which are really his has to be reckoned an indirect and deferred influence through a deutero-Pauline literature written in his name to apply his thought to new situations.

The precise occasions of the genuine Pauline letters are not easy to determine, as they have to be deduced from the letters themselves, and these rarely afford chronological information linking them to the apostle's life. To set them *faute de mieux* in the context of the narrative of Acts could be to get them out of focus, for the chronology of Acts is of the vaguest, and its narrative may be less a continuous sequence of events than the telescoping of traditions lying to hand in pursuance of the author's particular plan for his book and from his sub-apostolic viewpoint.

Thus 1 Thessalonians, a comparatively brief letter which is generally taken to be the earliest, itself suggests that it was written to a church composed of former pagans (1: 9; 2: 14), from whom Paul had been separated long enough for them to have become missionaries to, and a model beyond, Macedonia and Achaea (which Paul seems to have left, 1: 7 f.), for him to have made repeated attempts to visit them (2: 17 f.), and for some of their number to have died (4: 13 ff.). This does not fit easily with the Acts account of a brief mission to Jews and devout Greeks, nor perhaps with a dating of the letter during Paul's residence at Corinth which followed (Acts 17: 1—18: 5). The letter falls into three parts, an apologia for the original mission by appeal to its manner, content and results, arranged in alternating statements of Paul's activity and the Thessalonians' response (1: 2—2: 16), a rehearsal of his efforts to maintain contact with them (2: 17—3: 13), and an exhortation to follow his 'traditions', with special attention to prob-lems raised by eschatological expectations (4: 1—5: 24). None of this gives precise indication of the occasion of the letter, unless 'we would not have you ignorant' (4: 13) and 'But concerning' (5: 1)— a formula found in 1 Corinthians for introducing answers to questions he has been asked—imply that he had been led to write, despite the disclaimer that there is no need to do so (5: 1), by written or oral reports of anxiety about the end and in reply to actual questions about the status of Christians who have died before the parousia. In that case his original message will have been one of unqualified eschatology. Conversion was to a state of expectation of an imminent advent of Christ, who will deliver them out of the world (cf. Gal. 1: 4), and even when modifying this hope with what is perhaps the earliest statement in the New Testament of the resurrection of believers the stress is still on Christ as the coming one, whose own resurrection was to a position from which he is able to deliver at the judgement, and on Christians as those who are to preserve themselves in face of external and internal hindrances faultless to the end (1: 10; 3: 13; 4: 14–17; 5: 9–23). The lengthy and rhetorical apologia, which aims at distinguishing the apostle's mission from those of the familiar sophists and money-making charlatans, may then be a form of *captatio benevolentiae*; in order to gain a hearing for fresh instructions he first re-establishes communications with his readers after an interval by recalling his appearance among them, and reminds them that the sufferings which both have experienced in the interim are the lot of the Christian.

2 Thessalonians is difficult to place. In between an introduction and a conclusion which, while containing distinctive thoughts and expressions, are highly repetitive of 1 Thessalonians, there is a little apocalypse with a technical and cryptic vocabulary unparalleled in the Paulines (2: 3–12). This betrays the occasion of the letter, which is to lay down as partly known to the readers a necessary programme of preliminary events before the end in face of a belief, possibly engendered by a pseudo-Pauline letter (2: 2), that the day of the Lord is already present. Such a belief, however, is the opposite of what might be expected from 1 Thessalonians to have been current in the church there, though light might be thrown on it from the church in Corinth.

The Corinthian correspondence is, by contrast, lengthy, and represents a cross-section of a continuing dialogue, perhaps over a considerable time, between Paul and an exuberant, self-confident, even aggressive church. In the case of 1 Corinthians the occasion of writing is reasonably clear in the arrival, not necessarily simultaneously, of two types of information, the first being the reports, perhaps private, from 'Chloe's people' of discords and disorders in the church (1–4, 5–6?, 11: 17 ff.), and the second a letter from the church, perhaps brought by Stephanas, Fortunatus and Achaicus as its official bearers, the separate inquiries in which on sexual relations and asceticism, the eating of idol meat, worship, spiritual gifts, resurrection (?), the collection for the saints and the absence of Apollos, may be at least partly deduced from Paul's seriatim reply ('Now concerning the matters about which you wrote', 7: 1; 'Now concerning. . .', 7: 25; 8: 1; 12: 1; 16: 1, 12). That the inquiries were hostile is suggested by Paul's sense of being under fire (9: 3), and by the ambivalence of the positions he takes up. A tension not between Paul and particular opponents, but between him and the whole church, pervades the letter, and arises from their claim to a 'wisdom' which had expressed itself in banding under leaders (a typically hellenistic trait), and to a 'knowledge' which had brought them a condition of liberty and confidence both in relation to the world and within the church. An understanding of the letter turns on the question why Paul does not allow these attitudes to have their head, but applies to both of them the epithet 'puffed up' (4: 6, 18 f.; 5: 2; 8: 1; 13: 4). The 'wisdom' he dubs childish and egoistic in contrast to the folly of the gospel which negates the ego and glorifies not men but God, and in contrast to the mature spiritual wisdom which proceeds from the gospel, but upon which he does not enlarge; and in excited tones, sometimes with irony, sometimes with a volley of questions introduced by 'Do you not know?', he castigates the exaltation of leaders, the moral insensibility which goes with it, and spiritual disorder as the very opposite of a claim to be already living in the kingdom of God (1–6; 11: 17 ff.). The 'knowledge' he concedes, quoting with approval the Corinthians' own catchwords ('I (we) am free to do anything', you say, 6:12; 10: 23; You say 'It is a good thing for a man to have nothing to do with women', 7: 1; Of course we all 'have knowledge', as you say, 8: 1; Of course, as you say, 'a false god has no existence in the real world. There is no god but one', 8: 4;—so *NEB*). In each instance, however, he proceeds to introduce some qualifying consideration—expediency, the dangers of immorality and idolatry, seemliness, concern for the weaker brother, love, the building up of the church (7–14). The question thus arises of the occasion of the letter from the Corinthians to which 1 Corinthians is in part the reply, and of the nature and origin of the convictions expressed in it which Paul finds it necessary to modify. Was it simply a request for guidance on problems emerging from a (gnostic?) spirituality which had developed in Corinth since Paul's departure, or was it a hostile rejoinder to a previous letter from Paul in which he had told them 'not to associate with immoral men' (5: 9), and in which he may have put further checks on their freedom?[1] And were the attitudes which he sets out to modify those of an eschatological enthusiasm for which he had himself been responsible, and which he had shared? Certainly he bends his whole theological and pastoral energy to a dispute with lively contestants, and presses into service a wide variety of appeal— to scripture, words of the Lord, his own apostolic judgement, the custom of the churches, natural law, conventional philosophy and morality, custom and commonsense—with an elasticity and opportunism which receive classical expression in 9: 19 ff. It is this sustained energy, and not premeditated art or systematic thinking, which makes 1 Corinthians the first fine literary product of Christianity and the first manual of Christian casuistry, widely known among the early Fathers and recognised from the first as something more than an *ad hoc* reply.

2 Corinthians, which was not so soon or so widely known, exhibits one characteristic of Pauline writing carried to extremes. Side by side with passages which are so personal, agitated and allusive that the commentator is in despair to know what is being referred to, or even whether the language is to be taken as straightforward or as ironical and sarcastic, there are to be found some of Paul's most sublime, if paradoxical, statements of Christian truth and life. On the one hand there are abrupt changes of mood which it is difficult to know whether to attribute to the obscurity of the situation or to a combination into one of two or more letters—e.g. chs. 1–8 (*minus* 6: 14—7: 1), 9, where the outlook on the same subject is different from 8, and 10–13.[2] On the other hand there is greater unity of thought and feeling than perhaps in any other Pauline letter. Whatever the effect of 1 Corinthians may have been on the church at Corinth, the situation there had worsened. It is not clear whether this was due to the intrusion into Paul's sphere of certain influential Jewish figures who, though not mentioned in 1–9, are denounced in 10–13 as self-styled apostles of Christ and as ministers of Satan, nor who these 'superlative apostles' were—Judaisers, delegates from the Jerusalem church, gnostics, or a Christian version of itinerant prophets and wonder-workers[3]—nor

[1] So J. C. Hurd, *The Origin of 1 Corinthians* (London, 1965).

[2] G. Bornkamm, *Die Vorgeschichte des sogenannten Zweiten Korintherbriefes* (Heidelberg, 1961), has a slightly different analysis.

[3] For the first see H. Windisch, *Der Zweite Korintherbrief* (Göttingen, 1924) and others; for the second E. Käsemann, 'Die Legitimität des Apostels', *ZNTW*, XLI (1942),

whether they undermined Paul's authority or found it already undermined. A visit by Paul to Corinth had been a disaster, revealing the
whole church to be in rebellion, and was the occasion for an open
affront by an individual from which the whole church had not dissoci-
ated itself. It was followed by an ultimatum demanding punishment
of the offender and the submission of the church in a letter so severe
that Paul regretted having sent it. He is in anguish until he hears of the
successful outcome, which is treated retrospectively in 1–7. The hypothesis that this severe letter (2: 3–9; 7: 8–12) is to be seen in part in
10–13, where there is a sudden virulence of tone after 1–9, is probably
preferable to the alternative explanations (*a*) that fresh information of
the subsequent arrival of the false apostles had reached Paul while he
was writing, for he makes no mention of this, or (*b*) that these chapters
belong to a later situation caused by their arrival, for it is the whole
church which is still being addressed, and in terms which may mean
that he contemplated excommunicating it—an improbable sequel to
the reconciliation referred to in 1–7. Reading between the lines, the
accusations brought against him had been that he had shown himself
capricious, unscrupulous and a liar in his dealings with the church, too
unsure of himself to accept financial support as he had done elsewhere,
but also suspect in his appeals for money, effective as a letter-writer
and bold at a distance, but unprepossessing in appearance and ineffective
as a speaker, self-commendatory because lacking the proper credentials
and authority, and defective in religious experience. At times he is
stung to personal recrimination, but he sees these attacks as an assault
upon the gospel in his own person and in his apostolic labours; and they
draw from his antithetical cast of mind an apologia in terms of the
power, sufficiency and authority of God in the weakness, insufficiency
and lowliness of the apostle, of divine consolation in human tribulation,
of life in death, of the invisible in the visible, the inward in the outward,
behind which is a gospel of permanent, progressive and transforming
glory veiled only to unbelievers, and of a new covenant and new
creation in a Christ who is crucified through weakness but who lives
by the power of God.

Galatians and Romans belong closely together in respect of their
subject-matter and of their scriptural argumentation, in which the Old

52 ff.; for the third W. Schmithals, *Die Gnosis in Korinth* (Göttingen, 1965) and others;
for the fourth D. Georgi, *Die Gegner des Paulus im 2 Korintherbrief* (Assen, 1964).

Testament is appealed to against Judaism (most of Paul's Old Testament citations are found in them), but they differ markedly in form and tone. The 'different gospel', unspecified in 2 Cor. 11: 4, appears in Galatians as a demand for circumcision and for Judaism as the necessary supplementation of the gospel and as the perfection of what had been initiated by faith and the Spirit; and the place of the 'false apostles' of 2 Cor. 11: 13 is taken by 'false brethren' who make this demand. Apostleship is defended not in respect of the community over which it is exercised but as having God and not men as its source, and for the sake of the gospel with which it stands or falls. Despite the unique autobiographical passage, Gal. 1: 11—2: 16, 'the earliest continuous piece of church history', indeed because of it and of the highly personal, concentrated and polemical tone of the letter, the precise situation of Galatians is far from clear, and scholarly opinion remains divided between a date soon before, or some time after, the council at Jerusalem of Acts 15, between the inhabitants of the kingdom of Galatia and those of the regions around Pisidian Antioch as its recipients, and between 'Judaisers' from without, possibly from Jerusalem, and Gentiles from within as the cause of the trouble. Nor is it clear what circumcision would have meant for Gentiles, and in what circumstances its adoption could be spoken of as avoidance of persecution for the cross of Christ (6: 12). What does stand out clearly is the sharpness of the issue between Christianity and Judaism which Paul sees in the threatened defection not of a single church, but of the churches of a whole area, and the fierceness with which he deals with it. His contentions are that the law of Moses was always a secondary and subordinate instrument, with the negative function of establishing sin as transgression and men's imprisonment by it, and that it has now displayed its ineffectiveness for the attainment of divine righteousness by bringing about the crucifixion of Christ. To adhere to it as the mediator between God and man is to relapse into bondage to the elemental spirits which are no gods; it is to abandon the freedom of the Spirit which belongs to the children of God, who are the true children of Abraham, and to relinquish that trust in the sufficiency of God, which was already apparent in Abraham as the principle of God's dealings with men, and which has now been made effective by the gospel.

These and cognate issues are spelt out in Romans in greater detail, more methodically, and in calmer tones. It is, however, somewhat paradoxical that the longest and the most influential, because the most systematic, of Paul's letters should be the one which shows the least connection with those to whom it is addressed, and which it is the most difficult to see the reasons for writing. In the opening and closing chapters Paul writes to introduce himself, somewhat tentatively, tc a church which is not of his own creation but through which he is to pass on his way to Spain, to explain his plans, and to justify his encroachment on other men's ground. This, however, hardly accounts for the chapters of theological argument in between. There is manuscript evidence for the omission of the words 'in Rome' in 1: 7 (15), and for editions of the letter in which the present ending, the (Marcionite?) doxology 16: 25–7, followed after 14: 23 to conclude the letter (so Marcion?), or after 15: 33 to be followed by 16: 1–23 (so 𝔓46). These may be evidence of a desire to strip the letter of local elements and to make it general in its application, but they may also be held to indicate that at the point when he was about to leave the East as a mission field and to go via Jerusalem to the West Paul put out for general circulation where it was needed an authoritative statement of his position as apostle of the Gentiles (1: 5), and of the issues as he saw them in the light of his experiences with the Corinthian and Galatian churches; and that the Romans we possess is the form of the letter despatched to Rome as the church situated at the centre of the world and soon to lie in the rear of Paul's mission to Spain, to which ch. 16 has been added from the version sent to Ephesus, the central church in the Asia he is leaving behind. The issues were those of the new age of the world which had dawned; the revelation of the wrath of God by law upon all, Jew and Gentile, and of the salvation of a free grace received by faith; freedom from wrath, sin, law and death through union with the Christ who has died to sin and lives to righteousness; sonship of God through the Spirit which this freedom brings; the unexpected prior election of the Gentiles and the eventual speedy return of Israel; love and concern for the weaker brethren in the body of Christ. If this is a correct account of the genesis of the letter it is not unnatural, in view of Paul's past conflicts, that it should be cast, at least until the parenetical section beginning with ch. 12, in the diatribe form of debate with imaginary contestants, though the frequent disjunctions (e.g. 5: 12; 9: 1; 13: 1), if they are not to be taken as signs of later editing of the text, suggest that this form was beyond his capacities, and that the subject-matter was not suited to it.

Philippians and Colossians belong together as captivity epistles, though not certainly written during the same imprisonment, but in other respects they are widely different. Philippians presupposes intimate relations between Paul and the church addressed. They had heard of his imprisonment, had sent assistance by Epaphroditus, at whose subsequent illness, when they heard of it, they had written to express grief, and Paul promises the return of Epaphroditus, the despatch of Timothy, and a visit on his own part (4: 18; 2: 25–30; 2: 19; 1: 26). Such frequent exchanges, and the distances involved, have led to the questioning of the traditional view that the letter was written during Paul's imprisonment in distant Rome, and to the hypothesis of an earlier imprisonment in Ephesus unmentioned in Acts (cf. 2 Cor. 11: 23; 1 Cor. 15: 32). But the intercourse by letter may have been more extended. Polycarp (Phil. 3: 7) was aware of more than one Pauline letter to the Philippians, and serious difficulties in the text as it stands are removed if 4: 10–20 is taken by itself as part of a letter of thanks written (perhaps from prison, 4: 14) immediately on receipt of money, and not, as in its present position, some time after (cf. 4: 18 with 2: 25–30); and if 3: 2—4: 3, with its abrupt change of tone and subject, and its break of a natural sequence between 3: 1 and 4: 4, is taken as an extract from another letter written either earlier or later, and not necessarily from prison. Issues already met with in other letters appear in Philippians transfused by the particularly strong tie of pastoral affection between Paul and this church, and by his own position as a prisoner. The chief concern is still with the gospel, its beginnings in Philippi and its progress even in conditions of captivity (1: 3–18), with the arrangements and support which belong to it (2: 19–30; 4: 10–20), with faithfulness to it in the face of struggles and sufferings, which he now links with his own (1: 27–30; cf. 1 Thess. 2: 14), and with unity in the Church (2: 1–18). The eschatological note is still dominant (1: 6, 10; 2: 16; 4: 5; 3: 20), but with the modification that circumstances now compel Paul to contemplate the possibility of his own death (1: 20–4). In Philippi, as elsewhere, there has appeared a Jewish form of present perfectionism, disruptive, self-glorifying and libertine in its tendencies, of which he had warned them before (3: 18), and to which he now opposes a future heavenly perfection through

Christ as the coming saviour; but in the circumstances of peril and under the threat of death he lays a more complete stress than in 1 Cor. 15 on the necessity of the transformation of the body through resurrection in order to partake of it (3: 12–21). Colossians stands at the opposite pole, and some of its distinctive features have led to doubts of its authenticity. The Paul who writes here is at the furthest distance from any church he addresses, the (circular) letter to the Romans excepted, and it has been noted that the familiar Pauline address 'brethren' is absent.[1] Unknown to them personally, and to the neighbouring church in Laodicea, he has only been told of their faith (2: 1 f.; 1: 4). He writes, at least in part, to place his authority behind Epaphras, who is perhaps the church's founder and Paul's agent (if 'on our behalf' is to be read in 1: 8), and who is at any rate present with Paul along with others known to the church as his informant; and he takes responsibility for the form of teaching Epaphras has given them as being true apostolic tradition (1: 3–8; 2: 1–7; 4: 12 f.). There is still concern about the gospel, which, along with the Church, is now spoken of as universal (1: 6, 23; 4: 2–4), about the apostolic work, in which Paul's sufferings are now united to Christ's as their complement (1: 24—2: 5), and about unity and sanctity in the Church, though in this connection there is a formal passage (3: 18—4: 1) which does not sound like Paul but like a piece of traditional Christian catechesis reminiscent of Jewish or hellenistic household codes of behaviour. But the main part of the letter consists of an engagement, more specific than elsewhere, with a form of teaching which has some traces in other Pauline letters, but which is here called 'philosophy'. Its main outlines can be descried, despite frequent obscurities in the text and allusions of a semi-technical kind. It was Jewish but syncretistic, involving circumcision (probably), asceticism and cultic observance, and was bound up with reverence for 'elemental spirits', angels and heavenly intermediaries as arbiters of human destiny. In opposition to it the all-sufficiency of Christ is asserted more explicitly than elsewhere in cosmological terms; the universe is subservient to him and finds its coherence in him, who is the image of God, and in whom the divine 'fullness' dwells. The variations on the words 'all', 'fulfil' and cognate concepts are striking, and whereas in Philippians 'earthly things' are contrasted with the heaven from which Christ is awaited as saviour, here they are contrasted with

[1] E. Schweizer, *ZNTW*, XLVII (1956), 187.

the 'things that are above', which are to be sought where Christ now is, so as to appear with him in glory. The impression left is that the thought and language of the opponents has been appropriated and used to frame an answer in their terms.

Thus the Pauline letters reflect a highly distinctive mind engaged with a particular circle of churches, of whose subsequent development in the New Testament period only faint glimpses can be caught. How far it is possible to reconstruct from them aspects of a wider Christianity, hellenistic or Palestinian, with which Paul was conversant is a question of great fascination but also of great difficulty, for its answer hinges on the ability to distinguish what is Pauline from what is not, and in the case of one who was so versatile and sufficiently subject to prophetic inspiration to pen, for example, 1 Cor. 13, the dividing line is not easily drawn.[1] He shows little knowledge of, or concern with, the words of the earthly Jesus, but in the case of the eucharist and the resurrection appeals to tradition. There is considerable agreement that in Phil. 2: 5–11 he is quoting a hymn, perhaps from the Pauline milieu, and less agreement that in Col. 1: 15–20 a (baptismal) hymn is being used. In the course of expounding his own particular insights—justification by faith, the life 'in Christ'—he makes statements which have a traditional or credal sound, and where the vocabulary appears to be different from his own—Christological statements (Rom. 1: 3 f.; 10: 9; 1 Cor. 12: 3), soteriological (Rom. 3: 24 f.; 4: 25), eschatological (2 Cor. 5: 10; Rom. 14: 10; Phil. 3: 20), missionary (1 Thess. 5: 22; Rom. 13: 12 f.; 1 Cor. 6: 9 f.; Gal. 5: 21; Col. 3: 8, 18—4: 1). In his description of Christians as the Church in a particular place, and in his appeal to baptism and to the possession of the Spirit, he does not give the impression of writing as an innovator, though in his understanding of the Church as the body of Christ, of baptism as union with the death of Christ, and of the Spirit as the guarantee, he probably is.

POST-PAULINE EPISTLES

Of even greater consequence for the origin of the New Testament writings is the counter-question of Paul's subsequent influence on others. This is also difficult to answer, involving as it does disputed

[1] R. Bultmann, *Theology of the New Testament* (London, 1952), I, chs. II–III, makes a sustained attempt to do this.

matters of authenticity and literary dependence. That the predominance of the letter form in the New Testament was due to the example set by Paul is a tenable, though not a necessary, hypothesis, for these other writings are not real letters but various kinds of homily or tract with a more or less epistolary form, and for that there was wider precedent than Paul. As such they presented fewer problems for admission into the Canon, since, with one or two exceptions, they are written to a wide constituency and in more general terms on matters of common Christian concern. As a result it becomes more difficult to discern the identity of the author or of his audience, or the relationship between them, or the occasion and purpose of writing, and in them the number of traditional formulae increases. In various ways they testify to the growth of a literary consciousness in the Church.

Of immediate concern in this connection is Ephesians, over which scholarly opinion remains deeply divided between its being a genuine letter of Paul or the composition of an ardent Paulinist who writes to develop Pauline thoughts in a Pauline epistle of a general kind. The epistolary element is minimal. It is agreed that on textual grounds the words 'at Ephesus' are to be omitted from 1: 1, however the resultant address is to be rendered or reconstructed, so that even if Pauline it is for general circulation to 'the brethren...and all who love our Lord Jesus Christ' (6: 23 f.). These are otherwise unspecified except that they are Gentiles and unknown to Paul (1: 15; 3: 2)—and yet the same person, Tychicus, is to take the letter wherever it goes! (6: 21). The ascription 'to the Ephesians' perhaps arose from observation that otherwise there would be no letter from Paul to the chief church of Asia. While the epistle has its own distinctive message with vocabulary to match, most of its language has a Pauline stamp, but the extent of the similarity of its phraseology with Colossians has a parallel in the New Testament only in the Synoptic Gospels, and if Paul were the author he has repeated himself in a manner he has not done elsewhere (but cf. 1 and 2 Thessalonians). Its consistently elevated, even fulsome tone is predominantly one of adoration and meditation, and is in part the product of certain linguistic features such as the association of a noun with its cognate verb ('filled with all fullness'), of a noun with a related noun in the genitive ('the purpose of his will'), and the use of synonyms ('rooted and grounded'). These are already present in Colossians, but are here so recurrent as to constitute an established mannerism. Under their weight the over-long sentences tend to collapse, notably 1: 3–14, 'the most monstrous conglomeration of sentences in the Greek language'.[1] E. J. Goodspeed postulated, as both solving the literary problems of the epistle and as illuminating its text, the intention of the author to commend Paul as a writer and his letters at the moment when he himself was about to publish them for the first time as a corpus. There is no conflict with heresy, and no specific occasion is suggested by the epistle itself. There is a single theme, systematically worked out, which is to recall and extol the Christian dispensation. This dispensation, grounded as a secret before creation in the divine will and wisdom, has now been revealed as encompassing earth and heaven and as reaching to the end of things, which is not conceived as the parousia but as the summation of the universe in the cosmic Christ. Through his death, resurrection and exaltation it is effective for the deliverance of men from the evil powers and from heathen immorality into a present state with Christ 'in the heavenlies' (a favourite expression in the epistle), and for the reconciliation into unity of God and man, of the earthly and the heavenly, and of Jew and Gentile. The Church, which is spoken of always in the singular, is built upon the apostles, called 'holy', and the prophets, and plays a cosmic rôle as Christ's partner and fulfilment. The problem of the temporary exclusion and future return of the Jews discussed in Rom. 9–11 is not in view; for reasons undisclosed it is the Gentiles who have to be reminded that they have entered into Israel's inheritance. Within the Church with its single faith and baptism they are to grow together into the single man, Christ, and for this they are to maintain themselves free from their former ways and ignorance, and to wrestle with the evil powers in the strength of the divine armour. In this exposition key words such as 'mystery', 'dispensation' and 'fullness' are used in somewhat different senses from elsewhere in the Pauline letters, including Colossians, and represent on any view of the authorship a further extension of Pauline concepts. Some of the thought, notably on the Church and on the descent and ascent of Christ, has a gnostic flavour, and some of the language a liturgical ring, while for the first time, in 5: 14, an argument is supported by explicit quotation from one of the Christian (gnostic?) hymns which are referred to in 5: 19 and Col. 3: 16 as current in the Church.

[1] E. Käsemann, *RGG*, 3rd ed. II, 519.

Certain interests which appear in Ephesians—the Church as an object of faith, concern with its structure, with particular classes in it, and with a Christian upbringing (6: 4)—come to the fore in the Pastoral epistles, 1 and 2 Timothy and Titus, over whose character opinion is also, but less sharply, divided. Absent from Marcion's canon, probably because unknown to him, and absent, possibly, from 𝔓⁴⁶, their attestation before Irenaeus and Tertullian is confined to Polycarp (Phil. 4: 1 = 1 Tim. 6: 7, 10), and even there the similarities could be due to a common use of proverbial expressions. They form a unit both in displaying a common vocabulary, style, subject-matter and outlook which make them closer to each other than they are, singly or together, to any of the acknowledged Pauline letters, and in being addressed neither to churches (though the change from singular to plural in the closing salutations shows that the Church is still in mind), nor to private individuals, as with Philemon, but to individuals in their special capacity as agents of Paul in the discipline of churches, to which appeal was made in justifying their inclusion in the Canon. The 'extraordinarily patriarchal' manner in which Paul here addresses men as experienced as Timothy, who is otherwise co-author with Paul of most of his letters, and Titus, who was entrusted with the delicate mission to Corinth, is hardly to be accounted for by the proclivity of old age, since Paul would have been only a few years older than when he wrote Romans (Philem. 9 πρεσβύτης is probably to be rendered 'ambassador' rather than 'old man'). The situations presupposed are precise—Paul's temporary absence from Ephesus (1 Tim.), his departure from Crete after a mission there (Titus), and his imprisonment (in Rome?) after a visit to Rome and travel to the East (2 Tim.)—but it is agreed that they cannot be brought into harmony with Paul's life as it is supplied in Acts, but only with a release from a first imprisonment in Rome and subsequent missionary work in the East (in contradiction to the intention expressed in Rom. 15: 18–24), for which the Pastorals themselves are the only evidence. The high percentage of *hapax legomena* and of words uncharacteristic of Paul but characteristic of the literary *koine*, the flat style with its lack of Pauline particles and prepositions, and the evidence of the use of pagan rhetoric, compel those who would maintain the Pastorals to be Pauline to adopt the amanuensis hypothesis in the form propounded by O. C. Roller, that Paul did not dictate his letters in the ordinary sense, but gave a free hand to the secretary in the composition of what was to be said.[1] This hypothesis has difficulty in explaining why the amanuensis has not left his mark equally on other Pauline letters, and in accounting for such highly distinctive formulae in the Pastorals as 'the saying is sure' (1 Tim. 1: 15; 3: 1; 4: 9; 2 Tim. 2: 11; Titus 3: 8). The differences extend beyond a new style clothing familiar thought to the thought itself. Thus for the author Christianity is to be summed up as εὐσέβεια (1 Tim. 3: 16; 4: 7 f.; 6: 3 ff.; 2 Tim. 3: 5, 12; Titus 1: 1; 2: 12). This is a word which significantly is otherwise confined in the New Testament to Acts and 2 Peter and is rare in the Septuagint until the hellenistic-Jewish treatise 4 Maccabees, being the stock hellenistic word for religion in the sense of the pious performance of religious duties and reverence for established ordinances. It is found frequently in honorific inscriptions, sometimes in combination with σεμνότης = 'gravity' or 'respect', a word confined to the Pastorals in the New Testament. If on these grounds the Pastorals are judged pseudonymous writings, then the fictional historical settings with which they are provided (with or without assistance from genuine Pauline fragments), and the form in which they are cast as missives from Paul to his two lieutenants, argue a considerable degree of literary consciousness. The situation to which they point, probably in the late first or early second century, was one which gave rise to other New Testament writings also, where the major concern was the growing phenomenon of heresy, and, in the case of the Pastorals, with the closely related anxiety over a sufficient supply of leaders and teachers of the right calibre to meet it. How seriously the author took the heresy is seen in his somewhat awkward identification of it with the outburst of satanic wickedness prophesied for the last days (1 Tim. 4: 1; 2 Tim. 3: 1 ff.—there is no real evidence that he believed himself to be living in the last days). Apart, however, from 2 Tim. 2: 18 (there is no future resurrection—perhaps an echo of the spirituality opposed in 1 Cor. 15), he does not specify the heresy nor, unlike Paul, does he engage in discussion with it (indeed, he forbids this, 2 Tim. 2: 23; Titus 3: 9), nor does his positive teaching arise from any such engagement. It is said to consist of 'myths and genealogies', a combination found in Plato but here Jewish in character (1 Tim. 1: 4; 4: 7; 2 Tim. 4: 4; Titus 1: 14; 3: 9), in speculations and debates by professed teachers of law (1 Tim. 1: 7; 6: 4;

[1] *Das Formular der Paulinischen Briefe* (Stuttgart, 1933).

2 Tim. 2 : 23; Titus 3 : 9), and in antithetical statements of a false gnosis (1 Tim. 6: 20, unless this is a later addendum directed against Marcion). These descriptions may denote a speculative higher theology with dualistic tendencies based on an haggadic treatment of Old Testament texts (of which the references to Jannes and Jambres in 2 Tim. 3 : 8 may itself be an example), and an extension of the Jewish halakhic tradition. That the author is content to dismiss them as interminable, profane and fit only for old women may in part be due to his failure to understand them, while his wholesale condemnation of the heretics on moral grounds helped to establish the later principle of anti-heretical polemic that heretics are *ipso facto* immoral. Over against the heresy he sets 'the truth' which the heretics have spurned, and of which the Church is the pillar and bulwark. This also he does not specify—there is not here, any more than elsewhere in the New Testament, a handbook of what Christianity is—but refers to it in the general terms of a developing orthodoxy as 'the faith', 'the sound teaching' (an expression found in popular philosophy), and 'the deposit'; and in the alternating doctrinal and exhortatory sections into which these epistles generally fall there can be detected a wider range than elsewhere in the New Testament of Christological, soteriological and ethical statements which have the ring of traditional formulations, sometimes couched in hellenistic terminology (1 Tim. 1: 8, 15; 2: 5 f.; 3: 1, 16; 4: 9 f.; 2 Tim. 1: 9 f.; 2: 8 f.; 4: 1; Titus 1: 12; 2: 11 ff.; 3: 4 ff.). What is distinctive, however, of the Pastorals is that alongside the truth there stand as its guardians and transmitters the Church's ministers, whose ability, constancy and conduct are of vital importance, and they herald the later Church Orders in including in the instructions to various classes in the Church those to bishop, presbyters and deacons (1 Tim. 3: 1–13; 5: 1–22; Titus 1: 5—2: 10). The crucial questions of the author's time are the conduct of the Church, which now contemplates a continuing existence in the world, and the continuation of its apostolic basis in authentic teaching and reliable teachers. To meet its needs he addresses it everywhere (1 Tim. 2: 8) by way of letters to the apostle's intermediaries, to the one as ruling an established church (Ephesus), to the other as founding a new one (Crete), and in the case of 2 Timothy by presenting Paul not only as the source of truth and authority, but also as the paradigm of the true teacher and minister in his constant witness and patient suffering. C. K. Barrett makes the

further suggestion that the author had in mind to vindicate Paul in face of the bitter hostility of Jewish Christianity towards his memory, and of the misuse to which Gnostics had put his letters.[1]

Knowledge of Pauline letters and embarrassment over the handle they had given to some into whose possession they had come, are found within the New Testament itself in 2 Peter (3: 16), which, with the companion letter of Jude, reflects some of the same exigencies and reproduces some of the same features as the Pastorals, though at a different stage of development. 2 Peter, unattested in the second century, in the middle of which it may have been written, and still disputed in the third and fourth, is certainly and deliberately pseudonymous. Jude, which was widely accepted by A.D. 200, is possibly so, and appears to have been among the Christian writings which the author of 2 Peter knew in addition to a corpus of Pauline letters, 1 Peter and gospel traditions, and to have been utilised by him. Both are addressed to Christians at large, and in both the sole reason for writing is the presence in the Church of heresy prophesied for the last days (2 Pet. 3: 3, prophesied by the apostles themselves, Jude 17 f.). In both the heresy is associated with rebellion against authority (of the Church?), superiority to, rather than the cult of, angelic powers, and the dis-owning of Christ, and with gnostic claims—to freedom from cor-ruption (2 Pet. 2: 19), to separation of the spiritual and non-spiritual (Jude 19). In 2 Peter it is also associated with sophisticated myths, of which Jude's appeal to haggadic legend in the Assumption of Moses and his citation of 1 Enoch, both suppressed by the author of 2 Peter, may themselves be examples. In both the heretics, sectaries or apostates are not argued with but simply denounced as guilty of every kind of moral depravity, and are threatened with the fate of the worst Old Testament sinners. To the heresy is opposed an orthodoxy referred to as 'the traditional faith', 'the traditional commandment', 'the truth already possessed', or as 'piety' (εὐσέβεια), the reception of which establishes for those addressed a link with 'their' apostles (2 Pet. 3: 2) from whom it stems, and makes their own faith an apostolic faith. In 2 Peter, however, there is a specific issue, and in his treatment of it the author's standpoint becomes evident. The problem of the delay of the parousia, which lies not far below the surface of a number of New Testament writings and is met in them in a variety of ways, is

---

[1] *The Pastoral Epistles* (Oxford, 1963), pp. 13 ff.

here a subject of derision by the heretics in the form, 'Where is the promise of his coming? For ever since the fathers (apostles?) fell asleep, all things have continued as they were from the beginning of creation' (3: 4). This could be a mocking negative version of the positive gnostic assertion that there was no need of a parousia, since salvation, resurrection and the Spirit are present possessions. The eschatology which the author himself asserts, and which was to have immense influence after him, is neither a return to, nor a restatement of, the primitive eschatology of the appearance of the exalted Lord to complete his work in resurrection, judgement and consummation; it is instead a doctrine of the dissolution of the universe, of the certain and lurid punishment of all the sensual (*sc.* heretics), and of the reward of entrance into the kingdom as the motive of Christian living for all who are partakers of the divine nature. This is put out as being the apostolic eschatology on two grounds. It had been the repeated declaration, and is now in the epistle the last will and testament, of Peter, the apostle and eye-witness of the Transfiguration, an event itself proleptic of the parousia and confirmatory of Old Testament prophecy as pointing to the parousia, if only that prophecy is given an authoritative and not a private interpretation. It had also been the declaration of Paul in his letters, when these also are not allowed to fall into private hands, but are given an orthodox interpretation.

The previous epistle which the author of 2 Peter refers to, and which he may have used, is probably 1 Peter, to which he would then be an early witness along with Polycarp. This is a distinctive work of singular richness. It combines in a short compass and in a single comprehensive and balanced whole the basic elements of Christian belief (the doctrine of the Spirit excepted) which are found elsewhere in the New Testament in isolation and sometimes in exaggerated form. Thus the thought is primarily theocentric, proceeding from and returning to God as faithful creator, begetter of a new creation, gracious providence and impartial judge. Within this framework is the Christ, foreordained and anticipated in Old Testament prophecy, now at the last times the author of an effective and vicarious sacrifice, raised from the dead, Lord of Hades, and exalted in glory, yet also the object of imitation in his manhood; and the Church, the true Israel and holy people of God, into which men enter by a new birth, a saving baptism and faith, to live a pilgrim life 'in Christ', which looks to an imperishable salvation in heaven, but in which also good works are to be done, a positive attitude taken to the world, and appeal made to it to recognise goodness. The interrelated questions of the precise nature and occasion of this composition and of its authorship and destination are, however, matters of debate. The word 'composition' is used designedly, for the concrete and local elements belonging to a letter are minimal, and it does not appear in what relationship the author, who describes himself as co-presbyter with the presbyters and as their fellow-witness of the sufferings and glory of Christ, stands to the readers, in whose conversion he seems to have had no part (1: 12, 25); nor how the terms in which he addresses them as recent converts from heathenism (1: 14, 23; 2: 2, 10; 4: 3 f.) could apply automatically to all the Christian communities in an area comprising the greater part of Asia Minor. Indeed, it is difficult to envisage the mechanics by which a single letter would be taken round all the churches of such an area. The epistle has been described as an 'admirable essay in rhythmical prose of the Attic style',[1] and even a staunch defender of its authenticity observes that it is the lexicon of classical Greek which throws most light on its vocabulary and literary characteristics.[2] It can thus hardly be attributed directly to Peter, and the hypothesis of Silvanus as amanuensis suffers from the difficulties of all such hypotheses of separating the style from the man and of reducing the part played by the amanuensis' preceptor to vanishing point. In this case there is the further difficulty that if the same Silvanus is held to have had any part in penning the Thessalonian epistles there is no trace of any such style to be found in them. The main concern of the epistle is one of which there are brief glimpses in the Pauline letters and fuller indications in other New Testament writings, namely, the opposition which Christianity aroused from the outside world, and the suffering which is thereby the expected lot of the Christian. But what kind of suffering, at what period and where? In the view of some there is a marked sharpening of tone at 4: 12 ff., and the sufferings which have previously been spoken of in general and hypothetical terms are now imminent and precise. The language is technical ('when you make your defence at a judicial interrogation', 3: 15), and refers to state persecution 'for the name of Christ' or '*qua* Christian', to which Christians as such are now everywhere liable. In

---

[1] W. L. Knox, *Theology*, XLIX (1946), 343.

[2] E. G. Selwyn, *The First Epistle of St Peter* (London, 1946), p. 26.

that case the persecution cannot be that of Nero, which was confined to Rome, but is likely to be that of Trajan (the tradition that Domitian was a persecutor is dubious), and in Pliny's letter to Trajan some of the same language is to be found. The problem is then to explain why the author prefaced what he had to say in this specific situation by a homily in general terms, concluding with a doxology (4: 11). In the view of others the language is nowhere technical, but is conventional throughout, and none of the sufferings requires state persecution, but only social ostracism, Jewish hostility and mob violence to which Christians had been subject from the beginning. These were to be anticipated particularly in the 'last days', which for reasons undisclosed the author deems to be now upon the Church and the world (4: 7–19). This general character of the epistle has been related to the mention of baptism in 3: 21 and to other phrases which could gain an added point from a baptismal setting, and the whole epistle, or the first part of it as far as 4: 11, has been identified as a baptismal sermon, homily, address, liturgy, or the president's part at a paschal baptism. The more precise of these theories make it a very artificial composition, and hardly do justice to its unity of style as a recognisable piece of literature; but that the writer put what he had to say in familiar language is probable. Even the comparatively few allusions to baptism in the New Testament leave no doubt of its immense significance as the abnegation of the pagan world and as initiation into the holy people of God (in this epistle also as a rebirth, a thoroughly hellenistic conception), and if it was the case that doctrinal and ethical instruction followed rather than preceded baptism it may be that far more statements in the New Testament than we can now trace are in this broad sense baptismal in origin and character. In 1 Peter the sequence of doctrinal introduction followed by consequent exhortation ('therefore', 1: 13), the command to 'put away' (2: 1), the advice on relations to those outside and inside the Church, warnings of persecution to be expected, and all under the shadow of the end, together with its credal expressions, sometimes indicated by their participial construction, leave a strong impression of drawing heavily upon a formulated doctrinal and catechetical tradition. This may be the chief explanation for its comprehensive character mentioned above, though it is also possible that one of the contributory factors is the author's use of other New Testament writings, such as Romans and Ephesians.

At the opposite pole to 1 Peter in some respects is the Epistle to the Hebrews, for although it is also predominantly theocentric in thought, and exhibits some of the same concerns—suffering already experienced with perhaps more to come, the pursuit of peace and love of the brethren (φιλαδελφία), and the idea of pilgrimage, which is here worked up into a philosophy of Christian existence—it stands out as perhaps the most individual writing in the New Testament. Basic Christianity, defined as repentance from dead works, faith towards God, teaching of baptisms and laying on of hands, resurrection of the dead and eternal judgement (6: 1–2), is to be left behind in pursuit of the goal of perfection and of a higher knowledge to which the author wishes to lead his readers. Its attribution to Paul, which secured its place in the Canon in the East ($\mathfrak{P}^{46}$ includes it in the Pauline corpus), and eventually after considerable opposition in the West, is extraordinary, since its author would have been no more capable of writing the Pauline letters than Paul would have been of writing it, and the evident embarrassment which this attribution caused to the scholarly judgement of Clement and Origen at Alexandria, where the work would have been very welcome for its general character and semi-Platonic tone, illustrates the grip which the criterion of apostolicity had upon the Church. Neither the tradition found in Tertullian that the author was Barnabas, nor Luther's guess, recently revived, that he was Apollos, throws any light on the epistle, and they are plausible only if he has to be identified with one or other of the few figures with which our exiguous accounts of the early Church acquaint us. Whereas Paul distinguishes the letter from his spoken word, or sees the letter as bearing it (2 Cor. 10: 10 f.; cf. 2 Thess. 2: 15; 3: 14), the author of Hebrews calls his letter itself a λόγος παρακλήσεως, an 'exhortatory word' (13: 22). This is an expression used in Acts 13: 15 for the synagogue sermon, but it does not appear to belong to Judaism, and may be a Christian creation. Hebrews is too literary a work to be a sermon which could ever have been preached; we may perhaps compare the recently discovered Epistle to Rheginus, which is cast in epistolary form but without epistolary prescript, and has λόγος as its subtitle. The emphasis on what is being said and heard (2: 1; 5: 11; 6: 1; 8: 1; 9: 5; 11: 32), and the absence of the words 'writing' (γραφή) and 'to write' (γράφειν), indicate the orator rather than the writer, and Hebrews belongs within the tradition of rhetoric, which was one of

the bases of hellenistic education and culture. This is not only responsible for the epistle's form as a sustained and articulated argument with
the transitions carefully marked, and for its style with its periods,
rhythmical cadences, assonance and alliteration, and such rhetorical
expressions as 'one might even say' (7: 9), 'now the point in what we
are saying' (8: 1), 'and what more shall I say?' (11: 32); it also
governs the theology, for the central theme of the superiority of
Christ to all others—to angels, Moses, Joshua, the Old Testament
priesthood and sacrificial system—is built up by the constant use of
the rhetorical device of *synkrisis* or comparison specially fitted for this
purpose, and by the consequent use of the comparative ('how much
more. . .'). This is the only New Testament work which may be called
cultured and which smells somewhat of the lamp, and it invites analysis
in accordance with the criteria of hellenistic literary criticism. That
these analyses do not always tally is in part due to the fact that the
work is a blend of the hellenistic and the Jewish. It does not proceed
smoothly forward by philosophical argument, as for example the
somewhat similar 4 Maccabees, but by way of citation and exegesis
of scriptural texts, in which the author surpasses all other New Testament writers, and this inevitably breaks up the sequence. His scriptural
method has evoked the most diverse judgements, from contempt for a
fanciful typology and arbitrary use of proof texts to admiration for his
understanding of the inner meaning of the Old Testament. The citations are chiefly from the Pentateuch and the Psalms, generally in the
Septuagint version, with the point at times depending on the divergence of the Septuagint from the Hebrew, and the forms of citation ('it
says', 'God says') reflect a conception of the Old Testament as a
permanent living word, a book of promises with God for its author
awaiting its full realisation in Christ. The mode of exegesis varies.
In ch. 1 the superiority of Christ to angels is established by massing
seven texts from various sources in such a sequence as to reproduce,
with the aid of interpretative connecting links, a pattern of enthronement ritual—the king's adoption as his son by God, his presentation to
the heavenly powers, and his proclamation as lord—which in the view
of some scholars underlies other New Testament passages also (Phil.
2: 5–11; 1 Tim. 3: 16; Matt. 28: 18–20). In ch. 2 the significance of
Christ for his brethren is shown by an exegesis of Ps. 8 of the *pēšer*
type found in the Qumrân scrolls, in which a considerable passage of

scripture is quoted, and then words and phrases from it are taken up and expounded in the sense required. In ch. 4 the exegesis of Ps. 95 to show Christ as the giver of the sabbath-rest which Joshua had failed to give is in the manner of the midrash. But the author's thought as well as his method is a mixture of the Jewish and the hellenistic, and this blend determines the structure and tone of his book. Alongside an eschatological emphasis on the once-for-all nature of Christ's work at the end of the days, and on an appointed day when God will finally shake the earth, there is a semi-Platonic contrast between the earthly and the heavenly as shadow and reality, and related to this is a highly distinctive Christology in which Christ and his work are set forth in terms taken from the hellenistic conception of the heavenly man and divine hero. Thus Jesus (the human name is used frequently and given special stress) as man displays both sympathy with man's lot and piety towards God; in his labours (cf. Heracles) he utters intense supplications and learns obedience through suffering (here the author incorporates the Greek commonplace παθεῖν/μαθεῖν); he thereby qualifies as the effective pioneer and forerunner (ἀρχηγός, πρόδρομος) to the heavenly places, and as the agent (αἴτιος) of an eternal salvation, and is established as the eternal priestly mediator between heaven and earth. This latter, the high-priesthood after the order of Melchizedek, is the high point of the author's exposition, and appears to be a special piece of *gnosis* or higher teaching of his own devising from scripture. All this, however, is not just theology for its own sake. Whereas in the Pauline letters practical application tends to follow after the completion of the doctrinal sections, Hebrews is didactic throughout, and the argument is punctuated by passages of urgent exhortation which carry the main weight (2: 1 ff.; 3: 1 ff.; 4: 1 ff.; 5: 11—6: 20; 10: 19–39; 12: 3–13). In these the consequences of his teaching are pressed upon the readers, who, as the pilgrim people of God living by faith in the unseen, which is also the real, and sharing in the sufferings of the pioneer on the way to the city which has the foundations, are to be proof against the ultimate sin of apostasy. The readers form a distinct community whom he hopes to visit, but who they are, and in what precisely their temptation consists, his style does not make it easy to discern. It is an attractive hypothesis that he belongs to the hellenists of Acts 6, and that he reproduces the spirit of Stephen in his attitude towards the cult, but his treatment of his theme is too theoretical and bookish to allow firm conclusions that the Temple was, or was not, still standing at the time of writing, or that the readers are former Jews, or that 'to fall away from the living God' (3: 12) could mean reversion to Judaism. The greetings from 'those who come from Italy' (13: 24) could indicate that the community was in Italy, but if the letter was written after A.D. 64 it could hardly be in Rome, since they have not yet 'resisted to the point of shedding your blood' (12: 4).

Even more difficult to place in the spectrum of early Christianity is the Epistle of James. If it is a Christian document—and the paucity of specifically Christian sentiments has made it at least plausible to argue that it is not—'the twelve tribes in the Dispersion' to whom it is addressed cannot mean the Jews of the Diaspora, nor Jewish Christianity, with which its ascription to James (if the Lord's brother is intended) and its contents might seem to connect it, since that was predominantly Palestinian. It is plainly not a letter of any kind to anyone in particular; it is too disjointed and deals with too many subjects to be called, as by Jülicher and others, a sermon; and Harnack's description of it as a 'homiletic patchwork' amounts to admitting that it does not really qualify as a homily. It consists of a series of self-contained paragraphs of parenesis loosely strung together, and if some form of A. Meyer's thesis could be established that these are disquisitions based on the names of the twelve patriarchs, it would at least be possible to assign the work to a literary genre of which the Testaments of the Twelve Patriarchs would be another example.[1] It is eclectic in style and content. It combines a semitic Greek with an idiomatic Greek which cannot be that of translation, and contains the only instance, apart from Acts 15: 23; 23: 26, of the Greek form for beginning a letter (χαίρειν). Most of the paragraphs proceed by a series of aphorisms in the moralising imperative mood, but some (2: 1–13, 14–26; 4: 1–10) are formed by the more lively interrogative style of the diatribe. It has a wealth of similarities with other New Testament writings, probably reflecting a common Jewish background and an oral catechetical tradition rather than literary dependence, but some of its expressions, such as 'the implanted word', 'the cycle of nature', are hellenistic in origin. While it is possible to envisage a situation in a church for a discussion of the relation of faith and works (2: 14 ff.), we are hardly in a position to guess where and when Christians needed

[1] *Das Rätsel des Jacobusbriefes* (Giessen, 1930).

to be warned against excessive wealth, oppression of their labourers, and snobbery in their 'synagogues' (5:1–5; 2: 1–7). The 'epistle' was very slow to gain admission to the Canon, and it remains the odd man out, perhaps the biggest riddle of the New Testament.

THE SYNOPTIC GOSPELS

The division of the Canon into two very disparate classes of writings frequently raises the question whether to begin with the gospels as standing first, and as supplying by their narrative of the acts, teaching and passion of Jesus a basis for that message about him with which the epistles are concerned, or to begin with the epistles as having been written in some cases earlier than the gospels, and as reflecting the life of the churches which the message brought into being. In considering the emergence of the books of the New Testament there is much to be said for the latter course, for the writers of the epistles, even if they included traditional materials, were forging an immediate instrument for the purpose in hand, whereas the gospels were not immediate but end-products of a process of oral and literary tradition. Further, their analysis into separate units of tradition (*pericopes*), each with an independent life of its own and with its own particular point to make, has focused attention on the needs and interests of the churches, for which the epistles are some evidence, as factors in the formation, selection and transmission of these units. Nevertheless the connection between gospels and epistles is not obvious. None of the epistles presents a Christianity from which the production of the gospels was to be expected as the natural and inevitable outcome, since they are hardly concerned with the acts and words of Jesus, but rather with the eschatological drama in which men were now living as a result of the exaltation of the crucified Lord, and with prophetic and didactic utterance germane to that. Contrariwise, the gospels do not appear as the necessary basis for the Christian life as it is evinced in the epistles. Only in the case of the Fourth Gospel, which is written in the same language, and probably to meet the same needs as 1 John, is there a clear connection, and then only at the price of a transmutation of the gospel tradition itself into the later language of a church.

The transition from an oral tradition of the Lord's words such as can be traced in some of the Apostolic Fathers to a written gospel was, on the evidence of Papias, not without difficulties for some in the second century, but the acute problem came to be the existence of four approved gospels. εὐαγγέλιον, as denoting the message of the one God's final deliverance of men, was in the Christian vocabulary a singular word without a plural, and the original titles in the Canon were not 'the gospels of Matthew, Mark, etc.', but 'the Gospel, according to Matthew, etc.'. The Muratorian canon, which still speaks in this way ('the third book of the Gospel, according to Luke'), finds it necessary to give assurance that despite their differences the gospels teach one and the same faith, and Irenaeus has to justify a fourfold gospel by dilating on the mystical properties of the number four, while Tatian attempted in his *Diatessaron* to remove the problem altogether by scrambling the four into a single narrative. It is a question whether any of the evangelists ever contemplated his book standing alongside others, and not rather as the only gospel, at least in the constituency for which he was writing. When by a certain time all four were in existence and had become authoritative for some area or areas of importance, a virtue had to be made out of necessity, and they were justified on the basis of traditions associating the names attached to them with apostles—with Matthew and John, and with Peter and Paul as standing behind Mark and Luke—and they were eventually welcomed as supplying from a second-century point of view a multiple apostolic witness. These traditions do not, however, stand up well to examination. Papias' statement that 'Matthew made an orderly arrangement of the *logia* in the Hebrew dialect, and each one interpreted (translated) as he was able', if it refers to Matthew's Gospel (and the fact that he uses the phrase 'dominical *logia*' of the teaching of Peter reproduced by Mark suggests that it does), is plainly incorrect, as that Gospel is demonstrably not a Greek rendering of an Aramaic original, and its author's indebtedness to Mark makes it unlikely that he was an apostle. Papias' statement, which is the source of the later observations on Mark's Gospel by the Fathers, that Mark's lack of order was due to a faithful reproduction of Peter's unsystematic preaching, is a defence of what does not need to be defended if, with many scholars, Mark is seen to be a creative writer with a significant order of his own making, while the presence of Peter in the immediate background is precluded by some sections of Mark's Gospel and is demanded by none. The identification of Luke with Paul's companion, even if correct, has no bearing on his Gospel, which is derived from Mark and other sources but never from Paul, and the attribution of the Fourth Gospel from Irenaeus onwards to John the son of Zebedee has hindered rather than assisted the elucidation of its particular form, content and thought. In the dearth of reliable external evidence the questions of the transition from an oral tradition to written gospels and of the origins of these gospels have to be approached along different lines. Some of the answers commonly given, e.g. that the occasion of the writing of the gospels was the disappearance of the original eye-witnesses culminating in 'the death of the last apostle' John, or the decline of the expectation of the parousia which opened up a future existence of the Church in the world, or the lack of education amongst Christians which had prevented them from writing earlier, are not particularly convincing. Concern with the *autopsia* of eye-witnesses (which for Papias was a reason for continuing with oral tradition and not for writing) was a late and specialised phenomenon which went along with the idealisation of the apostles in the late first and early second centuries. In the New Testament it is found in Luke's preface for conventional reasons, and in the Fourth Gospel and 1 John in a peculiar form. The shape and character of the gospel units themselves suggest that long before they were written down they had passed out of the hands of any eye-witnesses there may have been, and into the hands of others as preaching and teaching units. The parousia hope, on evidence in the New Testament itself, did not uniformly fade, and in some areas was active beyond the time when the gospels were written,[1] while Christians who were expected to understand the Pauline letters can hardly have been uneducated. It is probable that no one reason or series of reasons will account for the emergence of all four gospels, and that there was a different reason for writing in each case, which can only be guessed at.

These questions were raised by the literary criticism of the nineteenth century when it returned to the synoptic problem, the problem of the agreements between the first three gospels, which had been treated by Augustine and subsequently forgotten. The partial solution of the problem in the priority of Mark's Gospel and the use of it independently by Matthew and Luke has lately been questioned in

[1] W. Marxsen, *Der Evangelist Markus, Studien zur Redaktionsgeschichte des Evangeliums* (Göttingen, 2nd ed. 1959), holds that Mark's Gospel was written to revive the hope.

respect of the logic of some of the arguments used,[1] but it has hardly been overthrown. It establishes a genetic relationship between the Synoptic Gospels, and at least suggests both imitation and criticism as possible motives for writing. The extent to which Matthew and Luke follow Mark's pattern and incorporate his material indicates that they approved the precedent he had set and took his work as normative, perhaps for want of any other; while their freedom in using it and their differences from it indicate that they were critical of its adequacy, at least for the purposes they had in hand, and that they intended to supersede it. The agreements between Matthew and Luke in non-Markan material, whatever their precise explanation, may also show dependence on precedents already set in the collection of material, and an intention to do something fresh with it within the framework supplied by Mark.

Form-criticism, which was broached by J. Wellhausen in his short commentaries and was developed chiefly by M. Dibelius and R. Bultmann, builds on the findings of literary criticism, and attempts to penetrate even further behind the finished gospels to the oral stages of the tradition by isolating originally self-contained units from the framework in which the evangelists have put them. The very fact that this can be done at all, and that the Synoptic Gospels, in contrast to the Fourth Gospel, are not only open to it but actually invite it, is significant in two directions. First, it means that whatever else the writing of a gospel may have entailed, it was in a measure a continuation of processes which had already been at work for some time in the churches. Even when it broke with tradition by bringing to an end its oral form and by incapsulating it at a certain point in its development, it did so in terms of the tradition itself. Thus Mark's book, which he connects closely with the εὐαγγέλιον, is made up largely of units which have already been shaped to be affirmations of some point in the gospel or controversial defences of it, while Matthew's, which as a whole is more of a teaching manual, contains a high proportion of material which has already been adapted for didactic purposes in the Church. That even Luke, who occasionally shows himself capable of writing otherwise, should also tell his story by this curious method of the juxtaposition of individual paragraphs from a pre-literary stage, is evidence

[1] B. C. Butler, *The Originality of St Matthew* (Cambridge, 1951) and W. R. Farmer, *The Synoptic Problem* (London, 1964).

that the tradition was so strongly established in this form that it could not be disturbed. Here individual authorship is at a minimum, and the Synoptic Gospels can be called literature only in a qualified sense.

Secondly, form-criticism opens the way to an exploration of the relation between the gospel traditions and their matrix in the faith and practice of the churches. This is a delicate matter, and there is plenty of room here for miscalculation, but it can hardly be denied that the relatively stereotyped forms of the self-contained units provide some indication of the practical aims governing the transmission of the tradition, and of the uses to which the separate stories have been put in the life of the churches concerned. Their concise form, in which the sharp point is generally some authoritative act or word of Jesus, suggests that they had functioned as miniatures of some aspect of the Christian message as their successive tellers had conceived that message to be. Each is concerned with a religious or theological theme rather than with historical detail or reminiscence as such, and with the possible exception of the core of the passion narrative they were held together not by any chronological framework, but as points on a circumference radially connected to a common, though not necessarily identical, centre. But on the evidence of the epistles this oral period was one of intense and varied theological development, and since the matrix of these stories of the deeds and sayings of the earthly Jesus was a post-Easter faith in him as the exalted and heavenly Lord and all that went with that, the question can be raised about any tradition of how far it had evolved or been moulded in the course of transmission to become a vehicle and expression of that faith.

It is a plausible hypothesis that behind each of the gospels stood an influential church responsible for its wide circulation and authoritative position. This, however, throws little light on the origins of the gospels, and attempts to be more precise, and to link Mark with Rome, Matthew with Antioch, Luke with Caesarea and John with Ephesus, rest to a greater or less degree on dubious external traditions or on disputable guesses from internal evidence. The crucial question is the basis upon which each evangelist, as a redactor of the traditions known to him, selected the materials he chose to include, and the principles upon which he arranged self-contained units which brought with them little or no suggestion of any relation to one another or of how they were to belong within a larger whole. Here, within the limits imposed by a reverence for the forms of the tradition, individual authorship is at a maximum. That the first three gospels are sufficiently similar to be printed in a 'synopsis' and to be called 'synoptic' must not be allowed to obscure the fact that out of identical materials and the same kinds of material the synoptic evangelists contrived such different products that it is debatable whether the word 'gospel', which derives from Mark's book, can properly be used to cover them all.

Once literary criticism had shown that Mark was, so far as we can tell, the first to give these pericopal traditions serial form, and that he was thereby the creator of a new genre distinct from the 'lives' (βίοι), 'acts' (πράξεις), or 'memoirs' (ἀπομνημονεύματα) which were current at the time for the narration of the life, deeds or teaching of a prominent person, his book has been allowed to stand in its own right and no longer under the shadow of Matthew's, as in Augustine's description of him as '*tanquam pedisequus*' ('like Matthew's footman'). In contrast to the oblivion into which it fell soon after its appearance it has received over the last hundred years the closest attention, yet without any great consensus of opinion in the search for the key to it. The most diverse views have been held of its purpose and arrangement—that it is primarily historical, and aims to trace a genuine sequence of historical cause and effect (F. C. Burkitt); that it is largely topical, with material arranged to illustrate different aspects of Christian truth (K. L. Schmidt); or that it is both (C. H. Dodd); or that it is numerological and typo-logical, with each cycle preparing for the next and the whole gospel prefigured in the part (A. M. Farrer); or that it was intended to provide a church with a lectionary for the calendar year (P. Carrington). Is the work 'the apostolic *kerygma*—Old Testament evidence and all—built up into a vivid narrative form',[1] and if so should the word *kerygma* be taken to mean that it was a missionary work addressed to outsiders? Or was it for internal consumption to explain Christians to themselves, or to arouse them to action in view of an imminent parousia in Galilee (W. Marxsen)? Was its emphasis on the passion of Christ and the disciple's suffering with him directed to those who at any time might expect to suffer martydom at Rome (A. E. J. Raw-linson)? Is it a simple, artless work in which it is fruitless to try to find any pattern, or a highly theological one to be classed with the Gospel of John (J. H. Ropes)? Was it a revolutionary departure from the

[1] C. F. D. Moule, *The Birth of the New Testament* (London, 1962), p. 92.

tradition, or a criticism of certain tendencies in the Church (E. Trocmé), or such a faithful transcript of tradition that its appearance may have made very little stir (R. H. Lightfoot)? It is evident from the diversity of scholarly opinion that something of the mystery and secrecy which are distinctive features of Mark's presentation of the acts, teaching and person of Jesus hangs over the book itself.[1] Its abrupt beginning is matched by an even more abrupt ending; it combines brevity with prolixity; its poor Greek serves a vivid narrative style; the forceful, pregnant utterances which provide the sharp points of the individual *pericopes* triumph over a general poverty of form. The predominance of stories of mighty acts of healing, exorcism, restitution and provision, the preference for teaching in the form of controversial dialogue, and the part played by the passion and the approach to it, leave a strong impression of the Gospel as one of divine power and authority in the epiphany of the Son of God who is also the Son of man, whose hiddenness, rejection and death are the predestined way to an ultimate sovereignty. But for whom all this was written down (the absence of citations from it in 1 Clement points away from Rome), at what date (except that it must be before the writing of the Gospels of Matthew and Luke), and for what purposes, remain obscure.

By contrast Matthew's Gospel approved itself quickly and permanently, and became in the eyes of the Church at large the Gospel *par excellence* and the norm of the others. This is shown by the frequency with which it is quoted from earliest times, and by the assimilation to its text of the text of others. Whether or not it was produced for liturgical or lectionary use, it certainly received it. It achieved its position because it tallied more closely with what the Church had come to wish its tradition to be, and with the ecclesiastical and catechetical interests which can be seen developing in the post-Pauline Catholic epistles. It was also a more direct continuation of some of the didactic motives which had been at work in the shaping of the traditional *pericopes*. It is correctly described as a fresh edition of Mark if equal force is given to both sides of the description, for it is at once the same kind of book as Mark and also vastly different. It is indebted to Mark for the outline and much of the contents of the Galilean ministry, although the order of events, particularly of the Markan miracles, can

[1] See T. A. Burkill, *Mysterious Revelation. An Examination of the Philosophy of St Mark's Gospel* (New York, 1963).

be altered, and its passion narrative is little more than a transcription of Mark's with legendary additions. Even the large amount of non-Markan teaching which is such a distinctive feature, and which often shows traces of previous application in the Church for homiletic purposes, frequently has its starting point in a passage taken from Mark, upon which it becomes a kind of targum or gloss by the addition of similar sayings. Yet the finished product is very different from Mark's. It is the gospel in the form of a catechetical manual, with all written out plain and heavily underscored by scripture. In contrast to the impetus in Mark of a succession of mysterious and powerful acts and controversies, its narrative almost stands still, and its impressiveness lies rather in the clarity, order and coherence of Jesus' authoritative words. The strongly Jewish flavour and bitterly anti-Pharisaic tone of the material, and the combination of a scribal manner with hostility to the scribes, suggest that it comes from a community, whether Jewish-Christian or one of the products of the Gentile mission referred to in 28: 19 f., which was still living close to rabbinic Judaism, and which had to justify before opponents from the Synagogue the impertinent and precocious claims to be the true Israel, and to possess in the words of the Messiah the true Torah. The closely knit character of some of its teaching sections may be the result not so much of the evangelist's skill in combining his sources as of a previous process of exposition and debate in his church, whereby sayings on a particular subject became associated, and appeal was made to the Old Testament to prove the case. These features are present in the composition of the book as a whole, which is punctuated at five points by a formal rubric 'It came to pass when Jesus had finished...that' terminating long and structured discourses (7: 28; 11: 1; 13: 53; 19: 1; 26: 1). Of these the first is the new Torah delivered on the mountain (5–7), the second a mission charge to the apostles (9: 37—10: 42), the third parables of the growth and nature of the kingdom (13: 3–52), the fourth instruction on life in the Church (18), and the fifth eschatological woes and apocalyptic discourse (23–5). They are mostly made up of non-Markan material but are attached to a Markan incident, and are separated from one another by layers of largely Markan narrative. They are enclosed between the story of a miraculous birth and infancy of Jesus and his passion and enthronement. The former consists of six episodes, all but one being annotated by an Old Testament text, and is introduced by a genealogy of sacred history from Abraham to Christ in six multiples of seven generations. Whereas Mark opens with 'The beginning of the gospel of Jesus Christ', Matthew begins with 'The book of the genesis of Jesus Christ' (cf. Gen. 5: 1), and while this probably refers to the following genealogy, or to the birth stories, it is not inapplicable to the whole Gospel, which is to a far greater extent than Mark's Gospel a 'book'. The word 'genesis' here, and the delivery of the discourse in 5–7 from a mountain after a baptism and testing in the desert, as was the Torah from Sinai, make it reasonable to suppose that the Old Testament Pentateuch or Hexateuch, with its discourses set within the context of saving acts of God, lies behind the arrangement of the work.

Perhaps no New Testament writing underwent a greater alteration of perspective as a result of its inclusion in the Canon than Luke–Acts, for this would appear to have involved the partition of an originally single two-volume work into two separate entities. The first was incorporated into the first part of the Canon to add its quota to the fourfold gospel, while the second—at a later date, to judge by the lack of evidence of its use until towards the end of the second century—came to occupy various positions in the second part of the Canon before settling in its present place between the gospels and the epistles. In the eyes of the second-century Church, Acts was important as providing a basis for legitimising both gospels and epistles, including Paul's, as apostolic; hence the tendentious statement of Irenaeus that Luke was 'not only the companion of, but the co-operator with, the apostles, but especially with Paul',[1] and the title given to the book in the Muratorian canon, 'the Acts of all the apostles', which Harnack called 'audacious' and Haenchen dubs 'an optical illusion'.[2] For these tasks in the Church, however, Luke's work was in one respect ill-designed, since it is possible that Luke–Acts is the only New Testament writing not intended originally for the Church at all but for a non-Christian public. The stylised preface (1: 1–4), which is unique in the New Testament and shows the author as wishing to stand within the Greek literary and historical tradition, dedicates the work to His Excellency Theophilus, who is probably not a Christian, and is to be distinguished

[1] *Adv. Haer.* III, 14, 1.
[2] For the first *The Origin of the New Testament*, p. 66; for the second *Die Apostelgeschichte* (Göttingen, 1957), p. 8.

from, and not included in, the 'us' of whom Luke writes. If the operative clause in the preface is to be rendered 'so as to give you authentic knowledge about the matters of which you have been informed' (so *NEB*), it establishes from the outset what is suggested by features in the Lukan passion narrative and by the repeated stress in Acts on the favourable attitude of the Romans towards Paul in contrast to the hostility of the Jews, that the whole work was intended as an *apologia* or defence of Christianity in the face of state suspicion of its treasonable character. It should be borne in mind, however, that an *apologia*, as later in the second century, was not confined to the negative task of defence, but could go over to attack, and one of the purposes of Luke–Acts was to commend Christianity as the most reasonable form of belief and the truest way of life for mankind. This design for a non-Christian public may be the reason for the fact that Luke's Gospel and Acts are the first Christian books to be found written on the rolls customary in the Graeco-Roman world and not, as was the usual Christian custom, in a codex, and for the fact that their text, especially that of Acts, exhibits more pronounced variations than in any other New Testament book, either because they were more open to such by being in the open literary market and not under the control of ecclesiastical usage, or because they were edited when taken over into the Church.[1] But by what process, then, they entered the Church's bloodstream to become part of Christian scripture cannot be known.

In another respect, however, Luke–Acts was well adapted to the outlook and purposes of the Church of the second century (in the early years of which it may have been written), since by its structure and very composition it gave expression to a Christianity which was apostolically based and which had a future in the history of the world. The other gospels, each in its own way, depict the life, death and exaltation of Jesus as the unique, eschatological event, in the light of which all life is to be lived, and the manner in which they end makes it inconceivable that their authors could take up the pen again to add a second volume. Luke is the only one to do so, and to conceive a historical work whose subject-matter, 'the things which have been accomplished among us' (1: 1), comprised not only the life, death and

[1] See C. F. D. Moule, *The Birth of the New Testament*, p. 92 n. 1, referring to the suggestions of C. H. Roberts and M. Dibelius.

resurrection of Jesus, but equally what had followed through the
Spirit in the Church; and in which not only the story of Jesus in the
testimony of the apostolic Church to Christ, but also its testimony to
itself and its formative years, were already epochs in the past. This
meant a radical change of perspective and a measure of schematisation.
Eschatology has receded into the background, its place taken by an
emphasis on the Christian movement commending itself irresistibly
to the world as manifestly the work of God. With an origin among the
pious in Israel, it attracts men and women of good will in all classes;
it extends beyond Israel to unite Jew and Gentile in a harmonious
fellowship; its character is symbolised by the arrival in the capital
of the Empire of its chief spokesman, a victim of persistent Jewish
hostility but kindly treated by his captors; and it is controlled by a
central and authoritative apostolic order which is taken back to Jesus
himself.

For this task Luke possessed a remarkable versatility. On the one
hand he has a strong sense for Judaism as a noble heritage once it is
shorn of its nationalist elements, and he is the most self-consciously
biblical of the evangelists in choosing often to write in the style of the
Septuagint. On the other hand he shows a delicate feeling for the
diversified strata of society, Greek, Roman and barbarian, and for the
ethos of towns and cities, and he can, when he chooses, write as a
literary artist in good Greek. He elected to perform his task not by a
flowing narrative but by reproducing in his first volume and in the
earlier part of his second the pericopal form of the Church's tradition.
He was in touch with a wider range of this than the other evangelists,
and it is probably in his preservation of it rather than in any profound
understanding of its meaning that his chief value lies. The rhetorical
reference to his predecessors as 'many' (1: 1) is probably not to be
pressed. In the composition of his first volume he had at least one
model, Mark; in his second, so far as we know, his special intentions
forced him to be a pioneer. His debt to Mark is of a different kind to
Matthew's. Within the Markan framework of the Galilean ministry he
has alternating blocks of Markan and non-Markan material, and in his
passion narrative he is more independent of Mark. The hypothesis
that he composed an earlier draft, 'Proto-Luke', from the material
he shares with Matthew and that peculiar to himself, which was then
supplemented from Mark's Gospel, cannot be said to have been

substantiated, and probably takes too little account of his editorial activity. His claim to write an 'orderly account' (1: 3) probably points to the smoother transitions provided between one *pericope* and another, and to an attempt to treat, where possible, one subject at a time, and to show one stage as following upon another. The distinctive feature, however, of the arrangement in both volumes is the use of the hellenistic literary convention of the travel story as the framework for the acts and teaching of the hero. The events of the birth of Jesus are not, as in Matthew, instances of the fulfilment of past prophecy, but occasions of the renewal of prophecy in Israel through the Spirit, which is also the hallmark of the earthly ministry of Jesus (4: 16 ff.). The gift of the Spirit is the content of the promise of the risen Lord (24: 49), and this provides not only a link with the second volume, but also something of a pattern for it in the rebirth of prophecy at Pentecost through the Spirit, who is the author of the Church's principal decisions in its life and mission.

The main key to the construction of Acts is to be found in what are represented to be the last words of Jesus on earth, the command to bear witness 'in Jerusalem and in all Judaea and Samaria and to the end of the earth' (1: 8). The testimony in Jerusalem occupies 1: 12—8: 1, that in Judaea and Samaria 8: 1—11: 18, and that to the end of the earth 11: 19 onwards, this last being articulated by the apostolic decree of freedom for the Gentiles (15) and by the first mention of Rome as Paul's goal (19: 21). The failure of source-criticism to establish written sources of any length underlying Acts has led to a form-critical or style-critical examination of the individual sections. The author's skill can be seen in his ability in the first twelve chapters to convey what he believes to be fundamental to, and typical of, the Church by the deployment of only some eighteen separate incidents with generalising summaries to link them, and by a change in the second part of the book to a form of narrative which is unique in the Bible for its continuity and variety, and for a graphic use of 'we' which brings the reader closer to participation in the events narrated. Throughout Luke shows himself a historian of a 'dramatic' type, who achieves his aim in a series of pictures, often of an impressionist kind. Unique also in the Bible is the careful articulation and relief of the narrative through speeches. These are in the main distributed between Peter and Paul as part of an elaborate parallelism which is drawn between these two principal figures, and they are diversified as to audience—to crowds or in the synagogue, to the authorities Jewish or Roman, before the leaders of the church of Jerusalem or Ephesus, to Gentiles simple or cultured. Here also the author shows himself at home in two worlds. The use of the speech to point the march and meaning of events was an established convention of Greek historiography, but it is the Old Testament which is the model for the form taken by the speeches in Acts, even by Paul's final speeches where the theme of *apologia* takes over. The question whether we are here in touch with authentic reminiscence, or with the gospel message which Luke knew in his own day and which he has, in accordance with Greek historical convention, put into the mouths of his characters according to the situation, is not unnaturally keenly debated, since it is these speeches which more than anything else lock the two parts of the Canon together, and they alone in the New Testament presume to give the basic outlines of the original Christian message.

THE JOHANNINE WRITINGS

There is finally a group of writings which require to be taken together, although the precise relation between them is not easy to determine. It comprises a gospel, a tract, a letter to a church, a letter to an individual and an apocalypse. While not without parallels with other New Testament documents, as, for example of the gospel with the synoptic tradition, of the tract with other anti-heretical 'epistles', and of the apocalypse with such passages as Mark 13, it also exhibits highly distinctive forms of thought and expression, and considerably extends the scope of Christian literature. It has been called 'the Johannine corpus', but it was never a corpus in the same sense as the Pauline corpus of letters, to be incorporated into the Canon as a single entity; and the name John, which came to be identified in tradition with that of the son of Zebedee, belongs to the least certain member of the group, the apocalypse, as does also the association of the Johannine writings with Asia Minor. The second and third epistles of John, the former addressed in somewhat high-flown language to a church on one of the themes of 1 John (if 2 John 7 is to be interpreted of a denial of the coming of Jesus in the flesh), and the latter a pastoral letter of introduction commending a certain Demetrius to a certain Gaius in face of the opposition of a certain Diotrephes to missionaries who had been sent out, are written by one who calls himself 'the presbyter'. This is a somewhat mysterious title, which appears in Papias and Irenaeus for those whom they regarded as direct disciples of the apostles and as repositories of the true tradition. If 'the presbyter' is also the author of Revelation he could be 'the presbyter John' referred to by Papias, but while there are affinities between Revelation and the other writings of the group which call for explanation, such as a triadic rhythm, a spiral form of exposition and a common stock of images and expressions, nevertheless the very marked peculiarities of Revelation are such that a common authorship can only be maintained if exceptionally heavy stress is laid on the hypothesis that its language and style are a deliberately artificial construction forced on the author by the content of the book. If 'the presbyter' is also the author of 1 John—and 2 and 3 John are too short to allow of conclusive evidence either way—then he has written partly on the same subject as in 2 John, but at greater length and to a wider but unspecified audience. If, with some scholars, the differences between 1 John and the Fourth Gospel in language and outlook (e.g. in eschatology) are held to be such as to require different authors, then the close similarities of vocabulary and style also require that they both come out of the same stable. Either one depends upon the other, and probably the evangelist upon the authoritative presbyter, or both belong to a 'Johannine' school which perhaps goes back to some authoritative figure. John 21, as a later addition to the Gospel, might point in the direction of such a school.

1 John is a writing of deceptive simplicity, and defies exact classification. Its range of words and ideas is restricted; its mode of exposition is cyclic almost to the point of monotony, and is effected through a juxtaposition of separate paragraphs whose sequence is not obvious. It is a letter to the extent that it is written in epistolary terms to an audience which can be addressed as 'children' and subdivided into young and old, but neither the overloaded introduction nor the exceedingly abrupt ending are those of a letter. The author's habit of juxtaposing without connection short rhythmical gnomic statements, either in the form of conditional sentences or introduced by the articular participle ('he who...', 'everyone who...'), imparts to the whole a generalising, even legal, tone, and attempts have been

made to see the origin of this in a *Grundschrift*. On the other hand he writes to a concrete and critical situation which pertains both to himself and to any he may be addressing, and which he treats in his antithetical manner as a matter of life and death, so that his writing is at once both tenderly and authoritatively pastoral and also fiercely polemical. The situation appears to have been the emergence within, and secession from, certain (unspecified) churches of a prophetic movement claiming a spiritual knowledge of God and Christ. This the author sees as the manifestation of the Antichrist of the last days because it denies the identity of Jesus and the Christ and the validity of the earthly life and death of Jesus. He meets the situation by appeal to a *gnosis* already possessed ('we know...', 'hereby we know...'), in which theology and ethics, the mission of the Son by the Father and freedom from sin and obedience to God's commandments, the love of God himself and love for the brethren, are inseparably connected. In doing this he not only produces the only abstract definitions in the Bible ('God is light', 'God is love'), but also appears to have gone a long way in taking over the language of his opponents (birth from divine seed, sinlessness, abiding in God) and giving it what he believes to be its true sense. In all this the epistle probably throws some light on the situation which led to the writing of the Fourth Gospel, and on the processes by which its material was shaped. For that Gospel is expressly written to show that eternal life is to be had in the belief that Jesus is the Christ, the Son of God (John 20: 30 f.), and the emphasis which is laid upon the 'flesh' of Jesus in relation to the Spirit leads to a crisis in which a great number of disciples secede from his company (6: 52–69). The words of Jesus are here presented in such a form as to have occasioned—so it would seem from the fugitive evidence—prolonged doubt in some circles in the early Church whether this Gospel had come down on the gnostic or orthodox side of the fence. Its purpose would therefore seem to have been to establish in the faith those already accustomed to it in semi-gnostic terms by means of a representation of Jesus in those terms.

It has something of the gospel form in that it starts from the Baptist, whose movement is treated in greater detail and polemically, and concludes with passion and resurrection narratives. While it includes activity in Galilee, most of the public ministry, which is sharply divided at the end of ch. 12 from the private discourses with disciples, takes place in Jerusalem, and has the more dramatic form of a conflict with 'the Jews'. Whether it was written in knowledge of one or more of the Synoptic Gospels, perhaps consciously correcting them, or on the basis of an independent (Judaean?) tradition, is still a matter of debate. It contains some material of the synoptic type such as miracles and *logia* (but not parables), but the former are carefully selected in number and for their symbolic value in pointing to Jesus as the true bread, light, life, etc., while the latter are not laid alongside *logia* of a similar kind but have become integral parts of closely knit and thematic discourses. These discourses make up the greater part of the work and give it its distinctive character and homogeneity. They are predominantly, if not entirely, of a hellenistic type, and although there is some progression of thought from one to another, they leave an impression of having been formed as separate entities, perhaps in the course of teaching or worship in a comparatively close knit and esoteric group. Their vocabulary and style are so much the author's own that detection of any sources is well-nigh impossible. They follow, with modifications, a certain pattern, in which misunderstanding of a word or phrase of double meaning sometimes plays an important part; and they expound in dualistic terms, whose possible provenance in sectarian Judaism the Qumrân Scrolls may illuminate, the eschatological realities of life, light, resurrection and judgement as already present in Christ. In some cases they are attached to a Jewish feast, and would appear to be concerned with its spiritual fulfilment in Christ. While the background of thought is complex, the book attains a remarkable unity by virtue of its Christology. Jesus speaks throughout in the accents of a self-conscious revealer, and the relationship between the Father and the Son, which runs like a thread through the narrative, is in the unique prologue carried back to an eternal relationship between God and the Word. Thus the gospel is transmuted into the terms of the religious experience to which it had given rise. Towards the end the anonymous figure of the Beloved Disciple emerges as a principal witness to the truth, and in the colophon in 21 : 24 is identified with the author.

Revelation is the only one of a number of Christian apocalypses to gain a permanent place in the Canon. Here the Church of Asia Minor is addressed as a whole through the persons of a symbolic number of seven of its churches, and is addressed not by a letter dealing with particular local problems, nor by an interpreted account of the acts and words of the earthly Jesus, but by an apocalypse of the last days, which is represented as committed directly by God to the exalted and heavenly Christ, by him through angelic mediation to John in prophetic visions, and by John to the Church in serial writing. Whatever elements of private visionary experience may lie behind the book, its complex unified structure, however difficult this may be to trace, its ordered movement as a single whole, and the relation of the parts to the whole, will not have been imparted in vision. They argue that a considerable process of rational reflection and conscious artistry has gone to its writing. A major clue to this process undoubtedly came to light in the recovery over the past hundred years of specimens of the apocalyptic literary tradition of Judaism, with its conventional devices of the summoning of the seer to heaven, the interpreting angel, symbolic animals, etc., and its preoccupation with numbers. This is not, however, the only clue, for in contrast to the pedestrian and derivative character of most apocalyptic writing Revelation manages to be a dramatic poem of considerable beauty, freshness and force. It is the only disciplined artistic work in the New Testament, and to this result not only conscious literary reminting of certain parts of the Old Testament, especially Ezekiel, Zechariah and Daniel, but also specifically Christian factors may have contributed. The choric odes which punctuate the heavenly scenes, like the scenes themselves, may owe something to the liturgical worship of the Church, which they certainly affected later. The conception of the whole as a letter, and its opening with letters to the seven churches, are unique in apocalyptic, and give it a pastoral realism. Though apocalyptic in form it is not, like much apocalyptic, a substitute for prophecy, but is itself prophetic and evangelical in content. The bizarre imagery is more controlled, and is given substance in being used not of some shadowy unknown future but to depict the cosmic lordship of Jesus as a known figure in the Church. After the seven preliminary messages there follows a theophany in which the exalted Christ takes from God the heavenly book, and from this a series of seven unsealings, seven trumpet blasts and seven bowls, each unfolding out of the one before, and each articulated by a heavenly scene, in which judgement and salvation are progressively developed in relation to the three staple elements of apocalyptic prophecy, the endurance of the elect, the reign of Antichrist and the victory of God.

Whether the book was called out by a specific situation is not clear. Its general theme, the part played in it by the martyrs, and the detachment of the Antichrist figure from the fall of Jerusalem and its attachment to Rome, suggest a situation of state persecution, which is taken as a presage of the end. The attempt to fix a date for this from the reference to emperors in 17: 10 f. has not, however, led to any consensus, and can hardly yield the reign of Domitian, which is the date supplied by Irenaeus, while in the letters to the churches there is reference only to a single martyr, Antipas at Pergamum. Whatever the situation may have been, there is a certain fitness in the position of Revelation in the Canon, despite the intense antipathy it aroused for long periods in certain quarters, and the melancholy history of its use and interpretation in the Church. It brings together into a single whole a number of separate concerns which are to be found in other New Testament writings, such as the threat of heresy in the last days, the danger of apostasy, the necessity of persecution, the tension between present and future, the coexistence of judgement and salvation, Christ as a figure of conflict, and the suffering but exalted Lord addressing his Church and ruling it until the parousia. It also compels attention to the scope, rôle and function of imagery in the whole Christian revelation and its literature.

CONCLUSION

The subsequent history and use of the New Testament writings after their 'publication' were governed less by the circumstances and needs of their several and varied origins than by the circumstances and needs of the churches of the second century. Their separation off from other Christian literature into a Canon to be the norm for the one Church of its preaching, teaching, polemic and worship, meant that they tended to be assimilated to one another and to be interpreted in terms of one another. The function of tradition, from which they had emerged or of which they had once been the accompaniments, was largely though not entirely taken over by the interpretation of them as scripture. The Canon itself, however, did not supply any principle upon which the books were to be treated or interpreted. K. Aland comments on the rationale of the New Testament offered by the Muratorian canon:

If one wanted to sum up in a formula the external principles which played a part in the choice of the canonical scriptures, one can only speak of the principle of 'having no principles'. From the Muratorian Canon, e.g., we can see how every emerging principle on which the choice has professedly been made is expressly repudiated again in words. The same state of affairs would, no doubt, become visible in all other lists of the Canon if they were not preserved in such brevity.[1]

Thus the books are not arranged chronologically, and it is no longer possible to date them in relation to one another with any confidence. Even if it were so, a purely chronological arrangement would leave out of account what might be of greater significance, the differences of ethos and development in the churches of the different areas concerned. An arrangement other than that required by the second-century conception of the Canon could have led to the retention of the connection between Luke's Gospel and Acts, and to the placing of John's Gospel alongside the Johannine epistles, and perhaps to other conjunctions such as that of the Epistle of James with Matthew's Gospel.

E. J. Goodspeed, in criticising the procedures adopted in *Introductions to the New Testament*, posed the questions: 'Does the literature of the New Testament reveal no clear pattern, no sweep of movement in its rise? Must its books be always so arbitrarily treated? Is there no broad literary principle that may reduce these reluctant units to a new and significant order?'[2] His own negative answer to the first two and affirmative answer to the last of these questions are however vulnerable at a number of points, as, for example, in the supposition that the publication of Luke–Acts was responsible for the collection of the Pauline corpus of letters with Ephesians specially written to act as an introduction to it, or that the letters to the seven churches in Revelation followed a Pauline model. It cannot be assumed that because these twenty-seven writings belong together in the Canon they are all capable of being related to one another, and on examination there appear to be too many uncertain factors of date, authorship, origin and milieu for this to be done. There is, indeed, overlapping, and some books have roots in others. The Synoptic Gospels are genetically related, though even this can be out of focus when Luke's Gospel is separated from Acts; so also are Jude and 2 Peter. Imitation of the Pauline letters was a major factor in the deutero-Pauline literature, and was probably a factor in 1 and 2 Peter, though dubiously so in the

---

[1] *The Problem of the New Testament Canon* (London, 1962), p. 15.
[2] *New Chapters in New Testament Study* (New York, 1937), p. 61.

case of James. Hebrews stands apart as distinctive, as do the Johannine writings, even if the Fourth Gospel is in some way related to the synoptic tradition and Revelation to the synoptic apocalypse. Certain similarities in different epistles may indicate the independent use of a common catechetical tradition or may be explained by a more genetical relationship and the dependence of one author on another.[1] The use of 'the *kerygma*' as an over-all term to denote a central message of the New Testament and a skeleton framework underlying it may be to some extent well founded; it is probably an over-simplification if the word *kerygma* or proclamation is extended to cover all, or the majority, of its books, or when such a *kerygma* is taken to be single rather than multiple. In relation to traditional positions, which went along with a doctrine of the unity of the Canon, historical criticism has often appeared to be largely negative. It makes a positive contribution, however, in so far as it legitimately brings to light the variety of the New Testament documents, of their backgrounds, intentions, sources and strata, as the starting point for a proper exegesis of them.

10. THE NEW TESTAMENT CANON

The Canon of the New Testament was the result of a long and gradual process in the course of which the books regarded as authoritative, inspired, and apostolic were selected out of a much larger body of literature. Such a process of selection necessarily involved both selectors and grounds on which the selection would be made. As far as we know, the early selectors were anonymous. We may suppose that they were leaders in the Christian churches, but we do not know their names or the dates at which selections were made. Only in the late second century does it become clear that such leaders as Irenaeus of Lyons and Serapion of Antioch are consciously discussing questions of canon, and when they do so they are relying primarily on older Church traditions. This is not to say that such individuals lacked influence upon the process of selection; it is to say that their influence was exerted in favour of prior views and contemporary consensus.

When we speak of selection it is clear that the process involves

---

[1] For the first view see P. Carrington, *The Primitive Christian Catechism* (Cambridge, 1940) and E. G. Selwyn, *The First Epistle of St Peter* (London, 1946), Essay II, and for the second F. W. Beare, *The First Epistle of Peter* (Oxford, 2nd ed. 1958), pp. 194 ff.

comparison between one book and another or among collections of books. The fact that the gnostic 'library' at Nag Hammadi includes books which may not have been gnostic in origin probably means that non-gnostic books were interpreted in gnostic ways by those who collected them. Similarly, the early Christian canonical collection implies that those who assembled or accepted it understood all the books as conveying essentially the same message. The books rejected from the Canon were rejected because they seemed to conflict with what the accepted books taught. Selection thus involved not only comparison among books but also comparison with a norm viewed as relatively fixed. Before this norm, among early Christians regarded as the faith of the apostles, reached a relative fixity of expression it was not possible for a definite Canon to come into existence. About A.D. 170, when opponents of the enthusiastic movement known as Montanism endeavoured to cut the ground from under it by rejecting the Gospel and Revelation of John, their own theological ideas had not incorporated Johannine insights, and their rejection of the Johannine books was destined to fall because the theology of the Church as a whole was coming to be increasingly Johannine. This is to say that the development of the Canon and the development of Christian theology were closely interrelated, and supported one another.

For this reason we cannot say that the gnostic gospels, revelations, and other books which were definitely rejected toward the end of the second century were necessarily written at a late date. They may well have been written early even though they came to be viewed as unorthodox and non-canonical only later. The question of canonicity or, to put it more historically, authority—since the term 'canon' was not used until the fourth century—did not and could not arise until the idea of orthodoxy had clearly arisen out of the second-century anti-gnostic debates.

Such a statement must, of course, be qualified in relation to several historical facts. First, except among the more extreme proponents of Jewish Christianity there was never any doubt about the major Pauline epistles, written by the chief apostle to the Gentiles to various churches and combined into one collection by the end of the first century. The three Synoptic Gospels were undoubtedly widely accepted early in the second century as the rival gospels (*According to the Hebrews*, *According to the Egyptians*, *According to Thomas*, etc.) were not. Secondly, some of the New Testament books were evidently intended for reading in more than one community (cf. Gal. 1: 2; Col. 4: 16; all the 'catholic' epistles), and the author of Revelation, writing to 'the seven churches in Asia' (1: 4), regards his book as analogous to scripture, for he claims that God will punish those who add to it or subtract from it (22: 18–19). Generally speaking, there was a common core of authoritative books, accepted by those Christians who were united at least (1) by their rejection of docetism, and therefore their maintenance of the historical reality of the life, death, and resurrection of Jesus, (2) by their acceptance of the Old Testament as containing God's revelation pointing toward Jesus, and (3) by their belief that God's revelation was accessible to all men without distinction, not to a spiritual élite only.

In the course of the anti-gnostic debates during the second century these positions were sharpened and carefully defined, but before that time there was at least an embryonic orthodoxy, and it was related to the common core of books which most Christians seem to have accepted. Proof that most Christians accepted them can probably be provided by the fact that gnostic teachers too made use of these books as well as of their own esoteric documents; presumably they would not have done so had not a consensus of earlier usage constrained them. This is to say that, at least in part, the process of canonisation was a process of recognising what had long been the actual situation. It would appear that the primary criterion was traditional usage among groups known to have held the traditional faith.

BEGINNINGS OF THE CANON

Though the New Testament as such emerged only in the life and thought of Christian communities in the second and third centuries, the books of which it consisted were known and used much earlier. During the apostolic age the Christian Bible consisted of the Old Testament alone—not that the Old Testament was precisely defined, but the main outlines were quite clear. In the writings of the apostle Paul there are no traces of any New Testament books. What Paul regards as authoritative, in addition to the Old Testament, is a rather vaguely defined group of oral traditions related to what Jesus had done and said. He obviously knew a good deal about the life of

Jesus; otherwise he could hardly have urged his converts to imitate him as he imitated Christ (1 Cor. 11: 1) or have stated that they imitated apostolic authorities and the Lord (1 Thess. 1: 6). In part, the traditions were presented within a chronological framework. We can see this framework not only in the list of resurrection appearances, beginning with Cephas and ending with Paul (1 Cor. 15: 5–8), but also in the tradition about eucharistic origins, which tells what the Lord Jesus did and said 'on the night when he was delivered up' (1 Cor. 11: 23). The fact that this tradition does not precisely agree with what we find in the gospels suggests that it was oral. Furthermore, the words which Paul uses about transmission in both these passages in 1 Corinthians are equivalent to the words used by rabbinical teachers in the same connection. In his letters there are also references to sayings of the Lord, though he gives them no historical context. In 1 Thess. 4: 15–18 he ascribes a rather detailed description of the Lord's return to a 'word of the Lord', and there are several examples in 1 Corinthians. 'The Lord commanded that those who proclaim the gospel should get their living by the gospel' (9: 14); 'to those who are married I proclaim —not I but the Lord—that a wife is not to be separated from her husband' (7: 10). In 1 Corinthians 7: 12 Paul explicitly differentiates what he is commanding from what the Lord commanded, and in 7: 25 he says that he has no commandment of the Lord in regard to 'virgins'. Therefore when he tells Corinthian prophets and 'spiritual' men that they should recognise that what he is writing is 'a command of the Lord' (14: 37) we must assume that he is not confusing his own authority with that of Christ; he must be relying upon some traditional saying of Jesus. Though he believed that Christ was alive in him (Gal. 2: 20) and that, as he instructed the Corinthians, he possessed the Spirit of God (1 Cor. 7: 40), he is not likely to have confused what he taught with what Jesus had taught—at least ordinarily! According to Acts 20: 35 he urged the presbyters of Ephesus to 'remember the words of the Lord Jesus, how he said "It is more blessed to give than to receive"'. This verse certainly proves that the author of Luke–Acts knew a saying of Jesus which he did not include in his Gospel; it probably shows that he knew that Paul was accustomed to refer to such sayings.

Though the Pauline epistles also contain many allusions to sayings of the Lord which we know from the gospels, it cannot be denied that Paul's basic concern is not with the traditions but with the new life in

Christ. 'Even if we have known Christ in human fashion, we now no longer so know him' (2 Cor. 5: 16). Paul's purpose was not that of collecting and compiling the traditions: it was that of transmitting some of them and interpreting their meaning to his converts. The task of compilation was left to the evangelists, and during the latter half of the first century various gospels came into existence. During the same period, the letters of Paul, which had been preserved either by their recipients or by Paul's assistants, were collected, and various other letters, Acts, and the Revelation of John were produced. What is probably the latest book in our New Testament is the epistle called 2 Peter, in which use is made of the little letter of Jude, perhaps the twenty-first chapter of John's Gospel, and a collection of Pauline epistles probably including the Pastorals (2 Pet. 3: 15–16). It would appear that the author of 2 Peter was conscious of the problem of the acceptance or rejection of various books. The author of Jude had clearly accepted such Jewish apocalypses as the Assumption of Moses and 1 Enoch; in the revised version provided in 2 Peter the clear allusions have been removed. When we find in 2 Peter clear references to 1 Peter (3: 1) and to 'all' the letters of Paul (3: 16), we are led to believe that something like a canon, at least of epistles, is being shaped. We should like to know the date of 2 Peter, but unfortunately we can only guess at it, placing it around the end of the first century or early in the second.

To determine what use was made of the various books in the late first century and the early second is very difficult. Early in the fourth century, Eusebius of Caesarea was concerned with precisely this problem, but his research method was both inexact and incomplete; he does not help us as much as we should wish. We still possess many of the materials he used, but they leave enormous gaps in our historical knowledge. From the years between about 90 and about 150 we have available only a letter and a sermon ascribed to Clement of Rome, a 'manual of discipline' called the *Didache*, seven letters by Ignatius of Antioch, a letter by his contemporary Polycarp of Smyrna, a treatise ascribed to Paul's companion Barnabas, an apocalypse by Hermas of Rome entitled the *Shepherd*, and fragments from Papias of Hierapolis. To some extent these documents can be classified by location (Rome: Clement, Hermas; Syria and Asia: *Didache*, Ignatius, Polycarp, Papias; perhaps Alexandria: Barnabas) and thus we can find out something about different local usages. To some extent they can also be classified by proximity to Jewish Christianity, but the lines between Jewish and Gentile Christianity in the early second century are not as sharp as scholars sometimes assume. In any case, all these documents were written in Greek by Christians. In order to say anything at all, we have to assume that the documents we possess are relatively representative of Christianity in the period, even though the fact that they were preserved proves that they were not representative of what came to be regarded as heresy.

The oldest document among them is the *Didache*, a manual produced in the name of the apostles probably in Syria between 70 and 90. Though it is difficult to be certain, the Didachist seems to have relied on oral tradition, called by him 'commandments of the Lord', as his primary authorities rather than upon written books. He considers these commandments to be essential to the Christian way of life: because of this status they must neither be added to nor taken away from (4: 13). He apparently takes them from tradition because the wording and order of these commandments usually varies from their synoptic forms as we have them. The teaching requiring love of God and neighbour (1 : 2 f.) is not identical with that either in Matthew (5 : 44, 46, 47; 7: 12) or in Luke (6: 31–3). This seems to indicate, as do the rest of the quotations, that he is either using oral tradition or quoting from memories of written books.

In either case, however, these commandments are part of the gospel tradition. From this tradition the Didachist derives, in addition to the commandment to love those who are against you (1: 3), the statement that 'the meek will inherit the earth' (3: 7; Matt. 5: 5), and the injunctions about baptism, fasting, prayer (7–8) and reconciliation (14: 2) as well as the eschatological materials of chapter 16. Further, the Didachist views this commandment-tradition as already anticipated in the Old Testament in 'ancient prophets' (11: 11) like Malachi (cited in 14: 3) and Zechariah (cited in 16: 7) and even in later Jewish writings like Ecclesiasticus (cited in 1: 6).

On the other hand, the Didachist probably knew the Gospel of Matthew and was referring to this book when he spoke of what Christians 'have in the gospel' or 'have in the gospel of our Lord', even though he views the oral or remembered forms of these commandments as primary. The last six chapters, especially, display a close relationship of the Didachist to the Gospel of Matthew. His teaching about apostles and prophets 'in accordance with the decree of the gospel' (11: 3) may be based on Matthacan passages. Indeed *Did.* 11: 7 is a clear allusion to Matt. 12: 31, and the end of the whole 'practical' section (15: 3–4), while containing no direct quotations from Matthew, sums up the teaching of Matt. 5: 22–6 and 18: 15–35. Chapter 16, though it may not be an original part of the document, is clearly based upon an apocalypse similar to Matt. 24.

Even the earlier chapters of the *Didache* display a close relationship to the Gospel of Matthew, although the closer wording of some passages to Luke may indicate that the Didachist quoted somewhat inexactly from memory. The sayings about turning the other cheek, going the second mile, giving your shirt as well as your coat, and not requesting back what has been taken from you (*Did.* 1: 4) have close parallels in Matthew (5: 39, 48, 41, 40) and Luke (6: 30), although, again, the order and wording is such that one cannot determine why they stand in this present form. In *Did.* 6: 1 there seems to be an allusion to Matt. 24: 4: 'See that no one makes you err' from this teaching. The chapters concerned with baptism, fasting, and prayer contain very definite quotations from the Gospel of Matthew. 'Baptize them in the name of the Father and of the Son and of the Holy Spirit' (7: 1) is surely an echo of Matt. 28: 19; the Didachist's injunction for the Christians not to fast with the 'hypocrites' is an exposition of the doctrine of Matt. 6: 16; the version of the Lord's Prayer in 8: 2 with the concluding doxology is certainly the prayer recorded in Matt. 6: 9–13. Further, *Did.* 9: 5, 'the Lord said, "Do not give the holy thing to the dogs"', is an explicit citation of Matt. 7: 6.

Our information leads us to say that the Didachist surely had close contact with the Gospel of Matthew or at least its tradition, but that he draws upon that tradition either from memory or from oral gospel tradition. We are led to say, then, that his primary authority must be tradition, whether oral or written, rather than documents considered as authoritative 'scriptural' documents.

Another important early witness to the prominence of oral tradition as well as written documents is Papias of Hierapolis in Phrygia, who apparently wrote during the early years of the second century. What he wrote is preserved only in fragments, chiefly in Irenaeus and Eusebius. In the preface to his *Exegeses* he stated that he tried to differentiate the valuable 'commandments given by the Lord to faith and proceeding from truth itself' (or 'from the Truth himself') from the less valuable materials derived from books. Since he had a high regard for oral tradition, he made an effort to discover what was taught by the elders or disciples of the Lord—men of the past (Andrew, Peter, Philip, Thomas, James, John, and Matthew)—from what men still alive were teaching (Aristion and the elder John). He explicitly referred to the composition of books by Matthew and Mark, but viewed a compilation by Matthew as originally written in a Hebrew dialect (and now extant in various translations), while he defended the Gospel of Mark as out of order, chronological or rhetorical, but containing everything that Mark had heard from Peter. Eusebius states that Papias also made use of 1 John and 1 Peter and related a story about a woman 'accused of many sins before the Lord' which was also to be found in the apocryphal *Gospel of the Hebrews*. Later Christian writers state that Papias also regarded Revelation with enthusiasm.

Papias' acceptance of oral traditions—including, according to Eusebius, 'strange parables and instructions of the Saviour'—and of apocalyptic eschatology accounts for the disappearance of his work. Irenaeus, who favoured millenarian views, quoted from him; Eusebius, who was more at home in the world, neglected his apocalyptic views while criticising him as unintelligent. For this reason we may suppose that the traditions collected by Papias were fairly primitive though unedifying to many later Christians, and that they reflected a form of Christianity close to Judaism which did not later survive. It may be doubted that he had anything like a 'canon' of New Testament writings.

Another Jewish Christian of this period was Hermas of Rome, whose *Shepherd* contains echoes not only of the Old Testament and apocalyptic writings but also of something like Matthew, Mark, and John, and probably the Epistle to the Ephesians. Once more, there is no trace of a canon, though Christian books evidently exist and are highly valued. What we find in Jewish Christian writings is a supremely authoritative Old Testament along with Christian writings which serve to interpret it for the Christian communities, but which are not, apparently, regarded as on the same plane.

Into a somewhat different category fall two documents ascribed to Clement of Rome. In 1 Clement, a letter from the Roman Christians to the Corinthians at the end of the first century, the Old Testament is the primary written authority, but the 'words of the Lord Jesus' are extremely important, and so is the letter which the apostle Paul wrote to the Corinthians at an early date. Clement also reflects the thought of the Epistle to the Hebrews, though we have no means of telling how he regarded the document, and there are echoes of various Pauline epistles as well. 2 Clement, actually a homily rather than a letter, contains echoes of synoptic traditions (and non-synoptic traditions as well), along with passages clearly influenced by some of the Pauline epistles. In one instance 2 Clement refers to a gospel saying as from 'scripture' (2: 4). This passage shows that the authority of gospel sayings was coming to be regarded as co-ordinate with that of the Old Testament. The category in which we should place 1 and 2 Clement is that of hellenistic–Jewish Christianity, in which the letters of Paul are valued highly (as not in the *Didache* or by Papias) and the possibility of a written authority beyond the Old Testament has arisen.

Beyond Judaism in the direction of hellenistic Christianity we find the letters of Ignatius of Antioch, Polycarp of Smyrna and 'Barnabas'. Ignatius almost certainly had a high regard for the Gospels of Matthew and John (perhaps also for that of Luke) and his letters are full of echoes from Pauline epistles, above all from 1 Corinthians, in which he found a religious-administrative viewpoint closely similar to his own. In both 1 Corinthians and Ephesians he found his own emphasis upon the unity of the Church. On the other hand, he never quotes from any New Testament documents as 'scripture', since he reserves the expression 'it is written' for two quotations from the book of Proverbs. In one letter (*Philad.* 8: 2) he gives a report of a debate he had with Judaising Christians. They apparently denied that Ignatius' views could be supported by the Old Testament: 'if I do not find it in the "charters" (ἀρχεῖα) I do not believe it in the gospel'. He replied, 'But it is written.' They abandoned the debate by stating, 'That is just the question.' He then affirms in the letter that for him the 'charters' are Jesus Christ, his cross and death and resurrection, and faith through him. Presumably this debate reflects the Judaisers' demand for Old Testament proof and Ignatius' refusal to enter into exegetical analysis. It indicates that for him and for them the primary authority had been the Old Testament but that he was beginning to be aware that Old Testament exegesis did not provide a fully adequate basis for theology. It was going to prove necessary to argue on New Testament grounds—but this stage had not as yet been reached.

The letter of Polycarp comes from a similar situation. The sayings of Jesus and Pauline epistles are authoritative for Christians, but they do not constitute the 'scriptures' which both he and his correspondents know. In one passage (*Phil.* 12: 1) he says that these scriptures include the sayings 'Be angry and sin not' and 'Let not the sun go down upon your wrath'. The first is from Ps. 4: 5 (LXX) and is combined with the second in Eph. 4: 26—a letter which Polycarp knew. It is likely, however, either that 'scriptures' means simply 'writings' or that Polycarp thought he was quoting from the Old Testament. Nothing else in what he wrote suggests that he viewed New Testament writings as scripture.

Finally, the Epistle of Barnabas clearly reflects not only the Old Testament but also Jewish apocalyptic writings and at least the Gospel of Matthew. It is most unlikely, however, that the author viewed any part of the New Testament as 'scripture'. We conclude that even among hellenistic Christians of the early second century the only scripture was the Old Testament, although for Barnabas the Old Testament may have included such documents as 1 Enoch, 2 Esdras, and 2 Baruch (*Ep. Barn.* 4: 3; 16: 5–6; 12: 1; 11: 9).

This is to say that as the early Church entered more fully into the Graeco-Roman world it placed an increasingly high value upon traditions about the Lord Jesus and upon the writings of the apostles, but the books of the apostles and their immediate successors were not yet viewed as scripture. The decisive step in this direction seems to have been taken among Gnostics and is first reflected in the remains of Basilides, who taught at Alexandria in the early years of the second century. The most complete and original account of his teaching has been preserved by Hippolytus, who wrote at Rome in the third century, and in it we find exegesis of the Gospels of Matthew, Luke, and John (introduced by formulae such as 'this is what the gospels mean when they say') and exegetical proofs based on Romans, 1–2 Corinthians, and Ephesians. These proofs begin with the formula 'as it is written' or, in one instance (Hippolytus, *Ref.* VII, 25, 3), 'it is written' (1 Cor. 2: 13). Basilides is therefore the first Christian to treat New Testament books explicitly as scripture.

A generation later, the attention of Christians was forcibly drawn to the question of canon by the dualistic Gnostic Marcion, who taught at Rome between 137 and 144. In Marcion's opinion the authentic teaching of Jesus had been distorted by his earliest Jewish disciples, who proclaimed the gospel among Jews and altered it for apologetic reasons. Paul, who had a special revelation of the risen Lord, recovered the authentic gospel, but his letters were later interpolated by Judaisers. Only Marcion was able to restore the original gospel, apparently in reliance upon Galatians, in which Paul describes himself as rebuking Peter on account of his Judaising tendencies. By virtue of an elaborate process of literary criticism Marcion removed interpolations from ten Pauline epistles (not including either Hebrews or the Pastorals) and from the one gospel which he accepted, a revised version of Luke. Presumably the rigour of Marcion's method resulted in considerable confusion among more orthodox Christians, who as we have seen had practically no conception of a New Testament Canon, whereas he actually did possess one *Gospel* and one (ten-letter) *Apostle*. Justin Martyr, who wrote at Rome soon after Marcion's exodus from the church there, never refers to the Pauline epistles, though he does clearly indicate that the Church had a plurality of gospels.

The Church was experiencing severe exegetical difficulties toward the middle of the second century. Many Gnostics were able to provide esoteric interpretations of Pauline epistles (in which, as the author of 2 Peter remarked, there were things difficult to understand) and of the gospels as well. Such a Valentinian Gnostic as Ptolemaeus, for example, frequently quoted from the epistles and made use of sayings of Jesus contained in Matthew, Mark, Luke, and John. None of the Valentinians seems to have used the word 'scripture', but this silence is probably due simply to the fact that few Christians used it except in relation to the Old Testament. Indeed, it was not until about 180 that a Christian writer came close to speaking of a New Testament book as scripture. Theophilus of Antioch (*Ad Autolycum*, II, 22) speaks of 'the holy scriptures and all the inspired men, one of whom, John, says "In the beginning was the Word and the Word was with God"'. Other passages clearly show that the gospel and the Pauline epistles are co-ordinate with scripture; but in a Jewish-Christian context Theophilus does not seem willing to identify the two groups of writings. The step of identifying New Testament books as scripture was finally taken by Irenaeus, a few years later. It is sometimes claimed that his New Testament included not only the four Gospels, Acts, thirteen

Pauline epistles (the Pastorals but perhaps not Hebrews),[1] 1 Peter, 1–2 John, and Revelation, but also 1 Clement and Hermas. It is clear, however, that when he speaks (*Adv. haer.* III, 3, 3) of 1 Clement as *scriptura* he means no more than 'writing', and the same conclusion is to be drawn from a similar reference to Hermas (IV, 20, 2).[2] Irenaeus occasionally used apocryphal traditions but he did not use apocryphal New Testament books.

By the end of the second century, then, Christians generally made use of a collection of books which included practically all those in use today. Irenaeus' writings contain no traces of James, Jude, 2 Peter, and 3 John; all but Jude are also absent from Clement of Alexandria, who unlike Irenaeus uses Hebrews; Origen employs all these New Testament books, and a few others. Before turning to the significance of the Alexandrian school, however, we should say something about the meaning of our evidence from the second century.

In regard to this period it is difficult to make positive statements in view of our lack of evidence. We have already indicated how few documents we possess from the period of the Apostolic Fathers. We should also point out that from the latter half of the century we have only some gnostic documents, mostly fragmentary, the writings of a few apologists (who certainly were not providing complete accounts of Christianity), and the anti-heretical treatise of Irenaeus. (Clement of Alexandria began writing in this century but the bulk of his production belongs to the third.) Most of the gnostic documents survive because they were quoted by orthodox writers; the other writings survive because their authors were highly regarded by later orthodox authorities. In other words, our information has a built-in bias towards orthodoxy and uniformity. We must assume that especially in the earlier years of the second century there was more diversity than appears in the extant evidence, and we must admit that when we trace a trend we do so only in regard to what later writers consciously preserved. In regard to the Canon this situation can conceivably lead us astray. In the fourth century the creator of a 'new Ignatius' filled his letters with the New Testament quotations he thought Ignatius ought to have provided. There is no reason for assuming that a similar distortion exists in regard to the documents we actually have, but there

---

[1] But cf. A. Rousseau *et al.*, *Irénée de Lyon. Contre les hérésies. Livre IV* (Sources chrétiennes, 100, Paris, 1965), pp. 281–2.   [2] *Ibid.* pp. 248–50.

is every reason to assume that second-century Christians used non-canonical documents to an extent greater than that reflected in what we possess. Two points clearly suggest this: (1) the loss of most of what Papias wrote, and (2) the hesitation of Serapion, bishop of Antioch about 190, as to whether or not he should approve the apocryphal *Gospel of Peter* (Eus., *H.E.* VI, 12, 3–6). It should be added that in the writings of most of the Apostolic Fathers and some of the apologists, not to mention Irenaeus, Clement, and Origen, there are quotations of sayings of Jesus not preserved in the canonical gospels. Some sayings doubtless came from oral tradition; others may well have been preserved in books. The gradual development of the Canon was a process of exclusion and it lasted at least to the fourth century.

On the other hand, it cannot be denied that there was a core of essential books which almost all Christians accepted and revered. This core consisted of at least the three Synoptic Gospels (arguments about the Gospel of John were carried on in the second and third centuries because of its incompatibility with the Synoptics), the major Pauline epistles, and Revelation (though this book's place was also debated). There was a basic picture of Jesus and his teaching; there was a basic understanding of what Paul taught. It was especially important that the gospels were read aloud at Christian worship (Justin, *Apol.* I, 67, 3). Because of this kind of reading the minds of Christians were regularly given formation in the direction of what Jesus had done and said, and they could differentiate a gospel regarded as authentically Christian by the community from others not so regarded.

At first, it would appear, the Christian gospels were regarded as practically self-explanatory. At any rate, we possess little explicit exegesis of them from an early period. It is possible to regard Matthew and Luke as examples of the exegesis of Mark, but rewriting is not quite the same thing as interpretation.[1] After a collection of the authoritative gospels had been made and they were in circulation together, difficulties arose. Marcion tried to solve the problem by using only one self-consistent gospel; Justin's disciple Tatian wove together one narrative out of the four and called it the *Diatessaron*. Others, like the Valentinian Gnostics, proceeded to provide rather detailed allegorical exegesis first of the prologue to John (Ptolemaeus), then of the whole book (Hera-

---

[1] Similarly the Pastoral Epistles constitute reinterpretations of Paul, and 2 Peter is a revised version of Jude.

cleon). These exegetical studies were imitated at Alexandria by Clement in his *Hypotyposes* (mostly lost) and by Origen in a vast series of commentaries. The gradual formation of a canon thus made necessary an attempt to provide authoritative exegesis of its contents. Such exegesis did not arise earlier, it would appear, because there was no real canon in existence.

SOME APOCRYPHAL DOCUMENTS

We have seen that early in the second century Christians had a high regard for oral tradition. This regard is reflected in the statement of Papias that he preferred materials from 'a living and continuing voice' to those from books; it also underlies the claim of his Gnostic contemporary Basilides to possess traditions from Peter's 'interpreter' Glaukias. The Gnostic Valentinus said he was instructed by Theodas, a disciple of Paul; Valentinus' own disciple Ptolemaeus wrote that the doctrine of the group came from apostolic tradition.

The earliest situation was thus one of conflict among rival oral traditions, although the existence of such books as the Pauline epistles and some of the gospels inevitably led to a conflict first between books and traditions and then between books and books. (I am assuming that in general the books which came to be regarded as canonical were prior to the 'apocryphal' ones. This seems to be the case as far as the extant literature is concerned, although of course it is possible that there were apocryphal books now lost. Discussion of them is not, however, very profitable.)

Among the earliest examples of apocryphal documents are four gospels: those *According to the Hebrews, According to the Egyptians, According to Peter*, and *According to Thomas*. Eusebius informs us that Papias made use of a story 'about a woman falsely accused of many sins before the Lord, which the *Gospel of the Hebrews* contains'. It has sometimes been supposed that this story is the one about the woman taken in adultery, found in manuscripts of the Gospel of John from the late fourth century, though not in earlier ones—but she was caught in one sin, not falsely accused of many. We simply do not know what the *Hebrews* story was. Fragmentary remains of this gospel show that it contained speculative and mythological reflections on the story of Jesus (in two instances the Holy Spirit is depicted as Christ's mother) and variant versions of gospel sayings, embellished apparently for the sake of vividness. There is no reason to suppose that this gospel contained older or more reliable accounts of Jesus' ministry than those in the Synoptic Gospels. Its title was doubtless meant to suggest that it was based on old tradition, though it may mean no more than that it was used by Jewish Christians—perhaps in Egypt.

The *Gospel of the Egyptians* is best known for a dialogue between Jesus and his disciple Salome (cf. Mark 15: 40), related by Clement of Alexandria. Jesus tells her that death is the consequence of birth, and that believers should 'trample on the garment of shame'. The two should become one, the male with the female neither male nor female; indeed the Saviour 'came to destroy the works of the female'. Whether or not this gospel was fully gnostic, rather than just extremely ascetic-minded, its author was on the way towards Gnosticism, even though the saying about the two becoming one also occurs in 2 Clement. The fact that the gospel is called 'according to the Egyptians' reminds us that in the second century, as far as our knowledge goes, Christianity in Egypt was exclusively 'heterodox'.

The *Gospel of Peter* is better known to us than *Hebrews* and *Egyptians*, for a fairly extensive section of it exists in a parchment book of the eighth or ninth century, found in Egypt in 1886–7. In this section there is an account of Christ's crucifixion and resurrection, almost certainly a paraphrased version of materials common to the four canonical Gospels. There are some important additions: (1) the rôle of Herod is emphasised; (2) Jesus is silent because he feels no pain; (3) he cries out, 'My power, my power, you have forsaken me'; (4) many details about his tomb are given; and (5) the guards see 'three men coming out of the tomb, and the two supporting the one, and a cross following them, and the head of the two reaching to heaven, and that of the one conducted by them surpassing the heavens'. A voice from heaven asks, 'Have you preached to those who sleep?' (cf. 1 Pet. 3: 19; 4: 6), and a voice from the cross says, 'Yes'. As in the case of *Hebrews*, the purpose of *Peter* is evidently to provide mythological, and rather unorthodox, additions to the traditional narratives. Indeed, Christ not only suffered no pain but also after stating that his power had left him 'he was taken up'. There is no real death of Christ—and this is why Docetists, as we know from Serapion of Antioch, used the book.

The only complete apocryphal gospel which we possess is the *Gospel of Thomas*, found in Egypt in a fourth-century Coptic version and in Greek fragments of the third century. This gospel, unlike the canonical Gospels, contains nothing but sayings of Jesus, sometimes in dialogue form. It begins with the programmatic statement: 'These are the secret words which Jesus the Living spoke and Didymus Judas Thomas wrote.' Jesus himself is depicted as saying, 'He who will find the interpretation of these words will not taste death.' The sayings provide a conglomeration of materials apparently taken from the Synoptic Gospels (perhaps also from John), from traditions reflected in *Hebrews* and *Egyptians*, and from what seem to be gnostic traditions. Whatever the origins of the materials may be, the author has placed them in a context which is indisputably gnostic.

From our brief review of these four apocryphal gospels (to which might be added the apocryphal acts, epistles, and revelations) it is evident that in the second century—from which all four come—Christians were confronted with a large variety of literature among which choices had to be made. The question of the formation of a canon was closely related to the question of defining Christianity itself. Only when it could be decided that something was really Christian, while something else was not, could Christians come to make definite decisions about the authoritative books. This means that the process was somewhat circular, or at least that the mode of procedure could not be stated with logical precision. One might say that 'Bible' and 'Church' grew up together.

THE OLD TESTAMENT

When we look through early Christian literature for evidence about the New Testament Canon we do not always recall how recently an authoritative Canon of Old Testament books had come into existence. To be sure, something of a nucleus of books universally accepted had long been utilised; its existence is attested not only by the writings of Philo and Josephus, by the Qumrân Scrolls, and by the writers of apocalyptic literature, but also by the Greek translations produced during and after the second century B.C. We may mention the statement by Josephus (*C.Ap.* I, 38–40) to the effect that there are twenty-two books 'rightly given credence'. The prologue to Ecclesiasticus had spoken of 'the law and the prophets and the other ancestral books'. According to 2 Esdras 14: 45–8 there were twenty-four books generally known, along with seventy others kept secret; the Babylonian Talmud (Baba Bathra 14*b*) mentions only the twenty-four. Apparently this number was accepted at a rabbinic council held at Jamnia in Palestine toward the end of the first century A.D., although among Christians in the second and third centuries, often close to Jewish sources, the number continued to vary. Apart from the question of how many books there were, what was clear to Christian writers was that Jews were able to speak of a rather clearly defined collection of accepted books which constituted their Bible. Those Christian writers who discussed the limits of the nascent New Testament were almost always concerned with the Old Testament as well.

We have already indicated that gnostic statements about the books of the New Testament provided impetus for their more orthodox opponents both positively and negatively. We should add that when, as was rather often the case, gnostic teachers rejected the Old Testament as the revelation of a god inferior to the supreme deity, they must have encouraged Christians to define the contents of the Old Testament with some exactness, and therefore to consider the New Testament as well.

AN EARLY ROMAN LIST

Among the most important documents in the history of the New Testament Canon is the 'Muratorian' fragment, so called because it was published by L. A. Muratori in 1740. It lacks a beginning, for it starts with the words *quibus tamen interfuit et ita posuit*—'at which he was present and thus he wrote them down'. Since what follows is 'third book of the Gospel, according to Luke', what has been lost must have described the work of the evangelist Mark, and the first book discussed must have been Matthew. The author explains that Luke was a disciple of Paul and wrote a gospel even though he too (like Paul) had not seen the Lord 'in the flesh'. Luke also wrote the Acts of 'all the apostles' in one book; the author thus rejects the apocryphal books of Acts current in his day. The Gospel of John is the fourth, and though it has a beginning different from those of the other three it sets forth the same basic Christian point of view. He lists thirteen Pauline epistles, not mentioning Hebrews at all, and also accepts Jude, 1–2 John, the

Wisdom of Solomon (!), and the Revelation of John. Beyond these books lie two about which there is some doubt. First, the author himself definitely accepts the *Revelation of Peter* although, as he says, 'some' will not allow it to be read in church. Second, he evidently knows people who publicly read the *Shepherd* of Hermas. He does not share their enthusiasm. The book is neither prophetic nor apostolic (compare Justin's statement that in the Roman church there were public readings from prophets or apostles), for it was produced in recent times when Hermas' brother Pius was bishop of Rome. (This statement, it would appear, definitely dates the fragment within the second century.)

There are also works which are universally rejected, or should be so rejected. These consist of Marcionite forgeries—the epistles to the Laodiceans and the Alexandrians and a book of psalms—and the treatises of the Gnostics Valentinus and Basilides and of the Montanists.

Of the New Testament books generally accepted toward the end of the second century—for example, by Irenaeus, whose relations with Rome were close—we miss only 1 Peter. Theodor Zahn offered the conjecture that a mention of it had accidentally dropped out[1], and in view of the whole history of the Canon we must assume that such is the case. It is unnecessary to explain the author's criticism of Hermas once we recognise that Irenaeus did not use the book as scripture (see above, p. 295).

The Muratorian list is in part polemical. When the author insists that the Gospels agree he may well have in mind the Alogi of Asia Minor, who were arguing that John contradicted the Synoptics. In describing Luke as not having seen the Lord, and also in upholding his authorship of Acts, the author is doubtless opposing Marcionites, as he is when he includes the Pastorals among Paul's letters. At the end of the fragment, as we have seen, the polemical element comes to the surface. At the same time, it must not be forgotten that there is also a rather simple and positive purpose. The author is insisting that the acceptable books reflect the common faith of the Church as based on the writings of the apostles and their companions. The document is polemical, but its polemic is based on what the author regards as apostolic tradition.

---

[1] *Geschichte des Neutestamenthichen Kanons*, II, 1 (Erlangen, Leipzig, 1890), p. 110.

THE SCHOOLS OF ALEXANDRIA

If we had only the writings of Irenaeus and the Muratorian fragment to consider, our picture of the development of the New Testament Canon would be considerably clearer than it becomes when we consider the evidence from the church of Alexandria. The beginnings of this church are shrouded in obscurity and for a long time the dominant influences in it seem to have been gnostic. Only when we reach the fragments of the shadowy Pantaenus (late second century) do we have evidence to show that questions about the Canon (e.g. who wrote Hebrews?) were under discussion, and only Clement—to some extent under gnostic influence—provides more adequate information.

It has only recently been realised how little we really know, in spite of a rather bulky literary product, about Clement's viewpoint. In 1960 Professor Morton Smith described a letter by Clement which he had discovered, and this letter makes plain the fact that at Alexandria no fewer than three versions of the Gospel of Mark were in circulation. First, there was the ordinary version known to all; secondly, there was a false version used by Carpocratian Gnostics; thirdly, there was a secret version, written by Mark himself at Alexandria and known only to the spiritual élite there. This statement shows that when we try to determine what Clement thought about the New Testament we are dealing only with what he thought was suitable reading for the mass of Christians, not for the inner group. This situation may well explain some of the vagueness of Clement's ideas about authoritative books. He knows that the Church as a whole accepts four gospels and four only. It is not quite certain that his own view is the same. He can quote the traditional saying of Jesus, 'Become approved money-changers', as from scripture (*Strom.* I, 177, 2), and can state that 'in some gospel it says, "Without grudging, the Lord commanded, My mystery is for me and the sons of my house"' (*Strom.* V, 63, 7). In his library, if not in church, there is a collection of apocryphal literature much more extensive than the canonical New Testament. He cites the *Didache* as scripture (*Strom.* I, 100, 4) and regards 1 Clement, Barnabas, Hermas, and the *Preaching* and *Revelation of Peter* as inspired. One may add that Clement was a private teacher and thus did not necessarily reflect exactly what the leaders of the church at Alexandria taught during his time. In view of the eccentric character of early Alexandrian Christianity (as compared, say, with the views of Irenaeus) we cannot be sure that he was less 'orthodox' than his contemporaries in this regard.

Origen, on the other hand, was self-consciously an ecclesiastical theologian. Unlike Clement, he expressed definite condemnation of several apocryphal gospels—those ascribed to Thomas, Matthias, and the Twelve, along with that *According to the Egyptians* (*Luc. hom.* 1). To be sure, he was less critical of the *Gospel of the Hebrews* and only gradually hesitated to use the *Acts of Paul*. Like Clement, he referred to the saying about approved money-changers not only as 'a command of Jesus' but also as being 'according to the scripture'. But in general he was much more cautious about accepting doubtfully authentic books, even questioning the authorship of Hebrews, James, Jude, 2 Peter, and 2–3 John.

Origen provides one of the best examples of the way in which literary criticism was being brought to bear on questions of authorship in relation to canonicity. At Alexandria Pantaenus had already argued that Paul wrote Hebrews but it did not bear his name because, as an apostle to the Gentiles, he refrained from making apostolic claims in writing to Jews. Clement held that Paul had written in Hebrew and that Luke had translated the epistle into Greek (Eus., *H.E.* VI, 142). Origen refined this theory by claiming that though Hebrews contains Paul's ideas it was actually composed by someone else, perhaps Luke or Clement of Rome, both disciples of the apostle (Clement because mentioned in Phil. 4: 3)—though he concluded that 'God alone knows' who wrote the letter (*H.E.* VI, 25, 14). In dealing with the vexing problem of the relation of John to the Synoptics, Origen actually insisted upon the striking differences between John and the others but reconciled them by urging that since the Holy Spirit had endowed the apostolic authors with perfect memories, the discrepancies were intentional and pointed toward the spiritual meaning underlying all the books.

We thus see that while literary criticism could be used by Marcion to restore the original pure gospel and by the Alogi to reject the Gospel of John, with other presuppositions—the defence of tradition —it could be used in a more conservative manner. Origen's own conservatism is evident in his defence of the story of Susanna against the convincing criticisms raised by his contemporary Julius Africanus, who had shown that plays on Greek words proved its Greek origin.

After Origen's time, Dionysius of Alexandria used literary criticism to show that one author wrote Revelation, another (the apostle John) the Gospel and First Epistle. Dionysius intended not to remove Revelation from the Canon but to prove to apocalyptically minded devotees of the book that it was less authoritative than the other books. He agreed with Origen that the Gospel was the most important book in the New Testament.

Undoubtedly the church's Canon at Alexandria was influenced primarily by considerations of what was being, or ought to be, included among the authoritative books of the Old Testament. Secondarily, however, it may well have been the case that the literary-minded Alexandrian Christians bore in mind the so-called 'Canon Alexandrinus', the list of poets, historians, and orators approved by Alexandrian grammarians. Such a list had been drawn up in the third to second centuries B.C. by the philologist Aristophanes of Byzantium and is definitely reflected in the writings of the Roman rhetorician Quintilian (first century A.D.). It is reflected in the treatise *Ad Autolycum* (III, 2) by the apologist Theophilus, who mentions (1) epic poets like Homer, Hesiod (he adds Orpheus and Aratus), (2) tragic poets like Euripides and Sophocles, (3) comic poets like Menander and Aristophanes, and (4) historians like Herodotus and Thucydides, and adds a list of philosophers including Pythagoras, Diogenes, Epicurus, Empedocles, Socrates, and Plato. Such a list certainly did not directly influence the ideas of Theophilus, or of any other early Christian, about the Canon; but the fact that the list existed provided another precedent for drawing up a list of New Testament books.

EUSEBIUS AND AFTER

The most important and influential early Christian writer on the question of the Canon was Eusebius of Caesarea, who intended to clarify the evidence about early usage as he wrote his *Ecclesiastical History* during the early years of the fourth century. To bring absolute clarity out of the changing opinions of earlier Christians would have been impossible, and Eusebius cannot be blamed for the rather imprecise picture he provided. Two categories he used—borrowing them from Origen—were quite definite. Some books, as he pointed out, were universally recognised among the authors whose works he knew (from

Origen's library at Caesarea). These included the four Gospels, the Pauline epistles (though Eusebius does not say how many there are), 1 John, 1 Peter, and perhaps the Revelation of John. He does not mention Acts but certainly accepts it. On the other hand, some books must definitely be rejected. These include the apocryphal gospels ascribed to Peter, Thomas, Matthias, and others, and the apocryphal *Acts of Andrew*, *John*, and others. The difficulty arises with 'intermediate states'. Some books he calls 'disputed' (James, Jude, 2 Peter, 2–3 John); others are more definitely 'spurious' (apocryphal books such as the *Acts of Paul* and the *Revelation of Peter*; writings of early Christians such as the *Shepherd* of Hermas, the *Epistle of Barnabas*, and the *Didache*). Possibly the Revelation of John should be called spurious rather than accepted, and the *Gospel of the Hebrews* may belong to this category too. In Eusebius' mind there is evidently considerable doubt about Revelation, and he has heard, though he is uncertain about the fact, that the Roman church does not accept Hebrews.

It is clear that Eusebius relied primarily upon Origen not only for his categories but also for their content. The disputed books were those about which Origen had raised questions; those rejected are those which Origen and others had rejected—except in the cases of two apocalyptic writings, *Barnabas* and Revelation, which Origen had used. Questions about Revelation had arisen at Alexandria after Origen's time, and one may suppose that the criticisms of that book were also being applied to *Barnabas*.

During the succeeding century or two attempts were made to create greater uniformity. Hebrews was gradually accepted at Rome and in the West; in the East the churches generally came to make use of Revelation. As late as the fourth and fifth centuries, however, there was one Christian church in which the Canon was rather different from the one accepted elsewhere. This was the church of Antioch in Syria, proud of its apostolic origin and convinced of the authenticity of its traditions. The letter of Serapion of Antioch, to which we have referred, shows that by the end of the second century Antiochene Christians were concerned with the authenticity of the books read in church, and it is significant that as we look through earlier writings from Antioch we find clear traces of rather careful usage of New Testament writings. Early in the second century Ignatius had apparently known several gospels and the major Pauline epistles, but in his letters there are no real traces of Acts, Hebrews, the Catholic Epistles, or Revelation. Theophilus of Antioch used these books and, in addition, the Pastoral Epistles, 1 Peter, 1 John, Revelation, and possibly Acts. When later Syrian Christians rejected the Catholic Epistles (except for 1 Peter and 1 John) and Revelation they were thus relying upon the ancient tradition of their church.

Indeed, it is significant that in the fourth century, when a Syrian Christian revised the letters of Ignatius and added several new ones, we find added some rather explicit New Testament quotations (of what Ignatius ought to have quoted) from Acts, the Pastorals, Hebrews, 1 Peter, and possibly 1 John, but not from the other Catholic Epistles or Revelation. Pseudo-Ignatius is faithful to the tradition of Antioch, the spirit (if not the letter) of which he rightly traces back to Ignatius.

Against the Antiochene limitations stood a general preference for common usage as against either local tradition or critical distinctions. 2 Peter had to accompany 1 Peter; if 2 Peter was accepted, why not Jude? 2–3 John went with 1 John, and Revelation with these letters and the Gospel. James too was widely accepted, and the more inclusive view ultimately triumphed. There were no good grounds in tradition for rejecting them, especially since the apostolic age was not often sharply differentiated from the sub-apostolic period and, in any event, church history was viewed synthetically rather than analytically.

It was still remembered, at least by scholars, that Paul had not written Hebrews, that Mark and Luke were not apostles (though the authority of their Gospels was derived from Peter and Paul), and that 2 Peter was rather different from 1 Peter. All these books, however, could be treated together as witnesses to the common faith of the Church in a way that the rejected books could not be treated. Though Marcionites continued to hold that their master had discovered the one true gospel and the only authentic letters of Paul, the Church as a whole was not impressed by the attempt to view Christianity as founded upon such a narrow base. The more inclusive Canon, with all its historical difficulties, kept Christianity from becoming an anti-Jewish Gnostic sect. Indeed, it can be argued that such inclusiveness, allowing for the preservation of insights both Jewish and Greek, was largely due to the work of those who gradually assembled the New Testament books. Unlike some of the Gnostics, they made use not of one gospel only but of four; to the major Pauline epistles they came to add both the Pastoral Epistles and Hebrews; alongside the Pauline letters they placed some or all of the Catholic Epistles. Viewed as an exercise in historical research, their idea that all these books were apostolic in origin or used from the earliest days of Christianity was mistaken. It seems undeniable, however, that they were right in regarding the accepted books as expressions of the apostolic spirit as it manifested itself under various circumstances. To say this is to say little more than what Papias said about the work of Mark in writing down what Peter had spoken in relation to the 'needs' of his hearers (Eus., *H.E.* III, 39, 15), or what Origen said about the composition of Mark, Luke, and Hebrews. To be sure, early Christians wrongly insisted that the New Testament books were rather mechanically inspired (Origen argued that the evangelists had been given absolutely exact memories and therefore disagreed in order to convey higher spiritual meanings). We should incline to describe the situation differently. The New Testament writings attest the rich diversity of early Christian thought; they stand in the way of excessively rigid 'orthodox' systems of theology while correcting the vagaries of those who seize upon one aspect or another of their expressions. Though many later Christians have sought for a canon within the Canon (following the lead of Origen, who insisted upon the primacy of the Gospel of John), the Church as a whole has been reluctant to follow them, preferring to allow for the diversities of the gifts given by the one Spirit.

This is to say that theologically and historically—as will have become evident in the course of this discussion—the position of the Council of Trent, at which all the books of the New Testament were recognised as accepted by the Catholic Church, seems more satisfactory than the idea of Luther that the Pauline gospel as he understood it was the key to the New Testament and that some non-Pauline books (Hebrews, James, Jude, Revelation) belonged to a kind of appendix to it. Luther was influenced by the Renaissance rediscovery of early Church history, but his grounds were primarily theological. In criticising his view we do not mean to say that all the New Testament books have been or are equally influential and authoritative. Certainly the theological insights of Paul and John, not to mention the historical Jesus who stands behind the gospel traditions, are more significant than the ideas of—say—Jude and 2 Peter. Even if it should be held that all canonical books are somehow equal (because all reflect the traditions of the earliest churches), some are obviously 'more equal' than others. The New Testament Canon, along with the writings of the Apostolic Fathers first recovered, for the most part, in the seventeenth century, provide the materials for a continuing historical–theological study, intended to ascertain not only what the revelation of God in Jesus Christ meant to the apostolic churches but also what its implications are today. To add to this Canon or to subtract from it nowadays would break bonds which unite modern churches and would make the historical development of the Christian tradition incomprehensible.[1]

We have tried to show that while there was considerable dispute in early Christianity over some of the New Testament books, the major writings were accepted by almost all Christians by the middle of the second century. Indeed, soon after the end of the first century we find the Pauline epistles and most of our four gospels well established, not only among the more 'orthodox' but in such Gnostic schools as those of Basilides and Valentinus. It is exciting to consider the criticism of various books by Gnostic groups and by the anti-Montanist Alogi. It is not clear, however, that their opinions were widespread. Historians love novelties and exceptional cases and they do not always pay enough attention to elements of traditional continuity in history. On balance, it would appear that the early history of the Canon, though certainly marked by diversity of judgement, was essentially a slow and gradual process of sifting, ratification, and rejection. In the course of this process, which went on in the continuing life of the Church as a whole, Christians came to recognise that the twenty-seven books now accepted represented classical responses to God's revelation in Christ.

11. THE NEW TESTAMENT TEXT

In the field of New Testament textual criticism, as in the study of the text of classical and post-classical Greek authors with which it is so intimately related, a great change of approach and method has taken place in the course of the present century. This may be described, without going into intricate detail, as a change from treating texts in abstraction as literary entities, to a method which views them in the context of history, and relates the changes observable in them to known

---

[1] Some of these points have been made by W. G. Kümmel, 'Sammlung und Kanonisierung des NT', *RGG*, 1 (3rd ed. Tübingen, 1957), 1136–8.

points in the history of their study and interpretation. The former method tended to seek the existence of specific different text-forms, and to explain their relationship by the hypothesis of definite acts of recension which either preserved or corrupted the original work of the author in question: hence one text was good, and the rest corrupt. The method which is supplanting it very often sees change coming about more imperceptibly, less at some given moment than over a period of time, and recensional activity as always a mixture of insight and error, so that the textually good and bad are to be found in all traditions, and spread in distribution over a far wider period.

FORMER METHODS

The former method owed much to the work of the great nineteenth-century philologist Karl Lachmann, who worked in the fields of the manuscript tradition of Latin classical texts, the New Testament and medieval German poetry. In the first and last of these fields he was often dealing with a tradition preserved in very few manuscripts, which not infrequently were close relatives one of the other. Dealing with such cases, he established a method of determining the *stemma*, that is, family-tree of the manuscripts, and demonstrating their descent from an archetype: a prime factor in the analysis was the identification of errors in copying from one manuscript to another, especially at the time of the change from uncial writing to minuscule. The later manu-scripts were *ipso facto* the worse (*recentiores deteriores*). The archetype was as a rule not extant, and the establishment of this point in the *stemma* owed much to the learning and acumen of the scholar expressed in conjectural emendation. In many of the works to which Lachmann applied himself the method has borne the test of time; in other cases, modern scholars would wish to emend his work in the light of other data than that which he knew or on which he relied. In the New Testa-ment, limiting himself to the aims of the eighteenth-century scholar Bentley, he sought, using the oldest manuscripts, versions and quota-tions in the earliest Fathers, to establish the text as known in the fourth century.[1] The method of Lachmann, to whatever literature it is applied, is known as the genealogical method. This was applied later in the

[1] *Novum Testamentum Graece* (1831); *Novum Testamentum Graece et Latine* (1842–50).

nineteenth century, when more materials were to hand, to the New Testament by the Cambridge scholars Westcott and Hort. So confident were they of its efficacy that they entitled their edition *The New Testament in the Original Greek* (Cambridge, 1881). This method has been enthroned within this discipline for almost a century, but we can now see that it has grave faults, especially in the realm of the New Testament. In the first place, while Lachmann's method was designed to deal with manuscripts and their readings, Westcott and Hort applied genealogical method to text-types: that is, dividing the witnesses to the text into several groups according to the most striking variants, they established the text of such groups, and arrived at a basically tripartite division of the evidence. Naturally, not all the witnesses to any one text-type always have the reading deemed to be original to that group. Hence the critics' basic material was the text-type, not the actual wording of the manuscripts. The three text-types, Neutral, Western and Syrian, in Hort's nomenclature, were treated as Lachmann had treated manuscripts. The Syrian text was relegated by a mixture of internal and historical evidence (which has not really stood the test of subsequent scholarship) to the position of Lachmann's *recentiores* and consequently ignored. Left now with two texts, the critics decided between them by criteria of internal probability, concluding on grounds of style that the so-called Neutral text was the original, and the Western text a corruption to be dated in early and careless centuries, just as a manuscript might be the work of a slipshod scribe. Further, because of the preliminary work of establishing the texts, Westcott and Hort were often basing themselves upon a single manuscript, the Codex Vaticanus (B), in which for them the Neutral text was best preserved. In this then they were leaning heavily upon their own judgement. In addition, they expressed themselves confident that the text of the New Testament had not been altered in any material respect from doctrinal motives.

After eighty years students of the text of the New Testament would dissent on all these grounds. They are no longer assured that they can establish particular texts as absolute and specifically defined entities. There are great areas of common tradition, but within these can be seen minor differences and movements. Certainly, even where a recension may with confidence be discerned it should never be treated as if it were a manuscript in the framework of a Lachmannian *stemma*. No one manuscript commands the modern critic's approbation as the best manuscript, and the effect of both stylistic and doctrinal motives in the history of the text has been widely acknowledged and its existence used in attempts to establish a text as close as possible to the original.

TWO AVENUES OF APPROACH

Having realised that there is no firm path by way of stemmatics to a knowledge of the text of the New Testament in its original form and in the course of its transmission, the critic finds that there are two main aspects of his research, the study of documents and the judgement of readings. We use here phrases penned by Hort himself, in a dictum which can be the slogan of the textual critic, 'knowledge of documents should precede final judgement upon readings' (Westcott and Hort, *The New Testament in the Original Greek*, II, 31). The study of documents treats of the origin and history of the manuscripts, of the text-types which they attest, and of interrelations between them, if these can be established. Since no one manuscript or text-type is any longer acknowledged as 'the best', the ideal should be that all manuscripts be thoroughly examined and their place in the history of transmission known. The judgement of readings will treat the variants revealed by this process—with full cognisance of the documents in which they are preserved—and will assess their claim to originality or the reason for their creation. This latter process and the establishment of a text by its means is known as 'rational criticism', that is, it is 'reasoned out', and not somewhat blindly and automatically pursued, as stemmatics has sometimes been in a degenerate form.

THE DESCENT OF MANUSCRIPTS

One of the greatest exponents of the study of documents a generation after Westcott and Hort was Kirsopp Lake. He wrote some words which express the ideal, however unattainable, for the textual critic working on this aspect of the field:

It is impossible to separate the history of the text from the general history of the church. The local history of a district, the monasteries of the country, local heresies and certainly local pronunciations and dialects with their variations at different times all act upon the text and are influenced by it in turn. The perfect textual critic will have to be an expert palaeographer and the possessor of a complete knowledge of all the bypaths of church history.[1]

He will also, as Lake's reference to the local dialects indicates, have to be concerned with the history of the Greek language in Roman and Byzantine times, and he will have to extend his purview to the attestation of the New Testament in other tongues. It is clear that this amounts to a counsel of perfection, but without it the task of establishing and elucidating the text is unlikely to be successful.

When Lake wrote he and some of his contemporaries were making the study of documents their prime concern, but the scientific exposition of this approach to a knowledge of the textual vicissitudes of ancient literatures has only been made more recently by an outstanding scholar of classical literature, the late Alphonse Dain, from whom we have the term 'codicology', i.e. the study of manuscripts in themselves, their interrelations and their place in the transmission of the text. His sketch of the descent of manuscripts, which is as applicable to biblical or pastristic documents as to those with which his research was primarily concerned, is as follows. The earliest fixed point we can know is that of the archetype or archetypes. These are the most ancient witnesses to the text of an author in the form in which it has been transmitted to us. There may be in any given case one or more traditions, and hence one or more archetypes. These are the result of the philological activity of the scholars of the Graeco-Roman world, pre-eminently in Alexandria, but also in other centres. The limits of the production of such work are approximately A.D. 100 and 450. From the period prior to the archetypes there may be material available in papyrus or in indirect testimony illustrating the choices facing the Alexandrian editors. The archetype was a manuscript produced officially and deposited in a library. From this were copied, and with it were collated, further manuscripts as required. We may, in any given case, possess a manuscript which has descended by accurate copying from the archetype, but such cases are few. More often we are faced with different strains of textual witness, all to some degree contaminated. Of such strains we may construct what Dain names (apologising for the cumbrous term) *le-plus-proche-commun-ancêtre-de-la-tradition*.

After the fifth century books became rare: there were in fact many losses from the store of extant classical (and also Christian) literature

---

[1] *The Text of the New Testament* (6th ed. rev. by Silva New, London, 1928), p. 10.

in this period. Various factors contributed to this, one which affected both classical and Christian literature being the century-long Iconoclastic struggle, in which the emperors of the Iconoclastic persuasion, as is so often the case with tyrants, showed themselves antagonistic to literature and literary activity in general. The end of the controversy in the eighth century brought a renaissance of learning and copying, producing the next significant stage in the history of Greek texts, the 'transliteration' from uncial to the newly created minuscule. Our earliest dated minuscule is from the year 835 and the period of transliteration extended to about A.D. 1000. Theological texts took first place, then philosophy, and literary texts came last, amongst which prose predominated over poetry, which Photius, for instance, at the beginning of the period, does not seem to have read. Apart from works on papyrus and in translation, our extant Greek literature is derived from the activity of this period. By palaeographical errors the stages of tradition anterior or subsequent to the transliteration may be traced. The official copy of the transliterated text forms a prototype: there may be a plurality of these according to the number of transliterations, and these too may be distinguished by palaeographical means. From the prototypes were copied other manuscripts, and against them were collated manuscripts of other traditions, into which distinctive readings of the prototype were inserted as marginal or interlinear notes. From these, and affected by marginal glosses and comments, arose mixed traditions of the text, as these distinct elements were copied as if they were all part of one continuous text. The penultimate cataclysm affecting the transmission of Greek literature is the sack and fifty-year domination of Constantinople by the Latins in the thirteenth century, when many precious manuscripts were destroyed and the activity of *scriptoria* came to an end. The Empire was fatally weakened by this barbaric episode but managed to survive for another two hundred years. In this last period many manuscripts were produced, some with all the scholarly material which the scribe could muster, others for private reading or for school teaching rather than for scholarly or official use. The growth of enthusiasm for Greek learning in the West and the growing threat of the Turk drove manuscripts and scribes to Italy and beyond. Many manuscripts of this final period are more calligraphical than anything else but, as Dain himself and Pasquali among others have shown, these *recentiores* are by no means necessarily *deteriores*. We can find a good tradition preserved in this period, and there are some instances of transliteration taking place in the earlier part of it.

PROBLEMS OF NEW TESTAMENT CODICOLOGY

In applying such an historical plan to the textual history of the New Testament there are evidently certain *mutanda*. While in many instances the philological choices of the Alexandrians may have purged classical texts of the faults which had invaded the tradition between original recension and archetype, we must take account, in dealing with religious documents, of the effect of theological development and of the deliberate alteration of readings which seemed to later eyes heretical, incomplete or prone to erroneous interpretation. Furthermore, there was no period when the production of biblical texts completely ceased, so that material from which the most carefully established traditions might be corrupted was always to hand and sometimes in great measure. The place of translations both in the establishment of texts and also in their transmission and corruption is far greater in the case of biblical documents. This is not unknown for classical writings, especially those of historians and philosophers, but even there the factors introduced by bilingual manuscripts are absent, whereas they are found at a very early time in the textual history of the New Testament.

Such an investigation has never been completed, although beginnings have been made: a prime factor in this is that 'the harvest is plenteous but the reapers are few'. The ideal would be to begin with the latest manuscripts and the text-types attested by them, and thence to work up the stream of transmission. The beginning was made by Lake and some of his contemporaries, notably Rendel Harris and Hermann von Soden. One of Lake's first works was on a group of manuscripts, now known as family 1.[1] This is a family, that is, a group in which some members have been copied directly from others, and which therefore possesses a clearly marked individual text, and other features in common apart from the text, such as style of decoration, series of chapter divisions, and the like. In subsequent years he and others added a few manuscripts to the group, but no further monograph was devoted to it. Rendel Harris, and later Lake and his wife, worked on the fascinating

[1] *Codex 1 of the Gospels and its Allies* (Texts and Studies, VII, 3, Cambridge, 1902).

Ferrar group of gospel manuscripts (so called after an earlier scholar who had published their text).[1] This group not only has a distinctive text and extraneous material,[2] but clearly was written in Calabria in the tenth and eleventh centuries, apart from one of its twelve members which was written in England in the fifteenth century. Von Soden worked independently on both these groups and claimed to identify several others. Since his results were published in a form difficult to use, and were linked to a general theory of the New Testament text which proved erroneous, little notice was taken of them, or subsequent checking made of his investigations. This is a pity because often, where his claims have been checked, he has proved to have been working on the right lines in this aspect of his research. Later the work of Josef Schmid[3] on the text of Revelation has revealed many families and groups of late minuscules with significant text. Much more analysis of this kind could profitably be undertaken.

One reason why such work has been neglected is that it did not prove a royal road to a clearer knowledge of the original text of the New Testament, which is the main interest, rightly or wrongly, of most of those who work in this field. If we consider the work on the Ferrar group and family 1, and the streams of broader research with which they were linked, we see some of the limitations of the codicological approach to the New Testament text. These are groups of minuscules, written somewhat after the period of transliteration. Either directly or through very few intermediaries they have each an uncial ancestor, the nearest-common-ancestor-of-their-tradition, that is, of their specific form of text. But we have no extant manuscript which corresponds to this point. Related to these groups (but not identical in text) are other manuscripts, amongst them the uncial Θ and the minuscule 565. These two are closely akin one to the other in text, and Θ perhaps represents a parallel or sister manuscript to the nearest-common-ancestor of 565. The archetypes of these related but distinct textual traditions would be manuscripts in the library at Caesarea, which Origen knew and to which Armenian and Georgian scholars and translators came for guidance. The Egyptian evidence for texts akin to

---

[1] *Family 13 (The Ferrar Group)* (Studies and Documents, XI, London, 1941).

[2] In many members of the group are to be found tractates on, for example, the lives of the apostles, the limits of the patriarchates, the symbols of the four evangelists. For a complete list see J. Rendel Harris, *The Ferrar Group* (Cambridge, 1900), p. 8.

[3] *Studien zur Geschichte des griechischen Apokalypse-Textes* (3 vols. Athens, 1955–6).

these, especially those on papyrus, would represent the pre-archetypal texts on which Caesarean philology had been at work.[1] A clearer single instance is to be found in the tenth-century minuscule 1739, a probable example of a carefully transliterated prototype. It is clear on both internal and external grounds that the archetype of this was a scholarly work of about the sixth century, and that the pre-archetype of the scholarly work itself was akin in text to the Chester Beatty papyrus of the Pauline epistles. It is clear then that while this research shows us much about Byzantine Christian scholarship, and somewhat less about the scholars and texts of the later patristic period, it does no more than hint at the situation prior to the conversion of Constantine and the peace of the Church. This should not deter the student from finding out all that can be known about documents and their antecedents, not only about the *scriptoria* which produced Byzantine manuscripts but also about those from which Egyptian papyri came, about the scholars of Christian antiquity, their aims and methods, and their adaptation of current philological procedures, about the libraries of antiquity and the monastic and patriarchal libraries in which their treasures are today preserved. This knowledge would be both interesting and important: knowledge of manuscripts and their antecedents suggests those which are most likely to preserve readings of value, but it does not absolve us from judgement of readings.

RATIONAL CRITICISM

The knowledge of documents, then, a codicological approach to the history of the New Testament text, while illuminating, does not solve every problem. There appears to be rich material at our disposal, several thousands of manuscripts and a number of ancient and fairly well-documented versions. In fact the richness is in part illusory, since many manuscripts have been destroyed in times of persecution and strife, and there have been many cross-currents, so that the lines of descent can no longer be traced. Hence while manuscripts must ultimately all be interrelated, their interrelation cannot be known, and reveals itself only in shared readings. Some of these are original, but many others are the result of various types of corruption, corrections

[1] See T. Ayuso Marazuela, 'Testo cesariense o precesariense?', *Biblica*, XVI (1935), 369–415.

in the eyes of those who made them on doctrinal, or frequently stylistic, grounds. Although the main lines of groupings of witnesses into text-types can be seen, no one text-type can be shown to be superior to the others in its readings in every respect. Thus it is always antecedently possible for the correct reading to have been preserved in but a few or even only one manuscript, or to have disappeared in the Greek tradition and to have been preserved only in a version. To identify and evaluate such readings we need 'rational criticism', and for this we need criteria. (A classical exposition of these may be found in M.-J. Lagrange, *Critique Textuelle*. II. *La critique rationelle* (Paris, 1935), pp. 33–9.) The basic principle, which has long been known, is that the original reading is that which explains the origin of the other readings. These may originate out of sheer error, if the original reading was open to some confusion of sight or sound through similar letters or pronunciations, or from grammatical correction of an original anacoluthon or solecism, or from stylistic correction of some phrase more common than learned or more Semitic than Greek, or from the theological need to make the sacred text more precise and certain in its doctrine. The practice of rational criticism and the definition of criteria such as these are no novelties in either the classical or the biblical field, but recently in both this approach has been revived. It is remarkable to observe how hard the old ways die: rational criticism and the arrival at an eclectic text by such methodology have been greeted with horror by non-specialists, either because the result is not based on an appeal to the majority of witnesses or because it may differ from the readings of some 'best manuscript' or even of some 'best text' ! While scholarship always needs those who will 'guard the guards themselves', our present circumstances justify the eclectic method, and in theory the text established by rational criticism is in no way suspect, although, like any man's hypothesis, such a text requires the judgement of his peers before it can in fact be accepted.

Elucidation of the text of the New Testament must approach its goal from this twofold direction. All that can be known of the text by means of tracing the descent of manuscripts and of text-types is a prime requirement, but no genealogical method can lead us to the original text. An informed recensional activity must take place and a text be provisionally established. Either aspect will influence the other and lead to a greater precision. Knowledge of manuscripts will suggest those which are more likely to preserve readings of value, and the acceptance of readings on 'rational' grounds will in its turn tell us something about the history of the documents in which those readings are found—at some time, they or their ancestors have been in contact with a stream of tradition less contaminated than others. To think that we have solved our problems is naïve: to despair is ridiculous in the light of the wealth of material and of available methods of investigation. What follows is a report both on material and method, and on the picture of the tradition of the text of the New Testament so far as we can see it at present.

MATERIALS PASSED ON IN THE LATER TRADITION

It will have become clear that we cannot confine ourselves to source material derived from the first five centuries of the Christian era. The text of the New Testament continued to change in the subsequent ten centuries, but as the rate of change was far slower than in the previous period, text-forms and manuscripts came into existence which often preserve, in whole or in part, traces or descendants of texts of the earliest Christian centuries. Sometimes the scholars of the Byzantine empire have been criticised by those of the present time because of their penchant for summary and compilation, for amassing the opinions of earlier ages rather than advancing the frontiers of thought and learning by independent research. Whether or not this criticism be well taken within any absolute frame of reference, it is unjustified within the limits of this study, for we still rely in a measure upon the reverence of Byzantium for antiquity, and upon the manuscripts which they produced, copied from ancient exemplars, so preserving for us the riches of other days.

We deal with this later material under the convenient traditional triple division of manuscripts, versions and quotations.

THE TEXT OF THE EMPIRE

The majority of manuscripts of the Greek New Testament are of Byzantine production, and most of these post-date the Iconoclastic controversy and the invention of minuscule. Amongst such late uncials and the minuscules, the majority attest a form of text which has received many names in the past century from textual critics, of which the least tendentious, however tautological, is the 'Byzantine' text. It has attracted little analytical attention apart from the work of von Soden, who examined it in some detail on the assumption that it was a major text-type directly descended from the original. He isolated differing forms within it. In chronological order of appearance (according to his conclusions) the main subdivisions of the Byzantine text are the K^1 text (represented in the gospels in V 461 Ω 028 and others), the K^x text (the majority of manuscripts unassignable to other texts), and the K^r text (Λ 1187 262 1573 1555 545). Other minor groups in the same scheme of nomenclature are K^i (EFGH), and K^a (family Π—a group later ascribed to another major text-type). Many of these groups have been studied by later scholars and their identification by von Soden confirmed, in some cases with modifications. Thus, K^r (according to von Soden the latest form of the Byzantine text to appear) has been shown to be a distinct entity. K^i has more recently been shown to be a unity, and its relationship to the Ferrar group has been more precisely analysed; while K^a was examined by Mrs Lake and shown to be a family, with the exception of Codex Alexandrinus, which she proved to be not a member of the family but a half-brother of the exemplar.[1] Within the K^x group von Soden himself made attempts to clarify the mass of evidence, on the one hand examining the manuscripts written by the scribe Theodoros Hagiopetrites, which are dated between A.D. 1278 and 1307 and, on a broader canvas, essaying the division of the type by an analysis of the form of the *Pericope Adulterae* (John 7: 53—8: 11) contained in the whole group. His analysis of the various forms of this *pericope* (of which he claimed to identify seven) was criticised by Lietzmann, and since then seems to have been neglected completely, apart from a recent study by Ulrich Becker (*Jesus und die Ehebrecherin*, *BZNW*, XXVIII, 1963) who has applied the methods of rational criticism to it, and who finds original, on intrinsic grounds, a form near to that which von Soden identified as original. Work on the lectionaries (an area neglected by von Soden) revealed an eighth form of text of this pericope.[2] There appears to be

[1] Cf. D. O. Voss, 'Is von Soden's K^r a Distinct Type of Text?', *JBL*, LVII (1938), 311–18; R. Champlin, *Family E and its Allies in Matthew* (Studies and Documents, XXVIII, Salt Lake City, 1966); Silva Lake, *Family Π and the Codex Alexandrinus* (Studies and Documents, V, London, 1936).

[2] A. P. Wikgren, 'The Lectionary Text of the Pericope, John 8: 1–11', *JBL*, LIII (1934), 188–98.

a field for further work here. It is clear that von Soden was using both of the methods which we have mentioned above as necessary for the elucidation of the data. It is a pity that his errors have been more rehearsed by his successors than his insights have been observed and the trails he blazed followed.

To examine the evidence relevant to the Byzantine text brings the student at once face to face with one of the major problems of the historian of the New Testament text. While he can often indicate times and places when and where certain text-forms were in use, he can rarely discover their time or place of origin. In this regard we find that neither the origin of the Byzantine text viewed as an entity nor the origin of its various sub-forms in the course of history is known. Its original recension (should we say archetype?) is frequently ascribed to Lucian of Antioch, and the ascription is turned to fact by frequent repetition, but as we shall see there is no direct evidence of any philological work by him upon the New Testament text. The Byzantine text goes back to the fourth century, as the Freer codex (W) shows by its text in Matthew and Luke,[1] but it was not dominant thereafter, as Hort and the succeeding generations were wont to state. Hort fixed the date of the incipient Byzantine text by its alleged use by John Chrysostom, but more recent examination of his quotations from Mark and Matthew has revealed a complex text-form in these gospels, which cannot be identified with any type specifically Byzantine or other,[2] and a like state of affairs seems to exist in the Pauline epistles used by him. The notorious uncertainty of the text of Chrysostom's works only increases the difficulties attendant upon the establishing of the New Testament text known to him and used by him. A more recent attempt to date the dominance of the Byzantine text by an investigation of the text known to Photius, patriarch of Constantinople in the ninth century, led to the surprising discovery that that learned and influential man used a text which, while it shows readings known in Byzantine manuscripts, is predominantly one of an older type.[3] Kirsopp and Silva

[1] H. A. Sanders, *The New Testament MSS in the Freer Collection*. Part I. *The Washington MS of the Four Gospels* (New York, 1912), pp. 46–63, 96–113.

[2] J. Geerlings and Silva Lake, 'Chrysostom's text of the Gospel of Mark', *HTR*, XXIV (1931), 121–42; and C. ·D. Dicks, 'The Matthaean Text of Chrysostom in his Homilies on Matthew', *JBL*, LXVII (1948), 365–76.

[3] J. N. Birdsall, 'The Text of the Gospels in Photius', *JTS*, n.s. VII (1956), 43–55, 190–8; *idem*, 'The Text of the Acts and Epistles in Photius', *JTS*, n.s. IX (1958), 278–91.

Lake suggested that the three main types of Byzantine text as analysed by von Soden might be the authorised texts of the dynasties of the Macedonians, the Comneni and the Palaeologi respectively, but they offer no evidence for this attractive assertion.[1] More recently, Zuntz asserts that 'the ecclesiastical text (by which he means the Byzantine text in its dominance in the later Eastern empire) is a product of the restoration of orthodoxy'[2] namely, after Iconoclasm, but he offers no precise evidence for the assertion, although admittedly a number of codicological facts point in that direction. The evidence of Photius does not however support this, and the lack of uniformity even after his time is shown, for instance, in the assertion of his pupil Arethas of Caesarea[3] that the reading of Rom. 3:9 in the most accurate and the oldest manuscripts is κατέχομεν περισσόν *l.* προεχόμεθα, a reading in fact not preserved in any extant manuscript although it has contributed to the conflate reading of D. The picture of a Byzantine patriarch sending for manuscripts from which to construct a text or to abstract readings may be convincing as an argument *a priori*, but we are hard put to substantiate it from precise data of history, strange as this may be.

The Byzantine text has many readings which appear conflate, and many evident rationalisations of cruces. Amongst examples of the former may be named Mark 9:49: πᾶς γὰρ πυρὶ ἁλισθήσεται καὶ πᾶσα θυσία ἁλὶ ἁλισθήσεται and Rom. 3:22: εἰς πάντας καὶ ἐπὶ πάντας. Amongst the latter are found, for instance, Mark 7:31: ἐκ τῶν ὁρίων Τύρου καὶ Σιδῶνος ἦλθεν εἰς τὴν θάλασσαν τῆς Γαλιλαίας, instead of the reading with ἦλθεν διὰ Σιδῶνος, which occasions a perplexing geography; and Rom. 7:25: εὐχαριστῶ τῷ θεῷ for the laconic χάρις τῷ θεῷ. However, it was an error of earlier years to dismiss the readings of this text as in all respects worthless. Many of them are not innovations. Zuntz is at pains to demonstrate that Byzantine readings may be ancient, and he declares with justice that Byzantine readings which recur in Western witnesses must be ancient, since the two streams of the tradition never met after the fall of the Western empire (pp. 55, 150). G. D. Kilpatrick in various essays has striven to show in accordance with the rational eclecticism so ably practised by him that Byzantine readings may be

---

1 'The Byzantine Text of the Gospels', *Mémorial Lagrange* (Paris, 1940), pp. 251–8.
2 G. Zuntz, *The Text of the Epistles*, Schweich lecture (London, 1953), p. 151 n. 1.
3 K. Staab, *Pauluskommentare aus der griechischen Kirche* (Münster, 1933), p. 654.

original.[1] For instance, the middle form of the future of ȝῆν was customary in hellenistic Greek, but was condemned by the Atticists: it is preserved in manuscripts of the Byzantine period, whereas manuscripts of the Alexandrian text-type have often rejected it and replaced it by the future active of the verb, which was deemed the pure Attic. Similarly, the verb εὐλαβεῖσθαι with the meaning 'to fear' was condemned by the Atticists of the second century. It is Byzantine manuscripts which preserve it, however, while manuscripts often regarded as in all ways preferable present an Atticising correction with φοβεῖσθαι. These considerations provide salutary correctives of the hard and fast categorisations of earlier generations. It is still however not unjustified to say that the Byzantine text in its entirety commends itself even less than other main text-types in their entirety as approximate representations of the original text. Original readings occur, but the original is not preserved here. This may be further illustrated from Revelation where the work of Josef Schmid has shown the existence of four main types of text, two ancient, two more recent in their present form. There are a number of cases where the more recent texts—and especially that called Koine by Schmid, in many respects equivalent to the Byzantine text here discussed—support the Codex Alexandrinus, our best manuscript witness to the text of Revelation, in original readings where other witnesses offer a corrupt text. Instances of this are 15: 3: ἐθνῶν *l.* αἰώνων and 2: 20: add σου post γυναῖκα (the latter reading is however rejected by Schmid as an error, but in the view of the present writer it is original). Many other instances given by Schmid bear upon the peculiarities of the grammar of the book, and convincingly prove their point without reference to exegesis. The Koine text of the book, as a whole, has on the other hand little to commend it. Some typical erroneous readings of this text are 12: 18: ἐστάθην *l.* ἐστάθη, by which the point of the account is obscured, and 22: 14 where an uncial error has produced ΠΟΙΟΥΝΤΕΣ ΤΑΣ ΕΝΤΟΛΑΣ ΑΥΤΟΥ out of ΠΛΥΝΟΝΤΕΣ ΤΑΣ ΣΤΟΛΑΣ ΑΥΤΩΝ.

The Byzantine text is properly the name of a text preserved in

[1] 'An Eclectic Study of the Text of Acts', *Biblical and Patristic Studies in Memory of R. P. Casey* (Freiburg, 1963), pp. 64–77; 'Atticism and the Text of the Greek New Testament', *Neutestamentliche Aufsätze. Festschrift für Josef Schmid* (Regensburg, 1963), pp. 125–37; 'The Greek New Testament Text of Today and the Textus Receptus' in *The New Testament in Historical and Contemporary Perspective* (Oxford, 1965), pp. 189–208.

manuscripts with continuous text, but other manuscripts contain the text of parts of the New Testament arranged according to their allocations for reading in public worship, which we term lectionary manuscripts. These have of late received particular investigation, especially in *Studies in the Lectionary Text of the Greek New Testament* (in progress. Chicago, 1933–). In these products of the Byzantine empire at its heyday a text has been discovered akin to older manuscripts and text-types of which we have evidence from the period before Constantine. Here is an instance of the conservatism of liturgy: a text apparently dating in its extant form from the fourth century has been transmitted with little change up to the time of the fall of the Byzantine empire. As already mentioned, the lectionaries preserve a form of the *Pericope Adulterae* otherwise unknown, and amongst many such ancient readings of the lectionaries may be mentioned Luke 11:13: ἀγαθόν *l.* ἅγιον read by the weekday lections with $\mathfrak{P}^{45}$ L, and the intriguing τὸν ἐκ πίστεως 'Ιησοῦν regularly read in lectionaries at Rom. 3:26 with much ancient support. Such readings are not necessarily original but their antiquity is not in doubt.

ANCIENT TEXTS IN LATER TIMES

The Byzantine church, however, not only preserved in the text it mainly used isolated readings of texts existing before the Christianisation of the empire, but in many instances copied and transmitted texts of more ancient type than those customary in its worship. Several striking examples of this have come to light in the course of the present century's researches, e.g. in the investigation of the Ferrar group (the more recent term Family 13 is now known to be, in strict terms, an inaccuracy). This investigation was undertaken in the first instance more from the palaeographical and codicological interest of the manuscripts concerned, but it led at length to a better understanding of the text of Origen and his day; and a text with which these manuscripts show the closest affinity came to light in the third-century papyrus of the gospels, $\mathfrak{P}^{45}$. Yet all the manuscripts in question, except one, were written in the eleventh century, and the exception comes from a Greek scribe resident in England in the fifteenth century. A group of similar importance and kinship is that known as Family 1, amongst which is numbered 1582, Athos Vatopedi 949. The scribe of this manuscript,

Ephraem the monk, copied another New Testament manuscript which amply illustrates the conservative genius of his age, namely, 1739 (Athos Lavra B 64). This manuscript preserves a critical work,[1] to be dated in the sixth century, in which is included an ancient text of the Paulines, which the learned compiler of Christian antiquity had identified in a manuscript source as corresponding closely to that used by Origen in his commentary on Romans and in other of his works. Taking this as his basis, he had collated the quotations and *lemmata* of Origen's commentary, and included these in his work as marginal and inter-linear variants. The text of Acts and the Catholic epistles is not Origenian, but the margins preserve fragments of Irenaeus and other Fathers. This rich repository of ancient lore has been copied, probably through one intermediary, with commendable accuracy by Ephraem. Twentieth-century scholarship has confirmed the Origenian affinities of the text utilised, while the Chester Beatty papyrus of the Paulines, $\mathfrak{P}^{46}$, has been shown to be a very close relation of the archetype from which the original scholar took his text of Paul. There are other traces of the same enriching act of *transcriptio* in the cousins-german of 1739, manuscripts 6 and 424. The latter has been collated against the proto-type of 1739, the noteworthy readings figuring as interlinear glosses, while manuscript 6 is probably an instance of a text derived from such a copy, in which some interlinear variants and some exegetical glosses from another source have found their way into the body of the text. 1908 and the two uncial fragments known as M are also related to Ephraem's work. Again, the Greek text of Acts in D has few supporters amongst Greek manuscripts, but where D is not extant, minuscules such as the twelfth-century manuscript 876 and the thirteenth-century manuscript 614 provide some of the material which would otherwise have been lost to us.[2] Although they do not correspond to D so closely as the other groups and manuscripts of Byzantine provenance which we have mentioned do to their ancient relatives, they represent scholarly activity of an earlier time.

[1] See E. Freiherr von der Goltz, *Eine textkritische Arbeit des achten bzw. sechsten Jahrhunderts* (Leipzig, 1899); G. Zuntz, *The Text of the Epistles*, pp. 68–84; J. N. Birdsall, *A Study of MS 1739 of the Pauline Epistles and its Relationship to MSS 6, 424, 1908, and M* (unpublished Ph.D. thesis, Nottingham, 1959).

[2] 876 is collated in K. W. Clark, *Eight American Praxapostoloi* (Chicago, 1941); 614 in A. V. Valentine-Richards, *The Text of Acts in Codex 614 (Tisch. 137) and its Allies* (Cambridge, 1934).

'SCHOLIA' AND 'CATENAE'

Nor should we omit to mention amongst the works of preservation due to Byzantium, the *scholia* and *catenae*. In marginal notes and inter-linear glosses (sometimes even incorporated in course of time into the text itself in error) and in marginal commentaries gleaned from many ancient sources now lost, the Byzantine scholars have not infrequently rescued information which the investigation of recent times has corro-borated. A striking instance of this is the marginal glosses giving variant readings and renderings from a source referred to as *To Ioudaikon*, which the investigations of Schmidtke and others have connected with an early Jewish-Christian gospel. The manuscripts which contain such *marginalia* often have a colophon indicating the collation of some manuscript in their ancestry with old exemplars 'in Jerusalem, in the Holy Mountain'. A large number of the manuscripts thus connected are of Calabrian origin; others come from the area of Trapezunt on the Northern coast of Asia Minor, both regions to which Christian scholars from Syria fled before the Muslim invasion. Schmidtke, the pioneer of the study of these manuscripts, has a brilliant codicological sketch of their origin and distribution,[1] but his work in this field has not been followed up. *To Ioudaikon* for instance is recorded as having omitted Matt. 16: 2 and 3, and the word εἰκῇ at Matt. 5: 22. *Catenae* also provide data of interest known to their compilers; much exegetical work of Fathers and heretics has been recovered from these sources, and occasionally we find notes of textual information otherwise lost. Such is the note on Matt. 27: 49 in manu-script 72, which has a marginal commentary[2] on this Gospel, largely drawn from the homilies of John Chrysostom, but which at this point deserts that source to declare that the 'chronologically arranged gospel of Diodoros, Tatianos and other holy fathers' inserts here the reading asserting the piercing of Jesus' side after his cry of dereliction but before his expiration. The reading is known to Chrysostom but he does not attribute it to any source, quoting it as the accepted text. Such a note might well have been attributed to the vagary of some scribe, although Vogels[3] made an attempt to link it with the omission of

---

[1] A. Schmidtke, *Neue Fragmente und Untersuchungen zu den judenchristlichen Evan-gelien* (Leipzig, 1911). [2] See Plate 22.
[3] 'Der Lanzenstich vor dem Tode Jesu', *BZ*, x (1912), 396–405.

John 19: 35 in a Latin gospel harmony. In a Coptic Manichaean homily edited in 1934, however, a series of references to the crucifixion of Christ is found in which the piercing of the side is referred to before the confession of the centurion.[1] Mani used the *Diatessaron* of Tatian, in which then, at that early date, the piercing preceded Jesus' expiring.[2] So one Greek source, probably written in a monastery near to Antioch in the tenth century, preserves ancient information, which only the chance discoveries of a later age have confirmed.

VERSIONS PRESERVED IN LATER TRADITION

What has been said of the Greek manuscript materials is true also of the versions. Many of the manuscripts on which we rely for our knowledge of their history and their bearing upon the history of the Greek text, are late. Some have been preserved because of their antiquity, some because tradition has associated them with a saint or attributed to them some spiritual efficacy. We have no Latin manuscript from before the age of Jerome, but our knowledge of the history of the Old Latin is not thereby too much impaired. Many of the Armenian and Georgian manuscripts reflecting early stages of the history of those versions are of the tenth century or later. The Ethiopic version is preserved in particularly late manuscripts, in common with much other literature in that tongue, and scholars have not infrequently dismissed the evidence of Ethiopic documents both of the New Testament and of other works for this reason. But critical study has shown the version of the Old Testament, however recent its manuscripts, to be a valuable witness to the Septuagint text, and recent discoveries, such as the Chester Beatty papyri of the Gospels and Acts, have sometimes shown the Ethiopic to have preserved ancient readings. An instance of this is the form of the apostolic decree (Acts 15: 20) which the Ethiopic version reads as a prohibition of 'idols, things strangled and blood', a reading disregarded until its appearance in the Chester Beatty papyrus suggested its antiquity and importance for the history of this difficult passage. The Slavonic and the Harklean Syriac versions also provide valuable information although both came into existence after the

---

[1] *Manichäische Handschriften der Sammlung A. Chester Beatty.* Bd. 1. *Manichäische Homilien*, ed. H. J. Polotsky (Stuttgart, 1934), p. 68.

[2] See C. Peters, *Das Diatessaron Tatians* (Rome, 1939), pp. 125–32.

limits of this period. The versions have not yet been fully sifted to yield all that they hold of value to the textual study of the New Testament.

MEDIEVAL PRESERVATION OF THE FATHERS

The study of later Fathers also helps to plot the course of the distribution of readings and text-types,[1] and the text of the works of early Fathers is not infrequently preserved in minuscule manuscripts. What has been suggested about the value of manuscripts of the New Testament of the later period is relevant here too. Information from authors and manuscripts even of the later centuries of the Byzantine empire is not to be treated as irrelevant in this field. Where then later materials are relevant to the discussions and descriptions which follow they will be laid under contribution.

FINDING THE EARLIEST FORMS OF NEW TESTAMENT TEXT

All modern hand editions rest upon the work of the great scholars of the nineteenth century, who all agreed in preferring a text which is related in some measure to the exercise of critical acumen amongst the Christian scholars of Alexandria. The exegetical school of Alexandria proved to be a means of constant supply of able scholars within that church right up to the Arab conquest. From its beginnings under Pantaenus and Clement it was committed to the utilisation of secular learning in the cause of Christ, and it is highly probable that the skills developed in the criticism of Homer and other Greek authors were turned to account in the textual problems which had arisen in the second century. It is however remarkable that we cannot link this putative activity with any known figure within that church. A shadowy Hesychius is mentioned by Jerome, but we know nothing more of him, and the dubbing of some particular text Hesychian, as German scholarship in particular has been prone to do, is a quite unjustifiable procedure.

The great Bentley intended, basing himself on the earliest uncials known to him and on the Latin Vulgate, to establish the text of the New Testament as it was in the age of the great councils. It was an

[1] See R. P. Casey, 'The Patristic Evidence for the Text of the New Testament' in *New Testament Manuscript Studies*, ed. A. P. Wikgren and M. M. Parvis (Chicago, 1950), pp. 69–80.

ambitious plan but failed rather because of Bentley's turbulent mastership of Trinity than because of inherent impossibility. What he failed to do and Lachmann attempted, Tischendorf, Hort and Weiss succeeded in doing, but all on various grounds, mainly internal grounds of readings judged to be good, claimed for their editions a close approximation to the original text. A theoretical answer by those who have preferred the other forms of text known to us has been hitherto that the text of Codex Vaticanus and its close allies is a 'recension', the direct result of critical sifting and evaluation by the Alexandrians. One of our latest acquisitions to the list of New Testament papyri, the Bodmer papyrus of Luke and John ($\mathfrak{P}^{75}$),[1] appears to have put this doctrine out of court for ever. It is a document which most palaeographers are willing to date in the eighth decade of the second century. Its text is essentially the same as that of B, which thus is objectively shown to have been in existence at so early a period. This fact cannot of course provide any sound reason for declaring that this text is older, better or nearer to the original than other texts: such views need to be argued on different grounds. The existence of papyri in the Bodmer collection, and of papyri in other collections of approximately the same date, with different text-forms, shows that the discussion must still be carried on on grounds other than the chances of evidence provided by archaeological discovery. For instance, the papyrus of John, also in the Bodmer collection ($\mathfrak{P}^{66}$),[2] to which some papyrologists have assigned the same date, but which may be somewhat later (early to middle third century), is markedly different in text from $\mathfrak{P}^{75}$.

We propose then in surveying the earliest period to look at a number of readings, selected because the evidence points clearly to an early date for their circulation, and to discuss whether on intrinsic grounds they can be considered original. In this discussion we shall be particularly concerned to perceive reasons for textual change which lie in the realm of doctrine and its development—the scandalous reading, the unharmonious reading (whether between the Synoptics or between the Synoptics and John), and the reading which in the course of years has lost its point. The doctrine of the Church suffered certain changes in the transition of Christianity to a Gentile environment, and

---

[1] *Papyrus Bodmer XIV–XV*, 2 vols. (Cologny-Genève, 1961).

[2] *Papyrus Bodmer II*, pub. by V. Martin (Cologny-Genève, 1956); *Supplément* (1958); *Nouvelle édition augmentée et corrigée avec reproduction photographique complète du manuscrit* (1962).

further change took place in the mid-second century which, as a time of debate and controversy, was more fluid than later centuries. The view has in fact been taken that to interpret the doctrinal situation of that period in terms of orthodoxy and heresy is to transpose those terms by anachronism. We know that Marcion altered the text of his scriptures to support his opinions; the Gnostics for their part were accused of this by their opponents, and although it is rather less simple to find clear instances of their activity, the manner in which the Coptic *Gospel of Thomas*[1] treats material akin to the Synoptics shows us something of what the Fathers were tilting against. In this gospel synoptic sayings or sayings allied to these are presented in a context which substantially alters their implications, sayings are collocated which originally (or at any rate in the synoptic tradition) are separate; while in other instances what we find is a distinct form of the synoptic sayings without any clear tendentious inclination. It would be an error to judge *a priori* that those whose views have moulded orthodoxy were immune from a similar *Tendenz* in their use of scripture.

THE VALUE OF VERSIONAL ATTESTATION

It is basic to the hypothesis of change in this period and to the method of tracing it that a reading may well have disappeared from the majority of Greek manuscripts, or at least from all collated manuscripts. It will often be from the concurrence of quotations in the Fathers and other early Christian writings, and of the text of versions, that we shall conclude that a reading was extant in the second century. Two outstanding textual scholars have argued that patristic quotations should carry far more weight than is customarily given to them in establishing the original text of the gospels—Friedrich Blass in respect of both Luke and John (*Evangelium secundum Lucam*, Leipzig, 1897; *Evangelium secundum Johannem cum variae lectionis delectu*, 1902), and M.-E. Boismard, who has devoted his work to John's Gospel alone in a noteworthy series of articles in the *Revue Biblique* between 1948 and 1953. Little impact seems to have been made by these discussions upon textual critics, but they demand a reappraisal. The place of the versions

[1] See, e.g., the discussion by R. M. Grant and D. N. Freedman, *The Secret Sayings of Jesus* (London, 1960), and B. Gaertner, *The Theology of the Gospel of Thomas* (London, 1961).

in tracing the history of the text and even in establishing the original text is more firmly fixed as part of text-critical procedure, particularly since Burkitt declared 'what right (have we) to reject the oldest Syriac and the oldest Latin when they agree?'.[1] Kilpatrick in his work on the Western text of the gospels has followed up this insight with various instances where the Western text is to be preferred.[2] One instance is at Matt. 4: 17, where the Codex Bobbiensis of the Old Latin and the two extant manuscripts of the old Syriac omit μετανοεῖτε and γάρ, and thus dissimilate the message ascribed to Jesus from that earlier ascribed to John the Baptist. In this reading these manuscripts have the support of early Fathers quoting the verse, but no Greek manuscript retains the shorter unassimilated reading. The ancient versions—and the Latin and Syriac are not the only ones worthy of attention here—are in their oldest forms indications of the oldest strata of the text. Such readings as we have mentioned are analogous to *Leitfossilien* in the rocks or tidemarks left by the ebbing sea. In using the versions for this kind of evidence we must be aware of their tendencies to paraphrase and to interpret in the earliest tentative attempts at translation, but all variants cannot simply be dismissed as instances of this. The tendency everywhere was towards greater conformity with the norms of the Greek-speaking Church, whatever these happened to be at the time, and where such conformation has taken place the primary versions, that is those rendered directly from the Greek, may help us to plot the developments which were taking place in the Greek in successive periods. Sometimes, however, the original state of a version's text has been obliterated by such conformation, and in this case the secondary versions, that is those translated on the basis of another version and not from the Greek, can, not infrequently, give insight into the history of that version from which they were taken and reveal the state of its text at the time when they were first translated.

THE VALUE OF THE 'DIATESSARON'

Most versions other than the Coptic, the Gothic and the Slavonic have provided examples of the widespread influence of the *Diatessaron* of

[1] P. M. Barnard, *Clement of Alexandria's Biblical Text* (Texts and Studies v, 5, Cambridge, 1899), Introduction by F. C. Burkitt, p. xix.
[2] 'Western Text and Original Text in the Gospels and Acts', *JTS*, XLIV (1943), 24–36.

Tatian, the second-century harmony put together by an Assyrian Christian converted in the West. This harmony had apparently already been lost sight of in the Greek world when Eusebius wrote his *Ecclesiastical History*, where he mentions the work (*HE*, IV, 29, 6) but confesses that he is unacquainted with the details of its compilation. Although its influence elsewhere was considerable and long persisting, it had everywhere disappeared before the modern period, until in the nineteenth century two documents came to light which still constitute the basis of more recent researches. These are an Arabic version, based on Syriac, but much conformed to the standard Syriac text even before translation, and the commentary of Ephraem the Syrian upon 'the Concordant Gospel' which was published in Armenian, and later in a Latin translation by a modern scholar. Since then, our knowledge has greatly increased and the problems of reconstructing the text of Tatian's work are much more clearly understood. Material has appeared in many Oriental tongues from the areas evangelised and influenced by the Syriac-speaking Church, and some small but significant traces in the Manichaean writings found in this century in Turkistan and Egypt; and a divergent stream of the tradition has been discerned and investigated in the West underlying gospel harmonies in Latin and in the languages of medieval Europe. There has been considerable scepticism (especially amongst English scholars) about the use of these materials for the textual criticism of the gospels, which may stem from the unjustified and over-enthusiastic procedure of Hermann von Soden, who used the Arabic *Diatessaron* as if it were an exact replica of Tatian's second-century text. But the progress of Diatessaric studies in the present century, culminating in the recent discovery and publication of about half of the Syriac original of Ephraem's commentary,[1] places us in a much more favourable position to assess the value of the data. In the course of this discussion we shall use our present information with confidence as well as caution, since light may thus be shed upon areas of textual growth and development of which we should otherwise be unaware.

It has been critical procedure to utilise the quotations of the Fathers and other early Christian writers to eliminate or to localise specific types of text. As we have intimated, it may be argued that yet greater

[1] S. *Ephrem. Commentaire de l'évangile concordant. Texte syriaque* (*MS Chester Beatty 709*), *édité et traduit par Dom Louis Leloir* (Dublin, 1963).

trust should be reposed in these witnesses to the state of the text in the earliest periods as guides to current scholarship in the establishment of the text. It has been too frequently suggested that in the majority of cases variations found in these sources are the result of paraphrase or of inaccurate memory, whereas it has subsequently proved to be the case that quotations thus dismissed are justified by manuscript discovery or by the investigation of the versions. But in dealing with quotations from the New Testament in first- or second-century authors two factors must be acknowledged, particularly in the case of the gospels. In the first place, as much recent discussion has revealed, oral tradition of materials parallel to those used by the original evangelists was still a living factor in the life of the Church and to this must be ascribed the fact that almost all the Apostolic Fathers quote the gospels in a textual form not exactly that known to us today.[1] If it comes as a surprise that we must say this of Clement or Ignatius, we may recall that Papias, at a later date than Clement and perhaps not contemporary even with Ignatius, declares that he prefers the living and abiding voice to the witness of written documents. In the second place, even as late as Justin, when an oral tradition may well have disappeared, the further enigmatic feature appears that he, and even Marcion, appear to have used a harmonised gospel text. Although the tradition mentions Ammonius and Theophilus as compilers of harmonies, to explain these features by reference to their names, even if we assumed their dates to be early enough, would be to explain *obscurum per obscurius*. We might perhaps include some quotations by Irenaeus in this category, since they are definitely from a harmonised text. It is a matter of uncertainty whether Tatian's work can have influenced his text, since their dates are close together. At present the only sound course appears to be to state the facts and our perplexity, and to hope that this line of research will be pursued by some able investigator.

THE FIRST CENTURY

Having discussed the sources of our information we may proceed to scan the data. Of the first century we know little, and in respect of the gospels we are dealing in large measure with a period before the writing down of the tradition. There is some reason to invoke a concept from

---

[1] H. Köster, *Synoptische Überlieferung bei den apostolischen Vätern* (Berlin, 1957).

the history of oral traditions as suggested by the study of the prophets, namely that it is a threat to the stability of the culture in which the oral traditions flourish which leads to their committal to writing. The gospels appear to date from the years around A.D. 70 when Jerusalem fell and Jewry entered a new period of its existence. At this time Christianity began to shake off the swaddling clothes of its Jewish birth and it would appear that it stabilised its traditions in the written gospels and in the gathering of the Pauline corpus of letters. It is clear that the three so-called Synoptic Gospels stand in close literary relationship one to another, although the classical two- or four-document hypothesis, as stated by Burkitt and Streeter and for long the orthodoxy of the British schools, is at present called in question on various grounds by a number of scholars. Basing themselves on that theory, however, certain scholars have attempted to discover the textual form in which Mark lay before the evangelists responsible for Matthew and Luke. It is probably indicative of the impossibility of a satisfactory ending to this quest that while one finds this *Vorlage* to be a 'Western' form of text, another discovers that it bore affinity to the 'Caesarean' group of witnesses.

Although the tradition was thus crystallised in the written gospels, it continued its separate existence orally. This continuing oral tradition was particularly active amongst the shrinking groups of Aramaic-speaking Christians of Jewish descent and affiliation who continued to exist east of Jordan and elsewhere. It may very well have been that there was also a Greek oral tradition. There have not been lacking scholars who have suggested that the divergences within the manuscript tradition of the gospels are to be accounted for by the influence of these traditions upon the written text. Since much material in the *Gospel of Thomas* akin to the synoptic material but not identical with it in detail has contacts textually with the text shown from Codex Bezae and with the traditions enshrined in Tatian's work, such theories are once again current coin. The Old Syriac is noteworthy for a number of linguistic features on which Burkitt and Black have commented. These are characteristic of Western not Eastern Aramaic, and may with great probability have links with an original tradition in a dialect akin to that of Jesus and his first disciples. No very striking variants partake of these features but their presence suggests the possibility that some of the peculiar variants in this version and its allies may come from a line of tradition not accounted for by direct methods of textual descent. An example of the possibility (not however attested in the Thomas or the Tatianic traditions, for evident doctrinal reasons) is the variation in the close of the genealogy of Jesus in Matt. 1:16 found in the Sinaitic manuscript of the Old Syriac version, which declares that 'Joseph to whom was betrothed Mary the virgin begat Jesus that is called the Messiah'. It is not only known in the Sinaitic manuscript but is also attested as late as the twelfth century in a comment of Dionysios bar-Salibi, who quotes the words as if they stood before him in the text, and then proceeds to expound the words 'the birth of Jesus the Messiah was thus' as an indication of the supernatural nature of the birth. While it is clear that the original of Tatian's *Diatessaron* did not include the genealogies, the Arabic version has genealogies from some other source, and it is of interest that this reading stands in one manuscript. Since the intention of the evangelist in this section is clearly to tell of the miraculous conception of Jesus, it might be thought incredible that he should introduce into his account a genealogy thus concluded: the presence of such a reading in the Sinaitic Syriac, we may then suggest, will derive from a West Aramaic tradition stemming ultimately from that group whom the Fathers call Ebionites, or some similar group, of whom we know that they taught a human parentage of Jesus. On the other hand, there is Greek attestation for such a reading in a document directed against the Jews, *The Dialogue of Timothy and Aquila*, of rather uncertain date, but presumably of ancient derivation even if it lies before us in a more recent form. The Ferrar group also appears to have contacts with a Greek reading of this kind. In the light of this it might be feasible to erect a contrary hypothesis that this is the original reading, in which case the evangelist would be envisaged as regarding his source as referring to the legal paternity of Joseph, not to his natural fathering of the child Jesus. The reading however would clearly be *lectio difficilior* and would in process of time be eradicated, the variations in the readings of the Ferrar group giving some indication of the way this came about. However, such a conclusion is not inevitable, and the view of an Aramaic origin for the variant may be supported from the further facts that the reading in the *Dialogue* is put into the mouth of a Jewish adversary of Christianity, while the Ferrar group has affinities with the Syriac gospels, which may be accounted for by the transporting of Syriac traditions from

Syria to Sicily and Calabria by fugitives from the seventh century onwards.

It is now clear from the evidence of the *Gospel of Thomas* that documents of Gnostic provenance may contain gospel material parallel to that of the canonical gospels. An instance of this is further to be found in the quotation from the synoptic 'cry of jubilation' (Matt. 11: 25–7; Luke 10: 21–2) which is attributed by Irenaeus to the Gnostic sect called Marcosians. Here, amongst other variants which reflect the highly uncertain textual state of the passage (to which we shall return), we read the Aramaic *Wah* in place of the Greek ναί—a cry of jubilation which well accords with the tone of the *pericope* and with the Lukan ἠγαλλιάσατο. The minuscule 1424 records a variant from *To Ioudaikon* in this *pericope*, and all versions and patristic quotations reveal numerous variations. It is one of the most striking passages to remind us that behind the text often confidently expounded there lies at points another, distinct and perhaps of great antiquity.

Traces of the Pauline epistles in their first-century state are not many. The variants which consist in the omission of the locative phrases in Rom. 1: 7 and 15 and in Eph. 1: 1 are in the view of many critics linked with the origins of these epistles as circular letters, or at any rate circulated to a wider audience than their immediate addressees. The traditions in which the place-names are found will reflect the specific copies sent to those churches. In the view of others, however, the variants are not original but date from the collection of the corpus, and are intended to make these specific letters universal in address. T. W. Manson, on the other hand, saw the hand of Marcion at work in the omissions, refusing the name of 'Pauline' to churches which had rejected his Paulinism.[1] Not unlinked with the omissions in Romans is the critical problem of chapter 16, and the very complex data about the position of the doxology (16: 25–7) and the absence of chapters 15 and 16 of Romans in the ancestry of the Graeco-Latin bilinguals D F G on the Latin side. These may have some light to shed upon the original form of the letter, but no very convincing arguments have yet been discovered after some years of study: the latest discussion concludes that these data are the result of a very early accidental omission, due to the loss of a *folium*, or some such hazard, and the subsequent attempts to mend the damage. 1 Clement 35 provides support for a

[1] 'St Paul's Letter to the Romans—and others', *BJRL*, xxxi (1948–9), 8.

variant otherwise known from B and the Vulgate at Rom. 1: 32. This creates an anacoluthon in the text, and accordingly most scholars would classify it as a corruption, and note the startling implication that corruption was at work very early in the Pauline text; but since anacoluthon is by no means unknown in Paul's writing where corruption is not suspected, it is possible that the text here demonstrated to be first-century is original, and that the grammatical forms elsewhere attested are corrections.

The Epistle of Jude is usually dated late within the range of composition of New Testament writings. It is characterised by a highly artificial style which might be the work of a writer unskilled in natural Greek and attempting to write in what is to him a fine style. Whether this is so or not is however strictly immaterial to the question of the complex variant in verses 22 and 23. The publication of 𝔓⁷² (of the third or fourth century) has focused attention on a form of these verses previously known in Clement of Alexandria and in the Syriac, Sahidic and Latin versions, and the origin of the variations may perhaps be found in the peculiar semantics of the verb διακρίνομαι, which normally bears the meaning of 'to be judged', but in the New Testament can have the meaning, unattested elsewhere, of 'to doubt' or 'to argue'. Is it the case that Jude, standing outside the main stream of primitive Christianity, used the term in its 'normal' sense, but later, when the letter was taken into the corpus of canonical writings, the 'biblical' meaning was assumed, and changes of order then became necessary because of the change in sense? If this were so, the form attested in the papyrus, which is best explained with the 'normal' meaning of the word, would be the original form or near to it, and the manifold other variants would be post-canonical corrections. This would be a further instance of versions and the quotations of a Father preserving the original text later confirmed by external and internal evidence.[1]

THE SECOND CENTURY

The second century is the period during which the Church begins to develop the forms which have become traditional in its doctrine and life. The early part of the century is marked by many variations and experiments which were later discarded, and it is not surprising that in

[1] See J. N. Birdsall, 'The Text of Jude in 𝔓⁷²', *JTS*, n.s. xiv (1963), 394–9.

textual matters there should be found a fluidity which disappears in later decades. It seems not improbable that there should be found readings where traces remain of an original which has suffered change in the processes of development. For this earliest period we are obliged to rely upon the versions and upon patristic quotations. Earliest amongst the Christian writers relevant to this inquiry is the heresiarch Marcion, of whose tendentiously edited Luke and Pauline corpus we still have no direct evidence but only the quotations made by Tertullian and Epiphanius, adversaries of his teaching in later generations. Much careful editorial work has been done on these by Zahn and Harnack, and more recently by Quispel and Higgins,[1] and in consequence we have a fairly clear knowledge of part of his gospel text, although it would be a boon indeed if some part of the original were to appear. Justin is the earliest orthodox writer to quote much of the gospel text. His work has occasioned much debate, since there are two factors which gravely complicate the issues. In the first place he quotes apocryphal material as possessing a status equivalent to that which was later defined as scripture; in the second place, in many places where he cites from the gospels his form of words suggests a harmony. Of Tatian, best known of the compilers of gospel harmonies, we have already given some account. We now possess so much material relevant to the reconstruction of the form and text of his *Diatessaron* that its study has become almost independent of New Testament textual criticism; we may however with care use its evidence for our purposes. Between the quotations in these three significant writers and editors, and the Old Latin and Old Syriac versions, with the Greek witnesses which in whole or in part concur with them, there is often to be found agreement in variants which indicate that at a very early period subtle changes of a doctrinal nature have taken place. Amongst these, and most instructive because of their evident doctrinal significance, are the variations within the *pericope* of Jesus' Cry of Jubilation (Matt. 11:25–7; Luke 10:21, 22). The divine address in all Greek manuscripts stands in Matthew as πάτερ κύριε τοῦ οὐρανοῦ καὶ τῆς γῆς while in Luke a form with the omission of καὶ τῆς γῆς is attested in $\mathfrak{P}^{45}$ and Marcion, and is

---

[1] T. Zahn, *Geschichte des Neutestamentlichen Kanons* (Erlangen and Leipzig, 1892), II, pp. 409–529; A. von Harnack, *Marcion. Das Evangelium vom fremden Gott* (2nd ed. Leipzig, 1924), pp. 40*–255*; G. Quispel, *De bronnen van Tertullianus' Adversus Marcionem* (Lyons, 1943); A. J. B. Higgins, 'The Latin Text of Luke in Marcion and Tertullian', *Vigiliae Christianae*, V (1951), 1–42.

reported in the uncial F by an eighteenth-century scholar, this part of the manuscript having since been lost. The Old Latin manuscripts, varying widely amongst themselves as they often do, reveal some discrepancies in Matthew: *b* reads *pater domine deus caeli et terrae, c, domine pater caeli et terrae, ff₁, deus pater caeli et terrae,* while *l* gives the short reading *pater caeli et terrae* which also stands in the text of *g₁*, although *domine* is added after *pater* between the lines by the scribe or his contemporary. In Luke, analogous variation is found in the Old Latin, amongst whose manuscripts *c f ff₂ i* read *domine pater caeli et terrae,* and *a, domine caeli et terrae*: Clement of Alexandria at this point has πάτερ ὁ θεὸς τοῦ οὐρανοῦ καὶ τῆς γῆς. Ephraem the Syrian commenting upon the *Diatessaron* at this point gives its text as 'father in the heavens', while specifying that 'the Greek' (probably the separated gospels, known to us now in the Curetonian and Sinaitic manuscripts) reads a form identical with that found in Matthew in all Greek manuscripts today. The data of these versions and quotations suggest the probability that the text has been subject to a series of honorific embellishments upon an original 'heavenly father' or 'father in heaven', which as we have noted is the reading of the *Diatessaron* as reported by Ephraem here. It is noteworthy that this is closely in line with Jesus' usual form of address to his God.

In the same passage, in the verses which treat of the secret of knowledge of the divine, it is well known that a perplexing transposition of terms is found in many Fathers and in a few Greek manuscripts and versions. Amongst the quotations, it is sometimes difficult to distinguish Matthaean from Lukan quotations: the Lukan, however, appear to have the form 'who is the Father (*or* Son)' while the Matthaean simply 'the Father (*or* Son)'. In the majority of Greek manuscripts these clauses stand in the following order: 'no one knows the Son except the Father and no one knows the Father except the Son and he to whom the Son wills to reveal it'. But patristic evidence provides us with a form of text attested by Marcion, Justin, Irenaeus, Tertullian, Ephraem, and many other Syriac and Latin Fathers and authors in which the Father–Son clause precedes the Son–Father clause so that the break in the logical structure is a harder reading. Amongst manuscripts it is found in Matthew in the uncials N and X, and in the Achmimic text of the Graeco-Coptic 𝔓⁶² (fourth century); in Luke in N once more, in U (related to X) and in the Old Latin manuscript *b*.

The minuscules 1424 and 477 (according to the apparatus of von Soden) have textually dislocated forms of the passage in Luke. Manuscript *a* of the Old Latin has only the Father–Son clause in Luke. Furthermore, it has not generally been observed by those who have discussed this crux that the Codex Bobbiensis of the Old Latin (which preserves our oldest ascertainable form of the version) presents palaeographical and textual corruption at this point, since in the text of Matthew here there is space for only one clause: the original has been erased and the second hand (that of a contemporary, probably the *diorthotes*) has written *filium nisi pater* with the words *neq. patrem quis agnoscit nisi filius* added in the lower margin. The lower text does not appear to have been deciphered and is probably illegible as is much of the manuscript. These data were made by Harnack (*The Sayings of Jesus*, E.T. London, 1908, pp. 272 ff.) the basis of an hypothesis that behind the form attested by the Fathers there was a stage in which only the clause asserting the Son's knowledge of the Father was to be found, the clause about the Father's knowledge of the Son being added (in Harnack's view already in the first century) to bring the whole passage into line with Johannine Christology. The inconcinnity of the resultant form found in the Fathers led at length to a further remodelling, producing the form now attested by the majority of witnesses. The three stages, on this hypothesis, are:

(*a*) No one knows the Father but the Son and he to whom the Son wills to reveal it.

(*b*) No one knows the Father but the Son and no one knows the Son but the Father and he to whom the Son wills to reveal it.

(*c*) The text as currently edited following the majority of manuscripts.

This hypothesis remains the only attempt to rationalise the data and if it is correct—and its rejection by many recent writers would seem to reflect their orthodox tendencies rather than a better explanation of awkward textual data—it reveals that the early second century was a time when the text was subject to alteration and corruption on doctrinal grounds arising from the theological unification of an originally heterogeneous tradition. If Harnack was unsuccessful in tracing its precise course in this instance, he nevertheless indicated with some success what factors have been at work in cases of this kind.

There are other cases which, while not of the far-reaching import of that just considered, show us a second-century text preserved only in outlying corners of Christendom. We may mention as similar to the case of Matt. 4: 17 above that of Mark 14: 4, where the omission of ἐπάνω is attested by three Greek minuscules, by *c* and *k* of the Old Latin and the Sinaitic manuscript of the Old Syriac. This gives a text which, as the absence of the adverb reveals, probably antedates the serious devaluation of the imperial currency in the late second century. To these instances may be added the interesting variant in Mark 8: 32 shared by *k*, the Sinaitic Syriac and one manuscript of the Arabic *Diatessaron*: here, in place of the past tense 'he spoke the word with boldness' we have 'he will speak the word with boldness', a clause which thus is to be understood as part of the first Passion prediction. It appears to presuppose an infinitive λαλήσειν instead of the imperfect ἐλάλει of our Greek texts, a variant not readily to be derived from transcriptional error. When Burkitt discussed this[1] he called it 'a neglected variant', and it remains so to this day, perhaps because the task also remains in the first place of elucidating its meaning if original (is it linked with a 'messianic secret'?), and secondly of explaining why it was transformed into the more banal reading which has been transmitted to us. Luke 9: 62 also lies before us in some witnesses— 𝔓⁴⁵ D lat vet Clem Al—in the form οὐδεὶς εἰς τὰ ὀπίσω βλέπων καὶ ἐπιβάλλων τὴν χεῖρα αὐτοῦ ἐπ' ἄροτρον εὔθετός ἐστιν εἰς τὴν βασιλείαν τοῦ θεοῦ, and the presence of this reading in diverse traditions in the third century makes it clear that it dates from the earliest period. In the place of the second participle, the Old Latin manuscript *b* reads the finite verb *mittit*, and in view of this Blass suggested that originally the clause εὔθετός ἐστιν. . .τοῦ θεοῦ was absent: Jesus' reply would then be tersely proverbial. This hypothesis has met with little remark, but it has the merit of considering variations within the manuscript tradition which other scholars have ignored.

Blass's theories were not limited to the Gospel of Luke, but also extended to the Gospel of John, where he contended that much greater weight should be given to the form of the quotations of the Gospel in the Fathers than other critics were willing to allow. This approach has been espoused in our own generation by M.-E. Boismard in the series of stimulating articles already mentioned. His position, which was reached on the basis of a very wide and careful collation of evi-

---

[1] 'St Mark viii. 32: A Neglected Variant Reading', *JTS*, II (1900–1), 111–13.

dence from the Fathers and from the versions, was that the critical text currently accepted is in many instances the end-product of an evolution which is revealed by these versional and patristic readings. The texts in question were, he postulates, in their original form succinct in the extreme: a second stage may be traced in which they have been expanded into a less laconic form: the third (which stands before us in our modern critical text) results from the conflation of the two. The main witness for the shortest form is Tatian, and support is often to be found in the Old Syriac, Old Latin, Georgian, Persian and Ethiopic versions. Codex Bezae sometimes supports it and 'manifest affinities' are to be found in the quotations of John Chrysostom and the Homeric paraphrase of the Gospel by Nonnus of Panopolis. Sometimes a Greek manuscript will preserve it, as in the case of John 13: 10, where 579, supported by Tertullian and by Tatian, as commented upon by Ephraem, reads ὁ λελουμένος οὐκ ἔχει χρείαν. The well-known variations in this verse all arise, in Boismard's view, from different supplementations of this excessively terse expression. Boismard recognises the existence of two other ancient forms of text in this Gospel, that represented in the Alexandrians, and that known in D and א, its ally in this Gospel. While there is certainly much material to support his theories, the publication in recent years of the first of the Bodmer papyri containing this Gospel has revealed some of the difficulties latent in them. In this papyrus, dated variously by experts between A.D. 175 and 225, a form of the Gospel is attested which sometimes agrees with the Alexandrian text, sometimes with the Bezan, with sporadic traces of the Tatianic *textus brevissimus*. Boismard seemed to envisage a process of recension jumping to and fro between the three, a very unlikely procedure, especially if it is not so much the readings as the men of that age responsible for them which are taken into consideration. Moreover, the date of the papyrus radically shortens the time allowed within the original hypothesis for the conflation of the two earliest text-forms. The situation has become even more problematical since the publication of the other Bodmer papyrus containing John, 𝔓75, which presents a text very closely akin to that of B. Are we to find the resolution of the questions now raised in reviving a sinister rôle for Tatian, and in placing the recensional activity suspected by Boismard not in the hinterland of the Alexandrian type, but in an abbreviating work by Tatian? On the other hand it has been pointed out by Zuntz (*Text of Epistles*, p. 275) that the application of grammatical and philological techniques to the elucidation of Christian scriptures, and perhaps to their critical restoration, is found amongst the Alexandrian Gnostics, whose works bore such titles as *Exegetica* and *Hypomnemata*. Can they have engaged in the expansion and conflation which Boismard's theory envisages? It may be of significance that certain of the Fathers considered the reading of the plural verb at John 1:13 to be an emendation of Gnostic *Tendenz*: the singular (referring to the Incarnate Word) was known to Tertullian, Hippolytus and Irenaeus, and is perhaps alluded to in Justin and even Ignatius. Its originality has been maintained by Boismard, and, on both internal and textual grounds, by Braun.[1]

We know little from direct sources of the text of Acts or of the Catholic epistles in the second century, but we can learn much of the Pauline epistles from what we know of Marcion's *Apostolos*. Two features deserve mention: first, that Marcion quite evidently emended the text in the interests of his own interpretations, since the emendations are patent and undisguised; secondly, the basic text from which he worked was already corrupt to some degree. Amongst readings generally thought to be patently tendentious changes are the omission of θεοῦ after ὀργή at Rom. 1:18 and of καὶ προφητῶν in Eph. 2:20. Marcion's supreme God was not the author of wrath, nor had he any hand in the inspiration of the Old Testament. Amongst the primitive corruptions, the most striking is that in 1 Cor. 14:19, where Marcion read πέντε λόγους τῷ νοΐ μου λαλῆσαι διὰ τὸν νόμον, which is otherwise unattested in Greek witnesses, but is known in the Latin Vulgate manuscripts D and Z (*quinque verbis loqui in ecclesiis in sensu meo per legem*). A history of corruption lies behind this reading, which has been elucidated by Zuntz (*The Text of the Epistles*, p. 230) as follows: the original reading is that preserved in the majority of Byzantine manuscripts, διὰ τοῦ νοός μου; this reading has on the one hand been corrupted at an early date to διὰ τὸν νόμον which has influenced Latin texts and is known from the 'Ambrosiaster' and Paulinus of Nola, and on the other, through the influence of adjacent passages, has been displaced by τῷ νοΐ μου. Marcion in fact has a text not only corrupt but also conflate! Yet the presence of the corruption διὰ τὸν νόμον in his text has the value to the

---

[1] ' "Qui ex Deo natus est" ', in *Aux sources de la tradition chrétienne. Mélanges offerts à M. Maurice Goguel* (Neuchâtel and Paris, 1950), pp. 11–31.

modern critic of demonstrating the antiquity of the original διὰ τοῦ νοός μου, which otherwise (at least to those unacquainted with the principles of rational criticism) would remain unrecognised because of its largely late Greek attestation.

Our attention has concentrated largely on two classes of variant, namely those arising from the alteration of the text in a doctrinal interest, and those which originated in the alteration of passages which had become obscure in the course of the development of Christianity. One other factor at least was at work during the second century, the elucidation of which we owe to G. D. Kilpatrick ('Atticism and the Text of the Greek New Testament'). This is change on stylistic grounds, and especially with reference to those criteria which were presented as normative by the Atticists of the second century. Against the background of this movement, and on the hypothesis of its effect on Christian scholars and scribes, many variants in tense, voice, mood and vocabulary become explicable. Thus although we lack specific evidence about variations of the verbs ἀγγέλλειν, ἀπαγγέλλειν and ἀναγγέλλειν, there is reason to think that ἀγγέλλειν, when it supplants either of the others, is an Atticism, and contrariwise, that ἀναγγέλλειν would be a word rejected by the Atticists. Similarly, when we find the passive aorist ἀπεκρίθη and the middle aorist ἀπεκρίνατο as variants, we may see the middle form as an Atticising correction. There was also, not only under the Atticists' aegis, a tendency to assimilate to Greek usage idioms deriving from the semitic languages, whether Hebrew (*via* the style of the Septuagint, deemed appropriate to sacred narrative) or Aramaic (*via* the oral tradition of the words of Jesus and his immediate disciples). The removal of such blemishes upon the Greek will account for the substitution of ἔφη for ἀποκριθεὶς εἶπεν in several gospel accounts, and possibly for the omission of the repeated third person pronoun when it reproduces the suffixes of the semitic languages.

The recognition of these factors, and the examination of variants at points where they may be deemed to have been at work, lead to an interesting conclusion, already adumbrated in the attestation indicated in the discussions of gospel variants and the epistolary text of Marcion, namely, that no one form of text has a monopoly of the original. Original readings may be discerned in the various witnesses to the so-called Western text, while the Byzantine text (brusquely dismissed by most exegetes since the days of Westcott and Hort) often reflects the putative original in both vocabulary and word-order. This indicates that all the major text-forms have their roots in the second century.

We are led to ask the reasons for these data in the text of the New Testament as attested in the second century. They have already been intimated in the discussion of particular variants and we summarise them here. In the first place, it was only during this period that the majority of writings of the New Testament achieved canonical status: in the early decades, side by side with the four gospels, others, later to be rejected, enjoyed the trust of Christians, while each of the four seems to have had at first only a regional vogue and circulation. It was inevitable that a certain amount of glossation and alteration should have taken place. This was not only in the interests of doctrine—indeed this happened far less than we might have expected. In the texts of Codex Bezae and the oldest strata of the Latin, and sometimes in the Old Syriac as well, we find in Luke and Acts a variant topographical and itinerary tradition (e.g. Luke 6: 17; 7: 17–19). As the Church began to assimilate the learning of the hellenistic world, as in the period of the Apologists, it is not surprising that prevailing stylistic canons should have made themselves felt, and that the language of the gospels in particular, and also the intentional peculiarities of Revelation, should have been subject to correction. It is also clear that a tendency existed from the first to harmonise the parallel accounts of the gospels: the earliest instances of this are perhaps better explained by the hypothesis of parallel oral traditions than by that of harmonisation of written documents. This may well account not only for the form of gospel material in the Apostolic Fathers, but also for Marcion's text of Luke at those points where it appears to have been harmonised to that of the other synoptics. By the time of Justin, however, there can be little doubt that the 'Memoirs' he knew were the gospels, and probably a harmony of them also. From the material common to Justin's quotations and the *Diatessaron* of Tatian it seems a not unlikely hypothesis that Tatian was indebted, to some degree at least, to his master's habitual text. The text of Irenaeus at the end of the century also shows the feature of harmonisation: it is not beyond the bounds of likelihood that Tatian's work was already known to him, or if not, that he knew whatever lies behind Justin's quotations. But, as Lagrange emphasised, one does not require a harmony in order to harmonise, and the Father who first stressed that a fourfold gospel is axiomatic in the Church may well have known all four gospels well enough to assimilate them to one another in his memory.

We do not know what part the organisation of the Church and especially the episcopate played in textual preservation and development. The century was a troubled time for the Church, as it made its way against the odds of prejudice and calumny, and there was no place for the reflection of the study. Bishops were no doubt content with what they had received; the main efforts of preservation were not philological, but directed against the outright falsities of the Gnostics and others. In large areas, however, so far as we can discern, even this aspect of debate is absent. The glossing activities of Marcion were opposed, but the work of Tatian does not appear to have aroused antagonism. Thus the harmonised and the contaminated traditions existed along with the tradition of the separated gospels, which in some cases displayed a text rather different from that transmitted in later generations. The corrupted texts also provide some information about this stage of development.

THE EARLIEST VERSIONS

Translation of the scriptures was already well under way by the end of the second century. Tertullian, the earliest of the Latin Fathers (born about A.D. 160, died after A.D. 220), in his gospel quotations most frequently translates for himself from the Greek, but his renderings reflect from time to time the form which we know from Old Latin manuscripts. The version known in the manuscripts, then, was in existence by the time Tertullian wrote. It has also been thought by scholars hitherto that Tertullian in quoting the Marcionite scriptures used a version of these rather than made his own translation. The most recent study of this material, however, has led to the conclusion that this is not so, and the existence of a separate Marcionite Latin version remains unproven, and indeed apparently without foundation. Another line of research has sought to connect the Latin gospels with the fortunes of the *Diatessaron*. It is clear at any rate that Tatian's work left its mark upon the Latin separated gospels in apocryphal additions and distinctive readings. It would seem likely then that the *Diatessaron* existed at an early period in Latin dress. The existence of such a form was demonstrated at length from the quotations of Novatian from the gospels. He was a contemporary and adversary of Cyprian of Carthage (who died as a martyr in A.D. 258), and probably met a martyr's end himself. Baumstark[1] found behind his quotations the marked influence of a Latin *Diatessaron*, which in its turn had been rendered from the Syriac without Greek intermediary. Traces of such a form of harmony have also been discerned in the medieval Dutch harmony, extant in three manuscripts, which the Dutch scholar D. Plooij investigated. This is directly based on a Latin harmony, but it seems clear that this had been rendered from Syriac. By the end of the second century, then, there already existed in Latin both separated gospels and a harmony. In Cyprian's quotations in the next century, and in the Codex Bobbiensis with which these are so closely allied, the separated gospels have already been corrupted in some places by the influence of the harmony, and by the time of Cyprian there was already a history of development within the separated gospels themselves.

The conclusion that behind the Old Latin there is to be found at points an Old Syriac strengthens the assumption that the gospel existed in Syriac dress by the end of the second century. There can be little doubt that the first form of the gospels in Syriac was the *Diatessaron*, since the Old Syriac known in two manuscripts, the Sinaitic and the Curetonian, shows many indications of the influence of a harmony text upon it. It is remarkable of course that Mesopotamia, with its many Jewish colonies into which the Christian gospel made its inroads, should have had to wait a hundred years for the literary impact of the gospels; hence there has seemed a certain historical likelihood, however contradicted by the textual evidence, that the separated gospels were very early translated, and that Tatian used them in the construction of the *Diatessaron*. A pointer in the direction of a solution which may account for both sets of data may be seen in the West Aramaic forms found in some passages of the Old Syriac separated gospels, some instances of which we now know to have been in the *Diatessaron* also. Do these belong to a strand drawn ultimately from an apocryphal gospel, which would be the first form of the gospel known to the Syriac church? To this the apocryphal additions so evident in all the strands of the *Diatessaron* tradition may be related. One further fact must be noted in this regard, namely, that we appear unable to identify the source of these apocrypha within any extant source. There are contacts with the Coptic *Gospel of Thomas*, with the

[1] *Oriens Christianus*. IIIᵉ Série, v (1930), 1–14.

Gospel according to the Hebrews, and with the *Protevangelium* of James. At all events the Syriac church had a gospel tradition related to the canonical gospels by the end of the second century, and through the work of Tatian in particular its influence was not limited to its homeland.

In dealing with the Coptic versions, the third of the primary versions, we are hampered by the absence of either documents or quotations of a period early enough to provide a basis for operations. Neither the manuscripts, by reason of date, nor the textual form of the documents which we do possess, can provide this basis. It is the opinion of some Coptic scholars that the Sahidic is from the second century, but others argue for the third. Certainly, Gnostic Christians were actively at work in Egypt in the second century and have some claim to be regarded as the first exegetes. We know from extant writings that their use of Christian writings embraced many of the books of the New Testament. Since many Gnostic writings are extant only in Coptic, it may be a reasonable assumption that they were responsible for the translation of the scriptures: Gnostic texts in the *Gospel of Thomas* which contain material akin to the Synoptics are often in agreement in their rendering with the canonical gospel texts known to us. A recently published Coptic gospel text reflects the converse state of affairs. Bodmer papyrus III contains a Bohairic version of John and Gen. 1–3.[1] It is a fourth-century manuscript (thus, incidentally, one of the earliest manuscripts of the version in that dialect), and shows signs of adaptation from an earlier Sahidic. Some of its readings clearly display a Gnostic tendency. If it were a primary translation in Sahidic, it could date back to the third century: if this was a rehandling of an already existing text, it might take us back as far as the second.

IRENAEUS

The most impressive figure of second-century Christianity, Irenaeus of Lyons, bridges the turn of that century into the third, and combines in himself features reminiscent of both. He is akin to the earlier second century by his preservation of primitive features of doctrine and text, and to the third by his comprehension of the faith as an intellectual

[1] *Papyrus Bodmer III. Évangile de Jean et Genèse I–IV, 2 en bohairique*, ed. R. Kasser, *CSCO*, CLXXVII, CLXXVIII (Cologny-Genéve, 1960); E. Massaux, 'Quelques variantes importantes de Papyrus Bodmer III et leur accointance avec la Gnose', *NTS*, v (1958–9), 210–12.

unity and his systematic attempt at presentation and defence. His witness to the New Testament text then is of the highest interest and importance, but to ascertain that text is no simple task. His work *Adversus Haereses* is not preserved in its entirety in the original Greek, and for the work as a whole we rely upon a Latin version, of which the probable date is the fourth century (rather than the late second century as has sometimes been thought). This is supplemented by fragments in Syriac, and for the fourth and fifth books (in which happily most of the scriptural quotations are to be found) by an Armenian version, the product of a period in which the Armenians slavishly followed the Greek model, to the detriment of Armenian style, but to the profit of subsequent textual scholars. This provides a cross-check on the Latin and helps us to see if that translator used the Latin version of the New Testament known to him in rendering the quotations of Irenaeus, or was faithful to the original Greek, which in most instances we can say that he was.[1] In Irenaeus' quotations from the gospels there are many instances of harmonisation within a text which is basically akin to the Old Syriac, the Old Latin and Codex Bezae. Von Soden and Kraft have explained this by the influence of the *Diatessaron*, or of a pre-Tatianic harmony, but Lagrange observes that quotations may not have been directly controlled by a written text, but may have been affected by memory and unconscious harmonisation.[2] It does not, however, appear as certain as some scholars would urge that the *Diatessaron* (to be dated about A.D. 170) could not have been known to Irenaeus by A.D. 185 when he wrote the *Adversus Haereses*: fifteen years seems adequate time for a work to travel from Rome to Gaul and to be known to Christians in that region. On the other hand, it is surprising that Irenaeus does not mention the harmonising work of Tatian in the account which he gives of him. We may be thrown back on the hypothesis of a pre-Tatianic harmony which Tatian also used as his model, but this awaits definitive investigation. No very detailed study of Irenaeus' witness to the text of Acts has been made. He frequently agrees with D and its allies, but we also find singular and sub-

[1] See K. T. Schaefer, 'Die Zitate in der lateinischen Irenaeusübersetzung, und ihr Wert für die Textausgabe des Neuen Testaments' in *Vom Wort des Lebens. Festschrift für Max Meinertz*, ed. N. Adler (Münster, 1951), pp. 50–9.

[2] See H. von Soden, *Die Schriften des Neuen Testaments* (Berlin, 1911–13), pp. 1615–20; B. Kraft, *Die Evangelienzitate des heiligen Irenaeus* (Freiburg, 1924); M.-J. Lagrange, *op. cit.* p. 177.

singular readings. A comparison with the text of Acts in the Chester Beatty papyrus does not give all the insight one might have hoped for, because of the fragmentary nature of that manuscript and the extent of Irenaeus' quotations from Acts, but one reading of Irenaeus previously unattested elsewhere is found in the papyrus (περιῆλθεν in Acts 10: 35). In the Paulines, Irenaeus usually supports the non-Alexandrians, and in many instances in readings which commend themselves, e.g. in a particularly striking example at 1 Cor. 10: 9, reading Χριστόν (in place of κύριον or θεόν) with D F G vulg, and many Fathers and ancient versions. In the Catholic epistles, Irenaeus has provided striking support for the reading known previously, apart from the margin of 1739, only in Latin dress at 1 John 4: 3 ὃ λύει τὸν Ἰησοῦν (in place of ὃ μὴ ὁμολογεῖ τὸν Ἰησοῦν), a reading which commends itself as original. In Revelation we have a very rich selection of variants, from which we find Irenaeus generally in agreement with the text of A and its ally C which is the most satisfactory textual tradition of this book which we have. In this instance, the Asian background of Irenaeus may have placed him in contact with a text closely related to the autograph.

THE THIRD CENTURY

For the early part of the third century our witnesses are Clement of Alexandria, Hippolytus of Rome, the Chester Beatty papyri and the Bodmer papyrus of John ($\mathfrak{P}^{66}$). In the gospels these witnesses remind the student once more of the wide divergences in gospel texts of this period. The Fathers attest broad agreement with the common voice of Codex Bezae, the Old Latin and the Old Syriac. Clement has been adequately studied, although there is room for a re-examination. Hippolytus, however, has been investigated only by von Soden, and however accurate his account may prove to be, it is vitiated throughout by the vagaries of his textual theory. Besides, so much of Hippolytus' work is extant only in Eastern Christian languages and was not accessible to von Soden that a new investigation is an urgent need. The Chester Beatty papyrus of the gospels ($\mathfrak{P}^{45}$) has been fully examined only in the Gospel of Mark, in which it shows a close affinity to the late minuscule groups Family 1 and the Ferrar group, and is more remotely connected with a text known to Origen and regularly used by Eusebius. Its Lukan text may well have the same characteristics, while in John it often shares readings with Codex Bezae, Codex Sinaiticus and the Old Latin. The Bodmer papyrus of John ($\mathfrak{P}^{66}$) has a distinctive text, which cannot be identified with that of any previously known witness—sometimes it is aligned to the text of B, sometimes to that of א and D, sometimes to variants known from Tatian and the versions.[1] Little of Acts is extant in $\mathfrak{P}^{45}$: what remains shows in its entirety a text not to be identified with any of the main types which have hitherto been analysed. The Chester Beatty papyrus of the Paulines ($\mathfrak{P}^{46}$) has, on the contrary, a striking affinity with B and 1739, which together often attest a text acceptable upon the principles of rational criticism as original. The Chester Beatty papyrus of Revelation ($\mathfrak{P}^{47}$) is dated somewhat later in the century than the other New Testament papyri of the collection, and preserves a text closely akin to that known from א. Although it is our earliest extant witness to this book, the text of this papyrus and of its uncial ally is corrupt at many points. In the Paulines and Acts, otherwise than in their text of the gospels, Clement and Hippolytus (so far, that is, as the latter's quotations have been examined) both agree far more with the Alexandrian text known in B 1739 and $\mathfrak{P}^{46}$ than with the other main early tradition known in the bilinguals and the Old Latin. When readings of the latter type, however, are found in these Fathers, they often confirm the view of rational criticism that such readings are ancient and perhaps original. In Revelation the balance of attestation in the two Fathers changes; Hippolytus quotes frequently and often displays readings known to us in C, whereas there are few traces of the book in Clement's writings, and what is found is textually neutral.

This brings us in point of time to the greatest figure in ante-Nicene Christian thought and scholarship, Origen, head of the catechetical school of Alexandria at an early age and later influential in Caesarea.[2] It is no matter for surprise that in the light of his important work on the text of the Old Testament, and because of his stature of mind and learning, scholars should have tended to credit him with a text-critical interest in the New also. His statement in his commentary on Matthew, a work dating from late in his life, seems to show that these opinions are ill-founded. He says: 'I did not think that I could do the same on New Testament texts without danger' (*Comm. in Matt.* xv, 14). He

---

[1] See M.-E. Boismard, 'Le papyrus Bodmer II', *RB*, LXIV (1957), 363–98.
[2] For Origen see v, 14.

was well aware of textual discrepancies between manuscripts in his own time,[1] but, to judge from the fact that in the Gospel of Mark at least he used different text-types at different times, he did not make any systematic study of these data, but used the manuscript which lay to hand. It is notorious that the hypothesis that he used one text-type in Alexandria and another after his move to Caesarea was based on faulty premises, although in spite of this the nomenclature of 'Caesarean text' is still with us and widely misinterpreted. Through his wide-ranging exegetical work his volume of quotation from the gospels is very large, and we also have from him a not inconsiderable body of textual material for the rest of the New Testament. In the Gospel of Mark, to which the attention of textual critics tended to be primarily directed in the twenties and thirties of this century, we find that Origen used two texts: one shares its main area of common ground with B and ℵ, and with other witnesses to their type of text, which because of its patristic attestation has come to be called Alexandrian; the other is attested by more recently discovered uncials, W and Θ, by many minuscules and by Eastern versions, particularly the Armenian and Georgian versions. The latter text was known and used by Origen both in Egypt and in Caesarea, while the former continued to be used by him for some time of his life in Caesarea, but the first investigators concluded in error that a transference from the one to the other could be clearly traced at the time of his migration. Hence, the name of Caesarean text came to be coined to indicate the text of Θ and its allies. However, the Chester Beatty papyrus of Mark ($\mathfrak{P}^{45}$), of Egyptian provenance, has this type of text. The term is therefore a misnomer. There are also some of Origen's works written in Caesarea in which his quotations from Matthew and John show such a close identity with the text in the manuscripts 1 and 1582 that this group of three may be said to constitute a family. It may be that the text of these gospels in 1582 has been deliberately constructed from the exegetical works of Origen, and does not represent a descendant of his habitual exemplar. The likelihood of this is suggested by the fact that the minuscule 1739, written by the same scribe Ephraem as 1582 and exhibiting a similar though much more extensive series of marginal notes, is a copy of a

---

[1] See B. M. Metzger, 'Explicit References in the Works of Origen to Variant Readings in New Testament MSS.' in *Biblical and Patristic Studies in Memory of R. P. Casey* (Freiburg, 1963), pp. 78–95.

manuscript of the Paulines in which a prologue expressly states that the text of Romans had been constituted from Origen's commentary in this way. The rest of its text, so the prologue states, was shown by collation to be closely related to his habitual text, and modern study has shown that this ancient critical observation was fully justified. With Origen and 1739, $\mathfrak{P}^{46}$ and B frequently agree, and in this part of the New Testament this text may be adequately described as Alexandrian, although the critical work which lies behind 1739 is more likely to be a product of Caesarean scholarship. Furthermore, whereas the Alexandrian text of the gospels is viewed by current scholarship as of variable quality, the text of the epistles as preserved in these witnesses is in the majority of places acceptable by rational criteria. In Acts Origen concurs with the representatives of this text-type, the 'old uncials' as they were termed by J. H. Ropes, but it is to be noted that neither 1739 nor the Chester Beatty papyrus ($\mathfrak{P}^{45}$) is a representative of this text-type in Acts. In Revelation, Origen's text is in agreement with $\mathfrak{P}^{47}$ and א, which, while often sharing good ancient readings with other witnesses such as A, shows by itself few acceptable ones, and many signs of ancient corruption, frequently in attempts to simplify by abbreviation. In addition to these conclusions reached from the study of the text quoted or commented upon by Origen, there is also a small number of passages where he shows knowledge of variations within the manuscripts of his day. In discussing these he shows little critical acumen, but rather a tendency to make use of all alternatives for edification. For the modern scholar the value of such cases lies not in Origen's choices but rather in the evidence which they provide of the textual situation within which Origen worked: many variants were known to him, through his connection with a wide range of Christian scholarship and tradition, which today are known only from versions or sporadically in minuscules. But in the case, at least, of the variant 'country of the Gergesenes' instead of 'Gadarenes' or 'Gerasenes' in Matt. 8: 28–32 or its parallels, it is probably the comment of Origen about the likelihood of the latter two readings known to him from manuscripts which has given rise to the former, since his knowledge of Palestinian topography led him to suggest Gergesa as a place traditionally alleged to be the scene of the stampede of pigs (*ad* John 6: 41).

Origen died shortly after the Decian persecution, *c.* 253, and this is an appropriate point at which to summarise the textual situation in the third century about fifty years before the peace of the Church. As we have seen, Origen knew, and at different times used, two different text-types, the Alexandrian and the Caesarean. Whereas the initial researches upon the latter tended to treat all witnesses involved as witnesses to one text, and to differentiate between them as 'strong' or 'weak', more recent scholarship has distinguished between the type known from the Chester Beatty papyrus and the minuscule families, and that known in Origen and from the uncials and the oriental versions. The former has been denominated 'pre-Caesarean' and deemed to be the raw material from which the latter 'recensional Caesarean' was created. At any rate, there are certainly two distinct texts formerly conceived of as one. Since the text of Family 1 is an aspect of the 'pre-Caesarean', and Origen knew the text of Matthew and John as represented in two manuscripts of that family, it might be true to say that he attests not two but three text-types. He also shows acquaintance with readings which are now known only from the Codex Bezae (e.g. at Luke 14: 19 the addition of καὶ διὰ τοῦτο οὐ δύναμαι ἐλθεῖν, cf. διὸ οὐ δύναμαι ἐλθεῖν of D against the absence of such a phrase in other traditions), or readings known only in versions, such as the omission of μετανοεῖτε and γάρ in Matt. 4: 17. A strictly regional distribution of text-types and readings, and any theory of local texts, seem to be ruled out of court by this evidence, and by the evidence from the preceding century which we have discussed.

Codex Bezae, a Graeco-Latin manuscript of the fourth or fifth century, was until fairly recently regarded as a *monstrum*, but now it must be looked on as a survival of a Greek text once widely spread.[1] It was found in Gaul, and some have held the opinion that it originated there; but the claims of South Italy, Sicily, Egypt and Jerusalem have all been more recently urged, and since all have a strong claim, it is very difficult to decide between them. South Italy and Sicily both have had periods when Greek was a spoken tongue there (and indeed dialects of Greek are spoken in both places still) and a continuous history of spoken Greek is required to account for the series of *marginalia* in Greek which characterise the manuscript, a continuity which is not provided by Gaul for so long a period as the data demand. However, the manuscript need not have originated in the West, since there

[1] The latest study of the MS., by E. J. Epp, *The Theological Tendency of Codex Bezae Cantabrigiensis in Acts* (Cambridge, 1967), gives an excellent bibliography.

are records of bilingual public lection in Jerusalem and Egypt. The extent of the distribution of the text known in Codex Bezae has led to the consideration of both places as serious candidates for its place of writing. Though the manuscript is an instance of a text once widely known, analysis has shown that it is not a pure representative of that text, for which we must frequently rely on Latin and Syriac witnesses. In Acts, Codex Bezae has been corrupted by the Alexandrian text of the old uncials (no equally thorough investigation has been made of the gospel text), and throughout, as the researches of Rendel Harris showed, the Latin text has acted upon the Greek and the Greek upon the Latin. Hence, neither as Greek text nor as Latin can this manuscript give its witness without cross-examination. We do not know how much further back the tradition of arrangement in double columns reaches, since it is our earliest example. Others are known mainly from the West, but there are Oriental examples—obviously, such bilingual manuscripts were not required in Greek-speaking lands after the division of Christendom. Several scholars in the past have attempted to explain the origin of the distinctive variants of the manuscript solely or primarily in terms of such interactions, whether of the Latin upon the Greek or of a putative Syriac: one theory took as its basis the format of the manuscript in which the lines are sense-lines and not a fixed number of letters. But neither palaeographical nor inter-columnar influence has explained all the enigmas in the manuscript. Its text has contacts with second-century heretics such as the Montanists and Marcion, and texts which we know to have been used by them. A highly harmonistic strain in the gospels has been noted, though not certainly proven to have any link with Tatian: an anti-Judaic tendency has been observed in the variants in Acts. Instances of the Greek text represented by Codex Bezae have come to light in two papyri, one of which supplements a lacuna in the manuscript which had previously to be filled from the Latin. No full inquiry has been made in the gospels to determine whether we have a Greek text extant which exactly represents that of which Bezae is a contaminated example. We have perhaps such a text in the first five chapters of the Freer codex. Or should it still be sought among the versions, for instance in the Old Latin manuscripts Bobbiensis or Palatinus? Both the Freer codex and these Latin manuscripts require a re-examination in the light of recent advances in textual theory and knowledge.

The Freer codex is to be dated in the fourth century. While it is akin to the Old Latin in the early chapters of Mark, elsewhere it is our earliest instance of the Byzantine text. While individual readings known from that text-type are to be found in the third century, especially in the Chester Beatty gospel papyrus, no Father or manuscript is known which attests the type in its entirety then.

In dealing with Codex Bezae we have already needed to mention the text of Acts in the third century, the evidence about which was admirably marshalled by J. H Ropes.[1] It is notorious that here we find two clearly differentiated text-types. Codex Vaticanus is a prime example of the text known in Alexandrian Fathers and Coptic sources; and attested also by many uncials and some minuscules. The other text is primarily known from Codex Bezae, in spite of some of the drawbacks and unanswered problems presented by this manuscript, and amongst the Fathers; it is attested by Tertullian, by other Latin writers, and by Irenaeus. Instances of the text in Greek are provided by $\mathfrak{P}^{38}$ and $\mathfrak{P}^{48}$; otherwise we have only a mixed text in some minuscules. The Old Latin provides several instances of the text in a pure form, e.g. the Fleury palimpsest, the Perpignan codex (preserved in the Bibliothèque Nationale at Paris), and the Codex Gigas (part of the booty of the Thirty Years' War, preserved in Stockholm). Old Syriac evidence is also known mainly in the commentaries of Ephraem the Syrian, preserved in Armenian. Most students of the problem have concluded that, taken as a whole, B is more faithful to the original, but that on the other hand the alternative tradition has preserved many original readings. The text attested by D and its allies is certainly very early: the reading τᾶς ὠδῖνας τοῦ ᾄδου for τ. ὠδ. τοῦ θανάτου (Acts 2: 24) is at any rate as early as Polycarp (Phil. 1: 2). Since the so-called Caesarean text in the gospels often appears to mediate between the extremes of other texts, such a text-type has often been sought or hoped for in the study of the text of Acts, but the data are either quite inadequate or plain contrary to the hypothesis. In the gospels the striking feature is that this early text known to Origen is preserved in late minuscules, in other Fathers and ancient versions, and has come to light amongst the papyri. While in Acts some minuscules preserve mixed texts mediating between the types known in uncial sources,

[1] F. J. Foakes Jackson and Kirsopp Lake, *The Beginnings of Christianity. The Acts of the Apostles.* III. *The Text*, ed. J. H. Ropes (London, 1926).

their text in no way corresponds to any papyrus text; Origen gives no alternative to the text of B, and other Fathers provide evidence so slender as to be useless for purposes of comparison. The text of the versions (which apart from the Old Latin have received too little attention) seems to bear no evident relationship to the minuscules, of which more could be studied. However, it can at least be indicated that in 1739, of which the text is known to be ancient, we have a text of Acts neither Bezan nor Alexandrian, but not Origenian, although the text of the Paulines is strikingly so. Some marginal notes in Acts refer to Irenaeus. It may have affinities with the Old Armenian: but this awaits further investigation.

The Catholic epistles are a strangely neglected area of textual study, perhaps because the problems are not so complex nor the data so multifarious as in the rest of the New Testament. The main sources of Greek evidence presenting the text known in early Fathers attest a form akin to that found in B and its allies, while a Byzantine form, later widely known, appears about the fourth century. However, $\mathfrak{P}^{72}$ (of about the fourth century) attests in Jude some readings unknown to the later Greek traditions but found in Latin, Sahidic and Syriac form and in Clement of Alexandria. It may be then that there was extant at an early period a third type of text in this epistle at least, which later disappeared and left only sporadic traces in the versions. The minuscules deserve closer attention than they have received, although *prima facie* they do not contain very much ancient material.

Only for the Pauline epistles are we as richly supplied with material for the pre-Nicene period as we are for the gospel text in that period. There are two basic types of text known, the first is that which is earliest attested in $\mathfrak{P}^{46}$, which has proved on examination to be a very carefully prepared text with many acceptable readings, and is also known in later witnesses such as B and its allies, and in the quotations of Origen. The tenth-century minuscule 1739 is also ultimately of Origenian provenance. The second[1] is that preserved in the Graeco-Latin bilinguals (the codices Claramontanus, Boernerianus and Augiensis—similar to Bezae in form and problems), which is also known in the Latin versions, partially in Syriac, and in early Fathers. There is no equivalent to the Caesarean text, as in Acts, in the sense that no

[1] Zuntz, *The Text of the Epistles*, pp. 84–148; H. J. Frede, *Altlateinische Paulus-Handschriften* (Freiburg, 1964).

early Father presents a text as yet unknown in the major manuscript sources, but the varying text of the minuscules has not yet been investigated in depth. It is clear from rational criticism that the Byzantine text has preserved acceptable readings known in earlier times but lost in the major streams of tradition, but the text-type itself is not attested in this period.

Revelation presents us with a different pattern of tradition than the other parts of the New Testament Canon. The uncertainties reflected in Eusebius' statements about the book's canonical status (*HE*, III, 25) have doubtless played their part in creating this distinctive situation. The Greek tradition separates into four main streams: that of the uncials A and C known also in 2344 and the commentary of Oecumenius; that known in ℵ and the Chester Beatty papyrus, attested by Origen; the Koine text attested in a majority of manuscript witnesses; and the text providing the *lemmata* of the commentary of Andreas of Cappadocian Caesarea. The two latter texts are not attested in the pre-Nicene period in their entirety, but they originated at a period earlier than the differentiation of the two other texts, and are not derivatives of them. Schmid has expressly denied the existence of any equivalent of the Bezan text, i.e. a text found in the early Greek Fathers and the versions but disappearing in the main stream of Greek tradition. The suggestion that such a text may however be discerned in the common readings of various minuscules with the versions[1] has not been fully investigated, but Kilpatrick has noted some places where the Armenian and Syriac (both having in this book hyperliteral renderings) have reproduced some peculiarities of syntax characteristic of the book, which have been corrected away in much of the Greek tradition.[2] This is probably an index of the high and untapped potential value of the versional tradition in this book in particular.

CHRISTIAN SCHOLARS AND THE NEW TESTAMENT

During the centuries before and after the peace of the Church, centres of instruction and Christian philology appeared, which seem to have had some relation to the preservation of the New Testament text, although it is difficult to say precisely what this relation may have been.

[1] J. Duplacy, 'Bulletin de Critique Textuelle du Nouveau Testament', *Recherches de Science Religieuse*, L (1962), 595. [2] *Vigiliae Christianae*, XIII (1959), 7–11.

The catechetical school of Alexandria is well known and it would seem that there was a similar institution at Caesarea; both were associated with Origen. Furthermore, at Alexandria even before Origen's day, and at both Caesarea and Antioch, outstanding men of learning gathered about them pupils who often succeeded them in their scholarly work. There seems to be a body of circumstantial evidence connecting the three main streams of Greek text which continued to exist after the turn of the fourth century with these three centres of Christian scholarship: what is lacking is firm evidence of the activity of the scholars in question in textual matters of the New Testament or, where their names are ostensibly linked with such activity, evidence of what precisely they may be deemed to have done on the text. It is clear that in the time of Origen all types of gospel text attested in his commentaries and other works were extant in Egypt, but subsequent teachers and leaders of Egyptian Christianity concur in their use of the Alexandrian text. In the rest of the New Testament there is no duality of witness from Origen, and the Alexandrian Fathers and Coptic versions of later date follow the pattern known in $\mathfrak{P}^{46}$ and other relevant documents discussed above. Up to the time of the Arab conquest, the nature of the Egyptian text remains in the main the same, although there is some relatively slight movement, particularly in the improvement of style perceived by Hort and designated by him specifically 'Alexandrian'. It does not seem too hasty an inference that a certain type of text commended itself to Alexandrian Christian scholarship on grounds which we can see to have had affinity with the philological principles of the classical scholarship of antiquity. (It should be interposed at this point in the interests of accuracy that for much of the data used in attempting to plot the pattern of the text in this period we depend upon the assertions of earlier scholars, especially of von Soden, which have not been checked or improved upon by subsequent generations. A need in this field is the collection and assessment of the citational material from the fourth century onwards: some few studies have been made, but the area as a whole has been neglected.) It is clear that Eusebius of Caesarea used in the gospels the Caesarean text-type in a form closely akin to that of Origen, but recensionally adjusted, as comparison with the papyrus and minuscule witnesses shows. Cyril of Jerusalem is also a witness to this type of text. To these, both in the gospels and in the other New Testament books, von Soden adds the name of Epiphanius of Salamis. In the Pauline epistles according to von Soden these three attest the text of the bilinguals and their related minuscule groups. Outside the Pauline epistles, it is to one such minuscule group that the renowned 1739 belongs, namely the group called I^{b2} by von Soden. The text of this group is not yet established and hence its affinities and worth are not yet known. It is customary to associate the explicit philological activity, upon which the text and apparatus of 1739 rest, with Caesarea. This is not a certain fact but is inferred from the reference in a marginal note on Jas. 2: 13 to a manuscript written by Eusebius in his own hand. Such a manuscript, together with the works of Origen with which the Pauline epistles might be compared, would most likely be found in the great library at Caesarea. If this conclusion were secure, it would emphasise that the usage of Fathers of Caesarean origin or education was not based upon tradition blindly followed, but had as its background work which compares well with the best methods of post-Renaissance learning, and that even if one text-type was mainly followed by them, others were known in circles of learning.

Attempts have been made to associate the great codices Sinaiticus and Vaticanus with Caesarea as their place of origin, but on rather slender data. In the first place, it would seem plausible after the palaeographical work of Milne and Skeat[1] that the same scribe has worked upon both manuscripts, scribe A of the Vaticanus being probably identical with scribe D of the Sinaiticus. Hence any datum bearing upon the origin of the one may well be valid for the other. The Sinaiticus has at Matt. 13: 54 for *Patrida* (homeland) the curious variant *Antipatrida* (an unknown word), which may spring from Antipatris, a place-name of the Caesarean region: similarly it has *Kaisareias* for *Samareias* at Acts 8: 40. Again, some of the corrections in the Sinaiticus, denominated C by the editors, were executed in the sixth century, and one of the correctors in the Old Testament laid under contribution a manuscript written by the martyr Pamphilus in prison. He was the teacher of Eusebius and an outstanding figure of Caesarean Christian learning. In the sixth century then the manuscript may have been at Caesarea, where such a treasured relic would be preserved with care. These points have some force, but a further which is sometimes urged

[1] H. J. M. Milne and T. C. Skeat, *Scribes and Correctors of the Codex Sinaiticus* (London, 1938).

is more dubious. Eusebius states that he produced for Constantine fifty copies of the scriptures, written in 'three, columns and four columns' and it has been proposed that the two manuscripts are part of this edition, being written respectively in four and three columns. But this does not follow, since this was not the only 'de luxe' edition commissioned by a rich patron. On the other side are two weighty points which argue for the Alexandrian origin of the Vaticanus at least (and the Sinaiticus probably comes from the same scriptorium): first, that the order of books is identical with that found in Athanasius' statements about the Canon of scripture, and secondly, that a striking variant in Heb. 1: 3 is known elsewhere only in a Coptic source.

Antioch produced a well-known school of exegesis, which in its emphasis upon the literal and historical meaning of scripture contrasted with the Alexandrian propensity to allegorisation.[1] Interest in the text is ascribed by tradition only to Lucian, an Antiochene teacher contemporary with Origen but one whose theological position contrasts in many respects with the Antiochene school as a whole. It is alleged by Jerome, however, that Syria used a text derived from the critical activity of Lucian, and while most of his references to this are in contexts where the Old Testament is in view, the presence of one such reference in the preface to the gospels suggests strongly that Jerome knew, or thought he knew, of work by Lucian upon the gospels and the rest of the New Testament. Lucian's work on the Old Testament is well known. Its characteristics were as follows: (a) supplementation of the Septuagint from the Hebrew, where the two differed; (b) double renderings of the Hebrew and conflate readings based on a different underlying Hebrew or a variant rendering; (c) explanatory additions; (d) substitution of synonyms, often Atticising. Those who believe that his work also produced the Byzantine text-type stress that analogous characteristics are to be found in that text. Certainly the text-type began to appear after his time, but it is a mistake to assert that it was uniformly dominant from the fourth century onwards. There are, however, many sub-varieties of the Byzantine as of other text-types; all text-types might well be described, as the 'Caesarean' has been,[2]

---

[1] See v, 15.

[2] J. E. McA. Baikie, as quoted in B. M. Metzger, 'The Caesarean Text of the Gospels', ch. 2 of *Chapters in the History of New Testament Textual Criticism* (Leiden, 1963).

as a process rather than a text. Within the variety can we perhaps determine that one definable text was produced by the work of Lucian? Streeter and Mrs Lake arrived independently at the guess that family Π (whose *stemma* Mrs Lake established) represents his work.[1] If this is so for the gospels we still do not know what tradition represents his work in other parts of the New Testament. Another early source of attestation of the Byzantine text-type is the Freer codex. It presents the remarkable phenomenon that its textual affiliation differs in different gospels or even parts of gospels. Mark is akin to the text of the Old Latin Codex Palatinus in its first five chapters, but in the rest of the Gospel to 'pre-recensional Caesarean'. Luke is partly Byzantine and partly Alexandrian in text, Matthew Byzantine, akin to von Soden's K^1, John is Alexandrian. According to its first editor, H. A. Sanders, there are throughout many traces of an underlying text closer to the type of the oldest versions, and later corrected to these norms. No thorough investigation of the text of this manuscript has been made since it was first discovered and published. The parts alleged to be Byzantine certainly differ in a number of significant respects from family Π. A fresh review might well cast new light on the origin of the Byzantine text-type.

Of Greek writers in this period other than Lucian, the Antiochenes Diodore, Theodore, Theodoret and (for some parts of the New Testament) Chrysostom use a text of Byzantine type—further definition of this would be welcome. Chrysostom both in the gospels and in the Pauline epistles frequently varies from the apparently normative text found in medieval manuscripts.[2] This fact warns us of the considerable amount of latent variation to be found even at a later period than this: for instance Andreas of Crete (seventh century) uses a text of John akin to D (had he found it in Crete or brought it from Jerusalem?), while the lectionary texts in some gospels and the citations of Photius (ninth century) have affinities with the 'pre-recensional Caesarean'. It is perhaps significant that the Cappadocians, of whom at least Basil was educated at Caesarea, have by contrast with the Antiochenes named above a text akin to the famous group of 'purple codices' (the

[1] B. H. Streeter, *The Four Gospels* (London, 1924), p. 579; Silva Lake, *Family Π and the Codex Alexandrinus* (Studies and Documents, v, London, 1936), p. 67.

[2] See p. 320 n. 2 and Seth K. Gifford, *Pauli epistolas qua forma legerit Joannes Chrysostomus* (Dissertationes philologicae Halenses, XVI, 1902).

uncials Rossanensis, Purpureus, Beratinus and Sinopensis) which have affinities with the Caesarean group of witnesses.

THE EUTHALIAN MATERIAL

At about the same time as Eusebius and Lucian were perhaps active in their respective spheres, philological activity of a slightly different kind was taking place, which sought not to change the actual text of the scriptures, but to provide an apparatus of explanatory summaries, references and text-divisions to aid the task of lectors in church and exegetes in the school. This material is known as the Euthalian material, and as it appears in most manuscripts is the end-product of a considerable process of evolution, which has not yet been adequately traced. It treats of Acts and the epistles, for which it provides a body of introductory summaries, a system of chapter divisions and subdivisions, and indications of Old Testament citations in the text. (There are both summaries and divisions of the gospels known from manuscript sources, but these are not linked with the Euthalian material, and even less is known of their origin.) In the original form of this apparatus the text was divided into sense-lines, in the terminology of ancient rhetoric, *cola* and *commata*. Euthalius, from whom it takes its name, is a shadowy figure, who appears to have been bishop of Sulki in Sardinia in the seventh century. If the addition of the name is not in some way erroneous, nor the identification with this bishop false, his part in the work cannot have been other than that of bringing to a conclusion and final edition the product of four centuries of effort. The minuscules 88 and 915 preserve a prologue to the material which in a personal statement names one Evagrius as the author of the work. The uncial H (which preserves the division into sense-lines and some material from the prologue) has only the initial EU of this name still extant. Chronological data about the date of the work are found in the *Martyrium Pauli*, which figures in many exemplars as part of the Euthalian material: two dates are given, at the end of the fourth and in the middle of the fifth century. However, since the *Martyrium Pauli* is absent from some important sources, we cannot take these dates as relating to the beginning of the gathering of the material, but simply to important stages in its evolution. Evagrius then will be a person of an earlier time, and two candidates amongst third- and fourth-century Christian scholars have been put forward—Evagrius of Pontus and Evagrius of Antioch. The uncial H and some early forms of the Euthalian material have a section intimating that the (*sc.* original) exemplar had been collated with a manuscript written by the hand of Pamphilus. This has led to the proposal of Evagrius Ponticus as the original author, a pupil of Origen and friend of Eusebius. ℵ and B (which as we have seen may have Caesarean connections) have a chapter division of Acts which may be related to the Euthalian material. This material has been handed down in Armenian, Georgian and Syriac versions, and Armenia in particular had close links with Caesarea as a centre of learning. But on the other hand there is evidence perhaps of a more certain kind for the other Evagrius, a friend of Jerome. An item of Euthalian material not found in all exemplars is an additional prologue, which refers to the author's composition of a commentary upon Luke, and speaks of Eusebius. There are some traces of such a commentary from Evagrius' hand, not unlike this prologue in style, and we know that Eusebius of Vercelli was a friend of his. This would bring the origin of this material into the Antiochene rather than the Caesarean orbit. There is external support for this identification in the discovery that the Gothic version of the epistles—of which all *manuscripts* date from before the seventh century—possesses a system of chapter division which is clearly the Euthalian. Since this version has very close links with the early Byzantine text-type, and this in turn with Antioch, we may suppose that the system of divisions has been taken over from a Greek exemplar at the time of translation. On the other hand, there is no trace of prologues or lists of Old Testament citations in the Gothic. Some scholars—despairing of the possibility of identification—have cut the Gordian knot by suggesting that the originator of the material was an unknown Christian grammarian. It should be emphasised that, whatever the resolution of this enigma, the presence of the Euthalian material in a manuscript does not indicate anything about the nature of its text: of the manuscripts which contain it some have a text of Byzantine type and others exhibit different types of text. To speak of a Euthalian recension is to go well beyond the evidence.[1]

---

[1] An up-to-date summary and discussion of the whole Euthalian question is still a prime requirement for students of these topics. The basic problems are still best grasped from the work of J. Armitage Robinson, *Euthaliana* (Texts and Studies, III, 3, Cambridge, 1895).

THE EASTERN CHURCHES

Meanwhile, the Eastern churches continued both to develop in their own ways, and also to endeavour to bring themselves more and more into line with Greek Christianity. The Christian faith had been planted in Syriac-speaking territory at an early date, and we have already discussed the importance of the *Diatessaron* in revealing, and in some cases perhaps in influencing, the text in the early centuries. Various dates have been postulated for the production of a translation of the fourfold gospel, called by the Syrians the 'separated gospels', *Evangelion da-Mepharreshe*. These lie before us in two manuscripts only, but there is much material in the scriptural quotations of ecclesiastical authors which has only of late been laid under contribution. This shows that the version was still revered as late as the twelfth century. It was already known to Ephraem in the fourth century, who calls it, by contrast with the *Diatessaron*, the 'Greek'. Burkitt wished to place its origins in the early third century, Lagrange much later.[1] This aspect of the problem seems insoluble. The designation used by Ephraem underlines the motive that produced the version, and which continued to be a prime factor in the history of scriptural translation and revision in the Eastern churches, namely the tendency and desire to bring their life and teaching more into conformity with current Greek orthodoxy. Evidently the Syrian church, at some time probably in the third century, was exercised by its lack of separated gospels and sought to remedy this by a version which retained much of the honoured wording of the *Diatessaron* but possessed a fourfold form. For this pattern Greek models would be needed: so far as we may judge these were found in manuscripts of the 'pre-Caesarean' type of text. Both W and Family 13 have contacts with the Syriac, which is in part at least to be explained by the recourse of Syrian churchmen to Greek centres of learning in search of guidance in biblical matters (another factor in the case of Family 13, as we have intimated, is the flight of Syrian Christians to the West at a later period). The *Diatessaron* continued to be used alongside the fourfold gospel until the fifth century. Then we find a firm ban upon it in the Syriac churches for which Rabbula was responsible: in the same period a similar wave of strong antagonism is seen in the

[1] See F. C. Burkitt, *Evangelion da-Mepharreshe* (Cambridge, 1904), II, pp. 212; M.-J. Lagrange, *op. cit.* pp. 205, 208.

action of Theodoret in Greek-speaking areas. Parallel to the separated gospels there was a version of Acts, strongly akin to the text of D and its allies, which we know from the work of Ephraem: there was also an early version of the Pauline epistles for which the evidence has not yet been fully collected or analysed. The standard version of the Syriac churches was and is the Peshiṭta, which was the text of Syriac-speaking Christians of all theological opinions and churchmanship, Chalcedonian, Nestorian and Monophysite, even after Chalcedon. It is essentially an Old Syriac text revised by a Greek Antiochian text. It has been customary since the work of Burkitt to ascribe to Rabbula the production of this version, since his biography accredits him with translation. More recently this view has been challenged by Vööbus (there had been other doubts previously expressed but unheeded), and he has raised a number of points of value for the discussion.[1] In the first place he claims that it can be shown that the Peshiṭta was in existence before the time of Rabbula, since BM MS. Add. 12150 (dated 411, a year before Rabbula became bishop) contains a Syriac version of the Clementine Recognitions in which the quotations from the New Testament have not been translated but taken from the current Syriac version, which proves to be the Peshiṭta. Secondly (though this point has been challenged), Rabbula himself in his translation of Cyril of Alexandria uses a form of the New Testament for his quotations which has Old Syriac affinities. Thirdly, the canon of the Peshiṭta is somewhat primitive; it lacks 2 Peter, 2 and 3 John, Jude and Revelation (that is, most of the *antilegomena* of Eusebius' discussion), and this may well reflect an earlier period than the fifth century. Fourthly, it would be truly remarkable if both Jacobite and Nestorian alike used with reverence a translation by a ruthless zealot of one party, and a turncoat at that.

The later versions of the Syrian Monophysites, known as the Philoxenian and the Harklean, take us well outside the limits of this discussion by the date of their respective appearances. According to Syriac tradition Mar Xenaia or Philoxenus, bishop of Mabbug, commissioned Polycarp to revise the New Testament in the sixth century. In the seventh century Thomas, bishop of Harkel, exiled to Egypt for his faith, worked in the monastery of the Enaton near Alexandria: some recent scholars deny the identification with a Syrian bishop and see as

---

[1] *Studies in the History of the Gospel Text in Syriac* (Louvain, 1951), chs. 4 and 5.

the author of this last of Syriac versions a humbler Thomas, deacon of Athanasius II.[1] It is still a matter of debate whether Thomas produced an entirely new version, or whether he only obelised and annotated the text of Philoxenus. For the gospels, Acts and the epistles of Paul, only one version later than the Peshitta is extant, and in most of its manuscripts is provided with the marginal notes and diacritical points which the prologue of Thomas claims as his work. In the Catholic epistles and Revelation, however, we possess two versions other than the Peshitta. Whatever the precise solution to the problem, both versions, though late, preserve material relevant to the study of earlier periods. The marginalia to Acts in the Harklean version cite ancient manuscript evidence from documents in the Enaton which materially increases our knowledge of the Bezan text of Acts. The version of Jude, thought to be Philoxenian, has affinities with recently discovered Greek texts, and the text of Revelation in both later versions assists the restitution of the history of the text of that book.

Armenia claims the honour of being the first kingdom to accept Christianity as its established religion: this came about with the conversion of Tiridates in the last decade of the third century or the earliest part of the fourth. It was an official conversion and it is uncertain how far the Armenian masses were at first affected. Certainly it was not until an alphabet was formed for the transcription of the language a hundred years later that effective translation of the scriptures could take place. The base of this translation was essentially Syriac, although its exact nature in the gospels—*Diatessaron* or *Evangelion da-Mepharreshe*—is still debated.[2] A major problem for the investigator of this question is that he must work largely from quotations, since the manuscripts of the Armenian canon derive without exception from a revision of the scriptures produced some time about the sixth century. This was indubitably revised to a Greek norm which seems to have had Caesarean affinities, and to have belonged within that wide affiliation to the form known to Eusebius and Origen. The Armenian bore marks of its Syriac parentage even after this, notably in the retention of the apocryphal Third Epistle to the Corinthians, which continued to be used

[1] R. Devreesse, *Introduction à l'étude des MSS. grecs* (Paris, 1954), p. 160 n. 1; and G. D. Kilpatrick, ʽΗ ΚΑΙΝΗ ΔΙΑΘΗΚΗ (British and Foreign Bible Society, 2nd ed. London, 1958), p. xvi.

[2] S. Lyonnet, *Les origines de la version arménienne et le Diatessaron* (Rome, 1950); A. Vööbus, *Early Versions of the New Testament* (Stockholm, 1954), p. 152.

liturgically until quite late. Revelation was not given canonical status in the Armenian church until the twelfth century, but was translated as early as the fifth century, and is preserved in a number of re-censions. Its earliest form is of interest to the student of the textual problems of the book as it bears a close relation to the Latin version known to the early commentators Ticonius and Primasius.

Georgia was converted during the fourth century, tradition has it by the agency of an Armenian slave woman, and whether these details are in any measure true or not, the tradition probably indicates the source of the Georgians' knowledge of Christianity and the Christian scriptures. These did not begin to be translated into Georgian until Mesrop, provider of an Armenian alphabet, also supplied the Georgians with an adequate means of transcription for their speech. Our earliest documents do not reach back further than the eighth century, but it is evident from linguistic data in many of them that we have in these sources traces of very early strata of the version's textual history. There is also available much citational material, but only a little has been done up to the present to elucidate its significance. An early hagio-graphical document, the Martyrdom of Eustathius of Mzkheta, of which a translation is to be found in D. M. Lang, *Lives and Legends of the Georgian Saints* (London and New York, 1956), ch. 6, suggests that a harmony or some sort of digest was the form in which the gospel story was known in the earliest days, but it would not appear that this was a direct form of the *Diatessaron*. Some five or six manuscripts and various fragments present us with the earliest form of the separated gospels in Georgian. These have attracted much attention since the so-called Caesarean text was first postulated, for it is clear that (in spite of further subdivision amongst themselves) their text is a witness to this text-type, and particularly to the recensional form represented in Θ and the minuscules 700 and 565, and in the quotations of Origen and Eusebius. But as with the Old Syriac and the Old Armenian, there is latent in the Georgian an older stratum akin to the Tatianic tradition due to Syriac and Armenian influences. Hence the Georgian has been used to trace the history of the Old Armenian and is also a source of *Diatessaron* readings.[1] In the tenth century and later the New Testament in Georgian was revised and supplemented largely through

[1] See A. Vööbus, *Zur Geschichte des altgeorgischen Evangelientextes* (Stockholm, 1953).

the labours of Georgian monks on the Bithynian Olympus and on Mount Athos, who strove to bring the scriptures into closer conformity with the Greek text of the day. It is in this dress that the Georgian New Testament is best known. The Georgian version of Revelation dates from this time, a form of the text and commentary of Andreas of Caesarea.[1]

A third Caucasian people, the Albanians, also received an alphabet from Mesrop, to supply scripture for their Christian church.[2] This church did not survive beyond the conquests of Islam, and all but few traces of the script have been lost, and there are no remains of the version known. The language has its probable modern descendant in Udish, a language spoken by the inhabitants of two towns in Azerbaijan. The Armenian scholar Akinian,[3] however, wished to interpret the reference to this people in Koriun's life of Mesrop in another sense, and to give to the saint the honour of supplying an alphabet to a Christian people whose monuments have not disappeared, and whose language is not at all unknown, namely the Goths.

THE GOTHS AND THE BIBLE

The Goths living in the Balkans came into contact with the Roman Empire at an early period, and there must have been Christians amongst them in the third century, since a bishop represented them at Nicaea. In the fourth century there were some links with the church in Cappadocia, and Wulfila was ordained bishop by Eusebius of Nicomedia. Through the influence of this contact and other factors, the Goths at length embraced the Arian interpretation of Christianity, which may have appealed to unsophisticated minds. Wulfila has traditionally the rôle, unchallenged by later scholars, of translating the scriptures into the language of his own people. The basic text-type of this version was that early Byzantine text which we have seen is to be putatively linked with Antioch and with Lucian, of which it is amongst the earliest monuments. But in spite of a marked literalness in rendering, so severe indeed at times that scholars have doubted whether certain

---

[1] Ed. I. Imnaishvili, *Ioanes Gamochadeba da misi t'argmaneba* (Dzveli K'art'uli Enis Kat'edris Shromebi VII, Tbilisi, 1961).

[2] G. Dumézil, 'Une chrétienté disparue: les Albaniens du Caucase', *Journal Asiatique*, CCXXXII (Série 13, T. XI) (1940–1), 125–32.

[3] See V. Inglisian, 'Das wissenschaftliche Leben der Armenier in der Gegenwart', *Oriens Christianus*, IVᵉ Série, III (1955), 110–11.

passages were intelligible to the hearers, it is not a simple task to use the Gothic for the reconstruction of the earliest form of the Byzantine text for, apart from the appearance of otherwise unattested readings, not unlike the readings sometimes found in John Chrysostom, there are additional complicating factors due to the migrations of the Gothic peoples. In their wanderings westward they were brought to Spain, Africa, Italy and Gaul, and for much of their time, before the Gothic kingdoms were at length destroyed in the sixth century, they were in closer contact with Latin than with Greek Christianity. All the manuscripts we have of the version are products of the Western Gothic kingdoms, and it is clear that the Old Latin version, which they presumably found in Africa, has influenced the text of their version, and left its mark externally in the Western order of the gospels, Matthew, John, Luke, Mark which is found in the one complete copy, the Codex Argenteus, preserved in Stockholm. It has even been shown that Gothic influence is to be discerned in one Old Latin manuscript, the Codex Brixianus; the attempt to show a like influence in the renowned Codex Palatinus has not met with much acceptance, however, and must be regarded as unproven.[1]

OTHER VERSIONS: ORIGIN AND SIGNIFICANCE

As we have intimated, other versions were made from those which have been mentioned.[2] Some of these were translated within the bounds of the period covered by this discussion, but insufficient critical work has been done upon them to enable us to discuss with any confidence the nature of their text and the course of their development. Such is the Ethiopic version, potentially of great interest textually, but without a critical edition, and very infrequently consulted. Syriac, Coptic and Arabic influences, as well as affinity with original Greek sources, have been recognised in its various parts at different times. The fortunes and affiliations of the Church in Ethiopia are doubtless reflected in this complexity. The Nubian version is only found in a

[1] G. W. S. Fridrichsen, *The Gothic Version of the Gospels* (Oxford, 1926); cf. the reviews of F. C. Burkitt (*JTS*, XXVIII, 1927, 90–7) and H. J. Vogels (*Theologische Revue*, XXVII, 1928, 17–18).

[2] See A. Vööbus, *op. cit.* (see p. 366 n. 2), and B. M. Metzger, 'The Evidence of the Versions for the Text of the New Testament' in *New Testament MS. Studies* (see p. 327 n. 1).

relatively few fragments, and these have not been closely analysed. The Christianity of Persia was rich and vigorous in the days before Islam, and gave birth to a number of martyrs and sages: the biblical remains in middle Persian, and in the related Sogdian of central Asia, have been very little studied, apart from the important versions of the *Diatessaron* recently edited. Some versions were made much later than the period which we are here reviewing. The Slavonic version in the East was made from the Greek after the tenth century. In the West there were various vernacular renderings, in Old English, Bohemian, Provençal and other tongues. None of these has been as deeply and thoroughly investigated as it might have been, and late and secondary though they are, there is textual information latent within them all. It is clear that in all of them, and particularly in the oriental versions, are reflected the varying circumstances of the Church and its fluctuating vigour under differing conditions of Christian supremacy and weakness. Many of them bear traces of revision, sometimes repeated, since all versions both in the East and in the West were affected by a desire, never entirely absent, to reach back to the Greek Church and the Greek scriptures regarded as normative. From this resulted glosses, corrections, even slavish imitations of Greek idiom. These were not always perhaps as instructive as they were intended to be, except for the very learned, but for the student of their history and of the history of the churches for which they were produced, this pedantry and its jargon can reveal details of incalculable value.

THE LATIN VERSIONS

The Latin, because of historical circumstances which it is unnecessary to rehearse, has been the most thoroughly studied of the versions. The manuscript material lies close to hand and there is great wealth of quotations in well-edited texts. Much of the pioneer work was done in the earliest days of philology, while the analysis awaited British scholars of the late nineteenth and early twentieth centuries for its execution. British scholarship has maintained its interest in the Latin versions, and has been responsible for a standard edition of the Vulgate,[1] but the investigation of the Old Latin, in which earlier British scholarship

---

[1] *Novum Testamentum Latine recensuerunt I. Wordsworth, H. I. White et alii* (Oxford, 1889–1954).

made great progress, has of late become the focus of research for German scholars in the Vetus Latina Institut of Beuron, where a rich collection of data made over many years is now in process of systemat-isation and analysis. The variety of the Old Latin has long been the object of comment. Jerome's observation that there were almost as many versions as manuscripts is often quoted, with Augustine's con-jecture that in the earliest days anyone with a smattering of Greek and a fancy for his own literary abilities turned his hand to translation. The editors of *Vetus Latina* have been criticised because of the complexity of their presentation when they sometimes give as many as five distinct types of text as the base for their apparatus criticus, but it may be argued that this perplexing variety within a scholarly presentation is a true reflection of the actual state of affairs, undisguised by any false over-simplification. The studies of the team of scholars working at Beuron have shown the truth of an older conclusion that the Old Latin is basically one version, successively revised both in language and style, and by correction from its original textual form to an agreement more and more with the norm of the Greek Alexandrian text-type. But not only was there much diversity of pace within this process of revision, so that one area might use an older form than another near by or far away, but also, and in part because of this, there was much overlapping and inbreeding, and this we find not only in manuscripts (where there is less cause for surprise since these are so often later than the heyday of their text), but also in quotations: hence we may conclude that it was a process which began very early in the history of the version. We have intimated above that Tertullian is the first writer to quote in Latin, and that his quotations, though often free and apparently translated directly from the Greek, show the marks of some reliance upon an existent version. Cyprian provides the oldest evidence which we possess of affinity with known manuscripts. In the gospels the affinities of his quotations lie with the codices Bobbiensis and Palatinus (*k* and *e*). In Acts, the Fleury palimpsest (*h*) preserves the form of Latin text known from Cyprian. In the Paulines however (Ephesians and Philippians having been studied at Beuron) we know of no manu-script preserving a form equivalent to his, and similarly in the Catholic epistles and Revelation. In both the gospels and the Paulines older and recent scholarship concurs in the conclusion that although Cyprian is the earliest evidence we possess, behind his text there stands already, as close study of it reveals, a history of development and revision, and perhaps even of contamination.

It was customary among the earlier investigators of the Latin texts to speak of a general twofold distinction between an African Latin and a European Latin, based primarily on differences in rendering rather than on variants. Much was made, and rightly, of the additional advantage possessed by the student of the versions, by contrast with the student of the Greek, in the second criterion of 'rendering' (i.e. translation of one Greek word by different Latin words) which enabled him to discern lines of descent otherwise hidden by identity of readings. From time to time there were attempts, based in part on this same criterion, to identify a third type, the so-called Itala (interpreting a laconic reference of Augustine,[1] which still remains an enigma). In the New Testament books they have studied, the Beuron investigators have distinguished a number of texts other than those found in the earlier African Christian writers, but they have eschewed any temptation to identify these with such enigmatic entities as the Itala, or even to express a correspondence and continuity between the text-types attested by the same author in different parts of the New Testament. Thus, in the Paulines they see as distinct the *D* text, found in the Latin column of the bilinguals Claromontanus, Boernerianus and Augiensis, and in the quotations of Lucifer of Cagliari (a text descended from the original Latin version by a line different from that which has produced the text attested by Cyprian), the *I* text known from Victorinus (late third century) to Cassiodorus (early sixth century), which differs from *D* in vocabulary but not in text, and the *V* text, that of the Vulgate, which was used by Pelagius and thus must have been in existence by the late fourth century at the latest. In the Catholic epistles they distinguish the text of Cyprian's quotations (*K*) from the later *C* text with which it is related: this is a late African text known in various African writers, but with little manuscript attestation. Sometimes this latter is known only in Augustine, and in these cases its siglum is *A*. This type of careful precision is one cause of their critics' irritation. *S* is a translation known mainly from the collection of texts called the *Speculum*, falsely attributed to Augustine. *T* is a very widely distributed text, known from some of the best Old Latin manuscripts of the

---

[1] *De doctrina christiana*, II, 22: 'In ipsis autem interpretationibus Itala ceteris praeferatur nam est verborum tenacior cum perspicuitate sententiae.'

Catholic epistles, namely the Freising fragments (*r*) and the Fleury palimpsest (*h*): it is especially noteworthy for the presence of the *Comma Johanneum* (1 John 5: 7) and other expansions of dogmatic content.[1] *V*, which in the Pauline epistles is a revision of a mixed *D–I* text, is in this part of the New Testament a text based on *S–T*.

In the case of Revelation, we still depend upon the older painstaking and detailed work of Vogels,[2] who concluded that the history of this book in Latin territory involved at least three distinct translations directly from the Greek. These are found respectively in the commentary of Primasius (sixth century, a text which is known less completely from earlier times in the quotations of Cyprian and the fragmentary attestation of the Freising fragments), in the commentary of Ticonius (a Donatist writer in the fourth century, whose work is partly lost in its original form but preserved in the eighth-century commentary of the Spanish Beatus of Libana and in other works), and in the Codex Gigas (*g*). The former two are both texts of African provenance, while the latter is known from many writers of European habitat, as well as in the manuscript source. The Vulgate is a revision, but some of its peculiar readings are known from as early as Tertullian, which might suggest another strand of translation. It is probable that when the work of the Vetus Latina project reaches Revelation some of these views will be modified: Dom Bonifatius Fischer, director of the work at Beuron, has indicated in various places that he considers that the use of 'rendering' to make hard and fast distinctions between different streams of textual tradition has gone too far, since an individual translator may often have varied his rendering of a word when it occurs frequently. However, as one may say with justice of research upon the Old Latin in general, even if 'this' proves not to be the case exactly as Vogels has defined it, at any rate 'something like this' is the state of affairs which more modern study will discover and define.

We have mentioned the Vulgate, but not yet Jerome:[3] this great scholar and controversialist has been traditionally credited with the retranslation, or in some cases revision, of the Latin Bible. We are not here concerned with the Old Testament, where Jerome started from the Hebrew of which he had considerable understanding, but used the

[1] See W. Thiele, 'Beobachtungen zum Comma Johanneum', *ZNW*, L (1959), 61–73.
[2] *Untersuchungen zur Geschichte der lateinischen Apokalypse-Übersetzung* (Düsseldorf, 1920).   [3] See v, 16.

Septuagint and other Greek translations as a guide in difficulty. His rendering of the gospels and of Acts represents a revision of an Old Latin base to the norm of an Alexandrian text-type. As regards the rest of the New Testament scholars have reverted to a view previously propounded at different times, namely that the version currently transmitted under Jerome's name is not his work, and it is doubted whether Jerome ever succeeded in bringing a revision of the whole of the New Testament to a satisfactory conclusion. The reasons for refusing to ascribe the translation of the Paulines and the Catholic epistles to Jerome are analogous to the reasons advanced against the authorship of the Peshiṭta by Rabbula: in the first place stylistic criteria, upon which the scholars of the Vetus Latina project have laid much weight; secondly, Pelagius, the contemporary and adversary of Jerome, attests the text now known from Vulgate manuscripts, so that the version must have existed before the time of Jerome; and in the third place Jerome himself by no means always quotes from the version traditionally attributed to him in these books.

The version stemming from, or attributed to, Jerome had its own complex development and history in the Middle Ages, which lie outside the limits of this discussion, but as in the case of the Greek manuscripts of the Byzantine period the monuments of the history of the Vulgate are not without value for our knowledge of the form of the text in its Old Latin dress, for a major factor of corruption has been the infiltrations of Old Latin readings into Jerome's text. In the centres of the old culture, such as Spain and Italy, and in the new areas of missionary expansion, such as Ireland, and later England and Germany, antiquarian and philological interests fostered the preservation and comparison of old texts, though the attempts at editing were not always successful. Similarly, the scholars of the *haut moyen age* in the West, while aware of the corruption of the current manuscripts, were not always able to purify them adequately by our standards. Their efforts and their failures have left a residuum of pre-Hieronymian readings from which we, with our distinct interests, can often benefit.

CONCLUSIONS

Thus a study of the history of the text of the New Testament in the earliest and formative period shows a number of different factors at work. In the first place, the New Testament documents have been open to the normal hazards of manuscript transmission. This is evident in some lines of descent: the text read by Tertullian at Heb. 6: 5 rested upon the omission of a line in his exemplar. It is still a matter of debate whether any places have been so affected in all lines of transmission: a plausible case for corruption might be made in John 3: 25, 1 Cor. 6: 5, Col. 2: 18, and Jas. 1: 17, to mention only some striking instances. Conjectural emendation, on which the classical scholar has not infrequently to fall back, has often been deemed unnecessary for the textual critic of the New Testament, but recently a number of scholars have conceded its propriety. Another debated factor is the influence of doctrine upon the text. It is understandable that many scholars, conscious of the sensibilities of fellow-churchmen, and often sharing those sensibilities themselves (whether from a consciously conservative standpoint or not), should have denied that any variant had arisen from alteration in the interest of some doctrinal issue. However, we have seen that there are instances where we run in the face of the evidence if we deny the presence of this factor in the development of the text. Many variants which can be traced to the second century bear the mark of the development of doctrine. Some of the earliest of these (e.g. the reading of the Sinaitic Syriac at Matt. 1: 16) belong rather to the history of the Canon or the prehistory of the book concerned than to textual criticism strictly conceived: that is, they may be recrudescences of strands of tradition not originally used in the composition of such a writing. But in other instances we see clear traces of the suppression of an original reading which appeared to support heterodoxy: we may mention Heb. 2: 9 where the reading χωρὶς θεοῦ (without God) has yielded to the innocuous χάριτι θεοῦ (by the grace of God) in the aftermath of the Nestorian and perhaps the Origenian controversies of later centuries. More subtle doctrinal influence has recently been discerned in the text-type of Acts known in D and its allies, many of its distinctive variants being held to show an anti-Judaic tendency. Many variants of a different kind have sprung from the closely related factor of interpretation: simplifications such as that at Mark 1: 41 ὀργισθείς (angry) to σπλαγχνισθείς (moved with pity), and expansions such as that of John 4: 9 οὐ γὰρ συγχρῶνται Ἰουδαῖοι Σαμαρίταις (Jews do not use the same vessels as Samaritans) —omitted in some ancient sources—stem from the desire to make the scripture simple and easily understood by the faithful. Lastly, we perceive that change has come about as a result of the history of the Greek language, both conscious changes from locutions deemed barbaric to others considered cultured, and unconscious changes such as arose through the disappearance of the dative case or the attenuation of the perfect.

In all the sources, manuscripts, ancient translations and the quotations in the Fathers is found an overwhelming richness of evidence for all these types of change. The course of change, the geographical distribution of certain main text-types, and the centres with which they may appear to be connected may all be plotted in general outline, and an over-all conception may be gained of the way in which the text grew and changed or, in some instances, was transmitted without significant change. In the later Middle Ages we can sometimes trace specific families of text in particular areas. But there is no royal road to establish the history in all its details: even where family texts may be discerned (and it may be that there are more than those hitherto identified), we find contamination coming from the text-type dominant in the medieval period. At an earlier period, many of the factors of change would imply recensional activity, but, as we have seen, it is very difficult to identify the men or institutions connected with this. Since this is so, it proves impossible to establish a purely stemmatological or genealogical method for tracing the history of the text or for establishing its most primitive form. Hence have arisen the two emphases which have come to the forefront in the last decade of textual studies of the New Testament. In establishing the text we need to resort to an informed and reasoned eclectic approach, since no one strand of tradition has preserved the autograph or its approximation. Secondly, we can at present gain the best insight into the textual data of the New Testament available to us if we regard it as the deposit of, and as a witness to, an historical process. In this field the interrelation of Church and scripture is very marked: we never encounter the New Testament except in the context of the life of the Church, its worship, institutions and doctrine, at specific points of time. We see in it, from the angle of textual criticism, not only the original record of events, but the ways in which the events were seen throughout the centuries. In this way we are again reminded of the point which has so often been made of late in New Testament study, both from an historical and from a theological standpoint, that we view the events of what is termed salvation history only through those who claim to know their own participation in it. This would be so even if we had the autographs; it is even more so when the text itself is no autograph but a moving stream. The task of textual criticism is the historical task of assisting in the discernment of first-century history through first-century documents, but it can only be prosecuted satisfactorily when the critic is vividly and constantly aware that the documents are seen through a series of stages of comprehension, stretching throughout the Middle Ages, and from Britain to Central Asia, from the North Sea to Ethiopia.

12. THE INTERPRETATION OF THE OLD TESTAMENT IN THE NEW

INTERPRETATION AMONG THE GREEKS

It is only the shortest books of the New Testament that do not contain numerous references and allusions to the Old. A very large majority of New Testament books quote the Old Testament explicitly, and often in such a way as to make it clear that their authors regarded the Old Testament as an authoritative body of literature which claimed the attention and obedience of Christians. It was used as the basis of theological argument and of ethical instruction. In their reliance upon this sacred literature the Christian writers followed directly the example of their Jewish contemporaries, who made similar use of the same Old Testament, and, somewhat less directly, that of many others in the ancient world who also looked for guidance and inspiration to ancient books. To understand the use of the Old Testament in the New it is necessary first to consider the use and interpretation of sacred texts in the ancient world generally; also, and more particularly, the Jewish use of the Old Testament.

There are few races that have not been familiar with some form of inspiration; that is, the apparent supersession of the powers of the human intellect by an extraneous force, resulting in extraordinary action or speech. Plato is perhaps not the most representative of Greeks, but the words he puts into the mouth of Socrates in his discussion with Ion the rhapsode state the matter fairly enough:

All the good epic poets pronounce all these beautiful poems not by art (ἐκ τέχνης), but being inspired (ἔνθεοι) and possessed, and it is the same with the lyric poets... For the poet is a light and winged and holy creature, and he can do nothing till he is inspired and out of his wits, and the mind is no longer in him. Until he has attained to this no man is capable of action and of giving oracles... Each man is able to do his work well only by divine destiny... They do not speak by art but by divine power (*Ion*, 533 E; 534 B, C).

Socrates goes on to argue that interpretation too is a matter of inspiration, though secondary and derivative.

Probably in fifth-century Athens poetry and drama suggested primarily the spoken word, and in a world that did not know printing this continued to be to some extent true, but as early as the New Testament period we find the literary study of written texts, and thus the crystallising of inspiration in lasting form. This is seen for example in the various collections of oracles, especially the Sibyllines, and the fact that Jews and Christians found it worth while to issue spurious Sibylline books in their own interests is good evidence for the importance attached to such literature.

The oracles delivered by the Sibyls, and notoriously by the Pythian priestess of Apollo at Delphi, were couched in obscure language—the result of natural caution on the part of those who issued them. Interpretation led into many pitfalls. Intentional obscurity, and the work of interpretation that it demanded, probably contributed to the view that the early poets too must be obscure and in need of elaborate exegesis. To this belief the poets themselves (granted belief in their inspiration) substantially contributed; for it could not be denied that, read on the surface, they often appeared to be dealing in a straightforward way with matters that were commonplace, earthly, human, and frequently immoral. Plato himself brought this charge against Homer. The third book of the *Republic* opens with a list of the grounds on which Homer and other poets must be banned from the ideal state. They inculcate the fear of death by grim descriptions of the underworld; they permit the gods to set the bad example of lying, and the heroes to show cowardice; they represent the gods as indulging in laughter, drunkenness, lechery, and corruption. All this Plato (through Socrates) can say, although he has always loved and reverenced Homer (*Republic*, X, 595 B); but truth is to be honoured more than any man (595 C), and for this reason the criticism must be made.

Thus the poets (or at least some of them, and even, with regret, Homer) must be banned; and yet 'poetic inspiration is divine and in its song, with the aid of the Graces and the Muses, it often attains to truth' (*Laws*, III, 682A). Plato can hardly be said to resolve this antinomy. It was resolved later by the allegorical method of interpretation.[1] In the first century B.C. or A.D. Heraclitus (fragment 1) made the point firmly: Homer was nothing but wicked, unless he allegorised.

The allegorical method was developed particularly by the Stoics. As P. Decharme says,[2] 'Ils enrôlèrent Homère et Hésiode dans leurs rangs'; this they did by allegorising their writings. The sacred books exist in their present form because the authors wished to stimulate thought. 'Why have they told in their myths of adulteries and thefts and the binding of fathers and other strange things? Or is this also worthy to be marvelled at, that the soul should, through the seeming strangeness, consider the words to be veils and believe the truth to be beyond speech?' (Sallustius, 3). Examples of allegorical interpretation are to be found not only in the Stoics, but in writers such as Plutarch. Thus Sallustius (4) has no difficulty in dealing with the tale that Kronos swallowed his children; it may be interpreted theologically ('god is intelligible, and all intelligence is directed to itself'), or physically ('the parts of time (χρόνος) are children of the whole').

The effect of this kind of interpretation is to emphasise the authority of the work interpreted, and at the same time to rob it of any serious historical meaning. It speaks only to the man who, by nature or special divine endowment, has the gift of penetrating its secret. It cannot be said that antiquity discovered any means of regulating the allegorical method and applying it with any kind of objectivity; the result was that each interpreter succeeded in reading out of his text the ideas that he had brought with him and placed within it.

INTERPRETATION OF THE OLD TESTAMENT IN PHILO

The interpretation by Greek thinkers of poetry and ancient myth forms a useful but distant background to the use of the Old Testament by New Testament writers. To the Greek philosopher, the existence of

---

[1] Anticipated by Plato himself (*Republic*, X, 605 A), and indeed by Theagenes of Rhegium, and other pre-Socratics.

[2] *Critique des Traditions religieuses chez les Grecs* (Paris, 1904), p. 352.

earlier literature was no more than incidental; at most it provided a useful confirmation of truths of which he was already persuaded on other grounds. It was helpful, but not essential, that he should be able to call on the support of those whose antiquity was counted to them for wisdom. A far closer parallel is provided by Jewish writers, for whom the ancient scriptures were a constitutive and generative element in their religious life. Their system of thought was (or at least was believed to be) not confirmed but created by their work on documents possessed of absolute authority. Judaism understood itself as a current practical exegesis of its Bible (together with such unwritten traditions as were believed to have been given, with the written Torah, to Moses on Sinai).

It can be truly said that Jewish interpreters are distinguished from Greek by the fact that they take their stand under the authority of, and profess to be controlled by, their scriptural text; yet it is possible to begin a consideration of Jewish use of the Old Testament with a Jew, Philo,[1] whose interpretative methods bear a marked resemblance to those of Stoics, Neo-Pythagoreans, and other Greek allegorisers. To these methods we shall return shortly; it is necessary first to note Philo's devotion to the plain, literal sense of the Old Testament.

To Philo, scripture means primarily the Pentateuch,[2] and for him no praise is too high to bestow on Moses as ruler and lawgiver.

I have formed the intention of writing the life of Moses, according to some the lawgiver of the Jews, to others the interpreter of the Sacred Laws, in all respects the greatest and most perfect of men, and to make him known to those who are worthy not to remain in ignorance. For though the fame of the laws which he left behind has spread through the whole world and reached the ends of the earth, not many know the man as he truly was (*De Vita Mos.* I, 1 f.).

Such reverence for Moses is equivalent to reverence for the sacred book, and in the same work Philo goes on to say:

They know this well who consult the sacred books, which, if he had not been such a man, he would not, under God's guidance, have composed and

---

[1] A contemporary of Jesus, spanning a period roughly from 20 B.C. to A.D. 45, and resident in Alexandria.

[2] It is instructive to count the biblical references in the Index to the Loeb edition of Philo: Genesis, 22½ pages; Exodus, 15½; Leviticus, 9; Numbers, 8; Deuteronomy, 10; the rest of the Old Testament, 5.

handed on to those who are worthy to use them, as the finest of their possessions, likenesses and copies of the patterns which are enshrined within the soul (*De Vita Mos.* II, 11).

In this reverence, the original Hebrew and the Greek translation are equal, as sisters (*De Vita Mos.* II, 40).

Philo was never anything other than a loyal Jew, and as such he repudiated those of his fellow-Jews who in their enthusiasm for a more spiritual interpretation of the Law overlooked its literal demands.

There are some who, taking the literal laws as symbols of matters belonging to the mind, are overpunctilious about the latter, but pass lightly over the former. Personally I should blame these men for their negligence, for they ought to have attended to both matters, a fuller examination of the things that are not apparent, and a blameless observance of those that are (*De Migr.* 89).

But though Philo is anxious that the Sabbath law, for example, should be literally observed (the discussions in *De Decalogo* and *De Specialibus Legibus* leave this in no doubt) and, in interesting contrast with Paul (1 Cor. 9: 9), treats the commandment not to muzzle the threshing ox as a 'gentle and kindly law' (*De Virt.* 146; but compare *De Spec. Leg.* I, 260), he is rightly known as an outstanding exponent of the allegorical method. There are, he says, statements in the Old Testament which it is impossible to understand literally. Quoting Gen. 2: 21 f. he comments: 'That which is said here is mythical (μυθῶδες). For how could anyone accept that a woman, or any human being at all, came out of a man's side?' (*Leg. All.* II, 19); and on Gen. 2: 8: 'To suppose that (God) planted vines, and olive or apple or pomegranate or other trees, would be sheer silliness which it would be hard to cure' (*De Plant.* 32).

The answer to such difficulties is to be found in allegorical interpretation. They are raised acutely by Gen. 4: 16, which refers to God's face.[1]

Let us consider whether we ought to take the matters in the books interpreted to us by Moses figuratively (τροπικώτερον), since the face-value of the words is much at variance with the truth. For if the Existent One (τὸ ὄν) has a face, and he who wishes to leave it behind can easily remove himself elsewhere, what ground have we for rejecting the impiety of the Epicureans, or the godlessness of the Egyptians, or the mythological ideas of which life is full?...(We must conclude that) none of the propositions set forth is to

---

[1] Hebrew, *pāním*; Septuagint, πρόσωπον.

be taken literally, and take the path of allegory (τὴν δι' ἀλληγορίας ὁδόν), which is dear to thoughtful men (φυσικοῖς ἀνδράσι) (*De Post. Caini* 1f., 7).

When the plain meaning of the text is impossible—and also in other places, where the plain meaning remains a possible alternative or additional interpretation—it must be allegorised. To say this however does not do justice to the diversity of Philo's treatment. His expositions (more than one of which may be applied to the same passage) are sometimes moral, sometimes philosophical, sometimes theological. Philo was at bottom a moralist, and liked to draw ethical lessons from his text. The obscure verse, Lev. 11: 42, which deals with clean and unclean animals, is interpreted in the light of the belief that the belly was the seat of lust and pleasure, and that the four feet might represent the four passions: 'He then who attends to the one thing, pleasure, is unclean, and so is he who moves upon all four (passions)' (*Leg. All.* III, 139).

Philosophically, Philo was an eclectic, who drew together out of Stoicism, Platonism, and Neo-Pythagoreanism whatever would serve his turn in commending Judaism to the Greek world. The Old Testament does not in fact teach any of these systems, and Philo could derive them from it only by allegory. Again, one example must suffice. Philo notes (*Leg. All.* I, 31) that the Old Testament contains two accounts of the creation of man. He explains this in Platonic terms: the man of Gen. 1: 27 is a heavenly man (οὐράνιος ἄνθρωπος), the idea of man that lies behind manhood in general, but the man of Gen. 2: 7, moulded out of clay from the earth, is earthy (γήϊνος), material man.

Philo also uses the allegorical method to bring out truths about the being of God. When Abraham (Gen. 18: 2) is visited by three persons, of whom only two went on to destroy the cities of the plain, the third was 'the truly Existent, who thought it fitting to be present to bestow good things through his own agency, but to leave it to his powers (δυνάμεσι) alone, acting as his agents, to effect the opposite, in order that he might be considered the cause of good things only, but not directly of evil' (*De Abr.* 143).

Philo knew that he was not the first allegorist, though how far he was familiar with the allegorists of Homer and other Greek writers is a disputed question. He can speak of the rules of allegory (τοὺς τῆς ἀλληγορίας κανόνας, *De Somn.* I, 73) as if they were well established; and we may recall his accounts of the Essenes and of the Therapeutae. In both groups the Sabbath sermon takes an important place (*De Vita Cont.* 31; *Quod Omn. Prob.* 82), and what Philo says of the Essenes he would probably have applied to both: 'For the most part philosophy is conducted among them, in emulation of the ancient manner, through symbols (διὰ συμβόλων).' It is worth while to recall too (cf. p. 381) those interpreters who, in Philo's view, went too far in abandoning the literal meaning of the text; there were Alexandrian Jews who introduced sheer paganism into their interpretation of the figures of the Old Testament.[1] The achievement of Philo in applying Greek methods of study to his biblical text, though open to severe criticism, compares well with that of his contemporaries and predecessors.

RABBINIC EXEGETICAL METHOD

How far Philo and the Alexandrians were in touch with the Palestinian exegetical tradition is a disputed question.[2] Philo's expositions of Hebrew words do not inspire confidence in him as a Semitic philologist,[3] but his etymologies are no wilder than those of the rabbis, and in no way disprove knowledge of colloquial Hebrew. The personal question is relatively insignificant; it is more important to note that, in exegesis as in other respects, Hellenistic and Palestinian Judaism stood closer together than is sometimes recognised.

Rabbinic exegesis was governed by *middôṯ*, or rules. In the oldest collection of these—ascribed to Hillel, though he listed rather than invented them—there were seven, as follows:[4]

(1) Inference drawn *a minori ad maius* (or *vice versa*).

(2) Inference by analogy, in which two passages were drawn together by means of a common word, or words.

(3) A family based on one member—a group of kindred passages, in which a feature peculiar to one member is taken to apply to all.

(4) A family based on two members: the same as (3), except that the feature is peculiar to two members.

(5) General and particular, particular and general. Here argument is drawn from one case to a group, or *vice versa.*

---

[1] Examples in C. K. Barrett, *From First Adam to Last* (London, 1962), pp. 56–9.

[2] See e.g. S. Belkin, *Philo and the Oral Law* (Cambridge, Mass., 1940).

[3] See e.g. *De Conf. Ling.* 129; *De Migr.* 13; *De Somn.* II, 250.

[4] For detailed references see H. L. Strack, *Introduction to the Talmud and Midrash* (Philadelphia, 1959), pp. 93 f. (and note 5).

(6) Interpretation by means of a similar passage elsewhere.

(7) Inference based on the context.

These *middôt* were expanded in the course of time. Thirteen were ascribed to R. Ishmael, thirty-two to R. Eliezer b. Yose the Galilaean. They were used in the production both of *hᵃlākôt* (rules for conduct) and of *haggādāh* (homiletical material). Thus the first of the *middôt* may be illustrated in both fields. Perhaps the most famous halakic application of the exegetical argument *a minori ad maius* occurs in the account of the discussion that brought Hillel himself to the presidency of the Council.[1] It was disputed whether the Passover offering 'overcame' the Sabbath (that is, whether the force of the Passover law was such that it justified the various kinds of work, not normally permitted on the Sabbath, that had to be performed if the offering was to be made). Hillel (who took the view that the Passover offering should be made on Nisan 14, even if that day was a Sabbath) gave first a twofold argument based on analogy with the *tāmîd* (the daily burnt offering), and then continued,

Further, the argument *a minori ad maius* applies. If the *tāmîd* offering, on account of which one does not become liable to the punishment of extirpation, overcomes the Sabbath [since it must be offered daily], is it not right that the Passover offering, on account of which one does become liable to the punishment of extirpation (Num. 9: 13), should overcome the Sabbath?

Hillel went on, characteristically, to add an argument from tradition. Here a *hᵃlākāh* is established by means of the first exegetical device (together with other arguments).

A second example will illustrate the use of the same exegetical principle but a different application of the Old Testament. R. Johanan b. Zakkai made use of Deut. 27: 6 ('Thou shalt make the altar of unhewn, *šᵉlēmôt*, stones') as follows:[2]

This means stones that establish peace (*šālôm*). See, the conclusion *a minori ad maius* applies. If God said, with reference to the stones of the altar, which neither see nor hear nor speak, because they establish peace between Israel and their Father in heaven, 'Thou shalt not lift up iron upon them' (Deut. 27: 5), how much more does it apply to him who establishes peace between two men, or between a man and his wife, or between two towns, or two

---

[1] Tos. Pesaḥim 4.1 f.; Pesaḥim 66a; p. Pesahim 6.33a.1.

[2] Mekhilta on Exod. 20: 25 (81a).

nations, or two governments, or two families, that no punishment shall come upon him!

In this moralising, haggadic, use of the Old Testament the rabbis stand not far away from Philo; even the exegetical methods employed are not widely different, and may well have come from the same source. The straightforward application of a text is the same the world over, and it must not be forgotten that this kind of interpretation (*pešaṭ*) was widely employed by the rabbis in addition to the more elaborate methods (*dîn*);[1] and the first of the *middôt*, which I have illustrated, is a simple logical principle which could occur independently to intelligent men anywhere. It is however possible to go further than this, and to trace a connection between the *middôt* and recognised principles of hellenistic rhetoric.[2] It is one thing to argue *a minori ad maius*, and another thing to recognise and describe the argument, and to classify it as one of a group of exegetical canons; and this both the hellenistic rhetoricians and the rabbis did. Parallels can be found to the other *middôt* in hellenistic sources; moreover, as Daube points out, the rabbis were engaged on the same task as the hellenistic rhetoricians and Roman lawyers. They possessed a body of sacred and authoritative literature which failed to cover all the cases that arose in practice; it was necessary to fill in the gaps, and to do so in a way that commended itself to logic, and thus gave to the supplements the same authority that the original material enjoyed.

The parallelism and dependence that can be demonstrated do not mean slavish imitation. The decisive steps were taken at a time when the development of Jewish law was proceeding with a great deal of inward vitality.

It is important to note that, when the Hellenistic methods were first adopted, about 100 to 25 B.C., the 'classical', Tannaitic era of Rabbinic law was just opening. That is to say, the borrowing took place in the best period of Talmudic jurisprudence, when the Rabbis were masters, not slaves, of the new influences. The methods taken over were thoroughly hebraized in spirit as well as form, adapted to the native material, worked out so as to assist the natural progress of Jewish law.[3]

[1] For the terminology see W. Bacher, *Die exegetische Terminologie der jüdischen Traditionsliteratur* (Hildesheim, 1965 (Leipzig, 1899 and 1905)), I, pp. 21 ff.; II, pp. 170 f.
[2] See D. Daube, 'Rabbinic Methods of Interpretation and Hellenistic Rhetoric', in *HUCA*, XXII (Cincinnati, 1949), 239–64; also 'Alexandrian Methods of Interpretation and the Rabbis', in *Festschrift Hans Lewald* (Basel, 1953), pp. 27–44.
[3] 'Rabbinic Methods', p. 240.

To the necessary development of the legal parts of the Old Testament in halakic decisions, and the homiletic expansion of it in moral exhortation, may be added more speculative interpretation, or expansion, which does not follow recognisable hermeneutical laws but is of some importance in the development of Jewish thought and contributes to the background of the New Testament use of the Old Testament. Outstanding examples are provided by the familiar Old Testament figures of Adam, Elijah, and the Son of man, which in later generations were developed in ways that bore little relation to the intentions of the authors of Genesis, Kings, and Daniel. It is indeed probable that much older mythological material lies behind the Old Testament account of the first man, and the Danielic vision of the cloud-man; but this mythical background cannot be simply identified with the mythical development of these figures. Adam, curiously, tended to become the ancestor of the Jewish people; Elijah, naturally (Mal. 4: 5), was seen as the forerunner of the Messiah, but also as the helper of the needy; the Son of man, in association with the patriarch Enoch, enjoyed a striking development through the Enoch literature to become eventually a more or less divine being. In all these developments, fantasy and the pressure of foreign mythology played their part; but the form, if not the substance, of Old Testament interpretation was always present.

QUMRÂN EXEGESIS

We have seen that Philo speaks of the allegorical expositions of scripture practised by the Essenes (cf. pp. 382 f.). Somewhat similar remarks are made by Josephus (*B.J.* II, 136, 142, 159), who records their devotion to the holy books of the ancients. If those scholars are right who take the Qumrân community to have been a group of Essenes, we are now able to learn from their own literature how their exposition of scripture was conducted. If, as some think, this identification rests on inadequate grounds, we have nevertheless in the Qumrân Scrolls a very important body of Jewish exegesis which considerably antedates the exegetical literature of the rabbis.

The Qumrân exegesis is far less subtle than that of Philo. It does, for example, contain a certain amount of allegory, but it is far cruder than Philo's, and is usually combined with the 'historical' kind of interpretation that will be referred to presently. Thus in the Damascus

Rule (VI, 3–11), Num. 21: 18 ('The well which the princes dug, which the nobles of the people delved with the stave') is quoted, and then explained.[1]

> The *Well* is the Law, and those who dug it were the converts of Israel who went out of the land of Judah to sojourn in the land of Damascus. God called them all *princes* because they sought Him, and their renown was disputed by no man. The *Stave* is the interpreter of the Law of whom Isaiah said, *He makes a tool for His work* (Isa. 54: 16); and the *nobles of the people* are those who came to dig the *Well* with the staves with which the *Stave* ordained that they should walk in all the age of wickedness—and without them they shall find nothing—until he comes who shall teach righteousness at the end of days.[2]

It is however particularly important that the Qumrân sectaries saw scripture being fulfilled in themselves and in the events that befell them. It was with reference to them that prophecy had been written down, and in their action that prophecy was fulfilled.

The interpretation put upon the Scriptures is primarily historical, not in the sense that it corresponds to modern conceptions of historical criticism and interpretation, but in the sense that everything is supposed to refer directly to the history of the group itself. Not only are events of the writers' own times interpreted in the light of Scripture; it is even more characteristic that the Scriptures themselves are interpreted in the light of recent events.[3]

This belief, in which the Qumrân community comes nearest to the New Testament Church,[4] rests upon the conviction that the present is the eschatological time, the beginning of the End, in which God's purposes, adumbrated in scripture, come to fulfilment.

It is in the context of biblical interpretation that the sect wrote down its own history, which it saw as the fulfilment of prophecy. To take one example only, but that perhaps the most notable, the Teacher of Righteousness and his unhappy fate are given as an 'historical' interpretation of Hab. 2: 8*b*, 15.

> *Because of the blood of men and the violence done to the land, to the city, and to all its inhabitants.*

---

[1] Translations of Qumrân texts are taken from G. Vermes, *The Dead Sea Scrolls in English* (Penguin Books, Harmondsworth, Middlesex, 1962).

[2] Vermes, pp. 102 f.

[3] Millar Burrows, *The Dead Sea Scrolls* (London, 1956), p. 248.

[4] See below, pp. 394, 399 ff.

Interpreted, this concerns the Wicked Priest whom God delivered into the hands of his enemies because of the iniquity committed against the Teacher of Righteousness and the men of his Council, that he might be humbled by means of a destroying scourge, in bitterness of soul, because he had done wickedly to His elect...

Woe to him who causes his neighbours to drink; who pours out his venom to make them drunk that he may gaze on their feasts!

Interpreted, this concerns the Wicked Priest who pursued the Teacher of Righteousness to the house of his exile that he might confuse him with his venomous fury. And at the time appointed for rest, for the Day of Atonement, he appeared before them to confuse them, and to cause them to stumble on the Day of Fasting, their Sabbath of repose.[1]

The decipherment of these, and similar, historical allusions is a problem of notorious difficulty, which cannot be attempted here. The point that must be noted is that the Qumrân sect not merely imitated the Old Testament in its own psalms (or *Hôdāyôt*) and apocalyptic works, but believed that Old Testament prophecies had been and were being fulfilled in its own history, and in the experiences of its leading members. Their interpretation of the Old Testament was determined by their conviction that they lived in the appointed time in which the words of the prophets became historical fact. This meant that they could handle the Old Testament with more confidence than some of their contemporaries, in that they were convinced that the Old Testament was about themselves.

Each of the two comments quoted above from the Commentary on Habakkuk begins with the word *Interpreted*, which translates the Hebrew *pēšer*, *interpretation*.[2] This word occurs once only in the Old Testament (Eccles. 8: 1), and does not appear to have been used by the rabbis as a technical exegetical term. The Aramaic equivalent is hardly more common. There is no doubt that the general meaning is *interpretation*, but only from the context can the method and manner of the interpretation be determined. A separate *pēšer* is supplied for each small unit of text. Paragraphs are not interpreted as wholes, though it occasionally happens that clauses are combined in defiance of the original connection (or lack of it). Continuity is thus provided not by the original sense and context, but by the new historical context

---

[1] 1QpHab IX, XI; Vermes, pp. 238 f.

[2] Normally with the pronominal suffix of the third person singular, *pišrô, its interpretation*.

into which the biblical material is introduced and in terms of which it is explained. Within the several units of text the allegorical method is used in order to apply the passage quoted to its new historical setting. The use of allegory is a fairly clear indication that the commentator has in fact begun with historical circumstances, and convictions regarding them, known to himself, and has imposed them on his text. Within this framework a number of methods are employed which recall those of Philo and the rabbis; for example, variant readings are used, and indeed seem sometimes to have been created by the interpreter who may from time to time have altered the vocalisation, and even the consonants, of the text before him, and one passage of scripture is interpreted by others.[1] It may be that the community thought the interpretations given to have been communicated supernaturally to the Teacher of Righteousness,[2] who could thus be said to have shared the inspiration of the prophet himself.

As we turn, however, to the New Testament, no observation about the use of the Old Testament in the Qumrân Scrolls is so important as that their authors believed that the prophets wrote not of their own time but of the time of the End, and that they, the community, lived at the time of the End, so that they themselves, and their deeds, were the fulfilment of scripture.

THE OLD TESTAMENT IN THE NEW:
(A) EXEGETICAL METHOD

Most of the writers of the New Testament were Jews, and all were children of their own age. It is therefore not surprising that their work bears many resemblances to that which we have now considered. It is true that the New Testament contains no formal and continuous commentary on any book of the Old Testament;[3] this serves to underline the fact that we owe the New Testament to a new and creative outburst of religious feeling and theological thinking, an event in which men were deeply conscious of the novelty and spontaneity of their ideas and experiences. Apart however from the absence of such

---

[1] See above; also F. F. Bruce, *Biblical Exegesis in the Qumran Texts* (London, 1960).

[2] 1QpHab vii: The Teacher of Righteousness, to whom God made known all the mysteries of the words of his servants the Prophets.

[3] See however pp. 405, 407 f., on Testimony Books.

extended expository material, the parallelism between the New Testament and contemporary Jewish use of the Old Testament is close. This will be considered first in respect of form.

In the New Testament, Old Testament material is often introduced without any citation formula, and sometimes without any indication that the Old Testament is being used. The wording of the Old Testament is taken over and woven into narrative or argument. Sometimes the context makes it clear that the Old Testament is employed, as for example in Stephen's speech in Acts 7. Here a good deal of Old Testament history is summarised and, as a glance in a copy of the New Testament where Old Testament words are printed in capitals or heavy type will show, there is frequent use of the wording of scripture, though it is not till verse 42 that a formal quotation occurs (*As it is written in the book of the prophets*...). Again, in 1 Pet. 2: 1–10, though only verse 6 (Isa. 28: 16) is marked down as a quotation (*It is contained in scripture*...), the application throughout the paragraph of language dealing with the people of God is sufficient to show that the Old Testament is being used. Often, however, if the reader were not familiar with the Old Testament passages involved, it would be impossible to pick them out from the apparently continuous material which the New Testament presents. There is a notable narrative example in Mark 15: 24: 'They divided his clothes, casting lots for them' (διαμερίζονται τὰ ἱμάτια αὐτοῦ, βάλλοντες κλῆρον ἐπ' αὐτά). This can be read as a straightforward account of the actions of the soldiers at the crucifixion. Matt. (27: 35) and Luke (23: 34) use similar words, and give no more indication than Mark that a quotation is involved. John, however (19: 24), refers specifically to a passage of scripture (γραφή), and the reader turns to Ps. 22: 18: 'They divided my clothes among them, and for my clothing they cast lots' (διεμερίσαντο τὰ ἱμάτιά μου ἑαυτοῖς, καὶ ἐπὶ τὸν ἱματισμόν μου ἔβαλον κλῆρον). It is now impossible to doubt that Mark 15: 24 was framed (either by Mark or by some earlier editor of the gospel tradition) in terms of the Old Testament, and that the reader was intended to pick up the allusion, even though the evangelist did not help him to do so. It was even easier for Old Testament material to be worked into hortatory and theological passages. Thus it would be easy to read Eph. 4: 25 f. ('Forsaking falsehood, speak truth, each man with his neighbour, for we are members of one another. Be angry but do not sin; let not the sun go down on your anger') without observing the references to Zech. 8: 16 ('Speak truth, each man to his neighbour'), and Ps. 4: 4 ('Be angry but do not sin'). There is, again, nothing to indicate that the last two verses of the Christological hymn of Phil. 2: 6–11 rest upon 1 Kings 19: 18 (Septuagint); Isa. 45: 23.

The use of the Old Testament in the New Testament is thus a much larger matter than direct, indicated quotation. There are, however, such quotations, and they are often marked out by citation formulas. Of these the most common reflect the fact that the Old Testament was known as a written book: *as it is written, for it is written,* and the like (καθὼς γέγραπται, γέγραπται γάρ). These recall the rabbinic use of *that which is written* (*kātûb*),[1] and hardly call for comment. Less common in the New Testament is the use of a verb of *saying* (e.g. καθὼς εἴρηται); this recalls the very common Hebrew *as it is said* (*šene'emar*). Both the New Testament writers and the rabbis on occasion personify scripture, as in such expressions as *Scripture says* (e.g. Rom. 10: 11, λέγει γὰρ ἡ γραφή; cf. *kātûb 'ômēr*). Its authors, or supposed authors, are also represented both as writing and as speaking; for example,

Mark 12: 36. 'David himself said in the Holy Spirit' (cf. Luke 20: 42, 'David said in the Book of Psalms').
Mark 7: 10. 'Moses said'; 12: 19 'Moses wrote'.
Mark 7: 6. 'Isaiah prophesied.'
Rom. 9: 27. 'Isaiah cried out' (κράζει).
Rom. 10: 20. 'Isaiah is so bold as to say.'

The supernatural element in scripture is more strongly stressed when its human authors are represented as mere mouthpieces for divine speakers; for example,

Matt. 1: 22. 'All this happened in order that what was spoken by the Lord through the prophet might be fulfilled.'
Acts 4: 25. '...who by the Holy Spirit said through the mouth of our father David...'[2]

Many Jewish forms and methods of exegesis recur in the New Testament.

(i) The New Testament employs allegory. An outstanding example occurs in Gal. 4, where Paul refers to the story of Abraham, and of the

---

[1] In such expressions as *kemāh šekātûb*.
[2] The Greek here is notoriously obscure, but the main point is not in doubt.

sons Ishmael and Isaac born to him by the slave Hagar and the free-woman Sarah respectively, the one in the course of nature, the other as the result of divine promise. 'These things', he adds, 'are allegories (ἐστιν ἀλληγορούμενα).'[1] The two women are covenants; their children are those who are born under the Law, and thòse who (as Christians) are born for freedom. Paul is not yet at an end, for he introduces also Mount Sinai in Arabia, the present Jerusalem, the heavenly Jerusalem, and the persecution of the freewoman's offspring by that of the slave. This is the most extended, but not the only, allegory in the New Testament.

(ii) Occasionally interpretations are found which are cast in a form akin to the *pēšer* form of the Qumrân commentaries. Perhaps the best example is the treatment of Deut. 30: 12 f. in Rom. 10: 6 f.

Do not say in your heart, Who shall ascend into heaven? that is, to bring Christ down; or, Who shall descend into the deep? that is, to bring Christ up from the dead.

This requires little modification to become:

Do not say in your heart, Who shall ascend into heaven? The *pēšer* of this is, Who shall bring Christ down? Do not say in your heart, Who shall descend into the deep? The *pēšer* of this is, Who shall bring Christ up from the dead?

(iii) At least two of the recognised methods of rabbinic interpretation occur in the New Testament.

(*a*) Arguments *a minori ad maius* are fairly common (and of course not only in exegetical discussions). These take various forms, but the transition from less to greater is usually based on a Christological fact or implication. Thus in Mark 2: 23–8 Jesus refers to the Old Testament incident (1 Sam. 21: 1–6) in which David and his followers, against the sacred regulation, ate holy bread from the sanctuary; since this was permissible it follows that the disciples of Jesus were free to pluck and eat ears of corn in circumstances (that is, on the Sabbath) in which this was not normally allowed.[2] A more formally theological example occurs at Heb. 9: 13 f. The former verse ('If the blood of bulls and

---

[1] For the verb cf. Philo, *De Vita Cont.* 28 f.

[2] Some see here a simple argument from analogy: in each situation this proposition holds, Necessity knows no law. Jesus' disciples, however, were not in serious need, and Matthew's insertion (12: 5 ff.) shows that he understood the argument to be of the *a minori ad maius* kind.

goats and the ashes of a heifer sprinkling those who have been defiled sanctify them with a view to cleanness of the flesh') does not quote a specific passage, but refers in Old Testament language to a number of Old Testament regulations;[1] the latter verse ('How much more will the blood of Christ...cleanse our conscience...') draws the Christian conclusion. 2 Cor. 3:4–18 should be noted here, for though it contains a complication of its own it provides a particularly clear illustration of the point at issue. Paul describes, with the frequent use of Old Testament language, Moses' descent from Mount Sinai after receiving the Law, when his face shone, so that he was obliged to cover it. The Law, in Paul's view, was a ministry of death (2 Cor. 3:7; cf. Rom. 7:10); if it was delivered in circumstances of such glory, how much more should the life-giving ministry of the Christian dispensation be accompanied by glory (3:8; cf. 3:17 f.). It should however be observed that that which transfigured Moses into a figure of glory was the Law, in Jewish estimation the central element of the Old Testament. Since the ministry of Moses pales into insignificance beside the Christian ministry, and is being done away (3:11), the Old Testament as a whole is seen to stand within the *a minori ad maius*. It is no longer one precept or institution that is transcended: the whole of sacred scripture is transcended by its fulfilment. 'Transcended' does not mean 'discarded', for the figure of Moses, and his writings, retain a transformed significance; this, however, is a matter that must be discussed below (cf. pp. 397, 408, 409 f.).

(*b*) The New Testament uses also the second of the *middôt* (*geʐêrāh šāwāh*). The best example of this occurs in Rom. 4.[2] Paul quotes Gen. 15:6, in which it is stated that Abraham's faith in God was counted (ἐλογίσθη) to him as righteousness. The question is, in what sense is the word 'counted' used? Paul answers this by means of a second quotation in which the same word is used. Ps. 32:1 ('Blessed is the man whose sin the Lord will not count', λογίσηται) shows that 'counting' and 'not counting' are not a matter of the balancing of good and bad deeds, but of forgiveness and reconciliation. Paul has now established the meaning of the disputed word, but sees the opportunity of drawing further use from his *geʐêrāh šāwāh*. The psalm he has

[1] Lev. 16:3, 14 f.; Num. 19:9, 17.
[2] See J. Jeremias, in *Studia Paulina*, ed. J. N. Sevenster and W. C. van Unnik (Haarlem, 1953), pp. 149 ff.

quoted is (he supposes) a psalm of David; David was a Jew; is then the blessing of forgiveness one that is confined to circumcised Jews? Not so, for the same verbal link allows us to return to Gen. 15, where righteousness is counted to Abraham while still uncircumcised.

(iv) Inevitably the New Testament uses also the simple and straight-forward (*pᵉšaṭ*; p. 385) kind of interpretation which was in use among Jews of every sort. The Old Testament is quoted because it says with authority what the New Testament writer wished to say. It furnishes, for instance, examples that are to be followed, such as that of Elijah, the man of prayer (Jas. 5: 17 f.), and Job, the man of endurance (5: 11), and others that are not to be followed, such as those of Cain the murderer (1 John 3: 12), and Esau the profane (Heb. 12: 16). Heb. 11 is worth noting because of a characteristic double emphasis: the Old Testament believers are held up as a pattern that should be copied, but at the same time it is observed that their witness, apart from its fulfilment, is incomplete (11: 39 f.; see below, pp. 409 f.).

The morality of the Old Testament is assumed, and its command-ments (notably the commandments to love God and the neighbour: Deut. 6: 4 f.; Lev. 19: 18) are repeated with added weight (e.g. Mark 12: 28–34, and parallels; Rom. 13: 8 ff.). Old Testament imagery, usually of a straightforward kind, is taken over and used in the same, or a very similar, sense. Examples are given below (pp. 404 f., 406 f., 409 f.).

(v) Finally, and most important, there is the parallel between the conviction which appears in the Qumrân writings that ancient prophecy was being fulfilled in the contemporary experience of a religious community, and the similar conviction which inspired the writers of the New Testament. It cannot however be said that this parallelism of conviction led to much formal similarity, because the Qumrân exegesis of prophecy in terms of current events is expressed in the *pēšer* form,[1] whereas the New Testament more often narrates the event, and adds that it happened in fulfilment of scripture.

---

[1] See the notable example of the Wicked Priest and the Teacher of Righteousness on pp. 387 f.

The New Testament

When the use of the Old Testament made by the New Testament writers is compared with that of their Jewish contemporaries, many formal resemblances, and some formal differences, appear. The same observation holds good with regard to substance as with regard to form. A simple pointer to this is provided by a comparison of the relative frequency of quotation of various parts of the Old Testament. The figures for Philo were given above (p. 380 n. 2); in the list of Old Testament references given in the Nestle edition of the New Testament, the Pentateuch occupies about seven columns, the Psalms five, Isaiah nearly five, the prophets as a whole (including Daniel) nearly twelve. The Pentateuch is still strongly represented (though Leviticus and Numbers make but a poor showing), but the Prophets and the Writings claim a much greater share of the interpreter's attention. The New Testament is less concerned with the legal, and much more concerned with the prophetic, element in the Old Testament, in both its religious and predictive aspects. This simple statistical observation, however, requires further analysis if it is to lead to useful consideration of the use of the Old Testament in the New.

The question from which this analysis may proceed is: What does the user of a sacred literature hope to find in his authoritative documents? For Jewish users of the Old Testament this question can be answered on the basis of the accounts given above. The rabbis turned to the Old Testament as the basis of the legal system which they created. Exact and scientific exegesis of the text made it applicable to new situations which were not contemplated by the original lawgivers, and permitted trained legal experts to draw out a full religious, civil, and criminal code capable of regulating the life of their own society. Philo, his mind stored with Greek speculative and moral theory, which he accepted as true, went to the Old Testament convinced that he would find this truth there—as he was able to do, by means of the allegorical method. He was thus able to prove to his own satisfaction, and for use in missionary propaganda, that the best Greek thought had been anticipated by Moses. The Qumrân exegetes found in the Old Testament predictions of events which took place in the life of their own sect, and thus were able to demonstrate both that the Old Testament was true prophecy (since it had manifestly been fulfilled), and that their sect was the messianic fulfilment of God's purpose for Israel, since its story could be found written (somewhat obscurely, it is true) in the pages of the Old Testament.

These statements are only approximately true. There is a speculative (and sometimes surprisingly mystical) element in the rabbinic use of the Old Testament, and the rabbis cherished the messianic hope of their people, and busied themselves with messianic texts. Philo, again, was more than a thinly disguised Greek philosopher; he was deeply concerned that the national law should be observed, and that in its literal sense; and occasionally (especially *De Praem*. 163–72) he expresses a straightforward hope for the glorious future of his people. The Qumrân sect separated itself from the main body of Judaism not on account of its messianism, but on account of a divergent interpretation of the biblical basis of the Law. Nevertheless, though it would be mistaken to draw clear-cut distinctions between the exegetical motivation of Philo, the rabbis, and the Qumrân *pēšer* commentators, it is correct to take the three exegetical lines that have been mentioned and use them as norms of the exegetical activity of the Jewish people. All reappear within the New Testament.

(i) New Testament writers use the Old Testament in order to establish regulations for the Christian life. Examples are numerous, and only a selection can be given here.

One important group deals with the relations between men and women. The treatment of marriage and divorce in Mark 10: 2–12 (and parallels) will serve as a useful starting-point, for it contains a discussion, which reflects legal exegetical controversy, of the Old Testament evidence. Quotation of Deut. 24: 1 suggests the permissibility of divorce; this however is countered by passages from Genesis (1: 27; 2: 24), which show that the original intention of God in creation was the permanent union of one man and one woman, so that revised legal procedure will exclude divorce. It is important that this principle is applied in Mark 10: 12 to a situation which the historical Jesus can hardly have envisaged,[1] and that Matthew (5: 32; 19: 9; cf. 1 Cor. 7: 15) shows that the prohibition was not understood in a strict legalistic sense. The subordination of women to men is grounded by Paul in the narrative of creation (1 Cor. 11: 3–12; cf. Gen. 1: 27; 2: 18,

---

[1] In Jewish law a wife cannot divorce her husband.

22 f.), though without formal quotation; the author of 1 Peter makes a different, moral and haggadic rather than theological and halakic, use of the Old Testament for a similar purpose when he notes Sarah's respectful way of addressing her husband (3: 6).

A second important field in which Old Testament material was used as the source and foundation of Christian legislation was that of the admission of the Gentiles, over which, as is well known, controversy raged in the middle of the first century. The controversy is presented in the New Testament by the side which ultimately caused its view, that Gentiles might be admitted to the Church without Jewish rites such as circumcision, to prevail. It is however evident that their adversaries must have based their argument on the Old Testament, and that they had ready to hand plenty of material which, at least on the surface, appeared to support them. From Abraham onwards, members of God's people were expected (if men) to be circumcised; the law was given to them that it might be kept. An almost unlimited number of Old Testament texts affirmed this. We possess (at least) two counter-arguments, and both of these are based on the Old Testament. Luke represents the Apostolic Council of Acts 15 as the scene of the decisive solution of the problem, and the debate is made to turn on James's quotation of Amos 9: 11 f. It is hard to believe that this quotation could have had the decisive force Luke attributes to it, especially as James is made to give it in the Septuagint form,[1] and the narrative of the Council raises other familiar historical problems; but presumably the quotation was thought by Luke and his contemporaries to be convincing, or at least to provide important confirmation of a position of the truth of which they were already satisfied.

The second justification of the admission to the Church of Gentiles as such is Paul's, and here a solid Old Testament foundation is provided. In Gal. 3, Paul conducts an argument to show that, though the Old Testament promised life to every one who does the things that are written in the Law (Lev. 18: 5), yet, by affirming that righteousness and life are to be had by faith (Hab. 2: 4), it implies that no one in fact does the things that are written in the Law, a conclusion that brings upon all men—Jews equally with Gentiles—the curse pronounced in

---

[1] B. Gerhardsson, *Memory and Manuscript* (Lund, 1961), p. 260 n. 3, is not convincing, if the intention is to suggest that James himself made use of the Septuagint variation in his interpretation.

Deut. 27: 26 upon every one who does not abide in all the things that are written in the book of the Law, to do them. Jews and Gentiles thus stand on the same footing before God, and the demand that Gentiles should become Jews by circumcision is not merely baseless but an affront to God. This is certainly not a modern argument, though it is far more profound than the mere citation of a concatenation of texts; it provides however a further example of the use of the Old Testament as the basis and source of Christian regulation and procedure.

Other matters of Christian usage and discipline were, at least in part, regulated by means of the Old Testament, which provided the basis for the requisite *hᵃlāḵôt*. How far were Christians obliged to keep the Jewish Sabbath? Various reasons were given for the new Christian freedom, of which one was the Old Testament precedent of David's freedom from similar religious regulations.[1] Were Christians permitted to eat food sacrificed to idols? Part of the answer is given by the quotation of Ps. 24: 1: since God assumes ownership of the whole earth and its contents it may be deduced that nothing is untouchable. Which is the more valuable gift, speaking with tongues or prophecy? The Old Testament shows (see 1 Cor. 14: 21) that the former will not lead to faith; it is therefore of little value, at least as an evangelistic agency. How ought the collection for the poor saints in Jerusalem to be conducted? The regulation for the collection of manna (Exod. 16: 18, quoted in 2 Cor. 8: 15) will supply the clue. Other Old Testament material is cited in 2 Cor. 9.

The nature of the Church and the basis of Church discipline are both founded in the Old Testament in the two allusions, in 2 Tim. 2: 19, to Num. 16: 'The Lord knows those who are his', and 'Let every one who names the name of the Lord depart from evil'. In the same epistle (3: 8), Church discipline is further strengthened by an allusion to Moses' treatment of his adversaries in Exod. 7 (with the addition of the apocryphal names Jannes and Jambres). Other New Testament books invoke other parts of the Old Testament for the same purpose, and Revelation makes particularly clear and forceful use of the figures of Jezebel and Balaam (2: 14, 20).[2] The appointment of a successor to Judas is given Old Testament grounding, and Paul uses the commandment of Deut. 25: 4 to justify the payment of apostles (1 Cor. 9: 9),

---

[1] See above, p. 392.　　　[2] On Balaam cf. also pp. 212 ff.

but apart from this surprisingly little use is made of the Old Testament in relation to the developing New Testament ministry—Christian ministers were neither rabbis nor priests.

There is in the New Testament far more halakic development, far more of moral and disciplinary regulation, than is sometimes recognised,[1] and much (though not all) of this is explicitly founded on Old Testament passages, from the principles of which rules relevant to the new situation of the new people of God are deduced. In this respect the New Testament writers stand close to their Jewish contemporaries. The outstanding difference lies in the fact, which is not always apparent, that, though the Law continues to provide a framework of argument, authority is found to lie elsewhere. This is expressed sometimes negatively, when (as in the argument quoted above from Gal. 3) the Law is used to prove its own incompetence. The positive counterpart to this negative argument is expressed most succinctly in Rom. 10: 4: Christ is the end of the Law. He is now the final authority under which the life of the people of God is lived.

(ii) The New Testament writers believed that the life, death, and resurrection of Jesus Christ, under whose authority they lived, had been predicted in the Old Testament. The events to which they themselves bore witness were thus the proof that they were living in the age of fulfilment. This is perhaps the most familiar aspect of the relation between the Testaments, and does not call for detailed illustration. All the main features of the story of Jesus are given Old Testament support.

Matthew[2] marks out the main features of the infancy narrative with quotations. The miraculous conception of Jesus fulfils Isa. 7: 14; he is born in Bethlehem, because so it is written in Mic. 5: 2; his parents flee, taking him with them, into Egypt, in order that later as God's Son he may be called out of Egypt (Hos. 11: 1), and thereby he escapes Herod's plot, which nevertheless is successful enough to provoke the lamentation of Jer. 31: 15. The modern reader may wonder whether the story was constructed on the basis of the Old Testament material; Matthew has no doubt that Jesus was the fulfiller of prophecy.

[1] See E. Käsemann, 'Sätze Heiligen Rechtes im Neuen Testament', *NTS*, 1 (1955), 248–60, reprinted in *Exegetische Versuche und Besinnungen*, 11 (Göttingen, 1964), pp. 69–82.

[2] In the Lukan infancy narratives the fulfilment of the Old Testament is differently expressed, through the use of Old Testament language in the hymns.

During his ministry, Jesus was notable as a worker of miracles (in fulfilment of Isa. 53: 4: 'He took our sicknesses and bore our diseases'; many other Old Testament passages are alluded to), and as a teller of parables (in order to fulfil the prophecy of Ps. 78: 2: 'I will open my mouth in parables'). Much more in the gospels is written in language that recalls the Old Testament, but the chief weight lies on the announcement that as the Son of man Jesus must suffer, for so it has been foretold. 'How is it written of the Son of man that he should suffer much, and be set at nought?' (Mark 9: 12). Many of the details are filled in. The combined hostility of Jews and Romans fulfils Ps. 2: 1 f. (Acts 4: 25 f.): 'Why did the Gentiles rage, and the peoples plot vanity? The kings of the earth stood by, and the rulers were gathered together against the Lord and against his Christ.' The betrayal by Judas was foretold not only by Jesus, but also in the Old Testament: John 13: 18 (Ps. 41: 9): 'He that eats my bread has lifted up his heel against me.' As the narrative continues, detail after detail is claimed as the fulfilment of prophecy: the division by lot of the clothes of Jesus (John 19: 24), his thirst (19: 28), the fact that none of his bones was broken, and that his side was pierced (19: 36 f.).

Paul is as certain that the resurrection took place 'according to the scriptures' as that the death of Christ was foretold (1 Cor. 15: 3 f.), but does not find it easy to give precise documentation. This was however supplied for example at Acts 2: 25–8, where a careful argument is given to support the exegesis. If David appears to refer to a promise that God's Holy One shall not see corruption, he cannot have been thinking of himself since the existence of his grave proves the corruptibility of his flesh; he must have been speaking of his greater descendant, Christ.

The events that follow and introduce the life of Christians, which rests upon the historic work of Jesus, are also documented. Christ ascended into heaven, as Ps. 68: 19 predicted (Eph. 4: 8). The gift of the Spirit was a fulfilment of the prophecy of Joel 2: 28–32 (Acts 2: 16). The Church is the Israel of God (Gal. 6: 16), and to it the epithets which had been used of the ancient people may now with even greater propriety be applied (1 Pet. 2: 1–10).

Not even the Qumrân manuscripts afford a list of fulfilments of scripture that can approach that which has now been outlined. It is clear that the first Christians believed themselves to be witnessing not a few preliminary tokens of God's fulfilment of his age-old purposes, but the central (though not the final) act to which all prophecy pointed. The process of fulfilment was focused upon the historic figure of Jesus: 'However many God's promises may be, in him is the Yes to them' (2 Cor. 1: 20). But because Christ was the focus of fulfilment, all who were in Christ were involved in it.

The Old Testament passages adduced in the New are of varying degrees of cogency. It is not easy, for example, to believe that Rachel's weeping for her children (Jer. 31: 15) had much to do with Herod's massacre of the innocents. Yet when this is said, it must be allowed that the use made of Old Testament passages in the New is surprisingly appropriate. The age of the New Testament was not an age of historical criticism; certainly it was not so in the orders of society in which Christianity spread most rapidly. Yet New Testament thinkers worked their way so successfully into the essential meaning of the Old Testament that they were sometimes at least able to bring to light a genuine community of thought and feeling between what had been experienced and said in the distant past, and the event of Jesus Christ. The 'argument from prophecy' may fairly be stated as an affirmation of the universal significance of Jesus.

(iii) It is the characteristically Philonic kind of exegesis that is hardest to find in the New Testament; and this is true even when we generalise, and look not simply for cases where Greek philosophy is sought and found in the Old Testament, but for those also in which any kind of contemporary thought is imported into the sacred text. This is not to say that New Testament exegesis of the Old Testament is always historical and sound—it has already been shown that this is not so. It is true, however, that New Testament interpreters commonly move within the same general framework of thought as the Old Testament itself.

A notable exception is perhaps to be found in the series of Christological terms which are qualified in John by the adjective *true* (ἀληθινός). Some of these are Old Testament terms—light, bread, vine. *Light* occurs in a context (John 1: 4 f.) which recalls the narrative of creation in Gen. 1; *bread* recalls the story of the manna; and the figure of the *vine* appears to be based on several Old Testament passages where the plant serves as a figure of Israel. The precise meaning that John gives to *true* is too large a question to be discussed here, but, at least in the view of some commentators, it owes something to the Platonic notion of the contrast between the real and the phenomenal. Thus the manna eaten by the Israelites in the wilderness serves as a figure of the true, heavenly bread given by God to men in his Son. So far as this exegesis is justified it may be said that we have an example of the reading of Greek philosophy into an Old Testament passage.

Many students of the New Testament have held that the same is true of the use of the Old Testament made by the Epistle to the Hebrews, which has been described as a Platonic reinterpretation of the original New Testament gospel. There is some superficial justification for this view in passages which speak of the Law as having a shadow of good things to come (10: 1; cf. Col. 2: 17), but it is in fact a misunderstanding of the epistle. The essential sense of its quotations is rooted not in Platonism but in apocalyptic.[1]

Old Testament material is indeed adapted in the New Testament to new circumstances; of this an outstanding example is the use of Old Testament passages (see pp. 397 f.) in the controversy about the admission of Gentiles to the Church. Many (though not quite all) of the passages used had originally no connection with the theme of the incorporation of non-Jews into the people of God; this however was the theme of the New Testament writers and, since it was imperative to them to prove their point out of the Old Testament, they read their opinions into the texts they used. Yet even here the New Testament exegesis is not wholly unprincipled. For example, in 1 Pet. 2: 10 the author draws on the language of Hosea (see 1: 6, 9; 2: 1, 23) to describe the Gentile Church: 'Who formerly were not a people, but now are God's people; who had not received mercy, but now have received mercy.' Now it is certain that in Hosea these words apply to Israel, who for her sins had been pitilessly punished so as to be no longer God's people, but would in the end be pitied by God so as to become his people once more. The prophecy had nothing to do with non-Jews, and is therefore, in a sense, misapplied in the New Testament. Yet in another sense it is used rightly, for it does state the principle that God's people exists as such only by God's mercy, and not at all in virtue of its own merits and qualifications; and this is the ground on which in the end Gentiles came to stand together with Jews as one people under the judgement and mercy of the same God.

[1] See below, pp. 408 ff.

It is here that we may make a distinction between the New Testament interpretation of the Old Testament, and that current in Judaism, which in many ways it very closely resembled. New Testament Christianity was aware of itself as a prophetic phenomenon. Its members were themselves inspired. This gave them a sense of kinship with the Old Testament writers. Deeper than this, however, was the fact that they conceived themselves to stand in fundamentally similar circumstances. The Law, the Prophets, the Psalms all arose out of situations in which men had become acutely conscious of the manifestations in history of God's judgement and mercy. This was often conceived in limited and limiting terms, but it was the creative factor which produced the various forms of literature. The New Testament literature itself was evoked by what its authors believed to be the supreme manifestation in history of the judgement and mercy of God, and the Old Testament manifestation and the New Testament manifestation interacted in mutual illumination. Sometimes this community of theme was expressed in too mechanically Christological a form, and reference to particular incidents in the life of Jesus was found where no such reference was intended. Even so, however, the community of theme is not robbed of its significance, and makes possible for the New Testament writers an understanding of the essential meaning of the Old Testament which it would be hard to parallel.

VARIETIES OF NEW TESTAMENT EXEGESIS

So far the New Testament has been regarded, in its treatment of the Old Testament, as a unit. This is a defensible, and indeed an indispensable, method. It is not however a final method, since in exegesis as well as in other matters there is much variety within the New Testament. Though, as has already been observed, all its authors view the Old Testament with respect, and quote it as an authority, some use it more than others, and in the various books different methods of interpretation and application are employed.

(i) *Synoptic Gospels and Acts*

These books contain a considerable number of Old Testament quotations, some of which have already been pointed out, which are adduced as prophecies fulfilled in the work of Jesus and of his disciples. An outstanding example is the quotation from Isa. 61: 1 f., which is used at Luke 4: 18 f. to bring out the meaning of Jesus' proclamation, and is sealed with the affirmation, 'Today this scripture has been fulfilled in your ears.' These quotations call for no further comment here. It is also however characteristic of the Synoptic Gospels to use, in teaching or narrative, Old Testament language without drawing attention to its source. In some passages this is unmistakable. Thus in the parable of the Wicked Husbandmen the steps taken by the owner of the vineyard are described as follows (Mark 12: 1): 'A man planted a vineyard, and put a fence round it, and dug a winepress, and built a tower, and let it out to husbandmen, and went away.' With this should be compared Isa. 5: 1–2: 'My beloved had a vineyard on a hilltop in a fruitful place. And I put a fence round it, and put in stakes, and planted a fine vine, and built a tower in the middle of it, and dug a winepress in it.' Even when allowance is made for the fact that the preparation and planting of a vineyard was necessarily a stereotyped procedure, it is impossible to doubt that, though there is no explicit reference to Isaiah, the language of the New Testament parable is based on that of the Old, and that the interpretation of the parable is thereby determined: in the New Testament, as in the Old, the vineyard is Israel (Isa. 5: 7).

With somewhat less confidence the miracle of Mark 7: 31–7 may be claimed as another example. The narrative records the cure of a man who is deaf and a stammerer (μογιλάλος). This is an uncommon Greek word, but it occurs in the Septuagint version of Isa. 35: 6: The tongue of the stammerers (μογιλάλων) shall be plain. The rarity of the word adds weight to the view that the Markan narrative was written with the Old Testament prophecy in mind; but there is no explicit reference to it, nor any suggestion that Mark himself saw a fulfilment of the Old Testament.[1]

The material we have now considered has not unnaturally given rise to the view that some at least of the gospel narratives arose as *miḏrāšîm* on Old Testament passages. This may be an exaggerated view, but the influence of the Old Testament on the form in which the traditions about Jesus were repeated should not be underestimated. It is salutary for the modern reader to recall Justin's intention (*Apol.* 1, 30) to

[1] See E. Hoskyns and N. Davey, *The Riddle of the New Testament* (London, 1931), pp. 167 f. A further example is to be found in Mark 15: 24; see above, p. 390.

demonstrate the divinity of Jesus Christ on the basis of his deeds, trusting rather to prophecies given before the event than to human reports. The gospel story as a whole differs so markedly from current interpretation of the Old Testament that it is impossible to believe that it originated simply in meditations on prophecy; it originated in the career of Jesus of Nazareth. But the earliest method of evaluating the theological significance of his life was to tell the story of it in terms of the Old Testament, and though the conviction that the story had been foretold arose before it could be documented (see Mark 9: 12; 14: 21; 1 Cor. 15: 3 f.; and see above, pp. 399 ff.) it is likely that when Old Testament material was adduced it contributed new details to the stories it was intended to illustrate.

A related suggestion (see further below, pp. 407 f.) is that already Testimony Books, or collections of Old Testament texts believed to have been fulfilled in the events of the New Testament, were in circulation in the New Testament period.[1] That such books existed at a rather later time is certain;[2] their existence in the first century can (in the absence of the books themselves) be no more than conjecture, but it is a reasonable conjecture, and is given some support by a special set of quotations peculiar to Matthew (1: 23; 2: 15, 18, 23; 4: 15f.; 8: 17; 12: 18ff.; 13: 35; 21: 5; 27: 9; cf. 2: 6). These are all introduced in similar terms, and do not follow the text of the Septuagint; it is possible that they were drawn by the evangelist from a special source.

The speeches in the early chapters of Acts are full of quotations; Stephen's in chapter 7 is little more than a summary of Old Testament history, and even Paul's speech at Athens in chapter 17 is not without its allusions. The quotations are on the whole of the kind that can broadly be described as 'messianic'; they are designed to illustrate and support that part of the preaching that asserts that in the life, death, and resurrection of Jesus the Old Testament scriptures were fulfilled, so that with him the new age began to dawn.

(ii) *John*

Like the Synoptic Gospels, the Fourth contains a number of straightforward proof texts; some of these have already been quoted. They are however relatively few, and to their fewness must be added the

---

[1] See J. R. Harris, *Testimonies*, I (Cambridge, 1916); II (1920).
[2] Notably the *Testimonia ad Quirinum* of Cyprian.

observation that from time to time John appears to handle the expectations of Judaism in a critical and even negative way. A notable example of this is John the Baptist's denial (1: 21) that he is to be identified with Elijah—an identification which the Synoptic Gospels make without hesitation (Matt. 17: 11 ff.; cf. Mark 9: 13; Luke 1: 17). It is characteristic both of John's ironical style and of his use of the Old Testament that he places on the lips of unbelieving Jews the Old Testament teaching that the Messiah would be of the seed of David, and would come from Bethlehem, the village where David was (7: 42); Jesus, therefore, who came from Galilee, could not, in their belief, be the Messiah. It is probable that John was aware of the tradition that, though Jesus was brought up in Galilee, he had been born in Bethlehem; he was thus representing Jewish unbelief as based on inaccurate opinion about Jesus' birthplace. Behind this point, however, appears to lie another: the earthly origin of Jesus, whether in Galilee or Judaea, is ultimately irrelevant, since he comes from God, and this divine origin determines the meaning and authority of his mission.

These observations, important as they are, do not lead to the conclusion that John had no use for the Old Testament; what they suggest is that he used it in a way of his own. It is his method to deal not so much with Old Testament texts as with Old Testament themes. One of the clearest examples is provided by his description of Jesus as the Good Shepherd (10: 1–16). In this passage, no part of the Old Testament is quoted, but no one familiar with the Old Testament can read it without recalling a number of places where similar imagery is used—for example, Pss. 23; 80; Ezek. 34; and not least the fact that David, the ancestor and prototype of the Messiah, was a shepherd. Without pinning himself to a particular prophecy, John takes up a central Old Testament theme, and familiar Old Testament language, and concentrates them upon the figure of Jesus. A similar example is to be found in John 1: 29, where the exegete who seeks the background of the description of Jesus as the Lamb of God does not need to decide too nicely between the Passover lamb, the lamb of the daily burnt offering, the lamb of Isa. 53, the goat of the Day of Atonement, and other Old Testament animals.[1] Whatever they suggest—all of them—in sin-bearing and sin-removing efficacy, Jesus was.

From this point another step may be taken. If Jesus truly *was* what-

---

[1] See C. K. Barrett, 'The Lamb of God', *NTS*, 1 (1955), 210–18.

ever lambs, shepherds, and the like may in the pages of the Old Testament suggest, he must have been more than the object of prophecy; it may reasonably be maintained that he was its subject too.[1] Here it must suffice to refer to two passages where this view stands out clearly. In John 12:41, after reference to Isa. 53:1 and 6:9 f., the evangelist comments, evidently with Isa. 6:1 in mind, 'These things Isaiah said because[2] he saw his glory.' The next words ('and he spoke about him') show that 'his glory' means Christ's glory; that is, the celestial figure whose glory Isaiah saw, and who entrusted to him his prophetic commission and message, was Christ himself. A similar point is made in John 10:34 f. After quoting Ps. 82:6 ('I said, You are gods'), John continues, 'If he called them gods to whom the word of God came...' But John has already (1:1 f., 14) identified Jesus with the word of God, and if this identification is to be taken seriously it must be concluded that Jesus, the Word, was in some sense involved in the Old Testament passage.

(iii) *Paul*

As examples given in the general discussion will have shown, Paul manifests so wide a range of the various uses of the Old Testament made by Christian writers that it will scarcely be possible to give special treatment of his peculiarities. He quotes isolated passages, which he held to be fulfilled in the gospel; he demonstrates the great themes of the Old Testament, and shows their significance in a Christian setting, as for example when he proves out of scripture the universal sinfulness of mankind (Rom. 3:9–20); he draws Christian $h^a l\bar{a}k\acute{o}t$ out of Old Testament data (e.g. 1 Cor. 9:9; see above, p. 398); and simply reiterates the Old Testament command of love, as Jesus himself had done (Rom. 13:8–10; Lev. 19:18; cf. Mark 12:31). Here two further points may be noted.

When taken with other New Testament writers Paul may be held to provide further evidence for the Testimony Book theory mentioned above (p. 405). Thus in Rom. 9:33 Paul places side by side Isa. 28:16 ('Behold, I lay in Sion a stone of stumbling and a rock of tripping'), and 8:14 ('He that believes in him—that is, in the elect corner-stone—shall not be put to shame'). There is no connection between the Isaiah

[1] For a full discussion of this theme see A. T. Hanson, *Jesus Christ in the Old Testament* (London, 1965).

[2] Accepting the reading ὅτι; the alternatives (ὅτε, ἐπεί) do not affect the point under discussion.

passages beyond the fact that each refers to a stone. In 1 Pet. 2: 4, 6, 8 the same passages are used (with the addition, in verse 7, of Ps. 118:22). Now it is possible that Paul and Peter independently set out to collect possibly messianic passages containing the word *stone*; it is possible that Peter had read, and borrowed from, Romans; but it is at least a reasonable hypothesis (though it can hardly be more than this) that Paul and Peter independently drew upon a ready-made collection of messianic texts, in which one subdivision was 'Christ as the Stone'.

It is perhaps more important to note that Paul raised in the sharpest form the Christian problem of the Old Testament (see p. 393). The use he made of the Old Testament is credible only on the part of one who believed it to be the word of God, whose authority must always be reverenced. This is backed up by explicit statements. It was the greatest privilege of Israel that they were entrusted with the oracles of God (Rom. 3: 1 f.). The law itself was holy, and the commandment it contained was holy, righteous, and good (7: 12). It was spiritual, that is, inspired by God's Spirit (7: 14). Yet it was also true that the Law was now fulfilled and completed: Christ was the end of the Law (10: 4). Moreover, Christians by definition were men who were no longer under the Law (6: 14 f.), which was unable to modify the covenant of promise, grace, and faith, which God had established—long before the Law was given—as the basis of his relation with his people (Gal. 3: 17). This paradox lies at the heart of Christianity, and Paul is content to leave it with his readers. Later generations were to demonstrate their inferior grasp of Christian truth by attempts to cut the knot of the problem—Barnabas, for example, by allegorising the gospel out of the most unlikely pieces of the Law, Marcion by rejecting the Old Testament altogether. Paul could not have accepted either of these expedients, and his example may suggest to theologians a wise caution. It will be better to hold firmly both elements of the problem than to eliminate either of them, or to be satisfied with too easy a synthesis.

(iv) *Hebrews*[1]

The origins of the allegorical method of interpreting a sacred text were discussed above (pp. 378 f.). It has often been maintained that Hebrews

---

[1] See C. K. Barrett, 'The Eschatology of the Epistle to the Hebrews', in *The Background of the New Testament and its Eschatology*, ed. W. D. Davies and D. Daube (Cambridge, 1956), pp. 363–93, especially pp. 391 f.

is a Christian attempt to apply this method to the Old Testament, and it is true that there are passages in Hebrews that suggest this view. The earthly tabernacle is described as a *parable* (9: 9); the true tabernacle is not made with hands, and is not of this creation (9: 11). It follows that whereas the copies of the heavenly things must be cleansed by the blood of bulls and goats and the like, the heavenly things themselves can be cleansed only by better sacrifices (9: 23), and that Christ did not enter into a man-made sanctuary, a mere antitype[1] of the true one, but into heaven (9: 24). The Law thus had a shadow of the good things to come (10: 1). It is however only on the surface that these passages suggest the Stoic method of allegory, and the Platonic contrast between the world of phenomena and the world of heavenly reality. The author's intention (especially in its relation to the Old Testament) is given by chapter 8, which contains in a long quotation from Jer. 31: 31–4 the prophecy of the new covenant; and the significance of *new* is underlined. 'If the first had been faultless, no place would have been sought for a second' (8: 7). 'By saying *new* he has antiquated the first; and that which is antiquated and growing old is near to disappearance' (8: 13). The theme of Hebrews is in fact not the relation between contrasting but parallel worlds of phenomena and reality, time and eternity, but (as with the rest of the New Testament) the fulfilment of Old Testament prophecy in time. Some of the verses quoted above themselves make this point. The tabernacle is a parable *for the present time* (9: 9). The Law had a shadow of good things *to come* (10: 1). Christ as the high priest now remains continuously in heaven until the time of his second coming (9: 28), but his self-offering, and his appearance before the Father in heaven, though in a sense they represent eternal truths, were once-for-all acts (e.g. 9: 24, 26). In its use of the Old Testament, Hebrews is nearer to common Christian usage than has sometimes been supposed.

Like Paul, the author of Hebrews also demonstrates the paradox that is involved in the Christian use of the Old Testament, but does so in a different way. We have already noted his conviction, which he shares with New Testament writers generally, that in Christ the promises and prophecies of the Old Testament were fulfilled. Yet in his account of faith he turns without hesitation to the Old Testament, and produces from it a long list of men and women who lived by faith.

---

[1] Hebrews appears to use τύπος of the original, ἀντίτυπος of the copy.

He agrees that they were seeking a homeland they had not found and did not yet possess (11: 14 ff.), and makes the claim that in his dealings with them God had in mind some better thing for us, so that they could not reach their goal independently of us (11: 40); yet he can say that Christians too are seeking the city that is not yet here but is still to come, and represent their life as a pilgrimage, or race, conducted in faith and hope (12: 1; 13: 14). He thus exposes himself to the questions, What difference did the coming of Christ make? What is the difference between life under the old covenant and life under the new?

The difference lies in the objective act of cleansing (1: 3) and atonement (2: 17) made by Christ, who, in his death, discovered eternal salvation for men (9: 12), and set them free from death and the devil (2: 14). Though they must still live by faith they have an assurance (10: 22), an anchor (6: 19), which Old Testament believers could not have. The pattern of the life of faith is the same in the New Testament as in the Old; but it is marked out more clearly, and there is no doubt of the goal to which it leads.

THE NEW TESTAMENT AND THE OLD

There is no single term that adequately describes the relation in which the New Testament stands to the Old. There is no doubt that New Testament writers viewed the Old as prophecy, and interpreted it as such; that is, they understood the Old Testament to predict certain events, which had duly taken place in the experience of Jesus or of the Church. There is no doubt that they employed the Old Testament also in a variety of ways that may be brought together under the term 'allegory'; that is, they believed that the Old Testament, or parts of it, contained hidden meanings that had been concealed from earlier generations but had now come to light with the Christian revelation.

It may be that along with these 'prophetic' and 'allegorical' interpretations of the Old Testament should be set a third, the typological. This may be distinguished from the other two in that it seeks correspondences between persons and events not (as allegory does) in meanings hidden in language but actually in the course of history, and looks not to the fulfilment of a prediction, but to the recurrence of a pattern.[1] The distinction is useful, but it is probably true that the most

---

[1] For this definition see H. Nakagawa, in *RGG*, VI (1962), 1095.

characteristic New Testament estimate of the Old sees in it a combination of typology and prophecy. The New Testament writers do see recurrence of patterns of divine activity (since the God of the Old Testament is also, in their belief, the God and Father of the Lord Jesus Christ); but the event of Jesus Christ, itself the fulfilment of the Old Testament as a whole (cf. 2 Cor. 1: 20), is for them so final and radical that after it no pattern could be simply reproduced.

It is doubtful whether any New Testament writer ever formulated for himself the question, What is the authority of the Old Testament? So far as they were Jews the question was one that could take care of itself. Of course, the Old Testament had the authority of the voice of God himself. This attitude was adopted in turn by Gentile converts to Christianity. Yet the attitude of Christians to the Old Testament was not the same as that of Jews. The change in attitude can be seen in a variety of lights: it was due to a new outburst of prophecy, which brought the interpreters nearer to those whom they interpreted; it was due to a new exegesis, which saw in the Law the end of a legal relationship with God; it was due above all to the conviction that Jesus himself was the fulfilment of the Old Testament, and thus the living and abiding word of God. Out of this complicated but creative attitude to the Old Testament scriptures a new scripture was born, in testimony to the incarnate Word.

CHAPTER V

THE BIBLE IN THE EARLY CHURCH

13. BIBLICAL EXEGESIS IN THE EARLY CHURCH

PRIMITIVE CHRISTIAN EXEGESIS

The exegesis of the primitive Christian Church was a direct and unself-conscious continuation of the type of exegesis practised by ancient Judaism in its later period. This Jewish exegesis had a number of traditional methods and characteristics which can all be recognised without difficulty when they are reproduced in early Christian exegesis, and some of them can be identified in the New Testament itself. The most important function performed by exegesis in ancient Judaism was the interpretation of the Law (Torah). The rabbinic schools set themselves the task of making the large collection of legal enactments, sagas, myths, stories, histories and cult material, which we call the Pentateuch, into a code of law capable of covering the whole life, inner as well as outer, cult as well as conduct, of communities of Jews living under quite different circumstances and in a much later age. In order to achieve this formidable task, they found it necessary to produce a complex and flexible technique of exegesis. Inconsistencies in the biblical text had to be explained away; errors, redundancies, absurdities, or anything shocking, indecent or unworthy of divine inspiration had to be removed. Every verse was regarded as potentially independent of the others and capable of interpretation without any reference to its context. It was necessary largely to ignore the historical background. Rules were made whereby the natural, historical sense of any text could be evaded, and sometimes a quite unnatural, symbolic sense could be read in. A cautious, Torah-directed form of allegory was born. Several examples of it can be found in the New Testament.[1]

The discovery of the Qumrân literature has opened to us another type of Jewish exegesis, the list of proof-texts. We can find this form in the *pēšer* treatment accorded to the book of Habakkuk and in the list of messianic proof-texts discovered in the caves above Qumrân.

---

[1] E.g. Gal. 4: 21–31; 1 Cor. 9: 9, 10. See IV, 12 for a fuller discussion.

That the early Christians used this 'proof-text' type of exegesis in the interests of their own messianic ideas is evident on almost every page of the New Testament. Then there was the tradition of *midrash*, the composition of edifying or doctrinaire enlargement or embroidery upon the text of sacred scripture, in the form of anecdote or of narrative or of the addition of circumstantial detail. This can be found in the Old Testament itself, in books such as Tobit, Esther and the History of Susannah, in many details in the books of Chronicles, and in the Genesis Apocryphon of the Qumrân literature. Traces of it can be found in the New Testament, e.g. in Stephen's speech in Acts 7 and at 1 Cor. 10: 2–4. This tradition of *midrash* may have influenced some of the early Judaeo-Christian apocalypses written pseudonymously under such great names as those of Enoch, Isaiah and Baruch, which have mostly survived in only a fragmentary form.

The early Christian Church, then, took over existing traditions of exegesis. But of course it used them for its own purposes, and this necessarily gave them a different appearance. The Christians were concerned to identify Jesus of Nazareth as the Messiah and to show that the last times had arrived with him. One of the results of this was a shift of emphasis from the Torah to the Prophets. It was difficult to find a specifically Christian interpretation of the ordinances of Leviticus, Numbers and Deuteronomy, even when the effort was made to use traditional methods in order to turn them into predictions of the Messiah and his Church. But the Prophets were much more promising material as sources of Christian doctrine, and could be made to yield all sorts of striking anticipations of Christ and his Church, again by traditional methods. The historical books were open to typology. This is a method of reading Christian significance into both events and persons in the Old Testament by seeing them as foreshadowings or types of Christ or of the events connected with his work and career. There is sufficient evidence from rabbinic messianic interpretation and from Jewish liturgy to assure us that this practice too had its roots in pre-Christian Judaism. Then the Psalms could be turned into a source of Christological ideas, as the Epistle to the Hebrews above all other books of the New Testament witnesses, by the device of allotting different passages in a number of suitable Psalms to different speakers or *personae*, one passage being attributed to God, another to Christ, yet another to the Church, and so on. This too had its Jewish antecedents:

the Jewish interlocutor in Justin's *Dialogue with Trypho* does not object to Justin handling the Psalms in this way, but only desires to substitute a different list of *personae* in them for Justin's; and rabbinic interpretation of the Song of Solomon along these lines can be traced to the first Christian century.

By far the greater part of Christian exegesis for a hundred and fifty years after the resurrection is of course exegesis of the Old Testament. There are some references to the words of Jesus, as when the *Didache* applies the *logion*, 'Give not that which is holy to the dogs' to the eucharist.[1] But the main exegetical preoccupation of the writers of this period is to show that the Law and the Prophets and the Writings are fulfilled in Jesus Christ, that they find their ultimate significance in him. The author of 1 *Clement*, in the tradition of that hellenistic Judaism which drew much of its inspiration from Stoicism, ranges over the Old Testament to find examples of good and bad conduct applicable to the Church of his day, and finds a prediction of the contemporary form of Christian ministry, not in the old Jewish priesthood, but in a passage of Isaiah,[2] and he sees a prediction of the blood of the Lord in Rahab's scarlet thread (13: 7 f.). The author of the *Epistle of Barnabas* devotes much space to a Christianisation of the Torah influenced by Alexandrian Judaism, but not by Philo. He reproduces an allegorisation of animals forbidden and permitted in the food-laws of the Torah obviously modelled on that of the *Letter of Aristeas*:[3] the 'good land' of Exod. 33: 1, 3 means Christ in the flesh;[4] the placing of the wool originally bound round the scapegoat on a thorny shrub is a type of Jesus.[5] And he expounds the mystical significance of biblical numbers,[6] again reproducing a Jewish tradition of exegesis. The author of 2 *Clement* sees in the 'den of robbers' of Jer. 7: 11 a figure of those who do not do the Lord's will and in Gen. 1: 27, describing God's creation of man and woman, sees Christ and the Church.[7]

This primitive Christian exegesis, with its cautious and still very Jewish allegory and its richly developed typology, finds its fullest and ablest exponents in two Fathers who wrote in the second half of the second century, Melito and Justin Martyr. Melito in his carefully constructed and highly rhetorical *Homily on the Pasch* draws out the

---

[1] Matt. 7: 6; *Did.* 9: 5.   [2] Isa. 60: 17; 1 *Clem.* 42: 5.
[3] *Ep. Barn.* 10: 8, 11.   [4] *Ibid.* 6: 8 f.   [5] *Ibid.* 7: 11.
[6] *Ibid.* 9: 8.   [7] 2 *Clem.* 14: 1–5.

analogies (or the fancied analogies) between the death and resurrection of Christ on the one hand, and on the other the events of the institution of the Passover and the Exodus from Egypt. His typology constantly lapses into allegory. He finds types of Christ, not only in the events associated with the Exodus, but all over the Old Testament, in Abel, in Isaac, in Joseph, in David, as well as in Moses and in the paschal lamb. Justin's exegesis is much more developed than that of any Christian writer before him. Not only does he use traditional types and images from the Old Testament Christologically, such as that of Noah's flood[1] and that of the promised land (*Dial.* 119, 8), but he is prepared to identify any object or incident in the Old Testament as a prediction of the Christian dispensation. Almost any references to a stick or rod, e.g. Moses casting the stick into the waters of Marah, Aaron's rod, the oak of Mamre, the rod and staff of Psalm 23, are indications of Christ's cross (*Dial.* 86, 1–6). We find first in Justin many 'proof-text' passages which occur again and again in later writers. Moses holding up his hands to secure success in war against Amalek,[2] and a passage from Jacob's song before his death (Gen. 49: 10–12), in which the 'sceptre' attributed to Judah, the reference to Shiloh, the foal bound to the vine and the washing of garments in wine provide great scope for allegory.[3] Another is the text from Lamentations, 'the breath of our nostrils, the anointed of the Lord, was taken in their pits'.[4] Even the 'wild-ox' (Septuagint 'unicorn') mentioned in Deut. 33: 13–17 becomes a prefiguration of the Cross (*Dial.* 91, 1–4). Justin also develops extensively a line of exegesis which occurs only occasionally and somewhat obscurely in the New Testament,[5] the identification of various persons and speakers in the Old Testament with the pre-existent Christ. He sees, for instance, Christ as one of the people included in the plural number of the verb in the statement 'Let us make man in our image',[6] as the person intended on a number of occasions when the Bible said that God appeared to someone or went up from someone or went down to see something, as one of the men who visited Abraham,[7] as the angel who wrestled with Jacob,[8] as the angel who

---

[1] *Dial.* 138, 2; cf. 1 Pet. 3: 20, 21. [2] Exod. 17: 10–12; *Dial.* 90, 4.
[3] *Apol.* 1, 32, 1–13, in a long list of proof-texts, and *Dial.* 52, 1–2; 53, 1–6; 54, 1–2.
[4] Lam. 4: 20; *Apol.* 1, 55, 5.
[5] E.g. John 12: 41; 1 Cor. 10: 4; 2 Cor. 3: 7–18. [6] Gen. 1: 27; *Dial.* 62, 1.
[7] Gen. 7: 16; 11: 5; 17: 22; 18: 1, 16, 21, 33; Exod. 6: 29. Cf. *Dial.* 56, 2–10; 57, 2; 58, 10; 59, 1; 60, 1; 61, 1; 127, 1–5. [8] Gen. 32: 22–30; *Dial.* 58, 6, 7.

appeared to Moses in the Burning Bush,[1] and so on. This type of interpretation was to have a long and vigorous history in later Christian
tradition. Justin also raids the Wisdom Literature to discover Christological material in the Old Testament. Not only does he exploit fully
the tradition of allotting *personae* in the Psalms, explicitly admitting
the suitability of this practice,[2] but he is the first to seize upon a text
which was later on to be at the centre of the Arian controversy. He
gives to Prov. 8: 22, 'The Lord possessed me (Septuagint 'created me')
in the beginning of his way', a Christological interpretation.[3] In this
he was followed a little later by the apologist Athenagoras.[4] Finally,
Justin supplies us with material (almost all of it consisting of proof-
texts) for reconstructing the early Christian tradition of explicitly
anti-Jewish exegesis. This material was destined to recur, little changed
or supplemented, in many anti-Jewish treatises during the next two
hundred years. We can find it in Tertullian's *Adversus Iudaeos*, in
Cyprian's *Testimonia*, even in parts of Athanasius' *De Incarnatione*,
and in many works by less famous authors.

Towards the end of the second century we find the beginnings of a
distinctive exegesis of the New Testament comparable to that which
Christians were already practising on the Old Testament. The New
Testament had by this time almost won its way to recognition as a
document possessing equal authority with the Old; writers are by
now beginning to quote it and refer to it more frequently and confidently than hitherto. But we may regard as certain the conclusion
that the New Testament was first subject to allegorising, not within
the bounds of the Catholic Church, but among the heterodox gnostic
sects which flourished outside the Church or only on its periphery, and
that orthodox Christian writers only adopted the allegorisation of the
New Testament by way of defence, in order to extract orthodox
doctrine from it.[5] The old idea, encouraged by Westcott and by
Harnack (who greatly exaggerated the influence and the significance of
Marcion), that the Gnostics rejected or wished to mutilate the books of
the New Testament, must be abandoned. The Gnostics on the whole
accepted such of the books of the New Testament as were in general

---

[1] Exod. 3: 4 ff.; *Dial.* 60, 4.   [2] *Apol.* 1, 36, 1.
[3] *Dial.* 61, 3–5.   [4] *Suppl.* 10, 3.
[5] This point, as regards the parable of the Good Samaritan at least, has been persua-
sively argued by W. Monselewski, *Der barmherziger Samaritaner* (Tübingen, 1967),
pp. 18–49.

circulation in the second century, and accepted them willingly, though they claimed the right to supplement them by their own secret traditions. It is among them that we can first discern the allegorisation of the New Testament. Tertullian tells us that 'allegories, parables and riddles' represent *par excellence* the heretics' way of interpreting the New Testament.[1] The Valentinians in Irenaeus' day regularly allegorised the parable of the Workers in the Vineyard.[2] The Gnostics interpreted the parable of the Foolish Virgins as referring to the five (deceptive) senses.[3] Carpocrates the Gnostic interpreted the sentence 'Thou shalt by no means come out thence till thou have paid the last farthing' (Matt. 5: 26) in an antinomian sense.[4] The Valentinians seem to have specialised in allegorising the Fourth Gospel.[5] The Naassenes, however, also allegorised this Gospel,[6] just as they allegorised the sayings of Jesus recorded in the Synoptic Gospels,[7] and the parable of the Sower.[8] Marcion himself violently rejected the use of allegory, but his disciples occasionally allowed themselves the use of it. They denounced the Jewish Law as 'an evil root' and 'an evil tree' (Matt. 7: 18)[9] and they interpreted the parable of the Unmerciful Steward to refer to the demiurge who is subject to evil passions.[10] We can observe the process of gnostic allegorising of the text of the New Testament taking place in the gnostic *Gospel of Philip*. This work interprets the 'wine and oil' poured into the injured man's wounds by the Good Samaritan as meaning their esoteric concept of *chrisma*,[11] and it gives its own gnostic meaning to the words of Jesus recorded in Matt. 5: 6 and Mark 15: 34[12] and to John 6: 53 f.[13] The Naassene Gnostics seem also to have specialised in producing an extraordinary jumble of texts from the Old Testament, the New Testament, Homer, Greek myth, and many other sources, allegorising freely in the process. For instance, they interpreted John 1: 3, 4 to suit their doctrine, and joined with it Gen. 44: 2, 4, 5, grotesquely allegorised, and a snatch from a drinking-song of Anacreon.[14] In this Clement of

[1] *Scorp.* 11, 4, *allegoriae, parabolae, aenigmata.*   [2] *Adv. Haer.* XI, 1.
[3] Tert. *De Anima,* 18, 4.   [4] *Ibid.* 35, 2.
[5] Iren. *Adv. Haer.* II, 11, 10.   [6] Hippol. *Ref.* V, 8, 4, 5, 6.
[7] E.g. Mark 10: 18 (par. Matt. 19: 17); see Hippol. *Ref.* V, 7, 26.
[8] *Ibid.* V, 8, 29, 30.   [9] Origen, *Comm. in Rom.* III, 6; *De Princ.* II, 5, 4.
[10] *Ibid. Comm. in Matt.* XIV, 13.
[11] *Gospel of Philip* (ed. Schenke), logion 117 (126); Luke 10: 34.
[12] *Ibid.* logion 69 (115–16) and 72 (116).   [13] *Ibid.* logion 23 (105).
[14] Hippol. *Ref.* V, 8, 4, 5, 6.

Alexandria, the most gnostic-minded of the Fathers, occasionally imitates them.

The Catholics responded to this gnostic enterprise by counter-allegory. The *Epistula Apostolorum,* a work of the second half of the second century which appears to come from the ill-defined frontier between Catholicism and Gnosticism, allegorises the parable of the Foolish Virgins: the five wise virgins are Faith, Love, Grace, Peace and Hope, and the five foolish are Knowledge, Understanding, Obedience, Patience and Compassion (foolish not in themselves but because they slept).[1] Tatian, an apologist writing in the seventh decade of the second century, quotes John 1: 5, 'the darkness comprehended it not', and interprets the text thus: 'the Word is the light of God, and the darkness is the uncomprehending soul',[2] an allegory reminiscent of the contemporary gnostic commentator Heracleon. Irenaeus allegorises the parable of the Good Samaritan as the fall of the human race among robbers (probably evil demons); the Lord had compassion on it, commended it to the Holy Spirit (presumably the innkeeper), gave it two pennies, with the image and superscription of the Father and the Son.[3] A similar allegorisation of this parable is found in Origen, attributed to 'an old man' (or 'a presbyter'), who may even be Irenaeus himself.[4] Here the injured man is Adam, Jerusalem is Paradise, Jericho is the world, the bandits are hostile powers, the Samaritan is Christ, the wounds are disobedience, the ass is Christ's body, the inn is the Church, and the Samaritan's promise to return refers to the parousia. Irenaeus also allegorises the parable of the Lost Sheep.[5] Tertullian (as we shall see) is no favourer of allegory, but even he admits that the passage about paying back the last farthing allegorised by Carpocrates could be taken to refer to slavery to the devil.[6] He tells us that the Catholics (at a period in his career when he is a Montanist, in opposition to them) thoroughly allegorise the parable of the Lost Sheep.[7] Hippolytus, at about the same time, allegorises the parable of the Unjust Judge: the judge is Anti-Christ; the widow is the Jews.[8]

The Gnostics, then, taught the Catholics to allegorise the New Testament. But this was not the only contribution which they made

[1] *Ep. Ap.* 43–45.   [2] *Oratio,* 13, 1, 2.
[3] *Adv. Haer.* III, 18, 2.   [4] *Hom. in Luc.* 34.
[5] *Adv. Haer.* III, 20, 3.   [6] *De Anima,* 35, 3.
[7] *De Pudic.* 7, 1–7.   [8] Hippol. *De Antichr.* 46 and 47.

to the history of Christian exegesis. We may safely credit them with two more inventions. Origen learnt from them some of his most revolutionary ideas about the transformation of primitive Christian eschatology. Irenaeus in one place remarks that to say that the heavenly and spiritual things which Christians enjoy are themselves types of other celestial things, and of another *pleroma*, is a typically gnostic idea.[1] But this is precisely what Origen does with his doctrine of the 'everlasting gospel' and the repetition in a higher form in the next existence or existences of all the main features of Christianity here and now. And generally we may suspect that Origen's habit of dissolving the eschatological language of the Bible into references to Christian experience, to the Christian's enjoyment of Christ or the Christian's spiritual or mystical life, was learnt from the same school. Further, there can be little doubt that the Gnostics invented the form of scriptural exegesis which we call the Commentary, even though Origen greatly expanded, developed and popularised it. The earliest Christian commentary on the Bible is the Commentary on St John's Gospel by the Valentinian heretic Heracleon, large fragments of which are preserved in Origen's own *Commentary on John*. Hippolytus' work on Daniel might be regarded as a Commentary, though it is better to class it as a series of expository sermons. But Heracleon's book appeared before this. We may consequently thank the Gnostics for one of the most fruitful and vigorous forms of Christian literature.

It will easily be perceived that it was possible for the men of the early Christian Church to interpret both Old and New Testaments in the way in which they did because they held a view of the text of the Bible which was essentially *oracular*. They were compelled, of course, to recognise that the Bible contained much history and that the gospels, for instance, at least on the surface had a narrative form. And generally speaking they respected both the history and the narrative. Even if the apocryphal gospels were anxious to add much edifying or appealing *midrash* to the story of Jesus, ultimately the Church did reject these gospels, partly because they were thought to mix narrative with *midrash*. Christian writers were also prepared to use the great figures of the Bible as examples and patterns of either good or bad behaviour. They were not always successful in choosing satisfactory figures for this purpose. The ancient Church, for instance, with almost complete

[1] *Adv. Haer.* IV, 32.

unanimity hit upon Job as the supreme instance of patience. This was nevertheless an attempt to use the Bible in its natural, unforced, original meaning. With the same intention, the early Christians would often use the sayings of the Wisdom Literature in their proper, gnomic sense, and used the Psalms as vehicles of worship and of individual devotion, employing them for that function for which they are most fitted and which has survived all the vicissitudes of criticism down to the present day.

But when all proper concessions have been made, it must be confessed that the early Christians did regard the function of the Bible as an essentially oracular one whenever they possibly could. The period in which Christianity grew up was one peculiarly favourable to oracles. The philosophical and cultural current had turned away from rationalism and ran towards an interest in the numinous, the mysterious and the miraculous. At the same time the old, immemorial sources of oracular wisdom had almost all fallen into decay. Delphi, Dodona, Delos, Ammon, Cumae were dumb. The time was in many respects ripe for a religion which claimed to possess mysterious, infallible oracles. Lucian in the second century sneers at the thaumaturgical adventurers who cashed in, or attempted to cash in, on the prevailing popular demand for mysterious supernatural communications, such as Peregrinus (who, it may be noted, went through a phase of being Christian) and Alexander, who ran a highly successful oracle in a small town in Asia Minor called Abounoteichos. But the reputations which these men gained and the popularity which they enjoyed are significant. The age in which the early Church expanded from being a tiny Jewish sect to being a universal religion was one that was interested in oracles, and the early Church found no difficulty in deciding that the Bible—and especially the Old Testament—was full of them.

It was the prophetical books and the Psalms which supplied them with their richest store of oracles. The Psalms exhibit many passages where the Hebrew is obscure and where even the perspicacity of modern scholarship cannot reconstruct the original meaning with any certainty. The early Church read these passages in a Greek translation which had been made by men who themselves often were not very good Hebrew scholars and who frequently followed the rule that in a case of difficulty logic and common sense must be sacrificed to fidelity to the original. Further, early Christian readers were obsessed with the conviction that the inspired writers must have known a great deal about Christ and Christian doctrine, and that the Psalms must represent in large part transcripts of conversations between God and Christ and the Church. The natural result was a great deal of gross misunderstanding and grotesque misrepresentation, some of which will be illustrated in later pages. We shall be content for the moment with only one example. Many early Christian writers, of whom Justin is the first, maintain that David wrote in one of his Psalms 'the Lord shall reign from a tree', and hail this as a particularly striking prophecy of the crucifixion. No such expression appears in any Psalm in either the Hebrew Canon or the Septuagint. We may conjecture that this illusion arose from some translator of the Psalms being faced with the phrase 'The Lord shall reign. Selah'. *Selah* is an expression occurring in some of the Psalms whose meaning is quite uncertain. It was probably unknown to this translator, who decided to transcribe it into Greek characters instead of translating it. If he had rendered this word as *xela* or even as *xyla*, it would not have been difficult for an earnest Christian reader to modify this into *xylou* and to add the preposition *apo*, thereby achieving the phrase *apo xylou*, 'from a tree', and manufacturing a prophecy of the crucifixion which was to be welcomed by Christian exegetes and finally even to find its way into Christian hymnody.

Very much the same conditions prevailed as far as the prophets were concerned. Here too there were many obscure passages indifferently translated, and in the case of this form of literature Christians had a peculiar interest in detecting Christological references. The writers in this case were prophets, predicters *par excellence*, and it was the duty of Christian exegetes to identify and clarify these predictions. That the utterances of the prophets had some reference to the circumstances in which the prophets were living was occasionally recognised, and occasionally their social and moral teaching is referred to and applied. But these aspects of the prophets were faint and insignificant in the minds of the early Christians compared with the predictive function which so deeply engrossed their attention.

We must, therefore, recognise that these were the presuppositions or, to be more honest, the limitations, which the early Fathers imposed upon themselves when they approached the Bible, and especially the Old Testament. No talk of the 'co-naturality' existing between the

Fathers and the scriptures and no admiration of the beauty or skill displayed in their typological and allegorical interpretation should be allowed to disguise the distorting effect which these ideas had upon their understanding of the Bible. And it should be recognised that the defects which have just been outlined were not confined to primitive Christian exegesis, nor can they all be laid to the account of Origen. They apply to the early as well as to the late period, they can be found in the 'Antiochene' tradition of exegesis as well as in the 'Alexandrian'. When Novatian, in his *De Trinitate* written in the middle of the third century, wishes to give a list of proof-texts for the status and functions of Christ, every single one of them is taken from the Old Testament.[1] Lactantius, introducing the prophets to pagan readers early in the fourth century, succinctly describes their function as *divinatio*.[2] Eusebius of Caesarea, writing for Greek-speaking pagan readers at about the same time, describes the messages given to the Hebrews from God through angels and by other means as 'peculiarly divine oracles... so that, inspired by God, they gained a vision of what was destined to happen as if it was present, and prophesied all things that were to happen to the race of men'.[3] He explicitly denies that the utterances of Moses and the prophets were concerned with contemporary history ('for they were not concerned with predicting matters which were transient and of interest only for the immediate future'), but dealt with a whole system of theology and Christology and with the remotely future coming of Christ.[4] In the same spirit Athanasius, in order to establish the eternity of the Son, can call as confidently on texts in Jeremiah to support him as he does on a verse from the Fourth Gospel.[5] Both are equally valid sources of Christian doctrine.

The method of identifying a second divine being in the Old Testament, in pursuance of these methods, was unsatisfactory and confusing enough. But confusion became worse confounded when any Father attempted to detect a *third* divine being there, in order to establish the existence there of the Holy Spirit. It was indeed a hopeless task, and few Fathers attempted it until the middle of the fourth century, and none very strenuously or methodically. Justin had identified the figure

---

[1] *De Trin.* 9 (pp. 29–30, ed. Fausset).   [2] *Div. Inst.* I, 4.
[3] *Praep. ev.* VII, 5, 1 (my translation).
[4] *Dem. ev.* V, *Praef.* 20–4 (my translation).
[5] *Orat. c. Ar.* I, 19; the texts are Jer. 2: 13; 17: 12 and John 14: 6.

of Wisdom in the Wisdom Literature with the Son, and the majority of the Fathers certainly followed this line. But Theophilus of Antioch identified it with the Spirit, and so did Irenaeus. Athanasius identifies it with the Son in his *Festal Letters* but with the Spirit in his *Letters to Serapion*. Irenaeus and Tertullian had spoken of the Son and the Spirit as the 'two hands' of God, explaining away thereby a frequent and embarrassing anthropomorphism in the Old Testament. Others had suggested that the 'beasts' which the Septuagint (mistranslating) had at Hab. 3: 2 placed on each side of God represented the Son and the Holy Spirit. But on the whole the ingenuity of the early Christian Fathers shrank from the task of establishing a consistent pneumatology by these exegetical principles, and their failure at this point was silently admitted until the much more satisfactory and realistic exegesis of the Cappadocian theologians in the second half of the fourth century changed the situation for the better.

One particular line of exegesis, however, which will illustrate not only the weakness but also something of the strength of early Christian exposition is worth studying in rather more detail. This is the interpretation of the Jewish Law. Very early on, the leaders of the Christian Church had decided that Gentile Christians must be exempt from observing the whole Torah, and in particular that they need not be circumcised. It is highly likely that until the Church emerged entirely from a Jewish into a Gentile milieu some ceremonial rules deriving from the Jewish Law were observed by Gentile Christians, even by Gentiles not living among or near Jews. But no attempt was made to observe the whole Law; after the Fall of Jerusalem in A.D. 70 it became impossible even for Jews to do so. The question gradually forced itself to the surface of the consciousness of the Church: what is to be done with the legal books of the Old Testament? They could not be abandoned nor suppressed in the spirit of Marcion. They could not be taken as literally binding. Yet most Christians felt obliged to regard the books of Exodus, Leviticus, Numbers and Deuteronomy as inspired scripture, to be treated with as much respect as the other books of the Bible and to be valued as oracular as much as they. The response of the writers of the Church to this dilemma took several forms. On the whole the commonest was to declare that the moral demands of the Law still applied to Christians but that the ceremonial precepts did not apply in their literal sense, and consequently should be allegorised. The earliest known explicit formulation of this view is to be found in the *Letter of Ptolemy*. Ptolemy was a mid-second-century Gnostic, and he wrote this letter to a female disciple of his called Flora. The fact that Ptolemy believes that the supreme God did not give the Law does not affect his claim to be the first exponent of this interpretation of the Law. His account of the subject is ingenious and surprisingly sensitive to historical fact. The Old Testament Law, he says, is composite. Some of it was given by a lesser god than the supreme God, some was added by Moses in order to prevent the hardness of the Jews' hearts from throwing over the Law altogether (and Matt. 19: 6 ff. is used to good advantage here). But the Elders (i.e. the rabbinic schools) contributed some of the Law also. Even the part that was given divinely was itself composite. There was the unchanging, perfect part which the Saviour came to fulfil (e.g. the Decalogue). There was the part imposed upon the Jews to prevent them committing worse sins (which contained such commands as the law of retaliation which Christians must regard as wrong); this part the Saviour entirely abolished. Thirdly, there was the spiritual part, which was allegorically fulfilled by Christ—everything to do with sacrifice, circumcision, fasting and festivals.[1] A view very like this (though not necessarily borrowed from Ptolemy) is that of Tertullian. The laws about forbidden foods were intended to produce self-control in eating; the complicated regulations about sacrifices were designed to prevent the Jews indulging in idolatry.[2] The *works* of the Law are abolished. The law that remains is the moral law.[3] Irenaeus in his discussion of the Law in Book IV of his great work produces similar sentiments. One curious by-product of this attitude to be found occasionally in the early Church is the idea that the laws which Moses gave after he had broken the original tablets upon which the Law was inscribed were an inferior, second legislation, sometimes called *deuterosis*, concerned only with sacrifices, feasts and ceremonies which are no longer binding. We find this idea hinted at in Ptolemy's letter,[4] and explicitly taught in the *Didascalia*, a work of the third century originating from Syria.[5]

We can also find several statements to the effect that all the Law is to be allegorised, because the Christian is freed from the yoke of the Law.

---

[1] *Ep. ad Floram* (PG, VII, 1281–1288; ed. G. Quispel, Paris, 1966, 4, 1–5, 15).
[2] *Adv. Marc.* II, 18, 2, 3. [3] *Ibid. De Pudic.* 6, 3, 4.
[4] *Ibid.* (PG, VII, 1285, ed. Quispel, 4, 8, 9).
[5] *Didasc.* (ed. and tr. R. H. Connolly), II, 12, 14; IV, 34; IX, 99; XXVI, 216–20.

Love, says Irenaeus, supersedes the 'wordiness' of the Law, and Christians do not need a prohibition against adultery or murder or coveting.[1] Novatian, while allowing that the ceremonial laws were intended to discipline the Jews, insists that now for the Christian all the Law is to be allegorised.[2] All the precepts of the Jewish Law, Lactantius maintains, 'were given in the form of a riddle so that they might be recognised as spiritual by means of the symbolism of fleshly things'.[3] Eusebius and Athanasius, though they have had the advantage (if advantage it be) of knowing Origen's more complex theories about the Law, echo the sentiments of Tertullian. The Law taken in its literal sense was intended for the Jews only. It now has to be allegorised.[4] Alongside these theories, however, and often among the same authors, there appears an interesting doctrine of which Clement of Alexandria and Origen were to make much more, that the Law had for the Jews an educative as well as a constraining function. For Irenaeus the Law provided, among other things, elementary moral and religious principles which Christ rather deepened and enlarged than repealed.[5] Tertullian can similarly say that the gospel is only distinguished from the Law 'because it marks progress from the Law, as something different from it but not foreign to it, distinct but not opposite'.[6] Eusebius can use very similar language.[7] Finally, many writers acknowledge that Christians do in fact have in some sense a law of their own and sometimes envisage the Old Testament as contributing to this law. We can find this conviction reflected in Tertullian's determined but unsuccessful attempts to transform the Sermon on the Mount and Paul's epistles into a system of law, in the tendency of the *Didascalia* to call on the Old Testament to contribute both to its ethics and its ecclesiastical law, in Cyprian's declaration that when God saved man through Christ 'he gave him a law in his restored state and ordered him to sin no longer, and also arranged that sin could be atoned for by good works',[8] in the *Canonical Letter* of Gregory Theodorus in the middle of the

---

[1] *Dem.* LXXXVII, 96. [2] *De Cib. Iud.* 3–7.

[3] *Div. Inst.* IV, 17: *per ambagem data sint ut per carnalium figuram spiritalia noscerentur.*

[4] Eus. *Praep. ev.* VII, 8, 39–40; *Dem. ev.* I, 3, 1, 2, 41, 42; I, 4, 6; Athan. *Festal Letters*, 19 (ed. and tr. Williams, pp. 119–27).

[5] *Adv. Haer.* IV, 17–28.

[6] *Adv. Marc.* IV, 11, 11: *dum provehitur ab lege, aliud ab illa sed non alienum, diversum sed non contrarium.* [7] *Dem. ev.* I, 6, 63–71.

[8] *De Op. et El.* I: *legem dedit sano et praecepit ne ultra iam peccaret.*

third century which draws extensively upon the Old Testament (and not least upon Leviticus) in the process of tidying up the bishop's see after the moral havoc caused by Gothic raids, and in the conviction of Lactantius that Christ has brought a new, eternal, law.[1] Gregory's letter can be said to mark the beginning of canon law, to be carried on in the next century by the canons of councils and by such documents as Basil's three *Canonical Letters*.

THE DEVELOPMENT OF EXEGESIS IN THE WEST

One of the most important new features in all Christian exegesis from the end of the second century onwards is the acceptance by the Church of the Fourth Gospel as fully authoritative. This Gospel was first used widely and confidently in gnostic circles, by Basilides (*c.* 130), by the *Gospel of Truth* (? *c.* 145), by Ptolemy, by Heracleon. It perhaps influenced some of the fragmentary apocryphal gospels recently found on papyri in Egypt. But recognition by the great Church came only slowly. Justin clearly knows the Gospel, but clearly does not give it equal authority with the others. Tatian and Theophilus of Antioch quote it but do not use it freely or extensively. No doubt its popularity in gnostic circles caused churchmen to be cautious about accepting it. It is Irenaeus who first uses John's Gospel without any restraint or caution. Indeed, he is careful (perhaps too careful to carry conviction) to supply it with an apparently unimpeachable chain of witness to its apostolic authorship. He was the first writer to realise—and it is a testimony to his penetration that he did so—that, far from being a gnostic document as it might appear at first sight to be, the Gospel is in fact a most effective weapon against the Gnostics. He accepted it wholeheartedly as authoritative. He quoted it frequently in his great work. His thought was deeply influenced by it. It is largely owing to the impact upon his mind of the Fourth Gospel that Irenaeus can be regarded as the first great theologian produced by the Christian Church. Henceforward it can almost be said without exaggeration that Christianity will be Johannine Christianity. And henceforward it is inconceivable that the doctrine of the Logos could be suppressed or abandoned as long as Christians are seeking for a Christology.

In most exegetical matters, however, Irenaeus is conservative and

[1] *Div. Inst.* IV, 17.

traditional. He is no lover of extravagant allegory. He reproduces many of the traditional examples of typology, such as Jonah being swallowed by the whale, though he does not refer this story to Christ's abode in the tomb, but to man's being swallowed by the devil, so that God through Christ should raise him up out of mortality into salvation.[1] The serpent in the wilderness (Num. 21: 8) was a type of Christ.[2] He excuses the daughters of Lot for committing incest with their father, but also allegorises the whole incident.[3] He allegorises the two categories of hoof-cleaving and cud-chewing animals in a manner reminiscent of the *Epistle of Barnabas* and Pseudo-Aristeas before him.[4] But there are limits to his use of allegory. In chapters 39–41 of the second book of *Adversus Haereses* he seems to be appealing to the ordinary, simple, obvious interpretation of the text of the Bible against the Gnostics' preference for the most recondite and far-fetched interpretations. And in one place he says that if anyone were to suggest that what the apostles said about God should be allegorised he would be quite wrong.[5]

Tertullian exhibits the same restraint, only to a greater degree. He will use traditional Christian allegory with moderation as when the Holy Land is allegorised to signify Christ himself.[6] But his experience of the allegorising practised by the Gnostics had made him wary of allegory as a general principle. He prefers the literal sense for the sayings of Jesus.[7] He does not give us any allegorisation of the food-laws of the Old Testament. He refuses to rely on the allegorisation of prophecies for his argument on behalf of corporeal resurrection.[8] In his late work *De Pudicitia* he formulates the dictum: 'But we prefer to find less meaning in the Bible, if possible, rather than the opposite',[9] and in his earlier *Adversus Marcionem* he had applied this rule admirably. This last work is indeed one of the finest pieces of scriptural exposition in Christian antiquity. He even understands the necessity of accepting the embarrassing particularity of the Old Testament revelation, including sacrifices, ceremonial purification and circumcision.[10] He insists more than once upon the necessity of taking passages

---

[1] *Adv. Haer.* III, 20, 3.   [2] *Ibid.* IV, 2.
[3] *Ibid.* IV, 48, 1.   [4] *Ibid.* V, 8, 2.
[5] *Ibid.* III, 12, 14.   [6] *De Res. Mort.* 26, 11.
[7] *De Anima*, XXXV, 2.   [8] *De Res. Mort.* 26, 1.
[9] *De Pudic.* 9, 22: *sed malumus in scripturis minus, si forte, sapere quam contra.*
[10] *Adv. Marc.* V, 5, 10.

in their context.[1] In short, Tertullian displays a strong commonsense in exegesis which one wishes had been more contagious among ancient expositors than it was.

Hippolytus early in the third century continues the tradition of cautious typology and allegory. Here, as in many other points also, he is greatly indebted to Irenaeus and to Justin. For him the prophets are a fruitful source of Christological doctrine, though he also relies greatly on the Fourth Gospel. On Isa. 45: 14, 'God is with you only' (Septuagint 'God is in you'), which his opponent Noetus had taken as a proof of his own Monarchian ideas, Hippolytus comments, 'In whom then is God but in Christ Jesus the Word from the Father and in the mystery of the incarnation?'[2] Cyprian too, in the middle of the third century, exhibits much the same tradition of exegesis. His *Testimonia*, which certainly contains material that Cyprian rather re-handled than composed afresh, reproduces traditional types, such as Jacob anointing the stone and the conduct of Moses during the battle against Amalek.[3] Elsewhere he again refers to this last incident,[4] and to the story of Moses sweetening the water of Marah with a stick.[5]

The third century also sees an increasing tendency for Christian writers to look to the details of the cultic ministry in the Old Testament as support or prefiguration for the structure of ministry in the Church of their day. Irenaeus does not exhibit this tendency. He appeals to the same prophetic authority for the ministry under the new dispensation as had Clement of Rome before him, Isa. 60: 17,[6] and he allegorises the priests and Levites of the Old Testament to mean 'all the disciples of the Lord who used to profane the sabbath in the Temple and are without blame'.[7] Tertullian, on the other hand, when he writes about the authority of the Christian ministry tends to draw his illustrations and his proof-texts from passages about the cultic ministry in the Old Testament.[8] The Syrian *Didascalia* can ordain that the bishop must be without blemish in body, 'for it is written, "See that there be no blemish in him that standeth up to be priest"'.[9] It also applies to the bishop the text 'Thou and Aaron shall bear the iniquity for your

---

[1] E.g. *De Praescr. Haeret.* 8, 1–4; *De Fuga in Persec.* 6, 1; 13, 2; *De Pudic.* 7, 3; 8, 10, 11; 9, 2, 3.

[2] *C. Noetum*, 4 (*PG*, x, 808 and 809, my translation). [3] *Test.* II, 16.

[4] *Ad Fort.* VIII. [5] *De Zelo et Liv.* 17.

[6] *Adv. Haer.* IV, 41, 2. See above, p. 414. [7] *Ibid.* V, 34, 3 (my tr.); cf. IV, 17.

[8] E.g. *De Exhort. Cast.* 7, 1–4. [9] IV, 32; Lev. 21: 17.

priesthood'.[1] And it bases the duty of the flock to support the bishop with offerings on the command to give tithes to support the Aaronic priesthood.[2] Perhaps the same tendency can be observed in the vague references to the Old Testament ministry to be found in the consecration-prayer of the bishop given in Hippolytus' *Apostolic Tradition*. But it is Cyprian who achieves the greatest extension of this exegetical principle in the West. For him the Christian bishop is no more nor less than a sacrificing priest of the Christian cult modelled closely on the sacrificial cult of the Old Testament. Though he never reproduces the direct correlation, 'bishop–priest–deacon equals High Priest–priest–Levite', his letters and treatises are studded with innumerable examples of a direct appeal to the legislation of the Pentateuch to support and clarify the authority and functions of the Christian ministry.[3] In consequence Cyprian contributed immensely to the development of the doctrine of ministry in the West.

Considering the great expansion of allegorical exegesis which took place in the Eastern Church during the third century, inspired by the work of Philo who himself drew directly upon the allegory practised by hellenistic philosophers and literary men, it is surprising to discover how freely Christian writers during this period denounced pagan allegorising. Earlier, Aristides and Tatian, both apologists, had attacked the tendency of defenders of pagan religions to explain the more embarrassing myths by allegorising them.[4] But it is curious to find Arnobius, writing a century and more later than these authors, at a time when the work of Clement of Alexandria and Origen in applying a precisely similar type of allegory to embarrassing passages in the Old Testament was widely known in the East, rejecting pagan allegory with unabated fervour, unconscious of the weakness of his position. 'This is an ingenious evasion,' he writes, 'but obvious to any fool.'[5] 'How are we to know that these (passages) are to be allegorised? Why should we accept this interpretation? Do you know the intention of the authors of these stories better than they knew it themselves?'[6] Eusebius of Caesarea, who was a devout disciple of Origen and who did much to clear Origen's memory of the imputations which were

---

[1] *Ibid.* VII, 86; Num. 18: 1.   [2] *Ibid.* VIII, 80, 82–4.

[3] In his *Epp.* alone, 3, 1, 1–2; 4, 4, 3; 59, 4, 1 and 13, 5; 65, 2, 1; 67, 3, 2, 3; 73, 8, 1.

[4] Aristid., *Apol.* III, 7; Tat., *Orat.* 21, 2.

[5] *Adv. Nat.* V, 36: *urbana est illa subtilitas, sed quibuslibet brutis patens,* and see the whole passage.   [6] *Ibid.* V, 33; cf. IV, 33 and V, 32, 34.

being made against it even in Eusebius' day, is aware of the thin ice upon which Christian apologists trod when they attacked the use of allegory, but this does not prevent him from maintaining the traditional Christian attitude. He appeals to Philo, to Pseudo-Aristeas, and to the Alexandrian Jewish writer Aristobulus as predecessors and authorities in order to justify Christian allegorising of the anthropomorphisms of the Old Testament.[1] And he quite openly poses the dilemma that if we are not to allegorise such trivial details as the flies, the bees, the razor, and the head and the hair of the feet mentioned in Isa. 7: 18–21 (Septuagint), then the only alternative is the quite unacceptable one of falling back on 'incongruous and incoherent fairy-tales'.[2] He appears to think that this allegorisation is quite a different thing from the application of allegory to pagan cult-stories, which he attacks as vigorously as does Arnobius.[3]

The Western tradition of exegesis showed its conservatism and caution, however, in another direction, and that is in its treatment of eschatology. The writers of the New Testament, with the exception of a few of the latest, such as the author of the Second Epistle of Peter, had all in some degree written under the influence of what has been aptly called 'realised eschatology'. In some sense for them the Last Time had already arrived, and this conviction played a great part in forming their thought. The earliest Christian literature of all, that which under the tutelage of Daniélou we have come to identify as Judaeo-Christian, very largely consisted of documents which were in the form of apocalypses, of which the canonical Revelation of St John the Divine is only one example (though the finest). The fact that the *Didache* still preserves a lively expectation of an early parousia, reproducing the primitive Christian cry of 'Come, Lord',[4] has usually been taken as an indication of its early date. But as time wore on, and the expected parousia did not take place, it became essential to make some adjustment in eschatological thought. The extent to which this necessity was making itself felt is evident from 2 Pet. 3: 3–10. As far as the formal mythological language of eschatology was concerned, the first adjustment made was to push the expected eschatological events into the indefinite future. The delay of the parousia also had

---

[1] *Praep. ev.* VIII, 10, 11–17.

[2] *Dem. ev.* II, 3, 94; the words translated are ἀτόπους καὶ ἀσυστάτους μυθολογίας.

[3] *Praep. ev.* I, 9, 26; II, *Praef.* 2 and 6, 16; and in III see 2, 1–5; 3, 1–11; 6, 1–6; 7, 1–5; 13, 10–24.   [4] *Did.* 10: 6.

other important results which do not concern us here, but from the point of view of exegesis we should note that the usual attitude of second-century writers is to take a selection of the rich store of eschatological images, myths and predictions afforded by both Old and New Testaments and to produce a relatively logical and consistent scheme of what might be called eschatological history out of them. The second coming would be followed by the resurrection of the just, which would be followed by the general resurrection, which would be followed by the last judgement, and thereafter there would be a final relegation of good and bad to their respective destinies. Any of the events before the last could be envisaged as occurring in a different order. This is the type of eschatological exegesis to be found in Justin and in Irenaeus. Eschatological language, with one or two interesting exceptions to be noted later, was taken literally. Of course, it proved impossible to take this language with exact literalness (how, for instance, could eternal darkness co-exist with eternal fire?), and different writers sometimes favour different orders for these events. But the rather naïve and unreflecting intention to transmute all formal eschatology into futurist eschatology and to take it literally is obviously there.

The Western writers of the third century continue this tradition of eschatological exegesis very little changed. Realised eschatology in any formal sense has completely disappeared. Tertullian tells us that the kingdom of God supervenes upon the general resurrection.[1] He has a rather confused scheme whereby physical death delivers each person to a kind of waiting-room for eternity, different spatial areas being reserved for the two kinds of people awaiting different destinies, and thereafter the conventional eschatological history follows in an order which sometimes varies. This is not a purgatory, but a kind of ante-room to heaven or hell. Hippolytus' eschatology is likewise primitive and uncritical, as his work *De Antichristo* amply shows. Novatian has an eschatological structure very like Tertullian's, even to the 'place whither the souls of the good and bad are conducted, feeling already the sentence that anticipates the coming judgement'.[2] Lactantius has a not dissimilar structure. He appears to envisage a time of troubles and apocalyptic confusion, a millennial kingdom and then

---

[1] *De Res. Mort.* 50, 2.

[2] *De Trin.* 1 (p. 6): *locus enim est quo piorum animae impiorumque ducuntur, futuri iudicii praeiudicia sentientes.*

the general resurrection and judgement.[1] All the Western writers of the third century, including Cyprian, make it quite clear that they believe in a physical hell. Tertullian finds the thought especially consoling. There are particularly vivid descriptions of a material hell and a material Paradise in *De Laude Martyrii* (20–1), an anonymous work of the mid-third century wrongly attributed to Cyprian.

One particular feature of this interpretation of the eschatological language of the Bible deserves a closer scrutiny. This is the expectation of a reign of Christ with his saints on earth usually for a thousand years or for multiples of a thousand years. The scriptural support for this expectation is scanty; it is virtually confined to Rev. 20: 4–6. But the theory clearly had some support in Jewish apocalyptic ideas already in existence in the first century. Papias, the second-century writer quoted by Eusebius in his *Ecclesiastical History*, had apparently derived it from such sources as these. Justin champions this theory and declares that all right-thinking Christians hold it, though he admits that there are some who do not.[2] Irenaeus when he wrote his *Adversus Haereses* was a warm advocate of it. The faithful will enjoy material benefits (including good meals) in a physical Jerusalem (not merely a spiritual city) on a miraculously fruitful earth. He alludes explicitly to Rev. 20, and to Papias.[3] He refuses to allegorise the passages presumed to refer to this millennial kingdom. The theory survived vigorously in the thought of Western writers right up to the fourth century. It can be found in Tertullian,[4] in Hippolytus,[5] in Lactantius,[6] and in the conservative-minded and rather uncultured Victorinus of Pettau at the end of the fourth century.[7]

This naïve and uncritical literalism in the acceptance of eschatological images and predictions in the Bible is among the Westerns modified by only one curious doctrine. This is the view that the contemporary Church *is* Paradise and that references to an ideal state of nature at peace and man in Utopia to be found in the Old Testament are to be referred allegorically to the Church as an empirical institution. This idea is to be found in Irenaeus, who refers to it in his *Adversus Haereses*,[8]

[1] *Div. Inst.* VII, 15, 20, 22–6.   [2] *Dial.* 80: 5.
[3] *Adv. Haer.* V, 33, 1–5 and 35, 1–12 and 36.
[4] E.g. *Adv. Marc.* III, 24.   [5] E.g. *Ref.* X, 34, 3 and *De Antichr.*
[6] *Div. Inst.* IV, 12; VII, 2, 20, 24, 25.
[7] *De Fab. Mund.* 6, p. 6 (*C.S.E.L.*); *Comm. in Apoc.* 20, 2, pp. 140, 142, 144 (*C.S.E.L.*).
[8] V, 20, 2.

even though he holds it along with a belief in the millennial kingdom. By the time he wrote his *Demonstration*, later in life, however, he had positively substituted it for a belief in the millennial kingdom.[1] The idea is also to be found in Tertullian and Cyprian, and appears in an inscription over the door of the baptistery of the fourth-century church in Ostia. It becomes one of the alternative interpretations offered in the third and fourth centuries by those writers in the Eastern Church who dislike the idea of a millennial kingdom. It is perhaps worth noting that one of the by-products of a belief in the millennial kingdom was a tendency to undertake careful computation of the chronology of events both before and after Christ; the idea plainly gave an impetus to the learned consideration of the history of salvation. This is evident in the work of Hippolytus, of Tertullian, of Sextus Africanus and of Lactantius.

EXEGESIS AFTER ORIGEN

The revolution which Origen effected in Christian thought was perhaps most lastingly demonstrated in the field of eschatology. Eschatological exegesis in the Eastern Church after the work of Clement of Alexandria and of Origen, and especially of the latter, could never return to the primitive unreflecting literalism whose persistence in the West we have just been considering. Literalism of any sort was always abhorrent to Origen, and millenarianism was peculiarly so. He campaigned vigorously against it all his life, and the same determination to suppress it is evident in his ardent disciples, Dionysius of Alexandria and Eusebius of Caesarea. Dionysius wrote against the millenarianism of a certain bishop Nepos whose see fell within the sphere of influence of the bishop of Alexandria, and Eusebius lost no opportunity of denying this theory in his *Ecclesiastical History*, even allowing himself to describe Papias as a fool.

Origen's chief motive in attacking millenarianism, as indeed in his enterprise in transforming eschatology, was the desire to commend Christianity to pagans who were well educated in philosophy, and to reconcile Christianity with contemporary philosophy, or at least to give it a philosophical grounding. It was impossible to reconcile an interpretation of Christianity in terms of Greek philosophy (even a

[1] LXI.

perfectly genuine and legitimate interpretation such as Origen was undertaking) with an ultimately Jewish eschatological frame of reference in which eschatological language was taken literally. It is only because Irenaeus, Tertullian, Hippolytus, Novatian, Lactantius and the other Western Fathers had never made any serious attempt to come to terms with Greek philosophy (though many of them had used it and some had discussed it) that they were able to continue the traditional, naïve literalism in accepting eschatological language. Origen, who was the most sophisticated and philosophically well-equipped Christian writer of the first three Christian centuries, dealt with the eschatological language of the Bible in two ways. In the first place, following the example of the Gnostics, he tended to allegorise it into the moral or spiritual or mystical experience of the Christian or of the Church. In the second place, even though at times he wrote as if he really accepted the Bible's eschatological language as referring to events which would take place in the future, he placed these events in so vast a vista of the pre-existence of souls before entering the material universe and of their encountering an indefinite number of new existences on quitting this world, that he reduced the urgency, the dynamic, and generally the significance of eschatology almost to vanishing-point.

The effect of this remarkable revolution upon Eastern writers after Origen is obvious. Dionysius of Alexandria, writing on the subject of the book of Revelation in the middle of the third century, does not indeed want to reject the book as unauthoritative, even though he does not think that it was written by John the apostle. But he confesses that he cannot pretend to understand it and suspects that it should be allegorised.[1] He certainly has no intention of taking it literally. Eusebius of Caesarea in the course of his works evinces a predilection for two interesting substitutes for eschatology. In his books written before the Peace of the Church, i.e. the end of the persecution started by Diocletian and the recognition of the Church by Constantine, he shows a constant tendency to interpret references in the Old Testament prophets which earlier might have been taken to refer to the apocalyptic time of troubles or to the millennial kingdom in quite a different sense. He regards them as predicting events of concern to Christians in the history of the Roman empire, the universal peace which Augustus had

[1] *On the Promises*, II–V (pp. 111–25 ed. Feltoe).

established at the time of Christ's birth, the Fall of Jerusalem, the revolt of Bar-Kochba, the dispersion of the Jews and the spread of Christianity throughout Europe.[1] After the Peace of the Church he cannot resist interpreting scriptural references to eschatological blessedness as referring to the happy state of the contemporary Church under imperial patronage. It is significant that in Athanasius' *De Incarnatione*, a general commendation of Christianity written for pagans in the second decade of the fourth century, a reference to eschatological doctrine appears only briefly, at the end of the treatise.[2]

It was only because Origen had introduced a sense of expansion and flexibility into biblical exegesis that such sweeping alterations in thought about eschatology could take place in the Eastern Church. This enlargement of scope and increase of confidence which is visible in exegesis after Origen was largely achieved by means of the introduction on the part of the Christian Platonists of Alexandria of a new tradition of allegory. This tradition was derived by them directly from Philo, and he had borrowed it from the writers and the philosophers of the hellenistic age. The latter had forged it as an instrument for interpreting both the text of Homer and the traditional Greek myths in order to bring them into accord with later and quite different religious and philosophical thought, while retaining a respect for their immemorial authority. Philo had applied this allegorical technique to the text of the Greek Pentateuch and occasionally to other parts of the Greek Old Testament as well. He knew very well the rabbinic methods of interpretation of his day, including both typology and allegory, and was ready to use them when they served his purpose. But it was precisely in his exegetical intention that Philo had differed from the rabbis. Their intention had been to accommodate the text of the Torah to a viable code of conduct, worship and life for the communities of Jews of their day. Philo's purpose was to interpret the Pentateuch in such a way as to demonstrate its support for his own particular philosophy, a synthesis of Platonism, Stoicism and late Judaism, so as to commend it to Greek-speaking philosophically well-educated pagans who might show an interest in Judaism. His was a typically Alexandrian enterprise. In consequence the end-result of his allegory was quite different from that of the rabbis. The surest test to distinguish different types of

[1] E.g. *Praep. ev.* I, 4, 2–4 and 5, 1, 2, 4, 5, 7; *Dem. ev.* III, 7, 31–6; VI, 18, 28 and 20, 20, 21; VIII, 3, 14, 15. [2] LVI, 1–5.

allegory is not to observe the technique itself, which is usually arbitrary and subjective in any form, but to look at the sorts of ideas which the allegorised text is made to produce. Under Philo's treatment, the Pentateuch produced moral, psychological and philosophical ideas. His treatment was specifically anti-historical. He did not want to dissuade Jews from the literal keeping of the Torah, but he did want them to ignore the literal sense and to concentrate upon a meaning which was as far as possible from the plain, surface meaning taken in its context.[1]

When, therefore, Clement of Alexandria and Origen introduced Philo's allegorical technique into the main stream of Christian exegesis they were bringing in something quite new. They were not, of course, the first Christians to show any influence from Philo. We can trace his influence in the work of Theophilus of Antioch, perhaps in that of Athenagoras, and probably in the thought of Hippolytus (the attempt to attribute some of Justin's ideas to Philo must be judged to have failed). But neither Theophilus nor Athenagoras was more than marginally concerned with biblical exegesis. Clement and Origen introduced the Philonic tradition of allegory consciously and systematically, Clement with a tendency to somewhat naïve reproduction of Philonic ideas and even phrases, Origen in a more indirect and well-assimilated way, but all the more effectively for that. Both these authors, of course, retain much of the traditional earlier Christian typology and allegory, but they put it in juxtaposition with the new Philonic tradition, and sometimes they suppress it in favour of the new allegory. In addition to conservative, Jewish-type allegory such as we find in the *Epistle of Barnabas* and Irenaeus and Tertullian, and to the primitive Christological types, there is now introduced a basically hellenistic, anti-historical kind of allegory which is designed to produce from the text to which it is applied general truths of morality, of psychology, of philosophy and, in the hands of Clement and of Origen, of a system of Christian doctrine which is steadily becoming more elaborate. For instance, when Clement of Alexandria comes to allegorise the parable of the Good Samaritan, examples of the earlier allegorisation of which we have already seen,[2] he finds that Christ is the Good Samaritan, the good physician who heals the evil passions which the demonic powers inflict upon us as wounds; he pours 'wine, the blood

---

[1] See also pp. 379 ff.   [2] See above, pp. 417 f.

of the vine of David', into our wounded souls; he binds us with love, faith and hope; he orders angels to look after us and gives them a great reward.[1] There follows from this treatment of the text the theory of the 'special sense' and of the three meanings of scripture, and many other exegetical consequences.[2]

The result of this new tradition of interpretation was to make the work of biblical exegesis at once more flexible and less controlled. The old 'proof-text' method of interpretation gradually disappeared. Its place was taken by the Commentary which, as it undertook to comment upon every phrase, indeed on almost every word, of the text dealt with, found it necessary to rely upon a technique which was capable (or was deemed to be capable) of extracting a Christian meaning, or a meaning relevant to Christian faith, from any and every part of the Bible. And, conversely, any desired meaning could be read into the Bible somewhere by this method. It is instructive to read Eusebius' *Demonstratio evangelica* and to observe the ease with which he can find the doctrines of the philosophers, and especially of Plato, his legal and ethical as well as his philosophical ideas, mirrored precisely (or precisely enough to satisfy Eusebius) in the Old Testament. This new method was particularly well suited for a great age of doctrinal articulation and development such as the fourth century, for it gave exegetes a certain detachment from the biblical text and freed them from a narrow biblicism which might have stifled or restricted doctrinal development and reflection upon the faith. But of course this new Philonic or hellenistic tradition of exegesis also brought the danger of subjectivity. It had precisely the defects which Arnobius and others had rightly discerned in its ancestor, pagan allegory. In the long run this danger has proved so disastrous that virtually all exegetes have now abandoned allegory of any sort. And even in the fourth and fifth centuries the Antiochene tradition of exegesis existed as a protest against this subjectivity.[3] But when Philonic allegory first entered the main stream of Christian exegesis it must have appeared to most of those who met it as a liberating influence. We have already seen that Origen's exegetical work, of which this new tradition was the centre, produced a revolution in Christian thought about

[1] *Quis Dives?*, 29.
[2] See *Cambridge History of the Bible*, Vol. 2 (1969).
[3] Cf. v, 15.

eschatology at a time when some adjustment of thought in this field was imperative.

Another change which Origen's influence upon exegesis caused was a wholly beneficial one. He raised the academic level of exposition. The interpretation of the Bible in published books became as the result of his work a learned activity. If we contrast Justin's exposition with that of Eusebius of Caesarea, for instance, we shall feel that we are comparing an amateur with a professional, even though we may find the professional uncongenial and uninspired. Justin can childishly accuse the Jews of corrupting the biblical text in those places where the Hebrew differs from the Septuagint, and can make gross errors of chronology about the Idumaean dynasty. Eusebius in his weightiest theological works freely refers to the translations of the Old Testament made by Aquila and by others, and is ready on occasion to prefer these readings to those of the Septuagint. And he has a good acquaintance with Pseudo-Aristeas, Philo and Josephus, and a very special interest in chronology. Origen's work resulted, indeed (as Daniélou has remarked), in a loss of spontaneity, of the original immersion in biblical thought and continuity with the primitive Jewish tradition in exegesis, of what might be called the first fine careless exegetical rapture. But it gained in breadth of vision; commentators would now, following Origen's example, range freely over the whole Bible in order to illustrate the meaning of a word or an image. It gained in depth of scholarship, in methodical, almost scientific, approach. It represented a gain in confidence and in flexibility.

Perhaps one of the examples of a loss of spontaneity and of original, undimmed insight is provided by the attempts of fourth-century writers to explain the reason for the crucifixion. The earliest centuries of the Church scarcely saw any coherent doctrine of the Atonement emerging. This was apparently not one of those subjects whose development and articulation were called for by the conditions in which the Church grew and expanded. When writers begin to give a systematic exposition of the Christian faith they exhibit some embarrassment on this subject. Arnobius, for instance, finds it very difficult to explain why Christ should have been crucified, and can only suggest that he was fulfilling a secret divine destiny whose origins we do not know; he does, however, appear to approximate to the thought that Christ was providing an example of unresentful compassion and generosity and a source of comfort to all who suffer.[1] But he has no conception of the Pauline doctrine of the scandal of the cross; far from being the centre of his doctrine, as it is with all the writers of the New Testament, Christ's death seems to him rather inconsistent with the rest of his Christology. This is even truer of other writers of the same period. Eusebius of Caesarea explains the death of Christ quite carefully in his *Demonstratio evangelica*, but always on the assumption that Christ is the master of the situation and at no time displayed anything approaching weakness, and he is particularly careful to insist that the Word who had assumed the man had no contact with death.[2] Earlier writers, not as conscious of the necessity of upholding a doctrinal tradition as Eusebius, had been less nice on this subject; Melito had accused the Jews of being 'murderers of God', and Tertullian had used the expressions *crux Dei* and *mors Dei* and was prepared to produce the paradox of *credo quia incredibile*. Athanasius, who reproduces several of Eusebius' reasons for the death of Christ, is quite as blind as he to the biblical witness that the cross is a scandal and labours hard in his *De Incarnatione* to prove just the contrary. He had a very firm grasp of the centrality of the Incarnation, but he failed to relate it to Christ's death in any way that could do justice to the evidence of the New Testament upon this point. Like Eusebius, he is deeply concerned to remove any impression that Christ displayed weakness. Hilary of Poitiers, the first of the Western writers to assimilate and exploit the heritage of Origen in the field of exegesis, does at times appear to appreciate, if not the tragedy, at least the paradox of the Incarnation and Atonement,[3] but his determination to iron out the scandal of the cross and to present a Christ without weakness goes beyond even that of Eusebius and Athanasius. Christ, he says, felt the assault of suffering, but not the pain of suffering (*impetum passionis, non tamen dolorem passionis*); it was as if a weapon were to pierce water or fire or air.[4] Christ did display thirst and sorrow and hunger, but only for the sake of others, not to satisfy his own needs[5] (a near-docetist sentiment already voiced by Clement of Alexandria). He could not have been pained by wounds because he healed wounds; he could not have been sad because he regarded the cross as glory; he could not have seriously desired that the cup of suffering should

---

[1] *Adv. Nat.* I, 62. [2] *Dem. ev.* IV, 12, 1–9 and 13, 1–10.
[3] *De Trin.* I, 15. [4] *Ibid.* X, 23. [5] *Ibid.* X, 24.

pass from him because he said 'Shall I not drink the cup which the Father gave me?' (Mark 14: 36; John 18: 11); he could not have felt deserted on the cross, because he knew that he would sit at the Father's right hand and later return again.[1] Concern for philosophical consistency, for the preservation of the impassibility of the incarnate Word, has here removed from the gospel its deepest appeal, that which had been for Paul its burning centre.

The great subject for exegetical activity in the fourth century, however, was that provided by the Arian controversy. In one sense, the whole controversy was about the interpretation of scripture. The Church of the fourth century asked of the Bible the single question, 'How divine is Christ?', and the answer which it received was an extremely confused one. The reason for the confusion was, of course, because the New Testament does not, for the most part, speak or think in the terms which are assumed by the question. But nevertheless the answer, once raised in as critical and public a way as Arius and his opponents had raised it, had to be answered. The attempt of the Homoean party to refuse to answer the question, by producing or championing creeds which declared that the Son was like the Father 'according to the scriptures', was bound to fail. The undecided question was, *how* much like the Father was the Son according to the scriptures? Those who drew up the many creeds and doctrinal formulae which were bandied about during this controversy would have been horrified at the suggestion that they were developing dogma. They would have claimed that they were simply interpreting the Bible, or rather reproducing the substance of the Bible in different words. Inevitably therefore the Arian controversy put a severe strain on the capacity for exegesis possessed by the Church. It showed up in a strong light the weaknesses of the Church's exegetical tradition. We gain an impression sometimes of ignorant armies clashing by night, of two blindfold men trying to hit each other. But in the long and tangled course of the controversy the theologians did learn at least one useful lesson about the Bible, as we shall see.

It is clear from the work of Eusebius of Caesarea that the subject which formed the centre of this controversy had been agitating the minds of Christian theologians for some considerable time before the controversy broke out. Writing his *Demonstratio evangelica* before

[1] *De Trin.* x, 28, 29, 30, 31.

the end of the persecution of Diocletian, several years before Arius began to publish those views which were to be the formal cause of the controversy, Eusebius pays a great deal of attention to questions such as the nature of the substance (*ousia*) of the Son, and his exact relationship to the Father and whether he was begotten out of nothing and before time began. The texts which he uses to establish his own particular views upon these subjects are for the most part the kind of Christological texts from the Old Testament which had already been used many times by his predecessors to prove the witness of the Bible to a second pre-existent divine or semi-divine Being in addition to the Father. He is particularly fond of using a text, to which we have had occasion to refer already as used by Justin and Athenagoras,[1] Prov. 8: 22, and the whole passage which includes it,[2] though of course the Christological doctrine which he reads into this text is markedly different from that which either Justin or Athenagoras, or indeed Lactantius, who had used it also,[3] derive from it. The hand of Origen is very visible in Eusebius' account. It is indicative of the weakness of the exegetical principles adopted by the Fathers that these four writers, living at different times and in different places, could confidently quote exactly the same text in order to support four quite different Christological theories.

But what had been merely a traditional Christological text with Eusebius became in the hands of the Arians the great touchstone of orthodox Christology, the foundation-text upon which they built their theology. Literally taken, the Septuagint translation of the most important line in this all-important passage reads 'The Lord *created* me the beginning of his ways'. The Arian theologians insisted that this text must be taken in (as they thought) its straightforward, plain, directly theological meaning. The subject of this passage was the Son or the Word. Nobody of any party denied this. Here, then, the Holy Spirit was expressly declaring that God had created the Son. Therefore they were justified in teaching that the Son was a created divine Being, inferior to God the Father in his nature or essence, but created before all other created things and both anterior and superior to them. This insistence upon the plain, precise, grammatical meaning of the words of scripture was a characteristic of the Arians and it gave considerable

---

[1] See above, p. 416. [2] *Praep. ev.* VII, 12, 5; XI, 14, 2–10; *Dem. ev.* V, 1, 8, 9.
[3] *Div. Inst.* IV, 6.

trouble to the pro-Nicene theologians. It is possible that this particular tendency marks the beginning of the 'Antiochene' tradition of exegesis, which is otherwise not much in evidence up to the middle of the fourth century, for the great authority to whom the Arians appealed in the early part of the controversy was Lucian of Antioch, a theologian who had been martyred in the persecution of Diocletian. Another man who may have contributed to form this 'Antiochene' tradition is Paulinus, who was bishop of Antioch before the Nicene Council of 325, and who indeed died before it took place. He was the subject of an attack for his Christological views by Marcellus, bishop of Ancyra, his contemporary, an anti-Arian writer who appeared early in the field in the controversy, and who was destined to suffer permanent exclusion from his see from 336 onwards because of his opinions.

Marcellus has usually been dismissed by those who write about the Arian controversy as so unreasonably extreme in his Christological views as to be scarcely worth consideration. But recent study has tended to go some distance towards vindicating him. His most observable characteristic appears to be opposition to Origenism and beyond this to the whole Logos doctrine as it had been developed in the form both of economic Trinitarianism since Justin on the one hand and of a graded Trinity since Origen on the other. His alternative Christology is awkward, and ultimately in its refusal of pre-existence to the Son perhaps indefensible. But he gave to those who wished to defend the Nicene viewpoint some of their most useful clues about exegesis, by propounding a quite new and original interpretation of Christological passages in the Old Testament. He took all the traditional texts hitherto universally assumed to apply to the pre-existent Word to refer instead to the incarnate Word, and especially to the human nature assumed by the Word. Thus Prov. 8: 22 'the Lord created me' would become a prediction that God would create a human body for the Word to assume, and Marcellus ingeniously pointed out that the Septuagint in the next line read 'before the age', not 'before the ages', and so, he claimed, predicted the new age which began with the Incarnation.[1] In like manner he took the text 'Let us make man in our image' (Gen. 1: 26) which had at least from the time of Justin been taken to imply the existence of a second divine Being present at creation, as a metaphorical way of declaring that a new man must be created in Christ

[1] Eus. *Adv. Marc.* I, 4 (*PG*, 24, 761); also II, 3 (*PG*, 24, 801, 804).

incarnate. It is as if a sculptor were to make a statue; first he designs it in his mind, and then says to himself, 'Come, let us make a statue'.[1] He interpreted in a similar way Ps. 110: 3, which had hitherto been assumed to refer to the pre-existent Word,[2] and many other passages which had formed the stock-in-trade of traditional Christology. He roused thereby in Eusebius of Caesarea and in those who held similar Christological views an intense exasperation which contributed towards the loss of his see, but he provided a line of exegesis which was unanimously followed by the champions of the orthodox viewpoint in the ensuing controversy (e.g. Eustathius of Antioch, Athanasius, Hilary, Epiphanius, Gregory Nazianzenus, Didymus, Basil, and Gregory of Nyssa). He appears to have been dimly aware of the unsatisfactory nature of much traditional exegesis in the interests of Christology, even though his particular solution contributed little or nothing towards remedying it.

Athanasius himself, the great champion of the Nicene doctrine, had inevitably to deal with the master-text, Prov. 8: 22. Indeed, this text forms the subject of the whole of Book II of his *Orations against the Arians*. He fortified the approach of Marcellus with a few extra arguments. He was anxious to take the Greek word usually translated 'created' (ἔκτισεν) as meaning 'renewed' or 'appointed', and he asks the Arians why, if in Prov. 9: 1 'Wisdom has built herself a house' they allegorise (i.e. take metaphorically) the word 'house', they cannot allegorise 'created' in the other text.[3] He even maintains, following an argument produced earlier by Marcellus, that the text 'The Lord by Wisdom founded the earth' (Prov. 3: 19) refers to the Incarnation, the 'earth' being allegorised to mean the incarnate Word.[4] Athanasius had also to deal with those texts adduced by the Arians where Christ is described as apparently showing weakness, ignorance, or fear, for the Arians took these as demonstrating the truth of their doctrine that the Son was liable to change, and not impassible. To prove Christ's ignorance they produced Mark 13: 32, 'Of that day and hour knoweth no man, neither the angels nor the Son'. Athanasius declares that Christ's ignorance is only apparent. It is of the nature of the flesh

---

[1] Eus. *Adv. Marc.* II, 3 (*PG*, 24, 793–6).
[2] *Ibid.* I, 2 (*PG*, 24, 740); II, 3 (*PG*, 24, 808).
[3] *Orat. c. Ar.* II, 46, 55, 56.
[4] *Ibid.* II, 73, 74; see also 75, 76 and *Letters to Serapion*, 2, 8 ff.

to be ignorant, but in fact Christ was not ignorant. Christ knows everything as Word, but does not know as man, so that omniscience and ignorance coexist in his mind. Athanasius frankly admits that he cannot think why the man should be described as ignorant at Mark 13: 32. As for the fact that Christ supplicated God and asked him for glory (John 17: 5), another text alleged by the Arians to show the limitations of the Word, Christ already possessed as Word what he asked as man.[1] As for Christ's apparent display of fear, the Word was, of course, not afraid.[2] But 'God, who is impassible, assumed passible flesh'.[3] It was the intention of the Word by allowing his body to endure these experiences to show us how to overcome them. By his cowardice Christ removed cowardice and enabled men no longer to fear death, not that he endured as a man in spite of fear, but that as God he destroyed his own human fear and hence ours.[4] Another text much used by the Arians was Phil. 2: 9, 10, where Paul appears to say that the exalted Name was bestowed on Christ as a reward for his virtue, and that Christ achieved divine status rather than originally possessing it. Athanasius contends that Christ started as equal with God, and that the humiliation and exaltation refer to his human nature only.[5] Athanasius ought logically to have conceded to the Arians that Christ's human nature was passible and liable to change (τρεπτός), but he denies even this. He says that after having had Adam as an example of changeable human nature what we needed was an example of a *man* who was unchangeable, and that we had in Christ.[6]

We cannot avoid the conclusion that in arguments with the Arians based on the Synoptic Gospels and on Paul Athanasius came off worst. In arguments based on the Fourth Gospel, as might be expected, he did much better. Indeed, much of his case and, for that matter, much of Hilary's as well, consists of playing off the Fourth Gospel against the first three. He uses this Gospel more than any other part of the Bible to refute the Arians, transposing into terms of 'substance' and 'nature' the unity in relationship of Father and Son between the first two Persons of the Trinity depicted in John's Gospel. The two great texts to which he recurs time and again are John 10: 30, 'I and the Father are one', and John 14: 9, 'He who has seen me has seen the

---

[1] *Orat. c. Ar.* III, 37, 39, 40, 42, 43.   [2] *Ibid.* III, 54.
[3] *Ibid.* III, 55.   [4] *Ibid.* III, 56, 57.
[5] *Ibid.* I, 37–41, 44, 47.   [6] *Ibid.* I, 51.

Father'. He describes these as 'like a fortification against all (the Arians') impious doctrine'.[1] The unity expressed in these two capital texts cannot simply be a unity of will, of love, of obedience and harmony such as all creatures owe their Creator. It must be deeper—one of substance.[2]

Athanasius also had occasion in one of his later works, the *Letters to Serapion on the Holy Spirit*, to deal with the biblical evidence for the consubstantiality of the Holy Spirit. He was facing opponents who by this time acknowledged the full divinity of Christ but rejected that of the Holy Spirit. The great proof-text in this question, both for the Arians and for their successors attacked by Athanasius, was Amos 4: 13. Passages from Eusebius of Caesarea, Basil, Epiphanius, Didymus, Gregory of Nyssa, Ambrose and Cyril of Alexandria make it clear what profound importance was attached by both sides to this text. It was only by using the Septuagint version and ignoring the Hebrew that this could be considered a theological passage at all (Didymus appears to have been the only Father who appealed to the Hebrew, and he only half-heartedly). Literally translated, the Septuagint ran, 'Because, behold, I am he who strengthens the thunder and creates spirit (or 'wind') and announces to man his Christ' (the last word a mistranslation for 'thought'). Athanasius' opponents claimed that this was a direct testimony from scripture to the createdness of the Holy Spirit. Athanasius immediately counters this by asking why, if they could agree that at Prov. 8: 22 the word 'created' does not imply the createdness of the Son, they cannot agree that here the createdness of the Spirit is not implied.[3] He maintains that 'spirit' in this passage does not refer to the Holy Spirit and that the mention of Christ in the passage means a reference to the Incarnation and to the spirit of man renewed by this event.[4] We may pronounce him to have got the best of an argument vitiated by false premises. Elsewhere in this work Athanasius ranges effectively over the Bible and especially the New Testament to describe the function of the Spirit, though he never succeeds in satisfactorily *defining* that function in the work of redemption. He finds it very difficult, as Basil and Gregory Nazianzenus were to find after him, to discover any biblical evidence to determine either the status of the Spirit or his relation to the two other Persons within

---

[1] *De Synod.* XLV. [2] *Ibid.* XLVIII.
[3] *Letters to Serapion*, I, 3. [4] *Ibid.* I, 4–9.

the Trinity. At one point, following a line of argument first found in Eusebius of Caesarea, he calls in contemporary baptismal practice to supplement the argument from scripture.

Hilary of Poitiers is, as has been said, the first Western Father to have absorbed and profited from the influence of Origen, and his exegesis consequently tends to be more in the Eastern than in the Western tradition. But he is quite capable of originality and does not adopt the Easterners' ideas without intelligence. He can, for instance, produce the idea that the Burning Bush seen by Moses is a symbol of the Church under persecution, and he is apparently the first to do so.[1] He inevitably handles the text Prov. 8: 22 at great length. Indeed, the whole of Book XII of his work *De Trinitate* is devoted to it. But he handles it in an interesting and perspicacious way, avoiding both the Arian and what might be called the Marcellan interpretations. He denies that it has anything to say about the generation of the pre-existing Word, though it does describe the activity of the Word in the universe. The reference to God 'creating' Wisdom he takes, as had all champions of the Nicene faith before him, as signifying the incarnate Word. But Hilary adds an interesting development of this idea: the appearance of the Word as incarnate began with Christ's activity in the Old Testament, when he walked with Adam in the garden (Gen. 3: 8), when he spoke to Cain, to Abel and Noah, when he addressed Hagar (Gen. 16: 7–13), when he accosted Abraham (Gen. 18: 2), wrestled with Jacob, spoke to Moses in the Burning Bush, and appeared to Isaiah (Isa. 6: 1 ff.; John 12: 41), to Ezekiel (Ezek. 37), and to Daniel (Dan. 7: 13, 14).[2] Most of the texts supporting his view of the generation of the Son came from the Gospel of John, but he does throw in Isa. 53: 8 and Matt. 11: 25, 27.[3] The text in the Fourth Gospel which the Arians most revert to, John 14: 28 ('The Father is greater than I'), he thus explains: 'Who will not allow that the Father is greater as the ingenerate is greater than the generated, the Father than the Son, as he who sends than he who is sent, as he who expresses his will than he who obeys it?'[4] But he will not allow the text to touch the consubstantiality of Father and Son. Elsewhere he explains this superiority of the Father over the Son as referring only to Christ in

---

[1] *De Trin.* I, 30.   [2] *Ibid.* XII, 36, 44–7.   [3] *Ibid.* II, 10.

[4] *Ibid.* III, 12: *et quis non patrem potiorem confitebitur ut ingenitum a genito, ut patrem a filio, ut eum qui miserit ab eo qui missus sit, ut volentem ab eo qui obediat;* cf. VI, 25; VII, 6; IX, 2.

his human nature.[1] As for Christ's ignorance, the apparent examples of this weakness are only exhibitions of a deliberate strategy of pretended ignorance deployed for our benefit.[2] We have already seen[3] how disastrously Hilary dealt with Christ's demonstrations of fear. Finally, it is interesting to note that Hilary uses very much the same texts to prove the co-divinity of the Son with the Father as Justin, and his successors, use to prove the pre-existence of a lesser divine Being beside the Father.[4] Once again we are struck with the inefficiency of a set of exegetical principles which can extract quite different meanings from exactly the same texts at different periods of the Church's history.

Before we leave this subject we must note one more interesting fact. The Arians had insisted from the beginning upon the necessity of taking the plain facts of scripture at their face value, as they saw that value. This was not ultimately a question of literalism or allegory, but of literalism or analogy. What the Arians were insisting was that the Bible does not speak analogously nor symbolically about God, but directly. When it described God as the Father and Christ as his Son, it could only mean that, like all fathers in human experience, God at one point cannot have been a father and, like all sons in human experience, Christ at one point must have been non-existent before he was begotten by the Father. The pro-Nicene theologians gradually realised that this could not be true, that if it was true it made nonsense of the biblical doctrine of God, and that the Bible speaks of God in language which is analogous, symbolical, but nevertheless true. This was one of the exegetical gains of the Arian controversy, and it is reflected in the theology of the Cappadocian Fathers later. Children, say the Arians, cannot exist unless they first do not exist; sons do not exist before they are born. Athanasius answers: architects cannot make things except out of previously existing material, and men cannot exist except in a place. Do we therefore argue that God, who made the world, made it out of previously existing material, and that because God exists he exists in a place?[5] The Arians also objected to the complete identification of the Son with the Word, for 'a human word is composed of syllables and simply signifies the meaning of the speaker and at once ceases and disappears'.[6] Athanasius answers as before, 'But

---

[1] E.g. *De Trin.* IX, 51.   [2] *Ibid.* IX, 58–67.   [3] See above, p. 439.
[4] *Ibid.* IV, 23–31, 35–41.   [5] *Orat. c. Ar.* I, 22, 23.   [6] *Ibid.* II, 34.

God is not like men'.[1] Similarly on the subject of the Spirit Athanasius had to deal with opponents who maintained that if the Spirit proceeds from the Father the Father has two sons, and if from the Son then the Father is the Spirit's grandfather. He answers these fools according to their folly. But he adds that the Father is eternally and uniquely Father and the Son similarly Son; humans who are fathers but also sons and sons but also fathers are not so appropriately father and son.[2] Shapland in his commentary on this passage points out that Athanasius had no objection to using human analogies for the Godhead, but insisted that the analogies are to be checked by each other and their scope is to be determined by scripture.[3] Hilary uses similar language. God, he says, cannot be exhaustively described in language because he exceeds all language and makes nonsense or contradiction of language: 'the highest knowledge is, so to know God that you may know him as not unknowable but indescribable'.[4] He warns against pressing the analogy of human birth too far; when we begin introducing the conditions of human birth, the analogy breaks down.[5] Even the traditional illustration of the production of the Son as fire lit from fire has its limitations. These corporeal images and analogies are given to support our weak faith and dim understanding, but they do not fully correspond to God's greatness.[6] Athanasius states the matter weightily and succinctly in his *Letter to the Monks*, written in 358, and prefixed to his *History of the Arians*:

I have not even been able to write what I imagine I was thinking; further, even what I wrote was less than what was in my thoughts, fleeting shadow of the truth though that was. . . All the same, even if it is impossible to grasp what God is, yet it is possible to say what he is not. We do know that he is not like a man, and that it is not right to imagine that anything transitory (τῶν γενητῶν) is in him. Similarly in regard to the Son of God, even if we are by nature very far from capable of grasping him, still it is possible and easy to condemn the suggestions of the heretics and to declare that the Son of God does not correspond to these.[7]

This hard lesson at least had been learnt by the end of the Arian controversy.

[1] *Orat. c. Ar.* II, 35.   [2] *Letters to Serapion*, I, 15, 16.

[3] R. B. Shapland, *The Letters of St Athanasius concerning the Holy Spirit* (London, 1951), p. 99.

[4] *De Trin.* II, 7: *perfecta scientia est, sic Deum scire ut licet non ignorabilem tamen inenarrabilem scias.*   [5] *Ibid.* VI, 9; VII, 28.   [6] *Ibid.* VII, 29, 30.

[7] *Ep. ad mon.* I, 2 (my translation).

CONCLUSION

The story of early Christian exegesis of the Bible which has here been unfolded has shown that in the first two centuries exegesis was cautious and conservative, not departing very far from the text of the Bible, not venturing much beyond a 'proof-text' type of exposition. But with the third century a change set in, at least in the biblical interpretation of the Eastern Church, which reached the Western Church a century later. Undoubtedly Christian exegetes surrendered much too readily to the seduction of the enchantress allegory who promised them an intoxicating freedom. Philonic allegory allied with the essentially oracular view of the biblical text inherited from Judaism resulted in a system of exposition which, as far as discovering what the Bible really meant was concerned, was highly inefficient, and even as a means of reading into the Bible what the exegete desired to find there was so open to abuse as to be almost useless. The reader of patristic literature is at times tempted to conclude that their assumptions and methods in dealing with the Bible were so utterly different from ours that in the field of biblical exegesis we have nothing significant in common with them.

But before we rush to this conclusion there are several facts which we ought to consider. The Fathers of the third and fourth centuries who, mainly under the influence of Origen, developed the use of allegory so widely were faced with a difficult and unavoidable task. By about the year A.D. 220 it was no longer possible for a Christian theologian presenting the Christian faith to an educated public, especially a Greek-speaking one, to content himself with a cautious reproduction of biblical terms and an invocation of a long list of proof-texts by way of expounding Christian doctrine. The rule of faith was being enlarged, a system, or at least a body, of doctrine was being formed. We can find this process in Irenaeus, in Tertullian, and in Hippolytus, to name only a few. In these circumstances a certain emancipation from a very literal and pedestrian observance of the text of the Bible was not only commendable, but essential. The move from teaching the faith by proof-texts to teaching it by a body of doctrines necessitated in one sense placing the Bible at a certain distance, looking at the wood as a whole instead of being bewildered by an investigation of the individual trees. This the use of allegory enabled the Christian exegetes to achieve, even though the price paid for this inefficient tool was a high one. But also during the third century another transposition, not unconnected with the other, was taking place. The Christian gospel was being transposed from a basically Jewish frame of reference and form to a basically Greek frame of reference and form. Much ink has been expended upon this subject ever since Harnack and Hatch brought it into the limelight at the end of the last century, and much indignation has been wasted upon it too. The theologians of the Christian Church had in fact no choice. They had either to effect this transposition, as far as possible without loss of any essential part of the Christian faith, or to abandon the defence and commendation of Christianity. Allegory, a technique for emancipating the exegete from bondage to the text, certainly played a useful part here too. Deeper learning, a greater sophistication in handling ancient texts, and above all an uninhibited use of contemporary philosophy were the other factors which contributed to this transposition. But it cannot be denied that allegory proved a useful ally here, though, as before, an ally who exacted a high price for aid.

Our perception of the inefficiency of early Christian exegesis (and 'inefficiency' is perhaps a better word for it than 'subjectivity') should not blind us to certain fundamental virtues which in a rough and ready way the Fathers did display in their interpretation of the Bible. In spite of the radical and indeed revolutionary ideas which Origen was capable of producing in the field of Christian doctrine, the Fathers did preserve what might be called the framework of the message of the Bible, the doctrines of creation, of the choice of the Jewish people by God, of the Incarnation, of the Atonement, of the resurrection and of judgement. They did not abandon what is today called the concept of *Heilsgeschichte*. They may have undervalued the historical books and the messages of the prophets to their contemporaries, but they did not reject or completely obscure them. And they understood perfectly well the necessity of defending and valuing the historical career of Jesus, even though they may have conceived of the humanity of Christ very unimaginatively. Origen in his *Commentary on John's Gospel* faces very honestly the existence of inconsistencies in the narratives in the gospels and does his best to reconcile them; the fact that he relegates some of them to the realm of purely spiritual and not historical truth serves to enhance his insistence upon the historicity of the others.

Eusebius of Caesarea in the third book of his *Demonstratio evangelica* produces a spirited and impressive defence of the authenticity of the gospels, appealing to the defects recorded of the apostles and to the human weaknesses of Jesus. Why, he asks, if the gospels are quite untrustworthy, did the evangelists not record that the arm of the man who struck Jesus during his trial was paralysed nor that the high priest Caiaphas who brought about the condemnation of Jesus was blinded? Why do they not say that no serious disaster overtook Jesus as a result of his trial, that he stood laughing at the court, or that his judges were afflicted by hallucinations, and so on?[1] Again, though we have seen some examples of how weakly the Fathers grasped the reality of the humanity of Christ, they often emphasised the reality of his human birth. Tertullian several times goes out of his way to underline the coarse reality of this birth: 'As soon as the security of the womb is broken he greets the light with tears...';[2] or again, after a superb passage painting the filthiness of human birth in Swiftian language, he turns upon Marcion and says, 'Do you disparage this honour paid to nature, Marcion? Well, how were you born yourself?'[3] Passages to the same effect, though not as fine, could be quoted from Irenaeus and Hippolytus.[4] Even the staid Hilary of Poitiers can write, 'The image of the invisible God did not disdain the humiliation of human origin, and experienced all the indignities of our nature by his conception, his birth, his squalling, his cradle.'[5]

Another important consideration is that, in spite of the oracular status which they accorded to the text of scripture, the more clear-sighted of the Fathers realised very well that its language did represent an accommodation of himself by God to the limited understanding of human beings. Origen, as is well known, very often stressed this idea and, characteristically, extended it to the length of saying that God was ready to deceive men for their own good. But we can find the concept of accommodation in Novatian, whom we cannot suspect of being influenced by Origen. 'The prophet was speaking about God

---

[1] *Dem. ev.* III, 5, 102, 103 and see the whole passage 81–110.

[2] *Adv. Marc.* IV, 21, 11: *statim lucem lacrimis auspicatus ex primo retinaculi sui vulnere.*

[3] *De Carn. Christ.* 4, 1–3: *hanc venerationem naturae, Marcion, despuis? Et quomodo natus es?*

[4] *Adv. Haer.* II, 22, 4 and *Ref.* X, 33, 15–17.

[5] *De Trin.* II, 24: *Dei igitur imago invisibilis pudorem humani exordii non recusavit, et per conceptionem, partum, vagitum, cunas, omnes naturae nostrae contumelias transcucurrit.*

at that point', he writes, 'in symbolic language, fitted to that stage of belief, not as God was, but as the people were able to understand... God therefore is not finite, but the people's understanding is finite; God is not limited, but the intellectual capacity of the people's mind is limited.'[1] Eusebius is a faithful enough disciple of Origen to agree with Plato that it is sometimes necessary for the lawgiver to lie in order to persuade people rather than coerce them, and to suggest that this is an explanation of the anthropomorphism of the Old Testament.[2] And Hilary can explain the language of Ps. 110: 3 ('From the womb before the daystar I begot thee') in much the same vein.[3] We have already seen how the pro-Nicene writers in the Arian controversy were driven to realise the symbolic and analogous nature of biblical language about God, simply through the necessity of wrestling with the Arians over their proof-texts.[4]

The Fathers of the early Church, therefore, were not without restraints upon the development of their scriptural interpretation, nor were they destitute of principles more satisfactory than those which led to some of the more serious misunderstandings of the Bible which have been considered in this discussion. At least from the time of Irenaeus, also, the Fathers were aware of one important truth. They knew what was their aim in handling scripture. It was not to produce an entirely consistent system of doctrine which would somehow fit in every little detail of the Bible, nor was it to set up a biblical literalism which would treat the Bible as one treats a railway timetable. It was to discover, and to preach and teach, the burden, the purport, the drift, the central message of the Bible. This is explicitly admitted by several Christian writers. Irenaeus describes this as the *hypothesis* of the scriptures, Tertullian as the *ratio*, Athanasius as the *skopos*. They are aware that their treatment of details may be open to question, and they often (especially Origen) put forward their speculative enough expositions with diffidence and modesty. But they realise that what matters is, what the Bible comes to, where the main weight of its evidence lies, in what direction its thought thrusts. In order to find this and to expound it they constantly take illegitimate short cuts and violate the

---

[1] *De Trin.* 6 (p. 20), ll. 2–5, 8–10: *parabolis enim adhuc, secundum fidei tempus, de Deo prophetes loquebatur, non quomodo Deus erat, sed quomodo populus capere poterat...non igitur mediocris est Deus, sed populi mediocris est sensus; nec angustus Deus, sed rationis populi angustus est intellectus habitus.*

[2] *Praep. ev.* XII, 31, 1, 2.   [3] *De Trin.* XII, 8.   [4] See above, pp. 447 f.

rules of probability and of historical commonsense. But one does gain the impression that though they were frequently wrong about the details they were usually right about the end result. For instance, the texts which Tertullian employs to refute the theological opinions of Praxeas are for the most part totally irrelevant to his purpose. But Tertullian's doctrine of God is on the whole much more consistent with the evidence of the New Testament than that of Praxeas. We may well deplore the futility of Athanasius' struggle with the Arians over texts which were useless to prove the truth of either case, but it is hard to deny that the doctrine of Athanasius was more faithful to the New Testament account of the significance of Jesus Christ than that of the Arians, whose fundamental trouble, one suspects, was that they could not believe that God really has communicated himself in Christ. It is worth recalling the observation of G. L. Prestige that what the Fathers really did was to interpret the whole Bible by the New Testament and to interpret the New Testament by the gospels.[1] They did indeed read their interpretation of the New Testament so thoroughly and indiscriminately into the Old Testament that they often deceive the modern reader into thinking that they have entirely deserted the Bible.

After all, in their exegesis the early Church theologians neither received the Bible as a 'Bible without notes' nor interpreted it in a vacuum. They received along with the Bible a tradition of interpreting it for a worshipping community and they proceeded to interpret it for a worshipping community. The study of the Bible as a scientific discipline to be carried on for its own sake was very far from their thought, and at all times has been, one suspects, a mere will-o'-the-wisp. This does not mean that the Fathers sacrificed everything for the sake of the edification of the faithful or for the consistent articulation of a doctrinal system. They sacrificed too much for these ends, but they were not unconscious of limits and controls on this process imposed by the Bible itself. Their purpose in exegesis was nevertheless purely practical, and we do not understand their exegesis until we understand this. They began the story of the Church's relations with the Bible, in which the Bible and the life of the Church were to interact for all the centuries to come, each correcting, deepening, fertilising the other. They inaugurated the Church's dance with the Bible, fancifully perhaps, but not irresponsibly, perhaps erratically, but at least gaily.

[1] *Fathers and Heretics* (London, 1940), p. 44.

14. ORIGEN AS BIBLICAL SCHOLAR

There was never a time when the Church was without written scriptures. From the beginning she had the Old Testament and it was for her the oracles of God. With it went also the message of Jesus, the preached gospel of the salvation which he had achieved, and the orally transmitted accounts of his life and teaching. By the end of the first century the bulk of our New Testament documents had been written. By the end of the second century there was general agreement about the writings which were to be received as making up the scriptures of the New Testament. There was no agreed list and different churches varied in detail over which books should be acknowledged; but the differences were marginal and unimportant in comparison with the fundamental measure of agreement. By the year 200 there was in practice a Christian Bible.

Origen's career spans the first half of the third century. In the year 203, at the youthful age of 17, he took charge of the catechetical school of Alexandria. He died, possibly as the result of torture received in persecution, about 254. He was the most versatile of all the scholars of the early Church; he was apologist and preacher, biblical commentator and philosophical theologian. In all these tasks his primary tool was the Bible. The Bible was there ready to his hand, but its boundaries were still ill-defined and its interpretation in dispute. Origen was forced to grapple more deeply than any of his predecessors with the questions, What constitutes the Bible? and How is it to be understood?

The works in which he deals most directly with the Bible (apart from the *Hexapla* of which we shall speak separately in a moment) are of three kinds. In the first place he composed a number of brief notes, or *Scholia* to give them the Greek name by which they are generally known, in which he dealt with points of particular obscurity or difficulty. Secondly, with the aid of stenographers provided by his wealthy friend and convert Ambrosius, he composed very full *Commentaries* on a number of books both of the Old and New Testaments. Finally, there are the *Homilies* or expository sermons which he preached during the later part of his life when he was ordained and living at Caesarea. These were based on the lessons read in church; the lessons followed one another in continuous sequence so that the series of *Homilies* often amount in practice to a more or less continuous exposition of a whole book. In the very last years of his life, when he was over sixty years old, so Eusebius tells us, he allowed these sermons to be taken down in shorthand as they were delivered.[1] There is thus a vast range of material in which Origen is involved in the task of biblical interpretation. The differences between these various kinds of writing are not as great as might at first seem likely. The *Homilies* are nearer to lectures than most modern sermons, and the *Commentaries* show more concern with the spiritual application of what is being expounded than most of their modern counterparts. Explanations of difficulties of the kind with which the *Scholia* deal are equally at home in either. Nor were the problems of biblical scholarship present to Origen's mind only when he was engaged directly in the work of commentary and exposition. The problems were always with him and are fully reflected in his devotional and apologetic writings also. The Bible and its true meaning was at the very heart of Origen's intellectual and spiritual life.

TEXT AND CANON

Origen was the kind of person, regrettably rare in Christian history, who appears to have been capable of entering into genuine dialogue with Jews. The obvious common ground for such debate was the Old Testament. But it would soon become apparent in any such discussion that the text used by the Jews and the Septuagint version used by the Church were not identical either in the books which they contained or in more detailed questions of precise text. The tendency of the Church controversialist was to claim that the Church's version was the true one and that any differences in the Jewish version must be due to deliberate falsification of the text on the part of the Jews. It was an easy way out but it was the death alike of serious scholarship and of genuine dialogue.

Origen approached the problem in a very different spirit. The question of the books to be admitted was not for him a matter of great difficulty. He knew which books were recognised by the Jews and was content to work within that frame for his discussions with them. But there were other books, treated by the Jews as apocrypha, which were in regular use in the Church. Origen saw no reason why the Church

[1] *H.E.* vi, 36, 1.

should be dispossessed of them just because the Jews did not acknowledge them and there was no Hebrew version in existence. Books like Judith, Tobit and the Wisdom of Solomon he was ready to use within the Church as freely and as authoritatively as any other part of the Old Testament. His readiness to do so was based quite simply on the fact that the Church accepted them and used them. They were the Church's scriptures.

It is a case of having it both ways, something that was always temperamentally congenial to Origen. But it is a natural and reasonable enough position. It is not quite so easy or so natural an attitude when Origen applies a similar principle to questions of textual difference. Here too he aimed to be as all-inclusive as he could. His general approach was a readiness to acknowledge both texts. On the one hand he recognised on scholarly grounds the priority of the Hebrew text. He saw too its importance for any fruitful conversation with the Jews.

I make it my endeavour [he wrote] not to be ignorant of their various readings, so that in my controversies with the Jews I may avoid quoting to them what is not found in their copies, and also may be able to make positive use of what is found there, even when it is not to be found in our scriptures. If we are prepared for our discussions with them in this way, they will no longer be able, as so often happens, to laugh scornfully at Gentile believers for their ignorance of the true reading which they have.[1]

But this did not mean that Origen was ready to dispense with the Septuagint text and advocate its replacement by a more exact equivalent of the Hebrew.

Are we [he asks] when we notice such things immediately to reject as spurious the copies in use in the Churches, and to tell the fellowship that they should put away the sacred books current among them and should cajole the Jews into giving us copies which will be untampered with and free from forgery? Are we to suppose that providence which has provided for the edification of all the churches of Christ through the medium of the holy scriptures has not taken proper care of the needs of those for whom Christ died?[2]

Origen was being realistic. The Septuagint was the Church's Old Testament. The tradition of its miraculous origins recounted in the *Letter of Aristeas* was widely believed. Its supersession was hardly a practical possibility. But Origen was not only acting from a sense

---

[1] *Ep. ad Afric.* 5.   [2] *Ibid.* 4.

of cautious realism. He was not only, not even primarily, a critical scholar. He too was a child of the Church. If the Septuagint was the Church's Old Testament, it must on theological grounds be an inspired text, its divergences from the earlier Hebrew notwithstanding. A proper recognition and authority had to be given to both.

Origen is careful to insist that this readiness to acknowledge both texts is not due to a desire to evade the work that might be involved in reaching a decision between them. The insistence hardly needed making. Even Origen's worst enemy (and he was never without enemies during his lifetime or after) could not have accused him of idleness. Even if we find it difficult to accept Epiphanius' estimate of 6,000 books from his hand, he was certainly a most prolific author. And of all his literary labours his work on the text of the Old Testament was the most extensive and the most exacting. What impressed his contemporaries and immediate successors most of all was that he learnt Hebrew for the purpose, a very rare undertaking for a non-Jewish scholar. His knowledge of the language was certainly limited, but it was sufficient to enable him to handle the Hebrew text and he was always ready to consult Jewish scholars on particular issues. With the aid of this rudimentary knowledge he undertook the enormous task of comparing the Septuagint text with the Hebrew and with other Greek translations. The other Greek translations were of interest to him not simply because of his limited knowledge of Hebrew but as being the texts actually used by the Greek-speaking Jews with whom he was in personal contact. He may be allowed to describe his objective and his method in his own words:

With the help of God's grace I have tried to repair the disagreements in the copies of the Old Testament on the basis of the other versions. When I was uncertain of the Septuagint reading because the various copies did not tally, I settled the issue by consulting the other versions and retaining what was in agreement with them. Some passages did not appear in the Hebrew; these I marked with an obelus as I did not dare to leave them out altogether. Other passages I marked with an asterisk to show that they were not in the Septuagint but that I had added them from the other versions in agreement with the Hebrew text. Whoever wishes may accept them; anyone who is offended by this procedure may accept or reject them as he chooses.[1]

[1] *Comm. in Matt.* xv, 14.

Origen is describing not simply his ambition but his achievement. The work, known as the *Hexapla*, covered the whole Old Testament. It was set out in six parallel columns. The first contained the Hebrew text, the second a transliteration of that Hebrew text into Greek script; the other four contained different established Greek versions, that of Aquila (the most literal rendering of the Hebrew), that of Symmachus, the revised Septuagint and finally that of Theodotion. The signs to which Origen refers as marking passages which he had added or which, in his judgement, ought to be omitted were not his own invention. They were drawn from the practice of classical grammarians in their work, particularly on the text of Homer. In addition to the asterisk (※) and the obelus (–, ‑̣̇, ÷) which marked the beginning of the passages added or to be omitted there was a third sign, the metabolos (/., ˙/., ˅), to mark the end of the passage so signified. The primary aim of the operation, as Origen's own description reveals, was to provide an improved version of the Septuagint text—one in which nothing would be lost and much would be gained.

The three Jewish translations of Aquila, Symmachus and Theodotion were well known. But Origen was not content to work simply with the easily accessible material. He made it his aim to unearth other less familiar versions also. One, he tells us, he himself found at Nicopolis near Actium; another was found in a jar near Jericho. So for the Psalms, and probably for some other parts of the Old Testament as well, he was able to set as many as seven different versions side by side.[1]

It has been estimated that the whole work must have covered about 6,500 pages. Little wonder that it was never copied in its entirety! It was available in the library of Caesarea until it perished there in the Moslem conquest of Palestine in the seventh century. Its primary aim had been to secure a revised Septuagint text. That part of it was therefore the one most used. It was used in particular for the correction of current texts, so that what has come down to us even in this case cannot be identified precisely with Origen's original fifth column. Among other modifications the critical marks indicating which passages were missing in the Hebrew or were additions to conform with the Hebrew were mostly omitted.

Origen's interest in securing a critical text was not confined to its value for apologetic work directed towards the Jews. He was preacher

[1] Eus. *H.E.* VI, 16.

as well as apologist and makes use of his critical studies in his preaching. His underlying text for the task of preaching is naturally enough the Septuagint, the version, as he puts it, 'which is familiar and current in the churches'. But he does not shrink from pointing out from time to time places where that text does not agree with the Hebrew or where it can be improved by comparison with the other translations of Aquila, Symmachus and Theodotion. Having done so, his readiness to have it both ways, coupled perhaps with a desire not to ride rough-shod over the religious susceptibilities of his congregation, asserts itself. He may be convinced that the Septuagint text is a result of faulty translation or scribal error. But he does not totally reject it for that reason. It is still the version familiar and current in the churches, and as such deserves to be expounded along with an alternative exposition based on the more original and accurate Hebrew text. Not only the additions but even the mistranslations of the Septuagint can be of spiritual profit in the providence of God.

Origen's attitude to the New Testament reveals the same underlying spirit of approach. In this case there was no agreed list of books, comparable to the Hebrew Canon, to serve as a basis. Nor does Origen show any particular desire for such a list. Clearly there are books to be rejected, but he does not feel any need for the line between the two to be a rigid and inflexible one. He is at his firmest with the gospels. The four already stood out firmly in tradition. Moreover, there were dangerously gnostic works like the gospels of Thomas or Basilides to be excluded. But even in the category of gospels there are borderline cases, like the *Gospel according to the Hebrews*, which he is very far from classing with the four but which he is prepared occasionally to use as a source acceptable to some and certainly not wholly unacceptable to himself. The epistles do not rank in his eyes as on precisely the same level as the gospels. They contain within themselves an explicitly acknowledged element of purely personal judgement—'to the rest I say, not the Lord' (1 Cor. 7: 12). This leads Origen to speak of them as at a slightly lower level of inspiration than the gospels. But it is not a distinction which reveals itself in the way he treats them in practice. They are a part of scripture and he uses them as firmly and as fully as the other parts. He knows that the authenticity of some of the epistles, such as 2 Peter, 2 and 3 John, is a matter of dispute but he does not appear to be unduly concerned about the fact. Other letters which did

459

not ultimately find their way into the Canon, like the epistles of Clement and of Barnabas, he quotes on occasion in a manner indistinguishable from his citations of scripture.

The acceptability or otherwise of a book bore only a very indirect relation to his own critical studies. On stylistic grounds he was convinced that Paul could not have been the author of the Epistle to the Hebrews, but this does nothing to undermine for him its rightful position among the accepted scriptures. Indeed the traditional but mistaken ascription of the authorship to Paul was in his judgement not wholly without point; though wrong in fact it did indicate a real and important affinity in thought between the Epistle and the Pauline writings. The nature of its contents and the longstanding tradition of its use by the Church were sufficient grounds of support. As with his defence of the books of the Old Testament apocrypha, the primary criterion by which he is guided is general acceptance by the Church. If that acceptance is substantial but less than universal, as for example with the *Shepherd* of Hermas, Origen is inclined to give the book the benefit of the doubt. He does not attempt to enforce his view on others, but if the book be sound in doctrine he will use it. For those who do accept it, it will be a useful additional source of edification. For those who do not, nothing vital will be lost; they will simply have to find their evidence and instruction from another source. But scripture is a rich enough mine to meet the needs of all.

Just as there was no official Hebrew Canon to provide the basic nucleus of a list of New Testament books, so there was no official Hebrew text to act as a check upon the New Testament text used in any particular church. But Origen was well aware that there were textual differences between the various existing copies of the New Testament. The passage which we quoted in description of Origen's work on the *Hexapla* was drawn from his *Commentary on Matthew* and was part of a discussion of how to deal with variants in the New Testament text. These have arisen, he claims, either through the carelessness of copyists or through the rashness of would-be emenders of the text. He is even prepared to suggest that the error may sometimes lie so far back in the past that every surviving manuscript may be wrong.

He did not undertake any major study of the New Testament text of the kind which he carried out in the case of the Old Testament. The ancient Latin version of the passage quoted from the *Commentary on*

Matthew makes him say that he would not dare to do such a thing; but the remark does not occur in the Greek text and cannot therefore be accepted with any confidence as genuine. In any event the nature of the task, with no equivalent of the Hebrew text to act as a norm, would have been a very different one. But Origen is still interested in the question of variants; he is still concerned to try to determine the original text. Where he does discuss the relative merits of variant readings, the criteria on which he bases his decision are not usually linguistic or textual but more often matters of historical or theological probability. Where there is no clear preference for one reading over the other on grounds of that kind, he is happy, as with the Old Testament, to suggest interpretations of both readings.

Both the quality and quantity of Origen's critical scholarship were enormously in advance of his contemporaries. Nor, as we have seen, was that scholarly skill something which he kept in a separate compartment of life, distinct from his office as a teacher or a preacher. Issues of textual criticism figure on occasion even in homilies delivered to gatherings of very ordinary and uneducated Christian believers. Yet such issues had in practice surprisingly little real effect on his biblical commentaries or sermons. He knew well the innate conservatism of his congregations. He had no desire to antagonise them unnecessarily by throwing doubt upon the text to which they were accustomed. They were slow enough already to see the inner spiritual message of the Bible and to order their lives in obedience to it without adding further stumbling-blocks of that kind. But this apparent contradiction between the energy devoted to textual scholarship and the comparatively little use apparently made of it in exposition was not solely an outcome of the problem of communication. The contradiction was also in Origen himself. It arose directly out of his understanding of the inspiration of scripture and the proper method of its spiritual interpretation.

INSPIRATION

Origen includes, as part of the fundamental deposit of faith, a part of the ecclesiastical tradition which he and the whole Church had received from the apostles, namely, the belief that the scriptures were written by inspiration of the Holy Spirit and have a deeper meaning than that which appears upon the surface of the record. These are the two fundamental convictions which guide and determine his own developed understanding of scripture.

About the method of inspiration Origen is not greatly concerned; it was the fact that mattered. The idea of inspiration by means of ecstasy, in which the normal processes of human consciousness are overruled and man becomes a passive instrument in the hands of the deity, was familiar to the pagan world, and is to be found in some contemporary Jewish and early Christian writers too. In arguing with Celsus, Origen can use or repudiate the parallel between the inspiration of the biblical writers and that of the Pythian oracle as it suits his purpose. But there is no doubt that his general view is opposed to the idea of inspiration as an automatic process. He is just as ready to describe inspiration as an activity of the Logos as he is to describe it as an activity of the Spirit. It is therefore to be thought of as a rational process—rational not in any narrow or restrictive sense of that word but certainly in contrast to that which is sub-rational. The character of divine inspiration is to clarify rather than to cloud, to heighten man's awareness rather than to diminish it. The author's natural powers may be enhanced to enable him to become the vehicle of spiritual truth, but he remains himself, an active conscious co-operating agent in the execution of God's purpose. The fact that the Word comes to him has its origin not in the will of man but in the will of God; but the Word does not force itself through him; he has to respond, and he can frustrate its purpose if he refuse to do so.

The peculiar personal characteristics of the different authors of the varying books of the Bible are not therefore irrelevant to the understanding of what they have written. John, the disciple whom Jesus loved, was well suited to be author of the most profound of all the gospels. But he was still a Galilaean fisherman and it is no matter for surprise that he does not always express himself with the clarity of a professional writer. Paul was the greatest of all the apostles; but he describes himself as 'unskilled in speaking' (2 Cor. 11: 6), and that fact is part cause at least of the obscurity of so much in his epistles and of the grammatical and syntactical inaccuracies to be found in them.

When Tatian first met the scriptures he regarded them as 'barbaric writings'. So they were by the canons of Greek taste. But this unattractiveness of the outward form was more than just a matter of a lack of aesthetic style and artistic merit. Those were not considerations that would have weighed very heavily with Origen. The unattractiveness that was a matter of primary concern to him was the unattractiveness of the surface meaning of so much of the Bible. Origen's two underlying convictions about the inspiration of the Holy Spirit and the hidden meaning of scripture belong closely together. Were it not for the latter, he would have to regard the former as demonstrably untenable. Treated simply as human laws, the laws of Moses compare unfavourably in Origen's judgement with the laws of Rome or of Athens or of Sparta. If he had to understand them in their plain and literal sense, he would blush to call them God's. The Song of Songs would have called still fiercer blushes to his cheeks had it not had a secret meaning into which he could escape; its surface meaning, he declares, is one palpably unworthy of God. Or again, how could he justify to Celsus the records of massacres commanded by God in Old Testament times or the words of the Psalmist 'O Daughter of Babylon, blessed is he who shall take hold of thy little ones and dash them against the rock' unless he could point to their hidden meaning?

But the difficulty went deeper still. It went beyond even the anthropomorphic language and the moral infelicities of the Old Testament. Scripture was not even free from factual error. So careful a student of the text as Origen could not help being aware of discrepancies between the different gospel records. The normal procedure of the early Church scholar was to explain these away by elaborate attempts to harmonise the conflicting accounts. That was a game which Origen could play when he wanted to as ingeniously as anyone else. But he did not believe that it could solve the problem entirely. Moreover, the factual truth of some recorded incidents was open to serious doubt on other grounds also, on grounds for example of their intrinsic improbability. In his *Commentary on John* Origen uses both arguments to demonstrate the literal falsity of the story of the cleansing of the Temple; doubts about the story are raised in his mind not only by the differences of the Synoptic and Johannine chronologies but also by the unlikelihood of one of so humble an origin as Jesus being allowed to do what he is reputed to have done. Thus the discrepancies between the different records and the historical implausibility of some of the incidents described are such that they might well undermine our whole faith in the trustworthiness of the gospels. They do not need to do so for one fundamental reason, namely, that the factual truth of the record is not always a matter of importance. Spiritual truth can be preserved in material falsehood. Differing factual accounts, which cannot all be true, may be intended to provide a richer range of spiritual meaning. If the surface meaning be unattractive we can be sure that there is a hidden meaning which is of primary importance. If the surface meaning be actually false we can say (though it is only very seldom that Origen in fact falls back upon this principle) that there is a hidden meaning which is not merely of primary importance but which is the only one that is true at all.

Inspiration therefore did nothing to ensure an attractive exterior to scripture. The scriptures had no form or comeliness that men should desire them. But that should not be a matter for surprise. The same had been true of the Word incarnate. It was not difficult to find parallel reasons to explain both cases. The divine Word took human form for the sake of those who by reason of the poverty of their spiritual insight could not aspire to an immediate appreciation of his divine nature. That is how God always works. He accommodates his revelation to man's capacity for comprehending it. That is how he has acted alike in the Incarnation and in the scriptures. Its effect is twofold. Negatively it means that God does not cast his pearls before swine. In not doing so he acts not only in the interest of the pearls but in the interest of the swine, since otherwise they might be guilty in their blindness and their ignorance of trampling blasphemously on the pearls of God's truth. This may at times be the conscious intention of the human author, as when in chapter 7 of the Epistle to the Romans Paul deliberately uses the word 'law' in a variety of senses without giving any indication of when he is moving from one sense to another so that his meaning will only be apparent to those who are seriously concerned with the deeper truths of God. Positively it means that God starts where we are. As a father uses baby language when talking to his infant child, so God attunes his speech to the level of our understanding. A father does not tell his child everything at once, nor express what he does tell him in adult language. When once we grasp that scripture is a tool for use in the process of God's education of mankind, then many of its difficulties begin to make sense and many of its most unpalatable features are seen to be of positive value. Even if we were capable of recognising and accepting the full truth about

God all at once (which is not in fact the case), it would still not be in our interest to have it presented to us in that way. Men remember better and value more highly knowledge for which they have had to dig hard and long than knowledge which is offered to them on a plate all ready for their simple acceptance. The difficulties which we encounter in the scriptures are spurs to greater effort in our search for spiritual knowledge, which would have been the more shallow had we attained it by any easier route. But the educational process involves not only hardship; it may even involve a measure of deception. 'O Lord, thou hast deceived me, and I was deceived' said the prophet (Jer. 20: 7); and he was speaking the truth. As the father may mislead his child in his own interest or the doctor deceive his patient for his own good, so too may God in working for our true good. Thus the imperfections of the outward form of scripture serve many purposes in the providence of God. They hide the truth from the spiritually flippant, while at the same time presenting it in a form which can start the beginner on the road of truth and lead him on gradually to the deeper truths as he is able to assimilate them.

Finally, the unattractiveness of the medium through which the word of God comes to men serves to ensure that the glory will be ascribed to the right quarter. If the Bible were simply the finest of books by ordinary accepted standards of judgement, then it would be in danger of receiving acclamation simply as a fine human achievement. But in fact, just as Paul being 'unskilled in speaking' could claim that the success of his preaching was due not to his oratory but to the power of God's spirit, so the scripture is another example of God entrusting his treasure to earthen vessels 'to show that the transcendent power belongs to God and not to us' (2 Cor. 4: 7).

DIFFERING SENSES OF SCRIPTURE

The presence of a deeper hidden meaning in scripture was therefore a necessity for Origen if he were to defend its inspired character; it was also the basis of his positive use of scripture for preaching and teaching within the Church. It was something on which he had to insist; but it was not something which he had to invent. It was, as he said, a part of the ecclesiastical or apostolic tradition which he inherited.

The early history of the church at Alexandria is largely unknown to us. The only orthodox writings that have come down to us from second-century Alexandria are the *Epistle of Barnabas* and the writings of Clement, but they are sufficient to show that an allegorical approach to scripture was to a very marked degree a particular characteristic of the church tradition there. But it was the apostolic even more than the ecclesiastical nature of the tradition which was of primary import- ance to Origen. In particular he justifies himself by the example of Paul. The principal illustrations which he quotes are the allegory of Sarah and Hagar (Gal. 4: 22–6), the interpretation of the Deutero- nomic law about the muzzling of oxen (1 Cor. 9: 9–10), the explanation of the Red Sea crossing in terms of baptism (1 Cor. 10: 1–4), the description of the law as a shadow of things to come (Col. 2: 17) and the understanding of the marriage ordinance in Genesis as a mystical reference to Christ and the Church (Eph. 5: 32). Further support was to be found in the whole approach of the Epistle to the Hebrews (sometimes treated by Origen as if Pauline in authorship, and always regarded by him as Pauline in spirit) and in the story of Peter's vision on the rooftop at Joppa. What tradition could be more apostolic than one which went back to the two greatest apostles of New Testament times? But in fact the tradition in Origen's eyes was even older than that. The prefatory words at the beginning of the long narrative psalm, Ps. 78 ('I will open my mouth in a parable; I will utter dark sayings from of old'), were evidence that the Psalmist had understood the historical accounts of Exodus and Numbers to contain a deeper hidden meaning. It was not only a matter of the New Testament writers' interpretation of the Old: the tradition was to be seen even in the Old Testament's understanding of itself.

It was naturally enough this Christian tradition going back to apostolic times and continuing in the life of the Church which Origen stressed. But the tradition itself was much broader than that. It had a long history in the Greek world where it had arisen for precisely the same reasons which made it so important to Origen. The Greek world had its sacred books too, of which the Homeric sagas are the most notable examples. With the passage of time their ideas and their ethics had become outmoded; yet men were loath to abandon them. So hidden spiritual or philosophical meanings were found in them which would enable them to be preserved without offence to the sensitive or religious mind. This was primarily the work of the Stoics and Origen explicitly refers to Chrysippus' use of this method of interpreting the Greek myths.

Nor were the Christians the first to apply such a method of interpretation to the scriptural text. That step had already been taken in hellenistic Judaism, most notably by Philo of Alexandria. With its help he had succeeded in reading all the tenets of contemporary philosophy out of (or more accurately into) the narratives and laws of the Pentateuch. But even Philo was not an innovator; he stands at the climax of a well-established tradition of interpretation in Alexandrian Judaism. Nor was Alexandria the only centre in which such an approach was to be found. The Palestinian rabbis were not such thorough-going allegorisers, but they too had found the necessity for some such method of interpretation in explaining the true meaning of such canonical books as the Song of Songs. The exegetical tradition in which Origen stood had a Christian form, but there was nothing exclusively Christian about it.

The particular manner in which Origen gives formal expression to his own way of interpreting the scriptural text is by the analogy of human psychology. Just as in man there is body, soul and spirit, so in scripture there is a threefold meaning—the literal, the moral and the spiritual. He finds support for this approach in various texts of scripture, especially in the Septuagint version of Prov. 22: 20 which reads: 'Describe these things in a threefold way.' Origen admits that there are occasions when this threefold pattern of interpretation has to be reduced to a twofold. (He sees scriptural illustration of this in the fact that the stone water jars at the marriage feast at Cana are described as containing two *or* three firkins apiece.) There are only two senses, he says, in those instances where the text has no literal or bodily meaning.

There is a strong case for reducing the threefold approach of Origen's theoretical formulation to a twofold, but it is not the case which Origen himself makes. It is true, as we have already seen, that he does on occasion feel bound to deny the reality of the literal meaning. But the real difficulty in the attempt to find meanings of scripture analogous to body, soul and spirit is the difficulty of drawing any clear distinction between soul and spirit, between the moral and the spiritual senses of scripture. In writing about human nature Origen normally follows the tripartite division of body, soul and spirit, but he does also use a dichotomous division, speaking simply of body and soul or of flesh and spirit or of inner man and outer man. This twofold form provides a closer parallel to his normal practice in the work of exegesis. He speaks most frequently in terms of a simple contrast between two senses. They can be described in many ways, the bodily and the spiritual, the literal and the figurative, the historical and the anagogical, but it is the same twofold contrast in each case.

Where he does make a difference between the moral and spiritual senses, he does not seem to be wholly consistent in the nature of the distinction which he draws. It appears in two main forms. On the one hand it is related to differing levels of spiritual attainment. The moral sense is the pure milk which is appropriate to those who are comparative beginners in Christian discipleship; the spiritual sense is the solid food which is suited to those who have progressed some way along the road of Christian maturity. In its second form the distinction is concerned rather with the content of the interpretation. The spiritual interpretation is that which relates to Christ and the great truths of God's saving dispensation, whereas the moral interpretation is one which relates to human experience. Two examples may serve by way of illustration of the second form of the distinction. The spiritual meaning of Noah's building of the ark concerns Christ and the Church; the moral meaning applies to the man who turns from the evil world around him and in obedience to the commands of God prepares an ark of salvation in his own heart. The spiritual interpretation of the story of Lot, Lot's wife and his daughters is in terms of the Law, of those who looked back to Egypt and perished in the wilderness, and of the Law's two offspring, Jerusalem and Samaria; the moral interpretation concerns the mind of man (Lot) which, even when it has left behind the flesh (Lot's wife), is still in danger of succumbing to the wiles of its two daughters, pride and vain glory.

It is impossible to equate these two forms of the distinction between the moral and the spiritual senses unless one were to say that Christian maturity was exclusively a matter of the fuller understanding of Christian truth and not at all a matter of growth in moral and spiritual experience. It seems rather that the distinction was a confused way of referring to different concerns with which Origen found himself having to reckon in his handling of the Bible. One concern was the need to adjust his teaching to the varied capacities—both intellectual and spiritual—of his hearers. There were many who were able to go beyond the mere literal sense (which did not always even exist) but who were incapable of appreciating or benefiting from the more intricate forms of allegorical interpretation. There was a sense of scripture that was appropriate to their needs. It stood in between the literal and the full spiritual senses. This was the midway category of the moral interpretation. But in addition Origen was also aware of differences of kind between the various figurative interpretations which he offered. The most obvious, though not the only, difference of this nature was that between interpretation in terms of the being of God and his self-revelation in history and above all in Christ on the one hand and interpretation in terms of the inwardness of Christian experience on the other. It is natural to think of the objective realities of the divine life as higher than the imperfect achievement of their assimilation into human life and experience. The former belongs to the highest category of spiritual mystery, the latter to a lower level of the 'soul' rather than the 'spirit' class.

Neither form of the distinction really requires or fits a threefold method of scriptural interpretation. Growth in Christian maturity is not a matter of two, or even three, clear stages. The Church is not divided into babes in need of pure milk and full-grown adults capable of digesting every species of solid food. There is every stage of adolescence and varying powers of digestion in between, and the sensitive preacher or interpreter will seek to adjust his manner of exposition accordingly. The other form of distinction is not really a distinction of exegetical method at all; it is a distinction of content, a distinction between the different kinds of Christian meaning which can be found in scripture. Once we embark upon such distinctions of content, there is no reason why we should stop at two. Nor does Origen in practice do so. He interprets Christ's cleansing of the Temple in a variety of ways. It is a sign of his own redemptive work, abolishing the Jewish sacrificial system and replacing it with his risen body, the Church. It is also a picture of the ever-necessary work of Christ in purging the Church of its corruption. Or again it may be interpreted in terms of Christ's coming to the individual human soul. Finally, it may represent the entry of Jesus into the heavenly Jerusalem and his freeing it from the spiritual hosts of wickedness in heavenly places. Thus the spiritual meaning may refer to Christ's redemptive work in the Incarnation, to

the continuing life of the Church militant, to the individual believer
or to the life of heaven. There is as good ground for distinguishing a
Christological, an ecclesiological, a mystical and an eschatological
sense as there is for the distinction between the moral and the spiritual.
Later systems of exegesis have in fact made full use of these more
elaborate distinctions. But again we must insist that the distinctions
refer to the content and not to the method of exegesis. Most of the time
Origen himself works in terms of two senses only, the literal and the
spiritual. It is only in that form that his system can be understood
consistently as a method of exegesis. The water-jars at Origen's feast
do not really hold two or three firkins apiece, but only one or two.

Origen, as we have seen, is quite explicit in his recognition that not
every passage of scripture has a literal sense. This statement can be
taken in a weaker or a stronger sense. Despite the great range of his
intellectual gifts Origen was totally lacking in poetic sensitivity. The
literal sense of scripture is for him the literally literal meaning of the
words. When the Psalmist declares that God's truth 'reaches to the
clouds', Origen feels constrained to insist that clouds cannot be
intended literally in such a saying; they must be interpreted spiritually
of those who are obedient to the word of God. The literal interpretation
of Zech. 4: 10 would imply that God had seven bodily eyes. Little
wonder that Origen insists that some passages have no literal sense in
that understanding of the phrase.

But he also meant more than that. He did also mean to say that some
passages, which have a straightforward and intelligible historical meaning, were at that level of understanding simply not true. On the face
of it they appeared to be factual statements, but in fact they conflict
with some other statement of scripture or they are morally unworthy
of divine revelation; we are therefore bound to conclude that in fact
they did not happen and the scriptural account is there solely for the
sake of its spiritual interpretation. The surprising thing is that once
having taken the big step of accepting this principle, Origen is very
reluctant to use it. We have seen the moral and spiritual meanings that
he drew from the story of the building of Noah's ark and the incest
of Lot's daughters. We might have expected him to be only too glad

to dispense with the literal historical meaning of such stories. But he does not. He recognises the difficulties which an acceptance of their literal sense raises and makes valiant attempts to overcome them. He admits that the measurements given for the ark appear at first sight totally inadequate to house fourteen specimens of every clean and four of every unclean animal in the world, but claims on the authority of a learned Jew that the cubits there mentioned are to be understood as geometric cubits and that therefore all the measurements need in practice to be squared. The behaviour of Lot's daughters might appear utterly shameless, but if they really believed that they and their father were the only survivors of a world conflagration might their conduct not have been a justifiable way of acting in the exceptional circumstances?

We find the same thing in the case of discrepancies between the different gospel records. Origen believes that one cannot fully solve the problem which they pose unless one is prepared to admit that some apparently historical and factual statements in the gospels are not historically and factually true. Yet in the great majority of cases he prefers to suggest the most far-fetched harmonising explanation rather than to apply the principle of non-historicity. The versions of the Lord's Prayer recorded by Matthew and Luke ought to be thought of as two separate prayers (with a certain amount of overlapping material) taught on two separate occasions rather than as two variant accounts of the same occasion or even as two variant accounts of the same prayer taught on separate occasions. It would be to impugn the reliability of the evangelists unjustifiably not to believe that there were two separate occasions, on one of which John the Baptist declared himself unworthy to carry his successor's shoes and on the other of which he spoke of himself as unworthy to untie them.

Thus in the stronger, and only really interesting, meaning of the idea, Origen is usually prepared to defend the truth of the literal sense. When we go on to ask what value he ascribed to it, we seem to be faced with a number of inconsistent assertions. For this there are two main reasons. The first we have already met. The concept of the 'literal sense' is not as straightforward as it seems. Apparent denunciation of it may have in mind only the weaker or more pedantic conception of literalism, and not be intended to apply to the second, historical or factual, conception. But there is another more important reason for Origen's apparent inconsistency. The exponents of the literal meaning whom he has in mind fall into two comparatively distinct groups. There are simple unintellectual believers who are scarcely capable of rising beyond the simplest understanding of scripture. Their literalism Origen is prepared, with some degree of protest, to tolerate. But there are also others of a Judaising tendency whose literalism is a more thought-out position and is linked with a desire to see the enactments of the Jewish law continuing to hold a place in the life of the Christian Church. When Origen has this kind of person primarily in view, his attitude towards literalism is very much less tolerant.

Very often even when Origen explicitly defends the historical truth of a passage it appears to be quite unrelated to what he regards as its real meaning. He points out to Celsus that the wells which the patriarchs are recorded to have dug did really exist; they can still be seen and are of an unusual and interesting design. But this has no bearing at all on what is for him the point of the passage. The real meaning of the passage, which he criticises Celsus for failing to recognise, is its figurative meaning which has to do either with the inner sources of spiritual refreshment or with that digging for the roots of things which constitutes natural philosophy. The great difficulty about so many of Origen's spiritual interpretations, as we shall see in more detail later, lies in this fact of their almost total lack of connection with the straightforward historical sense.

But the straightforward historical sense of scripture is not always as unpromising religiously as the well-boring activities of the patriarchs. Origen defends the historicity of the crucifixion but at the same time insists that its significance cannot be found in the bare historical fact alone.

The truth [he writes] of the events recorded to have happened to Jesus cannot be fully seen in the mere text and historical narrative; for each event to those who read the Bible more intelligently is clearly a symbol of something as well. Thus in this way his Crucifixion contains the truth indicated by the words 'I have been crucified with Christ' and by the sense of the words 'Far be it from me to glory except in the cross of our Lord Jesus Christ, by which the world has been crucified to me, and I to the world'. His death was necessary because 'the death he died, he died to sin once for all', and because the righteous man says that he is 'becoming like him in his death' and 'if we have died with him, we shall also live with him'.[1]

[1] *C. Cels.* II, 69.

Here Origen stands shoulder to shoulder with much recent thought. Bare facts by themselves, even if we allow that there are such things, are simply not interesting. They are only significant when they have become facts for someone, facts interpreted and applied in a human life—and at that point we are already beginning to move beyond the purely literal sense.

It is in his attitude to the Law that Origen's ideas about the literal sense find their most vigorous expression. In general he identifies the contrast between the literal and the spiritual, the letter and the spirit, with the Pauline contrast between law and grace. Within this context he firmly applies the text 'the letter kills' (2 Cor. 3: 6). The literal interpretation of the Law is the way of death. To follow it is to act not as a Christian but as a Jew; it is to frustrate the intention of Moses who knew all along the Law's hidden meaning and showed his contempt for the letter when he broke the tablets of stone. To teach the literal sense alone is to act like those lawyers who took away the key of knowledge, neither entering in themselves nor allowing others to do so.

When these sweeping denunciations are broken down into more detailed and specific form, they begin to appear slightly less violent. No law is to be understood in its literal sense alone; some laws, mainly the ceremonial laws, are not to be followed in their literal sense at all; but there are others, like the second half of the Decalogue, whose literal sense is directly binding on Christians. This is the law which is described in 1 Tim. 1: 9 as being 'not laid down for the just man but for the lawless and disobedient, for the ungodly and sinners'. Thus although it is binding on the Christian, it belongs so much to the prolegomena of Christian discipleship that it can still be regarded as a very inferior and incomplete form of revelation.

The formal inconsistency in Origen's attitude to the letter is most apparent when he is speaking about the New Testament. In one place he can insist that 'the letter kills' in the New Testament as surely as in the Old; in another he can say that those who follow the letter of the gospel will be saved. In the first instance he has in mind those who would take with full literalness the gospel injunction to pluck out an offending right eye or to cut off an offending right hand, or (like himself in his early youth) the suggestion that some men may make themselves eunuchs for the kingdom of heaven's sake. Those who take literally the instruction of Jesus to sell their garment and buy a sword are in danger of falling under the warning that those who take the sword will perish by the sword. They will find quite literally that even in the gospel the letter kills. But in the second case he has in mind the simple believers. They were in little danger of pressing home their literalism in the extreme form which Origen depicts in his illustrations of the letter's power to kill, but they were also unable and uninterested in following Origen into the deeper waters of mature spiritual understanding. They followed the gospel with a natural rather than a pedantic literalism. Origen cannot bring himself to approve them. They are, among other things, an embarrassment to him when explaining Christianity to the sophisticated pagan. He berates them at times and describes them as little better than Jews. But he is prepared to admit that they are better even if by only a little. The gospels are so designed by God that, while they have a deeper meaning, their simple meaning can suffice for the simple. If a man's literalism is the fruit of genuine simplicity then it can be for him the way of salvation. The more mature Christian may be convinced that the promise of Christ's coming on the clouds of heaven is to be understood exclusively in a spiritual sense, but he has no cause to be offended if the simpler Christian understands it of a literal coming on literal clouds. In practice Origen was obviously reluctant to believe that anybody could really be so poorly endowed or so spiritually unambitious as to justify their remaining content with the literal sense alone. But at least in theory he admits that in the case of the New Testament it was possible to do so and by that means still to derive an admittedly incomplete but none the less genuinely Christian meaning from it. The gap between the learned and the uneducated was greater in Origen's day than it is in ours, but the same problem of the coexistence of very different levels of understanding in the one community of the Church is still with us.

EVERY JOT AND TITTLE

The Holy Spirit was the real author of scripture. This fact guaranteed neither the stylistic quality nor the absolute historicity of the scriptural record. What it did guarantee was that when the true intended meaning had been laid bare, that meaning would be wholly true, the truth of

God rather than of man. And the word 'wholly' in that sentence has to be understood in the fullest possible sense. For Origen belief in the Holy Spirit's inspiration of scripture implied that it was true not simply in the broad, general drift of its teaching but in the most minute detail of its intended meaning. God does nothing in vain; just as men will have to give account at the day of judgement for every idle word that they have spoken, so every word of God has a purpose; there is not one jot or tittle of scripture that cannot bring spiritual profit to the man who knows how to read its true meaning aright. Thus Origen held to a view of verbal inspiration of a most rigorous kind. It was a common enough view shared alike by many earlier Jewish exegetes and by other Christian scholars too. But it was a view that was especially congenial to one who had Origen's eye for matters of detail and his relentless intellectual passion to seek out their full significance.

We have already seen how this concern for detail helped to make him a textual critic far in advance of his contemporaries. It drove him on to compare the text of the Septuagint at every point with that of the Hebrew original. It forced him to notice and record even the smallest variations of wording between the differing synoptic accounts of the same incident. It even sent him visiting the sites of the Holy Land to determine whether Bethabara or Bethany was more likely to be the true reading of the name of the place where John is said to have done his baptizing. So firm a belief in inspiration and so great a concern with the detail of the text might be expected to have given rise to a straightforward 'fundamentalist' insistence on the possibility of providing a completely reliable text which would be infallibly true at every level of understanding. But Origen was too honest in his scholarship and too Platonist in his spirituality ever to have adopted such an attitude. How could the declared despiser of the 'letter' of scripture also hold that inspiration applied to every jot and tittle of the scriptural record? The answer lies in the fact that when Origen insists that every jot and tittle is inspired, he means every jot and tittle of the intended meaning. The minutest detail is important, but it is the detail spiritually understood that counts.

The relation between these two types of concern for detail—the detail of the text and the detail of the spiritual interpretation—is a complex one, and is never clearly resolved in Origen's mind. In effect Origen tries to have the best of both worlds. If he can get back to the original Hebrew text, this can be important to him because even if the difference be only very slight that may yet be sufficient to reveal some new subtlety of spiritual meaning. But if he is unable to do so, the Septuagint text (being the form of scripture which God has given to the Church) can be used in just as detailed a way to provide precise spiritual meanings. Indeed even when the Septuagint text has been shown up as inaccurate by the Hebrew, its mistranslations can still be used to provide divinely intended spiritual meanings. If discrepancies between the differing accounts of the cleansing of the Temple show that they cannot all be literally true, this is a sign that the discrepancies must be intended to express different spiritual meanings, corresponding to the variety of ways in which God deals with the varied needs of different human souls. But such discrepancies are not needed to convince the exegete that there is a spiritual meaning to be found. He will expect to find it just as surely in places where it can be shown that recorded events did actually happen just as they have been described. If he can show that Bethabara, being nearer to Jordan, is more likely to be the correct reading in John 1: 28 he can then go on to point out how appropriate is its spiritual meaning, 'House of preparation'. But Bethany means 'House of obedience' and, even if not quite so closely linked in sense to the essence of John's mission, could have served the interpreter's purpose well enough. Origen's detailed textual work is not irrelevant to his fundamental goal of providing a spiritual interpretation of the text, because it can be used in the pursuit of that goal; but nor is it essential to that purpose, for in practice whatever text he has in hand could be made to serve his purpose.

The detail mattered, but it was the detail spiritually understood. How then did Origen detect the spiritual meaning in the details of the text before him? The process could take many forms. In the first instance it involved paying careful attention to the precise wording of a text. It is often possible, without indulging in allegory of any kind, to read a much more precise meaning into the words of a text than their author had ever envisaged when first writing them. Matthew's Gospel, says Origen, is the book of the *genesis* of Jesus Christ (Matt. 1: 1); Mark, 'realising what he was writing', describes his Gospel as the *beginning* of the Gospel of Jesus Christ (Mark 1: 1); Luke describes his Gospel as concerned with all that Jesus *began* both to do and to teach (Acts 1: 1). Thus all, in Origen's view, explicitly recognise that their accounts require the completion of John's Gospel, the most profound of the four.[1]

But individual words may also carry a deeper meaning which is distinct from and additional to their obvious sense. The Bible frequently explains the meaning of the names of people or of places in a way which coheres with the spiritual significance of that person's life or of the events recorded as happening at that particular place. Origen vastly extends the range of such interpretations. In doing so he could draw upon an established tradition of rabbinic exegesis. Most of his explanations seem to be drawn from written Jewish sources. The etymology on which they are based is often clearly wrong. But his suggested interpretations are not purely arbitrary. They are based on the very imperfect linguistic knowledge of his time and it was only with the aid of the Hebrew which he acquired so laboriously that he was able to draw as fully as he did upon the work of earlier scholars in this respect.

The interpretation of names is the most obvious example of a spiritual meaning attached to single words, but it is not the most important. Such interpretations may serve to underline the interpretation of a particular incident; they are not often determinative of the general nature of that interpretation. More important is the way in which Origen sees an allegorical meaning in the particular words or things which make up the substance of a biblical passage. We have already quoted Origen's interpretation of the story of Lot's wife in terms of the mind or spirit of man leaving behind the entanglements of the flesh. It probably appeared on first hearing to be a wholly arbitrary interpretation of the story. Origen would have denied such a charge. It is certainly not arbitrary in the sense of being an interpretation invented out of the blue solely to fit that particular story. Origen frequently claims that it is a general principle of scriptural interpretation that 'man' represents the higher element in human life, the man or spirit which is capable of attaining to a knowledge of God, while 'woman' represents the lower element. (Sometimes, it is true, he sees 'woman' as the flesh which has simply to be left behind by the spirit, and sometimes he sees her as the soul which is normally a downward drag on the spirit but which is capable of a true and fruitful union with it.)

[1] *Comm. in Ioan.* I, 6.

How did Origen derive such interpretations of many of the key concepts of scripture? Some he derived directly from scripture itself. Matt. 16: 12 states explicitly that when Jesus spoke about the 'leaven' of the Pharisees and of the Sadducees he meant their teaching. Origen observes: 'From this you will realise that whenever "leaven" is mentioned it stands figuratively for "teaching", both in the law and in those scriptures which come after the law.'[1] A word used metaphorically or parabolically with a particular meaning in one passage of scripture may be assumed to have that same meaning wherever it appears in scripture. But Origen was not dependent solely on such cases of explicit identification provided by scripture itself: his approach had a broader basis. Scripture speaks of an inner man and an outer man; it also speaks of the eyes of the soul and of men feeding upon the bread of heaven. Thus every detail of man's body and of his bodily activities has its spiritual counterpart. The words used in both cases are identical, but there is a world of difference between their meanings. The spiritual sense need not be restricted to those cases where the eyes are explicitly stated to be the eyes of the soul or the bread actually named the bread of heaven. Every reference to a part of the body or a bodily activity may be assumed to carry a reference to its spiritual equivalent. Nor need this principle of analogy be restricted to the sphere of the human. The whole world is God's creation and the invisible things are seen through the visible. If even a grain of mustard seed can be compared to the kingdom of heaven, then 'other things also may bear the appearance and likeness of things heavenly, not in one respect only, but in several'.[2] Scripture may not tell us explicitly that 'turtledove' signifies 'Church', but the absolute faithfulness of the turtledove to a single mate provides sufficient clue to its hidden meaning.

Every detail of scripture was redolent with spiritual meaning because everything, down to the smallest grain of mustard seed, had its spiritual counterpart in the invisible world. Thus Origen could convince himself that in producing an allegorical interpretation of even the smallest details of the scriptural text, he was not imposing a meaning of his own upon it. Just as man must read God's handwriting in the natural order, so he was reading the intended meaning of God's carefully chosen words in the oracles of scripture. But if Origen was able to

[1] *Comm. in Matt.* XII, 6.   [2] *Comm. in Cant.* III.

convince himself, he was not so successful in convincing all his contemporaries, let alone the modern exegete. His attempted justification of the search for spiritual meanings in scripture is not without a measure of attractiveness. But in reality it does very little indeed to reduce the arbitrariness of the process. The eyes of the inner man is a straightforward enough concept; but that the cheeks and the neck (Song of Songs 1: 10) mean modesty and obedience seems somewhat more artificial. But far more important is Origen's conviction that every passage of scripture, whatever its natural form, has a spiritual meaning of this kind. Names, parts of the body, human activities and ordinary objects of sense occur on every page of scripture. It is perfectly true that scripture itself shows that in some of these occurrences they are intended to convey a metaphorical or figurative sense But it is altogether another matter to deduce from that fact that they are always on every occurrence intended to convey such a figurative meaning. Exegesis of that kind has begun to lose touch with reality altogether.

We may return to John the Baptist's saying about the thong of his successor's shoes to illustrate the extent of the artificiality and the arbitrariness into which Origen can fall. A man's shoes are attached to the lower regions of his body; their spiritual meaning has therefore to do with Christ's mission to this lower earth. To untie his shoes' thongs is therefore to explain the mystery of the Incarnation and to distinguish between the detachable human nature and the eternal Word. Luke and John say nothing of stooping down to untie the shoes' thongs, suggesting thereby that the mystery of Christ's person may best be solved not by looking down and concentrating on the Incarnation itself but by looking up and contemplating the eternal Word. John, unlike the others, speaks only of one shoe's thong. The two shoes must therefore be distinguished, the one referring to the lowly incarnate life on earth and the other to the still lowlier descent into hell. It could be that by the time the Baptist spoke the words recorded in John's Gospel he had come to know the former but was still ignorant of the truth and meaning of the latter.

All this Origen says tentatively, but he does say it. The method has become so flexible that by means of it virtually any conclusion could be drawn from any passage of the Bible. But if the method is so flexible, what criteria controlled the nature of the conclusions which Origen actually did deduce from scripture? An important part of the answer to that question is Origen's conviction that scripture must always be consistent with itself, that the real meaning of every passage will be a part of the truth of the one Christian faith.

THE UNITY OF SCRIPTURE

If the Holy Spirit is the author of all scripture, it follows that every detail is significant since God does nothing in vain. But it also follows that the meaning of every part must be in full agreement with the meaning of every other part, since God never contradicts himself.

The issue was a living one. 'Failure to maintain a consistent harmony of interpretation from the beginning to end of the Bible', 'breaking the unity of spirit which is in all the scriptures'[1] was, for Origen, one of the distinctive marks of heresy. Above all it was the error of Marcion. Marcion is one of the very few early Christian scholars of the Bible who can merit mention in the same breath as Origen. He had the same forceful clarity of mind and something of the same pedantic scholarly literalism too. But his literalism was such that he jibbed altogether at the use of allegory. He was therefore unable to believe that Old and New Testaments were consistent with one another. If Origen had accepted his premises, he would have had to accept his conclusions. Marcion's error in theology was, in Origen's view, the inevitable outcome of his error in exegetical method.

Some degree of confirmatory link between the two testaments was possible, according to Origen, even at the straightforward level of literal meaning without recourse to allegory of any kind. The New Testament describes a number of incidents in the life of Jesus and of the apostles as the direct fulfilment of ancient predictions. Origen is ready to accept what the New Testament writings assert at its face value. Jesus was given a drink of vinegar mixed with gall as he hung on the cross. This was foretold in the words of the Psalmist (69: 21): 'They gave me gall for my meat and in my thirst they gave me vinegar to drink.' What other historical character, asks Origen, can the Jews produce who was given gall and vinegar in such perfect fulfilment of the prophecy?

But this direct fulfilment of literal prediction is never a matter of

---

[1] *Comm. in Ioan.* x, 42 and x, 18.

very great significance to Origen, it is never for him much more than an *argumentum ad hominem*. Even in the case of the vinegar and gall he emphasises that the real significance of the incident is to be seen in its allegorical interpretation. He shows a similar circumspection in his discussion of the fulfilment of the famous Zech. 9: 9 prophecy of the lowly king who enters Zion riding upon an ass. If the Christian should choose to stress the literal fulfilment of this prophecy in the triumphal entry of Jesus into Jerusalem, he lays himself open to the difficult challenge to show a literal fulfilment of the words of the succeeding verse about cutting off the chariot from Ephraim and the bow from Jerusalem. He will soon find that it is treacherous ground on which he has chosen to take his stand.

Nevertheless prophecy is for Origen a very important link between the two testaments. Its confirmatory value works both ways. The fulfilment of prophecy in the life of Jesus is not only important evidence for the reliability of the New Testament in the assumption which it makes about his messiahship and his divinity; it is not only the truth of the New Testament which receives support from the fact of prophecies fulfilled. The fact of their fulfilment is valuable confirmation also of the Old Testament in which the original prophecies are contained. Before the coming of Christ men might well have had reservations about the divine inspiration of some of the Old Testament. But Christ's coming has served to 'confirm for us the message of the prophets' (2 Pet. 1: 19, *NEB*). The concept of the fulfilment of prophecy is therefore both valid and important. But fulfilment in a direct and literal sense is only a very small part of it. Origen makes his point clearly in general terms in the *Contra Celsum*. 'Many prophets foretold in all kinds of ways the things concerning Christ, some in riddles and others by allegories or some other way while some even use literal expressions.'[1] Literal fulfilments of prophecy do exist, but they are the exception rather than the rule.

If the prophetic link between the two testaments was to be developed with the degree of thoroughness which the Church required, it could only be done with a large-scale use of figurative or allegorical interpretations. But the Old Testament does not consist only of prophecy, even in the more extended meaning which that term bore in Origen's day. Legal enactments, historical narrative and wisdom literature had

---

[1] *C. Cels.* I, 50.

also to be shown to be wholly consistent with the teaching of the New Testament. As we have already seen in relation to the Law, this could only be done very incompletely at the level of the literal meaning. Here figurative or allegorical interpretations were even more necessary if the apparent conflicts between the ideas of the two dispensations were to be overcome.

Modern scholarship has tended to draw a firm line of distinction between typological and allegorical interpretations of the Old Testament. The line has not always been drawn in the same way by different scholars, even where they are fully agreed about its crucial importance. Two features would generally be regarded as necessary components of a properly typological interpretation. In the first place it takes seriously the Old Testament law or the historical event in question as a word or act of God directly intended for and appropriate to its original historical setting. Secondly, the further meaning to which it points, that of which it is a type, must have a real connection with the initial but lesser meaning or purpose which it had in its original historical context. A typological interpretation of the Exodus, for example, is one which sees it as a real act of divine rescue of Israel out of Egypt and which also sees it as a type of Christian baptism because that too is an act of divine rescue, though rescue of a fuller and more perfect kind. To ask whether Origen's interpretation of the Old Testament is primarily typological or allegorical, commonly though it is done, is to ask the wrong question. It is not a distinction which he himself draws nor is it one which throws particularly helpful light on his exegetical method. Neither of the canons by which we have distinguished properly typological interpretations were matters of vital concern to him. We have already seen that he was in principle prepared to dispense with the original historical meaning altogether on occasion, even though he does not do so very often in practice. Similarly many of his figurative interpretations do have a close link in meaning with the original historical situation or incident, but equally certainly many others do not. They may stand anywhere on the scale from that which would satisfy the requirements of the strictest modern typologist to that which would tickle the fancy of the most imaginative allegorist. But Origen himself shows no sign of distinguishing his different figurative interpretations in that way.

His attitude to the lesser, preliminary meaning of the Old Testament is not consistent. At times the literal meaning of the Law is identified with those 'statutes that were not good' of which Ezek. 20: 25 speaks. At other times his conception of God as the great educator enables him to speak of them as having a thoroughly positive, even though incomplete, character. Before the coming of the true high priest and the true lamb of God, the sacrificial laws were like the sculptor's clay model: they served a positive purpose even though they are of no more use once the statue is complete. At one point, however, absolute consistency is to be found. However variable his judgements about the lesser, preliminary meaning of some parts of the Old Testament, the deeper meaning is always the full Christian meaning. Whether it involves the reversal of the apparent literal meaning or the fulfilment of it as an incomplete image, the true meaning will always be the meaning of the Christian gospel. Thus at the level which for Origen really matters all conflict is overcome. He makes his point forcefully in this way:

I do not call the law the Old Testament if I understand it spiritually. The law is only made the Old Testament to those who understand it carnally... But to us who understand it and expound it spiritually and with its gospel meaning, it is always new; both are New Testament to us, not in terms of temporal sequence but of newness of understanding.[1]

At the deepest level of all therefore we do not even have to think of reconciling two Testaments or of showing them to be complementary to one another. At that level they are not two at all but one. There is only the one truth of God, which is eternal and therefore ever new. The expressions of that truth in the Old Testament are hidden and obscure. But we must say more than that those expressions hint at the full truth or look forward to it. The eternal truth of God *is* the true meaning of every passage of the Old Testament. When Moses gave to the Jews their laws of circumcision and passover, of new moon and sabbath, he knew that the real meaning of what he was saying and doing had nothing to do with human bodies and the death of lambs but rather with the human heart and the sacrifice of Christ. John says that 'the law was given through Moses; grace and truth came through Jesus Christ' (John 1: 17). For Paul, Christ's relation to the law is primarily that of grace, that of redeeming man from an alien power;

[1] *Hom. in Num.* IX, 4.

for Origen, Christ's relation to the law is primarily that of truth, that of making intelligible what was always the law's true meaning and purpose. For a thoroughgoing Platonist like Origen this had to be so. The phenomenal world of historical occurrence might have a certain measure of significance; but the ultimate reality must belong to the changeless truth of the transcendental realm.

In the light of such a general understanding of divine truth, it is not difficult to see why the simple fulfilment of historical prediction should seem much less important to Origen than it appears to do to most of the New Testament writers. Even the broader fulfilment of 'types' is never allowed to rest at the purely historical level. The true meaning of the passover lamb is the sacrifice of Christ; but the sacrifice of Christ is not just his crucifixion under Pontius Pilate in Jerusalem. That too is a 'type', a 'type' of the heavenly sacrifice of Christ, which avails for the sins of every conceivable form of being, whether human, demonic or angelic. In the conclusion of a discussion of the meaning of the passover, Origen generalises this principle of final reference in scriptural interpretation with these words: 'We ought not to suppose that historical events are types of other historical events and material things of other material things; rather material things are types of spiritual things and historical events of intelligible realities.'[1]

Figurative interpretations are required therefore at every point, and not only with respect to the Old Testament in order to demonstrate its unity with the New. They are needed also to disclose the true meaning of the New Testament itself. For its deepest meaning cannot rest at the historical level. And since that deepest meaning pervades every section of the Bible, those passages which appear to be purely historical in character must have a deeper significance. Sometimes the figurative meaning of some part of the New Testament is itself developed in historical terms. As the Old Testament points forward to the dispensation of the New, so the New may point forward to the dispensation of the Church. When Jesus withdrew to a desert place on hearing of the death of John the Baptist (Matt. 14: 13), the mystical meaning of his action was a 'withdrawal from the place in which prophecy was attacked and condemned to the place which had been barren of God among the Gentiles in order that the Word of God might be among the Gentiles'.[2] But much more often and much more

---

[1] *Comm. in Ioan.* x, 18.   [2] *Comm. in Matt.* x, 23.

importantly the whole drama of New Testament history is seen as a type of the eternal truth, which may be expounded either in terms of present spiritual experience or more fully in terms of that heavenly Jerusalem already existing and one day to be entered into and enjoyed by the believer. What the law is to the recorded gospel, that the recorded gospel is to the eternal gospel.

THE PROBLEM OF EXEGESIS

Just before the start of the last section, we posed the question: with so apparently arbitrary a method of exegesis at his command, what actually determined the particular conclusions which Origen sets out in his writing and in his preaching? As at least a preliminary answer we suggested that an important controlling fact was Origen's insistence on the absolute unity of the message of scripture from beginning to end. It is an answer which Origen would readily have acknowledged. The exegete, he says, needs familiarity with the whole of scripture and a good memory. Then he can compare one passage with another, 'spiritual things with spiritual things' (1 Cor. 2: 13), and so 'by the mouth of two or three or more witnesses from the scripture may establish and confirm every word of God'.[1] In particular it was a valuable method for checking the acceptability of any suggested interpretation. But it is not the main line of answer which Origen would himself have chosen to give to our original question. The eternal gospel is a unity but it has many facets. The exegete has the task of seeing what facet of the ultimate truth is intended by each detail of the historical narrative. The criterion of the unity of scripture cannot answer that question for him. How can he be helped at this crucial point in the task of exegesis?

Origen's answer to that question is clear and is given many times over in differing forms. The Holy Spirit is the true author of scripture; the Holy Spirit therefore is the indispensable source of a true understanding of its meaning. John was enabled to write the greatest of all the books of the Bible not by virtue of any special intellectual or literary skill but by virtue of a specially close spiritual affinity to his Lord, which was symbolised by his reclining on the bosom of Jesus at the Last Supper; it is the same spiritual quality which is required of the

---

[1] *Comm. in Matt.* x, 15.

interpreter of his Gospel. As the Psalmist prayed to God to open his eyes that he might behold wondrous things out of God's law (Ps. 119: 18), so must we whenever we hear the scripture read. As the veil was taken away from the face of Moses when he turned to the Lord, who is the Spirit (2 Cor. 3: 13–17), so we must turn to the same source if we are to penetrate behind the veil of the literal meaning. As Jesus took his disciples privately into the house and explained his parables to them (Matt. 13: 36), so we must have him taking up his abode in our minds and souls if we are to be interpreters of the hidden truths of scripture.

Such an answer is the delight of the pious and the despair of the critical scholar. What is one to say of it if one wishes to be both at once? The suspicion with which the scholar is inclined to greet such an insistence is due to a fear that it may be used as a short-cut in a way designed to obviate the need for hard thinking, a fear that it may be thought to justify an appeal to intuition which will evade the drudgery of serious study and research. In the case of Origen such fears are without foundation. His conviction of the inescapable necessity of the Holy Spirit's guidance for the work of scriptural interpretation goes hand in hand with a readiness to pursue the most detailed textual or lexicographical research in the interests of a more precise exegesis. Just as in the inspiration of scripture the Holy Spirit does not bypass the human mind but enhances its capacities, so with its interpretation it is the divine Logos making his abode within the human mind who imparts to that mind the spiritual insight which it needs.

The spiritual illumination on which Origen insists so strongly is no substitute for scholarly method. The critical scholar has therefore no ground to protest in principle about that insistence, even though he may still properly reserve his right to criticise the detailed manner of its application. The Bible is more than a code of laws or a historical text-book: it is a book with a spiritual message for every generation. We give expression to that conviction when we call it 'the Bible' or 'Holy Scripture'. Just as there are no rules of thumb by which the literary critic can deduce the meaning of a poem from the past which he seeks to interpret to his own generation, so there are no absolute rules in the light of which the biblical expositor can ply his trade with confident assurance. In both cases it is reasonable to claim that the task cannot be fruitfully accomplished without a special endowment of spiritual insight. But the absence of laws is not the admission of licence. There are sometimes suggested interpretations of a poem of which one can say with confidence that they are wrong. They are too far-fetched for us to be able to agree that they are what the poem 'means', even in the most extended sense that can be given to that elusive term. That is certainly the kind of thing that one has to say with considerable frequency of Origen's exegesis. Sometimes what he writes is well expressed, doctrinally orthodox and spiritually profound, but in no sense the 'meaning' of the passage whose interpretation it claims to be. Origen's beliefs about the Holy Spirit's guidance did not lead him to skimp the hard work required of the would-be interpreter of the spiritual message of the Bible. But just as his belief in the Holy Spirit's authorship of scripture gave him a false expectancy that there were always detailed spiritual meanings to be found at every point within it, so his belief in the Holy Spirit's aid in the task of interpreting gives him at times a false confidence that he is in the process of finding them.

Many of Origen's critics would want to express these misgivings in a much more radical way. Indeed they began to do so in his own lifetime and have been doing so ever since. The substance of their charge is well expressed by the pagan Porphyry, but many a Christian has said the same thing both then and since. 'His manner of life was Christian...but in his opinions about material things and the deity he played the Greek, and introduced Greek ideas into foreign fables.'[1] Is it possible, one is tempted to ask, for someone so religiously devoted to the scriptures, so passionately concerned with the detail of their scholarly study and so wholly convinced of the truth and coherence of their teaching to be justly accused not merely of going astray in matters of detail but of a total misinterpretation of the substance of the scriptures? Many churchmen in the course of history have been guilty, some wittingly but the majority unconsciously, of proclaiming their own alien ideas under the guise of proclaiming the Christian gospel. But one does not usually expect to find such people in the ranks of the leading biblical scholars. It would be a strange irony if the greatest of all early biblical scholars should also be the supreme example of one who taught hellenistic philosophy and called it Christianity.

It would admittedly be strange, but that is no ground for saying that

[1] Eus. *H.E.* VI, 19, 7.

it would be impossible. It is not difficult to see how it could happen. Origen believed that his spiritual interpretations could be checked by their conformity with that Christian truth which is ever and always the same. But there is no such truth available to us in advance before the work of exegesis has been undertaken and therefore able to act as an independent check upon our performance of the exegetical task. The Church's tradition or rule of faith fulfils that rôle in part and it did have a sobering effect on Origen's exegesis. But the unified synthesis of Christian truth which Origen's method requires as a guide to his spiritual interpretations needed to be something far more comprehensive than the summary rule of faith. In practice it was Origen's total religious world-view, a blend of scriptural ideas, church tradition and religious Platonism. The Platonic spectacles through which he read the scriptures did colour everything that he saw there. That is not to say with Porphyry that he was simply introducing 'Greek ideas into foreign fables'. At times he does so; there are occasions on which with the aid of the allegorical method his Platonism was able to impose itself almost unaltered upon a text of very different meaning. But at other times that Platonism is radically modified by the scriptural record of the gospel of divine love, on which Origen had so firm a grasp.

It is not difficult today to recognise many of his errors and to show their cause. But we are in no position to sit in judgement on him with the scorn of a Porphyry or a Justinian, because the fundamental problem remains unsolved. The skills of textual and historical study, which Origen did so much to pioneer within the Church, have been so vastly developed that we can point out particular cases where he has gone wrong a thousand times over. But the task which Origen essayed of expounding the message of the Bible as a living and coherent whole remains. We are still faced with the problem of what we should regard as the ultimate frame of reference in the work of interpretation. If the Bible provided us with its own categories of interpretation, ready-made and adapted for our contemporary use, there would be no difficulty. But it does not. Perfect objectivity is a will-o'-the-wisp even at the historical level, let alone at the religious. The eye of the beholder has quite properly a constitutive rôle to play in the work of interpretation. The interpreter can do no other than try to present the intention of the text as it is seen through the medium of a particular mind and as it can be expressed in terms of a particular living culture. That Origen attempted to do. The nature of his achievement is that of a wayward genius. In matters of detail few if any interpreters can have shown themselves more penetrating, more subtle—or more wrong-headed. In the broad sweep of interpretation few if any interpreters can have shown so comprehensive or so profound a spiritual insight—or, we must add in line with Porphyry's judgement, so failed to do justice to the stark historicity and world-affirming aspect of the Bible. As an interpreter Origen fails. Not only is much of the detail of his work perverse, but at the broader level too he is often badly astray. But we for whom hermeneutics is a central issue of debate, in which we can see the nature of the problem better than the road to its solution, are in no position to cast the first stone.

15. THEODORE OF MOPSUESTIA AS REPRESENTATIVE OF THE ANTIOCHENE SCHOOL

Fourth-century Antioch was an outstanding centre of biblical scholarship and of ecclesiastical confusion. The former was not the primary cause of the latter, but the two were not wholly unconnected. Both characteristics were already features of the Antiochene scene in the third century. Paul of Samosata, bishop of Antioch in A.D. 268, was the first bishop to be excommunicated and deposed by a Church Council for unorthodoxy—and the first to defy that ban by staying on in possession of the Church's buildings until turned out by the civil authorities. Lucian, a presbyter at Antioch in the years after Paul's deposition, was probably the most learned biblical scholar (apart from Origen) in the whole history of the Church before Nicaea. Yet we know comparatively little of either of these men, for one was regarded as a heretic of heretics in his own right and the other as tarred with the same brush at one remove in his capacity as the supposed father of Arianism.

The leading figures of the Antiochene school of biblical scholarship in the fourth century were staunch upholders of the faith of Nicaea. Yet they probably stand much closer in approach to Paul and to Lucian than they would ever have been prepared to admit. There is the same emphasis on the biblical text, on historical fact and on the humanity of Jesus, which we can already detect in the scanty and biased accounts of Paul and Lucian. And it was the same feature of their fundamental approach—their beginning from below, their stress on the human aspect—which got them into trouble also with later standards of orthodoxy. As Lucian's school was seen in retrospect as a training ground for Arians, so the fourth-century Antiochene school in general came later to be regarded as a nursery for Nestorians. And for that reason we are faced once more with the survival in their original form of only a small proportion of the known works of the most prominent members of the Antiochene school.

This is particularly true of Diodore, the leading figure of the school in the middle of the century and bishop of Tarsus from 378. The scanty remains of his literary work are just sufficient to indicate the creative nature of his mind, but not enough to provide us with any detailed knowledge of his thought. We can, however, gain some understanding of his achievement from the writings of his two outstanding pupils, John and Theodore. John's great gift was that of preaching—as his nickname Chrysostom, or 'of the golden mouth', bears witness. The majority of his recorded sermons (and we have over 700 of them— Chrysostom was the one leading Antiochene scholar of that time to remain free of any suspicion of heretical taint) take the form of straight-forward scriptural exposition and reveal his firm grounding in the Antiochene tradition of exegesis. (Not infrequently, it has to be admitted, the sermons show a sharp break in continuity as Chrysostom moves on from exegesis to the pressing issues of contemporary society —a difficulty faced by every preacher who roots himself firmly in sober, historical exegesis.) Theodore's primary work is also revealed by his nickname—'the Interpreter' (like the name 'Chrysostom' it was given to him by posterity and does not belong to the period of his lifetime). Where Chrysostom is essentially the preacher who makes use of the work of biblical interpretation, Theodore is first and foremost biblical scholar and commentator. We shall, therefore, concentrate this study on Theodore exclusively as the greatest exponent of the Antiochene tradition in the specific field of biblical scholarship.

It would, however, be a gross anachronism to draw too sharp a distinction between Theodore the scholar and Chrysostom the preacher. Antiochene scholarship in general is a subject in which the lure of anachronistic judgements is an ever-present danger. It has many features which do have a genuinely modern ring about them, and it is easy to fall into the error of treating the Antiochenes as nineteenth- or twentieth-century critical historians with a number of surprising aberrations. But such an approach destroys the possibility of any true assessment of them. Theodore, as much as Origen, was a child of his age, though with a similar streak of originality and independence of judgement. He was born about the middle of the century, when the church of Antioch was a battleground of Arian and anti-Arian factions. He was ordained priest about A.D. 383—only a few years after the time when Antioch had had four rival bishops, Arian, old Nicene, new Nicene and Apollinarian. From 392 until his death in 428 he was bishop of the comparatively minor see of Mopsuestia in Cilicia. There he proved himself an energetic evangelist and pastor. He was also able to pursue the work of biblical exposition in comparative peace, but never out of touch with the practical needs of the Church for the defence of orthodoxy and the edification of the faithful.

Theodore himself draws a distinction between the office of the exegete and that of the preacher in the introduction to his *Commentary on John*. 'I judge the exegete's task', he writes, 'to be to explain words that most people find difficult; it is the preacher's task to reflect also on words that are perfectly clear and to speak about them. For the latter there are times when excess is valuable, but the former must give the meaning and do it concisely.' He goes on to say that the exegete must not be afraid of prolixity if it is needed, and that that is most likely to be the case when he has to deal with verses 'which have been corrupted by the wiles of heretics'. In other words the commentator is not to preach but he is to be a defender of orthodoxy—and that is natural enough, for in the judgement of Theodore and of his contemporaries orthodoxy and right exegesis were so closely related to one another as to be virtually identical.

In the light of this approach to the task of exegesis it is not surprising that Theodore's work should have been compact, comprehensive and strongly theological in character. His style is not particularly clear or attractive, but on the whole he keeps to the maxim he set out at the start of his Johannine commentary. He normally comments concisely verse by verse on the text, only prolonging his remarks where there is some point of obscurity or where the interpretation of the verse is a point at issue between orthodoxy and heresy. His commentary on John is approximately a quarter the length of Cyril of Alexandria's, and that on the Pauline epistles little more than one-tenth the size of Chrysostom's more homiletic treatment of the same set of letters. The comprehensiveness of his work as an exegete is shown by the fact that he appears to have written commentaries on almost every book of the Bible (exactly which books constituted his Bible we must consider in a moment). Most of these are lost. Theodore stood even nearer to Nestorius than Diodore and was the subject of explicit condemnation at the Fifth General Council of Constantinople in A.D. 553. The four commentaries that survive in any bulk are those on the Psalms (partly in Greek, partly in a Latin translation; incomplete, but fairly extensive remains covering the first 81 psalms), on the minor prophets (in the original Greek), on John's Gospel (in a Syriac translation) and on the minor epistles of Paul (in a fifth-century Latin translation). The first two of these are early works, almost certainly written in his twenties and before his ordination; the two New Testament commentaries are considerably later in date and belong to the early years of the fifth century. On the distinctive character of each, more will be said later. From that study too will emerge more fully the particular nature of that theological quality in Theodore's exegesis to which reference has already been made. For the moment it must suffice to insist that the emphasis on literal and historical interpretation, which is so much the most famous characteristic of Antiochene exegesis, did not in any way detract from the strictly theological character of the enterprise. Antiochene exegesis was no less theological (except in the very technical and somewhat misleading use of that word in which it is sometimes employed as a synonym for mystical) than its Alexandrian counterpart.

INSPIRATION

But first we must provide some of the evidence by which alone such assessments can be tested. For Theodore, as for all his contemporaries, the primary author of all scripture was the Holy Spirit. His work of commentary on the Psalms and on the minor prophets led him to pay more attention than the majority of early writers to the precise nature of inspiration. On one occasion he uses the celebrated image of the scriptural writer as the pen in the hand of the real author, the Holy

Spirit. But this fact should not be allowed to suggest that Theodore held a purely passive or instrumentalist conception of the human author's rôle. The passage in question comes in his commentary on Ps. 45, where the image of the pen and the writer arises naturally out of the text: 'My tongue is like the pen of a ready scribe'. In developing the analogy Theodore describes the Spirit as filling the prophet's mind with the ideas of revelation as the writer fills his pen with ink; his emphasis lies on inspiration as a special imparting of revealed truth. This general picture finds support in several other passages where Theodore speaks of the Holy Spirit providing the content of revelation and of the prophet (in co-operation with the Holy Spirit's aid) giving it appropriate form and expression. In any event Theodore's general understanding of grace was one which allowed plenty of room for the operation of human freedom, so that it is unlikely that his understanding of inspiration (which he certainly sees as a special case of divine grace) would have eliminated the human rôle altogether. Indeed the whole picture is remarkably similar to the general Antiochene conception of divine redemption. God, of his own prior divine initiative, has first provided the objective content (saving acts in the case of redemption; content of revelation in the case of inspiration); it is then a joint work of man and Holy Spirit together to work out the appropriate application of what God has provided.

All that we have said so far is developed by Theodore in terms of the Old Testament prophets and of David in particular, who was for him, as we shall see later, the prophet *par excellence*. It is not clear how far, if at all, this picture should be applied to the inspiration of the New Testament. One of Theodore's favourite examples is admittedly taken from the New Testament, namely, Peter's vision at Joppa. It included all the most distinctive features of the revelatory situation as he conceived it; it occurred in a moment of withdrawal from ordinary affairs and incorporated both visual and auditory phenomena (the vision of the great sheet full of all kinds of animals and the voice saying 'Rise, Peter, kill and eat'). Nevertheless there is never any suggestion that Theodore envisaged such a process to lie behind the writing of the New Testament documents. In fact all the evidence points against any such supposition. In dealing with the apparent discrepancies between the various evangelists' accounts of the Passion, Theodore (most unusually for his age) admits that there are real discrepancies which cannot be overcome by subtle harmonisation. These, he claims, involve only matters of secondary importance, such as the precise timing of events. In accounting for this fact (which he regards as not only not unduly damaging to the Christian claim for the historical reliability of the gospels but rather useful positive evidence that there was no collusion between the different evangelists), he argues that Mark and Luke were not themselves disciples and that their records have not therefore the precision or full evidential value of first-hand witnesses. Clearly in the writing of the gospels, at least, the human element was sufficiently real to allow for the inclusion of factual error in secondary matters through lack of fully adequate human sources of information. If the evangelists were in any sense 'pens', they were 'pens' with considerable powers of self-propulsion.

CANON AND TEXT

A man who can show that measure of independent critical assessment of the relative reliability of the various evangelists' accounts may be expected to have shown the same kind of judgement in such related topics as the determination of canon and of text. In both cases it is in relation to the Old Testament that the most interesting features emerge.

In the case of the canon our information comes in a tantalisingly incomplete and indirect form. Theodore's failure to give proper recognition to various biblical books was one of the charges laid against him by those who secured his condemnation more than a century after his death in 553. But they are not unbiased witnesses, and in most cases we lack the evidence that would be required to evaluate their accusation with any degree of confidence. He was accused of giving no place to Chronicles or Ezra; if that be true, he was simply acting in line with the early Syrian church. He was similarly attacked for rejecting James and the Catholic epistles; if that was his view, then in the case of 2 Peter, 2 and 3 John and Jude (and also Revelation) it was no more than the view of the general Antiochene tradition of his day and one which he shared with Chrysostom. James, 1 Peter and 1 John would be more surprising; it is true that he never quotes from any of them, but we have no knowledge of his actual opinions about them.

In the case of certain Old Testament books, however, the accusations brought against him at Constantinople are more precise and give some insight into the daring originality of Theodore's judgements. Proverbs and Ecclesiastes he is said to have regarded as useful works written by Solomon, who did not have the gift of prophecy but only the distinct spiritual gift of 'prudence'. There is nothing surprising about such a view in the light of Theodore's special understanding of prophetic inspiration. While it undoubtedly represents a lower evaluation of those two books as compared with the prophetic writings it need not imply any rejection of them from the Canon. Theodore's treatment of Job is more striking. Job was for him a historical figure, a model of patient endurance and uprightness. But the words of Job in the poetic sections of the book contain curses and complaints totally at variance with such a character. Theodore feels therefore that he has to choose between the Job of history and the author of the book, and opts for the former. The latter he regards as a learned pagan, an Edomite, who, to satisfy his own vanity, has written a work in which like the Greek tragedians he has fathered imaginary speeches on to historical personages. Theodore cites minor defects in the composition to support his view, such as the way the author makes God adduce the example of a fictional animal (Behemoth) in his address to Job and makes Job himself give his third daughter a name with pagan associations (an argument based on the Septuagint version of the name).[1] But despite this Theodore appears to have written a two-volume commentary on Job (dedicated to Cyril of Alexandria of all people) and does quote from the book of Job in other writings. His attitude seems therefore to have been one of drastic pruning, but to have fallen short of total rejection. Finally, in the case of the Song of Songs, Theodore rejects any spiritual interpretation; it is another writing of Solomon in which the absence of any special gift of prophecy is evident—that absence being clearly indicated in this case by the lack of any mention whatsoever of God. It is a poem written for the occasion of Solomon's marriage to his Egyptian wife, a marriage contracted to help safeguard Israel against external aggression. In the poem Solomon shows himself anxious to overcome any ill-feeling directed against his bride on grounds of her

[1] Job 42: 14. In the Hebrew the name is 'qeren happūk', meaning 'horn of eye-paint'; in the Septuagint it is Ἀμαλθείας κέρας, a proverbial phrase meaning 'horn of plenty', but referring in the first instance to the goat, Amaltheia, which suckled Zeus, from whose horn flowed whatever its possessor wished.

foreign extraction and dark skin. Theodore insists that such an interpretation is very far from treating the poem as immoral. (Why, he
asks, should Solomon have written a work of immorality when he
already had the opportunity of practising immorality as much as he
chose?) Even with this disclaimer, his view could hardly have failed
to give grave offence. He himself says that the Song is not appropriate
for public reading. Yet in his own eyes even this need not have implied
total rejection. It was still a morally acceptable work with a place in the
historical record of God's people.

Textual matters arise most frequently in the course of the *Commentary on the Psalms*. Theodore shows the scholar's instinct in his insistence that the Hebrew text, 'the language the prophet actually spoke',
must be regarded as fundamental. But he falls short of modern scholarly
standards in not being led on by that conviction to the acquisition of a
working knowledge of the Hebrew language for himself. In general,
therefore, he is dependent on the Septuagint. His respect for the
Septuagint is not based simply on grounds of current practice nor is it
wholly uncritical. It was not like the Syriac version, he argues, the
work of some unknown individual but rather of seventy respected
elders with a sound knowledge of the language. Its great merit is its
deliberate closeness to the original even at the risk of obscurity, in
contrast to its closest rival, the translation of Symmachus, whose gains
in clarity are sometimes at the cost of accuracy. Theodore recognises
that no translation can convey without loss the exact force of the
original, and that varying translations, some keeping nearer to the
original idiom, some giving more clearly the general intended sense,
can usefully supplement one another. To appreciate the proper sense
of a comparatively literal translation like the Septuagint he regards
some knowledge at least of Hebrew idiom and poetic form to be
necessary. A notable example, to which Theodore frequently recurs, is
the precise significance of the verb-tenses in the structure of the Psalms.
The Septuagint frequently gives the literal equivalent of the Hebrew
tense, when the context (and sometimes one of the other translations
as well) shows that that cannot be the intended force of the original.

Textual variants are seldom matters for comment in his New Testament commentaries. Where they are, his judgement is based wholly
on the suitability of the sense of the disputed reading, not on the
textual evidence. Thus in his commentary on Ephesians, for example, he

supports the reading of φρατρία against πατριά in 3 : 15 on the ground that there is no family kinship in the heavens, ἐπιφαύσει against ἐπιψαύσει in 5 : 14 on the ground of its greater suitability to the context and ἐπουρανίοις against ὑπουρανίοις (probably, though he does not explicitly say so, a Syriac reading, about which he is always highly scornful) in 6 : 12 on the ground that the latter would imply a total misunderstanding of man's spiritual position.

THE COMMENTARIES

But it was 'Interpreter' that was Theodore's nickname and it is as expounder of the meaning of the text rather than as determinator of its exact form that his primary claim to greatness lies. Before speaking in general terms of his quality and distinctive method as an exegete, we may best begin by surveying separately each of the four main surviving sets of commentaries.

(1) *Commentary on The Psalms*

The *Commentary on the Psalms* was a work of Theodore's youth. As with Origen, it is in this earliest work that we find many of his most original and striking ideas expressed in their most uncompromising form. He himself was later to express considerable dissatisfaction with it; in the only surviving fragment of his work *On Allegory and History* he confesses that he is painfully aware of imperfections in it arising from his inexperience at the time of its composition. Nevertheless, as we shall see, his later work does not show any serious divergence in method from this first commentary, and he himself continues to refer back to it in subsequent writings.

Much of the commentary consists of simple paraphrase, clarifying the meaning of the often obscure phraseology of the Psalms. For this purpose Theodore not infrequently cites other freer translations, especially that of Symmachus, as providing just that clarification of meaning which the reader of the Septuagint needs.

But interpretation involves more than mere paraphrase, and for this further work of interpretation Theodore takes as his starting-point the historical situation of the psalm which he is to expound. Now many of the psalms had traditional inscriptions or headings ascribing them to an author and frequently to a particular occasion in the author's life. Theodore does not regard these as having any authority; they carry credence for him only if they are substantiated by the text of the psalm itself. Theodore's aim, therefore, is to judge for himself on the basis of internal evidence what the historical occasion of each psalm must have been. He asserts without argument or discussion that David is the author of all the psalms. Moreover, he insists that each psalm is to be read as the words of David throughout. He is aware of a tradition, favoured by Jewish expositors, that some of the psalms may involve an alternation between differing spokesmen, taking the form for example of a dialogue between God and the psalmist. (The presence of a strong Jewish community at Antioch with its own tradition of Old Testament exegesis was an important influence both positively and negatively on the work of Theodore.) To this tradition he is violently opposed; he continually insists that no such change of spokesman ever occurs. Where it might appear to do so, the true explanation is normally to be looked for in a better understanding of some unusual or over-concise idiomatic form. Ps. 2: 3 'Let us burst their bonds asunder and cast their cords from us' certainly seems at first sight to involve the intrusion of a new spokesman, but in fact if you recognise that the word 'saying' is to be understood at the beginning of the verse (compare *AV* or *RV* with the Prayer Book version), there is no need to assume any change of spokesman at all in the course of the psalm. This stress on the unity and continuity of any single passage of scripture is a prominent feature of Antiochene exegesis and one which we shall find recurring in other contexts in Theodore's work.

Thus Theodore insists that the psalms are all David's and wholly David's. It might be anticipated therefore that he would have to find their historical occasion in every case completely within the experiences of David's life. But it is at this point that the most surprising feature in Theodore's interpretation of the psalms comes into play. For some psalms a setting in David's lifetime was certainly to be found (e.g. Pss. 6, 13 and 38 are related to the adultery with Bathsheba; Pss. 3, 22 and 70 to Absalom's revolt). But Theodore was equally convinced on the basis of internal evidence that the true historical setting of many of the other psalms belonged to a much later date. Not only did Psalm 72 refer to Solomon (its author according to the traditional headings) but there were others referring to the siege of Jerusalem in the reign of

Hezekiah, the capture of the city by Nebuchadnezzar, the captivity in Babylon, the return under Zerubbabel and, most striking of all, a substantial number relating to the time of the Maccabees. Psalm 51, for example, could not refer to the Bathsheba incident, despite the claim of its title, since verse 18 ('Rebuild the walls of Jerusalem') proves that it cannot refer to David's own day at all but rather to the time of the Exile. Psalm 35 refers to events in the time of Jeremiah as the existence of certain literary resemblances to the book of Jeremiah helps to substantiate. How could such a view be squared with belief in Davidic authorship? Theodore's answer is to treat David as the archetypal prophet who was given by the Spirit a vision of the future dispensation of God for his people. In the Psalms David does not merely foretell these future happenings, but speaking in the person (πρόσωπον) of those who will have to undergo them he expresses an appropriate response of confession, supplication or thanksgiving, thereby providing inspiration and guidance which would help those future generations to direct their lives appropriately when the time came.

The already remarkable character of this conception of the prophetic nature of the Psalter is further enhanced by its limitation (except for a very few cases) to the history of Israel before Christ. An understanding of the Psalter as prophetic of Christ, even if never worked out with the consistency upon which Theodore would have insisted, was after all a commonplace of Christian interpretation with its roots in the New Testament—its roots, one can even say, in the recorded preaching of Jesus and in Peter's first sermon at Pentecost. Theodore is not unaffected by this tradition. He does allow that three psalms within the compass of the commentary have a direct reference to Christ, being spoken prophetically by David in Christ's 'person' as others are spoken in the 'person' of the people of Israel at differing moments of her history. The three are Psalms 2, 8 and 45 (he appears to have interpreted Psalm 110 similarly but it falls outside the range of the surviving part of the commentary). In the case of Psalms 2 and 8, the main ground to which he appeals for relating them to Christ is their application to him in the New Testament. Yet this argument does not lead to the same conclusion in every case where the New Testament has applied the words of a psalm to Christ. Theodore's insistence on the need for a consistent and unified interpretation of each psalm is the nub of the difficulty for him. If David is speaking in the person of Christ in one verse of a psalm, he must be doing so throughout that psalm. Thus the Passion psalms, 22 and 69, cannot refer directly to Christ in the same sense as psalms 2 and 8. The final words of Ps. 22 (21): 1 in the Septuagint are οἱ λόγοι τῶν παραπτωμάτων μου ('the account of my transgressions') and are understood by Theodore as David's acknowledgement of his own sinful responsibility for God's forsaking of him; they could not possibly therefore have application to Christ; the psalm must be David's prayer at the time of Absalom's revolt. Psalm 69 contains four testimonies cited in the New Testament: verse 9 concerning the cleansing of the Temple in John 2: 17, verse 21 about the gall and vinegar at the crucifixion, verses 22–3 about the hardening of Israel in Romans 11: 9–10 and verse 25 about the replacement of Judas in Acts 1: 20. All these Theodore acknowledges, but goes on to ask whether the psalm in its original intention can really be referring to four such variant occasions. The basic meaning of the psalm has to do with the troubles and the treacheries of the Maccabaean age. In both cases the application to Christ is secondary, adopted by the New Testament writers not because they were prophecies of Christ but because they happened to be apt descriptions of what happened to him. In two cases the secondary nature of this application is made quite clear, says Theodore, by the way in which the New Testament author has consciously changed the original words of the psalm in order to make them fit better the situation of Christ's time. 'Ears' (more appropriate to the original occasion of a call to obedience at the time of the Babylonian captivity) in Ps. 40: 6 has been changed to 'body' in its citation in Hebrews; similarly 'received' in Ps. 68: 18 has been deliberately changed to 'gave' in Ephesians as more appropriate when reapplied to Christ and the gifts of the Spirit. Ps. 45 is to be applied to Christ throughout and not as by the Jews to a wedding of Solomon because its whole tenor (e.g. verse 6 'Your divine throne endures for ever and ever') shows that it concerns one above the rank of man. Ps. 72 on the other hand is to be applied to Solomon throughout and not as by some Christians to Christ; if one pays attention to the drift of the psalm as a whole and is not 'a slave to the letter' one will realise that verse 5 is not a prayer that '*he* may live while the sun endures' (which might seem to fit Christ better than Solomon) but rather that the peace and righteousness spoken of in verse 3 may so endure.

Theodore's treatment of Ps. 16: 10 does not fall precisely into either category. It is not a psalm about Christ, but an expression of David's trust that God will preserve him from his enemies; yet neither is it simply a case of reapplying words that fitted David's situation to a similar situation in the case of Christ. The words as applied to David were somewhat excessive, going beyond the bounds of natural description. They contained within themselves the hint of a further, fuller meaning so that their application to Christ is the proper completion of their total and true sense. In view of Hebrew idiom, Theodore points out, the tense of the verb is no guide in determining the application of such texts (cf. *RV* and *RSV* translations which in this case read 'Thou wilt not leave my soul to Sheol' and 'Thou didst not give me up to Sheol' respectively). This understanding of prophecy plays, as we shall see, a larger rôle in Theodore's treatment of the prophetic books themselves.

(2) *Commentary on the Minor Prophets*

Theodore's *Commentary on the Minor Prophets* was probably written shortly after that on the psalms. In it we find the same insistence on starting from the original historical situation of the prophets themselves and the same shrewd historical judgement in assessing those situations. Hosea, Joel, Amos and Micah are concerned with the threat of Assyria and the impending fall of Samaria in the eighth century; Obadiah, Jonah, Nahum, Zephaniah and Habakkuk belong to varying occasions in the ensuing century; Haggai and Zechariah prophesied at the time of the return from exile, and Malachi in the post-exilic period. The occasions of their prophesying were, therefore, closely related to some of the great moments in Israel's history, which David in the psalms had foretold. Their task was, as it were, to pick up and reaffirm the prophecies of David as the time for their realisation drew near. Thus the perspective of their historical vision was in general shorter than his, but it was by no means wholly restricted to their own day. If Amos' main task was to announce the impending danger of Assyrian invasion and captivity, it was also a part of his message to give assurance that God's purposes would not be wholly destroyed but that his grace would find expression in a future return from exile; if Zechariah's main task was to give assurance of God's favour to Zerubbabel and the people at the return from exile, it was also a part of his rôle to give warning of future troubles and unfaithfulness in the Macabbaean age

(Zech. 11:1—14: 11). Thus foretelling was a part of the prophets' rôle, but it was never arbitrary prediction; it always had a contemporary function as warning or encouragement to the people of the prophets' own time.

Theodore applies strictly his principle of seeking a consistent, connected interpretation of each book. He has nothing but scorn for interpreters who apply successive verses to Zerubbabel, to Christ and back to Zerubbabel again in expounding Zech. 9: 8–10. Since the prophetic books are not, like the Psalms, broken up into clearly separate units, there can in their case be no equivalent to the four psalms which relate directly to Christ. The only prophecy which is applied directly to Christ is the last prophecy of the last prophet, Mal. 4: 5–6, which is understood to refer to a coming of Elijah before Christ's second coming. Prophecies can only be referred to the incarnate Christ as a secondary reference, though it may be (in the sense defined in the case of Ps. 16: 10) a secondary reference which is also the necessary completion of the words' full meaning. Yet even this kind of application to Christ is comparatively rare. It is allowed only where New Testament precedent has already prepared the way. Even then, some well-known New Testament testimonies, where the New Testament application cannot be easily or intelligently related to the original Old Testament context, are simply ignored and the passage explained wholly in terms of its original Old Testament context (e.g. Hos. 11: 1, 'Out of Egypt I called my son'; Zech. 13: 7, 'Strike the shepherd, that the sheep may be scattered'). In other cases texts whose Christian reference was hallowed by tradition though not given in the New Testament are denied any such reference; Mic. 4: 1–2, 'It shall come to pass in the latter days that the mountain of the house of the Lord shall be established...', cannot in any sense be a type of the Christian dispensation, for its relation to Christian faith is one not of resemblance but of contradiction as the words of Jesus to the Samaritan woman in John 4: 21 make clear. It is predictive, but it is a prediction of the restoration of Jerusalem after the exile—even though in the light of A.D. 70 such an application requires, as Theodore recognises, interpreting the 'for evermore' in verse 7 to mean only 'for a very long time'.

In the end only five verses are given even a secondary Christian interpretation—Joel 2: 28, Amos 9: 11–12, Mic. 5: 2, Zech. 9: 9 and

Mal. 3: 1. (In the last of these the application is entirely to John the Baptist, even the words 'The Lord whom you seek will suddenly come to his temple' being referred to God's presence in the activity of the Baptist and not to a personal presence in Christ.) To these must be added the special case of the book of Jonah. The parallel between Jonah's three days in the whale's belly and Christ's three days in the bowels of the earth might not at first sight appear the kind of parallel which would have much appeal for Theodore. But it was a parallel of historical events (for Theodore never questions the historicity of the Jonah story) and therefore one falling within the range of acceptable historical typology. Moreover, Theodore succeeds in giving it an interpretation which takes in the whole Jonah story (not just the coincidence of the three days) and which gives point to the original incident in its own right as well as in its capacity as type. Jonah's experience was intended as a reassurance to the prophets that Israel's continuous rejection of God and of his message through them was no ultimate frustration of God's gracious purposes for the world; in spite of it God could still by miraculous means effect the conversion of the most unlikely Gentile nation. So with Christ was re-enacted the same sequence in its fullest significance: Jewish rejection, miraculous resurrection, conversion of the Gentiles.

But the direct prophetic message always stays for Theodore restricted to the period before the coming of Christ. And we may well ask why, since Theodore fully allows prediction of events well in the future such as the happenings of the Maccabaean age, he should not have allowed also direct prediction of events at the time of Christ also. The answer would seem to lie in his strong theological conviction of the radical nature of the break between the two ages or dispensations before and after Christ, which we shall meet as a prominent element also in determining the character of his New Testament exegesis. He always insists very strongly that Old Testament references to Holy Spirit are not references to the third person of the Trinity, who was wholly unknown to men before the coming of Christ, but are simply a way of speaking about God's grace or providential care. Zechariah's vision of a man on a red horse (1: 8) could not have been, as some maintain, a vision of the consubstantial Son, who was then wholly unknown; any Old Testament reference to a 'son of God' must always be understood at a human level to refer to one in a relationship of filial obedience to

God. Thus Theodore's historical sense, which was not in conflict with but an essential part of his theological sense, makes him (unlike the allegorists) interpret the Old Testament within the confines of its own place in the ongoing divine plan. Not only has this many advantages for Old Testament exegesis: it also enables Theodore to do greater justice to the newness of the New Testament.

(3) *Commentary on John*

Theodore's commentaries on the Old Testament show him as a scholar capable of acute historical observation. But they show him also as more than that. We see him developing there a general theory of remarkable complexity, ingenuity and originality which would be able to contain his historical insights and his sense of the religious purpose of the prophetic writings within a single scheme of an unfolding historical purpose of God.

In the Fourth Gospel he was faced with a writing which had for him a strongly historical and a strongly theological character. It had the fullest measure of historical reliability as a first-hand account, with greater attention to chronological exactitude than any of the other gospels. It was also composed with the express purpose of supplementing those other records by bringing out more fully the underlying theological truth, especially of Christ's divinity.

Theodore therefore takes very seriously the historical detail and chronological development of the Gospel record. This shows itself particularly clearly in his treatment of the faith of the disciples. When Nathanael greets Jesus as 'son of God' at the very outset of the ministry (1: 49), he cannot have meant it in the fully Christian sense but only with the human connotation of Jewish expectation. Even the acclamation of Thomas after the resurrection—'my Lord and my God' (20: 28)—must, on grounds of historical plausibility, have been a cry of gratitude to God rather than of immediate recognition of Christ's full divinity. (A piece of exegesis that was a serious rock of offence in 553.)

But if Theodore's strong historical sense leads him to portray for us 'disciples of history' with a very modern ring about them, it is no equivalent 'Jesus of history' whom he finds in the pages of the Gospel. Here the theological concern in Theodore's exegesis (a concern which he believed to be a paramount part of the evangelist's intention also) plays a determinative rôle. The Christ of the Gospel pages is the Christ of Antiochene orthodoxy—in other words a fully Nicene Christ of one substance with the Father, but one in whom there was a clear distinction between the rôles of the divine and human natures. This distinction dominates Theodore's exegesis. When Jesus says 'My Father is working still and I am working' (5: 17), the words can only refer to the full equality of the eternal co-creator Son with the Father; when he goes on to say that the Father will show the Son 'greater works than these' (5: 20), the words cannot possibly refer to the eternal co-equal Son but only to the human nature of the incarnate. Some such approach to a Gospel in which the two affirmations 'I and the Father are one' (10: 30) and 'the Father is greater than I' (14: 28) are to be found together is perhaps inescapable for any orderly system-atising mind. And that Theodore had in good measure, so that he carries through this analytic approach with relentless rigour. But Theodore, as we have seen, is a commentator who always lays stress on the continuity of a scriptural passage and who refuses to allow changes of speaker in the course of the interpretation of a psalm. What to us can easily seem a very artificial and discontinuous manner of interpretation in his handling of the Gospel did not seem to him to be such. The incarnate Christ was for him one person (Theodore was no Nestorian in intention), and if he speaks on different occasions on the basis of his distinct natures, he does not do so without purpose—a purpose intelligible in terms of Christ's own immediate historical situation. In 5: 17 (already quoted) he needed to refer explicitly to his divine nature in order to meet the charge that his healing work was a violation of the Sabbath. But when this only incensed the Jews (5: 18—'the Jews sought all the more to kill him because he. . .called God his Father, making himself equal with God'), his concern for their true good required that he change to a different tack and speak (as in 5: 20) in terms of his humanity, which was as much as they could grasp at that stage.

This relation of the Christological exegesis of the Gospel to the actual historical circumstances of the life of Jesus does not hold Theodore back from giving a wholeheartedly—indeed, one may even say, excessively—theological interpretation of the Gospel's teaching about the person of Christ. But in other ways a similar interpretation of some of the more symbolic aspects of the Gospel's teaching in terms of particular historical occurrences does seem to detract from a full apprehension of the theological depth of the Gospel. In 1:51 Jesus promises to Nathanael a vision of the angels of God ascending and descending on the Son of man; Theodore interprets this as a reference to the literal angelic visitations at the temptation, in Gethsemane, at the time of the resurrection and of the ascension. In 5:25 Jesus declares that 'the hour... now is when the dead will hear the voice of the Son of God, and those who hear will live'; Theodore refers simply to the widow of Nain's son, to Jairus' daughter and to Lazarus. In 14:18 and 28 Jesus promises to his disciples that he will come to them; Theodore finds the fulfilment of that promise in the historical happenings of the post-resurrection appearances. All these are characteristic of an approach which, however sensible and shrewd its comments, tends all too often to fall short of grasping the eternal dimension at the heart of the Gospel.

(4) *Commentary on the Pauline epistles*

It has sometimes been said that no one can be an equally sympathetic interpreter of Pauline and Johannine theology, that every theologian is born with either a Pauline or a Johannine bias. Certainly Theodore seems far more at home as an interpreter of the Pauline epistles. His characteristic attention to detail and concern for the continuity of thought in a scriptural passage are valuable assets in following out the intricacies of Pauline argument. But more importantly the theological character of Theodore's exegesis is in less danger of imposing itself upon the text which it is supposed to be expounding. In his commentary on the Fourth Gospel Theodore's theology tends to rest somewhat uncomfortably on the text which he is interpreting; but the sources of Theodore's own convictions lie closer to the Pauline text, leading to a more healthy interaction between theology and exegesis in this case. The heart of Theodore's religious vision is the conception of different ages. The age of the Old Testament was an age of incompleteness, of the law's impotence to provide a full salvation, of bondage to mortality and death; but it has given way to a new age of fulfilment, of the power of faith to do what the law was unable to do, of the gift of the Spirit as spirit of life and immortality. Into this new age man is translated by faith and baptism. Yet this is itself only a type, an image of that ultimate completion which lies in the final consummation of life beyond death. With such a conception Theodore is better enabled than most other writers of his time to do justice to the radical nature of Paul's gospel of salvation.

Yet the dangers inherent in the combination of the rôles of theologian and of exegete are also clearly evident. The point at which the ideas of Theodore and of Paul are most at variance is in Theodore's vigorous insistence on the dimension of man's freedom and his opposition to any strong form of predestinarian theory. And since right exegesis and right theology must coincide, Paul cannot have meant that God 'has mercy upon whomever he wills, and hardens the hearts of whomever he wills' (Rom. 9: 18); the words must be intended as words not of Paul himself but of the objector whom Paul is refuting. Similarly the words of verse 20 ('Who are you, a man, to answer back to God?') cannot be intended as a mere rebuke of man's questioning; they must rather be intended to show that man's ability to question in this way is an indication of his moral status and of the difference in his relation to God from that of the clay to the potter. Many may agree with the drive of Theodore's reasoning; some may wish his exegesis were correct; no one could seriously believe that it is.

Assessment

The commonest and easiest summary description of Theodore's exegesis is to call it 'anti-allegorical'. Such a description is fair and we may take it as a starting-point of our own summary, but its negative form should warn us that it can be no more than a starting-point. As already mentioned, only one fragment of his work *On Allegory and History*, directed particularly against Origen, has survived; but in commenting on Gal. 4: 24, where Paul describes his interpretation of the Hagar incident as an 'allegory', Theodore is at pains to emphasise that Paul's meaning of the word is very different from that of the so-called allegorists. Theodore's objection is to any interpretation which denies the historical reality of what the scriptural text records. Paul, he says, is involved in making a comparison and a comparison necessarily implies two realities. Paul is concerned with two historical occasions; he notes especially the 'as at that time...so it is now' of verse 29. To deny the historical character of Ishmael's persecution of Isaac and to say that its sole *raison d'être* was the allegorical meaning here given to it by Paul would lead, he says, to the absurdity of believing that the story was given by the author of Genesis solely because at a much later date certain defenders of circumcision were going to cause trouble to the Christians in Galatia. Moreover, to take a theologically more significant example, if Adam and the story of the Fall are to be denied historical reality, what are we to make of the factual way in which Paul normally speaks of Adam's disobedience and how would we have any knowledge of the theologically vital matter of the entry of sin and death into the world?

The great value of allegory to those who practised it was the way in which it made possible a theologically unified interpretation of the Bible as a whole. Theodore was as keen as any exegete to provide a theological exposition of that kind. How then does he achieve his goal while disallowing the most serviceable tool for the task? He does so in the main by his insistence on seeing the Bible as the record of a divinely intended and guided historical development. The Old Testament is to be read primarily as the account of God's gracious acts embodied in Israel's history. And the ultimate importance of that history is that it was designed in the purposes of God to provide the setting for God's supremely gracious act in Christ, by which the new age was realised as God's salvation made available universally. Thus, for Theodore, the Old Testament has to be understood first of all from within its own historical setting. And this Theodore achieves, not in the manner of a modern critical historian, yet often with great shrewdness and insight. But that is not for him the whole story. The Law and the Prophets are to be seen as type or shadow of the new dispensation in Christ. But this must always be done in a way which does not destroy the reality and purposiveness of the Old Testament history in its own setting. Moreover, the occasions where this further meaning is rightly to be found can be recognised from the nature of the Old Testament text itself; they will be occasions where the wording of the text expresses its immediate meaning 'hyperbolically', where the phraseology goes beyond what the immediate reference would seem to require. In such cases a further meaning with reference to Christ is properly to be discerned. Though Theodore seems to regard such cases as, by the standards of his own day, comparatively limited in number, this does not mean that he regards them as unimportant in substance. They are a vitally important element in that cement which gives a unifying meaning to scripture as a whole, without detracting from its essential character as the record of an unfolding historical development.

This stress on historical development is an undoubted source of strength to Theodore's exegesis of Old and New Testaments alike. But, like other aids towards a fully unified scheme of biblical interpretation, it too is not without its dangers. For it is in the light of this approach that he can find no satisfactory place in his canon for so much of the wisdom literature. The good historical sense and honesty of judgement which are such marked characteristics of his approach prevent him from finding not only allegorical meaning in them but even a prophetic or typological meaning which would fit them into that main stream of historical development in which, for him, the religious purpose of the Bible is to be found. This same single-minded determination to see the meaning of scripture in historical terms (not of course in a modern historicist sense but in terms of a divine purpose being worked out in history) also blinds him at times to nuances of thought within the New Testament, where the writer's imagination may on occasion be less firmly rooted in the dimension of history than Theodore's straitjacket requires. It is a failing at this point which is the primary weakness of his commentary on the Fourth Gospel.

But even Theodore needed other unifying categories in addition to that of historical development in his attempt to co-ordinate all his exegesis of the Bible in a single coherent pattern. Like the allegorists, he may think that he has found the categories he needs from within scripture itself, when in fact he deceives himself in so thinking. He objects to an interpretation of man's creation in the image of God in Gen. 1: 26 in terms of man's rôle of authority within the creation (which the ensuing verses in Genesis might seem to make quite plausible) on the ground that that rôle is not unique to man but belongs also to the angels. Being in God's image must be unique to man and, therefore, Theodore argues, it must refer to man's rôle as 'bond' of the cosmos, combining in himself the two realms of visible and invisible creation. Thereby he introduces into his exegesis of scripture as a whole (for it plays an important rôle also in his interpretation of the image concept in Pauline thought) an idea whose real roots are in a very different tradition of Greek culture. His historical bent may make this a less marked feature of his exegesis than it is in the case of the more allegorical Alexandrian scholars. But it does not eliminate it altogether.

Nor is he any more aware of its influence than they were. With obviously genuine sincerity, he expresses himself utterly amazed that so many people are unable to see that his interpretation of the image concept is the only possible meaning of the phrase as it figures in the pages of Old and New Testaments.

As with many other biblical commentators, his virtues and his vices are one. The same qualities which on one occasion lead him to valid and valuable insights (even against the whole tradition and trend of the exegesis of his time) may on other occasions lead him to an almost perverse inability to accept a line of exegesis which seems to cry out for acceptance (and this too he can do against the tradition and trend of his time). Perhaps the interpretation of scripture requires such a variety and flexibility of skills that no one man can ever hope to merit the title of 'the Interpreter'.

16. JEROME AS BIBLICAL SCHOLAR

Jerome was, next to Origen, the greatest biblical scholar of the early Church.

He was born, about 346, at Stridon, on the borders of Dalmatia and Pannonia. Both his parents were Christian: thus the young Jerome grew up with both a general knowledge of the Bible and some appreciation of its place in the life of the Church. They were also comparatively well-to-do, which meant that he was free to indulge his natural intellectual interests and his 'great ardour for learning'[1] for as long as and wherever he chose without the necessity for earning a living.

'In Latin', he wrote in the preface to the Vulgate Job, 'almost from the very cradle I have spent my time among grammarians and rhetoricians and philosophers.' Jerome was always prone to exaggeration. Nevertheless, it is not improbable that his formal education began at home under a private tutor.[2] When the Emperor Julian died in 363 he was a boy at school,[3] presumably at Stridon. Soon afterwards he went to Rome, together with his friend Bonosus, to sit at the feet of the celebrated grammarian Donatus.[4] Here he made his formal profession as a Christian and was baptized,[5] and embarked on the study

---

[1] *Ep.* 84, 3. [2] *Apol.* 1, 30. [3] *Comm. in Hab.* (*ad* 3: 14–16).
[4] *Chronic. Eus.* (under A.D. 358). [5] *Epp.* 15, 1; 16, 2.

of the Greek language and of Greek literature.[1] To this period must also be assigned the beginnings of his very considerable library, to which he was continually adding, and which he carried about with him wherever he went.[2]

From Rome Bonosus and Jerome moved into Gaul and took up residence at Trier, the provincial capital. Now appear the first signs of Jerome's interest in biblical and theological studies as distinct from classical. On the way the two friends had met Rufinus in Northern Italy, and at Trier Jerome copied for Rufinus two works of Hilary— his *Commentary on the Psalms* and his treatise *On Synods*.[3] After some three or four years the friends moved back to Italy and settled at Aquileia, where in association with several other like-minded young men they gave themselves up to the study of the Bible and the cultivation of the ascetic life. Among the group were Rufinus and Chromatius, afterwards bishop of Aquileia. Jerome's own first 'little work' dates from about this time. It was a commentary on Obadiah. In the preface to his later *Commentary on Obadiah*, written in 403, Jerome explains that it was allegorical, not historical, in approach: he excuses it as a work of his youth, of which he is now ashamed; and he goes on to elaborate the point with a story of how, despite his attempts to suppress it, a copy had recently turned up in the hands of a young man fresh from Italy, of the same age as himself when he wrote it, who lauded it to the skies. However, Jerome's hopes were ultimately realised. No known manuscript of it survives.

In 373 the group at Aquileia broke up, and Jerome set out for the East. At Antioch, in the year following, occurred what was probably the major spiritual experience of his life. In the middle of Lent he was attacked by a fever, and it was thought that he would die.

Preparations [he says] were made for my funeral: my whole body grew gradually cold, and life's vital warmth only lingered faintly in my poor throbbing breast. Suddenly I was caught up in the spirit and dragged before the Judge's judgement seat: and here the light was so dazzling, and the brightness shining from those who stood around so radiant, that I flung myself upon the ground and did not dare to look up. I was asked to state my condition and replied that I was a Christian. But He who presided said: 'Thou liest; thou art a Ciceronian, not a Christian. "For where thy treasure is there will thy heart be also."' Straightway I became dumb, and amid the

---

[1] Rufinus, *Apol.* II, 9.   [2] *Ep.* 22, 30.   [3] *Ep.* 5, 2.

strokes of the whip (for He had ordered me to be scourged)...I began to cry out and to bewail myself, saying: 'Have mercy upon me, O Lord, have mercy upon me'...At last the bystanders fell at the knees of Him who presided, and prayed Him to pardon my youth and give me opportunity to repent of my error, on the understanding that the extreme of torture should be inflicted on me if ever I read again the works of Gentile authors. In the stress of that dread hour I should have been willing to make even larger promises, and taking oath I called upon His name: 'O Lord, if ever again I possess worldly books or read them, I have denied thee.' After swearing this oath I was dismissed, and returned to the upper world.[1]

It is plain that Jerome did not interpret this oath too strictly. Rufinus reports that many years later he was to be found instructing the young in the classics.[2] To the very end it was his habit to season his writing with neat quotations from pagan authors. Nor, it seems, did he ever see anything incongruous (as Rufinus tartly pointed out) in referring to '*our* Cicero', '*our* Horace', or '*our* Virgil'.[3] Even so, in the light of this experience Jerome decided, for the time being at least, to turn his back on city life and seek seclusion among the hermits in the desert of Chalcis, east of Antioch.

Here he remained for four or five years, practising the most rigorous austerities and pressing forward with sacred study. He asked a converted Jew to teach him Hebrew: the first steps he found difficult; but he persisted, with ultimate success.[4] He made himself as 'eloquent' in the local 'Syrian tongue' as he had already made himself in Greek.[5] And meanwhile contact with the world was maintained by letter. In two letters he asks for books to be sent him;[6] and two more, addressed to Pope Damasus,[7] illustrate very aptly two of his more outstanding characteristics—his constitutional incapacity to keep out of controversy, and his almost grovelling respect for ecclesiastical authority.

The church in Antioch at the time was rent by schism. There were three claimants to the see, and Jerome was unable to make up his mind which to support. His own attitude was summed up in the slogan, which (he tells Damasus) was perpetually on his lips—'My man is the man in union with St Peter's chair'.[8] But all three claimants professed union.

---

[1] *Ep.* 22, 30 (trans. F. A. Wright, *Select Letters of St Jerome* (Loeb Library), pp. 127–9).   [2] Rufinus, *Apol.* II, 8(2).   [3] *Ibid.* 7.
[4] *Ep.* 125, 12.   [5] *Ep.* 17, 2.   [6] *Epp.* 5, 2; 10, 3.
[7] *Epp.* 15; 16.   [8] *Ep.* 16, 2.

Which of them did Rome accept? When Rome decided in favour of Paulinus, Jerome openly joined his party and, now back in Antioch, was admitted by him to the priesthood. It was probably now, too, that Jerome attended the lectures on scripture at Antioch of Apollinaris of Laodicea.[1] Certain it is that the end of this period in Antioch witnessed the appearance of his first controversial piece—the *Dialogue against the Luciferians*.

The year 381 saw him in Constantinople in the company of Paulinus, for the meetings of the Second General Council. Jerome eagerly seized the opportunity to attend the scriptural expositions of Gregory of Nazianzus.[2] He translated into Latin Eusebius' *Chronicle* and Origen's *Homilies on Jeremiah and Ezekiel*. He also wrote, at the request of Damasus, the first of his own short expositions of difficult scriptural words and passages. This was the treatise *On the Seraphim in Isaiah 6* (*Ep.* 18). In it Jerome based his interpretation on the Hebrew original and carefully compared with it the Greek versions of Aquila, Symmachus, and Theodotion, as well as the Septuagint, thus displaying a mastery of textual material, and opening up an approach that was altogether new in the Church of the West.

From Constantinople Paulinus and Jerome went on to Rome, together with Epiphanius, bishop of Salamis in Cyprus, to take part in the council held by Damasus in 382. Now began three years in the full glare of publicity. Damasus obviously valued Jerome highly. He not only used him as a confidential ecclesiastical secretary:[3] he also encouraged his biblical studies in a variety of ways and thereby set upon them the seal of official approval. Most important of all was the commission he gave Jerome to work on the Latin Bible. Precisely what form this commission took we do not know. From the Preface to the Vulgate Gospels (the first part of the work to appear) it is clear that what Damasus had in mind was a revision of the existing version(s) and not a fresh translation. It is also clear that it was to be a revision in the light of the Greek (from which, of course, the existing version(s) had been made). What is not clear is whether it was to be a revision of the whole Bible or of the New Testament only. The likelihood is that Damasus was thinking in terms of the whole Bible, even if he did not say so explicitly; and this is confirmed by the fact that Jerome produced

---

[1] *Ep.* 84, 3. [2] *De Vir. Ill.* 117; *Comm. in Eph.* (*ad* 5: 32).
[3] *Ep.* 123, 10; *Apol.* II, 20.

about the same time that he produced his revision of the gospels a revised version of the Psalms[1] (which, in the opinion of many, survives today as the so-called 'Roman Psalter'), and of some other Old Testament books as well.[2] At any rate, Jerome was now committed to an undertaking that was to occupy him on and off for upwards of twenty years and was to prove his most enduring title to fame.

Not that Jerome was without admirers in Rome besides Damasus. His reputation as a scholar had preceded him: he had speedily become the centre of a circle of high-born and wealthy Roman ladies, whom he influenced in the direction of his ascetic practices, and over whose studies in the scriptures he presided; and there were not a few among the general public who thought that when the time came he would make a suitable pope.[3] But when Damasus died in the spring of 385, Siricius, and not Jerome, was elected. The new pope did not hold him in such high esteem as had Damasus. Jerome determined to leave Rome for ever, and in August, once again, went East.

To begin with he had no definite plans. At Antioch he renewed his contact with Paulinus. At Antioch, too, he was joined by Paula and her daughter Eustochium, two faithful members of his Roman circle. Together they toured the holy places of Palestine and went down into Egypt. In Alexandria Jerome sat for a month at the feet of the aged Didymus the Blind[4] ('I questioned him about the things I found obscure in every part of scripture');[5] and the party visited the monks in the Nitrian desert. From Egypt they returned to Palestine and, in the autumn of 386, settled in Bethlehem, where Paula founded three convents for women, of which she was the Superior, and a monastery for men under the direction of Jerome. In Bethlehem they spent the remainder of their lives.

Jerome now embarked on his most productive period. He lectured on scripture daily and wrote continuously. Didymus' treatise *On the Holy Spirit* was translated, as were also more of Origen's biblical homilies. So was Eusebius' *Onomasticon*; and the translation of this prompted two works of Jerome's own—the *Book on Hebrew Names* and the *Book of Hebrew Questions on Genesis*. His series of extant biblical commentaries was started with the *Commentary on Ecclesiastes*,

---

[1] Preface to the 'Gallican' Psalter.   [2] *Ep. 32, 1.*
[3] *Epp. 45, 2, 3; 127, 7.*
[4] *Ep. 84, 3; Rufinus, Apol. II, 12.*   [5] *Comm. in Eph., Lib. I, Prol.*

to be followed shortly by commentaries on Galatians, Ephesians, Titus, and Philemon. And meanwhile, Jerome continued with his labours on the text of the Latin Bible. He prepared a second, and more thorough, revision of the Psalter (the so-called 'Gallican' Psalter) and applied himself to the remaining books in the Old Testament he had not already attempted. It is evident that he was now working on much stricter critical principles than he had been hitherto. The basic Septuagint Greek text was very carefully compared, not only with the Hebrew, but with all the other Greek versions too. From the library at Caesarea he obtained copies of the relevant parts of Origen's *Hexapla*.[1] And into the new Latin versions he began to introduce Origen's diacritical signs.[2]

How far Jerome actually progressed with this revision it is impossible to say. On a number of occasions he writes as if he finished it;[3] and he claims in one passage that he was still using it as the text for his daily lectures on scripture as late as 402.[4] But all that remains of it, apart from the 'Gallican' Psalter, is the version of Job, and the prefaces to Chronicles and the Books of Solomon (i.e. Proverbs, Ecclesiastes, and the Song of Songs). What undoubtedly Jerome found, as the work proceeded, was that it became more and more complicated and the result less satisfactory. Whatever intrinsic merits the Septuagint might have, and whatever authority it might have acquired in the Church, it was itself a translation and therefore secondary; it was, moreover, useless in controversy with Jews, who openly laughed at some of its renderings and quite rightly pointed out that they were a travesty of the Hebrew.[5] A satisfactory Latin version of the Old Testament could be made only on the basis of the Hebrew original. So Jerome decided to start afresh and produce his own translation of 'the Hebrew verity' (*Hebraica veritas*).[6]

Since his arrival at Bethlehem a Jew from Tiberias had helped him with his revision of Chronicles.[7] Another Jew (if it was another), named Baraninas, had come to him by night, 'like another Nicodemus', to teach him some more Hebrew.[8] And yet others were now called in

[1] *Comm. in Tit.* (ad 3: 9).
[2] *Praef. in Job* (Septuagint); Preface to the 'Gallican' Psalter. For an explanation of these signs see above, p. 458.
[3] E.g. *Ep.* 106, 2; *Praef. in Jos.*   [4] *Apol.* II, 24.
[5] *Ep.* 57, 11; *Apol.* III, 25; Preface to the 'Hebrew' Psalter; *Praef. in Esa.*
[6] E.g. *Ep.* 106, 9; *Apol.* II, 33.   [7] *Praef. in Paralip.* (Septuagint).   [8] *Ep.* 84, 3.

to assist in specific parts of the new venture: thus, he records having paid no small sum to a Jewish teacher of the highest possible reputation from Lydda to help him through the difficulties of Job ('though whether I really learned anything from him I do not know').[1] The books of Samuel and Kings were ready in 391; a third version of the Psalter (the 'Hebrew' Psalter) followed; then the Prophets and Job; and the whole undertaking was completed with the appearance of Joshua, Judges, and Ruth, towards the end of 404.

The beginning of that year was marked by the death of Paula. Jerome himself had still sixteen years of life and work in front of him. But he was getting old. A long time previously he had complained of failing eyesight and other physical infirmities, so that the employment of secretaries was a necessity, not a luxury.[2] In Lent 405 he was seized with another severe illness and again nearly died.[3] The sack of Rome in 410 not only involved Jerome in the loss of many of his closest friends: it also seemed the end of an era.[4] Refugees from the West streamed to the monastery at Bethlehem, and the organisation of relief meant that less and less time was available for study. Most of Jerome's work was now done at night, and his eyesight was so poor that even by day he could hardly read. Gradually he became as dependent on 'the voice of the brethren' for his reading as he already was on his secretaries for his writing.[5]

These last years witnessed the production of Jerome's major Old Testament commentaries—the Minor Prophets (finished 406), Daniel (407), Isaiah (404–10), and Ezekiel (410–14). Then came his last controversial treatise—the *Dialogue against the Pelagians* (416). The rate of output slackened, but the same vigour of mind, acidity of tongue, and mastery of the telling phrase, that characterised all his work, remained with him to the end. It is worth remembering in this connection that his immortal description of Pelagius as a 'dolt of dolts, with his wits dulled by a surfeit of his native Scotch porridge' (*stolidissumus et Scottorum pultibus praegravatus*) occurs in the preface to Book I of his *Commentary on Jeremiah*, which he never lived to finish. He died on 30 September 420.

[1] *Praef. in Job* (Vulg.).
[2] *Comm. in Gal., Lib.* III, *Prol.*, written in 387.
[3] *Ep.* 114, 1.
[4] *Comm. in Ezech., Lib.* I, *Prol.*
[5] *Comm. in Ezech., Lib.* VII, *Prol.*

JEROME AS A BIBLE TRANSLATOR

Jerome had an innate flair for languages. He lived at a time when the linguistic cleavage between East and West was deepening: few Christians in the East ever had known any Latin; and fewer and fewer in the West now knew any Greek. By his 'indefatigable' study of Hebrew[1] Jerome turned himself into a near-unique phenomenon at any period in the history of the early Church—a 'trilingual' (competent in Latin, Greek, and Hebrew).[2] In his youth he had also studied Aramaic (what he calls 'Chaldaic'), but he found difficulty with the pronunciation: however, he had persisted under the encouragement of 'a certain Hebrew'; although he had to confess that he always found reading Aramaic easier than speaking it.[3] By contrast, as a result of his sojourn in the desert of Chalcis he had become a fluent speaker of Syriac[4]—if that is the right modern equivalent for the 'Syrian tongue' to which he refers in a number of passages in various works.[5] He writes, too, as if he had more than a nodding acquaintance with 'Arabic'.[6] And in addition to these linguistic attainments, he had acquired, through his early training in the Latin classics, an exceptionally pure and incisive Latin style. He was thus possessed of every qualification that a successful translator could require.

His earliest works of translation were in all probability his versions of Eusebius' *Chronicle* and Origen's *Homilies on Jeremiah and Ezekiel*, completed in 381–2. To both authors he returned again. His admiration for Didymus prompted his translation of the book *On the Holy Spirit*, completed soon after the settlement at Bethlehem. His ascetic interests are represented by translations of the *Rule* and eleven of the letters of Pachomius, and his antiquarianism by translations into both Greek and Latin of the *Gospel according to the Hebrews*.[7] On several occasions he was asked by highly placed ecclesiastics in the East to provide Latin versions of their official or controversial correspondence.[8] And such was his reputation as a translator in the West that he was often credited with having translated many more authors than in fact he

---

[1] *Comm. in Gal., Lib.* III, *Prol.*   [2] *Apol.* III, 6.
[3] *Praef. in Dan.*   [4] See above, p. 512.
[5] E.g. *Praef. in Job* (Vulg.); *Comm. in Hier.* (*ad* 6: 6–7).
[6] *Praef. in Dan.*; *Praef. in Job* (Vulg.).
[7] *De Vir. Ill.* 2; *Comm. in Matt.* (*ad* 12: 13).
[8] E.g. *Epp.* 51; 92.

had: there was at one time a rumour current in Spain, for example, that he had translated Josephus, Papias, and Polycarp.[1]

But it is as a Bible translator that Jerome is most justly famous, and in particular as the translator of 'the Vulgate'. We now use 'Vulgate' to mean 'Jerome's Bible'. Yet this use, given universal currency by the Council of Trent, cannot be traced further back than the thirteenth century. In Jerome's day *editio vulgata* ('the common edition'), when applied to the Latin Bible, meant what we now call 'the Old Latin' as distinct from 'the Vulgate'—that is the popular Bible, which Jerome's work ultimately replaced; and it was in this sense that Jerome himself used the term.[2] When, however, in process of time, Jerome's new version had made its way and supplanted the Old Latin, *editio vulgata* naturally came to be applied to it rather than the Old Latin. But this is to anticipate.

Jerome did not set out at the start to produce a new Bible. As we have seen, he was set on his course as a Bible translator by Damasus. And Damasus commissioned him, so far as is known for certain, to produce a revised version of the Old Latin Gospels only. From the Gospels Jerome went on to revise the Old Latin Psalter, and then on to revisions of other Old Testament books—all on the basis of the Septuagint. The Septuagint he found increasingly unsatisfactory; and eventually he abandoned both it and revision altogether in favour of a completely fresh translation from the Hebrew. The whole process was spread over more than twenty years; and, when it was finished, the result was very much less a unity than we are apt to think. The versions of some books were fresh translations: others were merely revisions of existing versions. Some were based on Greek: others on Hebrew and Aramaic. Some, Jerome tells us, cost him much toil and anxiety:[3] others were dashed off with almost unseemly haste—as the Books of Solomon from the Hebrew, the translation of all three of which was completed in three days.[4] Of some books (e.g. Job) there were two versions: of the Psalms, it seems, three; and of yet other books (e.g. Wisdom) there were none. What, therefore, Jerome bequeathed to posterity in the field of biblical translation was made up of a variety of separate elements that differed, not only in character but also in

[1] *Ep.* 71, 5.
[2] E.g. *Comm. in Esa.* (*ad* 16: 14) (*Lib.* VI); *Comm. in Gal.* (*ad* 5: 24).
[3] *Praef. in Sam. et Reg.*   [4] *Praef. in Lib. Salom.* (Vulg.).

execution. It was also very far from identical with 'the Vulgate' that we know.

Attention has been drawn already[1] to the uncertainty that surrounds the extent of Jerome's revision of the Old Testament on the basis of the Septuagint. A similar uncertainty surrounds the extent of his activities in the New. About his having revised the gospels there can be no doubt. The gospels in the Vulgate exhibit a number of features of his translation-style: their text is in close agreement with the quotations in his epistles and other works written after 384; and they are preceded by a preface, which is unquestionably his, and which describes the circumstances in which the work was done. But with Acts, the epistles, and Revelation, it is otherwise. We might suppose antecedently that, having finished the gospels, Jerome would naturally go on to treat the other books of the New Testament in the same way; and on more than one occasion he writes as if he had ('the New Testament I have restored in accordance with the Greek').[2] There are, however, good grounds for regarding such a statement as one of Jerome's all-too-common exaggerations. For instance, one of his references to his 'New Testament' occurs in a reply to letters from Augustine;[3] but Augustine had referred only to his version of the gospels.[4] Indeed, Augustine seems to have used Jerome's gospels regularly since about the year 400, yet nowhere does he betray the slightest knowledge of the existence of a version by Jerome of any other book in the New Testament (although on three separate occasions he discusses various aspects of Jerome's work on the books of the Old Testament),[5] nor does he ever appear to quote the Vulgate beyond the gospels. Furthermore, although the Vulgate Acts, epistles, and Revelation are traditionally attributed to Jerome, there are serious difficulties in believing that they are in fact his. Certain features, characteristic of Jerome, are lacking in the Vulgate version of these books: the prefaces attached to them in the Vulgate are clearly not his; and the quotations from them in his writings frequently display such a wide divergence from the Vulgate as to make it almost impossible to suppose that they and the Vulgate have a common origin.

This last point may be illustrated by an example. In the left-hand

[1] See above, p. 515.   [2] *De Vir. Ill.* 135; *Ep.* 71, 5.
[3] *Ep.* 112, 20.   [4] Aug. *Ep.* 71, 6.
[5] Aug. *Ep.* 28, 2 (written 394); *Ep.* 71, 3–6 (written 403); *Ep.* 82, 34–5 (written 405).

column below is a quotation of Jas. 4: 13–16 from one of Jerome's letters, written in 415, only five years before he died; and on the right is the Vulgate version of the same passage:

Jerome, *Ep.* 133, 7, 2	Vulgate
Age nunc qui dicitis: hodie et cras proficis-cemur in illam civitatem, et faciemus illic annum unum, et negotiemur et lucre-mur; qui nescitis de crastino. Quae est enim vita vestra? Aura enim estis sive vapor paululum apparens; deinde dissipata. Pro eo quod debeatis dicere: si Dominus voluerit, et vixerimus, ut facia-mus hoc aut illud. Nunc autem exultatis in superbiis vestris: omnis istius modi gloria-tio pessima est.	Ecce nunc qui dicitis: hodie aut crastino ibimus in illam civitatem, et faciemus qui-dem ibi annum, et mercabimur et lucrum faciemus; qui ignoratis quid erit in crasti-num. Quae enim est vita vestra? Vapor est ad modicum parens; deinceps exterminabitur. Pro eo ut dicatis: si Dominus voluerit, et si vixerimus, facie-mus hoc aut illud. Nunc autem exultatis in superbiis vestris: omnis exultatio talis maligna est.

From this comparison there would seem to be only three possible inferences: *either* Jerome made the Vulgate version of James after he wrote *Ep.* 133 (i.e. between 415 and 420); *or*, if he made it before 415, he thought so little of it, when he wrote *Ep.* 133, that he was content to ignore it; *or* it is not his at all. There are very many examples of this kind, if we take into account the evidence of the quotations from the other books as well as James; and that evidence, taken as a whole, decidedly favours the third alternative as the best general solution. But whether we are entitled to go on from there and assume that Jerome never did revise Acts, the epistles and Revelation, or whether we ought to consider seriously the possibility that he did revise them, and that his revision has perished without trace, is another question.

The acceptance of Jerome's work by the Church took time. Only his revision of the gospels was at all widely accepted during his life-time. It had been commissioned by the pope, and this conferred on it a certain official status. But his work on the Old Testament was a private venture, undertaken either on his own initiative or at the request of his friends. It had in consequence to make its own way on its merits. Churchmen have always been conservative, and it is likely that not a little of the welcome accorded to his gospels was due to the fact that they were merely a revised version of the familiar Old Latin and not a fresh translation. When he went on to the Old Testament, the majority would doubtless have preferred him to continue along the same lines. Jerome, however, decided otherwise. He started on a revision of the Old Latin Old Testament and became increasingly concerned to secure the best Septuagint texts obtainable on which to base it.[1] But in the end he either gave it up before he had finished, or suppressed or lost the greater part of it if he ever did finish it.[2] His interests were now concentrated on his new translation from the Hebrew.

This 'Hebrew' Old Testament was not well received at first. Complaint was made that it was tainted with Judaism;[3] and it was alleged that Jerome, by abandoning the Septuagint as his base, had not only introduced all sorts and kinds of unnecessary changes, but had also cast aspersions on the inspiration of the Seventy.[4] Augustine, in particular, was concerned about the abandonment of the Septuagint and urged Jerome to think again: the 'Hebrew' version, he pointed out, was designed for reading in church: yet the Greek churches of the East would still use the Septuagint: any widespread use of the 'Hebrew' version in the West could, therefore, only result in the driving of an additional wedge between East and West—something to be deplored; and he concludes with the cautionary tale of how, when a progressive-minded bishop introduced Jerome's 'Hebrew' version of Jonah to his congregation at Oea in Tripolitania, the strangeness and unfamiliarity of it provoked a riot.[5] But it was ultimately a case of the survival of the fittest. In Gaul, Prosper of Aquitaine (*d. c.* 460) sang the praises of Jerome's new versions,[6] and Avitus of Vienne (*d. c.* 520) used the Old Latin for some books and Jerome for others. Pope Gregory the Great (*d.* 604) says the Roman church in his day used both the Old Latin and Jerome, though he himself preferred Jerome.[7] And not many years later Isidore of Seville (*d.* 636) could write of a well-deserved general preference for the new version on the ground that it was both more faithful and clearer, 'and inasmuch as it is the work of a Christian translator, truer'.[8]

About the ordering of Jerome's work into 'the Vulgate' as it is today we have no information. What indications there are point to Cassiodorus (*d. c.* 580) and to his monastery at Scylacium, on the toe of Italy. Cassiodorus is known to have busied himself with the text, copying, and arrangement of the biblical books for the edification of

[1] See above, p. 515.   [2] See *Ep.* 134, 2 in reply to Aug. *Ep.* 82, 35.

[3] E.g. Rufinus, *Apol.* II, 32–7.   [4] E.g. *Apol.* II, 24–35.

[5] Aug. *Ep.* 71, 3–5; cf. *Ep.* 82, 35.   [6] *De Ingrat.* I, 55–60.

[7] *In Job, Ep.* 5.   [8] *Etymol.* VI, 4, 5.

his monks, and it is as a constituent volume in the library of his monastery that we first hear of a 'pandect' (i.e. a complete Bible) containing Jerome's versions.[1] The earliest extant Latin pandect is the celebrated Codex Amiatinus, written in Northumbria *c.* 715; and Amiatinus has very definite links with Cassiodorus. But in any event, from the beginning of the eighth century onwards, apart from a few insignificant exceptions, the contents of 'the Vulgate' were fixed, namely: (i) Jerome's version of the Jewish canonical books (apart from the Psalter)—translated direct from the Hebrew; (ii) Jerome's 'Gallican' Psalter—a radical revision of the Old Latin, based on the Hexaplaric Septuagint; (iii) Jerome's free translations from the 'Chaldee'—i.e. Tobit and Judith; (iv) certain unrevised Old Latin 'ecclesiastical' books—Wisdom, Ecclesiasticus, 1 and 2 Maccabees, and Baruch; (v) Jerome's revised gospels; and (vi) Acts, epistles, and Revelation—revised by a person or persons unknown.

Questions of translation technique and details connected with the 'mechanics' of translation obviously occupied Jerome's mind continuously. One of his earliest works was his translation of Eusebius' *Chronicle*, and the greater part of his preface to it is devoted to a discussion of the principles on which a translation should be based and the problems that confront a translator. Translation, Jerome asserts, is a difficult, almost impossible, art to master. Languages vary so in their order of words, in their individual metaphors, and in their native idioms. The translator is thus faced with a choice between a literal, word-for-word rendering (which is certain to sound absurd and so be a travesty of the original) and something very much freer (in which case he is liable to be accused of being unfaithful). If anyone doubts this, let him try to render Homer word for word into Latin, and the result will be that 'the word-order will seem ridiculous and the most eloquent of poets scarcely able to speak'. Not even Cicero, despite his pre-eminence as a stylist, was entirely successful as a translator.[2]

To the discussion of the subject Jerome returned again and again. Sometimes his remarks are only incidental, as when he notes the difficulty of finding a suitable Latin equivalent for the Greek καταβολή in the phrase πρὸ καταβολῆς κόσμου.[3] At other times he was more explicit. As he anticipated, his translations proved a perpetual source of controversy. In 395, for example, he was accused of having falsified a

[1] *Inst.* I, 12, 3. [2] *Praef. in Chronic. Eus.* [3] *Comm. in Eph. (ad* 1: 4).

letter of Epiphanius to John of Jerusalem by a rendering into Latin that was thought to be unjustifiably free. Jerome defended himself vigorously by an appeal to the classical masters of translation (Cicero, Horace, Terence, Plautus), his predecessors in the Church (Evagrius, Hilary), and even the writers of the New Testament, all of whom, he pointed out, had in their various ways worked with similar freedom.[1] Everyone must recognise that a fine phrase in one language is not necessarily a fine phrase in another, if translated word for word.[2] The translator should, therefore, render sense for sense and not word for word.[3]

And this is what Jerome himself claims to do as a general rule, but he adds a significant exception—'except for the Holy Scriptures, where even word-order is a mystery'.[3] To what extent did he in fact make an exception in his versions of the scriptures?

His revision of the gospels was inevitably conservative. It was an early work: it was designed as a revision and not a fresh translation; and it was commissioned by the pope and was to receive the official papal *imprimatur*. So Jerome set himself deliberately to keep changes to a minimum and assured Damasus in his preface that he had 'used his pen with restraint'. Elsewhere he gives an instance: the Greek δοξάζειν is properly rendered in Latin by *glorificare*, but in the well-known passage in John 17 he says he has retained the Old Latin *clarificare* because he was unwilling to change what was read by the ancients when the sense was the same.[4] And inspection of the Vulgate gospels on the whole bears out his claim. We can see Jerome, the careful scholar, altering *azima* to *azyma* (because it corresponded more exactly to the Greek) or Beelzebul to Beelzebub (because this was the correct Hebrew form); we can see him changing finite verbs into participles because the Greek has participles (as *et congregans*...for *et congregavit*... at Matt. 2: 4); we can see him in such a verse as Mark 9: 15 emending an Old Latin text that was obviously corrupt; and we can see him replacing the traditional *panem nostrum cotidianum* in the Matthaean version of the Lord's Prayer by *panem nostrum supersubstantialem*. But relatively speaking the changes are few. What is remarkable about them is their inconsistency. Jerome tells us that he retained *clarificare* in John 17 because he was unwilling to introduce unnecessary alterations.[4] *Clarificare*, however, is the normal rendering

---

[1] *Ep.* 57, 5–10. [2] *Ep.* 57, 11. [3] *Ep.* 57, 5. [4] *Ep.* 106, 30.

of δοξάζειν throughout the second half of John—from chapter 12 to the end. Yet it is not always found after chapter 12: it is never found before chapter 12: nor is it found in Luke, Mark, or Matthew. There δοξάζειν is rendered by *glorificare*, or *magnificare*, or *honorificare*. To some extent inconsistencies of this kind may be explained as survivals from the Old Latin texts which Jerome saw no point in removing. Even so, a close inspection suggests that many of them are due to oversight rather than deliberate conservatism. He always worked in a hurry.[1] And in this gospel-revision his zeal seems to have flagged sadly as the work proceeded. He alters finite verbs into participles far more often at the beginning of Matthew than later: the Old Latin *pinnam* is corrected to the diminutive *pinnaculum* (= πτερύγιον) at Matt. 4: 5, but not at Luke 4: 9: *panem nostrum supersubstantialem* replaces *panem nostrum cotidianum* at Matt. 6: 11, but not at Luke 11: 3.

Naturally, it is in his version of the Old Testament from the Hebrew that Jerome's habits and characteristics as a translator of scripture are most apparent. In his youth he had found the style of the Old Latin prophets, when compared with the classics, 'harsh and barbarous'.[2] With this early judgement it is interesting to compare a passage written in Jerome's middle years, when he had completed his own version, not only of the prophets, but also of a number of other books of the Old Testament. Some of his youthful difficulties were due to faulty renderings on the part of the translators, but the major cause, he tells us, was his own wilfulness in comparing the scriptures with the classics: between scripture and classics there could be no comparison: no reader, therefore, should seek to find in his version any 'eloquence' of the kind that is found in Cicero: 'a translation made for the Church, although it may indeed have some literary merit, ought to conceal and avoid it, so as to address itself, not to the private schools of the philosophers with their handful of disciples, but rather to the whole human race'.[3] And it was presumably this idea that 'a translation made for the Church' (*ecclesiastica interpretatio*) was something special, coupled with the idea already mentioned that word-order in scripture could be a 'mystery',[4] that was responsible for such literalisms as *addiderunt autem filii Israhel facere malum in conspectu Domini* (Judg.

---

[1] *Praef. in Chronic. Eus.; Ep.* 117, 12.
[2] *Ep.* 22, 30.   [3] *Ep.* 49, 4.
[4] See *Ep.* 57, 5 (quoted above, p. 523).

3: 12), *homo homo de domo Israhel* (Ezek. 14: 4, 7), or *factum est verbum Domini in manu Aggaei prophetae dicens* (Hag. 2: 1).

On the other hand, Jerome affirms more than once that the principle of 'sense for sense' and not 'word for word' is as applicable to the translation of scripture as anything else.[1] This explains the considerable latitude he often allowed himself in the treatment of his original. The simple style of the Hebrew is varied, and its paratactic sentences repeatedly rearranged, in order to conform with more complex Latin idiom: proper names are sometimes translated rather than transliterated (as *Petra Dividens* at 1 Sam. 23: 28), or, if transliterated, perhaps supplied with an interpretative gloss (as *Benoni, id est filius doloris mei ...Beniamin, id est filius dexterae* at Gen. 35: 18); and the interpretative glosses are not confined to proper names (as *sebboleth, quod interpretatur spica* at Judg. 12: 6). But what is most remarkable is the variety of Jerome's renderings. Time and again he gives the impression that the last thing he would think of doing is to use a word or phrase twice in the same context if he could possibly avoid it. For example, a common Hebrew way of expressing emphasis is to add to the finite verb the infinitive absolute form of the same verb—as in *qārōaʿ 'eqraʿ* ('I will surely rend') at 1 Kings 11: 11: any normal translator into Latin would repeat the verb, and in this instance, perhaps, offer *scindens scindam*; but Jerome varies *disrumpens scindam*. Again, in Exod. 16 'the whole congregation of the children of Israel' is *omnis multitudo filiorum Israhel* in verse 1, *omnis congregatio fil. Isr.* in verse 2, *universa congregatio fil. Isr.* in verse 9, and *omnis coetus fil. Isr.* in verse 10. Similarly, Job's four messengers of woe differ in their Latin equivalents of 'and I only am escaped alone' (Job 1: 15, 16, 17, 19).

Jerome's version from the Hebrew is thus a curious mixture. In many respects it is conservative and in some places a slavishly literal rendering of the original. In other places we can discern the influence of the Old Latin and, behind the Old Latin, of the Septuagint or one of the other Greek translators (especially Aquila). Occasionally a piece of traditional Jewish lore obtrudes (as in the description of Goliath as *vir spurius* at 1 Sam. 17: 4, 23), or a passage may be given a definitely Christian 'twist' (as when 'I will joy in the God of my salvation' at Hab. 3: 18 is rendered *exsultabo in Deo Iesu meo*). Even Jerome's habit of variation in renderings poses a problem: some of the variations,

---

[1] *Epp.* 106, 29; 112, 19.

such as those given as examples in the preceding paragraph, are demonstrably studied; but others appear quite arbitrary—why should he prefer *verbum Domini* as a translation of 'the word of the Lord' in Jeremiah, but *sermo Domini* in Ezekiel? And even in this he is not consistent. The more closely one studies the version from the Hebrew the more one feels that, despite his theorisings, Jerome in practice translated very much as he happened himself to feel at any particular moment.

A fair specimen of the version is 2 Sam. 18: 28–33:

Clamans autem Achimaas dixit ad regem: 'Salve!' Et adorans regem coram eo pronus in terram ait: 'Benedictus Dominus Deus tuus qui conclusit homines qui levaverunt manus suas contra dominum meum regem.' Et ait rex: 'Estne pax puero Absalom?' Dixitque Achimaas: 'Vidi tumultum magnum cum mitteret Ioab servus tuus, o rex, me servum tuum; nescio aliud'. Ad quem rex: 'Transi', ait, 'et sta hic'. Cumque ille transisset et staret, apparuit Chusi, et veniens ait: 'Bonum adporto nuntium, domine mi rex. Iudicavit enim pro te Dominus hodie de manu omnium qui surrexerunt contra te!' Dixit autem rex ad Chusi: 'Estne pax puero Absalom?' Cui respondens Chusi: 'Fiant', inquit, 'sicut puer inimici domini mei regis, et universi qui consurgunt adversum eum in malum.' Contristatus itaque rex ascendit cenaculum portae, et flevit. Et sic loquebatur vadens: 'Fili mi Absalom! Fili mi Absalom! Quis mihi tribuat ut ego moriar pro te, Absalom fili mi, fili mi!'

Here may be noted, among other things: (1) the literalism *estne pax puero Absalom?* (in this instance repeated without variation); (2) the avoidance of parataxis in *cumque ille transisset et staret, apparuit Chusi* ...; and (3) the use of *cenaculum* for 'the chamber over' the gate— *cenaculum* is a favourite word of Jerome's, which does duty for six different words in the Old Testament as well as for ἀνάγαιον in the gospels.

JEROME AS A BIBLE TEXT-CRITIC

If it were not for the carelessness and waywardness of scribes there would be no need for text-critics at all. Jerome himself had copied manuscripts in his youth,[1] so that he could not have been unaware of the difficulty of making an exact copy. But this early experience seems to have mollified in no way his later strictures on the failings of others.

[1] *Ep.* 5, 2.

He was especially sensitive where his own writings were concerned. The preface to his translation of Eusebius' *Chronicle* shows him already apprehensive of the misrepresentation to be expected from 'the negligence of copyists'. In the preface to the 'Gallican' Psalter he complains that the text of his first revision had been hopelessly corrupted by contamination with the unrevised texts within four or five years of its issue ('so much more potent is ancient error than modern correction'). In 397 the wealthy Spaniard Licinius sent men of his own to Bethlehem to transcribe the more important of Jerome's works: Jerome inspected the results and 'repeatedly admonished them to compare their copies more carefully with the originals and correct the mistakes'.[1]

It was this inadequacy on the part of scribes, coupled with sporadic and isolated attempts at 'improvement', that was responsible for the chaotic condition of the text of the Old Latin Bible in Jerome's day. He could quite justly observe, when he set himself to fulfil the commission of Damasus and applied himself to the gospels, that 'there were almost as many texts as manuscripts': determination between them on a purely Latin basis was clearly impossible: in order to correct the mistakes of incompetent translators in the first place, the subsequent 'improvements' of confident but inadequate critics, and the additions and alterations of generations of 'nodding' scribes, resort must be had to the Greek original; and in his resort to the Greek Jerome claims that he had used 'only old' manuscripts[2]—because, of course, he knew well enough that the Greek manuscript tradition had suffered from scribes in much the same way as had the Latin, even though divergences between individual Greek manuscripts might not be either as many or as great.

How this programme worked out in practice may be seen partly from the Vulgate version of the gospels, and partly from the many observations on textual points that are scattered throughout Jerome's writings. At Matt. 5:22 the Vulgate reads *qui irascitur fratri suo* against the Old Latin *qui irascitur fratri suo sine causa*: Jerome, in his *Commentary on Matthew*, defends the omission of *sine causa* here and says that it had been 'added in certain manuscripts'. Conversely, at Luke 9:23 the Vulgate reads *et tollat crucem suam cotidie* against all Old Latins without *cotidie*: Jerome remarks that *cotidie* was found in 'the ancient copies'.[3] In neither of these instances does Jerome say expressly

[1] *Ep.* 71, 5.   [2] *Praef. in Quatt. Euang.*   [3] *Ep.* 127, 6.

that he is referring to Greek manuscripts; but, since there is no divergence between the extant Old Latin manuscripts in either instance, whereas the Greek are divided in both, it is a fair inference that he had Greek manuscripts in mind.

Sometimes, however, he is more explicit: the verses describing the appearance of the Strengthening Angel and the details of the Agony in Gethsemane (Luke 22: 43–4) are found 'in some copies, Greek as well as Latin',[1] and the story of the Woman taken in Adultery (John 7: 53— 8: 11) is found in John 'in many manuscripts both Greek and Latin'.[2] Occasionally he points out the doctrinal implications of a textual variant: the two words *neque filius*, for example, read by some texts at Matt. 24: 36, are (says Jerome) a godsend to Arians because they attribute ignorance to the Son: Jerome himself explains them as an addition 'in certain Latin manuscripts'; and he goes on to remark that they are not to be found in certain of the Greek manuscripts either, and significantly not in 'the copies of Origen and Pierius'.[3]

On other occasions he explains how he thought corruption came about. Thus, when dealing with the alternative readings *per prophetam* and *per Isaiam prophetam* in the introductory formula to the quotation of Ps. 78: 2 at Matt. 13: 35, he suggests that the evangelist wrote originally *per Asaph prophetam*, since Ps. 78 in the Hebrew text is ascribed to Asaph: an early copyist, not aware of this and not knowing who Asaph was, substituted the better-known Isaiah; and then at a later date another copyist, realising that the quotation was not from Isaiah, deleted *Isaiam* and left 'the prophet' unnamed. (Whether the reading *per Asaph prophetam* was in fact 'found in all the old manuscripts', as Jerome asserts in one of the places where he discusses the question,[4] or whether it was a conjecture of his own or someone else's, as he implies elsewhere,[5] is debatable. At all events it is not found in any extant manuscripts; nor did Jerome introduce it into the Vulgate.) But probably the most interesting of all his comments on the text of the gospels is his description of a passage that he says occurred 'in certain copies, and more particularly the Greek manuscripts',[6] at the end of Mark. The passage runs as follows:

[1] *C. Pelag.* II, 16. [2] *C. Pelag.* II, 17.
[3] *Comm. in Matt.* (*ad* 24: 36). [4] *Tract. de Ps. 77* (*ad* v. 2).
[5] *Comm. in Matt.* (*ad* 13: 35). [6] *C. Pelag.* II, 15.

Afterwards, when the eleven had sat down to meat, Jesus appeared to them and upbraided them for the unbelief and hardness of their heart, because they believed not them that had seen him rising. And they made excuse, saying, This age of iniquity and unbelief is under Satan, who through evil spirits alloweth not the true power of God to be apprehended. Therefore reveal thy righteousness now.

This is obviously an apocryphal expansion of Mark 16: 14, and it remained unparalleled until the discovery of the Greek Codex Washingtonianus (W) in the early years of the present century. It is worth noting that W gives, not only the excuse of the Eleven, but also a reply from Christ, so that Jerome may not have quoted the whole of what he found in his manuscripts. And he did not, of course, include it in the Vulgate.

A natural question is: Can the 'old' Greek manuscripts that Jerome used in the preparation of the Vulgate gospels be identified? The short answer is, No. Very often he preferred what modern critics call the 'ℵ B' or the 'β-type' text (as in his omission of *sine causa* at Matt. 5: 22, or his retention of *cotidie* at Luke 9: 23), yet by no means always (as in his rejection of *neque filius* at Matt. 24: 36). Frequently, no doubt, doctrinal and other considerations, apart from purely textual, determined his choice, so that it is difficult to be certain, in the absence of a direct statement, on what grounds in any instance his preference for a particular reading is based. Jerome was always arbitrary. But what is abundantly clear is that he shows no regular preference for 'Western' or 'δ-type' readings. And with this accords his deliberate rearrangement of the gospels in the Vulgate to agree with the customary Greek order as against the traditional Old Latin order (Matthew–John–Luke–Mark).[1]

Jerome's interest in textual problems in the rest of the New Testament may be illustrated by a brief summary of his comments on the following five selected passages from the Pauline epistles:

(1) At Rom. 12: 11 he rejects the reading *tempori servientes* in favour of *Domino servientes* (i.e. he reads τῷ κυρίῳ δουλεύοντες with the ℵ B text as against the Western τῷ καιρῷ δουλεύοντες).[2]

(2) At 1 Cor. 7: 35 he suggests that the absence of the last part of the verse in Latin manuscripts is due to the difficulty of translating the Greek.[3]

---

[1] *Praef. in Quatt. Euang.* [2] *Ep.* 27, 3. [3] *Adv. Iov.* 1, 13.

(3) At 1 Cor. 13: 3 he notes that the two Greek readings καυθήσομαι and καυχήσομαι differ by only a single letter. The right reading is καυχήσομαι ($\mathfrak{P}^{46}$ ℵ A B 33) although all Latins render *ardeam* (= καυθήσομαι: nearly all Greeks). Jerome accordingly renders *glorier*.[1]

(4) At Gal. 3: 1 some manuscripts read *quis vos fascinavit non credere veritati* and some simply *quis vos fascinavit*. Jerome sides with the latter on the ground that the Greek τῇ ἀληθείᾳ μὴ πείθεσθαι is found neither in 'Origen's copies' nor in 'the ancient manuscripts' (i.e. he sides with ℵ A B D* F G etc. against the majority of the Greeks).[2]

(5) At Tit. 2: 3 the Greek reading ἐν καταστήματι ἱεροπρεπεῖς is 'better' than that represented by the Latin *in habitu sancto*, though it is noteworthy that Jerome retains *in habitu sancto* in the text on which he is commenting (ἱεροπρεπεῖς is read by nearly all the Greeks, ἱεροπρεπεῖ by only C H** and a few cursives).[3]

So far as the text of the Septuagint was concerned, Jerome's attitude was conditioned entirely by his respect for the work of Origen. Because of his interest in the underlying Hebrew (and especially when his new translation from the Hebrew began to appear) Jerome was constantly under fire as a disparager of the Septuagint, and as constantly he felt called upon to vindicate himself.[4] He had no wish to disparage the Septuagint:[5] he admitted freely both its use by the writers of the New Testament and its place in the life of the Church.[6] But in course of time its text had been corrupted by copyists, in just the same way, and for just the same reasons, as had the text of the gospels.[7] The translators sometimes had misread or misunderstood their original, as when they read *hallᵉbānā...haḥammā* (the moon...the sun) at Isa. 24: 23 as if it were *hallᵉbēnā...haḥōmā* (the brick...the wall)[8] (although Jerome retracts this explanation a few pages later and maintains that the confusion was a purely scribal error!).[9] Some of them, too, had deliberately camouflaged their text: the translators of the Pentateuch, for instance, realising that their version was to be presented to King Ptolemy, a monotheist like themselves, had been at pains to conceal the more mystical parts and 'most of all those that announced the

---

[1] *Comm. in Gal.* (*ad* 5: 26); cf. *Comm. in Esa.* (*ad* 58: 3–4).
[2] *Comm. in Gal.* (*ad* 3: 1; 5: 7).   [3] *Comm. in Tit.* (*ad* 2: 3).
[4] E.g. *Praef. in Pent.*; *Praef. in Esdr. et Neh.*
[5] *Praef. in Sam. et Reg.*   [6] *Ep.* 57, 11.
[7] *Praef. in Paralip.* (Septuagint); *Praef. in Job* (Vulg.).
[8] *Comm. in Esa.* (*ad* 24: 21–3).   [9] *Comm. in Esa.* (*ad* 30: 26).

advent of Christ, lest the Jews should be thought to worship a second God as well':[1] indeed, 'whenever scripture witnessed to any sacred truth about the Father and the Son and the Holy Spirit, they either translated the passage differently or passed it over altogether in silence, in order both to satisfy the King and avoid publishing to all and sundry the mysteries of the faith'.[2]

But the errors in the Septuagint, however caused, could be detected and put right by reference to the Hebrew, assisted by comparison with the later Greek translations of Aquila, Symmachus, and Theodotion.[3] This had already been done by Origen in his *Hexapla*.[4] Jerome had seen and consulted the *Hexapla* at Caesarea,[5] and copies of the revised Septuagint column had been made and were used regularly in the churches in Palestine.[6] It was on this revised text of Origen's that Jerome's 'Gallican' Psalter and his other translations from the Septuagint were based.[7] And if anyone was puzzled by the differences between the 'Gallican' Psalter and their own Septuagint text of the Psalms, the answer was that they were using manuscripts of the corrupt 'common' text instead of manuscripts of the Hexaplaric text, in which the version of the Seventy was preserved 'uncorrupted and unstained'.[8] Thus, at Ps. 5 : 8 the 'common' text read κατεύθυνον ἐνώπιόν σου τὴν ὁδόν μου, but the 'Gallican' Psalter *dirige in conspectu* meo *viam* tuam, on the basis of the Hexaplaric reading κατεύθυνον ἐνώπιόν μου τὴν ὁδόν σου in conformity with the Hebrew and supported by 'the Three'.[9]

This respect for Origen and his work on the Hexapla conditioned also Jerome's attitude towards the Hebrew text of the Old Testament. The principle of correcting the Septuagint to conform with the Hebrew, as it was applied by Origen, involved the assumption that the Hebrew text of his day was the same Hebrew text that was known to, and used by, the Seventy (and, by implication, the same as the text of the original authors). Jerome shared this assumption. He may comment on the similarity of the Hebrew letters ד (*dālet*) and ר (*rēš*) and the possibility of confusion between them;[10] or he may cite an example of such

---

[1] *Hebr. Quaest. in Gen., Prol.*   [2] *Praef. in Pent.*
[3] *Hebr. Quaest. in Gen., Prol.; Praef. in Job* (Vulg.).
[4] *Comm. in Tit. (ad* 3: 9).   [5] *Brev. in Pss.*
[6] *Praef. in Paralip.* (Vulg.).
[7] Preface to the 'Gallican' Psalter; *Praef. in Job* (Vulg.).
[8] *Ep.* 106, 2.   [9] *Ep.* 106, 4.
[10] E.g. *Comm. in Ezech. (ad* 27: 15–16); *Comm. in Abd. (ad* 1).

confusion and propose (quite rightly most moderns would think) to read *haśśᵉdēmōt* at Jer. 31: 40 instead of *haśśᵉrēmōt*.[1] Or he may discuss Deut. 27: 26 in the light of its quotation by Paul at Gal. 3: 10 and conclude that Paul was correct in quoting 'Cursed is *everyone* (*kōl*) which continueth not in *all* (*kōl*) things that are written...': Paul knew his Hebrew Bible as well as anyone, and he is supported here, not only by the Septuagint, but also by the Samaritan: the Jews, Jerome conjectures, may well have excised 'everyone' and 'all' from the text for apologetic reasons.[2] (This last discussion, incidentally, is unusually interesting because it witnesses to Jerome's familiarity with the Samaritan. The extant Samaritan manuscripts of Deut. 27: 26, however, only read *kōl* once—in the second place. Did Jerome's Samaritan text really read it in both places, or did he, in his haste, fail to notice that it did not agree *exactly* with the Septuagint and Paul?)

Yet instances like this are rare. In spite of his grasp of text-critical principles and his constant censure of the Latin and Greek biblical texts of his day, Jerome found but little amiss with the current Hebrew text. This text, so far as we can see, was substantially the same as our own standard Massoretic text; and it is, therefore, to us all the more surprising that it never seems seriously to have occurred to him, either that it might have been at one time only one of several competing texts, or that it might be in any degree corrupt. The reason presumably was that, whereas Jerome's Latin and Greek manuscripts differed repeatedly and widely among themselves, his Hebrew manuscripts did not. In other words, except in the merest handful of passages, and then only in unimportant details, they posed no obvious textual problems. The *Hebraica veritas*, it must have seemed, was self-authenticating.

JEROME AND THE BIBLE CANON

The *Hebraica veritas* also influenced Jerome in another direction—namely, in his view of the extent of the Old Testament Canon.

The early Church read its Old Testament in Greek and as a matter of course accepted those books that were ordinarily read in the Greek-speaking synagogues of the Dispersion. When, however, at the end of the first Christian century, the rabbis in Palestine formally 'closed'

---

[1] *Comm. in Hier.* (*ad* 31: 38–40). The corrected reading means 'fields'; the Hebrew text *haśśᵉrēmōt* is of doubtful meaning.   [2] *Comm. in Gal.* (*ad* 3: 10).

the Canon and defined as 'canonical' only twenty-two books with an unimpeachable Hebrew ancestry, a difference was created between the Old Testament as it was understood in the Dispersion and the Old Testament of official Judaism.

In time all Jews everywhere conformed to the Palestinian ruling. But the Church was not affected: Christians still used, and quoted as scripture, books like Wisdom or Ecclesiasticus, which they had received as part of their Greek Old Testament; and, when the Greek Old Testament was translated into Latin, these books were naturally included. Christians, of course, were not blind to the differences between themselves and the Jews on this matter. Melito, at the end of the second century, on a journey 'to the east...to the place where these things were preached and done' (i.e. to Palestine), made special inquiries to find out the truth.[1] Origen, in the third century, emphasised the importance in controversy with the Jews of recognising the difference between 'their' Old Testament and 'ours',[2] and he listed 'the twenty-two books according to the Hebrews'.[3] Athanasius, in the fourth century, made a distinction between the 'canonical' books (i.e. those acknowledged by both Jews and Christians), the books 'that are read' (i.e. those acknowledged by Christians only), and the 'apocryphal' books (i.e. those rejected by both); and his list of 'canonical' books (with the possible exception of Esther) is the same as that in the 60th Canon of the Council of Laodicea.[4]

In the West we can see the influence of these Eastern authorities on the lists given by both Hilary[5] and Rufinus. Rufinus, in particular, follows Athanasius in his threefold distinction, though he calls his second class 'ecclesiastical' books: they are specified as Wisdom, Ecclesiasticus, Tobit, Judith, and the Books of the Maccabees; and all of them, he says, the fathers 'wished to have read in the churches, but not appealed to for confirming the authority of faith'.[6]

Jerome took a similar line about the place of the 'ecclesiastical' books in the Church—'as, therefore, the Church reads Judith, and Tobit, and the Books of the Maccabees, but does not receive them among the canonical scriptures, so also let it read these two volumes (i.e. Wisdom and Ecclesiasticus) for the edification of the people, but

[1] Eus. *H.E.* IV, 26, 13–14. [2] Or. *Ep. ad Afric.* 5.
[3] Eus. *H.E.* VI, 25, 2. [4] Athan. *Festal Letter*, 39.
[5] Hilary, *Tract. s. Pss., Prol.,* 15. [6] Rufinus, *Comm. in Symb. Ap.* 37–8.

not for confirming the authority of the doctrines of the Church'.[1] It may be that this statement is prior to Rufinus' (the relative dating is difficult); but what is important to notice is that, whereas Rufinus accepts a threefold division among books claiming to belong to the Old Testament, Jerome will admit only a twofold. For Jerome, in spite of what he says about the place of the 'ecclesiastical' books in the Church, there were no 'ecclesiastical' books as such: a book was either 'in' or 'out' of the Canon: it was either 'canonical' or 'apocryphal'. Like Origen, he was impressed by the futility of trying to argue with Jews from a different Canon, and he was clearly embarrassed by Jewish arguments discrediting, for example, the stories of Susanna and Bel and the Dragon which Christians read as part of the book of Daniel.[2] Hence he came (in theory at least) to champion the Hebrew Canon exclusively. There are twenty-two books in the Canon, he explains in the preface to his translation of Samuel and Kings, corresponding to the twenty-two letters in the Hebrew alphabet: these books are then listed by their Hebrew names; and any book that is not on the list is to be classed 'among the apocrypha'.

But the Latin Church looked with even less favour on Jerome's championship of the 'Hebrew' Canon than it did on his new 'Hebrew' translation. Under the influence of Augustine, who was anxious to maintain the tradition of the Western Church,[3] three successive councils in North Africa, in 393, 397, and 419, affirmed a Canon of the Old Testament based on the Septuagint. So did Pope Innocent I in 405—namely, five books of Moses, Joshua, Judges, four books of Kings, Ruth, sixteen books of the prophets, five books of Solomon, the Psalter, Job, Tobit, Esther, Judith, two books of Maccabees, two books of Ezra, and two books of Chronicles.[4] This has remained the official Roman Canon ever since, and it was left to the Reformers of the sixteenth century to revive the view of Jerome and segregate from the Church's Bible what is now regularly called 'The Apocrypha'.

Jerome, however, was not disinterested in apocryphal literature merely because it was apocryphal. He was aware of the existence of Enoch, even if he had no text of it, and he recognises it as the source of the quotation at Jude 14–15:[5] he can discuss the possibility that

---

[1] *Praef. in Lib. Salom.* (Vulg.).
[2] *Praef. in Dan.*
[3] Aug. *De Doc. Christ.* II, 8; *De Civ. Dei*, XVII, 20, 1.
[4] Innocent, *Ep.* 6, 7.
[5] *De Vir. Ill.* 4.

Paul's quotation at 1 Cor. 2: 9 was from the *Apocalypse of Elijah*[1] or that at Eph. 5: 14 from some other apocryphal book;[2] and he translated the *Gospel according to the Hebrews*[3] and on several occasions cited a noteworthy passage from it.[4] Nevertheless, apocryphal books as a class were dangerous. They were like 'the crazy wanderings of a man whose senses have taken leave of him' (*deliramenta*).[5] The younger Paula was to be brought up to

avoid all the apocryphal books, and if she ever wishes to read them, not for the truth of their doctrines but out of respect for their wondrous tales, let her realise that they are not really written by those to whom they are ascribed, that there are many faulty elements in them, and that it requires great skill to look for gold in mud.[6]

JEROME AS A BIBLE COMMENTATOR

Jerome's earliest work was a biblical commentary (the little *Commentary on Obadiah*, which has not been preserved); and biblical commentaries form the bulk of his writings.

He defines the purpose of a commentary thus: 'To explain what has been said by others and make clear in plain language what has been written obscurely.'[7] And scripture is full of obscurities.[8] Hence the need for a reliable guide.[9] Things in scripture that seem perfectly plain often conceal all kinds of unexpected questions.[10] There are many people who profess to be able to resolve these questions, but few can really do so.[11] Jerome himself does not claim to be in any way a 'master' of scriptural interpretation: he is no more than a 'partner' in study with others.[12] But what he does claim is that he has read as many different authors as possible, that he has plucked from them as many 'different flowers' as he can, and that he has distilled their essence for the benefit of his readers.[13] A commentary, if it is to be satisfactory, should always

---

[1] *Ep.* 57, 9; *Comm. in Esa.* (ad 64: 4–5).   [2] *Comm. in Eph.* (ad 5: 14).
[3] *De Vir. Ill.* 2; *Comm. in Matt.* (ad 12: 13).
[4] E.g. *C. Pelag.* III, 2; *Comm. in Esa.* (ad 11: 1–3).
[5] *Ep.* 57, 9; *Praef. in Pent.*; *Comm. in Esa.* (ad 64: 4–5).
[6] *Ep.* 107, 12 (trans. F. A. Wright, *Select Letters of St Jerome* (Loeb Library), p. 365).   [7] *Apol.* I, 16.   [8] *Ep.* 105, 5.
[9] *Ep.* 53, 6.   [10] *Comm. in Matt.* (ad 15: 13).   [11] *Comm. in Eccles.* (ad 1: 8).
[12] *Ep.* 53, 10.   [13] *Ep.* 61, 1.

repeat the opinions of the many, and say, 'Some explain this passage in this way, others interpret it in that: these try to support their sense and understanding of it by these proofs and by this reasoning'; so that the judicious reader, when he has perused the different explanations and familiarised himself with many that he can either approve or disapprove, may judge which is the best, and, like a good banker, reject the money from a spurious mint.[1]

This description of a satisfactory commentary was written in 402 in the context of Rufinus' criticisms of Jerome's *Commentary on Ephesians* and the substance of it was repeated some twelve years later with reference to Pelagius' criticisms of the same commentary.[2] It states very fairly Jerome's ideal as a commentator, even if he did not always realise it in practice. In his prefaces he not uncommonly lists the names of previous commentators and indicates the extent of his reliance on each of them: the result was thus partly his own, while in part he was indebted to others.[3] Rufinus objected that in the body of his commentaries the distinction between what was his and what was other people's was often far from clear and that it was extremely difficult to discover which, out of several interpretations given, Jerome himself preferred. Jerome's defence was a plea of 'humility': he had no desire to press his own opinions or to disparage others.[4] In fact, it is much more likely that his vagueness in this respect was due rather to his method in composing his commentaries and the speed with which he worked. It was his habit to read all the previous commentators first and then dictate,[5] sometimes so rapidly that his secretaries could not keep up with him[6]—he says he frequently got through 1,000 lines a day.[7] But in any case Rufinus had a point. It might not matter if the odd side-comment, such as the observation that only two birthdays are mentioned in scripture (those of Pharaoh and Herod), was taken over from a predecessor without acknowledgement;[8] but it was otherwise when two, or perhaps three, mutually inconsistent interpretations of the same passage were left side by side without any further discussion.[9]

---

[1] *Apol.* I. 16. [2] *Comm. in Hier., Lib.* I, *Prol.*; cf. *Comm. in Hier.* (*ad* 22: 24–7).

[3] *Comm. in Eph., Lib.* I, *Prol.*; *Comm. in Os., Lib.* I, *Prol.*

[4] *Apol.* I, 24. [5] *Comm. in Gal., Lib.* III, *Prol.*; *Comm. in Amos, Lib.* III, *Prol.*

[6] *Praef. in Chronic. Eus.*; *Ep.* 117, 12. [7] *Comm. in Eph., Lib.* II, *Prol.*

[8] *Comm. in Matt.* (*ad* 14: 6); taken from Origen, *In Matt.* X, 20 (*cf. Hom. in Lev.* 8, 3). [9] *Apol.* I, 21–9.

Not that Jerome was averse from criticising his predecessors when he felt so inclined. Origen, Pierius, and Apollinaris had all written on Hosea, either 'briefly' or 'at very great length'; but Jerome gives the impression that he had not greatly benefited.[1] Victorinus had written on Paul, but he was so immersed in secular learning that he 'knew nothing at all about the scriptures'.[2] Hilary was wrong in his interpretation of the word *Hosanna*;[3] and so were 'some' in thinking that David was called 'a man of blood' with reference to his wars.[4]

But Jerome's judgements on previous commentators were conditioned as much by personal as intellectual considerations (he was always especially concerned about a commentator's orthodoxy), and a judgement expressed on one occasion might easily be contradicted on another. Again and again he speaks of Origen in terms of the highest admiration;[5] but Origen was a heretic,[6] and Jerome's admiration for him, even as an expositor of scripture, was therefore limited.[7] So, too, was his respect for Apollinaris.[7] Rhetitius' commentary on the Song of Songs was stylistically 'sublime',[8] but it was full of the most elementary mistakes.[9] The commentary of Fortunatian on the gospels might be a 'pearl',[10] yet it was written in a 'rustic' style, and Fortunatian himself was 'detestable' because he had induced Pope Liberius to subscribe to heresy.[11]

And his opinions about the interpretation of particular passages were equally variable. An example of Jerome's contradicting himself within a few pages over a passage in the Old Testament has been cited already from his *Commentary on Isaiah*.[12] As an example from the New Testament may be cited his views on the meaning of 'holy city' at Matt. 27: 53. In a letter of 386, extolling the advantages of living in Palestine, Jerome assumes the natural interpretation and adds a warning against understanding it 'as the majority ridiculously do, of the *heavenly* Jerusalem'.[13] However, in a letter of condolence, written in 396, he has no scruples about deliberately misquoting 'at his resurrection many bodies of those which slept arose and were seen in the

---

[1] *Comm. in Os., Lib.* I, *Prol.*   [2] *Comm. in Gal., Lib.* I, *Prol.*
[3] *Ep.* 20, 1.   [4] *Adv. Jov.* I, 24.
[5] E.g. *Hebr. Quaest. in Gen., Prol.*   [6] *Ep.* 61, 2.
[7] *Ep.* 84, 2–3.   [8] *Ep.* 5, 2.
[9] *Ep.* 37, 1–3.   [10] *Ep.* 10, 3.
[11] *De Vir. Ill.* 97.   [12] See above, p. 530.
[13] *Ep.* 46, 7.

heavenly Jerusalem'.[1] In the *Commentary on Matthew*, written in 398, both interpretations are offered as alternatives.

Nowhere is Jerome's failure to observe consistency in interpretation more evident than in his attitude towards, and use of, allegory. His early commentary on Obadiah was allegorical, he tells us, because he had not yet appreciated the historical approach.[2] Yet, although he became increasingly suspicious of allegory as he grew older, he never ceased to regard it as legitimate, and in some cases necessary. In the preface to his *Commentary on Matthew* he more or less apologises for having included in it from time to time some of 'the flowers of the spiritual interpretation'. To take some passages in the Old Testament literally would be either absurd or unedifying:[3] Hosea cannot possibly be taken literally (for 'God commands nothing except what is honourable');[4] while to interpret Revelation literally would be to reduce it to the level of a purely Jewish tract.[5]

About the Christian application of the Old Testament Jerome had, of course, no doubts at all. Following the lead of 1 Pet. 3: 20 and a number of previous commentators he expounds the Ark as a type of the Church;[6] Joshua is a type of Christ;[7] and the forty-two stations of the Israelites in the Wilderness are emblematic of the Christian pilgrim's progress from earth to heaven.[8] More specifically many of the prophecies are directly applicable to Christ and Christian history: Jeremiah's prophecy about the Branch is a straightforward promise of the Advent of Christ;[9] the end of Joel foretells not only the Day of Pentecost and what followed from it, but also the destruction of Jerusalem;[10] and Isaiah's oracle on Damascus was fulfilled in the success of the Gentile Mission, the supersession of idolatry by the gospel, and the conversion of pagan temples into Christian churches.[11] Yet Jerome could be sceptical about some of the current interpretations along these lines: he will not admit, for example, that 'he will lift up an ensign to the nations' can be interpreted of the Cross and the Gentiles, on the ground that such an interpretation does violence to the context.[12]

[1] *Ep.* 60, 3.
[2] *Comm. in Abd., Prol.*
[3] *Ep.* 52, 2; *Comm. in Ezech. (ad* 47: 1–5).
[4] *Comm. in Os., Lib.* I, *Prol.*
[5] *Comm. in Esa., Lib.* xviii, *Prol.*
[6] *Lucifer.* 22.
[7] *Ep.* 53, 8.
[8] *Ep.* 78.
[9] *Comm. in Hier. (ad* 23: 5–6).
[10] *Comm. in Joel (ad* 2: 28–32, 3: 1–21).
[11] *Comm. in Esa. (ad* 17: 2–3), *Lib.* vii.
[12] *Comm. in Esa. (ad* 5: 26–30).

Jerome's commentaries thus offer the reader plenty of variety. Their outstanding characteristic is learning—sacred, secular, philological, textual, historical, exegetical, all mixed together. They preserve a mass of early exegetical matter that might otherwise have perished, and which through Jerome found its way into the commentaries of the Middle Ages. Not all of it is Christian. Regularly Jerome refers to information derived from his Hebrew instructors,[1] and phrases like 'the Jews think...' or 'the Hebrews say...' are not uncommon.[2] Thus, they are said to interpret 'the captivity of Jerusalem which is in Sepharad' as a reference to Hadrian's depopulation of Jerusalem in A.D. 132;[3] they think 'Malachi' is a name for Ezra;[4] and they cling to a very questionable interpretation indeed of 'the king of Tyre' in Ezekiel.[5] To all this Jerome added his own interpretations and a full measure of critical comments on all kinds of points as and when they happened to occur to him—the preface to book XVI of the *Commentary on Isaiah*, for instance, is used as the occasion for an extended discussion of the sources of Paul's quotation at Rom. 3: 13–18. But Jerome was not interested purely in critical matters: his exposition of Isa. 6: 9–10 shows him fully aware of the existence of theological difficulties, even if his aptitude for solving them did not match his obvious ability for dealing with the more critical questions.[6]

Undoubtedly Jerome's major contribution as a biblical commentator was the series of commentaries on the Old Testament prophets who, so far as the Western Church was concerned, provided him with a practically unworked field.[7] Like all his work, these commentaries suffer from the occasional irrelevant incursion into the realms of current ecclesiastical controversy, and they are also disfigured by some nasty exhibitions of petty spite and personal abuse. Nevertheless, they represent an achievement beyond the capacity of any of his contemporaries: they served as both a model and a storehouse for generations of subsequent commentators; and they can be read with profit, even today, especially by a student of the text. They contain, moreover, some excellent examples of Jerome's mature prose style.

[1] E.g. *Comm. in Eccles.* (*ad* 1: 14); *Comm. in Gal.* (*ad* 3: 14).
[2] E.g. *Comm. in Hier.* (*ad* 3: 14–16); *Comm. in Zach.* (*ad* 10: 11–12).
[3] *Comm. in Abd.* (*ad* 20–21).
[4] *Comm. in Mal., Lib.* I, *Prol.*
[5] *Comm. in Ezech.* (*ad* 28: 11–19).
[6] *Comm. in Esa.* (*ad* 6: 9–10).   [7] See *Comm. in Esa., Lib.* I, *Prol.*

We may conclude, by way of illustration, with three excerpts from the later part of the *Commentary on Jeremiah*, the last of Jerome's commentaries:

Haec dicit Dominus: invenit gratiam in deserto populus, qui remanserat gladio; vadet ad requiem suam Israhel. LXX: *sic dixit Dominus: inveni calidum in deserto cum his, qui perierant gladio; ite et nolite interficere Israhel!* Ridicule in hoc loco Latini codices ambiguitate verbi Graeci pro 'calido' 'lupinos' interpretati sunt; Graecum enim ΘΕΡΜΟΝ utrumque significat, quod et qipsum non habetur in Hebraeo. Est enim scriptum 'hen', quod Aquila, Symmachus, et Theodotio χάριν, hoc est 'gratiam', interpretati sunt; soli LXX posuere 'calidum', putantes ultimam litteram 'm' esse. Si enim legamus 'hen' per litteram 'n', 'gratia' dicitur; si per 'm', 'calor' interpretatur. Est autem sensus iuxta Hebraicum... Porro iuxta LXX haec intellegentia est...[1]

Haec dicit Dominus: vox in excelso audita est lamentationis, fletus et luctus Rachel plorantis filios suos et noluit consolari super filiis suis, quia non sunt. LXX: *sic dixit Dominus: vox in Rama audita est, lamentatio et fletus et luctus Rachel plorantis filios suos et noluit conquiescere, quia non sunt.* Nec iuxta Hebraicum nec iuxta LXX Matthaeus sumsit testimonium; legimus enim in eo post descriptionem infantum necis: 'tunc impletum est, quod dictum per Hieremiam prophetam dicentem: vox in Rama audita est, ploratus et ululatus multus Rachel flentis filios suos et noluit consolari, quia non sunt'. Ex quo perspicuum est evangelistas et apostolos nequaquam ex Hebraeo interpretationem alicuius secutos, sed quasi Hebraeos ex Hebraeis, quod legebant Hebraice, suis sermonibus expressisse. Rachel, mater Ioseph, cum venerit Bethlehem, subito partus dolore correpta peperit filium... Beniamin ... Quaeritur itaque, quomodo Matthaeus evangelista testimonium prophetae ad interfectionem transtulerit parvulorum, cum perspicue de decem tribubus scriptum sit, quarum princeps fuit Ephrathae, et nequaquam sit in tribu Ephraim, sed in tribu Iuda. Ipsa est enim et Bethleem διώνυμος, unde et nomina utriusque concordant; Bethleem vocatur 'domus panis', Ephratha καρποφορία, quam nos 'ubertatem' possumus dicere. Quia igitur Rachel in Ephratha, hoc est in Bethlehem, condita est... flere dicitur pueros, qui iuxta se et in suis regionibus interfecti sunt. Quidam Iudaeorum hunc locum sic interpretantur, quod capta Hierusalem sub Vespasiano... alii vero, quod ultima captivitate sub Hadriano... Dicant illi, quod volunt, nos recte testimonium sumsisse dicemus evangelistam Matthaeum pro loco, in quo Rachel condita est et vicinarum in circuitu villarum filios quasi suos fleverit.[2]

Haec dicit Dominus: quiescat vox tua a ploratu et oculi tui a lacrimis, quia

[1] *Comm. in Hier.* (*ad* 31: 2).   [2] *Comm. in Hier.* (*ad* 31: 15).

est merces operi tuo, ait Dominus, et revertentur de terra inimici—sive *inimicorum*
—*et erit spes novissimis tuis, ait Dominus, et revertentur filii ad terminos suos.*
Hoc iuxta litteram necdum factum est—neque enim decem tribus, quae in
civitatibus Medorum exsulant atque Persarum, reversas in terram Iudaeam
legimus—, sed iuxta spiritum et in passione Domini completum est et
hucusque completur, quando de toto orbe salvatur Israhel et Rachel dicitur:
'quiescat vox tua a ploratu et oculi tui a lacrimis!' Et est sensus: 'plorare
desiste—priora enim opera tua respexit Dominus—et revertentur filii tui
de terra inimici nec praesenti dolore tenearis! est enim spes in novissimis
tuis, ait Dominus, et revertentur filii tui ad terminos suos, quos habuerunt
patres eorum, Abraham, Isaac, et Iacob'. Melius autem de parvulis intellegi-
mus, quod mercedem habeant effusi pro Christo sanguinis et pro terra
Herodis inimici teneant regna caelorum et reversuri sint in sedem pristinam,
quando pro corpore humilitatis corpus receperint gloriosum. Ista est spes
novissima, quando 'iusti fulgebunt quasi sol' et infantes quondam parvuli
atque lactantes absque aetatum incremento et iniuriis ac labore corporeo
resurgant 'in virum perfectum, in mensuram plenitudinis Christi'.[1]

17. AUGUSTINE AS BIBLICAL SCHOLAR

Early in the year 391, just after his ordination (much against his will)
as presbyter of Hippo, Augustine addressed a letter to his bishop,
Valerius, begging for a little respite before taking up his duties, in
order that he might undertake a detailed study of scripture, as he had
been about to do when priest's orders had been forced upon him.

Perhaps there are some counsels in the sacred books—indeed, it is certain
that there are [he wrote]—which, if the man of God understands and accepts,
will enable him to perform his duties to the Church, or at least keep a clear
conscience in a wicked world so that, living and dying, he lose not that life
for which alone meek and gentle Christian hearts long. But how can this be
done except, as our Lord Himself says, by seeking, asking and knocking,
that is by prayer, study and penitence? It was with this end in view that I
sought through my brethren to obtain from your dear and venerable kind-
ness some little time—say until Easter—and to theirs I now add my personal
appeal.[2]

Valerius, a kindly man who was well aware what a treasure he had
found in his new presbyter, gave his consent, and Augustine in the
short time at his disposal—the last free time of his life—embarked

---

[1] *Comm. in Hier.* (ad 31: 16–17).　　　[2] *Ep.* 21, 4.

upon a course of reading of which the fruits were to be seen in the writings which he produced in the course of the next four decades.

Augustine's achievements as a biblical scholar and exegete can be appreciated only in relation to his childhood and general education. At the time of his ordination he had neither the solid foundation for scriptural exegesis provided by the regular reading of the Bible nor the scholarly accuracy produced by disciplined study. So far as we can tell, Augustine's religious instruction as a boy was of a superficial character. His mother Monica, although a saint, was not an educated woman, while his father Patricius was, for practical purposes, an unbeliever, and only became a catechumen towards the end of his life, when Augustine was about sixteen.[1] We can be sure that Monica went to church frequently and may fairly assume that she took her children with her; but Patricius' church-going would probably be confined to important occasions. In short, Augustine as a boy can hardly have known much of Christian family life, and his reference made soon after his conversion to the religion 'implanted in him in his childhood days'[2] ought not to be pressed. Monica certainly 'taught Augustine to pray and to hold in reverence the sacred name of Christ',[3] but it is doubtful whether she did much more, and if the schoolboy Augustine had been faced with the sort of inquisition to which Jane Eyre was subjected by Mr Brocklehurst, it is likely that his performance would have been even less distinguished than was Jane's on that unhappy occasion.[4] Nevertheless, the religious instruction of Augustine's youth had a permanent effect upon his attitude to the Bible. It was the Word of God. After his undergraduate conversion to philosophy, brought about by reading Cicero's *Hortensius*, it was to the Bible that Augustine turned, almost instinctively, in the hope of finding truth.[5] The result was bitter disappointment. By this time Augustine's rhetorical education had had its effect, and he was repelled alike by the style and obscurity of scripture and the unedifying details recorded of the lives of the Jewish patriarchs. In this unhappy state of mind he fell in with the Manichees, who assured him that the Old Testament could be disregarded, and that the New had been interpolated by Judaisers.[6] For a time this explanation satisfied him, even though the Manichees failed

[1] *Conf.* II, 3, 6.   [2] *C. Acad.* II, 2, 5. Cf. *De Util. Cred.* I, 2.
[3] R. L. Ottley, *Studies in the Confessions of St Augustine* (London, 1919), p. 5.
[4] Charlotte Brontë, *Jane Eyre*, ch. 4.   [5] *Conf.* III, 5, 9.
[6] *Ibid.* V, 11, 21.

to produce any uncorrupted versions of the scriptures. However, Augustine's increasing disillusionment with the sect during the period of more than nine years that he spent in it caused him to experience the greatest delight on hearing Ambrose's sermons at Milan, which explained that much in the Old Testament was to be understood in an allegorical sense.[1] Under Ambrose's influence, Augustine's difficulties about the Bible began to be resolved, and the process was accelerated by his discovery of Neo-Platonist philosophy in which (he persuaded himself) he could find confirmation of much that was in the Gospel of John.[2] On the eve of Augustine's conversion his friend Pontitianus, a professed Christian, was delighted to find him studying the epistles of Paul.[3] After his decision to seek baptism, Augustine approached Ambrose for advice about suitable reading and was (rather surprisingly) advised to read Isaiah—a work which he found to be too difficult for him at that stage, and which he accordingly set aside to study at a later date.[4] In fact, Augustine can hardly have undertaken much serious and detailed biblical study until just before his ordination. He read the Psalms during his retreat at Cassiciacum in the autumn of 386 with deep emotion, and was moved to tears by the hymns and canticles of the church of Milan,[5] but the writings which he produced in the first years of his life as a Christian are only relatively sparsely furnished with scriptural references.

However, from the time of Augustine's return to Africa in 388 the situation altered. His first book, begun and completed after returning to Thagaste, was *On Genesis against the Manichees* (*De Genesi contra Manichaeos*), in which he made use of the allegorical method of scriptural exegesis which he had learned from Ambrose in order to refute the Manichaean view of the Old Testament. In the years following Augustine's ordination a stream of biblical commentaries came from his pen[6] which reached its high point in the great series of sermons on the Psalms and the Johannine writings of the period 414–17,[7] upon

---

[1] *Conf.* v, 14, 24. [2] *Ibid.* VII, 9, 13.

[3] *Ibid.* VIII, 6, 14. Cf. *C. Acad.* II, 2, 5. [4] *Ibid.* IX, 5, 13. [5] *Ibid.* IX, 4, 8; 6, 14.

[6] *De Genesi ad Litteram liber imperfectus* (393–4); *De Sermone Domini in Monte libri II* (393–4); *Expositio quarundam propositionum ex Epistola ad Romanos* (394); *Epistolae ad Galatas Expositio* (394); *Expositio inchoata Epistolae ad Romanos* (394–5).

[7] *Enarrationes in Psalmos*; *In Ioannis Evangelium Tractatus CXXIV*; *In Epistolam Ioannis ad Parthos Tractatus X*. For a discussion of the dating of these works, see M. Le Landais, 'Deux années de prédication de saint Augustin', *Études Augustiniennes* by H. Rondet, M. Le Landais, A. Lauras and C. Couturier (Paris, 1953), pp. 9–95.

which his reputation as a preacher and exegete ultimately depends. The effect of this close and devoted application to the text of scripture in Augustine's early years as a priest and bishop may be seen in his later writings, both exegetical and controversial, with their constant citations which, on occasion, produce what is virtually a mosaic of scripture texts, perfectly welded together.

The Canon of scripture to which Augustine appealed and upon which he based his teaching was substantially that of the present day. The African Council of Carthage of 397, at which Augustine was present, recognised an Old Testament Canon which included the books of the Apocrypha (Ecclesiasticus, Wisdom, Tobit, Judith, Esther, 1 and 2 Esdras, and 1 and 2 Maccabees) and a New Testament Canon which included Hebrews (ascribed to Paul) and 2 Peter. This list is reproduced by Augustine in his treatise *De Doctrina Christiana* (II, 8, 13), and in the same work he gives a definition of what he regards as establishing canonicity: it is the authority of the majority of Catholic churches, and especially those of apostolic foundation and those which received the Pauline and Catholic epistles.[1] Augustine was aware that in his day there was still some hesitation among Catholic Christians regarding the reception of certain books of the Bible, and laid down the general principle that the books which command the greatest measure of support enjoy the greatest authority. Nevertheless, while allowing for degrees of authority in the books comprising the sacred text, Augustine made a clear distinction between what might be reckoned canonical and what might not. Towards the end of 419 he had to answer a certain Vicentius Victor, who had challenged the doctrine of the damnation of the unbaptized by appealing to the famous story of the African martyr Perpetua who, by her prayers, rescued her dead brother Dinocrates from a place of torment. Augustine, in his reply, was quick to point out that the *Passion of St Perpetua* was not canonical scripture and could not therefore be used to establish any point of doctrine.[2] Nevertheless African tradition, confirmed by African conciliar legislation, permitted the reading of the Passions of the martyrs in church on the anniversary of their martyrdom, and Augustine adhered to this practice at Hippo. The principle, however, remained: the Passions were not canonical scripture.

The actual text of scripture upon which Augustine exercised his

---

[1] *De Doc. Christ.* II, 8, 12.   [2] *De anima et eius origine*, I, 10, 12.

exegetical talent varied during the course of his life. During the third century A.D. a Latin version of the Bible had been produced in Africa which was frequently quoted by Cyprian, but there was no one official version. Augustine indeed deplored the multiplicity of translations circulating in Africa and recommended the *Itala* as being superior to all other versions.[1] The identity of this *Itala* has been the subject of much discussion which cannot be repeated here.[2] It would appear to have been a European version of the Old Latin translation used in North Africa in Augustine's time, but it does not seem possible to be more precise than this. In any case, from about 400 onwards, Augustine used Jerome's Vulgate revision of the text of the gospels in his church at Hippo and long passages from the Vulgate appear in his works after that date.[3] At the same time, in a manner which seems very strange to modern Western scholars, Augustine continued to the end of his life to regard as authoritative an Old Testament text based on the Greek Septuagint translation, and to depreciate Jerome's new translation based on the Hebrew. 'Their authority is of the weightiest', he wrote to Jerome in 394 or 395, *apropos* of the Septuagint translators;[4] he still held the same view at the end of his life, when he was concluding the *De Civitate Dei* in 426–7:

There were other interpreters who translated these sacred oracles out of the Hebrew tongue into Greek as Aquila, Symmachus, and Theodotion, and also that translation which, as the name of the author is unknown, is quoted as the Fifth Edition, yet the Church has received this Septuagint translation just as if it were the only one; and it has been used by the Greek Christian people, most of whom are not aware that there is any other. From this translation there has also been made a translation in the Latin tongue, which the Latin churches use. Our times however have enjoyed the advantage of the presbyter Jerome, a man most learned and skilled in all three languages, who translated these same scriptures into the Latin speech, not from the Greek, but from the Hebrew.[5]

Jerome was dead by the time Augustine wrote these words, which he would probably have regarded as an inadequate tribute to his life's work. Augustine's attitude was not, however, mere obscurantism. The

---

[1] *De Doc. Christ.* II, 15, 22.　　　　[2] Cf. above, p. 372.
[3] See C. H. Milne, *A Reconstruction of the Old-Latin Text or Texts of the Gospels used by Saint Augustine* (Cambridge, 1926), pp. xi–xxiii.
[4] *Ep.* 28, 2: *quorum est gravissima auctoritas.*
[5] *De Civ. Dei*, XVIII, 43.

general acceptance of the Septuagint by the Catholic Church undoubtedly counted for much in determining his preference, and, moreover, he was convinced that the translators of the Septuagint had been accorded a peculiar understanding of the text under the inspiration of the Holy Spirit.[1] To these considerations of principle was added another of pastoral expediency. When the bishop of Oea (Tripoli) rashly adopted Jerome's version of the book of Jonah for reading in church, his people broke into a riot on hearing the words: 'And the Lord God prepared ivy (*hedera*) and made it to come up over Jonah' (Jonah 4: 6) instead of the familiar gourd (*cucurbita*). The local Jews, on being consulted, declared, either from ignorance or spite, that the Hebrew original could only mean gourd, and the bishop was forced to return to the old reading.[2] Such an incident tended to confirm Augustine in his preference for retaining the traditional rendering.

Nevertheless, although Augustine preferred the Septuagint to other versions of the Old Testament, he did not invariably appeal to it and reject the aid of other translations. On the contrary, he was quite prepared to appeal to several different renderings of the same passage without making any attempt to discriminate between them, and without any consultation of the authoritative Septuagint. Thus, in discussing Ps. 118: 139 (*EVV* 119: 139), which read in his text: *My zeal has made me waste away* (*Tabefecit me zelus meus*), Augustine notes that other versions have: *Thy zeal*, while others again read: *The zeal of thy house has eaten me up*—a form which Augustine derives from John 2: 17.[3] Yet, oddly enough, Augustine makes no effort to consult the inspired Septuagint to decide the matter. So far as he is concerned, one form is as good as another for the purpose of preaching.

It might be supposed that whatever use Augustine might make of the Septuagint, he would certainly regularly refer to the Greek original when expounding the New Testament. This is not, however, the case,[4] and for two reasons. First, since Augustine lacked the easy familiarity with the Greek language of an Ambrose or a Jerome, any attempt to control his exegesis by reference to the original was a considerable effort, which he was not always prepared to make. Secondly, and more

---

[1] *Ep.* 28, 2, 2; *Enarr. in Ps.* 87, 10. 　　　 [2] *Ep.* 71, 3, 5.

[3] *Enarr. in Ps.* 118, 28, 2.

[4] See H. I. Marrou, *St Augustin et la fin de la culture antique* (4th ed. Paris, 1958), pp. 437 ff.

important, the exegetical principles upon which he worked did not impose upon him any necessity of constructing a critical text in the modern sense. For Augustine, it is not so much the words of the Bible themselves as the doctrine underlying the words which is important. The words express the doctrine, and if they declare it in various ways, there is no necessity to set one version against another, any more than it is necessary to prefer one exegesis of a given text to another. Indeed, Augustine specifically declares that he considers that the obscurities of scripture exist as part of the divine plan for disciplining the rebellious human mind.

Hasty and careless readers are led astray by many and manifold obscurities and ambiguities, substituting one meaning for another; and in some places they cannot hit upon even a fair interpretation. Some of the expressions are so obscure as to shroud the meaning in the thickest darkness. And I do not doubt that all this was divinely arranged for the purpose of subduing pride by toil and of preventing a feeling of satiety in the intellect, which generally holds in small esteem what is discovered without difficulty.[1]

It is this attitude which explains a feature of Augustinian exegesis which appears particularly strange to modern thought: his willingness to take the text as it stands (even if unintelligible, as his version frequently was, particularly in the case of the Psalms) and then expound it in a manner which appears to be mere fantasy, as when he applies the verse of the Song of Songs: *Thy teeth are like a flock of sheep that are shorn* (Song of Sol. 4: 2), first to the saints ('the teeth of the Church, tearing men away from their errors and bringing them into the Church's body, with all their hardness softened down, just as if they had been torn off and masticated by the teeth'), and then to the newly baptized ('laying down the burdens of the world like fleeces, and coming up from the washing, that is, from baptism').[2] For Augustine, such an interpretation was perfectly reasonable. It was the voice of God which had inspired holy scripture that he desired to interpret, rather than apprehend the mind of the men who wrote the biblical text.

Augustine's own views on scriptural exegesis are set out in the treatise *De Doctrina Christiana* (*On Christian Culture*—not 'doctrine' in the theological sense) which appeared in its final form only in 427, and which may therefore be regarded as representing his mature opinion. Augustine begins by making a distinction between *use* and

---

[1] *De Doc. Christ.* II, 6, 7.   [2] *Ibid.*

enjoyment. To enjoy a thing is to cleave to it for its own sake; to use it is to employ it as a means to obtaining what one desires to enjoy. The only true object of enjoyment is the Holy Trinity, and all other things are to be used to obtain that enjoyment, including the holy scriptures, which should be used to build up the supernatural virtues, Faith, Hope, and Love.

Thus a man who is resting upon Faith, Hope and Love, and who keeps a firm hold upon these, does not need the scriptures except for the purpose of instructing others. Accordingly, many live without copies of the scriptures, even in solitude, on the strength of these three graces... Yet by means of these instruments (as they may be called) so great an edifice of Faith and Hope and Love has been built up in them that, holding to what is perfect, they do not seek for what is only in part perfect—of course I mean so far as is possible in this life; for in comparison with the future life, the life of no just and holy man is perfect here.[1]

For Augustine the scriptures are only a means, albeit of the highest importance and divinely instituted, to come to God, so that we may love God for his own sake, and men in him for his own sake.

We should clearly understand that the fulfilment and the end of the Law and of all holy scripture is the love of an object which is to be enjoyed [namely God], and the love of an object which can enjoy the Other in fellowship with ourselves [namely our fellow men]... Whoever then thinks that he understands the holy scriptures or any part of them, but puts such an interpretation upon them as does not tend to build up this twofold love of God and of our neighbour, does not yet understand them as he ought.[2]

Any merely academic study of scripture is ruled out by this principle, including a great deal of modern critical research, which Augustine would probably have qualified by the opprobrious name of *curiositas*, pleasure in acquiring knowledge merely for its own sake.[3] Nevertheless, for the proper understanding of scripture with a view to increasing Faith, Hope and Love, some knowledge is necessary, and it is the character of such knowledge which is the theme of the *De Doctrina Christiana.*

All instruction is either about things or about signs; but things are

---

[1] *De Doc. Christ.* I, 39, 43.　　　　　[2] *Ibid.* I, 35, 39—36, 40.

[3] *De Vera Rel.* 49, 94: *Iam vero cuncta spectacula et omnis illa quae appellatur curiositas quid aliud quaerit quam de rerum cognitione laetitiam?*

learned by means of signs.[1] Among signs, words hold the chief place and to preserve them, writing has been invented.[2] However, because of the confusion of tongues, brought about as a punishment for sinful men at the Tower of Babel, even holy scripture, which brings a remedy to the disease of man's will, had first to be put forth in one language and afterwards translated into various tongues in order to become known to the nations and so effect their salvation.[3] But holy scripture is not only to be read, but also understood, and misunderstanding arises from unknown or ambiguous signs. Now signs are either proper (*propria*) or figurative (*translata*). Proper signs are those which indicate the objects which they were designed to point out. Thus the Latin word *bos* means an animal, the ox. Signs are figurative when by indicating one object they signify another, as when by saying *bos*, ox, we have in mind the preacher of the apostolic injunction: *Thou shalt not muzzle the ox that treadeth out the corn.*[4]

Ignorance of proper signs is remedied by a knowledge of languages, in particular of Greek and Hebrew.[5] Figurative signs, on the other hand, are to be understood partly by knowledge of languages, and partly by general education,[6] by a knowledge of history,[7] natural science,[8] dialectic,[9] and philosophy.[10] Augustine, in drawing up his programme for the education of the Christian exegete, makes use of the time-honoured image of the children of Israel coming out of Egypt and despoiling the Egyptians of gold and silver and raiment. In like manner, the Christian may despoil the heathen of their learning, and apply it to God's service in the study of scripture.

This, then, is Augustine's ideal of the training of the Christian biblical scholar and exegete, and at first sight he appears to provide a kind of charter for the Christian intellectual. In fact, this is very far from being his intention, and he takes good care to warn his readers 'not to venture heedlessly upon the pursuit of the branches of learning that are in vogue beyond the pale of the Church of Christ, as if these could secure for them the happiness they seek, but soberly and carefully to discriminate among them', and he quotes Terence's maxim, '*Ne quid nimis!*'—'Not too much!'—as a warning to the potential

---

[1] *De Doc. Christ.* I, 2, 2.   [2] *Ibid.* II, 3, 4—4, 5.   [3] *Ibid.* II, 5, 6.
[4] *Ibid.* II, 10, 15. Cf. *In Ioan. Evang. Tr.* 10, 7: *Boves erant apostoli, boves erant prophetae.*   [5] *De Doc. Christ.* II, 11, 16.   [6] *Ibid.* II, 16, 23.
[7] *Ibid.* II, 28, 42.   [8] *Ibid.* II, 29, 45.   [9] *Ibid.* II, 31, 48.
[10] *Ibid.* II, 40, 60.

curiosus.[1] Massive learning, in Augustine's opinion, is not necessary for the biblical exegete.

Furthermore, Augustine's programme, limited as it is, in his own case represents an ideal, rather than a standard which he actually reached. As a biblical scholar he was essentially self-taught, and self-taught within the framework of the conventional literary education of his day. His strongest qualifications were his own remarkable intellect, plus an increasingly profound acquaintance with the actual text of scripture, much of which he had learned by heart—a practice which he commends to others,[2] and which was in accordance with the methods adopted in the schools for the study of the classical authors, Virgil and Cicero. Otherwise Augustine's exegetical equipment was mediocre. He was ignorant of Hebrew, relying on the works of more learned men, though he had some notions of Punic, apparently still spoken in the Africa of his day,[3] which he could apply to the elucidation of a Hebrew word.[4] His knowledge of Greek is a more complicated question. Opinions vary from very little to a great deal, but the safest conclusion from the evidence of his own works is that he had a limited working knowledge of biblical Greek and, at the end of his life, a very slight working knowledge of patristic Greek. Since he had hated Greek as a schoolboy and had been able to make a perfectly good academic career in Latin-speaking Africa and Italy without any knowledge of the Greek language, Augustine's later knowledge, however limited, must have been the result of study during his life as a presbyter and bishop—an heroic achievement, in view of the unceasing demands made upon his time and energy. But such study could not make him at home in the language or a regular reader of Greek authors, and it is likely that the average theology graduate today knows at least as much Greek as did the great bishop of Hippo.

On the linguistic side, then, Augustine was seriously deficient. In terms of more general education he can best be described by Professor Marrou's phrase: *un lettré de la décadence,* a scholar of the cultural

---

[1] *De Doc. Christ.* II, 39, 58.   [2] *Ibid.* II, 9, 14.

[3] See M. Simon, *Recherches d'Histoire Judéo-Chrétienne* (Études Juives, Paris, 1962), pp. 30–100; J. Lecerf, 'Saint Augustin et les survivances puniques', *Augustinus Magister* (Paris, 1954), I, pp. 31–3.

[4] E.g. *In Ioan. Evang. Tr.* 15, 27: *Messias autem unctus est; unctus graece Christus est; hebraice Messias est, unde et punice dicitur ungue. Cognatae quippe sunt linguae istae et vicinae: hebraica, punica et syra.*

decline of the later Roman empire. He had received and had excelled in the standard education of a Latin-speaking Roman citizen of his day, an education which placed its emphasis on literary style and valued learning as a means to embellishing an oration rather than as something of value for its own sake. Thus history, on such a view, was mainly a matter of historical anecdotes, natural science a collection of curious facts (*mirabilia*), designed at once to display the erudition of the orator and, less consciously, to remind his hearers of the mystery underlying the visible order of things, and to move them to a sense of awe and wonder. Philosophy, so far as it was studied at all, was mediated at second hand by popularisers like Cicero and Seneca.

If Augustine's preparation for biblical exegesis had been simply that provided by his official education he would indeed have been poorly equipped. In fact, however, he had already before his conversion begun unconsciously to prepare himself for his future career, through the reading of the Neo-Platonist philosophers. Their value was twofold: they helped to destroy the last remnants of Manichaean materialism which haunted his mind, and they provided a metaphysic which appeared to harmonise with Christian revelation.[1] To these practical aids must be added the less easily ascertainable value of contact with profoundly religious minds, of which Augustine remained aware long after he had come to see the deficiencies of the Neo-Platonists as theological guides.

You proclaim the Father and his Son, whom you call the Father's Intellect or Mind [he apostrophised the dead Porphyry], and between these a third, by whom I suppose you mean the Holy Spirit, and in your own fashion you call these three gods...Oh had you but recognised the grace of God in Jesus Christ our Lord, and that very Incarnation of his, wherein he assumed a human soul and body, you might have seen it to be the brightest example of grace![2]

Similarly, in the *De Doctrina Christiana*, he commended the Platonists above all other philosophers to the attention of the Christian exegete.[3]

The influence of the Neo-Platonists upon Augustine's exegesis and indeed upon his whole theological development cannot be over-emphasised. At the very beginning of his Christian career they added independent testimony to the teaching of Ambrose that *the letter kills but the Spirit gives life* and 'helped to draw aside the mystic veil and

[1] *Conf.* VII, 9, 13, 14.   [2] *De Civ. Dei*, X, 29.   [3] *De Doc. Christ.* II, 40, 60.

open to view the spiritual meaning of what seemed to be perverse doctrine if it were taken according to the letter'.[1] At the end of his life Augustine was still quoting Plotinus when the Vandal armies were advancing across Africa.[2] The value of Neo-Platonism for Augustine was that it acted as a counterbalance to the literary training which he had received, with its minute attention to style and concentration upon the details of language. For the Neo-Platonist the visible world of phenomena was no more than an imperfect imitation, an exteriorisation of the intelligible world. Hints of this world can be found in sensible phenomena, and the wise man will look beyond these phenomena to the realities which they express. Such an outlook plainly favoured the allegorical interpretation of scripture, and reinforced the general tendency of the men of later Roman society to look for an occult, mystical significance in ordinary events.

In fact, however, Augustine diminished the allegorical element in his scriptural exegesis with the passage of the years, although he never wholly abandoned it. In the early work *On Genesis against the Manichees*, written while still a layman in 389, allegorical interpretation predominated to a degree which Augustine later regarded as excessive. Moreover, it had little effect upon the readers to which it was addressed, since the Manichees insisted on understanding the Old Testament (which they rejected) only in a literal sense. As a result, Augustine was forced to take up the problem again, first in the *Incomplete Literal Commentary on Genesis*, begun about 393 or 394 but never completed, and finally abandoned and replaced with the twelve books of the *Literal Commentary on Genesis*, written from 401 to 415, which were designed to settle any discrepancies between the biblical account of creation and natural science. This more literal approach to the Bible did not mean that Augustine had rejected the allegorical method of interpretation, but that he came, in the course of his Christian career, to attach an ever-growing importance to the biblical narrative, not in the sense of a slavish adherence to the actual words—we have already seen that any such attitude was alien to his mind—but as the record of God's plan of salvation, as divine history and prophecy.

---

[1] *Conf.* VI, 4, 6.

[2] Possidius, *Vita Augustini*, 28: *Et se inter haec mala cuiusdam sapientis sententia consolabatur dicentis: 'Non erit magnus magnum putans quod cadunt ligna et lapides, et moriuntur mortales'* (Plotinus, *Enneads*, I, 4, 7).

The key to this development is to be found in Augustine's attitude to the Church. It is within the Church that scripture is to be understood, it is by her authority that its truth is guaranteed. 'From whom did I derive my faith in Christ?...I see that I owe my faith to opinion and report widely spread and firmly established among the peoples and nations of the earth, and that those peoples everywhere observe the mysteries of the Catholic Church.'[1] So Augustine wrote to his friend Honoratus in 391, appealing to the Catholic Church as the guarantor of the scriptures. The passage of time served only to confirm his belief in the twofold authority, of scripture understood within the Church, and of the Church herself, portrayed in scripture as the People of God, the 'succession of the people devoted to the one God', whose history from Adam to John the Baptist is that of the Old Testament, and which is the image of the new people, whose life begins with the Incarnation and goes on until the Day of Judgement.[2] This notion, which occurs in the work *Of True Religion*, written in 390, is the prototype of the famous doctrine of the Two Cities, which finds its final development in the *De Civitate Dei*, where the last eight books (XV–XXII) are devoted to an exposition of the history of mankind, from Adam to the Second Coming, in terms of biblical history.

The characteristic feature of the development in Augustine's attitude to the Bible is this deepened sense of scripture as the history of God's saving work for man in the past, the present, and the future, until the Second Coming of Christ. It has been noted that history is the one aspect of Augustine's culture that Christianity seriously developed,[3] and the reason seems to be the development of Augustine's biblical studies. History, for him, is the record of human and divine actions.[4] Divine history is *res gesta*, the action of God in the past, and this is contained in the Bible in the historical books of the Old Testament and the writings of the New. But there is another element in the Bible: *res gestura*, what God will do.[5] This distinction is recognised by Augustine in his earlier writings—it is indeed an obvious one—where he explains that the scriptures may be expounded historically (*secundum*

---

[1] *De Util. Cred.* 14, 31 (tr. J. H. S. Burleigh).

[2] *De Vera Rel.* 27, 50.

[3] Marrou, *St Augustine et la fin de la culture antique*, p. 419.

[4] *De Gen. lib. imperf.* 2, 5. For what follows see R. A. Markus, 'Saint Augustine on history, prophecy and inspiration', *Augustinus* (Madrid, 1967), pp. 271–80.

[5] *De Agon. Chr.* 13, 15.

historiam) or prophetically (*secundum prophetiam*).[1] However, with the passage of time, Augustine ceased to emphasise this distinction between historical and prophetical texts and historical and prophetical modes of exposition, and by the time he came to write the *De Civitate Dei* in the last twenty years of his life, history and prophecy had for him become almost synonymous. The episode of Noah's drunkenness and its consequences (Gen. 9: 20–7) are 'all of them pregnant with prophetic meanings and veiled in mysteries'.[2] All the Bible, and not only the books of the prophets, is prophecy.

The object of the writer of these sacred books, or rather of the Spirit of God in him, is not only to record the past, but to depict the future, so far as it regards the City of God; for whatever is said of those who are not its citizens is given either for her instruction or as a foil to enhance her glory.[3]

Augustine's thought has therefore developed since his early days as a scriptural exegete. His exegesis is now less allegorical than typological and historical. His history is, indeed, selective. He distinguishes between historical investigation (*historica diligentia*) and divine inspiration,[4] and does not claim that all history is equally important as the revelation of God's dealings with men. He does, however, see in the sacred writings the record of God's revelation in time of his eternal purposes. In this respect, Augustine came to attribute to the temporal and the historical a far greater significance than a Neo-Platonist would do. In terms of outlook, if not in technique, Augustine represents a decisive factor in the history of Western biblical exegesis by his emphasis on the historical and typological.

There seems to be little doubt that a major influence in producing this development in Augustine's thought was his study of the Donatist writer Tyconius, one of the most interesting and original minds among Latin theologians of the fourth century. The greatness of Tyconius' achievement lay in his typological interpretation of scripture within a fixed pattern of thought: the struggle of the City of God, the members of the Body of which Christ is the Head, with the City of the devil, the infernal antitype of the Body of Christ. Tyconius expounded his views in his *Book of Rules*, giving seven rules for understanding Holy Scripture, which Augustine duly recorded in the *De Doctrina Christi-*

---

[1] *De Gen. c. Man.* II, 2, 3: *secundum historiam facta narrantur, secundum prophetiam futura praenuntiantur.*   [2] *De Civ. Dei*, XVI, 1.

[3] *Ibid.* XVI, 2.   [4] *Ibid.* XVIII, 38.

ana,[1] and in his lost commentary on Revelation, which can today be partially reconstructed from the quotations from it in other writers. The effect of Tyconius' work was to produce a type of exegesis which avoided crude literalism on the one hand and overstrained allegory on the other. Thus Tyconius rejected the old materialistic notion of a literal thousand-year reign of Christ with the saints after the first resurrection (Rev. 20: 4–6), regarding the Apocalypse as referring to the first resurrection which is effected by baptism, and the reign of the saints as the reign of the Church in the world to the end of time. It seems that he was instrumental in converting Augustine to his view, for Augustine at one time believed in a material reign of the saints on earth[2] but afterwards abandoned it.[3] Indeed, we may rank Tyconius with Ambrose as the major influence upon Augustine's theory of biblical exegesis, and it seems not unlikely that, in the long run, his was the stronger influence.

These are, however, the great outlines of Augustine's exegesis. It is desirable to look more closely, to determine his treatment of the Bible when instructing an African congregation.

Augustine's fundamental principle is that there can be no deliberate falsity in scripture, although God may permit different versions of the same episode by different authors. This is the issue underlying his famous dispute with Jerome over the interpretation of the apparent inconsistency in the behaviour of Peter at Antioch described in Galatians, when he first ate with the Gentiles and afterwards withdrew from them, and so incurred the rebuke of Paul (Gal. 2: 11–21). Jerome, following a tradition which looked back to Origen, had suggested that the dispute between Peter and Paul was, in fact, deliberately contrived, so that the Judaisers might be the more effectively rebuked in the person of the prince of the apostles. Augustine repudiated this sort of exegesis in the most emphatic language. 'It seems to me most disastrous to believe that the sacred books contain any deliberate lie,' he wrote, 'that is, that those men who preached and wrote the scripture for us in any way lied in their books',[4] and he pointed out that if the principle of deliberate deceit be once admitted, the whole authority of scripture is impaired and every man is left free to make his own

---

[1] III, 30, 42 ff. The *Liber Regularum* has been critically edited by F. C. Burkitt (Texts and Studies III, 1, Cambridge, 1894).   [2] *Serm.* 259, 2.
[3] *De Civ. Dei*, xx, 7.   [4] *Ep.* 28, 3, 3.

interpretation on the supposition that any passage may be a well-intentioned lie.[1] Augustine's remonstrance is not simply a plea for the apostles' honesty. It is a plea for honesty in the Christian exegete, for the sort of attitude which makes serious criticism possible. It does not exclude the possibility, which Augustine fully recognised, that discrepancies may exist between authors, that reported conversations may record the general tone rather than the actual words of the speakers,[2] and that individual authors, even if inspired, may differ in their order of narration.[3] Indeed, Augustine takes this for granted; but he rejects any attempt to avoid exegetical difficulties by the sacrifice of intellectual integrity. In this respect, Augustine has a remarkably modern approach to biblical criticism.

On the other hand, Augustine's attitude neither diminishes his respect for the authority of scripture as a whole nor does it impose upon him any necessity, when confronted by two apparently contradictory readings, to choose between them with a view to establishing the original text. On the contrary, as we have seen, Augustine is fully prepared to accept variant readings without any attempt to discriminate between them so long, at least, as they do not raise theological difficulties. Thus, during the Pelagian controversy, when he was concerned to defend the doctrine of the common participation of all men in Adam's primal sin, through their seminal presence in their progenitor's loins at the time of the Fall, Augustine notes that certain manuscripts of Romans have the reading: *death reigned from Adam until Moses, even over them that sinned in the likeness of Adam's transgression* (Rom. 5 : 14), in place of the more usual *had not sinned*. Since, however, this reading accords perfectly well with the doctrine that all men sinned in Adam, Augustine does not pursue the matter further.[4] Either reading is in conformity with Catholic doctrine and may, for that reason, be accepted.

Similar considerations seem to have governed a more famous piece of Augustinian exegesis: his notorious interpretation of Rom. 5 : 12: *in quo omnes peccaverunt*—'in that all sinned'—as if it were the equivalent of ἐν ᾧ πάντες ἥμαρτον—'in whom [i.e. Adam] all sinned'. In his numerous citations of this verse against the Pelagians, Augustine

---

[1] *Ep.* 28, 3, 5. On the whole dispute see J. B. Lightfoot, *St Paul's Epistle to the Galatians* (10th ed. London, 1890), pp. 128–32.   [2] *De Cons. Evang.* II, 12, 29.
[3] *Ibid.* II, 21, 51.   [4] *Ep.* 157, 3, 19.

never hesitates about the correctness of his understanding and never, so far as we can tell, thought of consulting the original Greek to see if it would bear the interpretation he placed upon it. The reason for this neglect seems clear. Augustine's exegesis was what he had learned in his early days as a Christian, and he never doubted that it was Catholic doctrine. This, he thought—wrongly as it happened—was the understanding of the universal Church. There was therefore no place for private judgement.[1]

The reasons for this apparently cavalier attitude to the text of scripture are simple enough. Augustine's general view of the authority of the Bible and the character of inspiration did not require the literal acceptance of any particular text but its understanding in the light of what the Church teaches. For Augustine the evangelists are Christ's hands,[2] not mere inert instruments, and they write their accounts at God's suggestion, not his dictation.[3] This attitude to the nature of inspiration helps to account for Augustine's refusal to be bound by any particular text, even though he regarded the Septuagint as having primary authority in the Old Testament, and explains why he felt no inclination to create a critical text in the modern sense of the term. His guide to understanding scripture is not biblical criticism but the authority of the Catholic Church.

Furthermore, Augustine's approach to scriptural exegesis is first and foremost that of a pastor, designed to instruct his congregation in the doctrine of the Church and to stir their minds to a greater warmth of devotion. In the fourth book of the *De Doctrina Christiana* Augustine writes at some length about the task of the preacher. He must, of course, be thoroughly well acquainted with scripture and draw upon its eloquence to support his own words,[4] but his sermon is primarily an act of worship, preceded by prayer and delivered without formal preparation,[5] *Domino donante*, by the inspiration of God.[6]

It is the duty of the interpreter and teacher of holy scripture, the defender of the true faith and the opponent of error, both to teach what is right and to refute what is wrong, and in the performance of this task to conciliate the

---

[1] See G. Bonner, 'Augustine on Romans v. 12', *Studia Evangelica*, v (*Texte und Untersuchungen*, 103, 1968), 242–7.

[2] *De Cons. Evang.* I, 35, 54.   [3] *Ibid.* II, 21, 51.

[4] *De Doc. Christ.* IV, 5, 8.   [5] *Ibid.* IV, 15, 32.

[6] *In Ioan. Evang. Tr.* 15, 1: *Ea quae dicturus sum Domino donante . . .*

hostile, to rouse the careless, and to tell the ignorant both what is occurring at present and what is probable in the future.[1]

It is this view of the function of the Christian preacher which helps to explain certain Augustinian exegeses which seem most extravagant to the modern reader. Thus, having taken for his text the words of the psalm: *Like as the hart desireth the water-brooks, so longeth my soul after thee, O God* (41: 2. *EVV*. 42: 1), Augustine proceeds to develop the theme into an exposition of a doctrine of mystical contemplation.[2] Abbot Butler, who quoted this sermon at length in his famous study of Western mysticism, considered that it would be

acknowledged by even the most objective exegete to be a noble piece of exegesis—a masterpiece of its kind. For however little it may express the real thought of the Psalmist, still, without doing violence to the text, it makes the words, with rare skill, serve as the basis of a statement of mystical doctrine forestalling the lines laid down by the great mystics of later times.[3]

This is true; but it nevertheless remains difficult for many modern readers to accept an exposition which bears so little relation to the thought of the original writer of the text. Nor is acceptance made easier when Augustine likens the thirst of the Psalmist for God to that which the hart was believed to conceive through destroying serpents— a piece of natural history which had been accepted by no less an authority than Origen, and which was to have a great future in the medieval bestiaries. 'The hart destroys serpents, and after the killing of serpents, it is inflamed with thirst yet more violent. The serpents are thy vices; destroy the serpents of iniquity, then wilt thou long yet more for the Fountain of Truth.'[4] Good allegory, no doubt; but poor zoology.

Again, Augustine's fondness for allegory combined with his reliance on a faulty Latin text based on the Septuagint produces some strange interpretations. In his version of Ps. 30: 21 (*EVV*. 31: 21) the Greek phrase ἐν πόλει περιοχῆς was rendered 'in a city of circumference' (*in civitate circumstantiae*) by the all-too-literal translator, instead of 'in a fortified city', which is the meaning of the Hebrew and, indeed, of the

---

[1] *De Doc. Christ.* IV, 4, 6.
[2] *Enarr. in Ps.* 41.
[3] Cuthbert Butler, *Western Mysticism* (3rd ed. London, 1967), p. 24.
[4] *Enarr. in Ps.* 41, 3. Cf. Origen, *Hom. in Cant.* 2, 11; *Hom. in Ier.* 18, 9.

Greek. Augustine, however, was perfectly satisfied with his version, and referred the phrase to the Gentile church, which is found on the circumference of the Chosen People.

There they were, the Chosen People, alone in the midst of the nations. But the prophet looks and sees the future Church of God established in all nations; and because all the nations surrounded the solitary people of the Jews like the circumference round the centre of a circle, he calls this Church of all nations that he foresees the city of circumference.[1]

Like Augustine's hart desiring the water-brooks, this understanding of the text is clearly too far removed from the original thought of the Psalmist to be congenial to a modern congregation. There is, however, no reason to suppose that Augustine would have abandoned it in the light of modern criticism. It served its purpose if it increased Faith, Hope and Love in the hearts of his hearers.

Even more disconcerting, however, is Augustine's fascinated pre-occupation with the hidden meanings, the *sacramenta*, of scripture. These are to be found everywhere: in the titles of the psalms,[2] in the names of men and places,[3] and, especially, in numbers.[4] There was nothing original in Augustine here. His contemporaries, pagan and Christian alike, attributed the greatest significance to numerology, and for Augustine and his congregation every number was a divine symbol, providing a key to the sacred text. Thus the six water-pots at the marriage at Cana in Galilee (John 2: 6) represent the Six Ages of the world, from Adam to the Last Judgement, and the sixth age begins with the coming of the Lord, who conforms our mind to his own image and turns water into wine as a sign.[5] The forty-six years needed to build the Temple at Jerusalem (John 2: 20) refer to Christ, the Second Adam, for the numerical value of the Greek letters of the

[1] *Enarr. in Ps.* 30, 3, 9 (tr. E. Hill).

[2] *Enarr. in Ps.* 29, 2, 6: *In hoc titulo est omnis spes, et universum sacramentum dissolvendae huius quaestionis.*

[3] *Enarr. in Ps.* 80, 2: *Interpretatio...nominis mysterium intimat occultae veritatis.* Cf. *De Doc. Christ.* II, 16, 23; 39, 59.

[4] See Marie Comeau, *Saint Augustin, exégète du quatrième Évangile* (2nd ed. Paris, 1930), pp. 127–42, and M. Pontet, *L'exégèse de S. Augustin prédicateur* (Paris, 1945), pp. 278–303.

[5] *In Ioan. Evang. Tr.* 9, 6. For the theory of the Six Ages, see C. W. Jones, *Bedae Opera de Temporibus* (Cambridge, Mass., 1943), p. 345; G. Bonner, *Saint Bede in the Tradition of Western Apocalyptic Commentary* (Jarrow Lecture 1966), pp. 14, 15.

name Adam is forty-six.[1] Again, one hundred and fifty-three, the number of the miraculous draught of fishes (John 21 : 11), is a triangular number, composed of the sum of the integers one to seventeen[2] and has therefore, according to Augustine's numerical theories, the same symbolical value as seventeen. But seventeen is the sum of ten (the Decalogue) and seven (the number of the Holy Spirit, who enables the elect to fulfil the law). Thus the 153 fishes symbolise the whole number of the elect, regenerated by the Holy Spirit. But there is a further calculation, which confirms this interpretation. One hundred and fifty-three is three times fifty with three added to signify the mystery of the Trinity. But the number fifty represents the square of seven—the number of the Spirit—with one added to show the unity of the Spirit whose operations are sevenfold and who was, moreover, sent to the disciples on the fiftieth day (the ancients counted inclusively) after the Lord's resurrection.[3]

This numerical interpretation represents Augustine at his most extravagant, and most readers will recoil before an exegetical ingenuity so subtle and fecund and, withal, so laboured and unconvincing. It would be unrealistic and even disingenuous to dismiss it as uncharacteristic—on the contrary, it reflects Augustine's taste and that of his age all too faithfully—but there is another, and more appealing, side to Augustine's use of allegory, when he interprets scripture typologically. An impressive example is provided by his treatment of the parable of the Good Samaritan,[4] which he originally understood as simple allegory[5] but later came to regard as typifying the whole story of man's fall and redemption, with Christ himself as the Samaritan and the wounded traveller as Adam.

The moon occurs in scripture figuratively for the mutability of human mortality. Therefore the man who fell among thieves went down from Jerusalem [which means 'Vision of Peace'] to Jericho, because Jericho is a Hebrew word which is interpreted in Latin as moon. He therefore who went

---

[1] *In Ioan. Evang. Tr.* 10, 12.

[2] See F. H. Colson, 'Triangular numbers in the New Testament', *JTS*, XVI (1914), 67–76.

[3] *In Ioan. Evang. Tr.* 122, 8. By a slip of the tongue, Augustine says ascension for resurrection.

[4] See Dominique Sanchis, '*Samaritanus ille.* L'exégèse augustinienne de la parabole du bon Samaritain', *Recherches de science religieuse*, XLIX (1961), 406–25.

[5] *De Gen. c. Man.* II, 10, 13.

down as though from immortality to mortality, and fittingly was wounded by thieves and left half-dead on the road, is Adam, from whom springs the whole human race.[1]

This interpretation which, although in recent years commonly rejected by New Testament scholars, now seems once more to be coming into its own, both conforms to Augustine's prophetic view of the Bible and, at the same time, indicates clearly his practice of expounding scripture in the light of the doctrine of the Church and as proof of that doctrine. It was for this reason that Augustine appealed to the parable of the Good Samaritan during the Pelagian controversy to illustrate the gratuitous character of salvation and to rebuke those who trusted in their own powers.

The influence of Augustine on the later biblical exegesis of the Latin Middle Ages was enormous. With Jerome, Gregory the Great and the Venerable Bede he was one of the four great authorities, and would probably have been reckoned the greatest of the four. Modern scholarship is likely to prefer Jerome, more learned if less brilliant, who sedulously acquired the solid foundation of accurate linguistic equipment which Augustine notably lacked. However, while doing justice to the very real achievement of Jerome, it is still possible to see in the work and teaching of Augustine on biblical exegesis an enduring quality which has a relevance for the interpreter of the Bible at the present day.

The most important feature of Augustine's biblical exegesis is its ecclesial quality. The Bible must be read and understood within the framework of the life and doctrine of the Christian community and not interpreted by mere private judgement, however learned. This does not mean, however, that on the Augustinian view we are bound to reject inconvenient critical considerations. Indeed, Augustine's doctrine of the character of inspiration left him free to display very considerable critical freedom in certain respects. Thus, having originally considered the Epistle to the Hebrews to be the work of Paul, he came in his old age to treat it as anonymous, while still recognising it as canonical.[2] There was no difficulty for Augustine here. The important consideration was that the Catholic Church recognised

---

[1] *Enarr. in Ps.* 60, 8. Cf. *Quaest. Evangel.* II, 19, where the whole theme is developed.
[2] See Odilo Rottmanner, 'St Augustin sur l'auteur de l'épître aux Hébreux', *Revue Bénédictine*, XVIII (1901), 257–61.

Hebrews as authoritative for the establishment of doctrine. Within this framework of authority critical faculties may be exercised, and it is for this reason that Augustine can make some judicious and candid remarks about the mistaken attribution to Jeremiah of a quotation from Zechariah in Matt. 27: 9.[1] Nevertheless, the Bible remains the book of the Church, and it is within the Church, the living, working, worshipping Christian community, that it must be understood.

With this ecclesial attitude to scripture goes a clearly defined attitude to its function within the Church. The aim of all biblical reading and study is to increase Faith, Hope, and Love, and the value of exegesis depends on the degree to which these supernatural virtues are developed. At a time when the literalism of an older generation is at a discount, and scholarly investigation—not infrequently marked by what appears to the secular historian to be a quite unwarranted degree of scepticism—often seems to add little to the understanding of the Christian life, Augustine's emphasis is a salutary one. In the last resort, all study of scripture must, for the Christian, be part of the life in Christ.

Finally, and arising from the foregoing, we must note the Christocentricity of all Augustine's exegesis. Christ is the guarantor and the interpreter of holy scripture, the witness from whom it derives its authority.

That in this faith the mind might advance the more confidently towards the truth, the Truth itself, God, God's Son, assuming humanity without destroying his divinity, established and founded this faith, that there might be a way for man to man's God through the God-man. For this is the mediator between God and men, the man Christ Jesus. For it is as man that he is the Mediator and the Way.[2]

This is Augustine the bishop, writing at the height of his powers; but the thought is no different from that expressed at the beginning of his Christian life while still a layman, when he warned his son Adeodatus that we are not to call anyone on earth our teacher, 'for One is our teacher who is in Heaven'.[3] Augustine's power, both as a preacher and as an exegete, lies in the fact that he was, in Frederick van der Meer's fine phrase, 'an unconditional Christian'. It is this which makes him,

---

[1] *De Cons. Evang.* III, 7, 29. See B. M. Metzger, *The Text of the New Testament* (2nd ed. Oxford, 1968), pp. 153, 154.

[2] *De Civ. Dei*, XI, 2.   [3] *De Mag.* 14, 46.

more than fifteen centuries after his death, supremely worth reading as a guide to the understanding, and still more to the application, of holy scripture.

18. THE PLACE OF THE BIBLE IN THE LITURGY

In his Encyclical Letter *Mediator Dei* of 20 November 1947 Pope Pius XII wrote, 'To go back in mind and heart to the sources of the sacred liturgy is wise and praiseworthy. The study of liturgical origins enables us to understand better the significance of festivals and the meaning of liturgical formulas and ceremonies.'[1] This research is important not only for the question of feast-days, but for the whole structure and content of Christian worship. It is impossible to understand or to appreciate the significance of any of the historical forms if the earliest endeavours to worship God in the Christian faith are ignored. But these endeavours did not arise spontaneously, for they had some connection with the earlier forms in use in Jewish Temple and synagogue. For information on this, the records of the Bible are of primary importance.

There is indeed one apparent complication, that the Bible as such was not in existence in the earliest years of the Christian Church, for the Canon of the New Testament was not settled till about the third century. Nevertheless the documents, both the Old Testament itself, and most of the constituents of the New Testament, were widely known, and are constantly referred to in the Christian literature of the second and third centuries. Apart from anything else, the large amount of surviving homiletical literature witnesses to the interest in and knowledge of the scriptures. It follows that the relation between the Bible and the worship of the early Church must be investigated. This should show not only the facts of the relationship, so far as information can be gathered, but also something of the attitude of the Church both to scripture and to the problems of worship.

The investigation must begin with the New Testament, though it provides less information than might be expected. But the earliest Christians were of Jewish origin, and were accustomed to the services held both in the Temple and in the synagogue. The latter were in many ways more influential, though some scholars are inclined to the view

---

[1] Catholic Truth Society translation, *Christian Worship* (London, 1963 ed.), para. 66.

that in fact the synagogue services had little influence on Christian worship.[1] Nevertheless there is in the New Testament some evidence of an hereditary connection. The main purpose of the synagogue was the reading and interpretation of the scriptures of the Old Testament, the Bible of the Jews, as well as prayer. Two lessons were read in the service. For the first the Pentateuch, usually referred to as 'the Law', was divided into fully one hundred and fifty portions which were read in continuous course, thus providing one lesson for each week in a triennial cycle. The technical name for each was *seder* or *parashah*, meaning 'section'. The second lesson, from the Prophets, was known as *haphṭarah*, that is, 'dismissal', as being the end of the reading. The lessons were first read in Hebrew and then translated into the vernacular Aramaic, and were followed by an explanation of their significance. This triennial cycle is known as the Palestinian cycle. Another in which the Law was read in one year is called the Babylonian cycle. Both point to the existence of lectionaries for the synagogue, and attempts have been made to apply them in the interpretation of New Testament writings.[2] The further suggestion has been made that a three-year course for the Psalter was made to correspond with the two courses of lessons. The number of psalms is 150, which along with the supplementary psalm in the Septuagint nearly equals the number of Sabbaths in three years and also the number of sections of the Law. Some writers have pointed to similarities in word or idea between a particular psalm and the readings for the corresponding day.[3] If this theory of the three-fold system, Law, Prophets, and Psalms, in a triennial cycle, could be proved, it would be very important for the attempt to trace developments in Christian worship. There has been however opposition to it, on the ground of lack of positive and sure information.[4]

The evidence of the New Testament indicates that the Old Testament scriptures were regularly read in the synagogue. Luke 4: 16 ff. shows that Jesus received the scroll from the ruler and read a passage from Isa. 61, and thereafter preached on its significance. The lesson from the Law would have been read before Jesus began. Acts 13: 14 ff. also speaks of the reading of the Law and the Prophets, followed by

[1] E.g. G. Delling, *Worship in the New Testament* (London, 1962), pp. 42 f., 92 f., etc.

[2] E.g. A. Guilding, *The Fourth Gospel and Jewish Worship* (Oxford, 1960).

[3] E.g. L. Rabinowitz, *JQR*, n.s. XXVI (1935–6), 349–68; N. H. Snaith, *ZAW*, N.F. x (1933), 304; A. Guilding, *The Fourth Gospel and Jewish Worship*, pp. 41 f., 81.

[4] E.g. Leon Morris, *The New Testament and the Jewish Lectionaries* (London, 1964).

an invitation given to Paul and his friends by the ruler of the synagogue to say a word of exhortation. In Luke 24: 44 Jesus says that everything written about him in the law of Moses and the prophets and the psalms must be fulfilled. Whether this refers to a threefold system of readings or only to the three parts of the Hebrew Canon is difficult to decide. It seems very probable that when the Christians met for their own Christian worship a similar pattern would be in use. The early Christian services thus retained a Jewish flavour, the Old Testament filling an important place in their worship, for it is certain that the Old Testament, and especially perhaps what was messianic in content, would be carefully studied and discussed. The Pauline letters, for example, contain many references to the Old Testament and knowledge of that scripture would be very helpful if not essential for the understanding of his presentation of the Christian message. It is then reasonable to believe that at the Christian meetings Old Testament passages were read, followed by their interpretation in the light of the teaching of Jesus Christ.

This style of exposition, the explanation and application of revelation in the light of the needs of a new age, is found in the Old Testament itself. In Deuteronomy, for example, Moses transmits what he has received from Yahweh, either to the people of Israel to whom the Law and its observance were of importance, or to Aaron who as priest had to know about matters of ritual observance. Similarly, according to Neh. 8, the book of the Law was read and the sense of the passage explained, so that all could understand it. Again, something like this took place in the Qumrân community, where there was a *doresh hattorah*, or interpreter of the Law, who shared some responsibility with the priest in the directing of the reading of the Book and the study of the Law.[1] The commentaries among the Dead Sea Scrolls may well have been records of expositions used in the Qumrân assemblies for study or worship. Much of the comment was an application of prophetic and other writings to the contemporary situation.[2]

Similarly when Christian services took shape they included the reading of scripture and its exposition (cf. 1 Tim. 4: 13). So far as the psalms are concerned, the New Testament does not provide direct evidence of their use in worship, but since they were used in Jewish

[1] G. Vermes, *The Dead Sea Scrolls in English* (Penguin Book, 1963), pp. 22, 81, etc.
[2] Cf. F. F. Bruce, *Biblical Exegesis in the Qumrân Texts* (London, 1960), ch. 1.

worship and appear very early in post-apostolic worship, it is likely that the practice was continuous throughout. The Old Testament thus remained influential in Christian faith and practice. But in New Testament worship it seems that other compositions could be read. Paul or the author of the letters apparently wished them to be read to the congregation (cf. Col. 4: 16; 1 Thess. 5: 27), and it is understandable that such documents would be highly esteemed. With the passage of time, as the Pauline corpus was gathered together, the letters would be regarded as increasingly valuable and even authoritative, and eventually became part of the Canon of the New Testament.

There has been discussion as to the nature of the early Christian services. Acts 2: 42–6 makes it clear that they met for the 'breaking of bread', usually interpreted as the Lord's Supper, and for 'prayers'. The question has been raised whether any such services were non-sacramental. Cullmann thinks that all the Christian services were sacramental, and that 'even if there had been a service which was exclusively a service of the Word, it would have been in any case an exception'.[1] But this seems very doubtful. Rather the evidence suggests that there were two different types of service. Gregory Dix[2] argued that the *synaxis* and the Eucharist were separate things with different origins, the former a continuation of the synagogue service and the latter of distinctly Christian origin from the Last Supper. Before long they came to be joined together as one service, though in the time of Tertullian they were still on occasion held separately. Thus he says, 'Either the sacrifice is offered, or the word of God is ministered' (*De Cult. Fem.* II, xi, 2).

Another question of importance is, how far liturgical expressions and forms are to be found in the New Testament. On this there has been much recent discussion. On the one hand it has been suggested that whole books of the New Testament have special liturgical import. Thus Matthew's Gospel might represent a collection of material to be read at worship-assemblies.[3] The Gospel of Mark might have connections with the Jewish lectionary tradition.[4] The Fourth Gospel might be connected with the Jewish lections in commentary form.[5] Some of

[1] *Early Christian Worship* (London, 1953), p. 29.
[2] *The Shape of the Liturgy* (London, 1945), p. 36.
[3] G. D. Kilpatrick, *The Origins of the Gospel according to St Matthew* (Oxford, 1946).
[4] P. Carrington, *The Primitive Christian Calendar* (Cambridge, 1952).
[5] A. Guilding, *The Fourth Gospel and Jewish Worship.*

the epistles have been regarded as homilies for Christian services. Thus
1 Peter has been explained as a baptismal address.[1] These suggestions
have not, however, met with wide acceptance. There is more agreement
on the idea that in the New Testament there are words and phrases
which have a liturgical significance and were used in worship-assemblies.
There are even short passages which may be fragments of liturgy,
some perhaps credal. For example, 'He was manifested in the flesh,
vindicated in the Spirit, seen by angels, preached among the nations,
believed on in the world, taken up in glory' (1 Tim. 3: 16). Other
possible passages are Eph. 5: 14; Phil. 2: 5–11; 1 Pet. 3: 15–22; 2 Tim.
2: 11–13. Further, there are words that are certainly used liturgically,
some of them of Semitic origin, *Amen, Hallelujah,* and *Maranatha,*
possibly derived from Old Testament worship. The doxologies that
appear in Revelation, and that at the end of the Lord's Prayer, have
found a place in the liturgies, but may well have been in liturgical use
before they were employed by the New Testament writers.

SOURCES

Before proceeding to examine the place of the Bible in the liturgy
beyond the first century, it may be useful to summarise the sources of
information to be used.

In the sub-apostolic period three useful texts are the Epistle of
Clement of Rome to the Corinthians (*c.* A.D. 96), Pliny's Letter to
Trajan (*c.* A.D. 112), and the *Didache,* whose date is doubtful but which
has been attributed to the period between A.D. 120 and 140. Unfortunately none of these is of much help for the place of scripture in the
services.

In the second century an important document is Justin Martyr's
account of the services at Rome in his *First Apology,* dated about A.D.
150. Tatian (*d. c.* A.D. 174) composed the *Diatessaron,* a harmony of
the four Gospels, but his only interest here is that in the Syrian liturgy
the harmony was read and was not displaced by the four separated
Gospels till about the fifth century. Ignatius in his epistles (A.D. 110–
17), and Irenaeus (*d.* A.D. 202) both refer to the Eucharist, but have
little to say about the use of the Bible there. The *Homily on the Passion*
by Melito of Sardis (*d. c.* A.D. 190) has some bearing on the subject.

[1] F. L. Cross, *First Peter, A Paschal Liturgy* (London, 1947).

There were in the third to the fifth centuries documents known under the generic term of Church Orders. Among the most useful are the *Apostolic Tradition* of Hippolytus, dated about A.D. 250, the *Testament of our Lord*, about a century later, and *Apostolic Constitutions*, two or three decades later still. Additional valuable sources are the *Sacramentary* of Serapion, bishop of Thmuis, about A.D. 350, the *Catechetical Lectures* of Cyril of Jerusalem, delivered in A.D. 347, and the *Pilgrimage of Etheria*, written shortly before A.D. 400. There are also references more or less extended in the writings of such leaders as Clement of Alexandria (A.D. 150–216), Tertullian (*d. c.* A.D. 240), Origen (*d.* A.D. 254), John Chrysostom (*d.* A.D. 407), Athanasius (*d.* A.D. 373), Basil of Caesarea (*d.* A.D. 379), Jerome (*d.* A.D. 420), and Augustine (*d.* A.D. 430).

THE EUCHARIST

Though originally the *synaxis* and the Holy Communion were held separately, they came to be joined together, and the first clear witness to this result is in the writings of Justin Martyr (*d. c.* A.D. 165), who gives two descriptions of the service in his *First Apology* (ed. A. W. F. Blunt, Cambridge, 1911, pp. 97 ff.). The first in chapter 65 describes a baptismal service followed by the Eucharist, and the second in chapter 67 explains a situation where *synaxis* and Eucharist are combined. But in both the point of juncture is quite clear, and in later days this was the dividing line between 'the liturgy of the catechumens' and 'the liturgy of the faithful'.

The Liturgy of the Catechumens

In this part of the service there were, as in Justin, lessons and sermon, but there was also psalmody, not mentioned by Justin, but frequently referred to by other writers, and prayers. These subjects require separate investigation.

The Psalms. Psalmody has always filled an important place in the worship of the Church. It was an inheritance from the Jewish Church. The liturgy of the Temple included psalms, and indeed the Psalter has been called the hymn book of the Second Temple. Some of the psalms were 'proper', being recited at specific times, especially at the great festivals. Thus the Hallel Psalms (113–18) were sung at the Passover, at the Feasts of Weeks, of Tabernacles, and of Dedication, and at the New Moon Festivals. Each day of the week had its proper psalm, which was recited both at the morning and at the evening sacrifice. It is believed that this custom was continued in the synagogue services. As already stated, it is possible that the Psalter was recited in triennial fashion.

Though in the New Testament few texts are relevant, many early writers speak of the use of psalmody. Clement of Alexandria on several occasions mentions psalm-singing (e.g. *Strom.* VII, 7). Tertullian speaks of the scriptures being read, psalms sung, an exhortation spoken, and prayers said (*De Anima*, 9, 4). In the writings of Jerome, John Chrysostom, Gregory Nazianzen, Athanasius, Augustine and others, there are many notices of psalm-singing in worship.

The position of the psalms was between the lessons. Tertullian's statement suggests this place, which is confirmed for the Cappadocian Church by Basil (*In Psalm.* 28), and by Ambrose for Milan (*Ep.* 22, 4, 7). Augustine frequently mentions which psalm was recited. Thus, he says, 'We saw this in the apostolic lesson; thereafter we sang a psalm, exhorting one another with one voice and with one heart as it ought to be.' He quotes Ps. 95, and continues, 'after these things the Gospel showed us the cleansing of the lepers' (*Sermo* X *de verbis apostoli*). And again, 'In the apostolic lesson thanks are given to God for the faith of the Gentiles. In the psalm we said, Restore us, O God of hosts, and let thy face shine that we may be saved (Ps. 80: 7). In the Gospel we are called to the feast' (*Sermo* 132). Augustine is interesting also from other points of view. On one occasion he instructed the lector to read a particular psalm on which he intended to preach, but the reader being confused a different psalm was read. Augustine felt that this indicated the will of God for that day—'we chose to follow in the error of the lector the will of God rather than our will in our proposal' (*In Psalm.* 138)—and so he changed the subject of his sermon. In a well-known passage in his *Confessions* (X, 33), he spoke of the power of the temptation to be moved by the singing rather than by the import of the words, and felt that in such a case it might be better not to hear the psalmody at all.

These references show that the practice of psalmody was widespread. It must have been popular, judging by the remarks of many writers. Basil for example addresses some who objected to the alternate or antiphonal method of singing and says, 'If on this account you avoid us, you will avoid the Egyptians, and you will avoid also both Libyans, Thebans, Palestinians, Arabians, Phoenicians, Syrians, and those who dwell near the Euphrates' (*Ep.* 207). No wonder Basil thought the objections to it were unreasonable. The method which the objectors apparently preferred was the older one, known as responsorial, in which one person, the cantor or leader of song, sang one verse or half-verse, while the next verse or half-verse was sung by all or by the choir. But the recital of psalms by the congregation fell on evil days, and it came about that the psalms were sung by cantor and choir, and the only part that remained to the people was some response such as *Alleluia* (cf. *Apostolic Constitutions*, II, 57, 5). This result was due to a large extent to the development of the Singers, who gradually became more important in the services. Jerome, *Comm. In Ephes.* (*ad* 5: 19), speaks of those 'to whom the office of singing belongs', and there are many other references, especially in the Church Orders. It was certainly to be regretted that the congregation lost this valuable exercise, the result being to some extent the weakening of the corporate sense of worship.

The Lessons. The lessons formed an essential part of the liturgy. One important point is that the service began with the lessons. There was for long no preliminary material such as prayers, and even in the days of Augustine this was still the case.

In Justin's description of the first part of the service (*Apol.* I, 67), he says that all in the towns or the country gather for the celebration. 'The memoirs of the apostles or the writings of the prophets are read as long as time permits.' Then the reader ceases and the president speaks, 'admonishing us and exhorting us to imitate these excellent examples'. The service then continues to the communion of the people.

Apparently two lessons could be read, one from 'the memoirs of the apostles', possibly a gospel or gospel passage known to Justin, and later perhaps incorporated in the canonical gospels, and the other from the 'prophets', generally taken to be a reading from the Old Testament. This order mentioned by Justin might not necessarily be that in which the lessons were read. In any case, whereas the synagogue lessons began with the Law as the more important and went on to the prophets as secondary, the Christian service reversed the order, putting the New Testament lesson and especially the Gospel last, this being always and everywhere regarded as the most important and valuable of all.

The lessons continued 'as long as time permits'. From this it appears that there was as yet no fixed lectionary. Whether this indicated *lectio continua*[1] is not certain, but it shows that the length of the lesson was not yet prescribed. Further, the lessons were read by a reader, not by the presiding minister. Was this the beginning of the custom of having a special reader or lector, as was the case later when the reader belonged to a ministerial order? Or was this merely a general term, not referring to a particular office, but simply to the fact that someone must read the lessons? The latter seems to be more probable at this date, though it was not long before the order of reader was well known.[2] Lastly, Justin reports the president as giving an address after the lessons were read. Evidently he spoke about what had been read, and took the opportunity of urging his hearers to put what they had heard into practice in their daily life.

Justin spoke of two lessons, but in later days there were often more than that, especially in the East. Thus, *Apostolic Constitutions*, belonging to about A.D. 380, in book VIII, 5, 5, mentions lessons from the Law, Prophets, Epistles, Acts and Gospels, while book II, 57, 5, speaks of the Law, the historical books, Job and the Wisdom Books, Prophets, Acts, Epistles, and Gospels, and says, 'let the lections be read two by two'. Many writers indicate the number of lessons read. Basil (*Hom.* 13) refers to three lessons, one from Isaiah, one from Acts and one from Matthew, and in another place (*Hom. de Lacizis*) again mentions three, from Proverbs, Epistles and Gospels. Augustine frequently in his sermons speaks of the lessons which have been read, sometimes only the Epistle and the Gospel, but at other times the Prophet also. On occasion the psalm seems to have been counted as a lesson (e.g. *Sermo 176 de Tribus Lectionibus*).

The Old Testament lesson was sometimes called 'the prophet' or 'the prophecy', as in *Apostolic Constitutions*. This lesson would be read not so much for itself, but rather as prophetic of the New Testament. The Epistle was normally the second lesson. This term covers the whole of the New Testament except the gospels. Sometimes the name

[1] For *lectio continua* see below, p. 572.   [2] See below, p. 574.

given to it was 'the apostle', because most of the readings came from the epistles of Paul. The lesson was heard in silence at the command of the deacon, not, as Chrysostom said, 'as doing honour to the reader, but to him who speaks to all through him' (*Hom. in 2 Thess.* 3). The Gospel was heard with still greater honour, the congregation being called upon to stand for it, and it was usually read not by the lector but by a deacon or presbyter. In some places candles were lit before the reading of the Gospel (Jerome, *Adv. Vigil.* 7). The so-called *Canons of Addai* of the third century give the direction, 'At the conclusion of all the scriptures let the Gospel be read, as the seal of all the scriptures; and let the people listen to it standing upon their feet, because it is the glad tidings of the salvation of all men.'[1]

How were the lessons selected? Were they chosen at random, or was there a scheme? The normal method was the straightforward reading of the whole of a particular book or a series of books, a system which received the name *lectio continua*, continuous reading. A variation of this occurred when a book of the Bible was chosen, but only selections in the order of the chapters were read, as chapters 1, 5 and 9, or when only verses of a chapter were chosen in their numerical order. A special method of reading was the selection of proper lessons suited to the day or season.

The first system was used in the reading of the Law in the synagogue, the only interruptions being in connection with the festivals. It is a natural way of reading because it gives a systematic view of, say, the events in the gospels or Acts, or of the argument in an epistle, and there is little doubt that this was the earliest custom. Some early manuscripts of the New Testament show marginal markings which reveal the length of the lessons. The series of sermons preached by some Fathers on books of the Bible suggest *lectio continua*. Thus, Origen delivered expositions of almost the whole Bible, book by book, and some five hundred of his homilies survive. Similarly Ambrose, Augustine, Chrysostom and others preached series of sermons in the same way. And even now, as in the *Roman Missal*, when the lesson does not open at the beginning of a gospel, the reader says, ' *Sequentia sancti evangelii...*', suggesting that the lesson is a follow-on from a previous reading.

The other system involves the selection of lessons suitable to

[1] Quoted by W. Cureton, *Ancient Syrian Documents* (London, 1864), p. 27.

particular circumstances, and therefore they are called 'proper'. It is natural that, say, at Easter, the narrative connected with the resurrection should be read. This custom would come about in line with the development of the Christian Year, though of this there is little evidence before the third century. Chrysostom is among the interesting writers in this connection. In one place (*Hom.* 73. *Cur in Pentecoste Acta leguntur*) he tells us that the reason for reading Acts before Pentecost was 'to give to men the evidences and proofs of that holy mystery (i.e. the resurrection) which completed their redemption'. Elsewhere he says that it was the custom to confine the reading of Acts and Revelation to the season between Easter and Pentecost (*In Acta Apost. Sermo* 4, 5), and that Genesis was read during Lent (*Hom.* 7 *ad Populum Antiochenum*). Augustine says that when the solemnity of holy days is interposed in the ordinary course, lessons pertaining to them should be read (*Sermo* 246). He refers to the reading of the resurrection narratives at Easter, the accounts in all four gospels being mentioned, and notes that Acts was read between Easter and Pentecost (*In Ioan. Evang. Tr.* 6, 18; *Sermo* 315). Ambrose speaks of reading the books of Job and Jonah in Passion Week: 'You have heard the book of Job read which is appointed to be read at this time', and adds, 'On the following day the book of Jonah was read in due course' (*Ep.* 20 *ad Marcellinam*). Origen says that Job was read then because this was a time of fasting and abstinence, wakening a feeling of fellow-suffering with Job, and further, the passion of Job was in great measure a type and example of the passion and resurrection of Christ (*In Job*). The *Pilgrimage of Etheria* at many points shows how suitable the lessons were to the festivals. Thus, on Palm Sunday the Gospel was from Matt. 21; on Good Friday it described the trial of Jesus; and at Easter the resurrection narratives were read (ed. M. L. McClure and C. L. Feltoe, pp. 63 ff.).

There seems to be little doubt that the use of proper lessons contributed to the making of lectionaries. Unfortunately the many problems connected with this subject have not, in spite of their great interest and importance, yet been solved. But if it could be accepted that by New Testament times the Jewish Church had some form of lectionary, it could reasonably be deduced that the Christian Church followed that example. Apparently no Sunday or weekday lectionaries survive from before about the fifth century. While there are, as noted above, many indications of what was read at certain seasons, especially at the great festivals, in fact no developed system seems to have been attained for some time. Attempts have been made to work out the lectionaries used by some of the great preachers, such as Ambrose and Augustine,[1] by drawing up a table of the Sundays of the year with the biblical material used from week to week. It appears however that these 'lectionaries' were very individual, and it is difficult to say how widely they were followed. In any case there is no suggestion that the same passages were used year after year, though this is one purpose of modern lectionaries.

The question of readers requires attention. Justin's reference in his *Apology* has been mentioned.[2] It seems that the reader was at first simply a member of the congregation, but by the beginning of the third century he was 'appointed', though apparently not yet ordained. *Apostolic Tradition* says, 'The reader is appointed by the bishop's handing to him the book, for he does not have hands laid upon him' (I, 12, ed. G. Dix, London, 1937, p. 21). It seems that they were sometimes young boys, perhaps in training for higher office in the ranks of the clergy. A little later we find the reader among the minor orders, and some of the Church Orders give interesting details about their appointment and duties. These seem to have varied considerably, though the main office was to read the lessons. But *Apostolic Church Order* 19 says that the reader must also be 'able to instruct or narrate' (διηγητικός).[3] It appears further that some acted as translators. Thus Eusebius (*De Mart. Palaest.* I, I) states that Procopius, martyred in A.D. 303, had rendered great service to the Church both as reader and as translator from Greek into Aramaic. Melito of Sardis begins his *Homily on the Passion*[4] by saying, 'The scripture of the Hebrew exodus has been read, and the words of the mystery have been explained.'[5] This seems to be a reference to the reader's part, but its actual significance is obscure. Some contend that the reader read the passage and then expounded it, 'the Hebrew exodus' meaning no more than 'the exodus of the Hebrews'. Others think that 'the Hebrew exodus' means

[1] G. G. Willis, *St Augustine's Lectionary* (London, 1962).
[2] See above, p. 571.
[3] A. J. Maclean, *The Ancient Church Orders* (Cambridge, 1910), pp. 86 f.
[4] Ed. Campbell Bonner, *Studies and Documents*, XII (Philadelphia, 1940).
[5] ἡ μὲν γραφὴ τῆς Ἑβραϊκῆς ἐξόδου ἀνέγνωσται καὶ τὰ ῥήματα τοῦ μυστηρίου διασεσάφηται.

'the exodus in Hebrew', that is, that the lesson was read in Hebrew and then translated. The problem is in the interpretation of διατετάφηται, whether it means only 'explained', or can mean 'translated' as well. So far there seems to be no agreement on the answer to this problem.[1] It was obviously important that the lessons should be understood by the people, and therefore, where necessary, translations were given, just as in the synagogue of old. Eusebius (*Praep. ev.* XII, 1) says that the scriptures 'were translated into all languages, both of Greeks and barbarians, throughout the world, and studied by all nations as the oracles of God'. Etheria gives definite witness to the translation taking place in the service of worship. 'Because all the lessons that are read in church must be read in Greek, [a priest] always stands by and interprets them into Syriac for the people's sake.' She adds that for speakers of Latin, the lesson is explained in Latin (VII, 5, ed. M. L. McClure and C. L. Feltoe, p. 94).

Not only did this lead to knowledge of the scriptures but, as not a few writers witness, also to conversions to the Christian faith. Augustine himself tells how he obeyed the command, *tolle, lege*, 'take up, read', and so became a dedicated Christian (*Conf.* VIII, 12, 29). The story of the conversion of Saint Anthony (Athanasius, *Vita*, 2; *Life of Saint Anthony* in *ACW*, X, London, 1950, 19 f.) is another witness to this influence of the Bible. Christians were not dependent only on the public reading of the Bible, for many were able to purchase copies of the Bible or of parts of it, so that there must have been much private reading. Several of the Fathers recommended that after divine service the lections heard in church should be read again at home, while Chrysostom sometimes announced the lessons to be read at the next service, advising the members of his congregation to read them and meditate upon them beforehand at home so that they would better understand his sermon (*Hom. in Ioan.* 41).[2]

The Sermon. Justin indicated that in his time the sermon followed the lessons,[3] and this seems to have continued as normal practice. Its purpose was the explanation of the Bible, usually one of the passages

---

[1] See the discussion in M. Testuz, *Papyrus Bodmer XIII* (Bibliotheca Bodmeriana, 1960).

[2] Further details on private reading in A. Hatnack, *Bible Reading in the Early Church* (London, 1912).

[3] See above, p. 570.

read, and its application to life. On occasion there were sermons on events commemorated in the festivals of the Christian Year, or on the life and example of a martyr. Sometimes the sermon would have for its subject a point of doctrine or of ethics. But in general these would be attached to a particular verse or passage of scripture. The course of sermons preached by some of the Fathers on books of the Bible have already been mentioned.[1] In many cases the sermons were prepared and written out beforehand. Sometimes they were recorded by stenographers. The surviving sermons of Jerome are mostly not complete, but consist of notes taken down by his hearers. Some sermons were delivered extempore, as on the day when Augustine had to change his subject unexpectedly.[2] Eusebius (*H.E.*, vi, 36, 1) tells us that Origen after reaching sixty years of age began to preach extempore.

Although the normal place for the sermon was within the Eucharist after the lessons, it is apparent that they were often preached at other times too, as Chrysostom shows (cf. *Hom.* 10 *ad Populum Antiochenum*). Similarly Augustine in the second sermon on Psalm 88 asks his hearers to attend to the remainder of the psalm about which he had been speaking in the morning. Preaching took place not only on Sundays but also on other days of the week, especially on the station days, Wednesday and Friday, according to the evidence of Tertullian (*De Orat.* 14, ed. and trans. by A. Souter, London, 1919, p. 34), and also on the anniversaries of the martyrs (cf. Chrysostom, *Sermones Quinque in Annam*). The greater festivals of the Christian Year, some of them occurring not on Sundays, afforded special opportunities for appropriate sermons. In Lent it seems to have been the custom in some places to have daily sermons, and the homilies on the book of Genesis preached by Chrysostom formed a series for that season. Frequently at morning or evening prayer there were sermons, and at a later period also in other daily offices, at some of which exposition of the scriptures as well as reading of lessons took place.[3]

In the earliest days of which there is record, it seems to have been the duty of the bishop to preach. Justin spoke of the 'president' delivering the homily, and many writers make it clear that the bishop must teach and be apt to teach. Indeed it was widely accepted that

[1] See above, p. 572.   [2] See above, p. 569.
[3] See below, pp. 582 f., for references in the *Pilgrimage of Etheria*.

preaching was one of the distinctive duties of the bishop. But as the Church increased there was need for others as well, and so presbyters came to be more and more eligible for this duty, as representing the bishop. Deacons too sometimes preached, and a large proportion of the sermons of Chrysostom belong to the years of his diaconate, and the same is true of Ephraem Syrus of Edessa (*d.* A.D. 399). A service might contain more than one sermon. A presbyter or more than one would preach, followed by the bishop. *Apostolic Constitutions* for example says, 'When a gospel is read, let the presbyters one by one, but not all, speak the word of exhortation to the people, and last of all the bishop, who is the pilot of the ship' (II, 57, 5).

The delivery of the sermon was regarded as very important. There is evidence that many preachers were listened to with keen appreciation, even on occasion with shouts of approval and loud applause. There is the well-known instance of Chrysostom rebuking his audience, arguing that applause was a bad and unseemly custom, and being nevertheless loudly applauded for the sentiment (*Hom. in Acta Apost.* 30, 3). On another occasion he suggested that the homily was less needful than the Bible itself. 'What need is there for a homily? All things that are in the divine scripture are clear and open' (*Hom. in 2 Thess.* 3, 4). Nevertheless he continued to preach. Some preachers however make it clear that the audience was not always as keen to hear or as well behaved as they should have been. Origen had to rebuke his hearers, among whom, he said, there were men whose main interest was in the things of this world, who even during service would carry out business transactions and indulge in worldly conversation, and women too whose real interest was not in the sermon or the service, but in gossip and scandal (e.g. *Hom. in Exod.* 12, 2; 13, 3). *Apostolic Constitutions* reveals that one of the duties of the deacon was to prevent nodding, whispering and sleeping (II, 57, 9).

The Prayers. The most important prayer was that which followed the sermon. Justin says that after the sermon 'we all stand up and offer prayers together' (*Apol.* I, 65, 67). The *Sacramentary* of Serapion has a prayer 'after rising up from the sermon' (ed. J. Wordsworth, p. 81). Cyprian refers to this prayer as *communis oratio*, common prayer (*De Dom. Orat.* 8. Cf. Augustine, *Ep.* 55, 18, 34). At times this prayer was in the form of a dialogue between the celebrant and the congregation.

Later it developed into the deacon's litany, which was a prayer for catechumens, energumens, competents, and penitents, prior to their dismissal from the service. (Cf. *Apostolic Constitutions*, VIII, 6, 1.)

An interesting question arises here, on the relation between liturgical language and the biblical text. This problem has been recently canvassed in relation to the Old Testament, and there is wide support for the view that in many cases there was liturgical priority. Much in Deuteronomy seems to reflect liturgical usage,[1] and many of the prayers recorded in Kings, Chronicles, Ezra, Nehemiah, Isaiah and Daniel are regarded as being modelled on customary liturgical forms. The prayer in Dan. 9: 3–19 has been called 'a liturgical gem in form and expression'.[2] The Psalter is of course a special case.

How far this applies to the New Testament has also been under discussion. Some have taken up the position that much of the biblical wording is an echo of the language of the liturgy. J. M. Neale argued for this in his essay on 'Liturgical Quotations'.[3] A. Baumstark in his *Comparative Liturgy* says on this matter, 'It may happen that in genuinely primitive *strata* of liturgical prose, where scriptural quotations or reminiscences might appear to exist, the language which the scriptural author himself used is, in fact, only the echo of liturgical language already established in the bosom of the most primitive communities.'[4] B. Botte[5] points out that the ancient texts are full of biblical allusions, and refers particularly to the prayers in 1 Clement 59–61.[6] F. E. Brightman has a long and valuable appendix in his book *Liturgies Eastern and Western* (pp. 553–67) in which he lists what he regards as biblical references in the liturgies. For example, he examines the liturgy of the eighth book of *Apostolic Constitutions*, and notices two hundred and seven quotations from or references to the Bible with twenty-one relative to the Apocrypha. It may well be that some of these are only apparent. But in any case there is here a witness to a correspondence between the biblical material and the prayers of the liturgies, though it is to be feared that the priorities cannot be finally determined.

---

[1] See G. von Rad, *Deuteronomy* (E.T. London, 1966), pp. 16 ff.
[2] J. A. Montgomery, *Daniel* (*ICC*, Edinburgh, 1927), p. 361.
[3] *Essays on Liturgiology* (2nd ed. London, 1869), Essay xv.
[4] *Comparative Liturgy* (3rd ed. B. Botte, tr. F. L. Cross, London, 1958), p. 59.
[5] *Ibid.* p. 59 n. 2.
[6] See *The First Epistle of Clement to the Corinthians*, ed. W. K. Lowther Clarke (London, 1937), pp. 82 ff.

The Liturgy of the Faithful

This part of the eucharistic service also has biblical connections. There were no lessons as such, but as the order developed psalmody was added at certain places.

The Offertory Chant sung during the Offertory procession, in which the bread and wine and other gifts were brought forward to the altar, seems to have been introduced at Carthage and at Hippo by Augustine, though against some opposition (*Retract.* II, 37). There is more evidence for psalmody at the communion of the people. This also is mentioned by Augustine (*ibid.*). Chrysostom speaks of it as a responsorial chant, the responses being sung by the newly confirmed, quoting Ps. 145: 15, 'The eyes of all look to thee; and thou givest them their food in due season' (*Expos. in Ps.* 144, 1). Brightman suggests that this may have been not a communion psalm, but part of the prayer of thanksgiving (*LEW*, pp. 475, 480 n. 32). Perhaps more frequently used was Ps. 34, either the whole psalm or part of it, this being due to the suitability of the eighth verse, 'O taste and see that the Lord is good'.

The Consecration Prayer is important here. The Salutation, which appears in various forms, frequently quotes Rom. 16: 20 (cf. Rom. 16: 24; 1 Cor. 16: 23), 'The grace of our Lord Jesus Christ be with you', or 2 Cor. 13: 14, 'The grace of the Lord Jesus Christ and the love of God and the fellowship of the Holy Spirit be with you all'. This is sometimes farced with additional words, as in *Apostolic Constitutions* (VIII, 12, 2). The Sanctus from Isa. 6: 3, 'Holy, holy, holy, is the Lord of hosts; the whole earth is full of his glory', is mentioned as early as 1 Clement, and is rarely missing. However, the second clause is usually expanded to 'Heaven and earth are full of thy glory'. *Apostolic Tradition* has no Sanctus, but this is unusual. *Apostolic Constitutions* directs that the whole people should say it together (VIII, 12, 13). Later it was sung by the clerics or the choir rather than by the whole congregation.

The Words of Institution[1] are normally recited within the Consecration Prayer, as a rule not exactly word for word. Indeed J. A. Jungmann says categorically, 'Our very first observation in this regard is the remarkable fact that the texts of the account of the Institution...

[1] Matt. 26: 26–8; 1 Cor. 11: 24–6.

are never simply a scripture text restated'.[1] The reason for this, he suggests, is that the Eucharist was celebrated long before the evangelists and Paul set out to record the gospel account. *Apostolic Tradition* quotes the words almost exactly, with the references to the bread and the wine close together. *Apostolic Constitutions* (VIII, 12, 16) adds only a few phrases. The *Sacramentary* of Serapion inserts between the words on the bread and the words on the wine, a passage which includes the prayer based on the *Didache*, 'As this bread has been scattered on the top of the mountains and gathered together came to be one, so also gather thy holy Church out of every nation and every country and every city and village and house and make one living catholic Church' (ed. J. Wordsworth, pp. 62 f.). In later days in the West the Words of Institution became much more important, being regarded as the consecrating formula, and therefore as necessary and invariable.

Finally, the Lord's Prayer was added to the Eucharistic Prayer from a date about which there is some doubt. Tertullian speaks of it, but does not say definitely that it was part of the Consecration Prayer (*De Orat.*, ed. A. Souter, pp. 19 ff.). Augustine points out that 'almost the whole church' concluded the Prayer with it (*Ep.* 149, 16), thus suggesting that he knew of places where this did not happen. According to Jerome, the Pelagians did not use it, regarding it as superfluous, and this was a deviation from general practice (*C. Pelag.* III, 15). Both Augustine and Jerome use the phrase 'make bold to say' this prayer, an introduction to the Lord's Prayer which became very common in later days. The early centuries give little information about other parts of the Eucharist, but it is evident that the service shows much dependence on the scriptures.

THE DAILY OFFICE

The details of the development of the Daily Office particularly in the earliest years of the Church are somewhat obscure, but by the third century there is more information. The Office itself owed its development to some extent to the growth of monasticism, yet the development began before monasticism was a real force. Many writers believe that it stemmed from the Jewish practice of morning and evening hours of prayer, which were an inheritance from the morning and evening sacrifices of the Temple. There are clear indications in the New

---

[1] *The Mass of the Roman Rite* (New York, 1953) II, pp. 194 f.

Testament that the Christians recognised the value and importance of definite hours of prayer. Thus, we read that Peter and John 'were going up together to the temple at the hour of prayer, the ninth hour' (Acts 3: 1), and again, 'Peter went up on the housetop to pray, about the sixth hour' (Acts 10: 9).

Whether these were regarded as obligatory hours for Christian prayer is another matter. However, Tertullian about the end of the second century mentions the hours which 'mark the divisions of the day, the third, sixth and ninth, which we may observe in scripture to be more solemn than the rest', but he also says that these times are different from the 'regular prayers which without any reminder are due at the coming of the light and the night' (*De Orat.*, 31, ed. A. Souter, p. 41). Somewhat earlier the *Didache* had spoken of prayer, especially the recitation of the Lord's Prayer, three times daily (8, 3), and Origen (*De Orat.* 12) mentioned prayer at morning, noon and night.[1] *Apostolic Tradition* (xxxvi, 2–6, ed. G. Dix, pp. 62–4) urges that a man should pray not only in the morning and at night, but wherever he may be he should pray at the third, sixth and ninth hours. Elsewhere (e.g. Cyprian, *De Orat. Domini*, 35) the same point is made, and it seems clear that morning and evening prayer were of long standing compared with the others. Many different reasons are alleged for the observance of these times, and that very fact makes the real reason obscure. The probability is that at first these hours were purely private, but later, especially with the development of monasticism, individuals grouped together and the services became more formal. One of the great matters in the Offices was the recitation of psalmody, but the reading of scripture was also important, though lessons were not read in them all from the first. The general practice was a form of *lectio continua*, except on festivals.

The writings of Basil (A.D. 316–79), especially the *Longer* and *Shorter Rules* (*PG*, 31, 889, 1079), give some information. Though he does not supply many details, it is clear that the services contained psalms, lections and prayers, and he says that 'a want of variety often produces slothfulness of mind, so that it becomes inattentive, while by changing or varying the psalms and the reading at each office our fervour may be rekindled and our attention renewed' (*The Longer Rule*, 37, 3–5).

[1] *Origen's Treatise on Prayer*, ed. E. G. Jay (London, 1954), p. 115.

The *Pilgrimage of Etheria* tells of her visit to Jerusalem in the latter part of the fourth century. She wrote a description of the services she attended there, including Matins, Terce, Sext, None and Vespers, in addition to the Sunday Vigil and the Eucharist, and some seasonal services at Epiphany, Lent, Easter and Pentecost. She says that in all the Offices psalms were recited, often responsively and with antiphons. She seldom mentions a particular psalm, but says that 'among all things it is a special feature that they arrange that suitable psalms and antiphons are said on every occasion, both those said by night, or in the morning, as well as those throughout the day, at the sixth hour, the ninth hour and at *lucernare*, all being so appropriate and so reasonable as to bear on the matter in hand' (II, 2, ed. McClure and Feltoe, pp. 51 f.). Etheria gives more detail about the lessons. They too are so chosen as to be apt for the occasion. At the service for the Sunday Vigil, that is, early on Sunday morning, the bishop takes the book of the Gospel and reads the narrative of the resurrection of the Lord (II, 1, ed. McClure and Feltoe, pp. 50 f.). In this way the connection of the Lord's Day with Easter is underlined. On Palm Sunday at the seventh hour the people go to the Mount of Olives, and at Gethsemane they hear the portions of the gospels relating to the events that took place there. She speaks too of the preaching of sermons, remarking that 'in order that the people may always be instructed in the law, both the bishop and the presbyter preach diligently' (IV, 3, ed. McClure and Feltoe, pp. 59 f.). Or again, on the fortieth day after the Epiphany 'all the priests, and after them, the bishop, preach, always taking for their subject that part of the Gospel where Joseph and Mary brought the Lord into the Temple' (III, 4, ed. McClure and Feltoe, p. 56).

Another important writer on the Daily Offices is John Cassian, who belongs to the same period. He too visited the East and has described in his *De Institutis Coenobiorum*, written about A.D. 420, the monastic services in Egypt and Palestine. He gives many interesting details in respect of the psalmody, the rules for which varied in different districts. So far as the lessons are concerned, he says that in Egypt the custom was to put the psalms into groups of twelve and after each group to read two lessons (II, 4, 5), one from each Testament. That from the New Testament was normally the *Apostolikon*, but on Saturday and Sunday and in the Paschal season, both lessons were from the New Testament. In Palestine the service of Nocturns contained psalms followed by three lessons (III, 8). On Sundays a more solemn and longer service of psalms, prayers and lessons was held (III, 11).

The custom of reading a passage from the gospels at the morning and evening Offices, and later at each of the Hours, spread through the various churches, and is regarded as having come from the habit, referred to by Etheria, of always reading a Gospel about the resurrection of the Lord at the beginning of the Sunday morning service. It should be added that in the developed Offices there were many short biblical passages known as *capitula* or little chapters, and many versicles and responses which were frequently quotations from the Psalter and other scripture. But little is said of these by writers in the early centuries.

THE OCCASIONAL OFFICES

The Occasional Offices do not require extended treatment. Particular lessons are seldom prescribed, though in some cases psalms are mentioned by number. The reason is that most of these Offices were attached to or part of other services. Baptism, Confirmation, Ordination, and the Consecration of Churches were from an early time closely associated with the Eucharist. Thus, according to most of the Church Orders, after baptism a person was at once confirmed, and the Baptismal Eucharist followed immediately. There is little indication of lections in the rites of Baptism and Confirmation, but the catechumenate, which might last for as long as three years (e.g. *Apostolic Tradition* II, xvii, ed. G. Dix, p. 28), was the period when the candidates received instruction on the tenets of the Christian faith. That instruction was on a biblical basis, normally given during Lent. Etheria says that the bishop 'goes through all the scriptures during these forty days, first literally, and then unfolding them spiritually' (VII, 2). During the vigil before the baptismal service, there were read such Old Testament passages as the narratives of the Creation, the Flood, the Passage of the Red Sea, and sections from the prophets, as well as portions of the New Testament. The formula of Baptism, '*N*. I baptize thee in the name of the Father and of the Son and of the Holy Spirit', was taken from the commission of Jesus Christ to his disciples as recorded in Matt. 28: 19–20. Some Orders speak of psalms to be sung at particular points in the baptismal service. Psalms 51 and 32 came to be regarded as specially suitable, the former before and the latter after the actual baptism. The Confirmation service does not seem to have contained lections or psalms as it led straight into the service of Holy Communion.

The rites of Ordination give little indication of scripture lessons. In *Apostolic Tradition* (I, ii, ed. G. Dix, pp. 2 ff.) the bishop who has been elected is 'ordained' by the bishops present, who lay hands on him, and thereafter he celebrates the Eucharist, laying his hand upon the offering, with all the presbytery, and says the Consecration Prayer. No indication of psalm or of lesson is given. The same is the case in the directions for the ordination of a priest, of a deacon, and of the minor orders.

The Church Orders provide no religious rites for Matrimony, though the Fathers of the Church had much to say about the meaning of Christian marriage.

In the references to the Burial of the Dead there is again little mention of lections. But there was psalmody, as in the funeral processions. Chrysostom gives as a reason for this, that if mourners were really assured that the dead were gone to a better life, they should not lament, and that their psalms should be to the praise of God for him who has been taken away (*Hom.* 30 *de dormientibus*). Jerome points out that the singing of psalms and hymns in a funeral procession was a Christian tradition (*Vita Pauli*, 16), and notes that at the funeral of the Lady Paula there was singing of psalms in Greek, Latin and Syriac (*Ep. ad Eustochium. Ep.* 108, 30). In some cases proper psalms are mentioned. Chrysostom notes Pss. 23 and 59 (*Hom. in Heb.* 4) and *Apostolic Constitutions* speaks of Ps. 116 (VI, 30, 1).

CONCLUSION

The worship of the early Christian Church was thoroughly impregnated with biblical thought and language. Scripture was regarded from the first not merely as a record of the mighty acts of God and of his gradual self-revelation in creation, providence and history and finally in Jesus Christ, but also as a living source of inspiration which never failed to nourish faith, to animate hope, and to make confidence more steadfast. Christianity asserted the divine intervention in history at the coming of Christ, and this led to the composition of the New Testament. But there were centuries of preparation for that intervention and their record was in the Old Testament. Hence it is that in the New

Testament there is a clear note of fulfilment, which underlines the importance and value of the events narrated in the Old Testament, as being not for their age alone, but for all time. Indeed, what Peter said on the day of Pentecost was typical of the whole attitude of the Church —'This is what was spoken by the prophet Joel' (Acts 2: 16).

Paul also strikes this note: 'Now these things happened to them as a warning, but they were written down for our instruction, upon whom the end of the ages has come' (1 Cor. 10: 11). And 1 Pet. 1: 12 says, 'It was revealed to them [the prophets] that they were serving not themselves but you, in the things which have now been announced to you by those who preached the good tidings to you.' Though the Old Testament was God's word, it was not in fact God's final word.

This was of course not an entirely new thing. Ezra for example (Neh. 8: 1–8) read the Law before the assembled people, and the Levites gave the interpretation so that the people could understand. Here was something already in the record, but it had a new application in the particular circumstances. Similarly in the Qumrân community, the mysteries of God had been recorded by the prophets, and the Teacher of Righteousness revealed to his followers the true interpretation (1QpHab VII, 1–5).[1] This process continued with new depth and urgency in the Christian Church. This attitude, looking at once to the past and to the present and to the future, is an underlining of the principles enshrined in the scriptures as being of permanent truth and cogency. The Church possessed the truth and had to apply and declare it.

Yet there was more here than mere fulfilment. There was a building-up of doctrine. As A. G. Hebert said, 'It is not that the prophets were inspired in a mechanical way to foretell various details of the life of Jesus; it is that the prophets, contemplating God's past and present acts of deliverance, give symbolical and poetical expression to great theological principles which find their full embodiment in Jesus the Messiah.'[2] It was the task and duty of the Church to proclaim and to expound these principles and to apply them to Christian life and worship. Hebert goes on to note the application by the Church of Ps. 114, 'When Israel went forth from Egypt', to the resurrection of Christ, and the use of the *Praeconium* for Easter Eve, in which the

[1] Cf. G. Vermes, *The Dead Sea Scrolls*, pp. 35, 37.
[2] *Liturgy and Society* (London, 1935), p. 216.

585

Exodus and the Passage of the Red Sea are symbols of the Lord's triumph over death. The use of the same extracts in the baptismal preparation,[1] as well as in the later texts of the Order of Baptism, is another application.

These great theological principles are recorded, if not dogmatically yet in essence, in the New Testament, but they were largely formulated and inspired by the common prayer and worship of the congregation. A. B. Macdonald has written,

> Even as, in after years, the canon of the Church's sacred Book was to be determined, not so much by the decisions of a few superior intellects as by a consensus of the general mind of the Church, so, in those early days, the main lines which Christian thought was to follow were laid down for it by the common mind of the believers, as it declared itself in their worship-assemblies.[2]

This common mind was reached through the reading, exposition and study of the biblical texts. The same process had a powerful effect in the rejection of many aberrations of thought, as well as the rejection of many apocryphal books. It was the constant recapitulation in worship of the divine plan and process revealed in the Bible that bound the Church to the truth.

There has in fact never been liturgy without the Bible, and Christian worship must continue to draw its inspiration from the same source. It has been said that 'liturgical progress is impossible apart from the biblical education of the Christian',[3] and that is why biblical study and liturgical study must not cease to go hand in hand. If the Church is to continue to be the Church, to be that institution which Christ founded and with which he promised to remain to the end of time, it must never be slack to proclaim the gospel of God, above all in the liturgy of word and sacrament.

[1] See above, p. 583.
[2] *Christian Worship in the Primitive Church* (Edinburgh, 1934), p. 200.
[3] *Parole de Dieu et Liturgie, Le congrès de Strasbourg* (Paris, 1958), p. 13.

BIBLIOGRAPHY

I. LANGUAGE AND SCRIPT

1. *The Biblical Languages*

Bauer, H. and Leander, P., *Historische Grammatik der Hebräischen Sprache* (Halle, 1918).

Bauer, W., *A Greek–English Lexicon of the New Testament and Other Early Christian Literature*, transl. and ed. by W. F. Arndt and F. W. Gingrich (Cambridge and Chicago, 1957).

Black, Matthew, *An Aramaic Approach to the Gospels and Acts* (3rd ed. Oxford, 1967).

Blass, F. and Debrunner, A., *A Greek Grammar of the New Testament and Other Early Christian Literature*, tr. and ed. by R. W. Funk (Cambridge and Chicago, 1961).

Dupont-Sommer, A., *Les Araméens* (Paris, 1949).

Moscati, Sabatino and others, *An Introduction to the Comparative Grammar of the Semitic Languages* (Wiesbaden, 1964).

Moulton, J. H. and Milligan, G., *The Vocabulary of the Greek Testament* (London, 1914–29).

O'Leary, De Lacy, *Comparative Grammar of the Semitic Languages* (London, 1923).

Turner, N., article on 'The Language of the New Testament', in *Peake's Commentary on the Bible*, ed. by Matthew Black and H. H. Rowley (London, 1962).

Turner, Nigel, *A Grammar of New Testament Greek*, by J. H. Moulton. III, *Syntax*, by Nigel Turner (Edinburgh, 1963).

Ullendorff, E., 'What is a Semitic Language?', *Or*, XXVIII (1958), 66–75.

2. *The Biblical Scripts*

Birnbaum, S., *The Hebrew Scripts* (London, 1954–7).

Bruce, F. F., *The Books and the Parchments. Some Chapters on the Transmission of the Bible* (London, 1950; 2nd ed. 1953).

Cohen, M., *L'écriture* (Paris, 1953).

Cohen, M., *La grande invention de l'écriture et son évolution*, 3 vols. (Paris, 1958).

Cross, F. M., Jr., *The Ancient Library of Qumrân* (New York; London, 1958).

Cross, F. M., Jr., 'The Development of the Jewish Scripts', *The Bible and the Ancient Near East: Essays in honor of William Foxwell Albright*, ed. by G. E. Wright (London, 1961), pp. 133–202.

Diringer, D., *Le iscrizioni antico-ebraiche palestinesi* (Firenze, 1934).

Diringer, D., *L'alfabeto nella storia della civiltà* (Firenze, 1937).

Diringer, D., *The Alphabet, a Key to the History of Mankind* (London; New York, 1948; 2nd ed. 1949, 1953, etc.; 3rd ed. in 2 vols., London, 1968).

Diringer, D., *The Story of the Aleph Beth* (London, 1958; New York, 1960).

Diringer, D., *Writing* (London, 1962).

Driver, G. R., *Semitic Writing. From Pictograph to Alphabet* (The Schweich Lectures, 1944) (London, 1948; rev. ed. 1954).

Février, J.-G., *Histoire de l'écriture* (Paris, 1948).

Gilyarevskij, R. S. and Grivnin, V. S., *Manual of World Languages and their Scripts* (in Russian) (Moscow, 1960).

Heuser, G., *Die Kopten* (Heidelberg, 1938).

Kahle, P. E., *The Cairo Geniza* (The Schweich Lectures, 1941) (London, 1947; 2nd ed. Oxford, 1959).

Kenyon, F. G., *Our Bible and the Ancient Manuscripts* (London, 1939).

Kenyon, F. G., *The Bible and Archaeology* (London, 1940).

Moorhouse, A. C., *Writing and the Alphabet* (London, 1946).

Moorhouse, A. C., *The Triumph of the Alphabet. A History of Writing* (New York, 1953).

Roberts, B. J., *The Old Testament Text and Versions* (Cardiff, 1951).

Ullendorff, E., 'Studies in the Ethiopic Syllabary', *Africa*, XXI (1951), 207–17.

Ullendorff, E., *The Semitic Languages of Ethiopia* (London, 1955).

Ullendorff, E., *The Ethiopians* (London, 1960).

Worrell, W. H., *A Short Account of the Copts* (Ann Arbor, 1945).

Würthwein, E., *Der Text des Alten Testaments* (Stuttgart, 1952; 2nd ed. 1963); English transl. of 1st ed. *The Text of the Old Testament* by P. R. Ackroyd (Oxford, 1957).

II. BOOKS IN THE ANCIENT WORLD

3. *Books in the Ancient Near East and in the Old Testament*

I *Material Form*

Černý, J., *Paper and Books in Ancient Egypt* (London, 1952).

Driver, G. R., *Semitic Writing. From Pictograph to Alphabet* (2nd rev. ed. London, 1954). [A useful survey of all writing materials and literary forms in the ancient Near East.]

Wiseman, D. J., 'Assyrian Writing Boards', *Iraq*, XVII (1955), 3–13.

II *The Scribal Art*

Gadd, C. J., *Teachers and Students in the Oldest Schools* (London, 1956). [Discussion of Sumerian school texts.]

Kraeling, C. H. and Adams, R. M. ed., *City Invincible* (Chicago, 1960). [Pp. 94–113 give summary of Egyptian (by J. Wilson) and Mesopotamian (by B. Landsberger) education and literacy.]

Kramer, S. N., *History begins at Sumer* (London, 1957).

Oppenheim, A. L., *Ancient Mesopotamia* (Chicago and London, 1964). [A survey of cuneiform literature with emphasis on traditional Mesopotamian scribal methods.]

Bibliography

III   Literature

Erman, A., *The Literature of the Ancient Egyptians*, transl. by A. M. Blackman (London, 1927). [Still the best general survey of Egyptian literature in translation.]

Lambert, W. G., *Babylonian Wisdom Literature* (Oxford, 1960).

Pritchard, J. B. ed., *Ancient Near Eastern Texts relating to the Old Testament* (Princeton, 1955). [Translations by specialists of myths, epics, legends, laws, histories, rituals, hymns, prayers, wisdom and other literature from Sumerian, Akkadian, Aramaic, Hittite and Ugaritic sources.]

Winton Thomas, D. ed., *Documents from Old Testament Times* (London, 1958). [A more restricted selection of texts than in Pritchard (see above), but with useful commentaries closely relating the documents with Old Testament literature.]

Wright, G. E. ed., *The Bible and the Ancient Near East* (London, 1961). [Essays on language, literature and religion including textual criticism.]

4. *Books in the Graeco-Roman World and in the New Testament*

Gerhardsson, B., *Memory and Manuscript* (Lund, Copenhagen, 1961).

Harnack, A., *Bible Reading in the Early Church*, transl. by J. R. Wilkinson (London, 1912).

Roberts, C. H., *The Codex* (Proc. Brit. Acad. XL, 1954).

Schubart, W., *Das Buch bei den Griechen u. Römern*, II (Berlin, 1921).

III. THE OLD TESTAMENT

5. *The Old Testament in the Making*

General works

Eissfeldt, O., *The Old Testament: An Introduction*, transl. by P. R. Ackroyd (Oxford, New York, 1965). [The standard work, with full bibliographical information.]

Anderson, G. W., *A Critical Introduction to the Old Testament* (London, 1959). [A readable short account of the literature.]

Driver, S. R., *Introduction to the Literature of the Old Testament* (Edinburgh, 9th ed. 1913 (1961)). [An older standard work, containing much basic information, though now inevitably somewhat dated.]

Lods, A., *Histoire de la littérature hébraïque et juive depuis les origines jusqu'à la ruine de l'état juif* (135 après J.-C.) (Paris, 1950).

Sandmel, S., *The Hebrew Scriptures. An Introduction to their Literature and Religious Ideas* (New York, 1963). [A modern Jewish approach to literary problems.]

Form criticism

Gunkel, H. and Begrich, E., *Einleitung in die Psalmen* (Göttingen, 1933). [The basic work, though limited in scope.]

589

Bibliography

Bentzen, A., *Introduction to the Old Testament* (Copenhagen, 1948–9, 5th ed. 1959). [Vol. I deals with form criticism.]

Koch, K., *Was ist Formgeschichte?* (Neukirchen, 2nd ed. 1967); English transl. by S. Cupitt, *The Growth of the Biblical Tradition: the form-critical method* (London, 1969).

6. Canonical and non-Canonical

General Works

Buhl, F., *Canon and Text of the Old Testament* (Edinburgh, 1892). [Particularly valuable for its ample references to rabbinic and patristic sources.]

Filson, F. V., *Which Books belong in the Bible? A Study of the Canon* (Philadelphia, 1957). [A lucid discussion of the problem of canonicity and of the status of the Old Testament and of the Apocrypha. Protestant standpoint.]

Hölscher, G., *Kanonisch und Apokryph. Ein Kapitel aus der Geschichte des alttestamentlichen Kanons* (Leipzig, 1905).

Mullen, T., *The Canon of the Old Testament* (New York, 1892). [An extended discussion and historical survey of differing ecclesiastical and sectarian attitudes to the Canon up to the nineteenth century. Roman Catholic standpoint.]

Ryle, H. E., *The Canon of the Old Testament. An Essay on the Gradual Growth and Formation of the Hebrew Canon of Scripture* (London, 1892). [Contains ample references to, and extensive citations from, rabbinic and patristic sources.]

Smith, W. R., *The Old Testament in the Jewish Church* (2nd ed. revised and much enlarged, London and Edinburgh, 1892).

Special Studies

Audet, J.-P., 'A Hebrew–Aramaic List of Books of the Old Testament in Greek Transcription', *JTS*, n.s. I (1950), 135–54.

Christie, W. M., 'The Jamnia Period in Jewish History', *JTS*, XXVI (1925), 347–64.

Eybers, I. H., 'Some Light on the Canon of the Qumrân Sect', *New Light on Some Old Testament Problems: Papers read at 5th Meeting of Die O.T. Werkgemeenskap in Suid-Afrika* (Pretoria, 1962), 1–14.

Jepsen, A., 'Zur Kanongeschichte des Alten Testaments', *ZAW*, LXXI (1959), 114–36.

Katz, P., 'The Old Testament Canon in Palestine and Alexandria', *ZNTW*, XLVII (1956), 191–217.

Östborn, G., *Cult and Canon: A Study in the Canonization of the Old Testament* (Uppsala Universitets Årsskrift 1950: 10, Uppsala and Leipzig, 1950).

Roberts, B. J., 'The Old Testament Canon: A Suggestion', *BJRL*, XLVI (1963), 164–78.

Sundberg, A. C., *The Old Testament of the Early Church* (Harvard Theological Studies, XX, Cambridge, Mass. and London, 1964).

Bibliography

7. The Old Testament Text

In addition to works mentioned in the footnotes, the following books and articles provide further information.

Cross, F. M., Jr., *The Ancient Library of Qumrân etc.* (2nd ed. New York, 1961), pp. 161–94.

Fitzmyer, J. A., 'The Use of Explicit Old Testament Quotations in Qumrân Literature and in the New Testament', *NTS*, VII (1960–1), 298–333.

Geiger, A., *Urschrift und Übersetzungen der Bibel in ihrer Abhängigkeit von der inneren Entwickelung des Judenthums* (Breslau, 1857, 2nd ed. 1912).

Gerleman, G., 'Synoptic Studies in the Old Testament', Lunds Universitets Ärsskrift N. F. Avd. 1 Bd. 44 Nr. 5 (1948), 3–35.

Greenberg, M., 'The Stabilization of the Text of the Hebrew Bible, Reviewed in the Light of the Biblical Materials from the Judean Desert', *JAOS*, LXXVI (1956), 157–67.

Jellicoe, S., *The Septuagint and Modern Study* (Oxford, 1968).

Orlinsky, H. M., 'The Textual Criticism of the Old Testament', *The Bible and the Ancient Near East, Essays in Honor of W. F. Albright* (London, 1961), pp. 113–32.

Rabin, C., 'The Dead Sea Scrolls and the History of the Old Testament Text', *JTS*, VI (1955), 174–82.

Roberts, B. J., *The Old Testament Text and Versions* (Cardiff, 1951).

Seeligmann, I. L., 'Indications of Editorial Alteration and Adaptation in the Massoretic Text and the Septuagint', *VT*, XI (1961), 201–21.

Segal, M. H., 'The Promulgation of the Authoritative Text of the Hebrew Bible', *JBL*, LXXII (1953), 35–48.

Skehan, P. W., 'The Biblical Scrolls from Qumrân and the Text of the Old Testament', *BA*, XXVIII (1965), 87–100.

Skehan, P. W., 'The Qumrân Manuscripts and Textual Criticism', *Suppl. to VT*, IV (1957), 148–60.

Sperber, A., 'Hebrew Based Upon Biblical Passages in Parallel Transmission', *HUCA*, XII–XIII (1937–8), 103–274.

Talmon, S., 'DSIª as a Witness to Ancient Exegesis of the Book of Isaiah', *ASTI*, I (1962), 62–72.

Talmon, S., 'Synonymous Readings in the Textual Traditions of the Old Testament', *Scripta Hierosolymitana*, VIII (1961), 334–83.

Textus, Annual of the Hebrew University Bible Project, I–III (1960–3) ed. by C. Rabin, IV–VI (1964–8) ed. by S. Talmon.

de Waard, J., *A Comparative Study of the Old Testament Text in the Dead Sea Scrolls and in the New Testament* (Leiden, 1966).

Würthwein, E., *Der Text des Alten Testaments, Eine Einführung in die Biblia Hebraica* (Stuttgart, 1952; 2nd ed. 1963). English transl. of 1st ed. *The Text of the Old Testament* by P. R. Ackroyd (Oxford, 1957).

Bibliography

8. Bible and Midrash: Early Old Testament Exegesis

Albeck, C., *Untersuchungen über die halachischen Midraschim* (Berlin, 1927).

Bacher, W., *Die Agada der babylonischen Amoräer* (Strassburg, 1878; 2nd ed. Frankfurt am Main, 1913).

Bacher, W., *Die Agada der Tannaiten*, 2 vols. (Strassburg, 1884, 1890; 2nd ed. 1903).

Bacher, W., *Die Agada der palästinensischen Amoräer*, 3 vols. (Strassburg, 1892–9).

Bacher, W., *Die exegetische Terminologie der jüdischen Traditionsliteratur*, 2 vols. (Leipzig, 1899, 1905). [Indispensable lexicon.]

Belkin, S., *Philo and the Oral Law* (Cambridge, Mass., 1939).

Bloch, Renée, 'Midrash', *Supplément au Dictionnaire de la Bible*, v (Paris, 1957).

Christiansen, I., *Die Technik der allegorischen Auslegungswissenschaft bei Philon von Alexandria* (Tübingen, 1969).

Daube, D., 'Rabbinic Methods of Interpretation and Hellenistic Rhetoric', *HUCA*, XXII (1949).

Geiger, A., *Urschrift und Übersetzungen der Bibel in ihrer Abhängigkeit von der innern Entwickelung des Judenthums* (Breslau, 1857). [A masterpiece far ahead of its time.]

Ginzberg, L., *Legends of the Jews*, 7 vols. (Philadelphia, 1909; 10th ed. 1954). [A compendium of exegetical traditions with valuable notes.]

Heinemann, I., *Darkē ha-'aggadah* [The Methods of the Aggadah] (Jerusalem, 1949).

Kahle, P., *The Cairo Geniza* (London, 1947; 2nd ed. Oxford, 1959).

Le Déaut, R., *Introduction à la littérature targumique* (Rome, 1966).

McNamara, M., *The New Testament and the Palestinian Targum to the Pentateuch* (Rome, 1966).

Mann, J., *The Bible as Read and Preached in the Old Synagogue*. 2 vols. (Cincinnati, 1940, 1966).

Rappoport, S., *Agada und Exegese bei Flavius Josephus* (Frankfurt am Main, 1930).

Strack, H. L., *Introduction to the Talmud and Midrash* (Philadelphia, 1931). [Translated from *Einleitung in Talmud und Midrasch* (5th ed. München, 1920; 1st ed. 1887). Out of date but not yet replaced.]

Vermes, G., *Scripture and Tradition in Judaism, Haggadic Studies* (Leiden, 1961).

Vermes, G., 'The Qumran Interpretation of Scripture in its Historical Setting', *Annual of Leeds University Oriental Society*, vol. 6 (Leiden, 1969).

Zunz, L., *Die gottesdienstlichen Vorträge der Juden historisch entwickelt* (Berlin, 1832; 2nd ed. Frankfurt am Main, 1892). [Pioneer work on post-biblical literature.]

Bibliography

IV. THE NEW TESTAMENT

9. The New Testament in the Making

Albertz, M., *Die Botschaft des Neuen Testamentes.* vols. 1–2 (I.1, Zürich, 1947, I.2, 1952).

Bultmann, R., *Die Geschichte der synoptischen Tradition* (Göttingen, 1921); English transl. of 3rd rev. ed. *The History of the Synoptic Tradition* by John Marsh (Oxford, 1963).

Bultmann, R., *Theologie des Neuen Testaments* (Tübingen, 1948); English transl. by K. Grobel, *Theology of the New Testament*, 2 vols. (London, 1952, 1955).

Dibelius, M., *Fresh Approach to the New Testament and Early Christian Literature* (London, 1936).

Fuller, R. G., *A Critical Introduction to the New Testament* (London, 1966).

Grant, F. C., *The Gospels, Their Origin and Growth* (London, 1959).

Kümmel, W. G., *Einleitung in das Neue Testament*, P. Feine and J. Behm (rev. ed. Heidelberg, 1963); English transl. of 14th rev. ed. *Introduction to the New Testament* by A. J. Matill, Jr. (London, 1966).

Kümmel, W. G., *Das Neue Testament. Geschichte der Erforschung seiner Probleme* (Freiburg/Münich, 1958).

Mitton, C. L., *The Formation of the Pauline Corpus of Letters* (London, 1955).

Moule, C. F. D., *The Birth of the New Testament* (London, 1962).

Munck, J., *Paulus und die Heilsgeschichte* (Copenhagen, 1954); English transl. *Paul and the Salvation of Mankind* by F. Clarke (London, 1959).

Rigaux, B., *St Paul et ses Lettres* (Paris, 1962).

Wilder, A. N., *Early Christian Rhetoric* (London, 1964).

10. The New Testament Canon

Aland, K., *The Problem of the New Testament Canon* (London, 1962).

Barth, C., *Die Interpretationen des Neuen Testaments in der Valentinianischen Gnosis (Texte und Untersuchungen* 37, 3, Leipzig, 1911).

Blackman, E. C., *Marcion and His Influence* (London, 1955).

Cross, F. L. ed., *The Jung Codex* (London, 1955).

Goodspeed, E. J., *The Formation of the New Testament* (Chicago, 1926).

Grant, R. M., *The Formation of the New Testament* (London and New York, 1965).

Grant, R. M. (with D. N. Freedman and W. R. Schoedel), *The Secret Sayings of Jesus* (New York and London, 1960).

Grant, R. M., *A Short History of the Interpretation of the Bible* (rev. ed. New York, 1964; London, 1965).

Knox, J., *Marcion and the New Testament* (Chicago, 1942).

Köster, H., *Synoptische Überlieferungen bei den Apostolischen Vätern (Texte und Untersuchungen* 65, Berlin, 1957).

Ruwet, J., 'Clément d'Alexandrie, Canon des Écritures et apocryphes', *Biblica*, XXIX (1948), 240–71.

Ruwet, J., 'Les apocryphes dans l'œuvre d'Origène', *Biblica*, XXIII (1942), 18–42; XXIV (1943), 18–58; XXV (1944), 143–66.

Smith, M., reported in *New York Times*, 30 December 1960.

Van Unnik, W. C., 'The "Gospel of Truth" and the New Testament', *The Jung Codex*, ed. F. L. Cross (London, 1955), pp. 79–129.

Van Unnik, W. C., ''Η καινὴ διαθήκη—a Problem in the early history of the Canon', *Texte und Untersuchungen*, 79 (1961), 212–27.

11. *The New Testament Text*

Convenient hand editions are:

Novum Testamentum Graece . . ., ed. E. Nestle et K. Aland (25th ed. Stuttgart, 1963).

Η ΚΑΙΝΗ ΔΙΑΘΗΚΗ (ed. G. D. Kilpatrick), British and Foreign Bible Society (2nd ed. London, 1958).

The Greek New Testament, ed. K. Aland, M. Black, B. M. Metzger, A. P. Wikgren (New York, London, Amsterdam, Stuttgart, Edinburgh, 1966).

In addition to the various works named in footnotes, which are worthy of perusal on points other than those specifically mentioned, the following works will also be found of value in pursuing the subject further.

Black, M., *An Aramaic Approach to the Gospels and Acts* (3rd ed. Oxford, 1967).

Clark, A. C., *The Acts of the Apostles. A Critical Edition* (Oxford, 1933).

Dain, A., *Les Manuscrits* (Nouvelle éd. revue Paris, 1964).

Hatch, W. H. P., *The Principal Uncial Manuscripts of the New Testament* (Chicago and London, 1939).

Hatch, W. H. P., *Facsimiles and Descriptions of Minuscule Manuscripts of the New Testament* (Cambridge, Mass., 1951).

Lake, K., Blake, R. P., New, S., 'The Caesarean Text of the Gospel of Mark', *HTR*, XXI (1928), 207–404.

Metzger, B. M., *The Text of the New Testament. Its Transmission, Corruption and Restoration* (2nd ed. Oxford, 1968).

Novum Testamentum Graece et Latine, ed. S. J. Merk. 9th ed. ed. S. J. Carlo Martini (Rome, 1964).

Pasquali, G., *Storia della tradizione e critica del testo* (2nd ed. Florence, 1952).

von Soden, H., *Die Schriften des neuen Testaments in ihrer ältesten erreichbaren Textgestalt hergestellt auf Grund ihrer Textgeschichte* (Berlin, 1911–13).

Vogels, H. J., *Handbuch der Textkritik des Neuen Testaments* (2nd ed. Münster, 1955).

Vogels, H. J., *Evangelium Palatinum. Studien zur ältesten Geschichte der lateinischen Evangelienübersetzung* (Münster, 1916).

Vööbus, A., *Early Versions of the New Testament* (Stockholm, 1954).

Zuntz, G., *The Text of the Epistles* (The Schweich Lectures, 1946) (London, 1953).

12. *The Interpretation of the Old Testament in the New*

Dodd, C. H., *According to the Scriptures* (London, 1952).

Ellis, E. E., *Paul's Use of the Old Testament* (Edinburgh and London, 1957).

Bibliography

Hanson, A. T., *Jesus Christ in the Old Testament* (London, 1965).

Harris, J. R. (assisted by V. Burch), *Testimonies*, Part I (Cambridge, 1916); Part II (Cambridge, 1920).

Lampe, G. W. H., and Woollcombe, K. J., *Essays in Typology* (London, 1957).

Lindars, B., *New Testament Apologetic* (London, 1961).

Moule, C. F. D., *The Birth of the New Testament* (London, 1962), ch. 4.

Selwyn, E. C., *The Oracles in the New Testament* (London, n.d. [1912], preface dated 1911).

Vischer, W., *The Witness of the Old Testament to Christ*, English transl. by A. B. Crabtree (London, 1949).

V. THE BIBLE IN THE EARLY CHURCH

13. *Biblical Exegesis in the Early Church*

Bonsirven, J., *Exégèse Rabbinique et Exégèse Paulinienne* (Paris, 1939).

Congar, Y., *Tradition and Traditions* (London, 1966).

Daniélou, J., *From Shadows to Reality* (London, 1960).

Daniélou, J., *The Theology of Jewish Christianity* (London, 1963).

Daniélou, J., *The Christian Gospel and Hellenic Christianity* (Paris, 1964).

Daube, D., *The New Testament and Rabbinic Judaism* (London, 1956).

Flesseman-Van Leer, E., *Tradition and Scripture in the Early Church* (Assen, 1955).

Grant, R. M., *The Letter and the Spirit* (London, 1957).

Grant, R. M., *The Earliest Lives of Jesus* (London, 1961).

Grant, R. M., *Gnosticism and Early Christianity* (Oxford, 1966).

Hanson, A. T., *Jesus Christ in the Old Testament* (London, 1965).

Hanson, R. P. C., *Allegory and Event* (London, 1959).

Hanson, R. P. C., *Tradition in the Early Church* (London, 1962).

Lampe, G. W. H. and Woollcombe, K. J., *Essays in Typology* (London, 1957).

Luneau, A., *L'Histoire de Salut chez les Pères de l'Église* (Paris, 1964).

Sanders, J. N., *The Fourth Gospel in the Early Church* (Cambridge, 1943).

Shotwell, W. A., *The Biblical Exegesis of Justin Martyr* (London, 1965).

Simon, M., *Verus Israel* (Paris, 1948).

Wiles, M., *The Spiritual Gospel* (Cambridge, 1959).

Wiles, M., *The Divine Apostle* (Cambridge, 1967).

14. *Origen as Biblical Scholar*

All general works on early Christian exegesis deal with Origen at some length: for these see bibliography to v, 13.

General introductions to Origen with useful sections on his exegesis are:

Bigg, C., *The Christian Platonists of Alexandria* (Oxford, 1886).

Daniélou, J., *Origen* (London, 1955).

The most important works devoted exclusively to Origen's exegesis are:

Hanson, R. P. C., *Allegory and Event* (London, 1959).

de Lubac, H., *Histoire et Esprit* (Paris, 1950).

15. *Theodore of Mopsuestia as Representative of the Antiochene School*

The following works on Theodore have useful sections on his exegesis:

Devreesse, R., *Essai sur Théodore de Mopsueste* (Vatican, 1948). [Especially for the Old Testament.]

Greer, R. A., *Theodore of Mopsuestia* (London, 1961). [Especially for John.]

Swete, H. B., 'Theodorus of Mopsuestia', in W. Smith and H. Wace, *Dictionary of Christian Biography*, IV (London, 1887), 934–48. [Especially for Paul.]

Works devoted exclusively to Theodore's exegesis are:

Pirot, L., *L'Œuvre Exégétique de Théodore de Mopsueste* (Rome, 1913).

Wickert, U., *Studien zu den Pauluskommentaren Theodors von Mopsuestia* (Berlin, 1962).

Editions of the Commentaries

The Psalms

Devreesse, R., *Le Commentaire de Théodore de Mopsueste sur les Psaumes (I–LXXX)* (*Studi e Testi* 93, Vatican, 1939).

The Minor Prophets

Migne, J.-P., *Patrologia Graeca*, LXVI, 105–632.

John

Vosté, J. M., *Theodori Mopsuesteni Commentarius in Evangelium Johannis Apostoli* (*Corpus Scriptorum Christianorum Orientalium: Scriptores Syri*, Series 4, Tomus III; Louvain, 1940). Greek fragments in R. Devreesse, *Essai . . .*, pp. 305–419.

Paul

Swete, H. B., *Theodori Episcopi Mopsuesteni in Epistolas B. Pauli Commentarii* (2 vols., Cambridge, 1880–2). Greek fragments in Staab, K., *Pauluskommentare aus der griechischen Kirche* (*Neutestamentliche Abhandlungen XV*, Münster, 1933).

16. *Jerome as Biblical Scholar*

Cavallera, F., *St Jérôme, sa vie et son œuvre* = *Spicilegium Sacrum Lovaniense, Études et Documents*, fasc. 1 and 2 (Louvain, 1922).

Favez, C., *Saint Jérôme peint par lui-même* = Collection Latomus, XXXIII (Brussels, 1958).

Grützmacher, G., *Hieronymus: Eine biographische Studie zur alten Kirchengeschichte* (Leipzig, Berlin, 1901–8).

Holworth, H. H., 'The Influence of St Jerome on the Canon of the Western Church', *JTS*, X, 481–96; XI, 321–47; XIII, 1–18.

Murphy, F. X. ed., *A Monument to Saint Jerome: Essays on some Aspects of his Work and Influence* (New York, 1952).

Rahmer, M., *Die hebräische Traditionen in den Werken des Hieronymus* (Breslau, Berlin, 1861–1902).

Bibliography

Roehrich, A., *Essai sur Saint Jérôme exégète* (Geneva, 1891).

Thierry, A., *Saint Jérôme: La Société chrétienne à Rome et l'émigration romaine en Terre Sainte* (Paris, 1867).

17. Augustine as Biblical Scholar

Bonnadière, A. M., *Biblia Augustiniana* (Études Augustiniennes, Paris, 1960–   ). [In progress.]

Bruyne, D. de, 'S. Augustin reviseur de la Bible', *Miscellanea Agostiniana* (Rome, 1931), II, 523–608.

Comeau, Marie, *Saint Augustin, exégète du quatrième Évangile* (2nd ed. Paris, 1930).

Hahn, Traugott, *Tyconius-Studien* (Studien zur Gesch. d. Theologie und Kirche, Leipzig, 1900).

Holl, Adolf, *Augustins Bergpredigtexegese* (Vienna, 1959).

Markus, R. A., 'Saint Augustine on history, prophecy and inspiration', *Augustinus* (Madrid, 1967), pp. 271–80.

Marrou, H. I., *Saint Augustin et la fin de la culture antique* (4th ed. Paris, 1958).

Meer, F. G. L. van der, *St Augustine the Bishop*, English transl. by B. Balteshar and G. R. Lamb (London, 1961).

Pontet, Maurice, *L'exégèse de S. Augustin prédicateur* (Paris, [1945]).

Rollero, Piero, 'L'influsso della *Expositio in Lucam* di Ambrogio nell'esegesi agostiniana', *Augustinus Magister* (Paris, 1954), I, 211–20.

La Expositio evangelii secundum Lucam *di Ambrogio come fonte della esegesi agostiniana* (Università di Torino, pubb. d. fac. di lettere e filos. x, 4, Turin, 1958).

Strauss, Gerhard, *Schriftgebrauch, Schriftauslegung und Schriftbeweis bei Augustin* (Beiträge zur Gesch. der biblischen Hermeneutik Nr 1, Tübingen, 1959).

18. The Place of the Bible in the Liturgy

Baumstark, A., *Comparative Liturgy*, 3rd ed. rev. by B. Botte, English transl. by F. L. Cross (London, 1958).

Brightman, F. E., *Liturgies Eastern and Western. I. Eastern* (Oxford, 1896).

Cullmann, O., *Early Christian Worship* (London, 1953).

Delling, G., *Worship in the New Testament* (London, 1962).

Dictionary of Christian Antiquities, ed. by W. Smith and S. Cheetham, 2 vols. (London, 1875, 1880).

Dictionnaire d'archéologie chrétienne et de liturgie, ed. by F. Cabrol, H. Leclercq and H. I. Marrou, 15 vols. in 30 (Paris, 1907–53).

Dix, G., *The Shape of the Liturgy* (London, 1945).

Dugmore, C. A., *The Influence of the Synagogue upon the Divine Office* (Oxford, 1944; reprint London, 1965).

Harnack, A., *Bible Reading in the Early Church* (London, 1912).

Hippolytus, *The Treatise on the Apostolic Tradition of S. Hippolytus of Rome*, ed. G. Dix (London, 1937).

Jungmann, J. A., *The Early Liturgy to the Time of Gregory the Great* (London, 1960).

Bibliography

Jungmann, J. A., *The Mass of the Roman Rite. Its Origins and Development*, 2 vols. (New York, 1950, 1953).

Lamb, J. A., *The Psalms in Christian Worship* (London, 1962).

Macdonald, A. B., *Christian Worship in the Primitive Church* (Edinburgh, 1934).

Maclean, A. J., *The Ancient Church Orders* (Cambridge, 1910).

Moule, C. F. D., *Worship in the New Testament* (London, 1961).

The Pilgrimage of Etheria, ed. and transl. by M. L. McClure and C. L. Feltoe (London, n.d.).

Quasten, J., *Patrology*, 3 vols. (London, 1950, 1953, 1960).

Serapion, *The Sacramentary of Serapion*, ed. J. Wordsworth (2nd ed. London, 1923; reprint Hamden, Connecticut, 1964).

Srawley, J. H., *The Early History of the Liturgy* (2nd ed. Cambridge, 1947).

ABBREVIATIONS

Acta Societ. Scient. Fennicae	*Acta Societatis Scientiarum Fennicae*, Helsinki.
ACW	*Ancient Christian Writers*, ed. J. Quasten, J. C. Plumpe, London.
Africa	*Journal of the International Institute of African Languages and Cultures*, Oxford.
AJSL	*American Journal of Semitic Languages and Literatures*, Chicago (Ill.).
Analecta Biblica	*Analecta Biblica*, Rome.
ANET	*Ancient Near Eastern Texts relating to the Old Testament*, ed. J. B. Pritchard, Princeton, New Jersey, 2nd ed. 1955.
ASTI	*Annual of the Swedish Theological Institute* (in Jerusalem), Leiden.
BA	*The Biblical Archaeologist*, New Haven (Conn.).
BASOR	*Bulletin of the American Schools of Oriental Research*, New Haven (Conn.).
Biblica	*Biblica*, Rome.
BJRL	*Bulletin of the John Rylands Library*, Manchester.
BSOAS	*Bulletin of the School of Oriental and African Studies*, University of London*, London.
BZ	*Biblische Zeitschrift* (Freiburg i. Br.), Paderborn.
CSEL	*Corpus Scriptorum Ecclesiasticorum Latinorum*, Vienna.
DOTT	*Documents from Old Testament Times*, ed. D. Winton Thomas, London, 1958, New York, 1961.
HTR	*Harvard Theological Review*, Cambridge (Mass.).
HUCA	*Hebrew Union College Annual*, Cincinnati (Ohio).
ICC	*The International Critical Commentary*, Edinburgh.
IEJ	*Israel Exploration Journal*, Jerusalem.
Iraq	*Iraq*, London.
JAOS	*Journal of the American Oriental Society*, Boston (Mass.), New Haven (Conn.).
JBL	*Journal of Biblical Literature*, New York, New Haven (Conn.), Philadelphia (Pa.).
JCS	*Journal of Cuneiform Studies*, New Haven (Conn.).
JNES	*Journal of Near Eastern Studies*, Chicago (Ill.).

Journal Asiatique	*Journal Asiatique*, Paris.
JQR	*Jewish Quarterly Review*, Philadelphia (Pa.).
JR	*Journal of Religion*, Chicago (Ill.).
JSS	*Journal of Semitic Studies*, Manchester.
JTS	*Journal of Theological Studies*, Oxford.
LEW	*Liturgies Eastern and Western. I. Eastern.* ed. F. E. Brightman, Oxford, 1896.
MGWJ	*Monatsschrift für Geschichte und Wissenschaft des Judentums*, Breslau.
NTS	*New Testament Studies*, Cambridge.
Or	*Orientalia*, Rome.
Oriens Christianus	*Oriens Christianus* (Leipzig), Wiesbaden.
PG	Migne. *Patrologia cursus completus.* (*Series Graeca.*) Paris.
Proc. Brit. Acad.	*Proceedings of the British Academy*, London.
PSBA	*Proceedings of the Society of Biblical Archaeology*, Bloomsbury (London).
Reallexikon f. Antike u. Christentum	*Reallexikon für Antike und Christentum*, Stuttgart.
RB	*Revue Biblique*, Paris.
RGG	*Die Religion in Geschichte und Gegenwart*, Tübingen, 1927–32, 1956.
Studia Evangelica	*Studia Evangelica.* Papers presented to the International Congress on 'The Four Gospels in 1957' held at Christ Church, Oxford. = Texte und Untersuchungen, 102. Berlin, 1968.
Textus	*Annual of the Hebrew University Bible Project*, Jerusalem.
Theology	*Theology*, London.
Vigiliae Christianae	*Vigiliae Christianae*, Amsterdam.
VT	*Vetus Testamentum*, Leiden.
Welt des Orients	*Die Welt des Orients.* Wissenschaftliche Beiträge zur Kunde des Morgenlandes (Wuppertal, Stuttgart), Göttingen.
ZAW	*Zeitschrift für die Alttestamentliche Wissenschaft* (*Giessen*), Berlin.
ZN(T)W	*Zeitschrift für die Neutestamentliche Wissenschaft* (*Giessen*), Berlin.

NOTES ON THE PLATES

1   The *Leviticus* fragments, like the other Palaeo-Hebrew fragments found in the Dead Sea caves, are written with ink on leather, and, from the point of view of palaeography, are unique. The majority of the letters are clear and neat, and there can be no doubt that this script represents a beautiful Palaeo-Hebrew literary hand, the first of its kind ever discovered. Reproduced by courtesy of the Shrine of the Book, Israel, D. Samuel and Jeane H. Gottesman, Center for Biblical Manuscripts.

2   Codex Orientalis 4445 is the earliest Hebrew manuscript preserved in England. This British Museum manuscript is undated, but belongs to the ninth century A.D. The majority of Hebrew manuscripts belong between the twelfth and sixteenth centuries. Reproduced by permission of the Trustees of the British Museum.

3   These fragments, belonging to the second century A.D., are the earliest (or among the earliest) extant Greek fragments of the Bible. The fragments, written on papyrus, were found in Egyptian refuse heaps, and are now in the John Rylands Library, in Manchester. Reproduced by permission of the Governors of the John Rylands Library.

4   Codex Amiatinus, dating from the early eighth century, is the leading manuscript of the Vulgate. It is an Anglo-Saxon production, and was written at the twin monasteries of Jarrow and Monkwearmouth; it was preserved in the Abbey of Monte Amiata (hence its name) in Tuscany, whence it passed to the Laurentian Library of Florence. Reproduced by permission of the Laurentian Library.

5   The best copy of the Harklean or Harklensian Syriac version of the Bible was made in A.D. 616 by Bishop Thomas of Harkel. The present manuscript, which was written in 1170, is in the Cambridge University Library. Reproduced by permission of the Syndics of the University Library, Cambridge.

6   A manuscript written in the famous scriptorium of the White Monastery (near Sohâg, in Upper Egypt, on the edge of the Libyan desert opposite Akhmîm). It is in the Sahidic dialect and is a fair example of the work done by Coptic monastic scribes in the sixth and seventh centuries. The manuscript is part of Sir Herbert Thompson's collection, purchased by him from the famous Egyptologist H. Hegvernat, and is now in the Cambridge University Library. Reproduced by permission of the Syndics of the University Library, Cambridge.

7   The sculptor depicts two scribes listing the spoil taken during an Assyrian campaign in Babylonia undertaken by Sennacherib, perhaps that against the Chaldaean tribes in 702 B.C.

The further scribe holds a hinged writing-board (see also Plate 8) and a stylus for writing the cuneiform script. The nearer scribe writes upon a leather, parchment or papyrus scroll with a brush-pen, probably using the Aramaic script. Other reliefs show Assyrian scribes writing with a stylus in the cuneiform script upon a clay tablet (e.g. sculpture of Teglakipileser III) or at work with the army on expeditions in the field (Shalmaneser III). *C.* 700 B.C. Reproduced by permission of the Trustees of the British Museum.

8   Reconstruction of the top three leaves of a series of sixteen writing-boards made of ivory, and, orginally, with hinges of gold. The inner surfaces were inlaid with wax on which could be written the cuneiform script used for Akkadian (Babylonian and Assyrian) or the alphabetic (Aramaic) script. According to the inscribed cover this text was a copy in Babylonian of a six-thousand-line series of omens made for the new palace library of Sargon II, king of Assyria.

This precursor of the later 'codex' and 'slate' was a more versatile writing material than the common clay tablet widely used throughout the Ancient Near East in the second and early first millennia B.C. Length 33·5 cm. 711 B.C. Reproduced from M. Mallowan, *Nimrud and its Remains* (London, 1966).

9   The fragments of carefully prepared papyri are palimpsests showing (right) the opening of a roll inscribed in large hieroglyphic characters with, to the right, a broken date column in which the name of the king is partially missing. An account of grain distribution in a cursive hieratic hand. The grid is ruled and (lower left) the table of detailed deliveries is marked in black ink and the balance of the account in red.

The lower centre fragment shows part of an account allocating meat rations to the king's mother.

From Abūsīr. Largest fragment: height 21 cm.; width 21 cm. Reproduced by permission of the Trustees of the British Museum.

10   This papyrus contains the whole of the 'Instruction of King Ameremhet' (I), the sheet shown beginning 'it was after supper, when the evening had come'.

Black and red ink are used. A number of inaccuracies by the pupil scribe have their correct forms drawn above. The same scroll includes other 'wisdom' literature in the 'Satire of the Trades', a work extolling the scribal profession by comparison with the hardships to be faced in other occupations. 'There is no vocation which is free of direction except that of the scribe; he it is who does the directing.'

19th Dynasty, *c.* 1250 B.C. Reproduced by permission of the Trustees of the British Museum.

11   This scroll is the widest known papyrus (19½ in.) and the longest (nearly 123 in.) of all the Theban recensions of the *Book of the Dead*. It contains more chapters (87), hymns, litanies and adorations to the gods, including Amen-Re' and Osiris, than any other extant text.

Written in well-formed clear hieratic characters with only rare errors, it also faithfully transcribes in black outline the full-page vignettes found in the older papyri. As it was prepared by, or for, a princess Nesitanebtashm, a royal priestess of

Amen-Re' at Thebes before her death in 940 B.C., it can be dated to within twenty years and thus provides a valuable authority on the writing, language, art and religion of Upper Egypt at the time.

From Deir al-Baḥri. E. A. Wallis Budge, *The Greenfield Papyrus in the British Museum* (1912). Reproduced by permission of the Trustees of the British Museum.

12 Report of proceedings before the native court in a dispute concerning inheritance between the offspring of the successive marriages of a certain lector-priest, Petetum, to Tshentesed and Ewe.

The text is part of the first plea of Tefhape, a son of Petetum. The proceedings cover dispositions made at court over a number of years until the time of the final transcript in year 11 of Ptolemy IV (Philometer)—June 170 B.C. It thus gives the only detailed account extant of proceedings before a native court in the Ptolemaic period.

From Asyut (Middle Egypt). Papyrus measures 285 × 32 cm. Sir Herbert Thompson, *A Family Archive from Siut* (1934), Text B; col. 3; p. 17. Reproduced by permission of the Trustees of the British Museum.

13 This fragment, Exod. 32:10–30, was published by P. W. Shekan (*JBL*, LXXIV, 1955, 182–7). He considered it to be probably in the 'Samaritan Recension', since it exhibits some deviations from the MT which it shares with the Samaritan. Judgement as to the affinity of the fragment with the Samaritan should be suspended, however, since the variants are mainly of a general orthographic and not of a specifically sectarian nature. Reproduced by courtesy of the Shrine of the Book, Israel, D. Samuel and Jeane H. Gottesman, Center for Biblical Manuscripts.

14 The Abisha Scroll at Nablus is the most famous copy of the Samaritan Pentateuch, deeply venerated by the members of the Samaritan community. It has now been more closely examined and an edition published by P. Castro in 1959; it appears that it is in fact medieval in origin, written by Abisha ben Pinhas in A.D. 1085. The effect of this re-examination is to raise considerable questions about the usefulness of the Samaritan recension, though it is true (see p. 193) that some readings of the Samaritan have also been found in Qumrân texts. Reproduced from P. Castro, *Séfer Abiša*, by permission of the Consejo Superior de Investigaciones Científicas.

15 This single sheet of papyrus of unknown provenance was purchased in Egypt by W. C. Nash, and was first published by S. A. Cook in 1903 (*PSBA*, XXV, 34–56). It contains the Decalogue (Exod. 20:2–17) and the Shema' (Deut. 6:4–5), and was probably used for liturgical purposes. Its text deviates somewhat from the MT and shows affinities with MS A of the Septuagint. Reproduced by permission of the Syndics of the University Library, Cambridge.

16 1Q Is^a—the First Isaiah Scroll from Qumrân Cave I—contains what is to all intents and purposes the full text of the biblical book of Isaiah. The well-preserved leather scroll contains fifty-four columns written in an early Square Hebrew book

hand, and may be dated in the first century B.C. Its text deviates in many instances from the MT, and in some cases was subsequently corrected by the scribe or by a second hand to tally with the MT. The corrections were inserted between the lines, and in some notable instances also vertically in the margins, probably because of lack of space. Reproduced by courtesy of the Shrine of the Book, Israel, D. Samuel and Jeane H. Gottesman, Center for Biblical Manuscripts.

17 The Habakkuk *pēšer* was discovered in 1947 among the first group of scrolls from Qumrân. It reveals that type of interpretation in which the statements of prophecy are seen by the Covenanters as referring to, and as fulfilled in, their own history and religious ideas (cf. pp. 226 ff., 387 ff.). The biblical text which is quoted in the commentary (the plate shows 1:10–15 with its *pēšer*) agrees in the main with the MT of Habakkuk, though it does deviate from it in some instances. Reproduced by courtesy of the Shrine of the Book, Israel, D. Samuel and Jeane H. Gottesman, Center for Biblical Manuscripts.

18 A. Díez Macho was the first to identify MS Neofiti I as a copy of the complete Palestinian Aramaic translation of the Pentateuch, which until then had been known by tradition as the Fragment Targum from sporadic insertions into the Aramaic translation attributed to Jonathan ben 'Uzziel (Pseudo-Jonathan). The language of Neofiti I shows clear affinities with the Palestinian Aramaic dialect. Internal evidence induced Díez Macho to date the formation of the Palestinian Targum in the second century A.D. It was based upon a Hebrew text tradition which deviated in some cases from the MT. Neofiti I is an early medieval manuscript containing a comparatively short text in which many of the late adumbrations that occur in Ps.-Jonathan are not yet found. Reproduced by permission of the Vatican Library.

19 This fragment comes from a scroll which contained the Greek translation of the Minor Prophets. The translation is much closer to the Hebrew MT than is the Septuagint or even the 'Three', or rather reflects a *Vorlage* which was practically identical with the Proto-MT. The editor of the fragment, D. Barthélemy, O.P., affiliates it with the καί γε group. Like this group, the Murabba'ât translation is characterised by the rendering of Hebrew *gam* by Greek καί γε. It appears to present a comparatively early Jewish translation of the Bible into Greek, a translation which preceded the destruction of the Second Temple in A.D. 70 and is even possibly of pre-Christian origin. Reproduced by courtesy of the Shrine of the Book, Israel, D. Samuel and Jeane H. Gottesman, Center for Biblical Manuscripts.

20 A page from a Hexapla MS which was discovered in a tenth-century palimpsest by Cardinal I. C. Mercati in Milan (Cod. Ambr. O. 39), and published by him (*Psalterii Hexapli Reliquiae*, Rome, 1958, fr. XIII, 2). The Milan MS also contains the other Greek columns of the Hexapla with a further collection of variant readings, but not the Hebrew column. Reproduced by permission of the Vatican Library.

21 This manuscript (British Museum Add. 14425) was part of a large collection brought to the Museum from a monastery in the Nitrian Desert of Lower Egypt

just before the middle of the nineteenth century. The manuscript contains Gen., Exod., Num. and Deut. (the plate shows Gen. 22:7–17), written in the old *Estrangelo* script (cf. p. 26). The first two books were written in A.D. 464 (the manuscript being dated to year 775 of the Seleucid era); this is the oldest known biblical manuscript which is exactly dated. The other two books are by a different scribe, probably of the same period. Reproduced by permission of the Trustees of the British Museum.

22 Uppsala MS Gr. 4 (899 in Aland's list of NT manuscripts); f. 49ᵛ showing Matt. 18:22, with a marginal scholion giving a reading from *To Ioudaikon* (see p. 325 of the text), also found in MS 566 (Leningrad, Public Library MS Gr. 54). It reads ' *To Ioudaikon* reads directly after "seventy times seven", "for even in the prophets, after they had been anointed with the holy spirit there was found word of sin" [or "sinful act"].' Reproduced by permission of the University Library, Uppsala, Sweden.

23 British Museum MS Harley 5647 (72 in Aland's list); f. 79ʳ showing the scholion on Matt. 27:49, discussed in the text on p. 325. Reproduced by permission of the Trustees of the British Museum.

24 Codex Bezae Cantabrigiensis (Cambridge University Library, No. 2.41) showing Luke 9:60—10:9 (f. 226b) in which occurs the reading of verse 62 discussed on p. 340. Reproduced by permission of the Syndics of the University Library, Cambridge.

25 Codex Sinaiticus (British Museum MS Add. 43725) showing f. 207ᵛ in which occurs the curious reading Ἀντιπατρίδα (Matt. 13:54) discussed on p. 359 in connection with the place of origin of this manuscript. Reproduced by permission of the Trustees of the British Museum.

PLATES

1   Palaeo-Hebrew: fragment of the Proto-Massoretic text of
Leviticus, from Qumrân, Cave I

2 Square Hebrew: a section of Leviticus from Codex
Orientalis 4445 (British Museum)

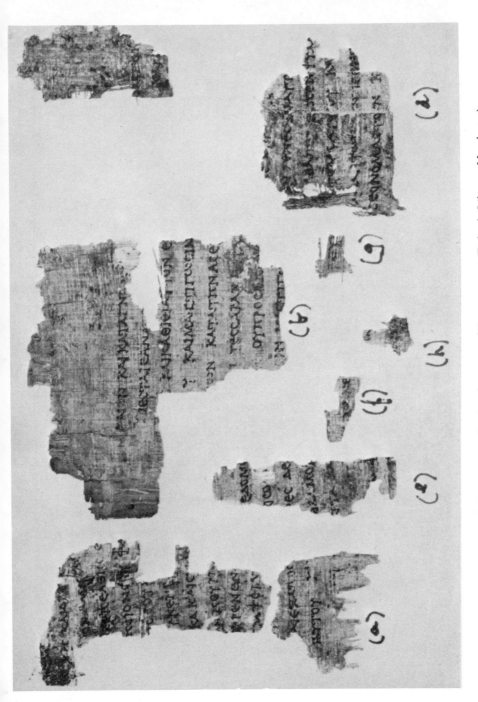

3 Greek: Rylands Papyrus 458, showing fragments of Deuteronomy (Rylands Library, Manchester)

4 Latin: Codex Amiatinus, showing Matt. 1:1–23
(Laurentian Library, Florence)

5   Syriac: a page from Add. MS 1700 (University Library, Cambridge)

6　Coptic: a page from MS Or 1699 (University Library, Cambridge)

7   Assyrian scribes at work, from a relief of Sennacherib in the British Museum

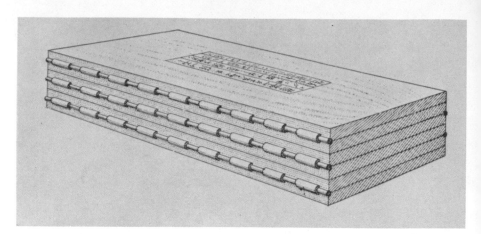

8 Assyrian ivory writing-boards of the eighth century B.C. (reconstruction)

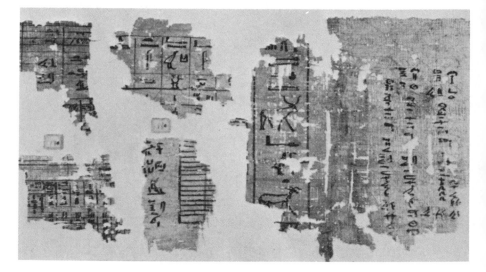

9 Fragments of Old Kingdom Temple accounts in hieratic,
5th dynasty, *c.* 2400 B.C. (British Museum)

10 Literary exercise in hieratic, 19th dynasty, *c.* 1250 B.C.
(British Museum)

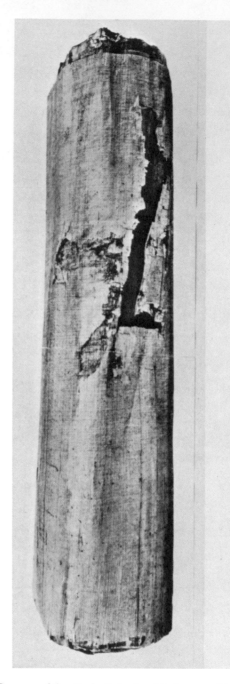

11 Papyrus of the *Book of the Dead*, before unrolling,
29th dynasty, *c.* 1000 B.C. (British Museum)

12   Review of Court proceedings, in demotic from
Asyut, 170 B.C. (British Museum)

13   A Palaeo-Hebrew fragment of Exodus, from Qumrân, Cave I

14 A Samaritan Pentateuch manuscript showing part of Deuteronomy

15   The Nash Papyrus (University Library, Cambridge)

16 Column XXXII of the First or Complete Isaiah Scroll from Qumrân,
Cave I (1 QIsᵃ), showing Isa. 38:8—40:2

17 The Habakkuk Commentary, columns IV–V, from Qumrân,
Cave I, showing Hab. 1:10–15

אלהי יעבד בדתחיל וה הספר עד אותרוהשלימי :
הוא ספר הקדיש נקרא תרגמ חומש ירושלמי :

בראשית · מלקדמין בחכמה ברא דיי שכלל
ית שמיא וית ארעא : והארץ : וארעא הות
תהיא ובהיא וצדי מן בר נש ומן בעיר וריקנא
מן כל פלחן צמחין ומן אילנין וחשוכא פריס על
אפי תהומא ורוח דרחמין מן קדם יי הוה מנשב
מנשבא על אפי מיא : ויאמר אלהים : ואמר ממ
דיי יהוי נהור והות נהור כגזירת ממריה : וירא
אלהים : וגלי קדם יי ית נהורא ארום טב הוא
ואפשר ממרא דיי בין נהורא לבין חשוכא :
ויקרא אלהים : וקרא ממרא דיי לטהורא איממ
ולחשוכא קרא לליא והוא רמש והוה צפר סדר
עבד בראשית יומ קדמאיי : ויאמר אלהים יהי
ואמד ממרא דיי יהוי רקיעא במיציעות מיא ויהוי
מפרש בין מיא ארעא לבין מיא עיליא : ויעש
אלהים : וברא יי ית רקיעא ואפשר בין מיא די
מן תחות רקיעא ובין מיא די מלעיל לרקיעא וה
והוה כן כמימריה : ויקרא אלהים : וקרא ממרא
דיי לרקישא שמיא והוה רמש והוה צפר סדר

1

Collegij Neophytorum Rom.

18 The first page of MS Neofiti I from the Vatican Library,
a Palestinian Targum manuscript, showing Gen. 1:1–8

19 Fragment of a Parchment Scroll from Wadi Murabba'ât in the Judaean Desert, showing the Greek translation of Zech. 8:19—9:4

20   A Hexapla fragment, palimpsest, showing Ps. 88:26–34 (Vatican Library)

21 Part of a Peshiṭta manuscript, showing Gen. 22:7–17 (British Museum)

22 Uppsala MS Gr. 4, showing a marginal scholion to Matt. 18:23
(University Library, Uppsala)

23   MS Harley 5647, showing a marginal scholion to Matt. 27:49 (British Museum)

ΟΔΕΕΙΠΕΝΑΥΤΩΑΦΕϹΤΟΥϹΝΕΚΡΟΥϹ
ΘΑΨΑΙΤΟΥϹΕΑΥΤΩΝΝΕΚΡΟΥϹ ϹΥΔΕ
ΠΟΡΕΥΘΕΙϹΔΙΑΓΓΕΛΛΕΤΗΝΒΑϹΙΛΕΙΑΝΤΟΥΘΥ
ϛ : ΕΙΠΕΝΔΕ ΚΑΙΕΤΕΡΟϹ ΑΚΟΛΟΥΘΗϹΩϹΟΙΚΕ
ΕΠΙΤΡΕΨΟΝΔΕΜΟΙΠΡΩΤΟΝ ΑΠΟΤΑΞΑϹΘΑΙ
ΤΟΙϹΕΙϹΟΙΚΟΝΜΟΥ ΟΔΕ ΙΗϹΕΙΠΕΝΑΥΤΩ
ΟΥΔΕΙϹ ΕΙϹΤΑΘΩΠΙϹΩΒΛΕΠΩΝΚΑΙΕΠΙΒΑΛΛΩΝ
ΤΗΝΧΕΙΡΑΥΤΟΥ ΕΠΑΡΟΤΡΟΝΕΥΘΕΤΟϹΕϹΤΙΝ
ϛζ : ΕΙϹΤΗΝΒΑϹΙΛΕΙΑΝΤΟΥΘΥ ΑΠΕΔΕΙΞΕΝΔΕ
ΚΑΙΕΤΕΡΟΥϹ ΟΒ ΚΑΙΑΠΕϹΤΙΛΕΝΑΥΤΟΥϹΑΝΑΔΥΟ
ΠΡΟΠΡΟϹΩΠΟΥΑΥΤΟΥ ΕΙϹΠΑΝΤΑΤΟΠΟΝΚΑΙΠΟΛΙΝ
ϛη : ΟΥΕΜΕΛΛΕΝΕΡΧΕϹΘΑΙ ΕΛΕΓΕΝΔΕΠΡΟϹΑΥΤΟΥϹ
ΟΘΕΡΙϹΜΟϹΠΟΛΥϹΟΙΔΕΕΡΓΑΤΑΙΟΛΙΓΟΙ
ΔΕΗΘΗΤΕΟΥΝΤΟΥΘΥΤΟΥΘΕΡΙϹΜΟΥΟΠΩϹ
ΕΡΓΑΤΑϹΕΚΒΑΛΗΕΙϹΤΟΝΘΕΡΙϹΜΟΝΑΥΤΟΥ
ϛθ : ΥΠΑΓΕΤΑΙ ΙΔΟΥΕΓΩΑΠΟϹΤΕΛΛΩΥΜΑϹΩϹ
ΑΡΝΑϹΜΕϹΟΝΛΥΚΩΝ ΜΗΒΑϹΤΑΖΕΤΕ
ο : ΒΑΛΛΑΝΤΙΟΝ ΜΗΠΗΡΑΝ ΜΗΥΠΟΔΗΜΑΤΑ
ΚΑΙΜΗΔΕΝΑΚΑΤΑΤΗΝΟΔΟΝΑϹΠΑϹΗϹΘΕ
οα : ΕΙϹΗΝΔΑΝ ΕΙϹΕΛΘΗΤΕΠΡΩΤΟΝΟΙΚΙΑΝ
ΛΕΓΕΤΕΕΙΡΗΝΗΤΩΟΙΚΩΤΟΥΤΩ
ΚΑΝΗΕΚΕΙΥΙΟϹΕΙΡΗΝΗϹΕΠΑΝΑΠΑΥϹΕΤΕ
ΕΠΑΥΤΟΝΗΕΙΡΗΝΥΜΩΝ ΕΙΔΕΜΗΓΕ
ΕΦΥΜΑϹΕΠΙϹΤΡΕΨΕΙΗΕΙΡΗΝΗΥΜΩΝ
οβ : ΕΝΑΥΤΗΔΕΤΗΟΙΚΕΙΑΜΕΝΕΤΕΕϹΘΟΝΤΕϹ
ΚΑΙΠΕΙΝΟΝΤΕϹΤΑΠΑΡΑΥΤΩΝ
ΑΞΙΟϹΓΑΡΟΕΡΓΑΤΗϹΤΟΥΜΙϹΘΟΥΑΥΤΟΥ
ΜΗΜΕΤΑΒΑΙΝΕΤΕ ΑΠΟΟΙΚΙΑϹΕΙϹ
ογ : ΟΙΚΙΑΝ ΚΑΙΕΙϹΗΝΑΝΠΟΛΙΝ
ΕΙϹΕΡΧΗϹΘΕ ΚΑΙΔΕΧΩΝΤΑΙΥΜΑϹ
ΕϹΘΙΕΤΕΤΑΠΑΡΑΤΙΘΕΜΕΝΑΥΜΕΙΝ
ΚΑΙΘΕΡΑΠΕΥΕΤΕΤΟΥϹΕΝΑΥΤΗ
ΑϹΘΕΝΟΥΝΤΑϹ ΚΑΙΛΕΓΕΤΕΑΥΤΟΙϹ

24   Codex Bezae Cantabrigiensis, showing Luke 9:60—10:9
(University Library, Cambridge)

25 Codex Sinaiticus, showing part of the Gospel of Matthew
with Eusebian sections (British Museum)

INDEXES

GENERAL INDEX

accommodation, concept of in early Christian exegesis 451–2, 464
Ahikar, story of 6
Akkadian 3, 4, 5, 33, 34, 36, 37
  cuneiform inscriptions 5
  literature 46–7
Aksum inscriptions 3
Alalakh 37, 42–4
Alexandria 59, 145–6, 149, 167, 295, 312, 314, 322, 360, 380 n., 435
  Alexandrian canon 141, 142–3, 145–6, 149, 304
  catechetical school 65, 350, 358, 454; see also Origen
  church of Alexandria 301–4, 327–8, 465–6, 509
  hermeneutical method 148, 327, 422, 492
  Alexandrian Judaism 48, 139, 141, 143, 145–6, 148–9, 383, 414, 467
  textual tradition 312, 322, 341, 350–6, 358, 361, 371, 374
  see also Clement of Alexandria, exegesis of New Testament, Origen
allegorical interpretation 47, 360, 379–80, 443, 447, 466–7, 476–8, 507–9, 538, 558, 560; see also Homer, Stoicism
  in ancient world 47
  of Old Testament 134, 215, 381–2, 386, 388, 395, 409–10, 412, 414, 429, 543
  in New Testament 391–2, 466, 507–8
  of Bible in early Church 296, 408, 415–18, 422–5, 427–30, 432, 434–7, 449–50, 469, 480–2, 488, 511, 552, 554–5; see also Ambrose, Augustine, Origen, Philo
Alogi, the 301, 303, 308
alphabet 12, 13, 23, 38, 366–8
  Aramaic 16, 26, 35
  Coptic 28
  Early Hebrew 12–15, 16

Ethiopic 28
  Greek 18–20, 160
  Latin 20–24, 160
  Phoenician 13
  Samaritan 12
  Square Hebrew 15, 16–17, 137–9, 534
  Syriac 24–7
  see also scripts, writing
amanuensis, hypothesis of in non-Pauline epistles 241, 254–5, 259
Ambrose 546, 569, 572–4
  as exegete 445, 555
  use of allegory 543, 551
Ambrosiaster, the 342
Amorite 4, 37
  Old-Amorite 3
Andreas of Caesarea 357, 368
Andreas of Crete 361
anonymity
  in ancient world 39
  in Old Testament 98, 110, 112
  in New Testament 63, 233, 561
anthropomorphism in Old Testament, in early Christian exegesis 423, 430, 452, 463
Antiochene scholarship 24, 305–6, 358, 360–1, 363, 368, 422, 489–91, 494, 505
  exegesis 437, 442, 490, 492, 498; see also Theodore of Mopsuestia
apocalyptic in New Testament 243, 284
apocalyptic literature 155, 157–8, 234, 299, 388, 402
  Jewish 10, 105, 115, 132–3, 201, 272, 281, 288, 291, 293; Assumption of Moses 257, 288; 1 Enoch 6, 10–11, 154–5, 288, 293, 413, 534; 2 Baruch 293, 413
  Judaeo-Christian 413, 430; Testaments of the Twelve Patriarchs 10–11, 264
  Christian 236, 277, 280–1, 288, 290

Apocrypha, the 28, 145, 148, 154, 156–7, 177, 192, 199, 455, 460
Christian use of 156, 534, 544, 578
apocryphal literature 533–5, 586
Jewish 27, 72, 104, 137, 148, 150, 155–7, 299, 455; *Apocalypse of Elijah* 535; Jubilees 28, 154–5
at Qumrân 152–3
Christian 295, 300, 302, 305, 337, 345, 366; *Acts of Andrew* 305; *Acts of John* 305; *Acts of Paul* 303, 305; *Preaching of Peter* 302; *Revelation of Peter* 301–2, 305; Third Epistle to the Corinthians 366
gospels 291, 296–9, 303, 305, 346, 419, 426
Apollinaris of Laodicea 513, 537
Apollinarianism 491
apologetic: Jewish 103, 227–8, 532
in Christian Church 133, 294, 458–9
apologia: in Acts 274, 277
in Pauline epistles 242–3, 246
apologists, the 236, 295–6, 344, 416, 429, 430, 454
apostles, the
apostolic authorship 235, 261, 266–84, 301, 303, 306–7, 426, 434
apostolic faith 257, 285
apostolic tradition 250, 253, 256, 274–5, 297, 301, 461, 465–6, 544
Apostolic Constitutions 568, 570–1, 577–80, 584
Apostolic Tradition 429, 568, 574, 579–81, 583–4
Aqiba, Rabbi 134, 174, 176, 206, 226
Arabic 2, 3, 26–7, 28, 331, 517
alphabet 26
version of *Diatessaron* 334, 340
Aramaic 2–8, 10, 12, 24–5, 36, 38, 154, 333–5, 343, 517–18, 564
alphabet 16, 26, 35
Apocryphon 6
language: biblical Aramaic 6, 161; East 6, 7, 333, *see* Syriac; Imperial 5–6; Jewish 6, 7, 169, 201; Old Aramaic 1, 5, 6; West 6, 333–4, 346
text of Old Testament 149–50, 158, 160, 166–7, 169, 176–7, 185, 188; of New Testament 266

Aramaisms in New Testament 10
Arian controversy as stimulus to exegesis 416, 440–8, 452–3, 489–91, 528
Aristides, apologist 429
Aristobulus, early allegoriser of Old Testament 430
Armenian 315, 331, 355–6, 366–8
manuscripts of New Testament 326
version of New Testament 351, 357, 363, 368
Arnobius, apologist 429–30, 437–8
Assyrian 3
law 42–3
literature 47, 80–2, 106
Athanasius 439, 452–3, 568–9
on Canon 360, 533
as exegete 422–3, 425, 443–5, 447–8
writings: *De Incarnatione* 416, 435, 439; *Letters to Serapion* 445; *Orations against the Arians* 443
Athenagoras, apologist 416, 436, 441
Atonement, development of doctrine of 438–40, 450
Atticisms in New Testament manuscripts 322, 343, 360
Augustine 371–2, 519, 521, 541–63, 568–74, 579–80
childhood and education 542–3, 550–1, 575
attitude to Church 553, 557, 561–2
as biblical scholar 267, 270, 541–3, 549–50, 556; commentaries 543–4, 552, 576; sermons 543–4
on Canon 534, 544
as exegete 542, 545–7, 549–52, 554–62
influence of Neo-Platonism 543, 551–2
authority
of ancient texts 39
of Old Testament 55, 92, 117, 133, 291–3, 304, 377, 380, 403, 408, 411, 416, 454, 553
of New Testament 59–60, 285–6, 307–8, 416, 553
of Bible 113, 232–3, 544, 555–7

Babylonian 3, 38
law 42–4
literature 46–8, 68, 71, 102, 106
Bar-Kochba, revolt of 15, 183, 226, 435

Barnabas, Epistle of 61
exegesis of Old Testament in 408, 414, 427, 436, 466
relation to New Testament Canon 288, 292–3, 302, 305, 460
Basil of Caesarea 426, 568–71, 581
as exegete 443, 445
as witness to text of New Testament 361
Basilides 301, 459
as witness to Canon of New Testament 293, 297, 308, 426
ben Sira, as witness to Canon of Old Testament 2, 110, 128–30, 147, 200
Bible
Greek 9, 11, 111, 138–40, 157, 168–9, 171, 198
Hebrew 135–6, 138–43, 169, 172, 182, 199, 228, 532
Latin 138, 157, 515, 518
bilingual manuscripts of New Testament 314, 335, 350, 353–4, 356, 359, 372; *see also* Codex Bezae
books
in ancient world 33, 48, 51–8
in Judaism 74, 156, 162
in early Church 63, 65–6, 233–5, 286, 289, 291, 296–7, 312, 391, 438; first Christian books 53–4, 55–7, 65, 233; *see also* proof-texts, *testimonia*
materials of 21, 30–5, 56–8; clay tablet 12, 32–4, 35, 37; codex 56–9, 62, 64, 131 n., 141, 175, 185; leather 12, 32, 51, 151; ostraca 14–15, 34; papyrus 12, 21, 30–2, 48, 51, 54, 59, 62, 151, 238, 312–13, 316; parchment 21, 53, 54, 57–9, 298; roll 48, 51–2, 53, 56–9, 131 n., 151, 274; stylus 21, 31, 32–3, 34; waxed tablet 21, 48, 53, 54, 58; writing-boards 34–5, 602, plate 8
sacred books: in ancient world 49, 377, 379, 466; in Judaism 50, 52, 186, 380; in early Church 233–4, 456, 541; *see* scriptures
boustrophedon writing 18–19
Byzantine scholarship 316, 318, 322, 325
text tradition of New Testament 319–24, 342–3, 355–7, 360–1, 363, 369, 374

Caesarea
scholarship 352, 358–9
textual tradition of New Testament 315–16, 333, 351, 353, 355–6, 358, 360–4, 367
Canaan 1, 2
Hebrew spoken in 1, 4
Canaanite 3, 4, 5, 13, 37, 68; elements in Old Testament 68
Canon 113, 199, 209, 234, 360, 544, 586
early canonical texts 40
of Old Testament 72–3, 79, 92, 113–59, 165–6, 173, 182, 299–300, 304, 421, 455, 459, 494–6, 532–4, 544; tri-partite Canon of Old Testament 114, 117, 130, 133, 135–9, 147–9, 157–9, 533–4, 565
of New Testament 57–9, 234–6, 239, 252, 254, 261, 265–6, 273, 277, 280, 282–308, 344, 365, 367, 375, 454, 459–60, 494, 544, 563; beginnings of Christian Canon 61, 66; four-fold Canon of the gospel 55, 58, 266, 273, 296, 298, 302, 306, 308, 344–5, 364, 459; Johannine literature 277; Paul-ine epistles 239–42, 253, 261, 283, 288, 333, 335, 566
Cappadocian Fathers 361, 423, 447; *see also* Basil of Caesarea, Gregory of Nazianzus, Gregory of Nyssa
Carpocrates 417–18
Carpocratian Gnostics 302
see also Gnosticism
Cassiodorus, work on Vulgate 372, 521–2
catechesis in New Testament 250, 264
catenae in New Testament manuscripts 325–6
Celsus 65, 462–3, 472; *see also* Origen
Christianity
Gentile 289
hellenistic 251, 292, 293
Jewish 285, 289, 292, 298
Palestinian 251
Christology 391–2, 403, 413, 415–16, 421–2, 426, 428, 436, 441–3, 470, 505
of Hebrews 263
Johannine 280, 339, 401
of Paul 251, 439
traditional 256

Chronicler, the 76, 88, 89–90, 92, 101, 112, 124, 129, 130, 218
Church, the
 its connection with the New Testament text 311–12, 336–7, 339, 345, 376, 453
 as guarantor of authority of New Testament, 553, 557, 561–2, 585
Church Orders, the 256, 568, 570, 574, 583–4
 Apostolic Church Order 575
Cicero 237, 511–12, 522–4, 542, 550, 551
citation formulae in New Testament 391
Clement of Alexandria 236, 439, 466, 568–9
 as exegete 417–18, 425, 429, 433, 436–7
 as witness to Canon of New Testament 295, 297–8, 302–3
 as witness to text of New Testament 327, 336, 338, 349–50, 356
Clement of Rome 54, 303, 428
 relation to Canon of New Testament 288, 291–2, 296
 as witness to text of New Testament 332
 1 Clement 234, 240, 271, 288, 295, 302, 335, 414, 460, 567, 578–9
 2 Clement 292, 298, 414
codex, Christian preference for 56–60, 62–4, 274
Codices
 Alexandrinus 142, 319, 322, 349, 352, 357
 Amiatinus 522, 601, plate 4
 Argenteus 369
 Augiensis 356, 372
 Bezae 324, 333, 335, 341, 344, 348–50, 353–7, 361, 365–6, 375, 605, plate 24
 Bobbiensis 330, 339, 346, 354, 371
 Boernerianus 356, 372
 Brixianus 369
 Claramontanus 356, 372
 Ephraemi 349–50, 357
 Freer 320, 351, 354–5, 361, 364
 Gigas 355, 373
 Palatinus 354, 361, 369, 371
 Sinaiticus 142, 341, 350–2, 357, 359–60, 363, 529, 605, plate 25
 Vaticanus 142, 310, 328, 336, 341, 350–2, 355–6, 359–60, 363, 529

Washingtonianus 529
codicology, in study of New Testament text 312, 315–16, 321, 323, 325
columns
 on cuneiform tablets 32–3
 on papyri 31, 51, 78, 151
 double in codices 354
 three or four in codices 360
commentaries on Bible 199, 389, 419, 566
 on law 145, 209, 211
 at Qumrân 65, 150, 155, 216, 226, 392, 396
 in early Church 373, 419, 437, 491–2, 535–6, 543
 medieval Jewish 192
community
 Christian books produced by 63–5, 236, 282, 286
 Bible interpreted in and for 453, 561–2
Coptic 27–9, 326, 329, 330, 346, 601, plate 6
 Bohairic 27–8, 347
 Sahidic 27–8, 336, 347, 356
 version of New Testament 338, 347, 355, 358, 360, 369
council of Jerusalem 247, 397
covenant, in Old Testament, as involving law 42–3, 93, 96, 109, 120
Covenanters, *see* Qumrân
Creation narratives 1, 40, 42, 70–1, 74, 108, 401, 552, 583
credal statements
 in New Testament 567; in non-Pauline epistles 260; in Paul 251
 in early Church 440
crises, as stimulus to literary activity 105–6, 108, 112–13
cuneiform 1, 12, 32, 34, 35, 36, 37; *see also* scripts
Cyprian of Carthage 345–6, 405 n., 416, 425, 432–3, 545, 577, 581
 as exegete 428–9
 Testimonia 416, 428
 as witness to text of New Testament 371–3
Cyril of Alexandria 492, 495
 as exegete 445
 as witness to text of New Testament 365

Cyril of Jerusalem 568
  as witness to text of New Testament 358

Damasus, Pope 512–14, 518, 523, 527
Davidic authorship of psalms 106
  at Qumrân 153
  in Theodore's exegesis 498–501
Dead Sea Scrolls 4, 14, 15, 16, 77 n., 182,
  219, 565; *see* Qumrân, Square He-
  brew
  '*Book of Study*' ('*Meditation*') 154
  Damascus Document 150, 154, 386–7
  First Isaiah Scroll 183, 188, 191, 224 n.,
    603, plate 16
  Genesis Apocryphon 207–8, 220, 413
  Habakkuk Commentary 225–6, 388,
    604, plate 17
  Manual of Discipline 154, 190
  Psalms Scroll 152–3
  Second Isaiah Scroll 193
  Testimony Scroll 58
  Thanksgiving Hymns (*Hôdāyôt*) 151,
    154, 190, 388
  War Scroll 154, 190
  Zadokite Documents 190
Decalogue 34, 42, 118–19, 144, 217, 424,
  473, 560
  Yahwistic Decalogue 120
Deutero-Isaiah 99, 110
Deuteronomy
  Deuteronomic Code 95, 121, 122, 209–
    10
  Deuteronomistic historian 121
  Deuteronomic material 75, 199, 212–13,
    466
  Deuteronomic writers 108, 112
diatribe, in New Testament epistles 238,
  248, 264
Didache 292, 302, 430, 567, 580–1
  exegesis in 414
  relation to Canon of New Testament
    288–90, 305
Didascalia 424–5, 428–9
Didymus the Blind 514, 517
  exegesis of 443, 445
Diodore of Tarsus
  as exegete 490, 492
  as witness to text of New Testament
    325, 361

Dionysius of Alexandria 304
  as exegete 433–4
divorce, law of
  in Old Testament 205–7, 209
  in New Testament 206, 396–7
doceticism 286, 439
Docetists 298
doctrine, Christian
  as related to development of Canon 285,
    299, 456, 460
  as related to development of New Tes-
    tament exegesis 416, 421, 437, 440,
    449–50, 453, 561
  as related to development of New Tes-
    tament text 311–12, 314, 317, 328–9,
    337, 339, 343–4, 375
duplicate texts in Old Testament 76–7, 86–
  90, 97, 100, 103–4, 106, 164, 214
Dura Europos 57, 217, 230
  roll-fragment 16

eclectic method of establishing New
  Testament text 317, 321, 376
editorial work
  in ancient world 38–40, 41, 45
  in Old Testament 76–7, 108, 160–1, 169
  in New Testament 11, 249, 274, 276,
    312, 359
Egypt
  origin of early Christian papyri 7, 55–8,
    62, 64, 315–16
  use of papyrus 30–1
Egyptian 36
  literature 46–8, 102
  words in Old Testament 2, 203–4
Elephantine papyri 6, 123
Eliezer ben Yose the Galilaean, Rabbi 221,
  384
Elohistic narrative (E) 73, 75, 91, 107–8,
  181
Ephraem the monk 324, 351
Ephraem the Syrian 331, 338, 341, 355,
  364–5, 577
Epiphanius of Salamis 457, 513, 523
  as exegete 443, 445
  as witness to Canon 138, 337
  as witness to text of New Testament 359
epistles, the 53, 235–6, 269, 294, 352, 362–
  3, 459

epistles (*cont.*)
    Catholic epistles 271, 286, 306–7, 324,
        342, 349, 356, 366, 371–4, 494,
        544
    Pastoral epistles 241, 254–7, 288, 294–5,
        296 n., 301, 307
    Pauline epistles 236–52, 267, 425, 460,
        492, 506–7, 529, 543–4, 565, 572; in
        Canon 257–9, 273, 285, 296–7, 300–1,
        307–8, 333; Marcion's use of 294,
        306, 335, 337; text of 62, 287–8, 316,
        320, 324, 335, 342, 349–50, 352, 356,
        359, 371–4, 462; witness to, in early
        Fathers 66, 254, 292–5, 305, 342–3,
        361, 365–6
Epistle to Rheginus 261
Epistula Apostolorum 418
eschatology 225, 289, 291, 387, 434–5
    in Old Testament 100
    in New Testament 242–3, 245, 249, 251,
        258, 263, 265, 272, 274–5, 278, 280
    in the early Church 419, 430–3, 437–8,
        470
Essenes 202, 221, 382–3, 386
Ethiopic (Ge'ez) 2, 3, 28, 157, 326, 340
    version of New Testament 369
    writing 28–9
Eucharist 241, 251, 287, 414, 566–7, 568–
    80, 582–4
Eusebius of Caesarea 54, 55, 58, 61 n., 65,
    443, 445, 452, 513, 514, 517, 522, 527,
    574–5
    Ecclesiastical History 304, 331, 432–3
    as exegete 422, 425, 429–30, 433–4, 437–
        41, 446, 450
    as witness to Canon of New Testament
        137, 288, 291, 304–5
    as witness to text of New Testament
        349, 357–60, 365–7
Eusebius of Nicomedia 368
Eusebius of Vercelli 363
Eustathius of Antioch, Antiochene exegete
    443
Euthalius 362
    Euthalian material 362–3
Evagrius of Antioch 363
Evagrius of Pontus 362–3, 523
evangelists, the 266, 268, 288, 307, 315 n.,
    451, 471, 494, 557, 580

exegesis 105, 378, 406, 411, 469, 476, 479,
    485, 488
    of Old Testament 68, 99, 189, 199–231,
        262–3, 380, 389–96, 400–3, 414,
        416, 504; Jewish exegesis 65, 199–
        231, 386, 391, 412, 414, 438, 475, 498,
        'applied' 202, 221–8, 'pure' 202–20,
        225; rabbinic exegesis 176, 208, 232,
        383–6, 392, 395–6, 412, 435, 477
    of New Testament 284, 293–4, 296–7,
        327, 347, 351, 362, 416, 503; early
        Christian exegesis 292, 324–5, 412–
        53, 467, 543; Gnostic exegesis 416–
        18, 434

Fleury palimpsest 355, 371, 373
form-critical analysis
    of Old Testament 67–8, 81–3, 91
    of New Testament 268–9, 276

Gamaliel II 217
genealogical method in study of New
    Testament text 309–10, 317, 376
genizah 56, 156
    at Cairo 16, 175
Gentiles, admission of, to Church 397–8,
    402, 423
Georgian 315, 367
    manuscripts of New Testament 326, 341
    version of New Testament 351, 363,
        367–8
Gezer calendar 4, 13
Gilgamesh 85
Gilgamesh epic 33, 40, 41, 42, 71
glosses of texts
    of Old Testament 76–9, 99, 194, 212, 525
    of New Testament 272, 313, 324–5, 344–
        5, 370
gnosis in New Testament 263, 279
Gnosticism 285–6, 298–300, 302, 418
    in early Church 244–5, 253, 256–7, 263,
        279, 302
    exegesis 329, 342, 345, 347, 416–19, 424,
        426–7, 434
    gospels: *of Philip* 417; *of Thomas* 55,
        285, 297, 299, 303, 305, 329, 333,
        336, 346–7, 459; *of Truth* 426, 459
    as witness to Canon of New Testament
        293–7, 301–2, 306, 308, 335

gospel, the 367, 402, 405, 450, 474, 483, 485, 487–9, 572
  as a new literary form 236, 279, 288
  as preached by early Christians 53–4, 61, 232, 290, 292, 294, 419, 440, 538, 580
  preached by Paul 233, 238–9, 244, 247, 249–50, 287, 407, 507
  written gospel 233, 265, 267, 272, 471
gospels, the 53, 235–6, 450–1, 453, 494, 570
  acceptance and circulation of 55, 296–7
  as division of New Testament Canon 265–9, 273, 459, 471, 518–20, 523
  separated gospels 345–6, 364–5, 367, 567; *see also* Tatian
  text of 287, 301, 323, 326, 329–33, 335, 337, 344–52, 354–5, 358, 360–2, 366, 371, 374, 400, 527–30, 545
gospels, apocryphal 299, 303, 305
  According to the Egyptians 285, 297–9, 303
  According to the Hebrews 285, 291, 297–9, 303, 305, 347, 459, 517, 535
  of Peter 296–8, 305
Gothic 330, 368
  version of New Testament 363, 369
  writing 24
Greek
  language 9, 154–5, 157, 259, 275, 289, 312, 336, 376, 511, 517–18, 549, 557; alphabet 18–20, 61; biblical Greek 7–9, 11, 550; hellenistic Greek 11, 322; Jewish Greek 7–11, 264; Koine Greek 7, 10–11, 254, 322, 357; New Testament Greek 7–11, 271, 310, 370, 461; semitisms 7–10, 264; words in Old Testament 2
  culture and literature: apocalypses 10–11; influence on transmission of Old Testament 166
  texts: of Old Testament 60–1, 148, 151, 167–70, 381, 420, 457, 513, 527–30, 532; of New Testament 266, 310, 313, 318, 324, 326, 329–30, 337–8, 345, 353–8, 364, 368, 372–4, 443, 546, 601, plate 3
Gregory the Great, Pope 521, 561
Gregory of Nazianzus 443, 445, 513, 569.
Gregory of Nyssa 443, 445
Gregory Theodorus 425–6

Habiru 1–2
haggadah 203, 207–8, 218, 220, 226, 230–1, 256–7, 384–5, 397
Hagiographa (Writings) as division of Old Testament Canon 115, 130, 131, 133, 135–43, 149–51, 155, 395, 414
halakhah 214, 221, 223, 229–30, 256, 384, 386, 397–9, 407
halakhic midrash 205
Hananiah ben Hezekiah, Rabbi 134, 156
hands, defiling, as indication of canonicity 114, 134, 156
haphtarah 201, 564
harmonisation
  of legal traditions of Old Testament 209, 212; *see also* exegesis of Old Testament
  of gospels 76, 326, 331–2, 337, 344–6, 348, 354, 367, 463, 471; *see also* Tatian
Hebrew 7, 12, 68, 78, 146–7, 150, 154, 156, 204–5, 291, 343, 383, 496, 512, 517–18, 549–50, 564
  biblical 18
  Early (Palaeo-) Hebrew 12–15, 601, plates 1, 13; alphabet 12–15, 16, 17 fig. A, 26; documents and inscriptions 12, 13
  influence on New Testament 11
  language of the Canaanites 1, 4, 68; of the Old Testament 1–2, 4, 11, 17
  Mishnaic 4
  modern 2, 4, 12, 16–17, 26
  original language of mankind? 1
  proto-Hebrew 4–5
  rabbinical 2, 4
  Square Hebrew script 12, 15, 16–17, 603, plate 2
  text of Old Testament 9, 50, 158–61, 166–73, 175–7, 180, 183–5, 189–90, 192, 202–4, 360, 373, 381, 420, 438, 445, 456–61, 475–7, 515, 521–6, 530–2, 545
  vocalisation 5, 17, 160, 175, 189, 389
Hebrews 261–4, 284, 402, 500
  authorship 241, 261, 264, 302, 460, 466, 561
  exegesis in 408–10, 413, 466
  position in Canon 240, 261, 292, 294–5, 300, 303, 305–7, 544, 561–2

Hebrews (*cont.*)
hellenism
  influence on Judaism 48, 166, 168, 182;
    on Church 66, 239, 263, 344
  Jewish hellenistic literature 177, 192,
    208, 255
hellenists in New Testament 263
Heracleon, gnostic, allegoriser 296, 418–
  19, 426
hermeneutics 148, 190, 386; *see also*
  allegory, exegesis, typology
Herodotus 87, 304
Hexateuch 273
'hidden' books as extra-canonical 155–7
Hilary of Poitiers 451–2, 511, 523, 533
  as exegete 439, 443–4, 446–8, 537
  De Trinitate 446
Hillel 206, 221–2, 383–4
Hippolytus of Rome, apologist 293, 418–
  19, 428–9, 431–4, 436, 449, 451
  Apostolic Tradition 429, 568
  as witness to New Testament text 342,
    349–50
historical interpretation of Bible 360, 386,
  492, 498, 503–6, 507–9, 511, 538,
  547, 553–4; *see also* Antiochene exegesis, Theodore of Mopsuestia
historiography 41–2, 44–6, 124–5, 277
history 44–5, 80, 109, 118, 124–5, 303, 549,
  551
  as record of God's acts 553–4
  Deuteronomic History 73, 92, 108,
    125
  of the Church 247, 307, 311–12
  of Israel 67, 73, 90–2, 108, 111–12, 165,
    499, 508
  'Succession History of David' 91–2
Holy Spirit, doctrine of 422–3, 445–6
Homer, allegorising of 378–9, 382, 417,
  435, 458
  criticism of 327
hymns
  in ancient world 40, 47
  in Old Testament 81, 99, 114, 568
  in New Testament 251, 253, 391, 399 n.
  in early Church 421, 484, 543

Iconoclastic struggle, literature suffers in
  313, 318, 321

Ignatius of Antioch 295, 332, 342, 567
  as witness to New Testament Canon
    288, 292–3, 305–6
  Pseudo-Ignatius 306
inspiration
  of Bible 459, 461–5, 475, 481, 486–7,
    492–4, 547, 554, 557, 561
  of Old Testament 117, 161, 166, 342,
    421
  of New Testament 53, 307
  of Septuagint 50
interpretation
  of Bible 427, 437–8, 440, 449–50, 452–5,
    461, 467–72, 475–8, 486–90, 535,
    537–8; unity of 480–5, 488–9, 499–
    500, 508–9
  of Old Testament 50, 68, 132, 149, 201–
    2, 206–16, 227–8, 231, 419; Jewish
    380, 412, 435; at Qumrân 154, 190,
    387–8; in early Church 52, 134, 291,
    377–412, 416; of units of Old Testa-
    ment 76–8, 83–4, 87–91, 98, 101–2,
    104–6, 110–11, 118, 127
  of New Testament 282, 314, 330, 342,
    375, 419, 453, 484
inter-testamental period 72, 112, 199, 217,
  223, 230
Irenaeus of Lyons 61, 64, 434, 451–2, 567
  Adversus Haereses 62, 348, 427, 432
  as exegete 418–19, 423–8, 431–2, 436,
    449
  as witness to New Testament Canon
    266–7, 273, 278, 282, 284, 294–6,
    301–3, 426
  as witness to New Testament text 324,
    332, 338, 342, 344, 347–9, 355
Ishmael, Rabbi 216, 221, 384
Israel as people of God 75, 79, 92, 95–6,
  109, 120–1
Itala 372, 545

Jahwistic narrative (J) 71, 73, 75, 91, 107–
  8, 181
James: *Protevangelium* 347
Jamnia, Synod of 133–5, 136, 145, 159,
  174, 177, 179, 300
Jerome 203, 510–41, 555, 561, 568–70,
  576, 580, 584
  acceptance by Church 520

Jerome (*cont.*)
  at Antioch 512–13, 514
  asceticism 511–12, 514, 517
  commentaries 511, 514–16, 527, 535–41
  on Canon 137–8, 157, 532–5
  as classical scholar 511–12, 514, 517
  linguistic knowledge 517
  as text-critic 203, 360, 371, 513, 526–32
  work on Bible translation 169, 373–4, 513–16, 517–26, 545–6
Johanan ben Zakkai 133–4, 384
Johannine literature 277–82, 285
Johannine theology 285, 426, 506
John Cassian 582–3
John Chrysostom 568–9, 572–3, 575–7, 579, 584
  as exegete 490, 492, 494
  as witness to text of New Testament 320, 325, 341, 361, 369
Josephus 2, 9, 131, 223, 228–30, 299, 386, 438, 518
  as interpreter of Old Testament 199, 204, 206–8, 213, 217–20
  as witness to Canon of Old Testament 114–17, 124–5, 136–7, 139, 146–8, 177
Judah ben Ilai, Rabbi 230
Judah the Prince, Rabbi 136, 227
Judaism 122, 157, 228, 247, 264, 275, 280–1, 291, 406, 435, 521, 533
  attitude to scriptures 48–52, 55, 115, 132, 168, 380, 396, 403, 412–14, 449
  hellenistic 11, 383, 414, 467
  orthodox 65, 133, 150, 152, 154–5, 183–4, 222, 226, 228–9
  Palestinian 139–40, 148–9, 159, 383
  Pharisaic 233
  rabbinic 145, 185, 190, 199, 272
  relation to Christianity 66, 234, 239
  Tannaitic 217, 384
Justin Martyr 404–5, 436, 447, 571, 576
  Dialogue with Trypho 414
  as exegete 414–16, 421–3, 428, 431–2, 438, 441–2
  First Apology 567–8, 574–5, 577
  as witness to Canon of New Testament 234, 236, 294, 301, 426
  as witness to text of New Testament 332, 337–8, 342, 344, 570

kerygma in early Church 55, 229, 270, 284
king-lists, as first stage of historiography 41, 44

Lachish letters 4, 14–15, 34
Lactantius 422, 425–6, 431–4, 441
languages
  of Old Testament 1–7; *see also* Aramaic, Greek, Hebrew, Syriac
  of New Testament 7–11, 312; *see also* Greek, Latin, Syriac
Latin 157, 517, 545, 558, 574
  alphabet 20–4
  Fathers of the Church 338, 345; *see also* Tertullian
  words in New Testament 53
  version of Old Testament 160, 169, 176, 185, 460, 515; of New Testament 326–7, 330–1, 336, 344–6, 348, 354, 367, 370–3, 530, 532–3, African Latin 372–3, European Latin 372–3; Old Latin version of Bible 169, 326, 330, 337–41, 345–6, 348–50, 354–6, 361, 369–74, 518, 520–5, 527–9, 545
law 42–6, 48–9, 50, 51, 61, 64, 65–6, 109, 115, 118, 120–1, 122–3, 133, 135–8, 150, 155, 156, 159, 199–200, 232–3
  in ancient world 42–6
  canon law 426
  code of law 94–6, 126, 199, 412, 486
  collections of laws 43, 70, 92 n., 93–6
  legal literature 44, 70, 80, 92–6, 118, 205–6, 386, 481
  ritual law 94
Law, the, in Old Testament
  attitude of New Testament 232–3, 235, 392–3, 397–9, 402–3, 408–9
  book found in Temple 120–1
  codes in Old Testament: Book of the Covenant 95, 120, 209–11; Deuteronomic Code 95, 199, 209–10; Holiness Code 95–6, 101, 122; Priestly Code 122–3, 199, 210
  as division of Old Testament Canon 94, 96, 109, 115, 133, 135–8, 146–50, 155–6, 159, 414, 478, 508, 564–5
  exposition by Ezra 95, 122–4, 144, 201, 565, 585
  oral Law 49, 50, 55, 222, 233

Law (*cont.*)
reverence for 48–51, 64–6, 118, 145, 199–200, 381, 387, 396, 412, 570–2
use of, in early Church 61, 423–5, 466, 468, 473, 482
written Law 49
lectionaries 361
in Church 270–1, 319, 571, 573–4, 582–3
in synagogue 564, 566, 573
lectio continua 571–2, 581
lectionary manuscripts 323
lectors, *see* readers in early Church services
lemmata in New Testament manuscripts 324, 357
lessons
in synagogue 564
in early Church services 454, 568–75, 576, 581–4
Letter of Aristeas 50, 146–7, 167, 178, 414, 456
Pseudo-Aristeas 427, 430, 438
letters, private 53, 236, 237–9, 252, 259, 281; *see also* Pauline epistles
Levi, Rabbi 208
Levites, as authoritative interpreters of Old Testament 75, 200–1, 221, 585
literal interpretation
of Old Testament 223, 380–1, 383
of New Testament 360, 427, 433–4, 441–2, 447–8, 452, 467–74, 480, 482–3, 486, 492, 552, 555
literature of Old Testament, history of development of 67–8, 81
literary analysis of Old Testament 73–6, 79, 91
liturgy 7, 152–3, 586
of Temple 130, 201, 563, 568
of synagogue 141, 201, 261, 563–4, 566, 569–70
in early Church 65, 232, 367, 563, 567, 570, 578–9
influence on Old Testament 99, 111; on New Testament 64, 323
liturgical forms in Old Testament 130, 578; in New Testament 253, 260, 271, 281, 566–7, 578
liturgical languages 25, 27
logia 55, 57, 61–2, 266, 280, 414

Lord's Prayer 290, 471, 523, 567, 580–1
Lucian of Antioch 65, 420
as exegete 360–1, 442, 489–90
as witness to New Testament text 173, 320, 368
Luke, Gospel of
authorship of 266–7, 269, 307
Marcion's use of 294, 296, 337, 369
position in New Testament Canon 273, 283, 289–90, 292–4, 300, 529
'proto-Luke' 275–6
structure of 268–9, 275–6
text of 10–11, 131, 289–90, 320, 328–9, 337–40, 361, 363, 471, 524
theology of 267, 274–5, 476
use of Mark 267–8, 271, 275, 296, 333
use of Old Testament 390
Luke–Acts 235
position in Canon 273, 283
purpose of 273–4
structure of 276–7
text of 59, 64, 274, 287, 344
theology of 274–6

Manichees 326, 331, 542–3, 552
Manichaean materialism 551
manuscript groups of New Testament 311–15, 317–19, 323–4, 326, 329, 333, 338–9, 351, 376
cursives 530
main groups: Family 1 314–15, 323, 349, 353; Family Π 319, 361; Ferrar group (Family 13) 315, 319, 323–4, 334, 349, 364
minuscules 313, 315, 318, 324, 327, 334, 339, 340, 349, 351–3, 355–9, 362
uncials 313, 315–16, 318, 324, 327, 338, 350–5, 357, 362–3
Marcellus of Ancyra, as exegete 442–3, 446
Marcion 296, 354, 408, 423, 451, 480
as witness to New Testament Canon 240–1, 248, 254, 293–4, 303
as witness to New Testament text 332, 335, 337–8, 342–5, 416–17
marginalia
in Old Testament manuscripts 186
in New Testament manuscripts 313, 324–5, 351, 353, 356, 359, 366

Mari texts 1, 42, 44, 70
Mark, Gospel of
  authorship of 235, 266, 269, 291, 307
  position in New Testament Canon 291,
    294, 300, 302, 369, 529
  priority of 267–8, 270–1, 272, 275, 296
  structure of 266, 268, 270–1, 566
  text of 7, 10, 273, 302, 320, 333, 349,
    351, 361, 524, 528–9
  theology 270–1, 476
  use of Old Testament 390
  use of in early Church 54–5, 59
Massada 156, 169, 183
Massoretic text 144, 163, 169, 170–81, 183–
    5, 188–93, 224, 230, 532
  Massoretes 160, 175
  proto-Massoretic text 173–4, 178, 198
Matthew, Gospel of
  authorship of 235, 266
  Jewish tone of 206, 272
  position in New Testament Canon 283,
    289–94, 300, 369, 529
  structure of 272–3, 566
  text of 56, 62, 131, 289, 320, 334, 337–9,
    351, 353, 361, 471, 524
  theology of 396, 399, 476
  use of Mark 266–8, 270–2, 275, 296, 333
  use of Old Testament 272–3, 276, 390,
    399, 405
  use of, in Church 268, 271, 566, 571
Megilloth (Scrolls) 111, 135, 141, 150
Mekhilta 211–12, 217, 222, 384 n.
Melito 439, 533
  as exegete 414–15
  Homily on the Pasch 414, 567, 574
  as witness to Canon 137
memoirs
  of the prophets 125
  of the apostles 236, 270, 344, 570
Mesrop, provides Armenian alphabet 367–8
messianic interpretation
  at Qumrân 412
  rabbinic 226, 396, 413
  in New Testament 405, 408, 413
middôt 221–2, 383–5, 393
midrash 6, 79, 157, 176, 199–231, 263
  '*al tiqrē*' midrash 187–9
  in New Testament 404, 413, 419
  Tannaitic 222, 229

millenarianism in early Church 291, 431–
    4, 555
ministry, development of doctrine 399,
    414, 428–9
Mishnah 114, 135, 201, 212, 216, 222, 224,
    229
Moabite 3, 5 n.
  Moabite Stone 87
Montanism 285, 301, 308, 354, 418
moral sense of scripture 382, 468–70
Murabba'ât 49, 51, 169, 183
Muratorian canon 240, 266, 273, 282–3,
    300–2

Naassene Gnostics 417
Nabataean 6
Nag Hammadi, Gnostic documents found
    at 285
narrative writing 552
  in ancient world 41
  in Old Testament 75, 86–92, 97, 105,
    107–8, 110–11, 137, 207–8, 481
  in New Testament 419
  in pseudepigrapha 157
Neo-Platonism 543, 551–2, 554
Neo-Pythagoreanism 380, 382
Nestorianism 25, 365, 375, 490, 505
Nestorius 492
New Testament
  literary criticism of 262, 267–8, 294,
    303–4
  units of tradition of 265, 267–71, 275–6,
    286–8, 375–6
Nicene theology 442–3, 446–7, 489, 505
nomina sacra in Christian manuscripts 60–
    1, 64, 66
notebooks
  in antiquity 54
  in early Church 53–7, 59
Novatian 434
  as exegete 422, 425, 431, 451–2
  as witness to text of New Testament
    345–6
Nubian version of New Testament 369–70
numerology
  in Jewish literature 281
  in New Testament 281
  in early Church 414, 559–60
Nuzi texts 44, 70

Oea, riot at 521, 546
Offices in early Church 576, 580–4
Old Testament, connections with ancient Near Eastern material 70–1, 79–81, 86, 93, 102–3
Old Testament
  different traditions 69, 71, 73–6, 85, 87, 90, 91, 106–7, 113, 120, 124, 161; *see also* text
  literature of 67–113
  types of literature in 67–71, 72, 79–105
  use of in New Testament 51–2, 62, 177, 213, 232–4, 246–7, 256, 262–3, 272, 362–3, 377, 379, 386, 389–411, 564; in early Church 53, 61, 286
Onias temple 223–5
oracles, collections of 378, 420, 462
  in Old Testament 77, 92 n., 97–101, 105, 109, 118, 127
  oracular view of Bible 419–20, 422–3, 449, 451, 454
Origen 446, 449–52, 454–89, 530, 568, 576–7, 581
  Commentaries 454–5, 497, 537, 572–3
  as exegete 351, 418–19, 422, 425, 429, 433–9, 454–5, 465–70, 485–9
  Hexapla 160, 177, 189, 454, 458, 460, 515, 521, 531
  Homilies 454–5, 513–14, 517
  use of philosophy 433–8, 487
  Scholia 454–5
  on text 65, 324, 349–53, 355–6, 358–60, 366–7, 455–61, 474–80
  witness to New Testament Canon 137, 156–7, 173, 189, 295–6, 303–5, 459–60, 533–4
orthodoxy, involved in development of New Testament exegesis 416
  Canon 285–6, 294, 299, 321
  text 364

Palestinian canon of Old Testament 141, 143, 145–9, 158–9, 199, 533–4; *see also* Alexandria
Palmyrene 6, 26
Pamphilus, teacher of Eusebius 359, 363
Pantaenus 302, 303, 327
Papias 58, 278, 288, 296, 307, 432–3, 518

preference for oral tradition 54, 61, 234, 266–7, 290–2, 297, 332
papyri of Old and New Testament 9, 48, 55–6, 59, 60, 66, 237, 316, 323, 328, 336, 350, 354–5
  Bodmer papyri 56, 328, 341, 347, 349–50
  Chester Beatty papyri 56, 60, 62, 63, 316, 324, 326, 349–53, 355, 357
  Egerton Gospel 56, 62
  Nash Papyrus 16, plate 15
  Rylands papyri 56, 63, plate 3
parousia 9, 242, 253, 257–8, 267, 270, 282, 418, 430
Paul, *see* epistles
Paul of Samosata, exegete 489–90
Paula 514, 516, 584
Pauline theology 225, 252, 506, 509
Paulinus of Antioch, 'Antiochene' exegete 442
Paulinus of Antioch, ordains Jerome 513–14
Paulinus of Nola 342
Pelagius 372, 374, 516, 536
  Pelagian controversy 556, 561
  Pelagians 580
Pentateuch 123–4, 128–9, 140, 143–6, 169–71, 236, 435–6, 467; *see also* Samaritan Pentateuch
  legal material 118, 120, 205, 412, 429
  literary analysis of 71, 73–6, 106–8, 181
  Mosaic authorship 74, 114–15, 380
  reading of 201, 564
  text of 191, 193–5, 209, 220, 435
  translations of 167, 176, 530
  use of in early Church 62, 262, 273, 395
Persian
  words in Old Testament 2
  Church 25
  version of New Testament 341, 370
personae, passages in Psalms allotted to 413–14, 416, 498–500, 505
pēšer technique of exegesis
  at Qumrân 102, 190, 226, 388, 396, 412
  in New Testament 262, 392, 394, 396
Peshiṭta 158–9, 192, 203–6, 216 n., 365–6, 374, 604, plate 21
Pharisees 117, 202, 206, 221–5, 233, 272; *see also* Judaism
  Pharisaic influence on Old Testament text 175

Philo 48, 50 n., 213, 228, 299, 414
  interpretation of Old Testament 379–
    86, 389, 392 n., 401
  use of allegory 429–30, 435–8, 449, 467
  witness to Canon of Old Testament
    148
  witness to text of Old Testament 204 n.,
    395–6
  Pseudo-Philo 213–14
philology in early Church 316, 320, 342,
  345, 357–9, 370, 374, 539
Philoxenus, bishop of Mabbug 365–6
Phoenician 3, 13
Photius, patriarch of Constantinople 313,
  320–1, 361
Pierius 528, 537
Pilgrimage of Etheria 568, 573, 575, 582–3
Pirke Aboth (Sayings of the Fathers) 201
Plato 49, 228, 255, 304, 377–9, 437, 452
  Platonism 382, 401, 435, 475, 484, 551;
    Christian Platonism 435, 488
  semi-Platonic tone of Hebrews 261,
    263, 402, 409
Pliny 30, 260, 567
  the Elder 56
Plotinus 552
Polycarp 61, 64, 355, 365, 518
  as witness to Canon of New Testament
    249, 254, 258, 288, 292–3
Porphyry as critic of Origen 487–9, 551
post-Pauline literature 251–65, 283
prayers
  in ancient world 47
  in Jewish practice 564, 580
  in early Church services 566, 568–70,
    576, 577–8, 580–1
Priestly Work (P) 71, 73, 91–2, 96, 107–8,
  112, 212–14
Primasius, early commentator 367, 373
Procopius, early translator 574
proof-texts
  from Qumrân 54, 233, 262, 412
  in New Testament 54, 405, 413
  in early Church 415–16, 422, 428, 437,
    445, 449, 452
prophecy 554
  in ancient world 48
  in Old Testament 96–102, 114–15, 118,
    127–8, 410, 481

  in early Church 51, 233, 245, 276, 279,
    398, 407
  fulfilment of, at Qumrân 102, 225–6,
    387–9, 394–6; in New Testament
    239, 258, 276, 394, 399–401, 403,
    409–11, 480–1, 585
Prophets, the
  appealed to at Qumrân 150, 155; in
    New Testament 564–5; by early
    Church 133, 159, 232, 395, 413–14,
    421, 508, 570–1
  as division of Old Testament Canon
    115, 129, 135–8, 149, 235, 403, 516
  Former Prophets 107–9, 135, 136, 140,
    142, 143, 164, 189, 194, 201
  Latter Prophets 109, 135, 136, 140, 142,
    143, 164, 201
  Minor Prophets 110, 125, 135, 136, 142,
    492, 501–4, 516
  prophetic literature 77–8, 80–1, 84, 96–
    102, 118, 119, 124, 125, 127–9, 130,
    137, 142, 236, 420–1
proverbs
  in Old Testament 46, 97, 103–4
  in New Testament 254, 340
psalmody
  pre-Israelite 68–9
  in Old Testament 67–9, 80, 83, 111, 157
  in early Church 564–6, 568–70, 579,
    581–2, 584
psalms 301, 466, 491
  in ancient world 46–7, 68
  in Old Testament 76–7, 82, 106, 119;
    outside Psalter 90, 97, 99, 130, 164;
    royal 83; wisdom 104
  at Qumrân 111, 151–3, 388
  quoted in New Testament 232, 262
Psalter 68, 77, 97, 111, 141, 151–3, 155,
  499, 578, 583
  use in early Church 130; 'Gallican'
    Psalter 515, 522, 527, 531
pseudepigrapha 72, 104, 146, 150, 155,
  167, 178, 199, 257, 264
  The Assumption of Moses 257
  Testaments of the Twelve Patriarchs 264
  from Qumrân 154, 157
  use in early Church 158
pseudonymity as claim to inspired authorship 132–3, 257, 413

pseudonymity (*cont.*)
  in New Testament 255
Ptolemy, Gnostic 294, 296–7, 424, 426
Ptolemy II Philadelphus 149, 167, 530–1
Punic 3, 550

Qumrân 73, 78 n., 143, 201, 223
  copying of manuscripts 49–50, 65, 184,
    190
  exegesis 216, 219–21, 224–5, 233, 386–9,
    394–6, 412–13, 585
  scrolls 111, 162, 182, 184–5, 189, 191–2,
    225, 280, 299, 400; *see* Dead Sea Scrolls
  texts 6, 49, 72, 133
  use of Old Testament 54, 190, 565
  witness to Old Testament Canon 124,
    149–57
  witness to Old Testament text 169,
    183–7, 189–93
  see also pēšer
quotations
  of Old Testament at Qumrân 190
  of Old Testament in New Testament
    131, 377, 390, 393–5, 397, 403–7, 409,
    532, 562
  from Fathers as witness to New Testa-
    ment Canon 271, 289–90, 292, 306;
    to New Testament text 309, 320, 329–
    32, 335–8, 340–1, 345–6, 355–7, 364,
    366, 370–2, 376, 416, 426, 494

rabbinic literature 51, 72, 94–5, 166, 169,
    226, 229
  quotations of Bible in 176, 192
Rabbula, authorship of Peshiṭta 364–5, 374
Rashi 74, 219
  Rashi-script 18
Ras Shamra 37, 42
  texts 3, 4, 68–9, 70, 72
readers, in early Church services 50, 362,
    570–2, 574
reading 313
  circulation of literature in early Church
    55, 63–5, 575
  knowledge of 48–9
  reading aloud 49–50, 54, 62
recital, as influence on Old Testament
    literature 119–20
Revelation 53, 100, 277, 280–2, 288, 315,

322, 349–50, 352, 366–8, 373, 398,
    538, 567, 573
  authorship 278
  nature of 157, 236, 281, 284, 344, 430
  position in Canon 234–6, 280, 282–3, 285–
    6, 291, 295–6, 301, 304–7, 357, 365,
    367, 434, 494
riddles, in Old Testament 46, 84–5
Rufinus 511–12, 533–4, 536

Sadducees 202, 223–5
Samaria, ostraca 14–15, 34, 69 n.
Samaritan
  canon of Old Testament 143
  community 15, 123–4, 143–5, 168, 170,
    178, 198
  Pentateuch 7, 123–4, 144–5, 169–70,
    172, 174, 178, 180–1, 192, 198, 215 n.,
    603, plate 14
  schism 112, 144
  text 163, 177, 185, 532
sanctuary legends 69–70, 88
scholia 325–6
scribes, in ancient world 14, 31–3, 35–40,
    42, 45; in Israel 40, 102, 122, 160–2,
    166, 168, 186, 194, 200–1, 221; in
    early Church 60–3, 65, 310, 319, 325,
    338, 343, 359
  scribal schools 35–6, 38, 50, 103, 181;
    Babylonian 36; Egyptian 35–6;
    Temple 38
  scribal techniques 49, 62, 65, 166, 184,
    186, 189, 362, 457–8, 515
scriptoria 35, 65, 185, 313, 316, 360
scripts 11–29, 42, 368
  Coptic 27–8, 601, plate 6
  cuneiform 12, 35, 36, 37
  cursive 5, 14, 16–19, 21–2, 26
  Egyptian demotic 28, 603, plate 12
  Ethiopic 28
  Greek 19, 458
  hieratic 35, 602, plates 9, 10
  hieroglyphic 35
  italic 24
  majuscule 21–2, 27
  minuscule 19–24, 309
  monumental (lapidary) 14, 16, 19, 21, 27
  Old Hebrew 12
  Samaritan 15, 145

scripts (*cont.*)
Square Hebrew 15, 16–17
uncial 19, 21, 28, 309
scriptures 114, 133–4, 147–8, 154, 232, 293, 345, 362, 366, 452, 460–2, 464–5, 487–8; *see also* Canon
of Old Testament 52–5, 58, 115–16, 124, 132, 136, 380, 400, 405, 411
of New Testament 64–5, 133, 239, 282, 293–4, 454, 456; copying of Christian scriptures 65–6
attitude of early Church to 50–3, 55
selection, of Christian literature 284–5; *see also* Canon of New Testament
Semitic languages 2–5, 7–8, 18–19, 24, 26, 160–1, 167–8, 343
influence on New Testament 7–8
letters of 18, 26
North Semitic 3, 13, 18–19
South Semitic 3, 29
syntax 4, 5, 8, 9
triliteral consonantal word-stems 4–5, 18
Septuagint (LXX) 148, 160, 188, 203, 227, 230, 275, 326
attitude of Jews to 50, 145
canon different from Hebrew 135–7, 139, 141–2, 145–6, 152, 199, 421, 534
differing text of 72, 124, 167, 170, 172–4, 178, 191–2, 204–6, 215, 223, 404–5, 423, 428, 438, 441–2, 467, 475, 495–7, 500, 513, 515, 521, 525, 564
influence on New Testament 8, 10, 343
language of 7–8
use of, in Church 50, 149, 158, 232, 262, 360, 374, 391, 397, 445, 455–9, 476, 518–19, 530–2, 545–6, 557–8
Serapion of Antioch 284, 296, 298, 305
Serapion of Thmuis, *Sacramentary* 568, 577, 580
sermons
in Judaism 383
in New Testament 264, 499
in early Church 260–1, 419, 454–5, 557, 568, 572, 575–7, 582
Shammai 206, 222
'Shepherd' of Hermas 64
relation to early Canon of New Testament 62, 157, 288, 291, 295, 301, 302, 305, 460

Sibylline books 378
signs, in understanding scripture 548–9
Siloam inscriptions 4, 14–15
Simon ben-Sheṭaḥ 38
Simeon ben Yoḥai, Rabbi 217
Slavonic version of New Testament 326, 330, 370
spiritual sense of scripture 464, 467–70, 472–9, 487–8, 495; *see also* allegory
stemma of manuscripts 309–10, 311, 361, 376
Stoics, development of allegory 379–80, 382, 409, 466
Stoicism 228, 414, 435
stylistics as involved in development of New Testament text 317, 343–4, 376
Sumerian 3, 33, 36, 44, 47
law 43
literature 41, 46–7
synagogue 66, 141, 261
language of 11
reverence for Law 48–50, 132, 171, 197
rift with Church 168–9, 272
synaxis 566, 568; *see also* Eucharist, liturgy, worship
Synoptic Gospels 9, 265–77, 280, 283–5, 296, 301, 303, 328–9, 333, 344, 347, 403–6, 417, 444
synoptic problem 267–8
synoptic tradition 289, 292, 329, 335, 463, 475
Syriac 2, 157, 356–7, 363–7, 369, 517, 575; *see* East Aramaic, Peshiṭta
alphabets 24–7
literature 24–5; Christian literature 7
translation of Old Testament 152, 160, 185, 192, 496
version of New Testament 330–1, 334, 336, 497; Harklean Syriac 326, 365–6, 601, plate 5; Old Syriac 330, 333–4, 337, 340–1, 344, 346, 348–9, 355, 365, 367, Curetonian 338, 346, Sinaitic 334, 338, 340, 346, 375; Philoxenian 365–6

Talmud 2, 16, 116, 140, 213, 219, 222, 229, 385
Babylonian 7, 156, 230, 300; Baba Bathra 116, 133, 136 n., 140 n., 141, 300
Palestinian 2, 217
Talmudic literature 12

Targums 6, 79, 201, 206, 213, 224, 229, 272
 Aramaic 7, 150, 178, 192, 201; Fragment Targum 176, 224
 Greek 201; Targum Neofiti 204–5, 215, 604, plate 18
 Palestinian 199, 203, 205, 218, 226, 230–1; Targum Onkelos 169, 176, 203–5, 214, 216; Pseudo-Jonathan 176, 211–12, 216, 219, 230
 Samaritan 7
Tatian
 Diatessaron (Harmony) 57, 76, 91, 266, 296, 354, 366–7, 426, 429, 567
 text of 330–2, 337, 367, 370
 as witness to New Testament text 325–6, 334, 337–8, 340–1, 344–8, 364, 418, 462
teacher in early Church 51, 256, 557–8
Teaching of Amenemope 102
Tell-el-Amarna letters 1, 4, 37
Temple (Jerusalem) 81, 224–5, 563, 580
 First Temple 38, 49, 69, 89–91, 95, 120–1, 159; Fall of 98, 101, 121, 165
 Second Temple 38, 51, 132, 143–4, 182, 217; destruction of 132, 168–70, 183, 186, 222
Tertullian 439, 451–3, 566, 568–9, 576, 580–1
 Adversus Iudaeos 416
 exegesis in 416–18, 423–5, 427–8, 431–4, 436, 449
 as witness to New Testament Canon 261
 as witness to New Testament text 337–8, 341–2, 345, 355, 371, 373, 375
Testament of our Lord 568
testimonia 53–4, 55, 58, 130, 233, 405, 407–8
Tetrateuch 73, 92, 108
text
 of Old Testament 72, 159–99, 350, 455–8, 460, 496, 508, 531–2, 578; textual analysis 161, 163, 168, 171, 172, 475; 'archetype' theory 173–5, 177–8; 'local texts' theory 181, 193–8; recensions of Old Testament 172, 177, 179–80, 182, 186, 193–6, 214, 'one-recension' theory 172–4, 176–7, 193, 196; 'vulgar texts' theory 177–81, 193, 197–8

 of New Testament 308–77, 460, 497; archetypes of New Testament texts 309, 312–14, 315–16, 320, 324; recensions of New Testament 309–10, 313–14, 317, 320, 328, 341, 353, 363, 367, 376, 578; Neutral text 310, Syrian text 310, Western text 64, 310, 321, 330, 333, 343, 529; textual criticism 308–12, 318, 329–31, 337, 350–1, 375–7, 461, 527–9, rational criticism 311, 317, 319, 343, 350, 352, 357
textual traditions
 in ancient texts 39–40
 of Old Testament 161–3, 169–70, 172, 176–81, 184–9, 192–4, 196–9
 of New Testament 309–10, 312–15, 318, 321, 349, 373
textus receptus of Old Testament 163, 169, 178–81, 183–7, 193, 198–9
Theodore of Mopsuestia 361, 489–510
 commentaries 491–2, 497–507
 as exegete 491–2, 497, 503–10
 as preacher 491
 as witness to New Testament Canon 494–6
 as witness to New Testament text 496–7
Theodoret, 'Antiochene' exegete 361, 365
Theophilus of Antioch, exegete 294, 304, 306, 332, 423, 426, 436
Thomas, bishop of Harkel 365–6
To Ioudaikov 325, 335, 605, plate 22
Torah 12, 38, 39, 44, 92 n., 109, 134, 135, 200–1, 209, 221–2, 380, 412–14, 423, 435–6; *see also* Law, the
 tôrāh 92, 94, 96, 103
 Torah-liturgies 119
 maintenance of 44
 reading of 18
 scrolls 17
Tosephta, the 224
tradition
 of authorship 38–40
 continuity of 40, 44, 55, 110, 113, 308, 466
 gospel tradition 251, 257, 265, 269, 289–90, 307, 390
 oral tradition: in ancient world 40; in Old Testament 74, 84–5, 90–1, 125,

tradition (*cont.*)
164–5, 182, 333, 380; of sayings of
Jesus 10–11, 54–5, 61, 265, 286–7,
289–91, 296, 343–4, 454; of gospel
267–8; in Church 234, 264, 297, 332
pre-Israelite 69, 71, 386
Rabbinic 39, 51, 131, 133, 201, 221, 384
written tradition: in ancient world 40,
49; in Old Testament 85, 90–1, 164–
5, 182; of sayings of Jesus 10–11, 61,
265, 290; of gospel 267, 332
translation as evidence of different texts
518, 522–6; *see also* versions
of Old Testament 160–2, 166–8, 192,
201
of New Testament 314, 345, 347, 364
in early Church services 574–5
transliteration from uncial to minuscule
313–14, 315–16
transmission of texts 39–40, 66, 135, 149,
166, 197
of Old Testament 50, 159, 161–2, 164–6,
168, 171, 179, 183, 187, 189–91, 194,
198, 221
of New Testament 197, 311–12, 314,
323, 375
Tyconius, Donatist theologian 367, 373,
554–5
typology
at Qumrân 190
in New Testament 262, 270, 410–11,
413–15
in early Church 422, 427–8, 435–6, 482–
5, 503, 509, 554, 560

Ugarit 42, 44
Ugaritic 3, 4, 47, 68
unity of scripture 480–5, 498, 505–6
Ur-recension of Old Testament 179–80,
193, 196
Ur-text theory 164, 174–7, 179–80, 193,
196

Valentinus, Gnostic 296–7, 301, 308
Valentinians 294, 417, 419
variant readings 556
in Old Testament 50, 72–3, 76, 106,
162–4, 168–72, 175–8, 183–5, 187–9,
191–3, 224, 389

in New Testament 64, 310–11, 316–18,
325, 327–9, 334–8, 340, 343–4, 349–
52, 354, 359–60, 375, 460–1, 496, 528
variae lectiones 160–1, 170, 172, 184,
187–9, 191–2
versions
of Old Testament 27–8, 160, 162–4, 174,
176–80, 183–4, 190–3, 199, 203, 326,
457–8; Aquila 160, 175, 203, 438,
458–9, 513, 525, 531, 545; Symmachus 160, 175, 188, 203, 205, 224,
458–9, 496–7, 513, 531, 545; Theodotion 160, 203, 205, 458–9, 513, 531,
545; *see also* Peshiṭta, Samaritan,
Septuagint, Vulgate
of New Testament 316–18, 326–7, 329–
30, 333–4, 336–8, 345–50, 354–8, 361,
363–74
Victorinus of Pettau 372, 432, 537
Vulgate 370, 372, 518–19, 527–9
Jerome's Prefaces 510, 513, 519
text of 327, 527–9
textual difference in 204–5, 336, 342
translated by Jerome 169, 192, 373–4,
518–23, 545

Wisdom literature 46–7, 157, 509, 571
in Old Testament 46–7, 97, 102–5, 416,
419, 423, 481
in New Testament 103
worship 568–86
use of Old Testament in synagogue 563–
4; in Church 565–6, 569–71
liturgical forms in New Testament?
566–7
use of New Testament in Church 323,
570–2
use of Bible in early writers 567–77
relation to biblical text 578–9, 586
writing 12, 19, 23, 44, 48, 52, 62–3, 234;
see also alphabet, scripts
knowledge of 13, 14–15, 35–8, 48–9,
58
reluctance towards, in early Church
233–4, 267
Wulfila, bishop of Goths 368

Yoḥanan, Rabbi 217

INDEX OF REFERENCES

OLD TESTAMENT

Genesis
  1 201, 401
  1–3 347
  1–11 41, 71
  1: 1–2: 4a 71, 74
  1: 26 442, 507
  1: 27 216, 382, 396, 414, 415 n.
  2 108
  2: 4b–25 71, 74
  2: 7 382
  2: 8 381
  2: 18 396
  2: 19 ff. 1
  2: 21 f. 381
  2: 22 f. 397
  2: 24 396
  3: 8 446
  3: 16 78
  4 131
  4: 7 78, 204
  4: 16 381
  5: 1 44, 273
  6–9 75
  7: 7 216
  7: 16 415 n.
  9: 20–7 554
  10 44
  10: 21 1
  10: 21 ff. 2
  11 1
  11: 5 415 n.
  11: 29 219
  12 218–19
  12: 6 144
  12: 10–19 86, 207
  12: 13 218
  12: 20 86
  14: 14 61
  15 394
  15: 6 393
  16: 7–13 446
  17: 22 415 n.
  18: 1 415 n.
  18: 2 382, 446
  18: 16 415 n.
  18: 19 37
  18: 21 415 n.
  18: 33 415 n.
  20 218

  20: 12 218–19
  20: 14 ff. 220
  22 69 n., 89
  22: 2 144
  23 44
  23: 3–18 88
  26: 6–11 86
  28: 11–22 69
  28: 11 70
  28: 12, 13 69
  28: 17 70
  31: 47 2
  32: 22–30 415 n.
  35: 18 525
  41: 43 2, 203
  41: 45 2, 204
  44: 2, 4, 5 217
  45: 8 204
  49: 10–12 415

Exodus
  2: 1–10 86
  2: 5 230–1
  3: 1–6 69
  3: 1–4: 17 81, 118 n.
  3: 4 ff. 416 n.
  4: 25–6 226–7
  5: 14 37 n.
  6: 29 415 n.
  7 398
  15: 1–18 68 n.
  16: 1, 2 525
  16: 9, 10 525
  16: 18 398
  17: 10–12 415 n.
  17: 14 37
  18: 21–2 37
  19–24 43
  20: 1–17 119 n.
  20: 1 118 n.
  20: 4–5 217
  20: 17 144
  20: 21 (24) 224
  20: 22–23: 33 95, 120
  20: 25 384 n.
  21: 2–6 209
  21: 7 209, 211–12, 222
  21: 8 212 n.
  21: 26–7 211

Exodus (*cont.*)
22: 26   34
23: 19   214
24: 1   118 n.
24: 3–7   37
24: 12   34, 118 n.
24: 15–18   118 n.
25: 16   34
32: 15 f.   118 n.
33: 1, 3   414 n.
33: 7–11   118 n.
34: 1   118 n.
34: 5–7   118 n.
34: 12–26   120 n.
34: 17   217 n.
34: 26   214
34: 28   118 n.
39: 14   37
39: 30   37

Leviticus
11: 42   382
16: 3   393 n.
16: 14 f.   393 n.
17–26   95, 101, 122
17: 1–9   122 n.
18   215
18: 5   397
18: 9   218
18: 20   215
18: 21   216
19: 18   394, 407
20: 2   215–16
20: 5   215 n.
20: 17   218, 248 n.
22   94
23: 39–43   123 n.
25: 40   211 n.
25: (39) 44–6   210
25: 45–6   212 n.
26: 1   218
26: 34   101
26: 43   101

Numbers
5: 23   31
9: 13   384
12: 1–8   118 n.
15: 17–21   222
16   398
18: 1   429 n.
18: 11 f.   222
19: 9, 17   393 n.
21: 8   427
21: 14   45

21: 18   387
22–4   212–13
22: 18   212
22: 22   212
22: 35   212
23: 3   212
23: 26   212
24: 1   212
24: 12 f.   212
24: 17   226
24: 24   226 n.
24: 25   212
25   213
31   93
31: 15 f.   213
31: 16   212
31: 25 ff.   93
31: 27   92

Deuteronomy
1: 15   37
4: 2   118 n.
4: 44   92 n.
4: 44–11: 32   95
5: 6–21   119 n.
5: 8–9   217
5: 21   144
6   43
6: 4   120 n., 394
6: 7   37
9: 9, 11, 15   118 n.
10: 1–5   118 n.
12–26   95
12: 15–28   122 n.
12: 32   118 n.
14: 21   214
15: 2   123
15: 12–18   210
15: 12   210
15: 17   210
17: 17   216
17: 18–19   200
17: 18   38
18: 3   222
18: 6–8   121 n.
18: 15–19   118 n.
18: 15–22   127 n.
18: 22   127 n.
22: 13 ff.   206 n.
23: 3 ff.   123 n.
23: 5–6   212–13
23: 12 ff.   206
24: 1   205–6, 396
24: 1–4   205, 207
25: 4   398

Deuteronomy (*cont.*)
26:5 1
27 95
27:4 144
27:5, 6 384
27:26 398, 532
30:12 f. 392
31:10–13 95
31:22 37
31:24–6 37, 38
33:13–17 415
34 201

Joshua
1:7–8 200
8:32 34, 37
9:23–5 44
10:13 47
13:22 212–13
22 93
22:8 92
24 43
24:1–28 119 n., 120
24:9–10 212–13

Judges
3:12 525
5:14 38
6:32 68 n.
8:14 38
9:8–15 46
12:6 525
14:5–9 84
14:14 84
14:18 85

Ruth
4 94

1 Samuel
2:1–10 68 n., 83
3:1 128 n.
3:10 70
5–6 87
7 83
10:11–13 38
10:11 f. 103
10:25 43
12:6–15 119 n.
17:4 525
17:23 525
19:18–24 125 n.
19:24 103
21:1–6 392

23:28 525
30 92–3
30:22 93

2 Samuel
1:18 47
2–24 89
2:4 93
2:12 69 n.
5:1–3 93
8:16 38
8:17 13
9–20 91, 107
11 218
12:1–4 47
14:4–11 94
18:28–33 526
20:8 9
20:25 13
21–4 77, 89–90
21:1–14 90
21:15–22 90
21:18–22 89
22 68 n., 76, 90, 164
23:1–7 76, 90
23:8–39 89–90
24 69, 76, 86, 89–90
24:1–9 87
24:1, 3 87
24:9 87
24:10–17 87
24:10 87
24:15 88
24:16*b* 87
24:18–25 87
24:24 88

1 Kings
1–2 91, 107
2:6 43
3:16–28 43
4:3 38
6–8 91
8:9 34
10 85
11:11 525
11:14 89
11:41 46
12:1–15 44
14:19 45
14:29 45, 91
19:18 391
19:19–21 125 n.
21 43
22:19–22 80

2 Kings
2: 1–18 125 n.
4: 12 125 n.
4: 25–31 125 n.
4: 38–44 125 n.
5: 6 32
5: 19–27 125 n.
6: 1–17 125 n.
8: 4 f. 125 n.
9: 1–10 125 n.
10: 1 38
14: 23–9 108
14: 25 110
16: 10–18 91
17 143 n.
18: 13–20: 19 164
18: 13–20: 21 97
19: 35 87
20: 20 14
22 f. 120 n.
22: 3–20 95
22: 13 95
23: 9 121 n.
23: 21–3 121 n.
24: 18–25: 21 97
24: 27–30 97
25: 1–22 164
25: 19 38
25: 22–6 97
25: 27–30 164

1 Chronicles
2: 55 38
9: 1 46
9: 39 69 n.
11: 10–41 89
12: 5 69 n.
16: 4 f. 111
16: 4 129 n.
16: 7 130
16: 8–36 164
20: 4–8 89
21–22: 1 69
21 76, 86, 88–9
21: 4, 5 88
21: 16 88
21: 25 88
21: 29–30 89
22: 1 89
22: 2–19 89
23–7 89
23: 31 129 n.
24: 1–19 150
25: 8 38
28–29: 9 89

2 Chronicles
3: 1 69 n., 89
9: 29 46
12: 15 46
16: 11 46
20 218
24: 20–2 131
32: 1–20 164
32: 3 f. 14
32: 18 1
32: 30 14
33: 14 14
34 120 n.
34: 18 38
35: 1–19 121 n.
36: 21 101

Ezra
4: 1–5 144 n.
4: 8–6: 18 1 n.
5: 6 38
5: 17 45
6 101
6: 1 38
7: 6 122 n.
7: 7 f. 123
7: 10 122 n.
7: 12–26 1 n.

Nehemiah
2: 10, 19 144 n.
4: 6 144 n.
8–10 133
8 95, 565
8: 1–9: 37 122–4
8: 1–8 585
8: 1 201
8: 7–8 201
8: 13–18 123 n.
10: 31 123 n.
11–12 44
13: 1 ff. 123 n.
13: 2 212–13

Esther
1: 22 32
2: 23 91
6: 1 91

Job
1–2 89, 111
1: 15, 16, 17, 19 525

Job (*cont.*)
21: 10 215
38 71
42: 7–17 111
42: 14 495 n.

Psalms
1 96, 104
1: 1–2 200
2 499–500
2: 1 f. 400
2: 3 498
3 498
4: 4 391
4: 5 293
5: 8 531
6 498
8 262, 499–500
13 498
15 119 n.
16: 10 501–2
18 68 n., 76, 164
19 96
22 152, 498, 500
22: 1 500
22: 18 390
23 406, 415, 584
24: 1 398
24: 3–6 119 n.
29 68
30: 21 558
31: 1 393
31: 2–4*b* 164
32 583
34 579
35 499
38 498
40: 6 500
40: 7 32
41: 2 558
41: 9 400
45 493, 499–500
45: 6 500
50: 7–23 119 n.
51 499, 583
51: 18 499
59 584
60: 7–14 164
68: 18 500
68: 19 400
69 500
69: 9 500
69: 21 480, 500
69: 22–3 500
69: 25 500

70 498
71: 1–3 164
72 83, 498, 500
72: 3, 5 500
72: 20 77, 111
74: 9 128n.
74: 12–17 71
78 466, 528
78: 2 400, 528
79: 2 f. 130
80 406
80: 7 569
81: 6–16 119 n.
82: 6 407
87 100
88 576
89 83
90 106 n.
91 153
95 263, 569
95: 7*b*–11 119 n.
96: 1–13 164
101 152
102 152
104 152
105 152
105: 1–15 164
106: 1 164
106: 47–8 164
107 152
108: 8–14 164
109 152
110 499
110: 3 443, 452
113–18 568
114 585
116 584
118–50 152
118 152
118: 22 408
119 96, 104
119: 18 486
119: 139 546
120–34 153
133 153
141: 5–10 153
144: 1–7 153
145: 15 579
147 152

Proverbs
1: 1 111
3: 3 52
3: 19 443
4: 31 46

Proverbs (*cont.*)
8: 22–31 71
8: 22 416, 441–3, 445–6
9: 1 443
10: 1 111
15: 8 150
22: 17–24: 22 102
22: 20 467
24: 23 111
25: 1 111

Ecclesiastes
1: 3 134
4: 2 134
8: 1 388
9: 2 134

Song of Songs
1: 10 479
4: 2 547

Isaiah
1–12 99
1 77, 99
1: 26 224
2 97, 100
2: 1 77 n.
2: 2–4 77, 100
3: 1 78
3: 2 ff. 18
5: 1–2 404
5: 1–7 47
5: 7 404
6 80
6: 1 ff. 446
6: 1 407
6: 3 579
6: 8 82
6: 9 f. 407, 539
7: 14 399
7: 18–21 430
8: 1–4 126 n.
8: 1 34
8: 14 407
8: 16 125–6
9: 19 189
10: 15 46
10: 19 38
12 99
16: 13 f. 127
19: 18 1
19: 18–19 222
21: 11 f. 84
23: 15 f. 84
24–7 98

24: 23 530
28: 4 47
28: 10 38 n.
28: 16 390, 407
28: 23 ff. 104
28: 27–9 98
29: 12 38
29: 16 46
30: 8 35
35: 6 404
36–9 97
36: 1–38: 22 164
36: 11 1
37: 36 87
38: 9–20 97
40–55 98–9, 110, 127–8
40: 3 202
41: 21–9 127 n.
42: 9 128
43: 9 127 n.
44: 24–6 127 n.
45: 14 428
45: 23 391
51: 9–11 71
53 406
53: 1 407
53: 4 400
53: 7–8 54
53: 8 446
54: 13 188
54: 16 387
56–66 98
60: 17 414 n., 428
61 564
61: 1 f. 404
61: 2 f. 128
62 100

Jeremiah
1–24 110
1 81
2: 13 422 n.
7: 11 414
8: 7 104
8: 8 31
10: 1–16 99
10: 11 2
17: 1 34
17: 12 422 n.
18: 18 103
20: 7 465
23: 18 118 n.
23: 22 81 n., 118 n.
25 72, 101, 110
25: 11 101

631

Jeremiah (*cont.*)
26–45 110
26: 16–19 100
29 101
29: 10 101
31: 15 399, 401
31: 31–4 409
31: 40 532
32: 7–25 44
32: 14 33
36 97, 126
36: 2 32
36: 10 38
36: 12–21 38
36: 23 31
39: 1–10 164
40: 7–43: 7 97
46–51 72
52: 1–27 97
52: 4–27 164
52: 25 38
52: 31–4 97, 164

Lamentations
2: 9 128 n.
4: 20 415 n.

Ezekiel
1–3 81
1: 1 102
2: 8–3: 3 52, 126 n.
2: 9 32
2: 10 31
3: 17–21 84
4: 1 34
4: 6 102
7: 26 103
9 81
9: 2–3 31
9: 11 31
14: 4, 7 525
20: 25 483
33: 7–9 84
34 406
37 446
40–8 100, 121–2

Daniel
2: 4–7 1 n.
2: 28 1 n.
4 72, 79
5: 7 38
7: 13, 14 446
8: 23–5 48
9 102, 225

9: 2 128 n.
9: 3–19 578
11: 3–4 48
11: 30 226 n.
12: 4 155
12: 9 155

Hosea
1: 6 402
2: 1, 23 402
9: 2 402
11: 1 399, 502
14: 10 105

Joel
2: 28–32 400
2: 28 502

Amos
2: 6–16 119 n.
3: 1 f. 119 n.
3: 7 81 n., 118 n.
4: 1–5: 17 101
4: 13 445
5: 18–6: 8 101
7: 1–8: 3 100
7: 1–3 100
7: 4–6 100
7: 7–9 100
7: 9 100
7: 10–17 100
7: 11 100
7: 14 ff. 81
8: 1–3 100
8: 4–14 101
8: 11 f. 128 n.
9: 11–15 101
9: 11 f. 397, 502

Jonah
4: 6 546

Micah
1–3 100
3 77
3: 9–12 100
4 97
4: 1–2 502
4: 1–4 77
4: 1–5 100
4: 7 502
5: 2 399, 402
6: 1–8 119 n.
6: 5 212
7: 7–20 68 n.

Index of References

Habakkuk
2: 2 35
2: 4 397
2: 8*b* 387
2: 15 387
2: 17 225
3 68 n., 97, 99
3: 2 423
3: 18 525

Haggai
2 92
2: 2 525
2: 10–14 94

Zechariah
1–8 110
1: 1 131 n.
1: 4–6 127 n.
1: 8 503

3 81
3: 1 f. 89
3: 7 81 n.
4 81
4: 10 470
8 101
8: 1–8 100
8: 16 391
9–11 110
9–14 110
9: 8–10 502
9: 9 481, 502
11: 1–14: 11 502
12–14 110
13: 7 502

Malachi
3: 1 110, 503
4: 4, 5 502
4: 5 386

APOCRYPHA

1 Esdras
3–4 73

2 Esdras
14 115, 133
14: 26 105
14: 45–8 300
14: 45–7 155
14: 45 139

Ecclesiasticus
24: 23 200
24: 33 128 n.
39: 1–8 201
39: 12 128 n.
44–50 128 n.
47: 9 f. 129 n.

48: 17–49: 10 110 n.
48: 20–5 128 n.
48: 24 f. 128 n.
49: 6–10 128 n.
49: 11 f. 129 n.
50: 27 128 n.
51: 13–30 77 n., 152

1 Maccabees
4: 46 128 n.
7: 16 f. 130
9: 27 128 n.
14: 14 128 n.

2 Maccabees
2: 13 130

PSEUDEPIGRAPHA

Letter of Aristeas
310, 311 147

Jubilees
12: 9 218
13: 11–14 219

23: 26 201
40: 10 204

1 Enoch
1: 9 158

QUMRÂN LITERATURE

1QS (Manual of Discipline)
VI: 6–7 200
VIII: 4–6 225 n.
VIII: 12–16 202
IX: 7 221 n.

CD (Damascus Document)
IV, 19–V, 2 216 n.
V, 2–6 216 n.
V, 7–11 219 n.
VI, 3–11 387
X, 4 ff. 154 n.
XI, 20–1 150 n.
XII, 22–XIII, 4 154 n.
XIV, 6–8 154 n.

1QM (War Scroll)
II: 1–4 150 n.

1QGA (Genesis Apocryphon)
XIX, 4–17 207
XX, 10–14 220
XX, 16–18 208 n.

XX, 22–3 208 n.
XX, 28–33 220

4Q Samᵃ 88 n.

1QIsᵃ (First Isaiah Scroll) 183, 188, 191, 224
cols. XXVIII, XXXII, XXXIII 78 n.

1QIsᵇ (Second Isaiah Scroll) 193

1QpHab. (Habakkuk Commentary)
VII 389 n.
VII, 1–5 585
VIII, 1 ff. 226 n.
IX, XI 388
XII, 3 ff. 225 n.

4QPsᶠ 152

11QPsᵃ 111 n., 151, 153–4
XXI–XXII 77 n.
XXVII 106 n.

11QPsApᵃ 153

RABBINIC LITERATURE

A. *Talmud and Mishnah*

A. Zar. (Abodah Zarah)
1: 8 218 n.
44b 217 n.

Y. A. Zar. (Yerushalmi A. Zar.)
III, 42d 217 n.

Ab. (Pirḳe Aboth)
3, 2 225 n.
3, 6 225 n.

Baba Bathra
13b 136 n.
14b–15a 116 n.
14b 140 n., 300

Berakot
64a 188

Beṣah
1 :6 222

Y. Gitt. (Gittin)
9, 10 206 n.
9, 50d 207 n.

Hull. (Hullin)
8, 1 214 n.
84 214 n.

Kidd. (Kiddushim)
1, 2 212 n.

Meg. (Megillah)
3 201
4, 9 216 n.

Bab. Meg. (Babylonian Megillah)
14a 219 n.

Y. Meg. (Yerushalmi Meg.)
4, 74d 201 n.
4, 75c 216 n.

Men. (Menahot)
13, 10 224 n.

Tosefta Men.
 13: 12–13 224 n.

Pesaḥim
 66*a* 384 n.

p. Pesaḥim
 6.33*a*.1 384 n.

Tosefta Pesaḥim
 4.1 f. 384 n.

Sanh. (Sanhedrin)
 7, 7 216 n.
 9, 6 215 n.

Bab. Sanh.
 69*b* 219 n.

Bab. Shabbath
 13*b* 156
 30*b* 156
 33*a* 188

Y. Ta'an. (Ta'anith)
 4, 68*d* 226 n.

Yadaim
 3, 5 114, 134

B. *Mekhilta*
 2, 169–70 227 n.
 2, 287 225 n.
 3, 18–19 211 n.
 3, 21 222 n.
 3, 24 211 n.
 3, 118 214 n.

C. *Midrash*

Gen. Rabbah
 40(41), 2 208 n.

Exod. Rabbah
 1, 22 207 n.

Deut. Rabbah
 2, 33 215 n.

Koh. Rabbah
 12: 12 157

NEW TESTAMENT

Matthew
 1: 1 476
 1: 16 334, 375
 1: 22 391
 1: 23 405
 2: 1–12 226
 2: 4 523
 2: 6 405
 2: 15, 18 405
 2: 23 405
 4: 5 524
 4: 15 f. 405
 4: 17 330, 340, 353
 5–7 272–3
 5: 5 289
 5: 6 417
 5: 22–6 290
 5: 22 325, 527, 529
 5: 26 417
 5: 32 206, 396
 5: 39, 40, 41 290
 5: 44, 46, 47 289
 5: 48 290
 6: 9–13 290
 6: 11 524
 6: 16 290
 7: 6 290, 414 n.

 7: 12 289
 7: 18 417
 7: 28 272
 7: 31–7 404
 8: 17 405
 9: 37–10: 42 272
 11: 1 272
 11: 25–7 335, 337, 446
 12: 3 48
 12: 5 ff. 392 n.
 12: 18 ff. 405
 12: 31 290
 13: 3 52 272
 13: 35 405, 528
 13: 36 486
 13: 53 272
 13: 54 359
 14: 13 484
 16: 2, 3 325
 16: 12 478
 17: 11 ff. 406
 18 272
 18: 15–25 290
 19: 1 272
 19: 2 206
 19: 4 48
 19: 6 ff. 424

Matthew (*cont.*)
19: 6 206, 396
19: 17 417 n.
21 573
21: 5 405
21: 42 48, 114 n.
23–5 272
23: 35 131
24 290
24: 4 290
24: 36 528–9
26: 1 272
26: 26–8 579 n.
26: 73 7
27: 9 405, 562
27: 35 390
27: 49 325
27: 53 537
28: 18–20 262
28: 19 f. 272, 583
28: 19 290

Mark
1: 1 476
1: 41 375
2: 23–8 392
7: 6, 10 391
7: 31 321
8: 32 340
9: 12 400, 405
9: 13 406
9: 15 523
9: 49 321
10: 2–12 396
10: 12 396
10: 18 417 n.
12: 1 403
12: 19 391
12: 28–34 394
12: 31 407
12: 36 391
13 277
13: 22 443–4
14: 4 340
14: 21 405
14: 36 440
15: 24 390, 404 n.
15: 34 417
15: 40 298
16: 14 529

Luke
1: 1–4 273
1: 1 274–5
1: 3 276

1: 17 406
4: 9 524
4: 16 ff. 201, 276, 564
4: 17 52
4: 18 f. 403
6: 17 344
6: 30 290
6: 31–3 289
7: 17–19 344
9: 23 527
9: 62 340
10: 21–2 335, 337
10: 34 417 n.
11: 3 524
11: 13 323
11: 50 f. 131
14: 19 353
20: 42 391
22: 43–4 528
23: 34 390
24: 44 f. 52
24: 44 130, 136, 232, 565
24: 49 276

John
1: 1 f. 407
1: 3 417
1: 4 f. 401
1: 4 417
1: 5 418
1: 13 342
1: 14 407
1: 17 483
1: 21 406
1: 28 476
1: 29 406
1: 49 504
1: 51 506
2: 6 559
2: 17 500, 546
2: 20 559
3: 25 375
4: 9 375
4: 21 502
5: 17, 18, 20 505
5: 25 506
5: 39 53
6: 41 352
6: 52–69 279
6: 53 f. 417
7: 42 406
7: 53–8: 11 319, 528
9: 23 529
10: 1–16 406
10: 30 444, 505

John *(cont.)*
10: 34 f. 407
12 279, 524
12: 41 407, 415 n., 446
13: 10 341
13: 18 400
14: 6 422 n.
14: 9 444
14: 18 506
14: 28 446, 505–6
17 523
17: 5 444
18: 11 440
19: 24 390, 400
19: 28 400
19: 35 326
19: 36 f. 400
19: 37 52
20: 28 504
20: 30 f. 279
20: 31 53
21 278
21: 11 560
21: 24 280

Acts of the Apostles
1: 1 476
1: 8 276
1: 12–8: 1 276
1: 20 500
2: 16 400, 585
2: 23 232
2: 24 355
2: 25–8 400
2: 42–6 566
3: 1 581
4: 25 f. 400
4: 25 391
6 263
7 390, 405, 413
7: 22 37
7: 42 390
8: 1–11: 18 276
8: 28, 30 49
8: 35 54
8: 40 359
10: 9 581
10: 35 349
11: 19 ff. 276
11: 26 24
13: 1 51
13: 14 ff. 564
13: 15 261
15 245, 276, 397
15: 20 326

15: 23 264
17 405
17: 1–18: 5 242
17: 11 53
18: 28 52, 54
19: 21 276
20: 35 287
23: 26 264

Romans
1: 3 f. 251
1: 5 248
1: 7 248, 335
1: 15 248, 335
1: 16 342
1: 32 336
3: 1 f. 408
3: 9–20 407
3: 9 321
3: 13–18 539 n.
3: 22 321
3: 24 f. 251
3: 26 323
4 393
4: 25 251
5: 12 248, 556
5: 14 556
6: 14 f. 408
7 464
7: 10 393
7: 12, 14 408
7: 25 321
9–11 253
9: 1 248
9: 18, 20 507
9: 27 391
9: 33 407
10: 4 399, 408
10: 6 f. 392
10: 9 251
10: 11 391
10: 20 391
11: 9–10 500
11: 25 237–8
12 248
12: 1 225
12: 11 529
13: 1 248
13: 8 ff. 394, 407
13: 12 f. 251
14: 10 251
14: 23 248
15 335
15: 18–24 254
15: 18–28 238

Romans (*cont.*)
15: 33 248
16 241, 248, 335
16: 1–23 248
16: 20 579
16: 24 579
16: 25–7 248, 335

1 Corinthians
1–4 243
1–6 244
2: 4 233
2: 9 535
2: 13 293, 485
4–6 239
4: 6 244
4: 18 f. 244
5–6 243
5: 2 244
5: 9 240, 244
6: 5 375
6: 9 f. 251
6: 12 244
7–14 244
7: 1 244
7: 10 287
7: 12 287, 459
7: 15 396
7: 25 244
7: 29 238
7: 35 529
7: 40 287
8: 1, 4 244
9: 3 244
9: 9–10 466
9: 9 381, 398, 407, 412 n.
9: 10 412 n.
9: 14 287
9: 16 233
9: 19 ff. 245
10: 1–4 466
10: 2–4 413
10: 4 415 n.
10: 9 349
10: 11 585
10: 23 244
11: 1 287
11: 3–12 396
11: 17 ff. 243–4
11: 23 287
11: 24–6 579 n.
11: 34 234
12: 1 244
12: 3 251
12: 28 51

13 251
13: 3 530
13: 4 244
14: 19 342
14: 21 398
14: 37 287
15 250, 255
15: 3 f. 232, 400, 405
15: 5–8 287
15: 32 249
16: 1 244
16: 12 244
16: 20 ff. 241
16: 23 579

2 Corinthians
1–2 238
1–7 246
1–8 245
1–9 245–6
1: 20 401, 411
2: 3–9 246
3 239
3: 4–18 393
3: 6 473
3: 7–18 415 n.
3: 7, 8 393
3: 11 393
3: 13–17 486
3: 17 f. 393
4: 7 465
5: 10 251
5: 16 288
6: 12 247
6: 14–7: 1 240, 245
7 238
7: 8–12 246
8 245
8: 15 398
9 245, 398
10–13 245–6
10: 10 f. 261
11: 2 239
11: 4 247
11: 6 462
11: 13 247
11: 23 249
13: 10 234
13: 14 579

Galatians
1–2 238
1: 2 286
1: 4 243
1: 11–2: 16 247
2: 7–9 238

Galatians (*cont.*)
2: 11–21 555
2: 20 287
3–5 239
3 397, 399
3: 1 530
3: 10 532
3: 17 408
4 391
4: 20 234
4: 21–31 412 n.
4: 22–6 466
4: 24 507
4: 29 507
5: 21 251
6: 16 400

Ephesians
1: 1 240, 252, 335
1: 3–14 253
1: 15 252
2: 20–2 225
2: 20 342
3: 2 252
3: 15 497
4: 8 400
4: 11 51
4: 25 f. 390
4: 26 293
5: 14 253, 497, 535, 567
5: 19 253
5: 32 466
6: 4 254
6: 12 497
6: 21 252
6: 23 f. 252

Philippians
1: 1–4: 9 240
1: 3–20 238
1: 3–18 249
1: 6–10 238
1: 6, 10 249
1: 20–4 249
1: 26 249
1: 27–30 249
2: 1–18 429
2: 5–11 251, 262, 567
2: 6–11 391
2: 9, 10 444
2: 16 249
2: 19–30 249
2: 19 249
2: 25–30 249
3: 1 249
3: 2–4: 3 249

3: 7 249
3: 12–21 250
3: 17–4: 9 239
3: 18 249
3: 20 249, 251
4: 3 303
4: 4, 5 249
4: 10–20 240, 249
4: 14, 18 249

Colossians
1: 3–8 250
1: 4, 6, 8 250
1: 15–20 251
1: 23 250
1: 24–2: 5 250
2: 1–7 250
2: 1 f. 250
2: 17 402, 466
2: 18 375
3: 8 251
3: 16 253
3: 18–4: 1 250–1
4: 2–4 250
4: 12 f. 250
4: 16 63 n., 240–1, 286, 566

1 Thessalonians
1–3 238
1: 2–2: 16 242
1: 6 286
1: 7 f. 242
1: 9 242
1: 10 243
2: 14 242, 249
2: 17–3: 13 242
2: 17 f. 242
3: 11–4: 18 239
3: 13 243
4: 1–5: 24 242
4: 1 237
4: 13 ff. 242
4: 13 242
4: 14–17 243
4: 15–17 238
4: 15–18 287
5: 1 242
5: 9–23 243
5: 22 251
5: 27 51, 240–1, 566

2 Thessalonians
2: 2 243
2: 3–12 243
2: 15 261
3: 14 261

1 Timothy
1: 4, 7 255
1: 8 256
1: 9 473
1: 15 255–6
2: 5 f. 256
2: 7 51
2: 8 256
3: 1–13 256
3: 1 255–6
3: 16 255–6, 262, 567
4: 1 255
4: 7 f. 255
4: 7 255
4: 9 f. 256
4: 9 255
4: 13 565
5: 1–22 256
6: 3 ff. 255
6: 4 255
6: 7, 10 254
6: 20 256

2 Timothy
1: 9 f. 256
2: 8 f. 256
2: 11–13 567
2: 11 255
2: 18 255
2: 19 398
2: 23 255–6
3: 1 ff. 255
3: 5 255
3: 8 256, 398
3: 12 52, 255
3: 15 114 n.
4: 1 256
4: 4 255
4: 13 52, 59

Titus
1: 1 255
1: 5–2: 10 256
1: 12 256
1: 14 255
2: 3 530
2: 11 ff. 256
2: 12 255
3: 4 ff. 256
3: 8 255
3: 9 255–6

Philemon
v. 9 254

Hebrews
1 262
1: 3 360, 410
2 262
2: 1 ff. 263
2: 1 261
2: 9 375
2: 14, 17 410
3: 1 ff. 263
3: 12 264
4 263
4: 3 ff. 263
5: 11–6: 20 263
5: 11 261
6: 1–2 261
6: 1 261
6: 5 375
6: 19 410
7: 9 262
8 409
8: 1 261–2
8: 7, 13 409
9: 5 261
9: 9, 11 409
9: 12 . 410
9: 13 f. 392
9: 23, 24, 26, 28 409
10: 1 402, 409
10: 19–39 263
10: 22 410
11 394
11: 1 9
11: 11 10 n.
11: 14 ff. 410
11: 32 261–2
11: 39 f. 394
11: 40 410
12: 1 410
12: 3–13 263
12: 4 264
12: 16 394
13: 14 410
13: 22 261
13: 24 264

James
1: 17 375
2: 1–7 265
2: 1–13 264
2: 13 359
2: 14–26 264
4: 1–10 264
5: 1–5 265
5: 11 394
5: 17 f. 394

1 Peter
1: 12   259, 585
1: 13   260
1: 14   259
1: 23, 25   259
2: 1–10   390, 400
2: 1   260
2: 2   259
2: 4   408
2: 6   390, 408
2: 7, 8   408
2: 10   259, 402
3: 6   397
3: 15–22   567
3: 15   259
3: 19   298
3: 20   415 n., 538
3: 21   260, 415 n.
4: 3 f.   259
4: 6   298
4: 7–19   260
4: 11   260
4: 12 ff.   259

2 Peter
1: 19   481
2: 19   257
3: 1   288
3: 2, 3   257
3: 3–10   430
3: 4   258
3: 15–16   288
3: 16   257, 288

1 John
3: 12   394
4: 3   349
5: 7   373

2 John
v. 7   277
v. 12   234

3 John
v. 13   234

Jude
vv. 14–15   158, 534
vv. 17 f.   257
v. 19   257
vv. 22, 23   336

Revelation
1: 4   286
2: 14   398
2: 20   322, 398
5: 2   52
9: 11   2
10: 8 ff.   52
12: 18   322
15: 3   322
17: 10 f.   282
20   432
20: 4–6   432, 555
22: 14   322
22: 16   226
22: 18–19   286

EARLY CHRISTIAN LITERATURE

Ambrose
Ep. 22, 47   569
Ep. 20 *ad Marcellinam*   573

Apostolic Constitutions
II, 57, 5   570–1, 577
II, 57, 9   577
VI, 30, 1   584
VIII, 5, 5   571
VIII, 6, 1   578
VIII, 12, 2   579
VIII, 12, 13   579
VIII, 12, 16   580

Aristides
Apol. III, 7   429 n.

Arnobius
Adv. Nat.
I, 62   439 n.
IV, 33   429 n.
V, 32, 33, 34   429 n.
V, 36   429 n.

Athanasius
De Synod.
XLV   445 n.
XLVIII   445 n.
Ep. ad Mon. I, 2   448 n.
Festal Letters
19   425 n.
39   533 n.
Letters to Serapion
1, 3   445 n.
1, 4–9   445 n.
1, 15, 16   448 n.
2, 8 ff.   443 n.

Athanasius (*cont.*)
  Orat. c. Ar.
    I, 19 422 n.
    I, 22, 23 447 n.
    I, 37–41, 44, 47 444 n.
    I, 51 444 n.
    II, 34 447 n.
    II, 35 448 n.
    II, 46, 55, 56 443 n.
    II, 73, 74, 75, 76 433 n.
    III, 37, 39, 40, 42, 43 444 n.
    III, 54 444 n.
    III, 55 444 n.
    III, 56, 57 444 n.
  Vita Ant. 2 575

Athenagoras
  Suppl. 10, 3 416 n.

Augustine
  Conf.
    II, 3, 6 542 n.
    III, 5, 9 542 n.
    V, 11, 21 542 n.
    V, 14, 24 543 n.
    VI, 4, 6 552 n.
    VII, 9, 13 543 n.
    VII, 9, 13, 14 551 n.
    VIII, 6, 14 543 n.
    VIII, 12, 29 575
    IX, 4, 8 543 n.
    IX, 5, 13 543 n.
    IX, 6, 4 543 n.
    X, 33 569
  C. Acad.
    II, 2, 5 542 n., 543 n.
  De Agone Chr.
    13, 15 553 n.
  De Anima
    I, 10, 12 544 n.
  De Civ. Dei
    X, 29 551 n.
    XI, 2 562 n.
    XV–XXII 553
    XVI, 1 554 n.
    XVI, 2 554 n.
    XVII, 20, 1 534 n.
    XVIII, 38 554 n.
    XVIII, 43 545 n.
    XX, 7 555 n.
  De Cons. Evang.
    I, 35, 54 557 n.
    II, 12, 29 556 n.
    II, 21, 51 556 n., 557 n.
    III, 7, 29 562 n.

De Doctr. Chr.
  I, 2, 2 549 n.
  I, 35, 39–36, 40 548 n.
  I, 39, 43 548 n.
  II, 3, 4–4, 5 549 n.
  II, 5, 6 549 n.
  II, 6, 7 547 n.
  II, 8 536 n.
  II, 8, 12 544 n.
  II, 8, 13 544
  II, 9, 14 550 n.
  II, 10, 15 549 n.
  II, 11, 16 549 n.
  II, 15, 22 545 n.
  II, 16, 23 549 n., 559 n.
  II, 22 545 n.
  II, 28, 42 549 n.
  II, 29, 45 549 n.
  II, 31, 48 549 n.
  II, 39, 48 549 n.
  II, 39, 59 559 n.
  II, 40, 60 549 n., 551 n.
  III, 30, 42 ff. 555 n.
  IV, 4, 6 558 n.
  IV, 5, 8 557 n.
  IV, 15, 32 557 n.
De Gen. c. Man.
  II, 2, 3 554 n.
  II, 10, 13 560 n.
De Gen. lib. imperf.
  2, 5 553 n.
De Mag. 14, 46 562 n.
De Util. Cred.
  1, 2 542 n.
  14, 31 553 n.
De Vera Rel.
  27, 50 553 n.
  49, 94 548 n.
Enarr. in Ps.
  29, 2, 6 559 n.
  30, 3, 9 559 n.
  30, 21 558
  41 558 n.
  41, 2 558
  41, 3 558 n.
  60, 8 561 n.
  80, 2 559 n.
  118, 28, 2 546 n.
Epp.
  21, 4 541 n.
  28, 2 519 n., 545 n.
  28, 2, 2 546 n.
  28, 3, 3 555 n.
  28, 3, 5 556 n.
  55, 18, 34 577

Augustine (*cont.*)
  Epp. (*cont.*)
    71, 3–6 519 n.
    71, 3–5 521 n., 546 n.
    71, 6 519 n.
    82, 34–5 519 n.
    82, 34 521 n.
    82, 35 521 n.
    149, 16 580
    157, 3, 19 556 n.
  In Ioan. Evang. Tr.
    6, 18 573
    9, 6 559 n.
    10, 7 549 n.
    10, 12 560 n.
    15, 1 557 n.
    15, 27 550 n.
    122, 8 560 n.
  In Psalm. 138 569
  Quaest. Evangel. II, 19 561 n.
  Retract. II, 39 579
  Serm. 10 *de verbio apostoli* 569
  Serm.
    132 569
    176 571
    246 573
    259, 2 555 n.
    315 573

Basil
  Ep. 207 570
  Hom. 13 571
  In Psalm. 28 569
  The Longer Rule, 37, 3–5 581

Cassian
  De Inst. Coen.
    II, 4, 5 582
    III, 8 583
    III, 11 583

Cassiodorus
  Inst. I, 12, 3 522 n.

Chrysostom
  Expos. in Ps. 144, 1 579
  Hom. In Acta Apost. 30, 3 577
  Hom. in Exod.
    12, 2 557
    13, 3 557
  Hom. in Heb. 4 584
  Hom. In Ioan. 41 575
  Hom. in 2 Thess.
    3 572
    3, 4 577

Hom. 7 *ad Pop. Ant.* 573
Hom. 10 *ad Pop. Ant.* 576
Hom. 30 *de Dorm.* 584
Hom. 73. *Cur in Pent. Acta leg.* 573
In Acta Apost. Serm. 4, 5 573
Sermones Quinque in Annam 576

1 Clement
  13: 7 f. 414
  35 335
  42: 5 414 n.
  59: 61 578

2 Clement
  2: 4 292
  14: 1–5 414 n.

Clement of Alexandria
  Quis Dives?, 29 437 n.
  Strom.
    I, 100, 4 302
    I, 177, 2 302
    V, 63, 7 302
    VII, 7 569

Cyprian
  Ad Fort. VIII 428 n.
  De Op. et El. I, 425 n.
  De Orat. Dom.
    8 577
    35 581
  De Zelo et Liv. 17 428 n.
  Epp.
    3, 1, 1–2 429 n.
    4, 4, 3 429 n.
    59, 4, 1 429 n.
    59, 13, 5 429 n.
    65, 2, 1 429 n.
    67, 3, 2, 3 429 n.
    73, 8, 1 429 n.
  Test. II, 16 428 n.

Didache
  1: 2 f. 289
  1: 3 289
  1: 4 290
  1: 6 289
  3: 7 289
  6: 1 290
  7–8 289
  7: 1 290
  8: 2 290
  8: 3 581
  9: 5 290, 414 n.
  10: 6 430 n.

Didache (cont.)
11: 3, 7   290
11: 11   289
13: 2   51 n.
14: 2, 3   289
15: 2   51 n.
15: 3–4   290
16   289–90
16: 7   289

Didascalia
II, 12, 14   424 n.
IV, 32   428 n.
IV, 34   424 n.
VII, 86   429 n.
IX, 99   424 n.
XXVI, 216–20   424 n.

Dionysius of Alexandria
On the Promises, II–V   434 n.

Epistle of Barnabas (Ep. Barn.)
1: 8   51 n.
4: 3   293
4: 9   51 n.
6: 8 f.   414 n.
7: 11   414 n.
9: 8   414 n.
10: 8, 11   414 n.
11: 9   293
12: 1   293
16: 5–6   293

Epiphanius
De mens. et pond. 23   138 n.
Pan. haer. VIII, 6, 2   138 n.

Epistula Apostolorum
43–45   418 n.

Etheria, Pilgrimage
II, 1   582
II, 2   582
III, 4   582
IV, 3   582
VII, 2   583
VII, 5   575

Eusebius
Adv. Marc.
I, 2   443 n.
I, 4   442 n.
II, 3   442 n., 443 n.
De Mart. Palaest. I, 1   574

Dem. Ev.
I, 3, 1, 2, 41, 42   425 n.
I, 4, 6   425 n.
I, 6, 63–71   425 n.
II, Praef. 2   430 n.
II, Praef. 6, 16   430 n.
II, 3, 94   430 n.
III, 2, 1–5   430 n.
III, 3, 1–11   430 n.
III, 5, 102, 103   451 n.
III, 6, 1–6   430 n.
III, 7, 1–5   430 n.
III, 7, 31–6   435 n.
III, 13, 10–24   430 n.
IV, 12, 1–9   439 n.
IV, 13, 1–10   439 n.
V, Praef. 20–4   422 n.
V, 1, 8, 9   441 n.
VI, 18, 28   435 n.
VI, 20, 20, 21   435 n.
VIII, 3, 14, 15   435 n.

H.E.
II, 15, 1   55 n.
II, 39, 1 f.   61 n.
III, 24, 5–7   55 n.
III, 39, 4   54 n., 234
III, 39, 15   307
III, 25   357
IV, 26, 13–14   533 n.
IV, 26, 14   137 n.
IV, 29, 6   331
V, 8, 2–4   55 n.
V, 20, 2   66 n.
V, 20, 7   61 n.
VI, 12, 3–6   296
VI, 14   303
VI, 16   458 n.
VI, 19 7   487 n.
VI 23, 2   65 n.
VI, 25, 2   137 n., 533 n.
VI, 25, 14   303
VI, 36, 1   455 n., 576

Praep. ev.
I, 4, 2–4   435 n.
I, 5, 1, 2, 4, 5, 7   435 n.
I, 9, 26   430 n.
VII, 5, 1   422
VII, 8, 39–40   425 n.
VII, 12, 5   441 n.
VIII, 10, 11–17   430 n.
IX, 17   208 n.
IX, 18, 1   227 n.
IX, 28, 2   231 n.
IX, 29, 4   227 n.
IX, 29, 7   227 n.

Eusebius (*cont.*)
  Praep. ev. (*cont.*)
    XI, 14, 2–10 441 n.
    XII, 1 575
    XII, 31, 1, 2 452 n.
    XIII, 12, 1 228 n.

Gregory the Great
  Ep. 5 521 n.

Hilary of Poitiers
  De Trin. I, 15 439 n.
    I, 30 446 n.
    II, 7 448 n.
    II, 10 446 n.
    II, 24 451 n.
    III, 12 446 n.
    IV, 23–31, 35–41 447 n.
    VI, 9 448 n.
    VI, 25 446 n.
    VII, 6 446 n.
    VII, 28 448 n.
    VII, 29, 30, 448 n.
    IX, 2 446 n.
    IX, 51 447 n.
    IX, 58–67 447 n.
    X, 23 439 n.
    X, 24 439 n.
    X, 28, 29, 30, 31 440 n.
    XII, 8 452 n.
    XII, 36, 44–7 446 n.
  Tract. s. Pss., Prol., 15 533 n.

Hermas: *Shepherd*
  Sim. IX, 15, 4 51 n.
  Vis.
    II end 64 n.
    III, 5, 1 51 n.

Hippolytus
  Apostolic Tradition
    I, ii 584
    I, xii 574
    II, xvii 583
    XXXVI, 2–6 581
  C. Noetum
    4 428 n.
  De Antichr.
    56, 57 418 n.
  Ref.
    V, 7, 26 417 n.
    V, 8, 4, 5, 6 417 n.
    V, 8, 29, 30 417 n.
    VII, 25, 3 293
    X, 33, 15–17 451 n.
    X, 34, 3 432

Ignatius
  Smyrn. 11: 3 64 n.
  Philad.
    8: 2 292
    10: 1 64 n.

Innocent
  Ep. 6, 7 534 n.

Irenaeus
  Adv. Haer.
    II, 11, 10 417 n.
    II, 22, 4 451 n.
    III, 3, 3 295
    III, 12, 14 427 n.
    III, 14, 1 273 n.
    III, 18, 2 418 n.
    III, 20, 3 418 n., 427 n.
    IV, 2 427 n.
    IV, 17–28 425 n.
    IV, 17 428
    IV, 32 419 n.
    IV, 41, 2 428 n.
    IV, 48, 1 427 n.
    V, 8, 2 427 n.
    V, 20, 2 432 n.
    V, 33, 1–5 432 n.
    V, 34, 3 428 n.
    V, 35, 1–12 432 n.
    V 36 432 n.
    XI, 1 417 n.
  Dem.
    LXI, 61 433 n.
    LXXXVII, 96 425 n.

Isidore of Seville
  Etymol. VI, 4, 5 521 n.

Jerome
  Adv. Iov.
    I, 13 529 n.
    I, 24 537 n.
  Adv. Vigil. 7 572
  Apol.
    I, 16 535 n., 536 n.
    I, 21–9 536 n.
    I, 24 536 n.
    I, 30 510 n.
    II, 20 513 n.
    II, 24–35 521 n.
    II, 24 515 n.
    II, 33 515 n.
    III, 6 517 n.
    III, 25 515 n.

Jerome (*cont.*)

Brev. in Pss. (*ad* 1 : 4)   531 n.
Chronic. Eus.   510 n., 522 n., 524 n., 536 n.
Comm. in Abd.
  Prol.   538 n.
  (*ad* 1)   531 n.
  (*ad* 20–1)   539 n.
Comm. in Amos
  Lib III, *Prol.*   536 n.
Comm in Eccles.
  (*ad* 1 : 8)   535 n.
  (*ad* 1 : 14)   539 n.
Comm. in Eph.
  Lib. I, *Prol.*   514 n., 536 n.
  Lib. II, *Prol.*   536 n.
  (*ad* 1 : 4)   522 n.
  (*ad* 5 : 14)   535 n.
  (*ad* 5 : 19)   570
  (*ad* 5 : 32)   514 n., 536 n.
Comm. in Esa.
  Lib. I, *Prol.*   539 n.
  (*ad* 5 : 26–30)   538 n.
  (*ad* 6 : 9–10)   539 n.
  (*ad* 11 : 1–3)   535 n.
  (*ad* 16 : 14),   *Lib.* VI   518 n.
  (*ad* 17 : 2–3), *Lib.* VII   538 n.
  (*ad* 24 : 21–3)   530 n.
  (*ad* 30 : 26)   530 n.
  (*ad* 58 : 3–4)   530 n.
  (*ad* 64 : 4–5)   535 n.
  Lib. XVIII, *Prol.*   538 n.
Comm. in Ezech.
  Lib. I, *Prol.*   516 n.
  Lib. VII, *Prol.*   516 n.
  (*ad* 27 : 15–16)   531 n.
  (*ad* 28 : 11–19)   539 n.
  (*ad* 47 : 1–5)   538 n.
Comm. in Gal.
  Lib. I, *Prol.*   537 n.
  Lib. III, *Prol.*   516 n., 517 n., 536 n.
  (*ad* 3 : 1)   530 n.
  (*ad* 3 : 10)   532 n.
  (*ad* 3 : 14)   539 n.
  (*ad* 5 : 7)   530 n.
  (*ad* 5 : 24)   518 n.
  (*ad* 5 : 26)   530 n.
Comm. in Hab.
  (*ad* 3 : 14–16)   510 n.
Comm. in Hier.
  Lib. I, *Prol.*   536 n.
  (*ad* 3 : 14–16)   539 n.
  (*ad* 6 : 6–7)   517 n.
  (*ad* 22 : 24–7)   536 n.
  (*ad* 23 : 5–6)   538 n.
  (*ad* 31 : 2)   540 n.

(*ad* 31 : 15)   540 n.
(*ad* 31 : 16–17)   541 n.
(*ad* 31 : 38–40)   532 n.
Comm. in Joel
  (*ad* 2 : 28–32)   538 n.
  (*ad* 3 : 1–21)   538 n.
Comm. in Mal.
  Lib. I, *Prol.*   539 n.
Comm. in Matt.
  (*ad* 12 : 13)   517 n., 535 n.
  (*ad* 13 : 25)   528 n.
  (*ad* 14 : 6)   536 n.
  (*ad* 15 : 13)   535 n.
  (*ad* 24 : 36)   528 n.
Comm. in Os.
  Lib. I, *Prol.*   536 n., 537 n., 538 n.
Comm. in Tit.
  (*ad* 2 : 3)   530 n.
  (*ad* 3 : 9)   515 n., 531 n.
Comm. in Zach.
  (*ad* 10 : 11–12)   539 n.
C. Pelag.
  II, 15   528 n.
  II, 16   528 n.
  II, 17   528 n.
  III, 2   535 n.
  III, 15   580
De Vir. Ill.
  2   517 n., 535 n.
  4   534 n.
  97   537 n.
  117   513 n.
  135   519 n.
Epp.
  5, 2   511 n., 512 n., 526 n., 537 n.
  10, 3   512 n., 537 n.
  15   512 n.
  15, 1   510 n.
  16   512 n.
  16, 2   510 n., 512 n.
  17, 2   512 n.
  20, 1   537 n.
  22, 30   511 n., 512 n., 524 n.
  27, 3   529 n.
  32, 1   514 n.
  37, 1–3   537 n.
  45, 2, 3   514 n.
  46, 7   537 n.
  49, 4   524 n.
  51   517 n.
  52, 2   538 n.
  53, 6   535 n.
  53, 8   538 n.
  53, 10   535 n.
  57, 5–10   523 n.

Jerome (*cont.*)
  Epp. (*cont.*)
    57, 5 523 n., 524 n.
    57, 9 535 n.
    57, 11 515 n., 523 n., 530 n.
    60, 3 538 n.
    61, 1 535 n.
    61, 2 537 n.
    71, 5 518 n., 519 n., 527 n.
    78 538 n.
    84, 2–3 537 n.
    84, 3 510 n., 513 n., 514 n., 515 n.
    92 517 n.
    105, 5 535 n.
    106, 2 515 n., 531 n.
    106, 4 531 n.
    106, 9 515 n.
    106, 29 525 n.
    106, 30 523 n.
    107, 12 535 n.
    108, 30 584
    112, 19 525 n.
    112, 20 519 n.
    114, 1 516 n.
    117, 12 524 n., 536 n.
    123, 10 513 n.
    125, 12 512 n.
    127, 6 527 n.
    127, 7 514 n.
    133 520
    133, 71 520
    134, 2 521 n.
  Lucifer
    22 538 n.
  Tract. de Ps 77
    (*ad* v. 2) 528 n.
  Vita Pauli
    16 584

Justin
  Apol.
    I, 14 234
    I, 30 404
    I, 32, 1–13 415 n.
    I, 36, 1 416 n.
    I, 55, 5 415 n.
    I, 65 67 577
    I, 67 570
    I, 67, 3 296
  Dial.
    52, 1–2 415 n.
    53, 1–6 415 n.
    54, 1–2 415 n.
    56, 2–10 415 n.
    57, 2 415 n.

    58, 10 415 n.
    59, 1 415 n.
    60, 1 415 n.
    60, 4 416 n.
    61, 1 415 n.
    61, 3–5 416 n.
    62, 1 415 n.
    62, 1 415 n.
    68, 6, 7 415 n.
    80, 5 432 n.
    86, 1–6 415
    90, 4 415 n.
    91, 1–14 415
    119, 8 415
    127, 1–5 415 n.
    138, 2 415 n.

Lactantius
  Div. Inst.
    I, 4 422 n.
    IV, 6 441 n.
    IV, 12 432 n.
    IV, 17 426 n.
    VI, 17 425 n.
    VII, 2, 20, 24, 25 432 n.
    VII, 15, 20, 22–6 432 n.

Mart. Pol. 27, 2 64 n.

Novatian
  De Cib. Iud. 3–7 425 n.
  De Trin.
    1 431 n.
    6 452 n.
    9 422 n.

Origen
  Comm. in Cant. III 478 n.
  Comm. in Ioan.
    I, 6 477 n.
    X, 18 480 n., 484 n.
    X, 42 480 n.
  Comm. in Matt.
    X, 15 485 n.
    X, 20 536 n.
    X, 23 484 n.
    XII, 6 478 n.
    XIV, 13 417 n.
    XV, 14 350, 457 n.
  Comm. in Rom. III, 6 417 n.
  C. Cels.
    I, 50 481 n.
    II, 69 473 n.
  De Orat. 12 581
  De Princ. II, 5, 4 417 n.
  Ep. ad Afric.
    4 456 n.

Origen (*cont.*)
  Ep. ad Afric. (*cont.*)
    5 456 n., 533 n.
  Hom. in Cant. 2, 11 558 n.
  Hom. in Ier. 18, 9 558 n.
  Hom. in Lev. 8, 3 536 n.
  Hom. Luc. in I 303
  Hom. in Luc. 34 418 n.
  Hom. in Num. IX, 4 483 n.

Polycarp
  Phil.
    1: 2 355
    4: 1 254
    12: 1 293
    13: 2 64 n.

Possidius
  Vita August. 28 552 n.

Prosper of Aquitaine
  De Ingrat. I, 55–60 521 n.

Ptolemy
  Ep. ad Floram
    (PG, VII, 1281–1288) 424 n.
    (PG, VII, 1285) 424 n.

Rufinus
  Apol.
    II, 7 512 n.
    II 8 (2) 512 n.
    II, 9 511 n.
    II, 12 514 n.
    II, 32–7 521 n.
  Comm. in Symb. Ap. 37–8 533 n.

Tatian
  Orat.
    13, 1, 2 418 n.
    21, 2 429 n.

Tertullian
  Ad Nat. 8 66 n.

Adv. Marc.
  II, 18, 2, 3 424 n.
  III, 24 432 n.
  IV, 11, 11 425 n.
  IV, 21, 11 451 n.
  V, 5, 10 427 n.
De Anima
  9, 4 569
  18, 4 417 n.
  35, 2 417 n., 427 n.
  35, 3 418 n.
De Carn. Christ. 4, 1–3 451 n.
De Cult. Fem. II, xi, 2 566
De Exhort. Cast. 7, 1–4 428 n.
De Fuga in Persec.
  6, 1 428 n.
  13, 2 428 n.
De Orat.
  12 581
  14 576
De Praescr. Haer. 8, 1–4 428 n.
De Pudic.
  6, 3, 4 424 n.
  7, 1–7 418 n.
  7, 3 428 n.
  8, 10, 11 428 n.
  9, 2, 3 428 n.
  9, 22 427 n.
De Res. Mort.
  26, 1 427 n.
  26, 11 427 n.
  50, 2 431 n.
Scorp. XI, 4 417 n.

Theophilus of Antioch
  Ad Autol.
    II, 22 294
    III, 2 304

Victorinus of Pettau
  Comm. in Apoc. 20, 2 432 n.
  De Fab. Mund. 6 432 n.

JEWISH AND GREEK LITERATURE

Herodotus
  Hist. II, 14 87

Josephus
  Ant.
    I, 12 146 n.
    I, 151 219
    I, 162 207
    I, 164 208

    I, 165 220 n.
    II, 91 204 n.
    II, 224 230 n.
    II, 238–53 227 n.
    III, 203 9
    IV, 253 206
    IV, 273 210 n.
    XIII, 68 223 n.
    XVII, 151 217 n.

Index of References

Josephus (cont.)
  B.J.
    I, 648–70 217 n.
    II, 136, 142, 159 386
    II, 184 ff., 217 n.
    IV, 334–44 131 n.
    V, 379–81 220 n.
    V, 380–1 208 n.
    VII, 432 223 n.
  C. Ap.
    I, 38–42 114 n., 136 n.
    I, 38–40 299
    I, 42, 43 116 n.
    II, 168 228

Philo
  De Abr. 143 382
  De Conf. Ling. 129 383 n.
  De Migr.
    13 383 n.
    89 381
  De Mut. Nom. 91 204 n.
  De Plant. 32 381
  De Post. Caini 1 f., 382
  De Praem. 163–72 396
  De Somn.
    I, 73 382
    II, 250 383 n.
  De Spec. Leg.
    I, 260 381

II, 85 21 n.
III, 30 f. 207 n.
De Virt. 146 381
De Vita Cont.
  28 f. 392 n.
  31 383
De Vita Mos.
  I, 1 f. 380
  II, 2–3 228 n.
  II, 11 381
  II, 40 381
Leg. All.
  I, 31 382
  II, 19 381
  III, 139 382
Quod Omn. Prob.
  81–2 50 n.
  82 383

Plato
  Ion 533 E; 534 B,C 378
  Laws III, 682 A 379
  Phaedrus 274 f. 49 n.
  Republic
    X, 595 B 378
    X, 595 C 378
    X, 605 A 379

Plotinus
  Enneads I, 4, 7 552 n.